Marriage and Divorce in America

Marriage and Divorce in America

ISSUES, TRENDS, AND CONTROVERSIES

Jaimee L. Hartenstein, Editor

BLOOMSBURY ACADEMIC
NEW YORK • LONDON • OXFORD • NEW DELHI • SYDNEY

BLOOMSBURY ACADEMIC
Bloomsbury Publishing Inc, 1359 Broadway, New York, NY 10018, USA
Bloomsbury Publishing Plc, 50 Bedford Square, London, WC1B 3DP, UK
Bloomsbury Publishing Ireland, 29 Earlsfort Terrace, Dublin 2, D02 AY28, Ireland

BLOOMSBURY, BLOOMSBURY ACADEMIC and the Diana logo are trademarks of
Bloomsbury Publishing Plc

First published in the United States of America 2023

Copyright © Bloomsbury Publishing Inc, 2026

Cover image © ClarkandCompany/iStockphoto.com

Library of Congress Cataloging-in-Publication Data

Names: Hartenstein, Jaimee L., editor.
Title: Marriage and divorce in America : issues, trends, and controversies /
Jaimee L. Hartenstein, editor.
Description: New York : Bloomsbury, [2023] | Includes bibliographical
references and index.
Identifiers: LCCN 2022053203 (print) | LCCN 2022053204 (ebook) |
ISBN 9781440868368 (cloth : alk. paper) | ISBN 9781440868375 (epdf) |
ISBN 9798216171973 (ebook)
Subjects: LCSH: Marriage—United States. | Divorce—United States. |
Marriage—United States. | Divorce—United States. | BISAC: SOCIAL
SCIENCE / Sociology / Marriage & Family | PSYCHOLOGY / Interpersonal Relations
Classification: LCC HQ519 .M357 2023 (print) | LCC HQ519 (ebook) |
DDC 306.810973—dc23/eng/20221201
LC record available at https://lccn.loc.gov/2022053203
LC ebook record available at https://lccn.loc.gov/2022053204

ISBN: HB: 978-1-4408-6836-8
PB: 979-8-2164-5218-8
ePDF: 978-1-4408-6837-5
eBook: 979-8-216-17197-3

Typeset by Westchester Publishing Services, LLC

For product safety related questions contact productsafety@bloomsbury.com.

To find out more about our authors and books visit www.bloomsbury.com
and sign up for our newsletters.

Contents

vi | **Contents**

Introduction

The institution of marriage and the dissolution of some of those same unions have become deeply threaded into the fabric of American life and society. The nuclear family was the most common family structure in the United States for its first two centuries of existence. Families were led by two parents—one male and one female with children. While this family structure remains a dominant one today, the blended family—a family with children from the current and all previous relationships—is the fastest-growing family structure in the United States. Family structures will continue to change as individuals, families, and society as a whole adapt and diversify in response to demographic, economic, and cultural changes. Laws, policies, and programs tailored to meet the needs of both families and individuals within those families, from senior citizens to toddlers, will need to adapt to these changing circumstances.

Divorce is one of the key contributors to the change in family structures that America has experienced, especially in the last half-century. The change to no-fault divorce laws in the late 1960s led to a marked increase in divorce proceedings, as parties no longer had to substantiate fault on the other party to obtain a divorce. In addition, child custody transitioned from children being considered property of their father to the "Tender Years Doctrine," in which mothers were considered the most important parent for the formative "tender" years of a child's growth. However, that one-size-fits-all philosophy has since given way to the "Best Interest of the Child Standard," which operates from an assumption that children with divorced parents benefit from strong, sturdy, and loving relationships with both.

The increase in cohabitation without marriage has led to fundamental changes in family structure as well. More and more people are cohabitating at younger ages as well as entering into multiple cohabiting relationships. Couples are also having children in nonmarital and/or cohabitating relationships in greater numbers.

This encyclopedia provides a one-stop general reference resource for understanding these broad trends and many other facets of divorce, marriage, and other committed partnerships. The contents provide an overview of the history and current state of marriage and divorce in the United States, including their many cultural, economic, political, legal, and religious facets, as well as information and insights into the dozens of factors—from childcare to in-laws to unplanned pregnancies to the legal system—that influence the trajectory of millions of American marriages, divorces, and other relationships every day.

A

Abortion

Abortion orbits around some of our most important and central values and arguments concerning the dignity of life, privacy rights, choice and autonomy, the moment of conception, and (parental) commitment. For a long time, this complicated issue has been one of the most intractable problems in American society, since it inextricably intertwines both moral values and medical facts. In modern terms, inside as well as outside the United States, the issue of abortion churns up major conflict between pro-choice and pro-life individuals, organizations, and lawmakers. Indeed, both camps can and do marshal a wide array of moral, philosophical, and medical arguments to advance their arguments.

From ancient times until today, the morality of medically assisting a pregnant woman to abort her fetus has been the subject of fierce debate. Ancient medical professional oaths forbade practitioners from carrying out abortions. The Hippocratic Oath, for instance, dictated—"I shall not give a woman an abortive pessary." A similar and stringent approach may be found in the Roman Catholic perspective, which has always treated abortion as a serious sin, whereas the Protestants' point of view has been much more complex and varied. Judaism takes a generally moderate view, allowing some abortions under several circumstances if there are justified moral appeals. Likewise, in Islam, there exists general permission to abort on medical and health grounds, but only up to a certain stage of pregnancy.

In the modern era, it should be noted that the vast majority of jurisdictions all around the globe massively regulate abortion to determine the conditions under which the estimated 73 million annual global abortions occur. Generally speaking, the most basic contemporary attitudes toward abortion can be divided into four main categories: a model of prohibition, a model of permission, a model of prescription, and a model of privacy. In the past, the early English common law was a model of prohibition, as it proscribed abortion after about the fourth month of pregnancy. Consequently, the 1861 British statutory abortion law defined any sort of action that causes an abortion as a felony. Likewise, over a jubilee, all the states in the United States treated any attempt to abort a fetus as a felony, excluding certain exceptions, such as the cases of rape and incest.

In 1973, two groundbreaking abortion decisions were handed down by the U.S. Supreme Court: *Roe v. Wade* and *Doe v. Bolton*. The common dominator of these central and substantial rulings was recognizing and legalizing, for the first time in American history, the right of the woman to abort her fetus, making abortion legal in all 50 states. This basic right is relevant only during the first trimester, the first three months when almost all induced abortions occur, and no law can restrict this right. During the second trimester, when fewer than 5 percent of all induced abortions are performed in the United States, the state may regulate abortion, only if it reasonably relates to the preservation and protection of the woman's health and life. After the point of viability, when the fetus is capable of surviving outside the womb, approximately at 23 to 24 weeks into pregnancy, a state has a compelling interest in protecting human life. Thus, states can regulate or even proscribe entirely a woman's right to an abortion once the fetus is considered viable.

This autonomous privilege is the pregnant woman's right, as the Supreme Court established in *Planned Parenthood v. Danforth* (1976). Sixteen years later, the U.S. Supreme Court ruled in *Planned Parenthood of Se. Pennsylvania v. Casey* (1992) that a person seeking to end her pregnancy does not need to first secure approval from her parents (if she is a minor) or from her husband (if she is married). In two additional landmark rulings, the U.S. Supreme Court handed down decisions about the late-term abortion procedure known to pro-life activists and their supporters as "partial-birth abortion" and known among medical practitioners as intact dilation and extraction, which is the standard safest surgical technique used for abortion after about 14 weeks. The first, *Stenberg v. Carhart* (2000), dealt with a Nebraska law that made performing "partial-birth abortion" illegal. The Court struck it down, finding that the Nebraska statute violated the Due Process Clause of the U.S. Constitution, as interpreted in its former rulings. But, seven years later, in *Gonzales v. Carhart* (2007), the Court upheld the federal Partial-Birth Abortion Ban Act of 2003, which makes it a federal

crime for doctors to perform certain late-term abortions, even if the health of the pregnant woman was endangered.

The year 2019 has been defined by some as a critical time for abortion rights, since during the first half of that year nearly 60 abortion restrictions were enacted in 19 American states, 25 of which would ban all, most, or some abortions, as many more have been introduced by state legislators. These statutes include gestational age bans, the "partial-birth abortion," not once even of a fetus that has or may have Down syndrome, however, have been challenged in court by pro-choice individuals and organizations, and many cases are continuing to wind their way through the U.S. court system. To summarize, 2019 alone reflected a dramatic deterioration of the basic human right to abortion.

In addition, the COVID-19 pandemic of 2020 profoundly jeopardized women's rights throughout the world. The year 2021 ended with the Texas Abortion Law (SB8) being effective as of September 1. This state law, which may be interpreted as the most prohibitive one, bans abortion after only six weeks of gestational age, even in cases of rape and incest. Not surprisingly, another 12 states have enacted similar "fetal heartbeat laws," prohibiting abortion once any embryonic cardiac can be detected. Also on September 1, 2021, the U.S. Supreme Court declined to block this law, consequently eliminating the entire abortion services in Texas.

On the other hand, there have been also numerous liberal global steps. Since 2017, Ireland, Chile, and South Korea have all legalized abortion. New Zealand moved to decriminalize abortion and, more generally, since the year 2000, a total of 27 countries broadened legal access to abortion.

Yehezkel Margalit

See also: Contraception; Donor Insemination; Planned Parenthood

Further Reading

Guttmacher Institute. 2020. "Unintended Pregnancy and Abortion Worldwide." https://www.guttmacher.org/

Planned Parenthood of Se. Pennsylvania v. Casey, 505 U.S. 833 (1992).

Post, Stephen G., ed. 2004. "Abortion." *Encyclopedia of Bioethics*, vol. 1. New York: Free Press.

Roe v. Wade, 410 U.S. 113 (1973).

Thomson, Judith J. 1971. "A Defence of Abortion." *Philosophy and Public Affairs* 1: 47–66.

Absent Father

A traditional family structure involves a married couple who are the caregivers of their biological offspring. However, the current norms are changing due to higher rates of divorce in the United States. As a result, the single-parent family is becoming more prevalent. In the early 1960s, children were born within wedlock. Today, we are seeing more women bearing a child out of wedlock and raising the kids as single mothers (Pew Research Center). This literature aims to delve into similar inferences of the absent father phenomenon.

In older times, a father was perceived as the breadwinner of a family and a mother was limited to the role of homemaker. However, this arrangement has taken a drastic shift since more women are seen in the workforce these days. The institution of marriage has also lost its importance in the new era. This has adversely affected the family structure in America. Divorce and separation have become a norm in the United States due to which the single-parent family is common.

Researchers suggest that one in three kids from the United States grows up in a fatherless home. The kids who are brought up in such households often experience a psychological crisis when they reach adulthood. The consequences are even worse for children who have to deal with an emotionally absent father. Emotionally absent fathers barely participate in their child's day-to-day activities, hardly involved in their studies or other activities.

While an absent father is predominantly a result of parental separation, additional elements like children born out of wedlock and the death of a father also contribute to this issue. Children who are brought up in such a family situation have frequent trust issues in relationships. Being part of a single-parent household, the child hardly gets parental attention since the mother is the sole breadwinner and is dependent on others for childcare.

According to the United States Census Bureau (2011), it is observed that children hailing from absent-father households are more likely to be living below the poverty line. Eighty percent of all children in Black families are susceptible to living apart from their fathers. These results create additional stress on the child's mother financially as well as psychologically, particularly when the mother was dependent on the father for finances. Poverty is not the only consequence of the absent father phenomenon. Several other dimensions like substance abuse, anxiety issue, emotional development, and overall personality development of a child are affected due to the absence of a father in the home. In addition, the children from absent-father households are susceptible to behavioral problems from early childhood. A compilation of several data points is presented below to understand the adverse effects caused by a father's absence.

Education: Even though an absent father does not have any adverse effect on the cognitive skills of a child, those children are still observed to be less enthusiastic about higher education and are subjected to unemployment. This is also a result of the mother being the sole breadwinner.

Relationship and stability: Because these children miss getting care and lessons from their father, they tend to suffer from trust issues in a relationship. They are more likely to have a broken marriage in the future.

Emotional well-being: The presence of both parents in the life of a child is of vital importance. However, a father's presence is more crucial when it comes to raising a boy. Studies in the area of sociology have proven time and again that kids who grow up without a father experience anxiety into adulthood. They experience feelings of abandonment and are emotionally vulnerable.

Substance abuse: The majority of children who become addicted to drugs are from unstable families. This is more frequently observed in boys as they require a father to understand them physically, emotionally, and psychologically while growing up.

Teen pregnancy: Daughters who are brought up in father-absent homes are more likely to get pregnant in their teens. They miss a fatherly figure at home and seek that love outside in the form of a partner.

Apart from the above-listed concerns, there is one more critical aftereffect of this phenomenon. It is the increasing crime rate in the United States. Youngsters are majorly a part of such an increase in crime, and it is not at all because of social, economic, or racial problems. It is an outcome of father absence. Certain solutions can be implemented to lessen this issue, such as:

1. Organizing a Fatherhood Forum in the cultural meets.
2. Partnering with educational institutes to increase fathers' involvement in child mentor programs.
3. Offering counseling sessions to children who are dealing with an absent father in their homes.
4. Make the father responsible for child support, financially as well as emotionally.
5. Get in touch with The Responsive Fathers Program which offers peer support and parenting skills to new fathers to help them lead their families.

It is noteworthy to mention President Barack Obama's speech on Father's Day 2011, during which he spoke from his heart out about the changing times in the family arena and about absent fathers specifically. He made it very clear that parental responsibility is of utmost importance and that a father cannot run away from his commitments when it comes to his children. Also, a book published in 1994,

Fatherless America—Confronting Our Most Urgent Social Problem by David Blankenhorn, takes a look at this situation in the United States. It focused on the literature surrounding the significance of a father in a child's life, principally when it comes to bringing up a son.

The statistics point to the soaring percentage of women nurturing fatherless children, indicating a profound shift in the family arrangement and fatherhood. It is crucial to keep this situation in check so that the next generation lives a quality family life. In order to overcome this tough situation, we probably need a flexible family policy in place.

Archana Kamaal

See also: Absent Mother; Maternal Gatekeeping; Nonresidential Fathers

Further Reading

Blankenhorn, David. 1994. *Fatherless America*. New York: Basic Books.

McLanahan, Sara, and Irwin Garfinkel. 2000. *The Fragile Families and Child Well-Being Study*. Madison, Wisconsin: Institute for Research on Poverty, University of Wisconsin-Madison.

Schlomer, Gabriel L., and Hyun-Jin Cho. 2017. "Genetic and Environmental Contributions to Age at Menarche: Interactive Effects of Father Absence and LIN28B." *Evolution and Human Behavior* 38 (6): 761–769. doi:10.1016/j.evolhumbehav.2017.06.002.

Absent Mother

Absent mothers are a growing phenomenon in today's family culture. This absence can be due to a tragic departure due to death, failing to give enough time to the children due to multiple responsibilities, or being emotionally absent due to relationship issues with a partner. Millennial women are highly pressurized due to the modernization of technology and the responsibility of being a breadwinner. Additionally, the rise in single motherhood has made the situation even graver in the United States. In fact, statistics show that single motherhood is becoming a norm in America.

The life of a child being raised by a single mother can be quite challenging. Children yearn for attention and motivation at every stage of their lives. The U.S. Census Bureau (2022) states that more than 80% of all single parents in the United States are single mothers. This puts considerable pressure on the mother to earn for her family. Hence, mothers need a strong support system, such as grandparents or a daycare, to help them with their children.

Since time immemorial, mothers have been perceived to be caregivers who understand their children both emotionally and physically. However, times are changing. The adverse effects of an absent mother on the well-being of children are being researched extensively. The presence of a mother in a child's life is imperative to their development, especially in the first five years (California Department of Education, 2000). During this period, if kids have to deal with an absent mother, it leaves them agitated and sad as they need motherly love and care in this crucial stage of development.

The term "absent mother" is itself extremely heavy. It does not imply only physical absenteeism, but it invariably includes an emotionally absent mother as well. The modern woman is well-known for her multitasking skills.

However, these skills have started to take a toll on the overall well-being of children. It is widely seen that kids who are parted from their mothers at a young age are more susceptible to depression. In addition, children raised solely by a father were found to have anxiety problems along with a low level of self-confidence. Moreover, an emotionally absent mother triggers issues in children's psychological health.

Being emotionally shut down is common in American culture and exacerbated by a lack of work-life balance (Cori, 2017). This implies that a mother is present but absent emotionally. For instance, she might not be easily approachable as she may be continuously caught up with watching TV, working, or on a mobile device. These recent technological distractions create a communication gap between parents and children. Sometimes, a mother may be so involved socially that she hardly makes time for her kids. Such absent mothers prove to be difficult for a child.

All these factors play a huge role in the declining emotional well-being of a child. Despite a mother being present at home, the child fails to get the nurturing warmth from its mother. This gives rise to a rejected feeling which stays with the child forever if it is consistent. Such kids are more prone to depression and anxiety into their adulthood. Low self-esteem along with addictions becomes a part of their life.

An emotionally absent mother may cause her child to become more frustrated. Children of emotionally absent mothers tend to seek more attention by turning into troublemakers. Most of the time it is observed that they are just replicating the detached relationship they experienced with their own mothers. A mother plays an imperative role in the emotional development of her child. And surprisingly her role doesn't end there. She continues to be a nurturer throughout her children's teenage years and into adulthood.

It recently has been observed that counselors and therapists are getting increased visits from emotionally disturbed adults. These developments were not because they came from disturbed families but, rather, they were due to present yet emotionally absent mothers. The unavailability of their mothers from an emotional perspective continued to affect these people into adulthood. In addition, these adults were prone to experiencing trust issues later in life, suffered from anxiety and sleep disorders, and found themselves often unable to cope during trying times.

Despite all this, there are ways to help children cope with such situations. It is suggested that friends and close family members of a child dealing with an absent mother take active roles in that child's upbringing, remaining vigilant as to their needs. It is also important that it is stressed to the child that their mother's absence is not their fault and that they are loved.

In a nutshell, if a mother remains unavailable during her children's development those children will try to find that love in other places, such as their peers or romantic partners. Their constant wish to feel loved and accepted may land them in extreme situations where they fail to distinguish between right and wrong. Adults who were deprived of care and nurturing from their mothers are more likely to become addicted to drugs. However, if a person has a strong bond with other family members, the effect of an absent mother is minimized to a large extent. Absence due to untimely death can't be overcome. However, in the case of emotionally absent mothers, a few measures can be taken into consideration.

To avoid such instances, a mother may teach small routines in the present lifestyle. She must try to keep a work-life balance and be present with her child in times of need. A child's need to feel connected must be fulfilled by giving ample time for open communication, which is the key to developing successful social relationships. Restricting screen time such as refraining from using mobile phones during meal times should be put into practice. This will help to create quality time between mother and child. Children's needs are simple: they simply need to feel loved and accepted. A little motivation from a caring mother will go a long way in fostering a successful adult.

Archana Kamaal

See also: Absent Father; Maternal Gatekeeping; Nonresidential Mothers

Further Reading

Cori, Jasmin Lee. 2017. *The Emotionally Absent Mother.* New York: Experiment.

Hernandez, Donald J., Arlene F. Saluter, and Catherine O'Brien. 1993. *We The American—Children.* Washington, D.C.: U.S. Dept. of Commerce, Economics and Statistics Administration, Bureau of the Census.

Ackerman Institute for Family Therapy

The Ackerman Institute for Family Therapy is an institute for couple and family therapy in New York City. The mission of the Ackerman Institute is to provide (1) on-site family therapy services through its clinic, (2) on-site training programs for mental health and other professionals, and (3) research on new treatments.

In terms of on-site services, the Institute offers couple and family therapy, divorce mediation, and various resources for families. The Institute's on-site clinic is licensed by the State of New York Office of Mental Health. In terms of on-site training programs, the Institute runs workshops, core courses, short courses, community training, social work programs, international training, and webinars. Finally, the Institute's current clinical research topics include adolescents and their families, children with special needs, fathers, foster care and adoption, money and family life, and substance use disorders.

The Ackerman Institute also offers free resources on its website. For example, the Ackerman Podcast explores issues in family therapy, the blog covers relevant topics, and the website offers a 150-page guide to parenting.

Nathan W. Ackerman founded the Institute in 1960. He was a psychiatrist and trained as a classical analyst, but in the 1950s, he pioneered a new type of therapy when he began seeing his patients with their families as a group on the theory that it is rare for mental illness to occur in only one family member. Ackerman also started audiovisual documentation of clinical work that later became used in family therapy training.

After Ackerman died, Donald Bloch became director of the Institute in 1972. Under his leadership, the Institute expanded its clinical training program, developed a large family therapy clinic, and started a series of projects aimed at creating new approaches to difficult clinical problems, such as chronic illness.

In 1990, Peter Steinglass became the next director of the Institute. During his years at the helm, the Institute organized its work into the following centers: (1) The Center for the Developing Child and Family, (2) The Center for Families and Health, (3) The Center for Work and Family, (4) The Center for Substance Abuse and the Family, and (5) The Center for Children and Relational Trauma. These centers typically provided direct services to families in the specified specialty area, as well as professional training for therapists and related professionals.

In 2006, Lois Braverman became Ackerman Institute's next director. During her tenure, the Institute relocated from its Upper East Side location of over five decades to its current state-of-the-art facility in the Flatiron District of New York City. New research projects also began during this time, including the Gender and Family Project, which provided gender-affirmative services, training, and research; the Children with Special Needs Project, which offered specialized family therapy services to families with children with developmental disabilities; and the Foster Care and Adoption Project, which worked to preserve and enhance family connections while also focusing on a child's need for safe and permanent attachments.

Gisselle Acevedo became the Institute's fifth and most recent president in 2018. She has committed her time as president to helping serve mental health care professionals and bringing innovative perspectives to health care. Under her leadership, the Institute is continuing to offer services to families as well as training and research on the issues facing families today, including substance use and financial concerns.

Margaret Ryznar

See also: American Association for Marriage and Family Therapy; Gottman Institute; National Council on Family Relations

Further Reading

Ackerman, Nathan W. 1966. *Treating the Troubled Family.* New York: Basic Books.

Ackerman, Nathan W., Donald Bloch, and Robert Simon. 1982. *The Strength of Family Therapy: Selected Papers of Nathan W. Ackerman.* New York: Brunner/Mazel Publisher, Inc.

Ackerman Institute for the Family, https://www.ackerman.org/

Addiction (Non-substance)

Most people who are experiencing some difficulty with addiction also experience interpersonal difficulties in some form. Much research has studied the impact of addiction to substances (drugs and/or alcohol) on individual romantic relationships, but less is known about the impact of compulsive sexual behavior, problematic pornography use, and gambling on relationships. A lack of widespread research does not mean that these are not important topics to understand. More research into these topics will lead to a better understanding and identify ways to protect against some, or all, negative effects of these behaviors.

Many people participate in gambling without any serious negative consequences. Estimates put the rates of problem gambling across the world at 2–3% and research suggests that each of these individuals with problem gambling in turn directly impacts approximately 8–10 other people (Kourgiantakis, Saint-Jacques, and Tremblay, 2013). A gambling disorder is an addictive disorder characterized by dysregulated and recurrent gambling behaviors that can generate clinically significant levels of distress and impairments in functioning according to the Diagnostic and Statistical Manual (DSM-5). However, problem gambling is often referred to as gambling behaviors that do not meet full diagnostic criteria in the DSM-5 but still result in serious consequences for the individual and others in his or her social support system or community.

According to research summarized by Kourgiantakis and colleagues in their 2013 systematic review, most research that looks at the effects of gambling on the family have focused on romantic partners. Spouses reported a lack of awareness or understanding of gambling, consequences for the spouse on the individual, family, and social level when a member of the family had problems with gambling, and that effective coping skills helped mitigate the negative effects of problem gambling. Some of the specific consequences noted were that spouses often became aware of the family member's gambling problem after the behavior or problems had become quite severe (e.g., financial losses or devastation). In addition, once the spouses or partners had become aware of the individual's gambling problems, they were likely to report physical (e.g., headaches, insomnia, or overeating) and emotional (e.g., loss of trust, relational strain, distress, and/or isolation) problems. Beyond the partner relationship, Kourgiantakis and colleagues (2013) also summarized how an individual's gambling behaviors can impact their children. Both adult and non-adult children reported negative impacts from their gambling parent's behavior, including physical and

emotional unavailability, loss (of home, trust, relationships, etc.), food insecurity, and emotional and behavioral problems, such as depression and conduct problems (Kourgiantakis, Saint-Jacques, and Tremblay, 2013).

One area of hope threaded through the literature on problem gambling and relational impacts was that those who received support from their partners or other family members had better recovery outcomes. When family members were involved in treatment with the individual who had gambling problems, the individual with the gambling problem was more likely to stay engaged with treatment and more likely to successfully complete treatment when compared to those in treatment without a supportive family member (Kourgiantakis, Saint-Jacques, and Tremblay, 2013). While gambling may negatively impact the family during an active problem, working together to overcome the problem gambling may help the damaged relationships to heal.

Just as there is a distinction between problem gambling and a gambling addiction, there are also differences in sex-related behaviors. While sexual partners may have different sexual drives and needs, some individuals experience persistent difficulties controlling intense urges or impulses which result in repetitive sexual behavior over an extended period (e.g., six months or more). This behavior causes marked distress or impairment in personal, family, social, educational, occupational, or other important areas of functioning and can be classified as compulsive sexual behavior (Kraus et al., 2018). Although this behavior does not rise to the level of an addiction as classified in the DSM-5, the previously mentioned criteria were proposed and ratified for inclusion in the International Classification of Disease (ICD-11) as an impulse control disorder.

More research is needed to fully understand the development of and treatment for compulsive sexual behavior. The age of onset appears to be in early adolescence or young adulthood, and it occurs in approximately 5% of adults, although this prevalence rate varies by specific subsets of the population (e.g., it is higher in LGBT samples, sexual trauma survivors, and samples of military veterans; Cooper, Houchins, and Kraus, 2018). The specific impact on relationships cannot be currently qualified given the difficulty in measuring behaviors—the specific definition proposed for ICD-11 was only ratified in June 2019 and compulsive sexual behavior is likely underreported due to the shame and guilt associated with many of the behaviors.

According to the researchers who proposed the ICD-11 definition (Kraus et al., 2018), there are concerns about over-pathologizing of sexual behaviors that are not disordered. Individuals with high levels of sexual interest and behavior who do not exhibit impaired control over their behavior but do experience significant distress and/or those individuals who do not experience impairment in functioning should not be diagnosed. High sex drive, shame, or guilt alone are not diagnostic of compulsive sexual behavior. Additional research is needed to accurately assess prevalence, gender differences, and overall impact on romantic relationships.

One area where research has been conducted into the impact of certain behavior on relationships is pornography use. Overall, it is noted across many studies that the more frequent the use of pornography within a romantic relationship, the lower the relationship satisfaction. Samuel Perry, a researcher who studies the impact of pornography use on relationships, has conducted several research projects on this subject, both cross-sectional and longitudinal. In his work, he has found that the negative effect of pornography use on marriages through longitudinal study was almost exclusively on the male partner. Female married partners who reported using pornography at the first time point were more likely to report increases in their marital satisfaction at the second time point. The marriages that were the most severely impacted by one partner's use of pornography were ones where the men reported viewing pornography at least once a day, which may indicate a deeper problem with pornography use such as compulsive sexual behavior.

Pornography use among Americans, especially young Americans, is on the rise (Perry and Davis, 2017). This may be due to factors such as accessibility and availability. They noted that in individuals below the age of forty, 60–70% of men and 30–40% of women reported viewing pornography in a given year, with rates dropping to 45% for men and 15% for women for any given week. Both Perry and Davis suggested that little attention has been paid to relationship stability when considering pornography use, and the results from their longitudinal study affirmed the idea that early use of pornography (by age) and greater use frequency were more likely to lead to a romantic break-up between the baseline assessment and six-year follow-up. In their study, men who were viewing pornography were more likely to experience a relationship break-up than women who were using pornography. Some longitudinal work has found that Americans who viewed pornography were more likely to have positive views about sex outside of a relationship. Perry and Davis also summarized the findings of several research studies that suggest that female partners whose male partners viewed porn without them developed feelings of jealousy or inadequacy, which in turn decreased their sexual desire, feelings of intimacy, sexual attraction to their partner, and self-esteem.

The majority of research on pornography use has found negative effects overall on relationships but this has largely taken place in research on one partner viewing pornography alone, and not considered the impact of viewing pornography together (Perry and Davis, 2017). Some research conducted on viewing pornography with one's partner has found perceived relationship benefits. This included an increase in the perception of sexual quality. It is noted, however, that men who use pornography alone far outnumber male/female partnerships who use pornography together. Solitary pornography use may cause the other partner to feel insecure or betrayed, which may be made worse if the pornography-viewing partner is dishonest or hiding the behavior from their partner.

Overall, research on gambling, compulsive sexual behavior, and pornography use highlights the importance of open communication and understanding of individual boundaries within relationships. Engaging in a specific behavior may not be problematic on its own, but a pattern of behavior that causes problems—individually

and interpersonally—may disrupt and sometimes end relationships. Treatment approaches often mirror traditional substance use treatment (Kraus and Sweeney, 2019), and the findings from research on all three of the covered topics indicate a need for increased education for adolescents, emerging adults, and single and partnered adults on healthy relationship skills in general, as well as the impacts of other factors on those relationships.

Koriann B. Cox, Arielle A. J. Scoglio,
and Shane W. Kraus

See also: Addictions, Drugs and Alcohol; Divorce, Causes/Risk Factors of; Infidelity; Marital Separation; Pornography

Further Reading

Cooper, Ilana, Houchins, Joseph R., and Kraus, Shane W. 2018. "Personality and sexual addiction." In *Encyclopedia of Personality and Individual Differences*, 1–4. Switzerland: Springer Nature.

Kalischuk, Ruth G., Nowatzki, Nadine, Cardwell, Kelly, Klein, Kurt, and Solowoniuk, Jason. 2006. "Problem gambling and its impact on families: A literature review." *International Gambling Studies* 6, no. 1: 31–60.

Kourgiantakis, Toula, Saint-Jacques, Marie-Christine, and Tremblay, Joël. 2013. "Problem gambling and families: A systematic review." *Journal of Social Work Practice and Addictions* 13, no. 4: 353–372. https://doi.org/10.1080/15332 56X.2013.838130

Kraus, Shane W., Briken, Peer, Krueger, Richard, and First, Michael B. 2018. "Compulsive sexual behaviour disorder in the ICD-11." *World Psychiatry* 17, no. 1: 109–110. doi:10.1002/wps.20499

Kraus, Shane W., and Sweeney, Patricia J. 2019. "Hitting the target: Considerations for differential diagnosis when treating individuals for problematic use of pornography." *Archives of Sexual Behavior* 48, no. 2: 431–435.

Perry, Samuel L. 2017. "Does viewing pornography reduce marital quality over time? Evidence from longitudinal data." *Archives of Sexual Behavior* 46: 549–559. doi:10.1007/s10508-016-0770-y

Perry, Samuel L., and Davis, Joshua T. 2017. "Are pornography users more likely to experience a romantic breakup? Evidence from longitudinal data." *Sexuality & Culture* 21: 1157–1176. doi:10.1007/s12119-017-9444-8

Addictions, Drugs and Alcohol

Currently, in the United States, it is estimated that approximately 24.6 million Americans have used illicit drugs during a 12-month period. This statistic has been instrumental in creating a renewed interest in determining the causes and effects of addiction on the individual as well as those on the greater society (National Institute on Drug Abuse, 2015). To appropriately delve into this subject, it is important to understand what constitutes addiction through the history of drug use and regulation, defining addiction and differentiating between it and abuse, identifying substances of abuse and their effects on the individual, and finally understanding the effects of addiction on families and couples.

It is important to understand that drug use has been a part of the human condition for millennia (Inaba and Cohen, 2011; Kuhn, Swartzwelder, and Wilson, 2014; Laxmaiah et al., 2018). The first recorded use and misuse of opioids can be seen as far back as 5000 years ago (3500 B.C.E) in Mesopotamia, modern-day Iraq, Kuwait, eastern Syria, and south-eastern Turkey, with the cultivation and extraction of the alkaloids of the poppy plant (Inaba and Cohen, 2011; Kuhn, Swartzwelder, and Wilson, 2014; Laxmaiah et al., 2018). The use of psychoactive substances transcended culture, religion, gender, and time, including modern times (Inaba and Cohen, 2011; Kuhn, Swartzwelder, and Wilson, 2014; Laxmaiah et al., 2018). In the United States in the mid-1800s it was not uncommon to find over-the-counter medications that included opium, heroin, morphine, and cocaine, these were often referred to as "tonics" or "patent medicine" (Inaba and Cohen, 2011; Laxmaiah et al., 2018). Throughout the Victorian era, it was quite common for average people to use laudanum recreationally, this alcohol-based tincture included 10% powdered opium, and was marketed as a panacea for a multitude of ailments (Inaba and Cohen, 2011; Kuhn, Swartzwelder, and Wilson, 2014; Laxmaiah et al., 2018). Interestingly enough, Americans could buy reusable syringes from the Sears Roebuck catalog, along with heroin, opium, and marijuana-based "patent medicines" (Inaba and Cohen, 2011). Until the passage of the Pure Food and Drug Act of 1906, patent medicine manufacturers did not have to list what ingredients were in their medicinal tonics that were marketed to consumers for a multitude of ailments (Inaba and Cohen, 2011). To illustrate the presence of drugs in our society, one of modern Americans' favorite carbonated beverages Coca-Cola, contained up to 5 mg of cocaine (until 1903) and was marketed as a brain tonic, luckily today Coca-Cola has had the cocaine removed although it still uses the coca leaves for flavoring (Inaba and Cohen, 2011). From 1906 on, the United States began to see value in regulating substances and ingredients that Americans were consuming and began doing so.

The first such government regulation regarding the manufacture, sale, or distribution of drugs began in 1914 with the passage of the Harrison Narcotics Tax Act. With this, the United States outlawed the importation, production, sale, and distribution of opium or coca leaves, and their derivatives. Before this, it was common for Americans to use these substances quite regularly and without concern. This was followed by the Volstead act of 1920 via the 18th Amendment which prohibited the sale, use, importation, or manufacture of any alcoholic beverage this is colloquially known as prohibition. In 1933, the 18th amendment was repealed via the 21st amendment effectively ending prohibition, this was followed in 1937 by the Marijuana tax act, which banned the cultivation, importation, production, and use of cannabis (Inaba and Cohen, 2011; Kuhn, Swartzwelder, and Wilson, 2014). In 1970, the Comprehensive Drug Abuse Prevention and Control Act otherwise known as the Controlled Substances Act was enacted (Inaba and Cohen, 2011; Kuhn, Swartzwelder, and Wilson, 2014; Laxmaiah et al., 2018). This act developed five "schedules" to classify and regulate all psychoactive substances within the United States, with it was the creation of the Drug Enforcement Administration in 1973 (Inaba and Cohen, 2011; Kuhn, Swartzwelder, and Wilson, 2014; Laxmaiah et al., 2018). Please note that this is a quick illustration of the history of the regulation of drugs and alcohol within the United States and not a comprehensive history.

What is addiction? Well, that is a multi-faceted question, the most commonly accepted definition of addiction comes from The National Institute on Drug Abuse (NIDA) which falls under The National Institutes of Health (NIH). NIDA defines addiction as, "a chronic, relapsing disorder characterized by compulsive drug seeking and use despite adverse consequences. It is considered a brain disorder because it involves functional changes to brain circuits involved in reward, stress, and self-control, and those changes may last a long time after a person has stopped taking drugs" (NIDA, 2018, para. 1). While others such as the *Diagnostic and Statistical Manual 5*, which is referred to as the DSM 5, identify addiction as a substance use disorder or a substance-induced disorder, we will only look at substance use disorders in this entry (American Psychiatric Association, 2013).

Think of addiction or substance use disorders in the following ways: each substance we ingest acts on the brain's reward system, the system involved in reinforcing desired behaviors that have evolutionarily kept our species alive—eating, reproduction, etc. This system also acts on the production of memories, good, bad, or indifferent. When these substances are used, they act on this system to create a positive activation of the reward system, associated good memories tied to the use, and a disruption of the typical biological and neurobiological functioning of the individual. Like all diseases that most people are familiar with such as: diabetes, heart disease, or asthma, addiction impacts the normal healthy biological functioning of the person, as the body moves into a dysregulated state caused by the substance of choice. Long-term effects can be serious and affect every major organ system within the body, which in turn can lead to long-term impairment and even death

(Inaba and Cohen, 2011; Kuhn, Swartz-welder, and Wilson, 2014).

The DSM 5 is used to define what constitutes *substance use* or *dependence*, terms are clinically appropriate and as such should be used in place of "addiction" within the clinical framework, but within this context, addiction will be used interchangeably. The DSM 5 places the following diagnostic criterion for substance use or dependence.

1. Taking the substance in larger amounts or for longer than you're meant to.
2. Wanting to cut down or stop using the substance but not managing to.
3. Spending a lot of time getting, using, or recovering from the use of the substance.
4. Cravings and urges to use the substance.
5. Not managing to do what you should at work, home, or school because of substance use.
6. Continuing to use, even when it causes problems in relationships.
7. Giving up important social, occupational, or recreational activities because of substance use.
8. Using substances again and again, even when it puts you in danger.
9. Continuing to use, even when you know you have a physical or psychological problem that could have been caused or made worse by the substance.
10. Needing more of the substance to get the effect you want (tolerance).
11. Development of withdrawal symptoms, which can be relieved by taking more of the substance.
(American Psychiatric Association, 2013, pp. 490–491)

To be diagnosed as having a substance use disorder an individual must meet at least two of the criterion as stated above, the DSM 5 includes severity qualifiers. These severity qualifiers are: mild, 2–3 symptoms are present, moderate, 4–5 symptoms are present, or severe where 6 or more symptoms are present. An important aspect of addiction is developing a tolerance for the substance of choice. Tolerance is defined as when drugs of abuse are used repeatedly over time with increasing amounts needed to obtain the "high." During this use, the body begins to require more of the drug than was initially used to achieve the "high" or inebriation. At this point, the individual has developed a tolerance for their drug of choice, and more of the drug is required going forward (National Institute on Drug Abuse, 2007, para. 1).

It is important to note that as humans, we are each individually unique in physiology, which affects our tolerance. Each individual is unique, which accounts for the differing levels of addiction in our society (Inaba and Cohen, 2011; Kuhn, Swartzwelder, and Wilson, 2014). Addiction has no single factor that researchers can pinpoint, yet it has been determined that the more risk factors an individual has the more likely they will use and possibly become addicted to particular substances (Inaba and Cohen, 2011; Kuhn, Swartzwelder, and Wilson, 2014). Risk factors vary, but can include: a family history of addiction, social environment, mental health history, life stressors, and individual resilience or stress tolerance (Kuhn, Swartzwelder, and Wilson, 2014).

Within the United States we generally have four social designations of substances: prohibited drugs (e.g., heroin), tolerated drugs (e.g., marijuana), instrumental drugs (e.g., oxycodone), and celebrated drugs (e.g., alcohol). Depending on where the drug falls along this continuum impacts the user's perception of the drug, and this has been found to contribute to how addiction takes root. Drugs that are commonly abused fall under a series of classifications: cannabis or marijuana; depressants such as alcohol; hallucinogens such as LSD or psilocybin mushrooms; inhalants such as nitrous oxide; opioids such as heroin or its relative oxycodone; and stimulants such as cocaine (Inaba and Cohen, 2011; Kuhn, Swartzwelder, and Wilson, 2014).

Why are these designations important? As stated previously, how an individual perceives the substance of choice impacts their usage and views on them. Based on this, it is important to understand the life cycle of addiction. The life cycle of addiction is cyclical in nature, where first use is usually innocuous and without addictive intention. This first stage is either celebratory, initiative (to be one of the group), or out of curiosity. This moves on to more frequent use with mild side effects (e.g., hangovers), then on to justification of use with more consequential side effects. During this time, the individual begins to develop cognitive defenses for their use, then the individual starts to identify with their drug of choice. At this point, the individual starts to detach from their previous world and begins to spend more time within their substance-related world. The individual may or may not start to test control at this point, ideations of "I can quit anytime," etc. Increasing negative side effects and consequences begin to affect the individual, resulting in possible deception and/or theft to obtain drugs. Often this is followed by a resolve to quit, which the person truly believes they can and will do. Then the individual returns to the first stage (Inaba and Cohen, 2011; Kuhn, Swartzwelder, and Wilson, 2014).

Anthony Rivas

See also: Addiction (Non-substance); Pornography

Further Reading

American Psychiatric Association. 2013. *Diagnostic and statistical manual of mental disorders: DSM-5*. Arlington, VA: American Psychiatric Association.

Inaba, Darryl, and Cohen, William E. 2011. *Uppers, downers, all arounders: Physical and mental effects of psychoactive drugs*. Medford, OR: CNS Productions, Inc.

Kuhn, Cynthia, Swartzwelder, Scott, and Wilson, Wilkie. 2014. *BUZZED: The straight facts about the most used and abused drugs from alcohol to ecstasy*. New York, NY: W.W. Norton.

Laxmaiah, M., Sanapati, J., Benyamin, R. M., Atluri, S., Kaye, A. D., and Hirsch, J. A. 2018. "Reframing the prevention strategies of the opioid crisis: Focusing on prescription opioids, fentanyl, and heroin epidemic." *Pain Physician* 21, no. 4, 309–326.

National Institute on Drug Abuse. 2007. "Definition of tolerance." Retrieved from https://www.drugabuse.gov/publications/teaching-packets/neurobiology-drug-addiction/section-iii-action-heroin-morphine/6-definition-tolerance

National Institute on Drug Abuse. 2015. "Nationwide trends." Retrieved from https://www.drugabuse.gov/publications/drugfacts/nationwide-trends

National Institute on Drug Abuse. 2018. "Drug misuse and addiction." Retrieved from https://www.drugabuse.gov/publications/drugs-brains-behavior-science-addiction/drug-misuse-addiction

Adoption

To adopt is defined by Merriam-Webster as a process by which one chooses "to take by choice into a relationship." Based on the juvenile justice system's idea of *parens patriae* (principle that allows court to act as the parent of a child or other individual who needs protection), adoption is a possibility when it is in the best interest of the child. Some types of adoption include familial or stranger adoptions and closed, open, and semi-open adoptions. With adoption, all legal parental rights are given to the adoptive parent(s) and terminated from the birth parent(s). An adoptive family may choose to adopt domestically or internationally, depending on their financial resources. International adoption has increased in popularity since the end of World War II, which has led to sweeping changes to legislation regulating the adoption of children. Also, there are now legal avenues to non-traditional adoptions, including interracial, single-parent, and LGBTQI+ adoptions, that were not previously available.

Closed adoption simply means that there is no contact between the adoptive parent(s) or child(ren) and the biological parent(s). In some jurisdictions, this is more strictly regulated than in others; however, adoption agencies in those strict jurisdictions may allow adopted children to place a waiver in their file to allow contact should someone in the birth family wish to make contact. This assures a mutual desire to meet. Open adoption allows continual contact between the adoptive and biological families at their discretion, which could even include the families spending time together. This is relatively common when someone meets a pregnant woman who is looking to vet the adoptive family before relinquishing her rights to the child or in familial adoptions. Semi-open adoptions also allow contact; however, that contact is handled through an intermediary agency or person instead of direct contact between the families (Children's Service Society, n.d.).

Another piece of information regulated by jurisdiction is the way birth certificates are handled. In some, the birth certificate would have the names of the biological parent(s) redacted, and the names of the adoptive parent(s) entered. In others, a completely new birth certificate might be created with the adoptive parent(s) listed as the birth parent(s). The latter can cause a variety of problems for the adopted child, though, in that they lose all access to family medical and cultural history. There also may be trauma associated with an accidental discovery later in the life of the adoption.

Historically, adoption was not something that happened with regularity (or some regulation) until into the 20th century unless there was a familial tie to the biological family. It simply did not occur to childless couples to adopt due to a desire to maintain lineages. International adoption was never considered until after World War II when so many children were orphaned because of the war (Carlson, 1988, pp. 321–322); however, celebrities in the United States have increased the popularity of this process. Celebrities such as Angelina Jolie, Ewan McGregor, and Madonna have all adopted children from outside the United States, but others do sometimes engage in the international process because it is perceived as easier and less expensive than domestic adoption. While this may or may not be accurate, depending on various fees for legal counsel, home inspections, prenatal care (in the case of some open adoptions), etc., both processes are lengthy and expensive. Generally, an agency is used in the international process, which will help prospective adopters decide if they want to adopt from a country affiliated with The Hague Adoption Convention. When both parties are from Convention countries, there are some increased protections and help to ease the adoption process (Bureau of Consular Affairs, 2019).

According to the American Adoptions website, domestic adoptions can cost as little as $2,000 to as much as $40,000 depending on what avenue the adopting family chooses, while international adoption fees vary depending on the country of origin. Many children available for adoption in the United States are foster care children instead of newborns, and some prospective adoptive parents are unwilling or unable to take on a child with a background that includes abuse or neglect. Most foster care agencies facilitate free or low-cost adoptions, but rarely have newborn babies available.

Due to the types of environments many foster children experience, these children are considered by many to be special needs. This is a broad, overgeneralized term, though. Some foster children have behavioral problems, but many are just older than newborns and not preferred by prospective families. Other children available for adoption, both domestically and abroad, may be available due to developmental delays of varying severity. An adoptive family must weigh all factors, including their support system, access to services, and financial situations before considering this type of adoption so that the children may receive the best care available. The judge who will ultimately decide the adoption case will also consider these factors. *Parens patriae* is central to this entire process and means that the government (or those acting on behalf of the government) works to protect those that cannot do it for themselves. In the case of a child, this is an important distinction as children are unable to control their environments.

Legislation has changed over the decades with regard to adoption and continues to do so. At one time, it was not legal for a single parent to adopt, for one race of adoptive parents to take on children of a different race, or for members of the LGBTQI+ community to adopt. As public opinion changes, so does the legislation, though, lawmakers will continue to address changes to legislation through the lens of the child's best interest. Federal law sets the stage for individual states to write jurisdiction-specific statutes (Katz, 1964, p. 27). Before international adoption became a commonly accepted practice, there was no legislation; however, the federal government, in conjunction with immigration services, has to be involved. A child must be eligible for adoption in their home country, and eligible to come to the United States, and the adoptive parents must be approved to complete the adoption process in the country of origin and the United States for the process to be completed (Carlson, 1988, p. 320). As different countries open their borders for international adoption, American legislation has to be continuously updated to include any international relations issues that may impact the process. International adoption from developing countries and domestic adoptions from impoverished communities has continued to trend upward in the 21st century. Overall, adoption seems to be much more accepted by the community at large than in the past, which makes it easier for all involved parties.

Perhaps the most overlooked aspect of adoption is the lifelong impact that adoption has on those involved. A parent or couple goes through the trauma of giving up or losing a child. A parent or couple introduces this unknown child into their home and must make decisions for that child that include things such as their own marriage decisions, school choices, medical care, social situations and supports, and financial resources. The child, though, will have a variety of issues with which to come to terms. If they are told of their adoption early, they may or may not experience some displacement and a desire to seek out their origins. If they are not informed of their adoption and find out accidentally, it can cause a rift in the parent-child relationship that may be irreparable. Others may seek out and find their birth mother (most common) and develop healthy relationships with this extension of their family or encounter a birth parent who wants nothing to do with them, resulting in rejection. Most children will, at the very least, express curiosity about their biological families; however, many will outgrow that curiosity or simply decide it is unimportant. Much like a biological child's relationship with their parents, too many variables influence the outcome to make sweeping assumptions about how adopted children and their relationships will develop over the life course.

In conclusion, access to support, social services, medical care, and financial resources all play a role in adoption. This is true regardless of the type of adoption or the race, gender, development, or national origin of the child(ren) being adopted. Children orphaned during times of war have increased the popularity of international adoption, which is the easiest it has ever been with legislative updates. Conversely, there are incentives for adopting domestically such as federal funding to the state governments for adopting out foster care, special needs, and particular aged children. Some may see adopting children in need of homes from within their country to be a personal incentive, although others will not consider that to be an issue. Most adoptive parents are in their 30s and 40s due to pursuing careers, long years attempting to conceive, or, perhaps, having and raising biological children first. This seems to indicate more stabilized environments, both financially and emotionally. Regardless, adoption is an extremely personal choice and must be considered with due diligence, and, perhaps because of this, it may be a conscious decision to have children in a way that having biological children is not.

Jennifer M. Miller

See also: Child Custody; Shared Custody

Further Reading

American Adoptions. n.d. "Comparing the costs of domestic, international and foster care adoption." Accessed November 5, 2019, https://www.americanadoptions.com/adopt/the_costs_of_adopting.

Bureau of Consular Affairs. 2019. "Adoption process." Accessed November 30, 2019, https://travel.state.gov/content/travel/en/Intercountry-Adoption/Adoption-Process.html.

Carlson, Richard R. 1988. "Transnational adoption of children." *Tulsa Law Journal* 23, no. 3: 317–377.

Children's Service Society. n.d. "Types of adoption." Accessed November 15, 2019, https://cssutah.org/services/adoption /looking-to-adopt/types-of-adoption /?gclid=EAIaIQobChMIor-0t_iX5gI -VUv_jBx2JhAw-EAAYASAAEgJPIPD _BwE.

Katz, Sanford N. 1964. "Community decision-makers and the promotion of values in the adoption of children." *Social Service Review* 38: 26–41.

Merriam-Webster Dictionary Online, s.v. "Adopt." Accessed December 2, 2019, https://www.merriam-webster.com /dictionary/adopting.

Adoption of Stepchildren

Adoption of stepchildren is one of the most common forms of adoption within the United States. Among all other adoption types, this specifically refers to the process wherein a stepparent is granted equal legal authority and guardianship to the biological child of their birthparent. This process can occur in both married and unmarried partnerships. Often arising because of birthparent divorce, separation, or death of one parent, adoption of stepchildren is an underrepresented area of research in comparison to the general adoption literature. The 2010 United States Census indicated that of the 64.8 million children under the age of 18, four percent were stepchildren and two percent were adopted children (U.S. Census Bureau, 2014). The 2020 Census data on United States demographics and household structure is set to be released in 2023. Although the figures are not concrete,

estimates have shown that only around five percent of children living with one birthparent and one stepparent go through the process of becoming an adopted stepchild (Stewart, n.d.).

Collecting data can be challenging because the census does not explain the different types of adoptions that occur in families. Therefore, adoption of a stepchild often gets misrepresented. For example, the U.S. Census Bureau (2014) provides space on the census forms to indicate "adopted children" but does not provide space for indicating the family relationships that the children are being adopted into (e.g., adopted by a stepparent, adopted by two non-biologically related parents, etc.). This is significant in that it limits the research that can be done on this unique population. As a result, the process of adopting stepchildren is often initially viewed through the legal lens with secondary considerations given to the social-emotional impacts on the child and family.

Blended families, adoption by relatives, or kinship adoption are phrases often used interchangeably within social and political spheres to represent the action of adopting stepchildren. The process of adopting stepchildren is similar to adopting non-stepchildren. For the process to be a legal stepchild adoption, the law requires that both biological parents give consent for the stepparent to assume the legal rights and responsibilities of the birth parent (Stewart, n.d.). This is one barrier that likely contributes to the low number of stepchild adoptions, as birth parents may work together to share custody of their child. Although a stepparent may fill the role of a child's biological parent, they cannot assume legal guardianship until both birthparents provide consent. An exception to this is if one birth parent is not fulfilling their parental duties for at least two consecutive years. Similarly, if one parent's rights have already been terminated by the state then they also no longer have a right to consent. If this is the case, then the remaining parent can consent to the adoption unanimously.

An additional stipulation is that the stepparent and biological parent must be married. In 2015, the Supreme Court ruled that all same-sex couples could access marriage, which included the opportunity of stepparent adoption (lbgtmap.org). A Second Parent Adoption is also an option for people not married; however, only certain U.S. states offer such a possibility. Second Parent Adoption is a type of adoption where the adoption does not require marriage. Ultimately, the adoption process can vary in its legal stipulations and requirements from state to state. For example, some states require that once a child reaches a determined age (usually between 10–14 years old), they too must consent for the adoption to continue. Ultimately, it is best to check with the local state adoption laws for more specific information.

In addition to the legal process, the adoption of stepchildren is an impactful social and emotional process for the family as well. In traditional adoption, the child is the new family member to an existing family culture. In the adoption of a stepchild, the stepparent is the newcomer, bringing their own historical family culture to the family culture of the biological family. As a result, family units with adopted stepchildren face the unique challenge of developing a new and evolved family dynamic. Children in this scenario will also be tasked with navigating the loss of one of their birth parents and the

associated addition of a new parent. This process can be challenging and is often best navigated through the support of community programs and family therapy.

Conclusively, despite the lack of statistics, stepchildren are being adopted by stepparents. Families are legally coming together as blended families, merging social and emotional family norms. Local state laws have made it possible for stepparents to choose to expand their families and make happier households.

Brian Hannigan and Vanessa Perocier

See also: Adoption; Blended Families; Stepfamilies; Stepfamilies, Developmental Stages; Stepfamilies, Laws and Policies

Further Reading

"Foster and adoption laws." Movement Advancement Project. Accessed March 30, 2021, https://www.lgbtmap.org/equality-maps/foster_and_adoption_laws/second_parent_adoption_laws.

Kaldwell, J. 2019. "Should I adopt my stepchild?" Retrieved from https://adoption.com/should-i-adopt-my-stepchild#:~:text=The%20adoption%20of%20a%20stepchild,allow%20the%20stepparent%20to%20adopt.

Pylyser, Charlotte, Buysse, Ann, and Loeys, Tom. "Stepfamilies doing family: A meta-ethnography." *Family Process* 57, no. 2: 496–509. https://doi.org/10.1111/famp.12293.

Steward, Susan D. n.d. *Stepchildren adopted by their stepparents: Where do they fit?* Iowa State University. https://paa2007.princeton.edu/papers/71568

"Unique issues with stepparent adoption." Creating a Family. Accessed April 11, 2018, https://creatingafamily.org/adoption-category/stepparent-adoption-unique-issues/.

U.S. Census Bureau, Kreider, Rose M., and Lofquist, Daphne A. 2014. Adopted children and stepchildren: 2010 § (2014). https://permanent.fdlp.gov/gpo106859 /p20-572.pdf

"Who may adopt, be adopted, or place a child for adoption." 2020. Washington, DC: U.S. Department of Health and Human Services, Administration for Children and Families, Children's Bureau. https://www.childwelfare.gov /pubPDFs/parties.pdf.

Adults and Illness

Millions of spouses and other relationship partners shoulder long-term caregiving responsibilities for loved ones when illness, disability, or age-related problems appear in their marriage or relationship. A 2015 report released by the National Alliance for Caregiving and the AARP found that approximately one in ten caregiving situations in America revolves around a spouse. In some cases, these relationships grow stronger, nurtured by love, patience, and a capacity to reset marriage expectations—especially when the caregiver in question has a strong support network and stability in other aspects of daily life. For example, gender roles and family responsibilities sometimes change dramatically when serious and/or long-term illnesses or disabilities appear. "Spouses need to pause and recognize that their marriage has changed completely and may never return to the way it was," explained psychologist Diana Denholm. "If the sick spouse is still able to communicate, I always recommend that couples talk about the changing relationship openly and honestly, and as soon after it starts changing as possible" (Wynn, 2016).

But the challenges associated with long-term care of spouses and other life partners are considerable, not only in terms of demands on time and effort and household financial resources—all of which can contribute to stress on the caregiver's health—but in feelings of isolation and depression that sometimes accompany a new or intensified or long-time role as caregiver for a wife, husband, partner, or another family member (as in elder care situations, for instance). Studies have also found that spouses perform more tasks and assume greater physical and financial burdens when they become caregivers than adult children placed in the same role for a parent.

Mental health experts emphasize that caregiving often has a cumulative quality, as months of repetition and isolation take their toll. "For unpaid caregivers, the burnout comes from the combination of performing physically and mentally exhausting work, coordinating care and medications, managing their own jobs and families, and navigating the bureaucracies of care and finance," summarized journalist Anne Helen Peterson. "Compassion fatigue and secondary traumatic stress, with symptoms ranging from depression to insomnia to substance abuse, are widespread and largely undiagnosed" (Peterson, 2021).

Studies have also repeatedly confirmed that men are considerably more likely than women to end a marriage if faced with caregiving responsibilities for their spouse. One 2009 study published in *Cancer* followed more than 500 people who had either cancer or multiple sclerosis for five years; it reported that women requiring caregiving from a spouse were six times more likely to be separated or divorced than men in the same situation (Wynn, 2016).

As expected, caregiving arrangements in marriage and other long-term relationships become much more common as couples age—during their transition into retirement and fixed incomes. But although many couples have the financial resources and acumen to secure long-term care insurance or high-quality in-home care for spouses and partners requiring care, millions of others face financial limitations that can make caregiving seem like the only choice.

"Many adults have no plan at all [for long-term care], or assume that Medicare, which currently kicks in at age 65, will cover their health costs," wrote Peterson. "Medicare, however, doesn't cover the long-term daily care—whether in the home or in a full-time nursing facility—that millions of aging Americans require. For that, you either need to pay out of pocket (the median yearly cost of in-home care with a home health aide in 2020 was $54,912, and the median cost for a private room in a nursing home was $105,850) or have less than $2,000 in assets so that you can qualify for Medicaid, which provides health care, including home health care, for more than 80 million low-income Americans" who have an average wait time of more than three years before they can secure a place in the program (Peterson, 2021).

Christine Slovey

See also: Marriage and Legal Planning

Further Reading

Graham, Judith. 2019. "When caring for a sick spouse shakes a marriage to the core." *Kaiser Health News.* https://khn.org/news/when-caring-for-a-sick-spouse-shakes-a-marriage-to-the-core/ (accessed February 14, 2022).

Mitric, Julia. 2014. "As a husband becomes caregiver to his wife, a marriage evolves." *NPR—All Things Considered.* https://www.npr.org/sections/health-shots/2014/07/04/325810067/as-a-husband-becomes-caregiver-to-his-wife-a-marriage-evolves.

Ornstein, Katherine A. 2019. "Spousal caregivers are caregiving alone in the last years of life." *Health Affairs.* https://www.healthaffairs.org/doi/10.1377/hlthaff.2019.00087 (accessed February 14, 2022).

Peterson, Anne Helen. 2021. "The staggering, exhausting, invisible costs of caring for America's elderly." *Vox.com.* https://www.vox.com/the-goods/22639674/elder-care-family-costs-nursing-home-health-care.

Rolland, John S. 2018. *Helping couples and families navigate illness and disability: An integrated approach.* New York: Guilford Press.

Wynn, Paul. 2016. "How to balance being a caregiver and a spouse." *Brain & Life.* https://www.brainandlife.org/articles/succeeding-as-a-spousal-caregiver-means-knowing-when-to-ask/ (accessed February 14, 2022).

Age Differences in Relationships

Significant age disparities exist in many romantic relationships. Many studies have been conducted on age differences in heterosexual, married couples. Historically, researchers have documented a general tendency for males to prefer younger females, and that the age gap between older men and younger women can be twenty years or even more (Buss, 1989, pp. 3–5). According to the 2013 U.S. Population Survey, the highest percentage of relationships feature age disparities of one year or less (33.2 percent). The second highest were those with two or three years between them (20.4 percent), and the third highest were those with four or five years (13.3 percent); husbands tend to be older among all groups. This trend is reflected in some Western European countries as well. The perspective on age differences has changed over time, as mental age does not necessarily correlate with chronological age. A current perspective predicts that a healthy, positive relationship is not linked to a chronological age gap (Brings and Winter, 2019).

Explanations for age differences in relationships vary by culture, but sociologists Albert Eseve, Clara Cortina, and Anna Cabré studied long-term patterns of marital age differences in Spain; this has suggested that people seek partners based on rational choice theory (RCT), according to where they live (Casterline, Williams, and McDonald, 1986, p. 353). In other words, people select partners as a function of their immediate needs. If a decent, stable income is an important variable in someone's life, since older men tend to earn more than women, RCT should reflect the age difference, as women date or marry older men to meet their financial security needs (Casterline, Williams, and McDonald, 1986, p. 355). The researchers proposed that analyzing demographic trends in a specific society will yield a good prediction of age differences in marital relationships among races, ethnicities, and subgroups. Each race and group prioritize cultural values, which can play an instrumental role in selecting a partner: this can similarly result in age differences if shared by others with similar interests. Gender ratio, trends in the workforce, and power dynamics also act to influence age disparities in relationships.

Men who marry younger women have been a dominant trend across cultures, but the opposite seems to be a growing phenomenon as well; this happens more frequently when wealth and physical attractiveness are factored into the equation (Brings and Winter, 2019). Several case studies have indicated why women may desire younger men (Schwarz and Hassebrauck, 2012, p. 447). Reporters Felicia Brings and Susan Winter evaluated approximately 200 relationships and found that younger men were often attracted to age, maturity, and intellectual status. The fact that women live longer on average is a turn on for younger men and this in turn may play a role in their increased longevity. It, particularly for women, is positively associated with sex appeal, so the trend has remained steady. Medical research, reported by Ian Sample (2010), suggests that women seven to nine years older than their husbands or partners have a higher mortality rate than other women; this may indicate that a large age gap in a couple affects the life expectancy of both genders, positively or negatively.

Social expectations across cultures have been associated with age differences in relationships as well. Psychologists Belisa Vranich and Laura Grashow noted that approximately 12 million women in the United States report being happily married to older men, but preferences can also be related to stereotypes or the perception that age gaps are generally seen as socially acceptable. The "half-age-plus seven rule"—is about dating someone whose age is half your own, plus seven, or the social rule defining the youngest age one may date with socially acceptable age—which is perceived as a social prejudgment of age disparity but is still deemed "acceptable" in Western Europe and the United States (Vranich and Grashow, 2008, p. 16). Any substantial difference in gender, demographic trends, or cultural norms contributes to the age in relationships, and, as such, continued research and population data are necessary for better documentation.

Seungyeon Lee

See also: Marital Expectations; Marital Success

Further Reading

Brings, Felicia, and Winter, Susan. 2019. "Men confess: 22 reasons why younger guys fall for older women." *Today*. Accessed March 11, 2019, https://www .today.com/health/men-confess-22-reasons -why-younger-guys-fall-older-women -t74731

Buss, David M. 1989. "Sex differences in human mate preferences: Evolutionary hypotheses tested in 37 cultures." *Behavioral and Brain Sciences* 12, no. 1: 1–14.

Casterline, John, Williams, Lindy, and McDonald, Peter. 1986. "The age difference between spouses: Variations among developing countries." *Population Studies* 40, no. 3: 353–374.

Esteve, Albert, Cortina, Clara, and Cabré, Anna. 2009. "Long term trends in marital age homogamy patterns: Spain, 1922–2006." *Population* 64, no. 1: 173–202.

Sample, Ian. 2010. "Marrying a younger man increases a woman's mortality rate." *The Guardian*. Accessed May 12, 2019, https:// www.theguardian.com/science/2010 /may/12/marrying-younger-man-woman -mortality

Schwarz, Sascha, and Hassebrauck, Manfred. 2012. "Sex and age differences in mate-selection preferences." *Human Nature* 23, no. 4: 447–466.

U.S. Census Bureau, Current Population Survey. 2013. "Married couple family groups, by presence of own children under 18, and age, earnings, education, and race and Hispanic origin of both spouses." *U.S. Census Bureau, Current Population Survey, 2013 Annual Social and Economic Supplement*. Retrieved December 13, 2017, https://www.census .gov/hhes/families/files/cps2013/tabFG3 -all.xls

Vranich, Belisa, and Grashow, Laura. 2008. *Dating the older man: Consider your differences and decide if he's right for you*. Massachusetts: Adam Media.

American Association for Marriage and Family Therapy

The American Association for Marriage and Family Therapy (AAMFT) is the professional association for the field of marriage and family therapy. AAMFT recognizes that relationships are fundamental to the well-being of individuals, couples, families, and communities and represents the professional interests of more than 50,000 marriage and family therapists in the United States and Canada (AAMFT, n.d.). AAMFT strives to advance the profession of marriage and family therapy through research, development, education, and ethical and training standards.

One of AAMFT's primary purposes is to regulate the field and practice of marriage and family therapy (MFT). AAMFT develops standards for graduate education, training, clinical supervision, and clinical practice. Clinical fellows and members of AAMFT have met the highest standards of their profession for education and clinical experience. A second purpose is to advance

MFTs' professional identity and legiti-macy (Bowers, 2007). The field of Mar-riage and Family Therapy is a licensed mental health profession that diagno-ses and treats mental disorders along with facilitating therapeutic relational work in couples and families as well as individuals.

AAMFT, formerly the American Association of Marriage Counselors (AAMFC), was founded in 1942 and originated in the marriage counseling movement (Gurman and Fraenkel, 2002, p. 200). Before this, the field of family therapy considered couple therapy to be an entirely separate profession. AAMC evolved into AAMFT with two goals: to regulate the standards of training and practice of the marriage and family ther-apy profession and to develop an inde-pendent, separate, and distinct, mental health profession. In 1949, AAMFT began to explore licensing marriage therapists. AAMFT invested millions of dollars and countless hours in the regula-tion of the field of marriage and family therapy, ultimately leading to the profes-sion's federal recognition and widespread popularity.

In 1963, California became the first state to regulate MFTs. Michigan and New Jersey followed in 1966 and 1968, while AAMFT continued to build the professional literature. The Com-mission on Accreditation for Mar-riage and Family Therapy Education (COAMFTE) was established in 1974 by the AAMFT Board of Directors to establish the profession's core compe-tencies and training standards. In 1978, COAMFTE was recognized by the U.S. Department of Health Education and Welfare (now the U.S. Department of Education). Throughout the 1970s and 1980s, AAMFT sought recognition as the accrediting body in MFT education and training.

The MFT profession experienced explosive growth in the 1980s, thanks to a formalized legislative grant program that helped AAMFT enact licensure law. The MFT scope of practice was officially defined at this time as the diagnosis and treatment of mental disorders, which allowed MFTs to receive reimbursement from insurance companies. Several other mental health professions, such as clini-cal psychology and counseling, fought against this established scope of MFT practice.

The Association of Marital and Family Therapy Regulatory Boards (AMTRB) was incorporated in 1987 with the sup-port of AAMFT. This independent reg-ulatory board developed the first model of the Code of Ethics as well as the Marriage and Family Therapy National Exam. The AAMFT Model Marriage and Family Therapy Licensure Act sets standards of education for train-ing programs and establishes experience requirements for licensure in each state. As of 2009, all 50 of the United States and the District of Columbia have licensure standards.

As of 2020, AAMFT membership exceeds 50,000 and includes six different levels: Clinical Fellow, Pre-Clinical Fel-low, Allied Mental Health Professional, Pre-Allied Mental Health Professional, Student, and Affiliate. The association offers opportunities for members to earn continuing education hours and hosts a national conference for MFTs each year. AAMFT is led by an Executive Director and a Board of Directors that is elected by the clinical membership.

Katie Nick and Kristina S. Brown

See also: Association of Family and Conciliation Courts; Divorce Education; Parent Education Programs; Relationship Education

Further Reading

American Association of Marriage and Family Therapy. n.d. "About AAMFT." Accessed February 8, 2020. https://www.aamft.org/About_AAMFT/AAMFT.aspx.

Bowers, Michael. 2007. "The making of the MFT profession: Standards, regulation." *Family Therapy Magazine.*

Gurman, Alan S., and Fraenkel, Peter. 2002. "The history of couple therapy: A millennial review." *Family Process* 41 (Fall).

Annulment

Annulments, like divorces, terminate a marriage. If a marriage ends through an annulment, however, it is as if the marriage never existed. This is because an annulment is a court's way of saying that, due to some fatal flaw in the formation of the marriage, the marriage was never actually created.

The concept of annulment in American law comes from the English ecclesiastical (church) courts, which prohibited divorce under any circumstances. Annulment was the only way to end a marriage, and only if the church found that the marriage had not been properly formed, to begin with (Grossman and Guthrie, 1996, p. 309). In the United States, divorce has always been available, but up until the mid-1900s, most states had very restrictive divorce laws (Abrams, 2013, pp. 659–60). Depending on the state, annulments were sometimes easier to obtain than divorces.

With the rise of no-fault divorce over the past 50 years, however, some legal scholars argue that annulments are an antiquated way to end a marriage and are no longer necessary. In many states, courts can divide marital property and debt and award alimony in annulment cases, just as they would in divorce cases. Thus, for many people, there is no practical difference between ending their marriage through divorce or annulment. Nowadays, a person may have religious or moral motivations for seeking an annulment (Grossman and Guthrie, 1996, pp. 325–26), but obtaining a no-fault divorce is almost certainly an easier task.

There are very few grounds, or court-accepted reasons, for seeking an annulment. Contrary to what may be portrayed on television, annulments are now quite rare and often difficult to obtain. They are generally not available to parties who simply regret a hasty marriage and are looking for a quick and easy way to dissolve it. For instance, just because a marriage has not been consummated does not mean it is eligible to be annulled.

An annulment is only available when a fatal impediment to forming a lawful marriage existed at the time the parties married. In these circumstances, an annulment declares the marriage void or voidable. A void marriage never existed in the first place. A voidable marriage is one in which an impediment existed at the time of the marriage but is valid unless one of the spouses seeks to have it declared invalid. The following types of marriages are usually considered void from their inception: (1) incestuous marriages, where the parties are too closely related to each other, either by blood or marriage; and (2) bigamous marriages, where one of the parties is already married to someone else. It is not necessary to get an annulment if a marriage is void because it was never formed in the first place, but many people choose to go through the court process so they have documentation or proof that the marriage was invalid. The following circumstances usually make a marriage voidable: (1) one of the parties to the marriage was under the age of consent at the time the parties married; (2) one of the parties was mentally incapacitated in some way at the time of the marriage and thus unable to consent to the marriage; (3) the parties did not have mutual assent to marry because they did not give serious thought to it or married as a joke; (4) one spouse is impotent (unable to have sex); or (5) one spouse lied to the other about something essential to the marriage to convince that person to marry him/her (this is often called fraudulent inducement to marry).

Like much of family law, the law of annulments varies by state, including the grounds for requesting an annulment and the proof required to prove those grounds. While there have been calls to reform or repeal annulment law, annulment statutes persist in every jurisdiction.

Shannon Roddy

See also: Divorce, Process of; Divorce, Types of; Divorce Pre-1950

Further Reading

Abrams, Kerry. 2013. "The End of Annulment." *Journal of Gender, Race and Justice* 16, no. 3: 681–704.

Cotter, David M. 2004. "Misrepresenting or Concealing Prior Marital History as a Ground for Annulment." *Divorce Litigation* 16, no. 12: 219.

Grossman, Joanna, and Chris Guthrie. 1996. "The Road Less Taken: Annulment at the Turn of the Century." *The American Journal of Legal History* 40, no. 3: 307–330.

Anti-miscegenation Laws

Anti-miscegenation laws in America derive from a history loaded with racial disparity. The earliest recorded interracial marriage, between John Rolfe and Pocahontas in 1614, was revolutionary and had supporters. Following this union, however, Virginia started punishing interracial relationships and ultimately outlawed the practice. Between 1630 and 1640, there were two cases in Virginia in which a white man was punished for initiating a relationship with a Black woman. By 1691 Virginia had legally prohibited interracial marriage.

Nine states and the District of Columbia have never had anti-miscegenation laws. Some states' anti-miscegenation laws restricted people of all different races from being married. Others restricted whites from marrying non-whites. In 1850, California restricted whites from marrying Blacks or those who were mulatto. In 1908, Oklahoma restricted Blacks from marrying non-Blacks. Louisiana banned marriage between Black people and Native Americans in 1920. In 1935, Maryland banned marriage between Blacks and Filipinos.

As those laws indicate, anti-miscegenation laws in America were not only passed hundreds of years ago, when racist attitudes and beliefs were so pervasive that slavery was officially sanctioned, but also well into the twentieth century. During the late 1800s and early 1900s, academicians, scientists, and members of the general public believed that there was a connection between biological factors, racial groups, and social problems. Cesare Lombroso, in the late 1800s, focused on the biological factors involved in crime and concluded that criminals had atavistic qualities that led to their criminality; essentially, he believed that criminals had more primitive genetics. Forced sterilization took place in many English-speaking countries during the late 1800s and early 1900s, and in the 1930s and early 1940s, Germany's Adolf Hitler used these ideas to justify separating people by race and ethnicity and, ultimately, putting Jews and others he deemed to be inferior to death.

Despite the reality of mixed-race relations, various state laws defined race with specific terms that were often left undefined. For instance, in Virginia in 1924, the anti-miscegenation law placed everyone into the categories of "white," "colored," or "non-white." In many states, laws made mention of "indians," "mulattoes," or "malays," without adequately defining these terms. Still, other states would declare that someone was Black because they were 1/8 or 1/16 Black. Ultimately, the "one drop rule" became a way to define the lines between white, Black, mulatto, or Native American. The one-drop rule stated that for a person to be considered truly white, a person was required to have no ancestral influence of a different race—or in other words, not a single drop of non-white blood coursing through their veins.

Intermixing of the races was consistently taboo throughout colonial and early America. Upon the issuance of the Emancipation Proclamation following the Civil War, laws and social mores continued to make interracial marriage virtually nonexistent. In the 1883 case *Pace v. Alabama*, for example, the Supreme Court determined that Alabama's anti-miscegenation statute was constitutional. In this case, Tony Pace (a Black man) and Jane Cox (a white woman) received two years in prison for "living together in a state of adultery." This ruling held for nearly 80 years and was not overturned until 1964 in *McLaughlin v. Florida*. In this case, an interracial couple was living together and received a 30-day sentence. The Supreme Court of the United States ruled Florida's anti-miscegenation law unconstitutional.

Outside of the court system, several constitutional amendments have been put before Congress to ban interracial marriage. Following the conclusion of the Civil War, in 1871, Andrew King, a Democrat from Missouri, proposed the criminalization of these marriages nationwide. King argued that an amendment was needed because the interpretation of the fourteenth amendment of the Constitution deprived the States of the power to prohibit the intermarriage of the white and colored races. Despite an impassioned attempt at passing this amendment, it did not continue through the House Judiciary Committee. Although the legislative branch made several attempts to influence the racial allowances of marriage, the issue was predominantly contained within the court system. Two of the most monumental rulings are *Perez v. Sharp* and *Loving v. Virginia*.

In 1948, The California State Supreme Court struck down an anti-miscegenation law in *Perez v. Sharp*, ruling that it violated the First and Fourteenth Amendments. Andrea Perez (a Mexican American woman) and

Sylvester Davis (an African American man) had applied for a marriage license and were denied. The law was overturned by the California State Supreme Court in a split 4–3 decision. *Perez v. Sharp* was the first case in the 20th century to negate a state anti-miscegenation law. In 1948, 30 of the 48 states had anti-miscegenation laws.

Another, even more, momentous ruling, was *Loving v. Virginia* (1967). This U.S. Supreme Court decision struck down all state laws forbidding interracial marriage. In 1967, 16 states had anti-miscegenation laws. In this case, Richard (white) and Mildred (Black and Native American) married in 1958 in Washington, D.C. (where interracial marriage was legal). After moving to Virginia, however, they were indicted for violating Virginia's anti-miscegenation laws. They pleaded guilty and were each given a 1-year jail sentence which was suspended on the condition that they leave the state and not return as a couple for 25 years. By 1963, the Lovings tried to have their sentences vacated. Specifically, Richard and Mildred Loving claimed that Virginia's anti-miscegenation law violated the 14th Amendment. Ultimately, in 1967, the Supreme Court ruled 9–0 in their favor. The legal arguments made in the *Loving v. Virginia* case would later be used by those who supported the legalization of homosexual marriage.

Since 1967, all states that had anti-miscegenation laws on the books have repealed the legislation. Alabama was the last to do so in 2000. Even then, however, barely 60 percent of the voters were in favor of repealing their anti-miscegenation laws; 40 percent were against it.

Daniel W. Phillips III and Morgan
Watkins Murray

See also: Interfaith Marriage; International Marriage; Interracial Marriage; Socioeconomic Status and Marriage

Further Reading

Anomaly, Jonathan. 2018. "Defending eugenics: From cryptic choice to conscious selection." *Monash Bioethics Review* 25(1–4): 24–35.

Stein, Edward. 2004. "Past and present proposed amendments to the United States Constitution regarding marriage." *Washington Law Review* 82(3): 611–685.

Swenson, Sue. 2019. "New eugenics, old problems." *Journal of Policy and Practice in Intellectual Disabilities* 16(2): 141–143.

Whitman, James. 2018. *Hitler's American Model: The United States and the Making of Nazi Race Law.* Princeton, NJ: Princeton University Press.

Arranged Marriage

Arranged marriage is an agreement in which the bride and groom are matched by others, predominantly by parents and/or other family members. It has been a historically common practice across the world up until the early twentieth century (O'Brien, 2009, p. 40) and still exists in contemporary societies (Reis and Sprecher, 2009, p. 113). Several factors have encouraged the practice of arranged marriages, such as family inheritance issues, cultural and religious beliefs, politics, upholding traditional values, a strong tie among certain ethnic groups, and/or age limits. In some cases, professional matchmakers or companies have assisted in finding a potential spouse for an individual. A prenuptial agreement, a written contract created by the bride and groom before marriage that sets out the property and financial rights of the two parties in the event of divorce or death, can be discussed with close family members. In most cases, however, arranged marriage is based on mutual trust between the bride and groom and their respective families (Ghimire et al., 2006, p. 1181). If both parties feel that trust no longer exists, they are likely to file a divorce by seeking professional help. Arranged marriages are prominent in several cultures, including those in regions of East and Southwest Asia. The practice is much less prevalent—but still does occur—in Western Europe and the United States, primarily among particular immigrant groups (Fish, 2010). Marriage is seen as an important foundation, so arranged marriages have extremely clear parameters that emphasize family alliances and specify financial rights and obligations.

Four types of arranged marriage have been predominant for many years: autonomous marriage, self-selected marriage, consensually arranged marriage, and forced-arranged marriage (Ghimire et al., 2006, pp. 1181–1182). Autonomous marriage is a form of agreement between the bride and groom. Self-selected marriage is also an agreement between the bride and groom, but they tend to seek advice on potential issues before the wedding. Parents and families share practical advice and help the arranged marriage as needed, but the bride and groom decide what is necessary for any legal agreement. Both autonomous and self-selected marriages are chosen if the bride and groom are consenting adults. Consensually arranged marriage takes place when the individuals are introduced, with their parents' or legal guardians' recommendation and consent. This can be refused if one party thinks the marriage may not work, but in some societies, parents or legal guardians also have the right to object to it—especially if the bride or groom is not a consenting adult. Engagement and marriage are considered to be contracts, in which both parties must agree to the terms. Forced-arranged marriage is a situation in which the bride and groom do not have a choice. Parents, legal guardians, and/or family members have full authority to specify how, when, and under what conditions the marriage should proceed. In consensual and forced-arranged marriages, the bride and groom have the least (or almost no) power to share their opinions; this type of arranged marriage elicits public attention when legal separation or divorce is necessary (Anitha and Gill, 2009, pp. 165–167). Arranged marriages continue to establish and maintain familial and societal expectations.

Arranged marriage is not uncommon in the United States—if the definition of "arranged" includes unions of teens who must secure the approval of parents or other guardians before marriage. According to a 2016 study from the Pew Research Center and the American Community Survey, approximately five out of every 1000 individuals between 15 and 17 years old are legally married. The rate of teen marriage varies, depending on the state in which the couple lives, but data indicate that teen marriage is generally higher in southwestern areas of the country, including Texas, Oklahoma, Arkansas, Nevada, and California. Several states allow minors to legally marry with judicial and parental consent. CBS News reporter Shanika Gunaratna studied child marriage and noted that 27 states do not specify a minimum age, below which a minor would be prohibited from a legal or legitimate marriage (Ganaratna, 2017). Teen pregnancy is a consideration when proceeding with obtaining a legal marriage as well. In Florida, for example, age minimums can be waived by judges issuing marriage licenses if one of the parties to the marriage is pregnant (McClendon and Sanstrom, 2016).

A handful of ethnic groups in the United States still practice one of four types of arranged marriage, but certain issues continue to escalate. Journalist Eleanor Bader provided a case study of a Jewish-American woman in an arranged marriage, which was based on her mother's will. The woman thought the groom was the "right" fit, as they were each part of a Jewish-Orthodox community: they were married soon after, but several years of domestic abuse ended this connection (Bader, 2013). Women from certain religious and ethnic backgrounds (e.g., Jewish-Orthodox, Hindu, Muslim, and Sikhs) are also more likely to be pressured into arranged marriages. Some maintain a positive marital relationship, while others experience domestic violence, lack of proper education, and financial difficulties.

Seungyeon Lee

See also: Diversity in Marriage; Marriage, Financial Implications

Further Reading

Anitha, Sundari, and Aisha Gill. 2009. "Coercion, consent, and the forced marriage debate in the UK." *Family Legal Studies* 17: 165–184.

Bader, Eleanor J. 2013. "Arranged marriage is a U.S. issue." *News Analysis.* Accessed April 20, 2013. https://truthout.org/articles/arranged-marriage-is-a-us-issue/

Fish, Jefferson M. 2010. "Arranged marriage: Billions of people live in arranged marriages. Why?" *Psychology Today.* Accessed on April 27, 2010. https://www.psychologytoday.com/us/blog/looking-in-the-cultural-mirror/201004/arranged-marriages

Ganaratna, Shanika. 2017. "The 'ugly' reality of child marriage in the U.S." *CBS News.* Accessed May 5, 2017. https://www.cbsnews.com/news/child-marriage-in-the-u-s-surprisingly-widespread/

Ghimire, Dirgha J., William G. Axinn, Scott T. Yabiku, and Arland Thornton. 2006. "Social change, premarital nonfamily experience, and spouse choice in an arranged marriage society." *American Journal of Sociology* 111, no. 4: 1181–1218.

McClendon, David, and Aleksandra Sanstrom. 2016. "Child marriage is rare in the U.S., though this varies by state." *Factank: News in the Numbers.* Accessed November 1, 2016. https://www.pewresearch.org/fact-tank/2016/11/01/child-marriage-is-rare-in-the-u-s-though-this-varies-by-state/

Myers, Jane E., Jayamala Madahill, and Lynne R. Tingle. 2005. "Marriage satisfaction and wellness in India and the United States: A preliminary comparison of arranged marriage and marriage of choice." *Journal of Counseling & Development* 82, no. 2: 183–190.

O'Brien, Jodi. 2009. *Encyclopedia of gender and society*, *1*, pp. 40–42. Thousand Oaks, CA: SAGE Publications.

Reis, Harry, and Susan Sprecher. 2009. *Encyclopedia of human relationships*, pp. 113–117. London, UK: SAGE Publications.

Association of Family and Conciliation Courts

The Association of Family and Conciliation Courts (AFCC) is a multidisciplinary, international, professional organization composed of judges, attorneys, clinicians, parent educators, mediators, and other family court professionals. AFCC members work in a variety of settings in the public, private, and non-profit sectors, but all share a central goal to help resolve family conflict in healthy ways. AFCC serves not only as a professional membership organization, offering training and support for its members but also as an educational resource for professionals and the public. Amongst their more high-profile activities, AFCC maintains a prestigious academic journal, produces practice guidelines, and hosts interdisciplinary task forces.

AFCC offers professional training through conferences and seminars. For over 50 years they have hosted an annual professional conference bringing together leaders in the legal and mental health fields to address continuing and emerging issues in family courts. For over a quarter century they have also hosted a bi-annual Symposium on Child Custody evaluation and issues. In addition to these long-running programs AFCC has hosted interdisciplinary trainings with the American Academy of Matrimonial Lawyers, the National Council of Juvenile and Family Court Judges, and local and regional training events throughout the United States, Canada, and Australia.

For over half a century, AFCC has published a quarterly academic journal.

Launched as *Conciliation Courts Review* in 1963, the journal now known as *Family Court Review* is described by the publishers as "the leading interdisciplinary academic and research journal for family law professionals" (Wiley Online Library, 2020). Editorial management of the journal is through the Hofstra Law School Center for Children, Families, and the Law, adding both academic rigor and expertise to the publication.

Through their Center for Excellence in Family Court Practice, AFCC has served as a coordinating body for collaborative endeavors and interdisciplinary initiatives across all fields of family law. AFCC has worked in collaboration with the National Council of Juvenile and Family Court Judges on domestic violence issues; the Institute for the Advancement of the American Legal System on resources for lawyers, litigants, and non-legal professionals; the American Bar Association Family Law Section and the National Council of Dispute Resolution Organizations on Standards of Practice for Family and Divorce Mediation; multiple law schools on diverse issues such as improving family law education, mediation, and other forms of alternative dispute resolution; and even state judicial branches to implement empirically-based screening instruments (a project which eventually became a semi-finalist in the Kennedy School of Government Innovations in American Government Awards). Drawing on interdisciplinary resources from within their own membership AFCC has also published guides for educators working with separating, divorcing, and never-married parents and their children; profiles of exemplary and innovative family court programs; and multiple professional guidelines related to child custody evaluation, parenting coordination, and court-connected therapy.

In all of this work, AFCC remains dedicated as an organization to helping children and families by finding healthy solutions to family conflicts. Running through all aspects of the organization is a clear belief in the ability to achieve the best possible outcomes through collaborative work at all levels of the justice system and support of self-determination for families who access it.

Aaron Robb

See also: American Association for Marriage and Family Therapy; Divorce Education

Further Reading

Association of Family and Conciliation Courts. 2016. *Guidelines for Use of Social Science Research in Family Law.* Madison, WI: Author. Retrieved February 4, 2020 from www.afccnet.org/Resource -Center/Practice-Guidelines-and -Standards.

Association of Family and Conciliation Courts. 2020. "About AFCC." Accessed December 22, 2020. www.AFCCnet.org /About/About-AFCC.

Family Law Education Reform Project. 2020. "About the FLER Project Website." Accessed December 22, 2020. https://www.flerproject.org/?q=node/12.

National Council of Juvenile and Family Court Judges. 2020. "Child Custody and Supervised Visitation." Accessed December 22, 2020. https://www.ncjfcj .org/family-violence-and-domestic -relations/child-custody/.

Wiley Online Library. 2020. "Family Court Review An Interdisciplinary Journal." Accessed December 22, 2020. https:// onlinelibrary.wiley.com/journal/17441617.

Attachment Theory of Love

Couples come to therapy with a variety of concerns. According to Doss, Simpson, and Christensen (2004), the most common issues reported are communication-related concerns and lack of affection, financial and childrearing stressors, followed by divorce and separation concerns. Communication issues range from lack of communication, communication difficulties, or miscommunication of feelings. In many cases, communication difficulties can be related to attachment styles. A therapeutic intervention named Emotionally Focused Therapy (EFT) began with Leslie Greenberg (1979) and was further developed by Sue Johnson (1985) to help connect couples who are struggling with connection and intimacy. EFT is a short-term, structured, therapy intervention that can be effective in working with couples presenting with attachment-related issues. Marital distress is often accompanied by rigid and repetitive interactional patterns; these patterns become a sort of dance, a habit for which we find ourselves stuck in that role. Couples can feel stuck or frozen. When the disconnect occurs, certain reactions can develop, such as the removal of love, complaining, expressing contempt, and/or staying in a defensive position with the partner. John Gottman (2002) studied couples' interactional patterns and found behaviors that are marriage-ending: criticism, defensiveness, contempt, and stonewalling (or withdrawing emotionally from interacting) (Gottman, 2013). He called these behaviors the Four Horseman. Gottman said that couples are not able to connect if they are absorbed by a negative state, meaning they are stuck in this internal pattern of responding to their partner. Partners then get into a pattern of pursuer/distance, where one partner chases and the other feels chased. These patterns relate to our earlier forms of interactions with our primary caregivers, and how our internal attachment system formed. Emotionally Focused Couples therapy is a process of moving couples from a state of disconnection to a place of connection and emotional bonding by addressing underlying attachment dysfunction and healing attachment wounds.

Within relationships, our perception of love, connection, and safety is understood through the lens of Attachment Theory. Rene Spitz, who observed both abandoned infants in hospitals and failure-to-thrive infants, was among the first to contribute to this body of research. These babies often had their basic needs met, such as food and water, but were unable to thrive and at times did not survive infancy.

Scientist Harry Harlow's experiment with rhesus monkeys demonstrated that despite the monkey going to the wire figure for basic needs, it spent the majority of its time with the cloth monkey for comfort. Based on these observations, and Darwin's evolutionary theory, John Bowlby founded attachment theory.

Evolutionary theory explains attachment as necessary due to the nature of our species' vulnerability in infancy; protection is needed physically and psychologically for the species to make it to reproduction age and to pass on its genetic makeup (Simpson and Rholes, 2017). The protection requires extended interactions that require an attachment system in place for the caregiver to want to protect the young.

Simpson and Rholes (2017) further elaborate that this system "motivates young individuals to seek out physical and emotional proximity to their primary caregivers, especially when they are distressed" (1). Therein, at our foundation, there is a need to seek safety and comfort when distressed and vulnerable.

Attachment theory began with the work of John Bowly in 1958 and continued with Mary Ainsworth in 1967 when she researched the interactions of mothers and their infants in what she called a strange situation. Attachment research has continued, with the strange situation replicated many times over. The research from John Bowlby's work on attachment found several patterns of responses to separation, including protest, despair, and detachment. An early collaborator of Bowlby was Mary Ainsworth. Her experiment elaborated on Bowlby's work and included observations of mother and infant interactions, her famous experiment "The Strange Situation" identified these consistent patterns of attachment responses. Ainsworth observed parent and child interaction, observed the child's reaction when separated from the mother, and then again upon the reunion. She noted that the child often used the mother as a secure base to explore and to come close if a stranger entered. She then asked her mother to leave and then re-enter. It was during the process of separation and reunion that the child demonstrated their stress response to the separation, reaction to the "stranger," and if they were able to use their mothers as a source of comfort upon return. Upon the return of the mother, on both occasions, there were four observed behaviors directed at the mother: proximity and contact seeking; contact maintaining; avoidance of proximity and contact; and resistance to contact and comforting.

Mary Ainsworth (1967) found that infants and children develop styles or patterns of attachment in response to their caregivers. The style of attachment is secure, insecure, or disorganized. Two primary styles of insecurity are dominant in most parent/child relationships: ambivalent and avoidant. Children presenting with insecure attachment were unable to use the parent as a safe base and in the ambivalent attachment style, the infant would respond to the parent with frustration, anger, or hurt (resistance to contact/comfort); with avoidant attachment style, the infant would respond to the parent in a sullen and disconnected manner (avoidance of proximity/contact). While the majority of children—nearly 70%—were securely attached, the other nearly 30% demonstrated insecure attachment; with most of that percentage broken into two primary types of insecure attachment: anxious-ambivalent and anxious-avoidant with a small percentage of disorganized attachment. Disorganized attachment occurs in situations with severe abuse and neglect, where the child has developed odd or inconsistent behaviors in response to the caregiver. In cases of abuse and neglect, the inconsistent and negative response created confusion for the child and the abuse increased the child's stress response. According to Ringel and Brandell (2012), this style was "characterized by contradictory behavior patterns" such as avoidance, freezing, or dazed behaviors and interrupted movements and expressions (80). In all three cases of insecure attachment, the child has high levels of cortisol, a hormone released in a stress response.

The caregiver/child separation creates anxiety in the child's response. The securely attached children were able to take comfort from their parents, or another caregiver in their parents' absence, and use them as a secure base to decrease their anxiety. The children with an anxious attachment style were unable to take comfort from their parents, and the anxiety remained. When the parent is consistently warm and responsive, the child learns that the parent can serve to alleviate stress and anxiety. Attachment patterns are necessary for the protection of vulnerable youth. Proximity to caregivers offsets the distress, allowing the youth to focus on other developmental life tasks (Simpson and Rholes, 2017). During a stress response, children are to use their parents as a secure base to seek comfort and safety, this helps them manage their stress response and increases the oxytocin (the bonding hormone) that alleviates the stress response. Once comfort has eased the distress signal, the attachment system turns off, and the child can focus on other tasks. When security is not achieved through the relationship, the system remains activated and anxiety remains. When the caregiver is inconsistently responsive, the child learns that they cannot rely on the caregiver and thus the anxiety response remains. This attachment pattern continues into adulthood. Kids with an anxious-ambivalent attachment style demonstrate overt levels of anger and protest toward caregivers when distressed, these children have an outward expression of their distress. In adult relationships, the outward expression of distress is aimed at the partner in behaviors described by Gottman such as defensiveness and the pursuer response. Kids with anxious-avoidant attachment demonstrate levels of disengagement with distress, these children have an inward expression of their distress. In adult relationships, this presents Gottman's stonewalling, emotional detachment, and distance responses in the relationship.

Attachment styles affect all relationships, including how we react to our family of origin, friends, and later romantic relationships. Through these relationships, it shapes an individual's understanding of themselves through an internal working model, in other words how the individual views themself, others, and relationships in general. This influences how we connect, communicate, and how we see our role with friends and partners. People with a secure attachment style have an internal working model of themselves as confident and others as relatively dependable and well-intentioned, and they can rely on others in times of stress. They often find satisfaction, trust, commitment, and dependence in relationships. Those with an anxious-ambivalent style view themselves as unsure, misjudged, but well-intentioned; and others as unreliable or unwilling to commit. They find themselves less able to trust in relationships and experience less satisfaction, and therefore they have an imbalance of dependence in those relationships. Lastly, those with an anxious-avoidant style have an internal working model of undeserving, cynical, and standoffish, and others as unreliable or over-eager to commit. This attachment style tends to be more reserved and distant in relationships, experiencing less trust, commitment, and dependence.

This attachment system is maintained through a system referred to as a working model and this working model is activated during times of stress and distress (Simpson and Rholes, 2017). Specifically, internal, external, or chronic stress activates this response system, and in marriage/relationships, this internal activation is what Gottman referred to as absorbed by a negative state. According to Simpson and Rholes (2017), two dimensions underlie the adult romantic relationship: avoidance and anxiety. Securely attached individuals' response to stress is to lean on their partner for comfort. Individuals with anxious-ambivalent attachment react to distress individually, often uncertain or reactive in their response to their partner. Finally, anxious-avoidant attachment styles have a heightened emotional reaction and pull away from their partner during times of stress.

Individuals with secure attachment find their needs met with others who are securely attached and Emotionally Focused Therapy aims at this goal of connection and attachment. Insecure attachment styles find their counterpart with attachment style, the two mechanisms of coping tend to repeat or reaffirm patterns from childhood with one distant reserved partner and one reactive. This inward and outward pattern of distress management continues with a pursuer/distance relationship dance.

However, it is important to note that attachment styles are fluid and thus can change through newly learned behaviors. The challenge is that in times of stress, we tend to revert to earlier forms of coping. In romantic relationships, as challenges develop and intimacy deepens, a stressful event (for example, a disagreement) can lead to a stress response and when the stress response is triggered, it coincides with our attachment stress response.

Meaning, if one partner feels stressed *and* disconnected, they may respond in a reactive or disconnected manner. This earlier attachment response heightens the anxiety response and the individual is in the same pattern of self-protection, unable to use the partner as a safe base. In a securely attached relationship, the partners can use the support of the other to minimize the stress response.

Attachment is a fluid process; within relationships, we adjust our patterns of response. However, these newly learned patterns require practice, meaning that anything new takes a little while before it is automatic. In times of stress, attachment elicits the same stress response and it is common to react in much the way we are familiar while forgetting new patterns of response. In a stress state, there is something called the "amygdala hijack" which refers to an amygdala response, reactive to immediate sensations in immediately identifying threats to safety. As our brain filters sensory information, a part of our brain, the amygdala, is responsible for reacting to that stimulus rather quickly. This, again, is an evolutionary response. During stressful times, the pre-frontal cortex, which is responsible for executive functioning (planning, logic, self-regulation, focus) is not as active. In addition, the hippocampus (memory) is not as active. We operate on "auto-pilot" and in the stressful state, respond quickly by "muscle memory," patterns of behavior when practiced become muscle memory, like driving, we remember and our body remembers. The practice of new attachment styles requires time and practice before it can become our new "muscle memory." The stress state can often linger if during childhood there was frequent exposure to stressors. This rewires our brain to react quickly and automatically to stress. The "fight or flight" response to stress is initiated as part of the sympathetic nervous system response. Part of learning the new behavior is to initiate the parasympathetic nervous system, which allows other bodily functions to resume (eating, sleeping, engaging the pre-frontal cortex).

According to Kunce and Shaver (1994), adult caregiving behaviors include four characteristics: proximity, sensitivity, control, and compulsive caregiving. These patterns of reactivity to stress persist from childhood, whether it is in our caregiving response or our internal response to anxiety and fear.

These behaviors, when encouraged and practiced, help mend the discord within marriages. The ability to be vulnerable with a partner and develop trust that the partner is well-intentioned is the key to deepening intimacy.

Love necessitates intimacy. Intimacy can take two forms: emotional and sexual. Within relationships, the latter can often be confused with lust. However, for longevity in relationships, the balance between emotional and sexual intimacy is the key to a deeper and long-lasting relationship. Brené Brown (2010), a researcher investigating connection, found that empathy and vulnerability are important in all relationships. The initial wound was that the primary caretaker was inconsistent or unsafe, therefore the pattern in future relationships is to protect the self, and therein vulnerability is not easily explored. In taking risks in intimacy and vulnerability, we develop a new meaning and a new working model of ourselves within relationships.

The emotional state of lust and infatuation can further drive those with an insecure attachment to continue the cycle of engagement and retreating since that emotional state is inconsistent. This does nothing to alter the internal or external working model of relationships but rather continues the cycle of response.

In contrast, love is seen as an intimate relationship that involves the sharing of thoughts, emotions, and ideas, challenges our working model, and allows us to alter our attachment style within this dimension. It is within the state of vulnerability that allows the other to feel the comfort and proximity that allows the attachment system to turn off and relieves anxiety and fear, thus challenging the adult working model.

This consistent process allows the attachment system response to move to a more secure attachment style.

As the adult attachment patterns soften, and the partner learns to communicate their feelings and be vulnerable with their partner, this allows the relationship to deepen which therein deepens the level of intimacy experienced by both partners both sexually and emotionally. The key is maintenance of this model consistently for the working model (both internal and external) to shift and change. As partners communicate, sharing feelings and thoughts openly, they develop a better sense of what the other needs and therein change their caregiving response. As our working model changes, it alters how we see ourselves, ourselves within a relationship, how we view relationships, and how to respond to others' needs. The therapeutic intervention that addresses this phenomenon is in repairing attachment wounds, such as in Emotionally Focused Therapy.

Bita Ashouri Rivas

See also: Love, Connection, and Intimacy; Love at First Sight; Styles of Love; Triangular Theory of Love

Further Reading

Brown, Brené. 2010. *The Gifts of Imperfection: Let Go of Who You Think You're Supposed to Be and Embrace Who You Are.* Simon and Schuster.

Crowell, Judith A., and Everett Waters. 1994. "Bowlby's Theory Grown Up: The Role of Attachment in Adult Love Relationships." *Psychological Inquiry* 5, no. 1: 31–34.

Dillow, Megan R., Alan K. Goodboy, and San Bolkan. 2014. "Attachment and the Expression of Affection in Romantic Relationships: The Mediating Role of Romantic Love." *Communication Reports* 27, no. 2: 102–15.

Doss, Brian D., Lorelei E. Simpson, and Andrew Christensen. 2004. "Why Do Couples Seek Marital Therapy?" *Professional Psychology: Research and Practice* 35, no. 6: 608.

Galinha, Iolanda, Costa Oishi, Shigehiro Pereira, Cicero Wirtz, and Roberto Esteves. 2014. "Adult Attachment, Love Styles, Relationship Experiences and Subjective Well-Being: Cross-Cultural and Gender Comparison between Americans, Portuguese, and Mozambicans." *Social Indicators Research* 119, no. 2: 823–52.

Gottman, John Mordechai. 2013. *Marital Interaction: Experimental Investigations.* Elsevier.

Greenberg, Leslie S. 1979. "Resolving Splits: Use of the Two Chair Technique." *Psychotherapy: Theory, Research & Practice* 16, no. 3: 316.

Johnson, Susan M. 2019. *The Practice of Emotionally Focused Couple Therapy: Creating Connection.* Routledge.

Kunce, Linda J., and Phillip R. Shaver. 1994. "An Attachment-theoretical Approach to Caregiving in Romantic Relationships." In K. Bartholomew and D. Perlman (Eds.), *Attachment Processes in Adulthood,* pp. 205–237. Jessica Kingsley Publishers.

Naar, Hichem. 2013. "A Dispositional Theory of Love." *Pacific Philosophical Quarterly* 94, no. 3: 342–57.

Péloquin, Katherine, Audrey Brassard, Marie-France Lafontaine, and Phillip R. Shaver. 2014. "Sexuality Examined Through the Lens of Attachment Theory: Attachment, Caregiving, and Sexual Satisfaction." *The Journal of Sex Research* 51, no. 5: 561–76.

Ringel, Shoshana, and Jerrold R. Brandell. 2012. *Trauma: Contemporary Directions in Theory, Practice, and Research.* Cengage.

Shaver, Phillip R., and Cindy Hazan. 1988. "A Biased Overview of the Study of Love." *Journal of Social and Personal Relationships* 5, no. 4: 473–501.

Shpall, Sam. 2018. "A Tripartite Theory of Love." *Journal of Ethics & Social Philosophy* 13, no. 2: 91.

Simpson, Jeffry A. 1990. "Influence of Attachment Styles on Romantic Relationships." (Interpersonal Relations and Group Processes). *Journal of Personality and Social Psychology*, 59(5), 971–980.

Simpson, J. A., and W. Steven Rholes. 2017. "Adult Attachment, Stress, and Romantic Relationships." *Current Opinion in Psychology*, 13, 19–24. doi:10.1016/j.copsyc.2016.04.006

B

Bachelor Parties

The term "bachelor party" is commonly used in the Western tradition. In the United States (and some Western European countries), it is often known as a "stag party." Australians call it "a buck's night," which refers to a party for a soon-to-be-married man. It refers to a celebration among the groom's male friends and brothers, connoting the end of bachelorhood. The history of bachelor parties began as early as the 5th century BCE in ancient Greece, but it later passed through several Western countries, including the United States. The original meaning of bachelor is "a young knight-in-training." It was first mentioned in Chaucer's *The Canterbury Tales*, and was later introduced as a bachelor's party, that is, a "jolly old party."

A groom's close male friends (and male siblings) coordinate this party before the wedding ceremony, which can vary from a half-day to a week. References to this term were made in the 19th century as "stag nights" (Bradshaw, Bishop, and Tetsuo 2007). The party traditionally involved a black tie, hosted by the father (or the equivalent) of the groom, along with plenty of food, creating strong male bonding, and a toast for his son. The tradition continues, but some prefer it to be called a casual gathering among males, while others host a getaway trip. Las Vegas, Nevada, is one of the popular U.S. destinations for a bachelor party in the modern tradition. In the United Kingdom, people refer to "stag weekend trips" in which men take part in several outdoor activities. This is often seen as a merry-go-round party for vacation trips. Canadians also refer to them as stag parties, similar to Americans.

A bachelor party is often interpreted as the end of single manhood, so Anglo-style bachelor parties have become more risqué, e.g., female strippers and a hostess serving alcoholic beverages, even dancing before, clubbing activities, etc. Prostitutes are often expected as an integral part of celebrating manhood. The German tradition includes a similar event of breaking ceramics and the removal of all evil spirits, followed by a funny costume contest. In South Africa and other countries, the party is more to provide sex education for the groom, as the primary wedding goal is to soon have children. A bachelor party is less common in Asian culture but has become more popular in East and Southeast Asia. Sensation-seeking activities, like skydiving and rock climbing, are popular events for bachelor parties around the world.

The common theme of a bachelor party is a farewell to being single and preparing the groom for his wedding day. Different cultural expectations exist, but the entire day is memorable, as men are fueled by a steady stream of screaming, laughter, and alcohol. The modern trend of bachelor parties is to stay within the groom's comfort zone, having a relaxed milieu to celebrate the last moments of his single life.

Seungyeon Lee

See also: Bachelorette Parties; Wedding Party

Further Reading

Bradshaw, Graham, Bishop, Tom, and Tetsuo, Kishi. 2007. *Special Sections, Updating Shakespeare.* Ashgate Publishing, Ltd., p. 174.

Chaucer, Geoffery. 1990. *The Canterbury Tales.* Simon & Schuster, pp. 1342–1400.

Bachelorette Parties

Bachelorette parties (also known as "doe," "hen," or "stagette" nights) are events where people (primarily women) gather to celebrate the upcoming wedding of a female friend or family member. Modeled after bachelor parties, these events celebrate upcoming nuptials but also frequently orbit around or mock stereotypical ideas that marriage involves giving up freedom (sexual and otherwise). This is accomplished by activities like performances from an exotic dancer or scavenger hunts where brides-to-be solicit phone numbers, underwear, kisses, or more from random men. There is usually a good deal of alcohol consumption, and the bride-to-be is often dressed up with a veil or other novelty items which identify her as "the bachelorette."

Bachelorette parties can give brides-to-be a feeling of "equality" with their future husbands. Research finds that some women did not like the idea that only men got a fun night out with their friends before their wedding; they saw the bachelorette party as leveling the playing field entering into marriage (Montemurro 2006). Bachelorette parties also provide evidence of changing roles in marriage. Before women had

these parties, pre-wedding celebrations were limited to bridal showers which celebrated the domestic role and only focused on what women gain in marriage. In contrast, bachelorette parties ritually acknowledge that many women have had relationships or sexual encounters before marriage and that they, too, give something up when committing to a monogamous relationship.

There is evidence that bachelor parties date back to Ancient Rome, where men would celebrate upcoming nuptials with parties characterized by excess and debauchery. In North America, bachelorette parties came along much later, with the term coined in the early 1980s, though the practice probably emerged in the 1960s. These early parties were small, often informal affairs with women gathering for an evening to go out for drinks or a night on the town. Popular culture shows bachelorette parties in films like *Shag* and *Bachelor Party*, in the 1980s, which is also the decade where the term began appearing in popular press articles.

Bachelorette parties are not just North American events. In Finland, for instance, there is a custom called *polttarit*, practiced by both men and women, where engaged people go out and perform dares (like soliciting a kiss from a stranger in exchange for money). In Scotland, there are hazing type-rites called "blackening" in which brides and grooms are kidnapped by friends and then decorated in costumes or with mixtures of mud, grease, or other substances, as well as women-only hen parties which feature similar structures to bachelorette parties.

In North America and the United Kingdom, bachelorette parties increased in popularity and prevalence in the 1990s and early 2000s as industries developed to support and encourage such events and word spread about their practice. Weddings became more lavish, and celebrations extended beyond the ceremony to months of preparation and festivity. Bachelorette parties went from a simple night out to dinner to multi-location events, with pre-parties at someone's home—complete with suggestive games. Businesses like nightclubs and exotic entertainment clubs increasingly offered "party packages" for brides-to-be and their friends. As bachelorette parties extended from single-day events to destination trips for some wealthier brides, tourist destinations ranging from New York, Las Vegas, and Portland, Maine promoted themselves as hotspots for brides-to-be and offered bachelorette-party-themed getaways.

The popularity and number of social media sites like Facebook and Pinterest also functioned to institutionalize bachelorette parties, as brides-to-be and their friends share images and ideas for parties. This not only inspired but reinforced the idea that having a bachelorette party is a typical part of the pre-wedding process.

Beth Montemurro

See also: Bachelor Parties; Bridal Showers; Wedding Industry

Further Reading

Montemurro, Beth. 2006. *Something Old, Something Bold: Bridal Showers and Bachelorette Parties.* New Brunswick, NJ: Rutgers University Press.

Tye, Diane. 2018. "Edible Men: Playing with Food at Bachelorette Parties." *Western Folklore* 77, no. 3/4: 221–247.

Tye, Diane and Ann Marie Powers. 1998. "Gender, Resistance, and Play: Bachelorette Parties in Atlantic Canada." *Women's Studies International Forum* 21: 551–561.

Young, Sheila M. 2019. *Prenuptial Rituals in Scotland: Blackening the Bride and Decorating the Hen.* Lexington Books.

Bankruptcy

While many factors can contribute to a decision to file for bankruptcy, one of the most common factors is divorce. When bankruptcy is being considered, whatever the marital status, it is important to consider various options. Some of these include which type of bankruptcy to file (Chapter Seven or Chapter Thirteen), the timing of filing (before divorcing or after the divorce is final), and the lasting impacts on marriage, divorce, and the families and children involved.

There are times, for various reasons, that married individuals file for bankruptcy. These reasons can include unexpected unemployment, failure of a business, large debt incurred from credit card purchases, or larger-scale economic factors, such as the housing crash of 2009 and the ensuing Great Recession.

Declarations of bankruptcy, though, are also sometimes filed during or after a divorce. During divorce settlements, both assets and liabilities are divided in some way between the two parties. In addition to the division of these, each party's income will now decrease from a joint income to a single income, which can be a significant economic loss. The decrease tends to be more significant for women, who on average earn less than men, even for the same job. This phenomenon is sometimes called the feminization of poverty. A few reasons behind the feminization of poverty include disadvantages for women in the job market and their greater likelihood of taking primary responsibility for childcare. Many times, the lower household income that comes with divorce triggers an increased inability to cover debts and potentially additional expenses like alimony or child support. These various factors can place individuals in financial straits that make them more likely to explore bankruptcy.

The two most common types of personal bankruptcy are Chapter Seven and Chapter Thirteen. Chapter Seven bankruptcy is instituted when parties can pay some of their debts back through liquidation of non-exempt assets, like the sale of vehicles, investments, boats, etc. Part of the debt may be reduced or eliminated, but an agreed-upon sum is paid, in full, through a payment plan or a combination of both. Chapter Thirteen bankruptcy is a complete absolution of the majority of debt. An agreed-upon percentage of the debt will be paid to creditors through a payment plan, typically three to five years. The rest of the debt is removed if the payment of the percentage is completed within the agreed-upon time frame. If the payment is not completed, the full balance of debt returns to the filer. Bankruptcy filings remain on the filer's credit report for months or years, depending on the situation. For example, personal bankruptcies typically remain on credit reports for seven to ten years. This reality can make it difficult for filers to secure big loans for purchases of homes or home remodeling projects, automobiles, small business investments, and the like (although people who declare bankruptcy can also begin rebuilding their credit score immediately after filing).

Individuals considering divorce must decide on when to file for bankruptcy—either before or after the dissolution of the marriage. This decision can depend on the urgency needed to file and the circumstances surrounding the relationship. Filing jointly can be more cost-effective for all parties involved; one lawyer fee versus two, one court fee versus two, and one filing fee versus two. However, there are times when the need to initiate divorce proceedings, such as cases where domestic violence or abuse is a factor and personal safety is a priority, may preclude filing jointly.

While bankruptcy in marriage and divorce is primarily an economic function, there are social implications for the families involved. There continues to be a negative connotation and stereotype around filing bankruptcy. Some people considering bankruptcy expressed fear of being labeled as lazy or deadbeat. Additionally, divorce has its stigmas tied to social norms and religious beliefs.

Sarah Alkire

See also: Division of Assets; Divorce, Economic Consequences (Personal); Economic Independence

Further Reading

Danikas, Alky. 2008. "Bankruptcy, Personal." In *Encyclopedia of Social Problems*, edited by Vincent N. Parrillo. California: SAGE Publications, pp. 71–72.

Fisher, Jonathan, and Angela Lyons. 2005. "Till Debt Do Us Part: A Model of Divorce and Personal Bankruptcy." *Review of Economics of the Household* 4: 35–52. https://doi.org/10.1007/s11150-005-6696-0

Mann, Laura. 2015. "'Til Debt Do Us Part': The Interplay Between Bankruptcy and Divorce." *GPSolo* 32, no. (4): 47–50.

Masi de Casanova, Erynn. 2008. "Divorce." In *Encyclopedia of Social Problems*, edited by Vincent N. Parrillo. California: SAGE Publications, pp. 247–248.

Peterson, Janice. 1987. "The Feminization of Poverty." *Journal of Economic Issues* 21, no. (1): 329–337. https://doi.org/10.1080/00213624.1987.11504613

Sullivan, Teresa, Elizabeth Warren, and Jay Westbrook. 1995. "Bankruptcy and the Family." *Marriage & Family Review* 21, no. 3–4: 193. https://doi.org/10.1300/J002v21n03_10

Blended Families

A blended family is a family where two adult partners bring their children from previous relationship(s) to their new relationship. The term blended family is often interchangeably used with the term stepfamilies. However, these terms may not exactly refer to the same type of family structure. For example, in blended families, both adults are stepparents to their spouse's biological child(ren), whereas in stepfamilies only one adult may bring a child(ren) from a previous relationship(s) into the new relationship. The former is specifically referred to as a complex stepfamily (i.e., a stepfamily that contains stepsiblings or half-siblings); the latter is a simple stepfamily. Regardless of these types, both blended families and stepfamilies involve children from prior unions.

According to a 2015 report by Pew Research Center, approximately 15% of children ages 18 and younger in the United States are living with two parents, one of whose current marriage is remarriage, whereas 6% of the children in cohabiting adult households are stepchildren (Kennedy and Fitch 2012, 1489). These numbers may vary by different demographic factors. For example, among children living with (re)married parents, 17% of Hispanic and Black children are living in blended families, while only 7% of Asian children are living in these families, leaving the majority of them staying with both biological parents (Pew Research Center 2015).

The term blended family defines neither the marital status of adult partners nor the residential status of the family members. It is important to note that not all blended families or stepfamilies are formed through remarriage after the loss of a previous spouse from death or divorce. With the increasing share of cohabiting couples, remarriage is no longer a precursor to constituting blended families. Also, remarried families do not necessarily involve children from prior unions; divorced individuals who do not have pre-existing children may remarry a new partner whose marriage is either a first-marriage or higher-order marriage (second or third) and may not have any child(ren) before the current union. The residential status of a blended family or stepfamily members is contingent on custody arrangements of the children from previous unions, meaning that they may or may not reside together full-time, most of the time, or part-time. Given that the marital status of adult partners and the residential status of family members are additional information beyond the definition of blended families or stepfamilies, a more specific term may be used to describe various conditions of these families. For example, a nonresidential stepmother family in remarriage implies that the current relationship of the adult partners is a second marriage to at least one of them and stepchild(ren) resides somewhere else than with his(her) stepmother and biological father.

Blended families experience unique challenges as they develop and maintain their relationships. American sociologist Andrew Cherlin referred to stepfamilies as *incomplete institutions* to illustrate some of these challenges. He cited an absence of appropriate terms to explain or define relationships in stepfamilies, as well as no to little institutional social support (e.g., medical systems, school systems) available. Cherlin also argued that social policies and family laws were constituted based on a nuclear family ideology, thus being unclear and unsupportive to affect the everyday life of stepfamily members (e.g., confusion about how stepparents discipline their stepchildren) and that norms and rules about stepfamilies are relatively scarce (Cherlin 1978, 642–646). Although nontraditional families are common and outnumber traditional families (i.e., families based on a nuclear family ideology) these days, and it has been over 40 years since nontraditional families as *incomplete institutions* were documented, many blended families still experience similar challenges in our society (Ganong and Coleman 2017).

Blended families also are known to experience stress due to the structure of family relationships; compared to first-marriage families, biological parent-child relationships precede couple relationships. This difference contributes to unique issues in blended families. For example, blended families generally experience stress related to family dynamics (e.g., loyalty conflicts, difficulty building a solid couple bond), adjustments (e.g., building a shared family history and rituals), emotional difficulty (e.g., a loss of one parent, feeling guilt), and negotiation of expectations among stepfamily members (e.g., the role of a residential stepmother in the presence of the biological mother) (Ganong and Coleman 2017, 251). These challenges may be associated with a higher risk of relationship dissolution among couples with stepchildren. Challenges in blended families, however, often vary depending on the stage of the family life cycle that they are experiencing. For example, while parenting may be the most challenging task for stepparents in blended families with young children, that is not as much of an issue in later-life stepfamilies. In this stage, as stepchildren are already adults and have their own children, other issues (e.g., stepgrandparent–stepgrandchild relationships, inheritance, health issues) may be more relevant to them than to stepfamilies in other family life stages. Given that blended families have unique family issues that are discussed above, practitioners believe that it is normal to take several years to establish a stable, successful stepfamily (Ganong and Coleman 2017).

Regardless of the previous challenges discussed, blended families are resilient and have strengths. For example, stepfamily members enjoy diverse family relationships, support systems, and new opportunities to learn from each other and how to adapt to new environments and others (Coleman, Ganong, and Gingrich, 1985, 585–586). To be able to build successful stepfamily relationships, family members must negotiate ambiguous and unclear rules, roles, and expectations among themselves through clear communication (Ganong and Coleman 2017, 240). This may be particularly true for blended families that are formed following divorce. In this case, both biological parents may still be involved in their children's lives as active coparents between households. This possibly creates more complex family dynamics, role confusion among stepparents, and loyalty conflicts among stepchildren, which requires family members to have clear, yet flexible boundaries.

Research on the effects of stepfamily living on children indicates that overall, children of stepparents are more likely to experience various negative outcomes compared to children living with both biological parents due to relationship issues (e.g., loyalty conflict, negative relationship with a stepparent) and stress associated with family transitions. For example, researchers found that children living with stepparents reported lower academic achievements (Tillman 2008), more emotional problems (Laubjerg, Christensen, and Petersson 2009), and a higher risk of involvement in substance use (Mandara, Rogers, and Zinbarg 2011) than children in first-marriage families. Scientific evidence of the effects on stepfamily living on children needs to be interpreted with caution, however, because most stepchildren adjust well (Ganong and Coleman 2017). Researchers emphasize that there is a wide array of factors that may make differences within the group of children living in blended families. For example, researchers found that stepchildren's lower stress level was associated with greater closeness with both residential biological parents and stepparents while stepchildren's higher stress level was associated with greater closeness with nonresidential biological parents (Jensen, Shafer, and Holmes 2017). The findings of this study indicate that stepchildren's positive relationships with both residential parental figures may help with a smooth family transition and adjustment, yet loyalty conflict that stepchildren may experience among multiple parental figures may be a source of stress.

Due to the increasing number of cohabiting couples and blended families headed by gay and lesbian couples, blended families are also becoming more complex and varied than ever before (Ganong and Coleman 2017).

Youngjin Kang and Kwangman Ko

See also: Coparenting and Divorce; Stepfamilies, Developmental Stages

Further Reading

Cherlin, Andrew. 1978. "Remarriage as an Incomplete Institution." *American Journal of Sociology* 84, no. 3: 634–650.

Coleman, Marilyn, Lawrence H. Ganong, and Ronald Gingrich. 1985. "Stepfamily Strengths: A Review of Popular Literature." *Family Relations* 34, no. 4: 583–589.

Ganong, H. Lawrence and Marilyn Coleman. 2017. *Stepfamily Relationships: Development, Dynamics, and Interventions* (2nd ed.). New York: Springer.

Jensen, Todd M., Kevin Shafer, and Erin K. Holmes. 2017. "Transitioning to Stepfamily Life: The Influence of Closeness with Biological Parents and Stepparents on Children's Stress." *Child & Family Social Work* 22, no. 1: 275–286. https://doi.org/10.1111/cfs.12237.

Kennedy, Sheela, and Catherine A. Fitch. 2012. "Measuring Cohabitation and Family Structure in the United States: Assessing the Impact of New Data from the Current Population Survey." *Demography* 49, no. 4: 1479–1498.

Laubjerg, Merete, Anne, M. Christensen, and Birgit Peterson. 2009. "Psychiatric Status among Stepchildren and Domestic and International Adoptees in Denmark: A Comparative Nationwide Register-based Study." *Scandinavian Journal of*

Public Health 37, no. 6: 604–612. https://doi.org/10.1177/1403494809105799.

Mandara, Jelani, Sheba Y. Rogers, and Richard E. Zinbarg. 2011. "The Effects of Family Structure on African American Adolescents' Marijuana Use." *Journal of Marriage and Family* 73, no. 3: 557–569. https://doi.org/10.1111/j.1741-3737.2011.00832.x.

Pew Research Center. 2015. "The American Family Today." Accessed July 1, 2019. http://www.pewsocialtrends.org/2015/12/17/1-the-american-family-today/

Tillman, Kathryn. H. 2008. "'Nontraditional' Siblings and the Academic Outcomes of Adolescents." *Social Science Research* 37, no. 1: 88–108. https://doi.org/10.1016/j.ssresearch.2007.06.007.

Bridal Showers

The first documented bridal showers in the United States happened among upper-class brides at the time of the Industrial Revolution. Although wedding gifts were given before this time, showers seem to have started in the late 1800s (Pleck 2000). The purpose of the shower was to help women stock their "trousseau"—the linens and clothing needed in the early days of marriage. Being able to host or give a shower was a sign of class status and a way to show a connection to other wealthy families. Among those upper-class women, gifts shifted over time from necessities like sheets and towels to luxuries like silver. Magazines like *Ladies Home Journal* provided information about planning wedding showers which it touted in 1904 as a "new ritual." In the early 1900s, showers became a more common practice, with documentation of their practice among employed women (Howard 2008). It was

around this time that weddings began to become more lavish among those who could afford to have such celebrations, as businesses and industries promoted and encouraged conspicuous consumption. Bridal showers followed suit.

In the early days, bridal showers were described as "informal" and often surprises for the bride-to-be. Around the 1930s, bridal showers filtered down from the upper class and were practiced among middle- and working-class women as well. In the 1940s, mainstream magazines like *Look* and *Life* advertised household products as "perfect" for wedding shower gifts. In the second half of the twentieth century, books exclusively focused on planning bridal showers began to be published. When these books were snapped off bookshelves, publishers quickly took notice and began publishing greater numbers of such books. During this period, bridal showers had a "typical" format where guests gathered in the afternoon and mingled in a reception hall, church hall, restaurant, or someone's home. They had light refreshments or a meal and then guests watched while the bride-to-be opened and displayed her gifts. Bridal showers were understood as opportunities for families who were going be joined together by marriage to unite, get to know one another, and begin to see themselves as one family.

Bridal showers remain a constant in the pre-wedding process. Since their origin, these events were women-only. Given the focus on domesticity and the separation of public and private life as Western societies industrialized bridal showers were rituals of femininity that reinforced traditional gender roles. The soft goods and items for cooking and cleaning commonly given at bridal showers were for the wife-to-be and so the husband-to-be's presence was unnecessary. This framework underscored the idea that husbands and wives had different roles in marriage—and that wives were responsible for domestic/household work.

In the 1990s and early 2000s, when traditional gender roles and responsibilities underwent increasing challenges from women and (some) men, "couples showers" were increasingly practiced among middle-class and upper-middle-class couples, although some research suggests these were supplements rather than replacements for traditional bridal showers (Montemurro 2005). This research also finds that men's presence resulted in very different experiences—including the addition of alcohol and more of an evening "party" atmosphere, where gifts are secondary to the social experience.

Beth Montemurro

See also: Bachelor Parties; Bachelorette Parties; Wedding Industry

Further Reading

Braithwaite, Dawn O. 1995. "Ritualized Embarrassment at 'Coed' Wedding and Baby Showers." *Communication Reports* 8, no. 2: 145–157.

Howard, Vicki Jo. 2008. *Bride's Inc: American Weddings and the Business of Tradition.* Philadelphia: University of Pennsylvania Press.

Montemurro, Beth. 2005. "Add Men, Don't Stir: Reproducing Traditional Gender Roles at Modern Wedding Showers." *Journal of Contemporary Ethnography* 34, no. 1: 6–35.

Montemurro, Beth. 2006. *Something Old, Something Bold: Bridal Showers and Bachelorette Parties.* New Brunswick, NJ: Rutgers University Press.

Pleck, Elizabeth. 2000. *Celebrating the Family: Ethnicity, Consumer Culture, and Family Rituals.* Cambridge, MA: Harvard University Press.

C

Celibate Marriage

Celibate marriage is also known as sexless marriage or celibacy in marriage. In religious literature, celibacy is referred to as a voluntary abstention from sex. For example, the celibacy of Catholic priests implies religious commitment and devotion. Today, however, the term celibate marriage usually has little to do with religion. Celibate/sexless marriage can be understood as one in which there is little or no sexual relations exist between the two marital partners. Although the conceptual definition of celibate marriage can be easily fathomed, the operational definition of "little" sex has generated much debate. After all, definitions of sex vary, and every relationship is different. What is considered "little" for one individual may be "too much" for another.

The operational definition of a sexless marriage is tied to the frequency of sex. A common definition of a sexless marriage is having sex nine or fewer times per year (Kuster 2016, 70–72). It is estimated that 15% or more of married Americans are in sexless marriages (Snyder 2018). However, the percentage of celibate marriages can fluctuate depending on the definition and sample. Frequency of sex declines with the progression of marital duration and one's age. Individual's sexual dysfunction/disorder, mental illness, physical health, erectile dysfunction, and menopause or premenopausal symptoms may also affect the frequency of sex in marriage (İlhan et al. 2017, 815–817). Not surprisingly, relational factors such as marital conflict and negative interpersonal behaviors between spouses (related to perceived inequities in the division of household chores, for instance) have also been shown to influence the frequency of sexual activity within marriage (Gillespie, Peterson, and Lever 2019, 11–15). Moreover, extramarital affairs can lead to sexless marriages, as the cheating spouse's sexual needs are fulfilled outside of the marriage. When such affairs are discovered, it is also common for the non-adulterous spouse to refuse to engage in sexual intimacy with the unfaithful partner. Finally, children frequently have an enormous impact on a couple's sexual activity. Having sex once a month may be perceived as deprivation for a healthy, happy, and childless couple in their 20s with high relationship satisfaction, financial security, and a good support system. However, having sex once a month may sound like an impossible retreat for a sleep-deprived couple that is under financial strain or grappling with health problems in their infant.

The path to the sexless state in marriage is varied. For some couples, sexual activity gradually decreases over time, whereas other couples may have had very little sex to begin with. Some couples' sexual activities seemed to stop suddenly, while no observable pattern could be identified for other couples. Most individuals in involuntarily celibate relationships utilized various coping strategies (e.g., masturbation) to deal with their unmet sexual needs and wants. Decreased sexual activity in marriage may be short-term, such as following surgery or childbirth, or it may be chronic and a result of a complex mix of factors. Discrepancies in sexual desire are a commonly mentioned problem among couples. Recent research has found that sexual desire is not experienced by everyone. Asexuality—the nonexistence of sexual attraction and desire—has received increasing attention from researchers who have, unsurprisingly, found that asexual individuals are more comfortable with celibate relationships than people with higher levels of sexual desire and feelings.

Sexual intimacy is an important element in marriages and is often seen as a barometer of relationship quality. However, sex may not be the most essential part of every marriage. Furthermore, sexual frequency does not guarantee sexual satisfaction. In other words, a celibate marriage is not necessarily a threat to marital stability if both spouses are satisfied with the quality of their relationship and agree on the inactivity in their marital chambers. Conversely, dissatisfaction and discontentment can arise when one or both spouses are unhappy or frustrated with the sexual relationship they have.

Celibate marriage is complex and can be perceived as problematic, and there is no easy way to address issues in sexless relationships. Depending on the causes of sexual inactivity, treatment and interventions such as sexual communication training, medical intervention, couples' therapy, and individual counseling can be employed. Even though sexually explicit material and content flood media and society, candid discussions about sex remain a challenge for many couples, and relationship education is needed to equip individuals with knowledge and skills for marital success. Hence, couples will be able to understand human sexual behaviors, communicate openly and effectively, and make educated and informed decisions about their relationships.

I. Joyce Chang

See also: Attachment Theory of Love; Love, Connection, and Intimacy; Sexual Compatibility

Further Reading

Dahlen, Heather. 2019. "Female Sexual Dysfunction: Assessment and Treatment." *Urologic Nursing* 39, no. 1: 39–46. https://doi.org/10.7257/1053-816X.2019.39.1.39.

Gillespie, Brian Joseph, Gretchen Peterson, and Janet Lever. 2019. "Gendered Perceptions of Fairness in Housework and Shared Expenses: Implications for Relationship Satisfaction and Sex Frequency." *PLoS ONE* 14, no. 3: 1–18. https://doi.org/10.1371/journal.pone.0214204.

İlhan, Gülşah, Fatma Verda Verit Atmaca, Meryem Kurek Eken, and Hürkan Akyol. 2017. "Premenstrual Syndrome Is Associated with a Higher Frequency of Female Sexual Difficulty and Sexual Distress." *Journal of Sex & Marital Therapy* 43, no. 8: 811–821. https://doi.org/10.1080/0092623X.2017.1305030.

Kuster, Elizabeth. 2016. "The Cure for Sexless Marriages." *Prevention* 68, no. 7: 70–79. https://www.preventionaus.com.au/article/the-cure-for-a-sexless-marriage-565345.

Ševčíková, Anna, Jaroslav Gottfried, and Lukas Blinka. 2021. "Associations among Sexual Activity, Relationship Types, and Health in Mid and Later Life." *Archives of Sexual Behavior*, August. https://doi.org/10.1007/s10508-021-02040-6.

Snyder, Stephen. 2018. "Why Sexless Marriages Happen and 1 Way to Prevent

Them." https://www.today.com/series/one
-small-thing/why-sexless-marriages
-happen-how-prevent-them-t124738.

Twenge, Jean, Ryne A. Sherman, and
Brooke Wells. 2017. "Declines in Sexual
Frequency Among American Adults,
1989–2014." *Archives of Sexual Behavior*
46, no. 8: 2389–2401.

Child Abuse

The abuse of children is not a recent phenomenon. Modern conceptualizations of
abuse vary from country to country and
even regionally within a country. Culture
plays a large role in what is deemed to be
an appropriate way to discipline a child
and where the line is drawn between discipline and abuse. What the legal system
and society consider to be abusive behavior can vary. While extreme cases of child
abuse garner a consensus that what has
occurred is abuse, it is the less extreme
scenarios where people differ in their definitions of what is abusive and what is not.
For this reason, there are minimum guidelines and definitions for what is considered
to be abuse and neglect at the federal level
in the United States although each state
can make more restrictive laws as they see
fit. The Child Abuse Prevention and Treatment Act (CAPTA) sets the minimum
guidelines at the federal level, which is the
starting point for all state-level legislation
on child abuse. CAPTA was originally put
into place in 1974 but has gone through
several reauthorizations over the decades.
The 2019 passage of the Child Victims
Act in New York allows victims up to 55
years of age to seek prosecution of their
perpetrators. This allows for prosecution
where there had previously been a statute
of limitations that often-limited victims
of child sexual abuse from reporting once

they reach a certain age, which may not be
when they are ready to report (Knoll 2019).

Child abuse can be an action or inaction. Abuse, or action, is the most commonly referenced type of child abuse.
Neglect, or inaction, is less often thought
about but can nonetheless have significant impacts on the well-being of victims.
Indeed, regardless of whether a child is
being abused or neglected, there can be
serious ramifications at the moment and
potentially throughout their lifetime.
The four categories of child maltreatment that are recognized by the Centers
for Disease Control (CDC) are: neglect,
emotional abuse, physical abuse, and
sexual abuse. While each category will
be discussed individually, it is important
to understand that more than one may be
present at any point in a child's life. For
instance, in situations involving physical
abuse, emotional abuse is also present.

Neglect

Children are dependent on proper emotional care and attention, good nutrition,
and safe living conditions to grow and
thrive. The absence of any of this can constitute neglect. At the most basic level, children need food of proper nutritional value
regularly, have clean clothing that fits them
and is seasonally appropriate, and live in
stable housing that is structurally sound
and has electricity and running water.

Nationally, neglect is the most common
form of child maltreatment, accounting
for 75% of child abuse cases in 2017 (United
States Children's Bureau 2017). Some children so victimized live in homes without
running water or electricity, which can
mean no heat in the winter (environmental neglect). There may be concerns not
only about the safety of the structure that
they live in but also about the cleanliness

(household sanitation). Beyond the living situations, some children also face situations of food scarcity and insecurity which can lead to hunger and malnutrition (physical neglect). Some school-aged children are heavily dependent on meals that are offered for a free or reduced cost from their schools. This means that children are going to school hungry and often not getting regular meals at home. Some children do not have clothes that fit, are not prepared for seasonal weather changes like extremely cold winters or are unable to maintain proper hygiene due to circumstances at home.

While neglect is the most commonly identified form of child abuse nationally, it is important to note that this is also in part because it is easier to identify. It is easy to see when a child is not properly clothed, is not washing or bathing regularly, or is constantly hungry or malnourished. With that being said, there is a difference between willfully neglecting a child and having a lack of resources to provide for their needs. While the legal system may not always make this distinction, many parents or caregivers do the best they can to take care of their children, but still do not have enough financial support to meet basic needs. In most cases of neglect, the primary caregivers, typically the mother, is identified as the predominant perpetrator. This is due in large part to mothers being those that are most often tasked with the care of children.

Emotional Abuse

Of all of the categories of child abuse and neglect, emotional abuse is the hardest to prove but can be the most damaging. Emotional abuse comes in several forms, including name-calling and derogatory or demeaning language, threats of physical

harm, and unrealistic expectations (such as the parent who puts intense pressure on children to perform athletically or academically) are all forms of emotional abuse. The latter is a big reason why children's sports teams and leagues have implemented firm rules about parental behavior at sporting events.

In addition to emotionally abusive behavior, there is also emotional neglect that occurs. This can take the form of denying a child comfort, attention, or affirmation—or giving attention to one child at the cost of the other.

Emotional abuse and neglect have lasting impacts but are often the most difficult to prove. In many states, the legal standard for charging someone with emotional abuse is that their abusive behavior has to have caused significant psychological harm. Meaning, that due to the emotional abuse directed at a child, they have developed depression, anxiety, etc. This means that the burden of proof in emotional abuse cases is often higher than those involving other categories of child abuse.

Physical Abuse

Physical abuse is an action that is taken against a child that often, but not always, leaves a physical mark. Perpetrators may use their fists or feet to hit or kick a child, but they may also rely on objects such as belts, switches, paddles, or other objects that are within reach. Injuries as a result of physical abuse can include spiral fractures, broken bones or skull fractures, burn marks from cigarettes or cigars, immersion burns from being held in scalding water, or bruising in the shape of hands or other objects. Not all injuries that children sustain are a result of abuse, so it is important to highlight the difference between accidental and intentional injury.

Sexual Abuse

While sexual abuse does not comprise the highest type of child abuse nationally, in some states it is the most frequently reported and confirmed form of child abuse. This discrepancy can often be explained by the high-profile child sexual abuse cases in a state, changes in mandated reporting laws, and the focus of educational efforts. For instance, following the trial of Jerry Sandusky and the sanctions against Penn State, Pennsylvania lawmakers created more prescriptive mandated reporting laws and focused more education and resources on sexual abuse awareness. This was meant to address breakdowns in reporting processes and require direct reports to designated authorities of suspected child abuse as opposed to the previous requirements to report to managers. This put the decision-making into the hands of those who have specialized training in child abuse and child welfare. Even before this change in mandated reporting laws, Pennsylvania consistently had the highest number of reports and confirmed cases of child sexual abuse. This statistic was replicated annually, sometimes with more than 60% of cases in a given year confirmed to be cases of child sexual abuse (Pennsylvania Department of Public Welfare 2010).

Rates of child sexual abuse are higher for young girls than boys. One in nine girls will experience sexual abuse by the time they reach the age of 18 in comparison to one in 53 boys (RAINN n.d.). However, it is important to keep in mind that gender socialization and roles can play a key role in the underreporting of the sexual abuse of boys. Just like we see with intimate partner violence in adults, society does not often see young boys as being vulnerable to this type of abuse and does not encourage them to report in the same way that girls are encouraged to do so. Sexual abuse can include inappropriate conversations or picture taking, sexting, fondling, or sexually caressing a child, and engaging in sexual acts with a child (under 18 years of age).

Perpetrators in these cases are often overlooked because they don't fit common stereotypes of a sexual predator or child molester. While many people think the most common perpetrator in child sexual abuse cases is a stranger (personified by notions of unkempt and homely men driving vans), the reality is that 90% of victims in child sexual abuse cases know their perpetrator (RAINN n.d.). It is a family member, family friend, neighbor, teacher, or someone that the family trusts that is most likely to be abusing the child. While it is important to teach children to be safe around strangers, they also need to be taught that certain actions are always inappropriate no matter who is engaging in them.

Regardless of the type of child abuse a child may be experiencing, it is important to note that parents, relatives, significant others of parents, and other adults who are in their lives (as coaches, teachers, or youth organization leaders, for example) are those who are most likely to be abusive or neglectful to a child. While laws are becoming more comprehensive in capturing what child abuse is and what mandated reporting looks like, further work is needed. Reporting suspected child abuse is key to reducing the problem.

Melanie L. Duncan

See also: Cycle of Violence; Intimate Partner Violence

Further Reading

Centers for Disease Control. "Child Abuse and Neglect Prevention." Accessed on September 2, 2019. https://www.cdc.gov/violenceprevention/childabuseandneglect/index.html.

Child Welfare Information Gateway. "Child Abuse & Neglect." Accessed on September 2, 2019. https://www.childwelfare.gov/topics/can/.

Crosson-Tower, Cynthia. 2014. *Understanding Child Abuse and Neglect.* New York: Pearson.

Knoll, Corina. 2019. "'I Can Still Smell Him': For 4 Legislators, the Child Victims Act Is Personal." *The New York Times.*

Pennsylvania Department of Public Welfare. 2010. "2010 Pennsylvania Department of Public Welfare Annual Child Abuse Report." Accessed on October 5, 2019. http://www.dhs.pa.gov/cs/groups/webcontent/documents/report/p_011342.pdf.

RAINN. n.d. "Children & Teens: Statistics." Accessed on September 2, 2019. https://www.rainn.org/statistics/children-and-teens.

United States Children's Bureau. 2017. "Child Maltreatment 2017." Last modified 2018. https://www.childtrends.org/indicators/child-maltreatment

Child Custody

Until the mid-19th century, men almost unquestionably maintained full custodial rights over children, leaving mothers with no claims to custody. An increased focus on the importance of motherhood and the protection of children led to social and legal changes during the mid- to late-1800s. Married women gained the right to own property, a few gained custody of their children in divorce, and what was in "the best interest of the child" was a question asked for the first time in cases of divorce and custody (Mason 1994, 60–62).

Divorce rates rose steadily from the early 1900s well into the 1970s. Facing a continual uptick in custody disputes, courts began relying on input from the mental and behavioral health fields for guidance around what was in the best interest of children. What the mental and behavioral health fields presented to family courts was mainly based on a theory with some broad generalizations from the limited and problematic research available at the time. *Beyond the Best Interest of the Child* (Goldstein, Freud, and Solnit 1973/1979), for example, was a primary source of information for courts despite being heavily critiqued and relying almost entirely on psychoanalytic theory without tying to the research of the day. Criticisms of early research on children of divorce included lack of generalizability, focus on highly distressed, white, middle-class families, and over-reliance on reports by mothers (Luepnitz 1978; Roman and Haddad 1978, 105).

Legislation about child custody gradually moved toward gender-neutral policies throughout the 1970s and 1980s, shifting from assumed sole custody going to mothers with weekend visitations for dads to a preference for joint or shared custody arrangements. The specifics of joint custody vary widely as do the living arrangements within these agreements. Parents may have joint physical and legal custody where parents share time and decision-making power. Alternatively, custody arrangements may have a primary physical custodial parent with the majority of the parenting time but shared legal custody meaning all medical, educational, and religious decisions for the child(ren) must be agreed upon by both parents. In terms of residence, parents with joint custody might have separate homes between which the children are shuttled or there might be a primary home for the child(ren) by which the parents come and go as dictated by the agreed-upon parenting schedule (i.e., nesting arrangement). Finally, sole physical and legal custody given to a single parent still happens, but it is not the family court's preferred arrangement.

To provide children with representation in the divorce process, guardians ad litem (GAL) or guardians were introduced into the family courts in the 1970s (Mason 1994, 190). The required profession of the representative varies by state as does the role of the GAL. Some states utilize lawyers; others make use of minimally trained volunteers. Judges appoint GALs in many states, but some allow for them to be retained privately by parents. Roles of a GAL may include conducting interviews; analyzing information; creating custody reports; advocating for children's interests throughout custody proceedings; and offering testimony and subpoenaing witnesses at hearings.

Divorce literature and family courts have and continue to assert the importance of children maintaining relationships with both parents, preferably through cooperative coparenting and relatively equal parenting time (Braver and Lamb 2018). This assertion disregards newer research which suggests that children's post-divorce adjustment and overall well-being are best when the arrangement closely matches the pre-divorce parenting arrangement (Poortman 2018). Children's well-being appears lower in custody arrangements where a child's time is divided equally between parents, but one was the main caretaker during the marriage or if caretaking was equally divided, but a single parent is awarded primary physical custody (Poortman 2018). Additionally, there is support for the consideration of parenting quality (O'Hara et al. 2019) and the quality of the parent-child relationship (Sandler et al. 2008) when making decisions about custody and parenting time. Despite this evidence, research suggests that a majority of children, even those who experience intimate partner violence and/or a high-conflict divorce, are placed in joint custody arrangements (Forssell and Carter 2015).

Due to the high number of multi-household families with various custody arrangements in place, the "stay at home" orders associated with the COVID-19 crisis that unfolded in 2020 had an especially unique impact. What was already a complicated process for families was exacerbated. That is, in most instances, social distancing and shelter-in-place orders did not directly impact custody orders; therefore, it was up to coparents to continue to coordinate parenting time throughout the pandemic. While we are unable to go into depth here about the different complexities that COVID-19 had on custody arrangements, we will highlight one solution families, more than ever, may utilize if there are disruptions to in-person visitations: virtual visitation.

"Virtual visitation" includes the combination of using telephone, videoconferencing, instant messaging or texting, and other internet tools to supplement in-person visitation (Flango 2003). Using these various forms of technology to communicate between the non-custodial parent and child(ren) is increasingly being supported in family law, with some families going as far as to ask the judge to prescribe virtual visitation rights and schedules (Shefts 2002). To optimize the benefits of virtual visitation coparents must consider the developmental stage(s) of their child(ren) and capabilities for using technology, availability, and access of technology for family members, and perceptions about engaging in virtual visitation.

Rachel M. Diamond and Rachel D. Miller

See also: Divorce, Process of; Intimate Partner Violence

Further Reading

Braver, Sandford L. and Michael E. Lamb. 2018. "Shared parenting after parental separation: The views of 12 experts." *Journal of Divorce and Remarriage* 59, no. (5): 372–387. https://doi.org/10.1080/10502556.2018.1454195

Flango, Carol R. 2003. *Virtual visitation— is this a new option for divorcing parents?* Retrieved from: https://ncsc.contentdm.oclc.org/digital/collection/famct/id/227/

Forssell, Anna M. and Åsa Carter. 2015. "Patterns in child–father contact after parental separation in a sample of child witnesses to intimate partner violence." *Journal of Family Violence* 30, no. (3): 339–349. https://doi.org/10.1007/s10896-015-9673-2

Goldstein, Joseph, Anna Freud, and Alfred J. Solnit. 1979. *Beyond the best interest of the child.* New York: The Free Press. (Originally published in 1973).

Luepnitz, Deborah. A. 1978. "Children of divorce—A review of the psychological literature." *Law and Human Behavior* 2, no. (2): 167–179. https://doi.org/10.1007/BF01040389.

Mason, Mary Ann. 1994. *From father's property to children's rights: The history of child custody in the United States.* New York, NY: Columbia University Press.

O'Hara, Karey L., Irwin N. Sandler, Shadrlene A. Wolchik, Jenn-Yun Tein and C. Aubrey Rhodes. 2019. "Parenting time, parenting quality, interparental conflict, and mental health problems of children in high-conflict divorce." *Journal of Family Psychology* 33 no. (6): 690–703. https://doi.org/10.1037/fam0000556

Poortman, Ann-Rigt. 2018. "Postdivorce parent–child contact and child well-being: The importance of predivorce parental involvement." *Journal of Marriage and Family*, 80 no. (3): 671–683. https://doi.org/10.1111/jomf.12474

Roman, Mel and William Haddad. 1978. *The disposable parent: The case for joint custody.* New York: Holt, Rinehart and Winston.

Sandler, Irwin N., Jonathan Miles, Jefferey Cookston, and Sanford Braver. 2008. "Effects of father and mother parenting on children's mental health in high- and low-conflict divorces." *Family Court Review* 46, no. (2): 282–296. https://doi.org/10.1111/j.1744-1617.2008.00201.x

Shefts, Kimberly. R. 2002. "Virtual visitation: The next generation of options for parent-child communication." *Family Law Quarterly* 36: 303–327.

Child Marriage

Child marriage, or marriage below the age of 18, has a long history in the United States dating back to the colonial era. Child brides have always vastly outnumbered underage husbands because historically the primary qualifications for marriage for girls and women have been their fertility, physical attractiveness, and ability to keep a home—only the first attribute delimited by age—whereas men have, until relatively recently, been measured by their ability to support a household, which required the financial stability that usually came with higher age. While child marriage's prevalence has been on a steady decline since the 1950s, recent debates about states' minimum marriageable ages and the deleterious health effects of minor marriage have brought renewed attention to the phenomenon in the early 21st century.

From the beginnings of European colonization of what became the United States, minors have been marrying—and some lawmakers have been attempting to limit their ability to do so. The marriageable age in English colonies was first regulated by common law, which set the minimum ages of 12 for girls, and 14 for boys. Catholic doctrine, which regulated those in Spanish and French colonies, set minimum ages of 11 and 13 for girls and boys, respectively. Most colonies also passed statutory laws of their own to govern minors' ability to marry, either raising the marriageable age or mandating parental consent, not usually out of concerns for child welfare, but instead to preserve filial deference to parents' wishes and parental rights to the labor of their children, which were severed after marriage.

While precise accounting of those who married as minors did not emerge in most areas of the country until the late 1800s, in earlier periods child marriage was most common in regions with demographic imbalances between men and women that encouraged men to seek out younger brides. It was also more common in areas of the country least touched by state bureaucratization and the development of schooling; that is, regions where citizens were far less aware of their birthdays and the increasing significance of calendar age, meaning that they were often unaware of their precise chronological ages.

Beginning in the mid-19th century, two trends brought greater attention—and resistance—to child marriage. The first was a greater understanding of childhood as a stage of life where children's innocence should be preserved, their minds should be broadened through education, and they should be protected from the adult responsibilities of work, sex, and marriage. The second trend was a shift in the understanding of marriage away from an economic union to one based on love and the complementarity of duties between husband and wife. Many Americans, including women's rights advocates, clergy, and those in the newly developed field of social work, worked to end child marriage because they saw it as adverse to new understandings of childhood *and* of marriage and because those who married young were more likely to divorce.

At the turn of the 20th century, just as these adults were working to protect children from what they perceived as the harms of premature marriage, children themselves were recognizing the benefits of early marriage, which legally emancipated them from their parents, entitled them to keep their own wages and inheritances, and legalized the sex that young people had with their elders after the passage of statutory rape laws beginning in the 1880s. Until the mid-20th century, it was remarkably easy to marry illegally below the age of consent (through lying, forgery, etc.), and judges almost always affirmed that marriages contracted illegally remained valid. This fundamental conflict between minors seeking marriage and adults hoping to protect minors *from* marriage continues to this day.

Over the course of the 20th century, rates of minor marriage steadily decreased across the United States, except in the late 1940s and 1950s. This 15-year period following World War II, during which Americans were particularly enamored of domesticity, produced the Baby Boom, the lowest average age of first marriage for the century, and large numbers of pregnant teenage brides marrying in order to legitimize their pregnancies. In 1960, 6.64% of girls aged 15–17 were married; by 2010, that percentage had dropped to 0.44% (Syrett 2016, 256). Until the 1950s, minor marriage had been most common among African American girls, who were nearly twice as likely to be child brides as white girls. Beginning in the 1950s, white and Latina rates of minor marriage overtook Black rates, especially as African Americans became decreasingly likely to marry at all after mid-century.

Throughout U.S. history, minor marriage has always been most common in rural areas, especially the South and the West. Minor brides in the 20th and 21st centuries have also always been more likely to be working-class or impoverished, often without many opportunities aside from marriage. Today, there is also a significant overlap between marrying as a minor and conservative religiosity, marriage seen either as the entrée into sanctioned sexual relations or the "solution" to pregnancy out of wedlock.

Between 2000 and 2015, at least 208,000 minors married in the United States, 87% of whom were girls (Tsui et al. 2017). Sociologists and demographers demonstrate that those who marry as minors are more likely to drop out of school than are their unmarried counterparts. They are more likely to be abused in their marriages and to suffer from both mental and physical health problems, though it remains unclear whether marriage itself or the underlying poverty that may have made marriage appealing, leads to these outcomes (Le Strat et al. 2011). Marriages contracted by minors are also much more likely to end in divorce than adult marriages. Studies also demonstrate that those who marry as minors continue to be more likely to be impoverished and are just slightly more likely to be girls of color (though not African American) and immigrants than those who wait until reaching 18 years of age to marry (Koski and Heymann 2018, 61).

In the early 21st century, several activist groups, including Unchained at Last and the Tahirih Justice Center, have been lobbying state legislatures to close the legal loopholes that allow children to marry below the age of 18, usually with parental or judicial permission or if the prospective bride is pregnant. While they have been successful in a handful of states, they have also met with substantial pushback, both from conservative lawmakers who see marriage as a fundamental right and also want to protect parental oversight of their children, and from more liberal lawmakers who note that some minors marry to escape from abusive homes (either natal or foster) via marriage.

Nicholas L. Syrett

See also: Dowries

Further Reading

Koski, Alissa, and Jody Heymann. 2018. "Child Marriage in the United States: How Common Is the Practice, and Which Children Are at Greatest Risk?" *Perspectives on Sexual and Reproductive Health* 50, no. 2: 59–65.

Le Strat, Yann, Caroline Dubertret, and Bernard Le Foll. 2011. "Child Marriage in the United States and Its Association with Mental Health in Women." *Pediatrics* 128, no. 3: 524–530.

Syrett, Nicholas L. 2016. *American Child Bride: A History of Minors and Marriage in the United States.* Chapel Hill: University of North Carolina Press.

Tsui, Anjali, Dan Nolan, and Chris Amico. 2017. "Child Marriage in America: By the Numbers." *Frontline.* http://apps.frontline .org/child-marriage-by-the-numbers/

Child Support

Child support is financial support provided from one parent to the other to assist in the everyday expenses of raising a child. When parents separate, either due to divorce or a break in a relationship, the allocation of financial responsibility to care for the child must be addressed. Some parents can reach an agreement regarding a feasible arrangement to ensure the child's basic needs are met. Unfortunately, not all parents can reach an agreement amicably, and court intervention is required. One common theme across states is that both parents share the responsibility of financially supporting their children. In most states, parents are obligated to support their children until age 18 or graduation from high school. However, some states like Oregon and New York have established laws that require parents to financially support their children through age 21.

If parents are unable to resolve how they will financially support their children upon the termination of their relationship, the parent seeking financial support will have to file a motion with the appropriate court. To begin, a parent must initiate a domestic action or an action with the child support division of the courts of the county in which the parents live. If a parent moves out of state or lives out of state, there are usually court-provided resources to assist the parent seeking to obtain the child support from the out-of-state parent.

There are several common factors the courts consider when determining a child support order. Each state in the United States has established its own guidelines that are used to calculate the child support court order. The cost of living, which is different in each state, is one of the main factors that impacts the formula. Likewise, tax-filing status can impact the support obligation as well. For public policy reasons, if you pay fewer taxes, then it is assumed you have more available income to pay child support. The gross income of each parent, including taxable and non-taxable income, is often used as the starting point of calculating child support.

The approximate time the child spends with each parent is also a factor that makes a large impact on the support obligation. For example, if all other factors remain the same, a parent who has a child only 10% of the time is going to pay more child support than a parent who has custody 40 or 50% of the time. There are software programs available that use the financial and custody information of both parties to automatically calculate the state guideline child support amount. Some states provide calculators on their websites that allow a party to determine the approximate child support amount based on their current financial circumstances.

Both parents must make every effort to financially support the child. If one parent is not working or working "under the table," some courts will require the non-working parent to show proof of efforts to find work. A court can also impute or assign income to a party if the court finds that it is appropriate. Other parents who are either self-employed or work for cash must provide alternative proof of income or income ability. Tax returns can also be used as proof of income for purposes of support.

A parent seeking child support should gather several pieces of information to seek child support. Pay statements and documentation showing the estimated income of each party are almost always required before a Court can establish a child support order. Throughout the process, each parent will have the opportunity to present evidence to the Court regarding each parent's total financial circumstances before the Court will make a child support determination. However, a parent must not ignore notices from the Court. Once a court has determined the other parent has received proper notice as required by law in that jurisdiction the Court will proceed with making child support orders whether the other parent provides documentation and/or shows up at the scheduled hearing or not. It is the responsibility of each party to ensure they provide the Court with all appropriate information requested.

After the Court makes child support orders, the parent seeking to receive the child support can take steps to ensure the support is paid. Child support can be directly taken from the paying parents' paycheck, either once a month or allocated per pay period. A specific order to garnish wages can be obtained when requested. These orders are then sent directly to the employer of the paying parent. It then becomes the responsibility of the employer to ensure it withdraws and disperses it on a timely basis. Some states have the support funds sent to a disbursement unit that then sends the money to the receiving parent. For example, if the paying parent is in the military the Department of Finance and Accounting Services will be sent the wage withholding order for the child support obligation of the military member and ensure the payment is taken directly out of his or her monthly salary benefits.

When one parent receives state welfare assistance, the county will first try to collect from the other parent funds to cover the assistance the state is providing. These policies are crafted to ensure that the state is not providing financial assistance in cases when the other parent is capable of providing adequate support for the child. Sometimes, these types of cases result in the payor parent repaying the state or county that assisted the parent in receiving support.

Lastly, child support has unique characteristics compared to other debts or obligations. A parent receiving child support cannot waive child support, though child support can be set at $0 and reserved for further determination at a different time. Child support cannot be wiped away if a paying parent files for bankruptcy. Thus, if a parent is behind in a child support obligation it will continue to grow—especially since interest payments accrue. If a parent is behind in child support, interest can be added to the amount past due as a penalty for not paying the support obligation on time. In California, the interest rate for any outstanding child support is 10% annually. Sometimes if the paying parent owes a large sum of money, that parent can ask for a payment plan to pay the amount of child support that is outstanding and remains unpaid depending on how much is owed and the specific financial circumstances of the paying party. Each state has its own state-mandated rules regarding the collection of arrears on child support.

State-sponsored services like child support divisions of the Court have additional resources available to ensure a parent meets his or her child support obligations. For example, the state can intercept tax refunds from the IRS to pay a child support obligation if a paying parent is behind on his or her obligation. Some states have also authorized agencies to impose other penalties, including suspensions of driver's licenses and professional licenses or restrictions on international travel (listing the child support owing parent on a no-fly list) and passport renewals. Therefore, it is always best to ensure child support is paid timely and to keep good records of all payments made.

Amanda J. Hill

See also: Child Custody; Parenting Plans and Custody Arrangements; Shared Custody

Further Reading

McFarland, Saundra T. and Nicholas Hill. 2014. "The Impact of Child Support Laws on the Measured Outcomes of Children." *Journal of Legal Issues in Business* 3.

National Conference of State Legislatures. http://www.ncsl.org/research/human-services/child-support-homepage.aspx

Sorenson, Elaine. 2016. *The Story behind the Numbers: The Child Support Program is a Good Investment.* Office of Child Support Enforcement, Administration for Children & Families, U.S. Department of Health and Human Resources.

Child Support Calculations

This entry summarizes the framework governing child support calculations throughout the United States. While there are several different models and all states differ in the details, all state models are driven by a federally mandated structure. This federal framework demands mathematically calculable awards that create consistency and efficiency across courtrooms, judges, and families. These guidelines apply in a gender-neutral fashion and without regard to marital status.

The modern model for calculating child support is perhaps best understood in contrast to historic approaches. Historically, family law judges had great discretion to fashion orders on a case-by-case basis seeking results that were "just" or "reasonable." That discretion still dominates much of the spousal support and property distribution frameworks in family law, as other entries in this volume highlight. These discretionary models created inconsistency and uncertainty, both of which undermined settlement and increased conflict. These historic models also encouraged "forum-shopping" whereby litigants could shop different courts or different judges to hope for better results. Historic models were also gendered, presuming that the duty of support sat on the father alone and, historically, only imposed a duty of support on *married* fathers. When child support was inadequate or nonexistent, the caregiver would likely need support from public benefits programs.

The federal government then intervened to tighten and transform child support frameworks. The Child Support Enforcement Amendments of 1984 required states to develop child support guidelines and provided federal grants for compliance. Under this law, there were no particular guideline requirements established and consequently, variability persisted. While the law required that the guidelines be made available to judges, they were not binding. The law launched some early enforcement mechanisms (such as wage withholding), paternity establishment procedures, reporting and data collection procedures, and incentives for state recoupment efforts.

The Family Support Act of 1988 made several additional changes to the child support framework. The amendments strengthened enforcement mechanisms, further mandated wage withholding, and set up collection programs through the Office of Child Support Enforcement. The law notably required states to develop guidelines for consistent mathematical awards that would be presumptive awards, unless there were deviations justified by written findings of fact that the presumptive award would be unjust or inappropriate. States had to revisit the sufficiency of the award amounts every four years.

Each state began modifying their state guidelines in response. Today, state guidelines can differ in what "counts" as income. For example, variability exists on whether disability payments or personal injury awards are qualifying income. States may impute income to those who are voluntarily unemployed or under-employed. States do not impose $0 awards, setting a higher minimum. Most jurisdictions put an upward bound on the award in the application of the guidelines. Income exceeding the guidelines may be the basis for a deviation.

The majority of states apply an Income Shares model to their child support guidelines. This model treats the two parents as one economic unit and calculates their gross monthly income. It attempts to approximate the standard of living that existed in marriage, but it applies to non-marital families too. Gross monthly income is broadly defined to include all income from all sources, except means-tested government assistance. States can include "offsets," which are reductions in gross monthly income for prior family support awards.

The Income Shares model then identifies what percentage each parent contributes to the total gross monthly income. The state publishes a standardized chart denoting exactly how much the state has determined is the proper award amount for the number of kids in a household with that gross monthly income. The state then allocates the award at the same percentage of the parents' respective contributions to the monthly income. Thus, if one parent earned 75% of the total gross monthly income and the other 25%, and if the presumptive award was $2,000, then one parent would be assessed $1,500 of the child support award and the other $500.

There is then a mechanism to deviate from the presumptive award if the judge concludes that the presumptive award would be unjust or inappropriate. Deviations are often based on extraordinary medical, dental, or educational needs or the independent wealth of the child.

This model has been critiqued heavily because it treats two individuals as one economic unit when they are not actually an economic unit. This creates uncomfortable disincentives for the lesser-earning spouse to increase their economic earning power because to do so would decrease their child support. These models have also been critiqued for the inability to set a gross monthly income at $0, leaving parents who are incarcerated, disabled, hospitalized, or unemployed continuing to accrue child support debt while unable to pay it. This model does not generally account for caregiving time, which does not then value the non-economic costs of childrearing.

A smaller number of jurisdictions have adopted the Percentage of Income model for calculating child support. The Percentage of Income model only takes into consideration the noncustodial parent's income when making the calculations of child support. Seven states use this method of calculating child support.

When calculating child support under the Percentage of Income model, the noncustodial parent's income is first calculated. The state's designated statutory table then reveals the percentage of the noncustodial parent's income that is relevant to the presumptive award. This number varies based on the number of children and is used to determine the presumptive support award. If the non-custodial parent earned $2,000 monthly, that number would be used to determine the appropriate percentage based on the number of children. If the noncustodial parent has only one child making that amount, for example, the parent's percentage would be 17% and that parent's obligation would be $340 a month. This model also allows for deviations to the presumptive award for extraordinary medical, dental, or educational needs.

The Percentage of Income model has its own critiques. With this model, this presumptive award negatively affects lower-income obligors because a large percentage of their monthly income could be used toward paying child support, especially if that parent must pay toward more than one child. This presumptive award also assumes that all parents will pay the same amount regardless of whether the custodial parent earns an income or not. Moreover, this presumptive award creates an assumption that the noncustodial parent could pay this amount without sacrificing their minimal standard of living. This model does not consider the economic status or economic stability of the custodial parent. If the noncustodial parent has a significantly lower economic status than the custodial parent, the non-custodial parent may have to forgo their own economic stability to assist the other parent unnecessarily. Even with this potential lack of economic stability, the non-custodial parent's income may fluctuate, meaning that the amount of support to the custodial parent could drastically drop at points.

Only a couple of jurisdictions have adopted either the Melson formula or the Delaware model of calculation. This formula is a more complicated version of the Income Shares model. Created by a Delaware Family Court, this model incorporated several public policy judgments. Designed to ensure both parents' basic needs are met in addition to the children, only three states currently use this model: Delaware, Hawaii, and Montana.

The Melson formula involves a three-step calculation. First, the net income of each parent must be calculated. Under this formula, the court looks at take-home pay when considering net income. Significantly, a self-support reserve is subtracted from the net income. The concept of the self-support reserve stems from the critique that a person cannot support another if their own basic support needs are unmet. Second, each individual's remaining income identifies a presumptive award of child support. Third, an additional percentage of the income remaining tacks onto the presumptive award, but only if the parent holds any additional income following the first two computations.

While the Melson formula does incorporate policy considerations that could protect lower-income obligors by ensuring each parent protects finances for *their* basic needs, criticisms of this model still exist. This model allows for great inconsistency in the support obligations. With this inconsistency in the payment obligations, this model also creates the possibility of higher individual obligations to maintain the child's status of living if the parent's income is higher.

These varying models are also backed up by a robust child enforcement system, which is addressed in a separate entry. These child support obligations are imposed until the child reaches the age of majority (as set by state statute). Child support calculations are thus directed by federal law with great variability at the state level.

Jamie R. Abrams and
Nickole Durbin Félix

See also: Child Custody; Parenting Plans and Custody Arrangements; Shared Custody

Further Reading

Child Support Enforcement Amendments of 1984, Pub L. No. 98–378, 98 Stat. 1305 (Aug. 16, 1984) (codified as amended in scattered sections of 42 U.S.C.).

Child Support Guideline Models by State, Nat'l Conf. Of State Legislatures (Feb. 20, 2019), http://www.ncsl.org/research/human -services/guideline-models-by-state .aspx.

Family Support Act of 1988, Pub. L. No. 100–485, 102 Stat. 2343 (Oct. 13, 1988) (codified as amended in scattered sections of 42 U.S.C.).

Family Support Act of 1988, Inst. for Res. on Poverty 15, 15–18 (1989), https://www .irp.wisc.edu/publications/focus/pdfs /focl14e.pdf.

Childcare and Eldercare

According to numerous research studies and government reports, childcare and eldercare constitute two of the most significant challenges for marriages and other relationships to navigate. Seeing to the needs of dependent children and declining elderly parents often requires considerable sacrifices of financial resources, time with a spouse or partner, career opportunities, and investments in other relationships with friends or family. In 1981, sociologist Dorothy Miller coined the term "the sandwich generation" to describe adults who are caring for their own children while also caring for elderly parents. The number of American adults living in this circumstance has been growing for the last few decades. According to a 2021 Pew Research Survey, 23% of American adults now find themselves providing care for their younger children and aging parents simultaneously.

Childcare Challenges

Broadly speaking, childcare is any service provided to watch over a child or children. Sometimes these arrangements do not have a financial component to them, as with childcare provided by other family members or friends. Other childcare arrangements require financial outlays on the part of families. Babysitting services, day care for infants and toddlers, and camps for older children during school breaks are common childcare arrangements that cost money to use.

Millions of American parents who work outside the home struggle when seeking affordable, quality childcare. Federal programs do exist that help poor families pay for childcare—often so a parent can go to work—but child welfare advocates contend that they are badly underfunded. The Childcare and Development Fund (CCDF), the federal government's chief source of childcare funding, is so underfunded that it only reaches one out of seven eligible families. "This leaves the burden of paying for childcare primarily on families who struggle to afford the true cost of care in most communities. Families are extremely price sensitive, with childcare often taking up one-third of more of their monthly budget and forcing families to consider a price above many other variables," noted a 2021 report from the Center for American Progress, a liberal public policy group (Workman 2021).

Childcare for infants and toddlers is a year-round expense. Meanwhile, a 2021 YouGov/Bankrate survey found that 45% of parents with childcare needs during the summer, or other times when schools are on break, planned to assume credit card debt to pay for it. That same survey estimated that the per-child cost of summer childcare for those families at $834 (Johnson 2021). Parents of school-age children get some relief during the school year. However, if both parents work full-time jobs, many still find themselves paying for care to cover the hours between the end of the school day and the end of the work day.

Researchers and marriage counselors alike agree that the cost and logistics of childcare, as well as the guilt that some parents feel at not being a "stay at home" parent, often put a strain on marriages, relationships, and other coparenting arrangements. This is especially true in heterosexual relationships where there is, traditionally, a marked imbalance in the division of caregiving duties, with female partners often managing the lion's share of both childcare and eldercare.

Childcare, however, does proceed along generally predictable lines as children grow older and become more independent. Eldercare, on the other hand, "is an unpredictable, variable event that can occur suddenly during a loved one's health crisis, or creep up slowly as a relative's health and functioning decline" (Dobkin 2007).

Eldercare Challenges

According to a 2020 AARP study, about 41.8 million people in the United States (16.8% of the population) provide care or significant assistance to an adult over the age of 50. "Of those caregivers," noted *Vox*, "28 percent have stopped saving, 23 percent have taken on more debt, 22 percent have used up their personal short-term savings, and 11 percent reported being unable to cover basic needs, including food. The average age of someone providing care for an adult is 49, but 23 percent are millennials [born between 1981 and 1996] and 6 percent are Gen Z [born between 1997 and 2012]. Sixty-one percent are women, and 40 percent provide that care within their own homes, up from 34 percent in 2015. A lot of these caregivers are really, really struggling" (Peterson 2021).

Prohibitive costs and concerns about the quality of care in professional facilities drives families to absorb the responsibilities themselves. Many adults find themselves in caregiving roles for their parents at a time when they are in mid-career or even approaching retirement. The demands of caring for parents with greatly diminished physical or mental faculties in in-home settings can be so great that caregivers feel forced to take early retirement to ease the strain of their responsibilities, which results in further financial strain. One 2011 MetLife study estimated that people 50 and older who retired early because of eldercare responsibilities would lose an average of $300,000 over their lifetime in wages and Social Security benefits (Conlon 2019).

Eldercare experts emphasize that the financial expense of caring for a parent or other elderly relative—which is often dauntingly high—is only one aspect of the burden. Eldercare often requires attending to basic needs of nutrition, medical care, hygiene, and home upkeep, all while the caregiver tries to simultaneously maintain other aspects of their life related to work and family. Most are entirely unprepared for the type of nursing care that older adults require.

Looking to the future, researchers warn that demographic trends related to lower birth rates mean that the ratio of potential adult caregivers to elderly people is going to continue to drop. "In 2010, there were about seven people between the ages of 45 and 64 available to care for every person over the age of 80, but that ratio is shrinking. By 2030, that ratio is expected to be about four to one, and by 2050, it's expected to be three to one" (Conlon 2019).

Organizations and agencies, such as Caregiver.org, the National Caregiver Alliance, and federal, state, and local agencies on aging are focused on raising awareness, providing support to caregivers, and advocating for more government resources to address the issue.

Christine Slovey

See also: Adults and Illness; Children and Illness; Marriage, Financial Implications

Further Reading

American Psychological Association. 2008. "Sandwich Generation Moms Feeling the Squeeze." https://www.apa.org/topics/families/sandwich-generation.

Conlon, Rose. 2019. "The Financial Toll of Caring for Aging Parents as an Only Child." Marketplace.org. https://www.marketplace.org/2019/09/25/the-financial-toll-of-caring-for-aging-parents-as-an-only-child/ (accessed February 7, 2022).

Dobkin, Leah. 2007. "Why Childcare and Eldercare Are so Different." Workforce.com. https://workforce.com/news/why-child-care-and-elder-care-are-so-different (accessed February 7, 2022).

Glenn, Evelyn Nakano. 2012. *Forced to Care: Coercion and Caregiving in America.* Cambridge, MA: Harvard University Press.

Jacobs, Barry J. 2019. "Keeping Your Marriage Strong While Caring for a Parent." AARP. https://www.aarp.org/caregiving/life-balance/info-2019/keeping-your-marriage-strong.html (accessed February 7, 2022).

Johnson, Allie. 2021. "Poll: Many Parents Will Put Summer Childcare on a Credit Card This Summer." BankRate.com. https://www.bankrate.com/finance/credit-cards/summer-childcare-survey/.

Miller, Claire Cain. 2019. "Why Mothers' Choices About Work and Family Often Don't Feel Like Choices at All." *New York Times.* https://www.nytimes.com/2019/08/29/business/economy/labor-family-care.html (accessed February 7, 2022).

Miller, Dorothy A. 1981. "The Sandwich Generation: Adult Children of the Aging." *Social Work*, 26, no. 5.

Peterson, Anne Helen. 2021. "The Staggering, Exhausting, Invisible Costs of Caring for America's Elderly." Vox.com. https://www.vox.com/the-goods/22639674/elder-care-family-costs-nursing-home-health-care (accessed February 7, 2022).

Solitto, Maria. 2015. "9 Ways Caring for Parents Is Different than Caring for Children." AgingCare.com. https://www.agingcare.com/articles/caring-for-parents-versus-caring-for-children-120215.htm (accessed February 7, 2022).

Workman, Simon. 2021. "The True Cost of High-Quality Childcare Across the United States." American Progress. https://www.americanprogress.org/article/true-cost-high-quality-child-care-across-united-states/ (accessed February 7, 2022).

Child-Inclusive Mediation

Mediation is one process of alternative dispute resolution that is often viewed as being the least conflictual and allowing the individuals to have the most control and influence over the resolution process. Mediation has found a place in the family court system internationally in various forms as an alternative to the traditional court process where a judge decides the parenting plan for the parties involved. Mediation allows individuals to determine what is best for themselves and their families. Self-determination is widely considered the core principle of mediation (Alfini 2008). Child-inclusive mediation has developed over time as one form of mediation that reflects this core principle of self-determination by providing the children a voice in the mediation process. When children can participate in the mediation process, it can assist parents in understanding the sometimes-complex issues surrounding parenting time arrangements through the perspective of their children.

Since the United Nations Convention in 1991, children participating in the divorce or separation process have been protected as a right of the child. Even with these children's rights outlined, children do not always participate directly in the process. Their participation can also be in the form of someone representing the child or in multiple other ways (Lansdown 2011). The options for how children can participate in the mediation process vary widely across the United States and internationally. This can be an attorney coming to represent the children, or parents both agreeing to meet with the children together and mutually speaking to them to get their point of view. If a parent represents a child in mediation, it should be mutually agreed upon by both parents in mediation. In some cases, parents can mutually agree to speak to the child(ren) together and take their children's opinions to the mediation session.

Children adapt to divorce better when their parents manage the separation process in a low-conflict way (Amato and Keith 1991; Kelly and Emery 2003). Mediation and other alternative dispute resolution processes work to include children's perspectives in an attempt to keep conflict low. Unfortunately, research on the effectiveness of including the child's voice in this process is minimal. This means that most of the information practitioners have about the effectiveness of different child-inclusive mediation processes come from personal practice experience.

At the 2002 Association of Family and Conciliation Courts Conference (AFCC), a survey was conducted with the participants, and they were asked to rate eight different methods of children sharing their voice in the dispute resolution process. The method that was rated as the healthiest for children to share their opinion in the process was for the child to be interviewed privately by a mental health provider, such as a social worker, child therapist, or psychologist. The provider works with the parents as well as possibly interview the child with the parents. In this style of child-inclusive mediation, the mental health provider often brings the information back to the mediation session or shares it with the parents. The same participant survey ranked the most damaging way to obtain the opinions of the child is having a child testify in court with a judge (Birnbaum 2009). While there are multiple methods in how a child gets to express their preferences, there are clearly ways that family court professionals perceive as less harmful and impactful on the child. In fact, when child-inclusive mediation or alternative dispute resolution involves the child, it can be an empowering process for both the child as well as the parents.

If the mediation process does not include someone to represent the child in mediation, the mediator may assist a child in different methods. The mediator's role in assisting the child to express their thoughts about the parenting plan can be as simple as interviewing both parents and the child individually. In some cases, mediators may determine that it would be helpful to bring the child in with the parents during the mediation session when an issue is being discussed. These topics could be preferences in after-school activities. Sometimes children can provide insight into where they prefer to have exchange locations. For older children, direct input on the parenting plan can be helpful. These issues can be items such as where the exchange point can be, bedtime routine, or other items personal to them. Sometimes mediators may ask

the child or children to participate in the finalization of the agreement.

There are many factors for a mediator to consider before deciding to use the child-inclusive mediation approach. Ruth Sinclair explains that the potential participation of children in mediation has four dimensions (Sinclair 2004). These include: (1) the level of engagement in participating in the mediation; (2) the goal of the decision-making that involves children; (3) the actual participation activity in the mediation; and (4) the emotional development of the children. Sinclair states that the things to consider when deciding whom to involve the mediation process include age, gender, culture, economic and social circumstances, and the possible disabilities of the participating children.

In 2001, the American Bar Association House of Delegates developed the Model Standards of Practice for Family and Divorce Mediation. The model outlines guidelines to follow when involving children. The consent of parents and any court-appointed representative(s) should be obtained after the mediator outlines the possible participation and the process. When exploring this possible participation with the parents and any representative, the mediator should outline what all options are available to the child for possible participation in the process (Birnbaum 2009).

While the American Bar Association has provided this model as a general outline, these guidelines still do not provide specific information about conducting the interviews and the actual interview process as a mediator. Many mediators who are willing to do child-inclusive mediation understand that children will often try to please each parent and can be coached to answer the way they feel their parents want them to answer. This is why the mediator needs to be trained to understand children and their developmental stages. Not all states require mediators that work with children to be trained in child-inclusive mediation. Depending on the state a mediator is practicing in, they may not have this important training. It is important when selecting a mediator to know the skills and background they have.

For example, children closer to ages 9 or older are better candidates to participate in mediation because of the decreased chances of manipulation by parents as well as being able to articulate their wants and needs. But not all children at this age may be able to participate in the same way depending on their emotional development. However, there could be developmental or emotional issues that would make the child being considered for participation not appropriate for mediation. The mediator should know how to assess the child appropriately.

Children can be represented by their own legal representative. This could be an attorney acting as an advocate, as a guardian ad litem, or as a friend of the court. A child could have a child specialist representing them, such as in the process of Collaborative Family Law. The places that use Collaborative Family Law are using a method that both attorneys agree to work together to solve the family issues in the least conflictual way possible. The children can express what they feel is important and child evaluations by a neutral third party can also add to the full picture of the family dynamics.

There are best practice recommendations for child-inclusive mediation. While other models referenced earlier have addressed the issues of age and child development, best practice models also address the importance of obtaining the child's consent, ensuring the child's safety, and making sure they fully understand the concept of confidentiality. Interviewers also need to understand the importance of the ability for mediators understanding the ability to overcome barriers that can be created by language and other diversity issues. While child-inclusive mediation still varies throughout the world, professionals are seeing the positive impact on how the children and parents can jointly participate in this process together.

Tonya Ricklefs

See also: Communication between Parents and Children in Divorce; Divorce Mediation

Further Reading

Alfini, J. J. 2008. "Mediation as a calling." *South Texas Law Review* 49.

Amato, P. R., and Keith, B. 1991. "Parental divorce and the well-being of children: A meta analysis." *Psychological Bulletin* 110, no. 1: 26–46. https://doi.org/10.1037/0033-2909.110.1.26

Birnbaum, Rachel. 2009. "The voice of the child in separation/divorce mediation and other alternative dispute resolution processes: A literature review." Department of Justice Canada.

Kelly, J. B., and Emery, R. E. 2003. "Children's adjustment following divorce: Risk and resilience perspectives." *Family Relations: An Interdisciplinary Journal of Applied Family Studies* 52, no. 4: 352–362.

Lansdown, Gerison. 2011. "Every child's right to be heard." *Save the Children UK*.

Sinclair, Ruth. 2004. "Participation in practice: Making it meaningful, effective and sustainable." *Children in Society* 18, no. 2: 106–118.

Children and Illness

Although 90% of parents report their child to be in excellent or very good health, during the 2017–2018 school year, over 44% of children missed between 1 and 3 days of school because of illness (Child and Adolescent Health Measurement Initiative 2018). Young children experience many common diseases throughout their course of development. They may contract common illnesses such as sore throat, ear pain, urinary tract infection, skin infection, pain, common cold, bacterial sinusitis, and cough. Children in school settings are also at an increased risk of transmitting communicable illnesses due to the close-quartered nature inherent to schools (White et al. 2001). However, these effects of common diseases often may be eased by practicing good hygiene, such as hand washing (White et al. 2001).

Despite the data regarding positive parent perception of their children's well-being, the number of school-aged children experiencing chronic illnesses is ever-increasing, ranging from 10–30% (Lagor et al. 2013). Chronic illness means a health condition requiring ongoing medical intervention, including epilepsy, arthritis, cancer, asthma, chronic pain, cardiac issues, and sickle cell disease. Both children with chronic illnesses and their close friends and family members have social-emotional needs or clinical illnesses, such as depression and anxiety. As such, mind-body health approaches, such as mindfulness-based techniques, are gaining empirical justification for addressing many physiological and psychological outcomes in children with chronic illnesses and their immediate and extended family (Kabat-Zinn and

Nhat Han 2009). Psychoeducational programs have been mounting in number and gaining effectiveness in improving the psychological impacts on families with children with chronic illnesses. Positive outcomes of these interventions include symptom reduction for a variety of chronic diseases, including epilepsy, seizures, respiratory disorders such as asthma, and pain management.

When a child receives a medical diagnosis, especially a chronic or life-threatening one, this illness may become a stressor for the family system. Family stressors, or family stress, is a term addressing the disruption in the typical functioning patterns of the family (Boss 1987). When a family faces a chronic illness of a child, such as cancer, couples report a variety of perspectives related to their marital satisfaction, some of which are positive, others negative (Long and Marsland 2011). The marriage quality can change throughout the child's illness as parents may prioritize the needs of the child over that of their spouse. Interestingly, a large subset of parents with children facing a cancer diagnosis have indicated that they face ongoing marital problems (Long and Marshland 2011). It is critical to consider the potential negative implications illness can place on the family system, specifically the stress and emotional toll. Parents may also experience "role overload," as they take on additional responsibilities and chores to support the family during the stressful period (Major 2003). Mothers have historically been likely to serve in a caretaking role. At the same time, fathers are less likely to be involved in caring for the child who is ill. At the same time, spouses may rely on each other for support (Long and Marshland 2011). Overall, the effects of a chronic childhood illness possess the ability to impact the family system. Such impacts may vary depending on the system and family members' typical response to stressors.

In addition to learning how to cope with changes to the family system, families must also consider ways to assist their child in experiencing chronic illness. One of the best ways parents and families can aid their child is to provide developmentally appropriate guidance and support around treatment management and self-advocacy. A critical part of treatment management is for parents to teach their child how to take over their medication regime. Achieving the developmental milestone of self-management is often directly connected to the parent-child relationship (Armstrong et al. 2011). Children can learn from their parents exactly how to manage their medications. Eventually, the child will be ready to oversee their medications on their own. Despite this connection, research has identified very few psychosocial interventions that teach adolescents how to properly manage their medications, emphasizing why learning from parents is critical. Only two interventions use a theoretical lens, adapted from versions of Multisystemic Therapy (MST) (Ellis et al. 2005) and Brief Strategic Family Therapy (BSFT-D) (Wysocki et al. 2007). Even still, these findings are limited to diabetes. These limitations highlight the need for research to help children independently manage their chronic illnesses, whether the child lives in a house with married parents or has parents who are divorced.

Many psychosocial interventions for children with chronic illness involve the child solely (e.g., Cognitive Behavioral Therapy, Motivational Interviewing). A comprehensive review of the literature suggests better outcomes, such as better long-term health from chronically ill children, if the family system engages in therapy together as opposed to the child just individually receiving support (Distelberg et al. 2014). Past research has investigated methods involving family systems therapy and its effectiveness for the child and their family (Distelberg et al. 2014). Mastering Each New Direction (MEND) is a biopsychosocial intensive outpatient program providing mental health treatment for children with chronic illness and their families (Distelberg et al. 2014). MEND increases adherence to medication and treatment regimens as well as disease outcomes and stress on the families. At the same time, MEND affects functional measures related to the family system, such as physical, emotional, social, and cognitive functioning, as well as worry, communication, daily activities, and family relationships. MEND is an exciting endeavor, as very few programs exist that involve both the child and the family. Results investigating the benefits of MEND demonstrate significant improvement regarding physical, emotional, social, cognitive, and school functioning for the child, and evidence reduced levels of negative impact on the family system (Distelberg et al. 2014).

Emily Winter, Melissa A. Bray, and Rachel Baumann

See also: Adults and Illness; Childcare and Eldercare; Death of a Child

Further Reading

Armstrong, Bridget, Eleanor Race Mackey, and Randi Streisand. 2011. "Parenting behavior, child functioning, and health behaviors in preadolescents with type 1 diabetes." *Journal of Pediatric Psychology* 36, no. 9: 1052–1061.

Boss, Pauline. 1987. "Family stress." In *Handbook of marriage and the family.* Boston, MA: Springer, pp. 695–723.

Child and Adolescent Health Measurement Initiative. 2018. *2017–2018 National Survey of Children's Health (NSCH) data query.* Distributed by Data Resource Center for Child and Adolescent Health supported by the U.S. Department of Health and Human Services, Health Resources and Services Administration (HRSA), Maternal and Child Health Bureau (MCHB). https://www.childhealthdata.org/browse/survey

Distelberg, Brian, Jackie Williams-Reade, Daniel Tapanes, Susanne Montgomery, and Mayuri Pandit. 2014. "Evaluation of a family systems intervention for managing pediatric chronic illness: Mastering Each New Direction (MEND)." *Family Process* 53, no. 2: 194–213.

Ellis, Deborah A., Maureen A. Frey, Sylvie Naar-King, Thomas Templin, Phillippe Cunningham, and Nedim Cakan. 2005. "Use of multisystemic therapy to improve regimen adherence among adolescents with type 1 diabetes in chronic poor metabolic control: A randomized controlled trial." *Diabetes Care* 28, no. 7: 1604–1610.

Kabat-Zinn, Jon, and Thich Nhat Hanh. 2009. *Full catastrophe living: Using the wisdom of your body and mind to face stress, pain, and illness.* New York: Random House.

Lagor, Anne F., Dahra Jackson Williams, Jennifer Block Lerner, and Kelly S. McClure. 2013. "Lessons learned from a mindfulness-based intervention with chronically ill youth." *Clinical Practice in Pediatric Psychology* 1, no. 2: 146–158.

Long, Kristin A., and Anna L. Marsland. 2011. "Family adjustment to childhood cancer: A systematic review." *Clinical Child and Family Psychology Review* 14, no. 1: 57–88.

Major, Debra A. 2003. "Utilizing role theory to help employed parents cope with children's chronic illness." *Health Education Research* 18, no. 1: 45–57. https://doi.org/10.1093/her/18.1.45

White, Catherine G., Fay S. Shinder, Arnold L. Shinder, and David L. Dyer. 2001. "Reduction of illness absenteeism in elementary schools using an alcohol-free instant hand sanitizer." *The Journal of School Nursing* 17, no. 5: 248–265.

Wysocki, Tim, Michael A. Harris, Lisa M. Buckloh, Debbie Mertlich, Amanda S. Lochrie, Nelly Mauras, and Neil H. White. 2007. "Randomized trial of behavioral family systems therapy for diabetes: Maintenance of effects on diabetes outcomes in adolescents." *Diabetes Care* 30, no. 3: 555–560.

Children with Exceptionalities

During the 20th century the divorce rate increased; nearly 50% of married couples experience divorce, therefore, approximately half of children experience parental divorce in the United States. Research has shown that children of divorce have to deal with a variety of mental health outcomes including anxiety, depression, attention problems, and aggressive behavior. Also, they are more likely to suffer from low levels of self-efficacy, self-esteem, social support, and coping behaviors. Children who face parental divorce or separation are more likely to have eating disorders as opposed to children with intact families Also, these children are less likely to attend and graduate college, and more likely to marry children of divorce, affecting the educational outcomes of their offsprings (Price 2010).

Interestingly, studies on children who experienced parental divorce are more likely to have children when they were adolescents and before marriage, and they are more likely to divorce in their own marriages compared to children from intact families. Children with exceptionalities which have various difficulties such as learning, emotional, behavioral, and required special attention and services might have more adverse outcomes than children without special needs as consequences of the divorce of parents. Forty percent of children younger than 16 face parental divorce in their families and 30% of these children have special needs (Sneed, May, and Stencel 2000). Therefore, this means there are millions of children with special needs who might experience parental divorce. During or after the divorce, children with special needs have more aggression, loss of toilet training, loss of academic and social skills, self-injury, hopelessness, thoughts about suicide, and emotional outbursts or running away. In these kinds of situations, children who have special needs may react different than typically developed children since their needs and coping abilities vary.

Unlike parents of special needs children, research stated that parents of gifted children are less likely to divorce than parents of typical children. In addition, the difference between academic success for gifted children of divorced parents, gifted children from intact families, and children with average intelligence from divorced parents is examined by Kraynak (1997). In this study, gifted children from intact families have more successful academic performance than children from divorced parents. In that case, we can say that divorce has a negative impact on gifted children' academic success.

In their meta-analysis, Risdal and Singer (2004) found that parents of children with special needs are more likely to detach an average of 5.97% more compared to the parents of typically developing children. Also, these parents have more marital conflict than other parents. More studies found higher divorce rates and lower relationship satisfaction among the parents of special education children compared with the parents of children without special needs. Different factors might also correlate with these results, such as the educational level of both parents, the number of children, race, ethnicity, etc. Interestingly, while the divorce rate decreases when the child reaches adolescence, for the parents of children with Autism Spectrum Disorder (ASD), the rate of divorce does not decrease (Hartley et al. 2010). Being a parent of a child with ASD might have a negative impact on the healthy communication between the couple which can potentially increase the divorce rate. Researchers found that parents who have adolescents diagnosed with attention deficit/hyperactivity disorder (ADHD) are more likely to divorce than parents of typically developed adolescents, as the latency to divorce is shorter when compared with the parents of typical adolescents. In their analysis, race/ethnicity, maternal/paternal education, and paternal antisocial behavior are significant predictors for latency to divorce (Wymbs et al. 2008). A similar finding indicated that mothers of adolescents who have ADHD are more likely to divorce or live separately from the fathers than mothers of typically developing adolescents (Barkley et al. 1991).

Marriage

Marital satisfaction is crucial for a healthy relationship and improved parenting efficacy. It is also correlated with lower levels of depression and parenting stress. Research found that parents of children with ASD have lower parenting efficacy than parents who have children without special needs. In addition, parents of children with special needs have more marital problems and their quality of marital life has been found lower than parents of children without special needs because of the difficulty of handling children with special needs (Hartley et al. 2017). High levels of stress can have an adverse effect on marital relationships and it affects the marriage and divorce among parents of special needs children. Parents of special needs children have greater risk to be divorced (Hartley et al. 2010) compared to peers who have typically developing children. To increase marital satisfaction, avoid stress as much as possible. Sharing the childcare and household responsibilities would also be beneficial.

The parenting stress in families of children with ASD, ADHD, and ASD+ADHD were compared to parenting stress among parents of typical children by Miranda, Tarraga, Fernández, Colomer, and Pastor (2015). The highest level of parenting stress was observed in parents of ADHD children and the lowest level of parenting stress was found in parents of typically developing children. It is evident that having children with special needs can be overwhelming for parents and the high level of stress might influence their marriage and personal life as they need to adjust their life's routine to care for the child. The parents of children with special needs should reserve more time, effort, and resources for the well-being of their children. The difficulties might weaken the relationship among family members and increase the level of parental depression.

Seyma Intepe-Tingir

See also: Childcare and Eldercare; Children and Illness; Divorce Education; Marriage, Financial Implications

Further Reading

Barkley, Russell A., Mariellen Fischer, Craig Edelbrock, and Lori Smallish. 1991. "The adolescent outcome of hyperactive children diagnosed by research criteria—III. Mother–child interactions, family conflicts and maternal psychopathology." *Journal of Child Psychology and Psychiatry* 32, no. 2: 233–255.

Hartley, Sigan L., Erin T. Barker, Marsha Mailick Seltzer, Frank Floyd, Jan Greenberg, Gael Orsmond, and Daniel Bolt. 2010. "The relative risk and timing of divorce in families of children with an autism spectrum disorder." *Journal of Family Psychology* 24, no. 4: 449.

Hartley, Sigan L., Leann Smith DaWalt, and Haley M. Schultz. 2017. "Daily couple experiences and parent affect in families of children with versus without autism." *Journal of Autism and Developmental Disorders* 47, no. 6: 1645–1658.

Kraynak, Audrey Rericha. 1997. "The relationship of children's intellectual ability and adjustment to parental divorce." PhD diss., ProQuest Information & Learning.

Miranda, Ana, Raul Tárraga, M. Inmaculada Fernández, Carla Colomer, and Gemma Pastor. 2015. "Parenting stress in families of children with autism spectrum disorder and ADHD." *Exceptional Children* 82, no. 1: 81–95.

Price, M. S. 2010. *The special needs child and divorce: A practical guide to handling and evaluating cases.* Philadelphia, PA: American Bar Association.

Risdal, Don, and George H. S. Singer. 2004. "Marital adjustment in parents of children with disabilities: A historical review and meta-analysis." *Research and Practice for Persons with Severe Disabilities* 29, no. 2: 95–103.

Sneed, Raphael C., Warren L. May, and Christine S. Stencel. 2000. "Training of pediatricians in care of physical disabilities in children with special health needs: Results of a two-state survey of practicing pediatricians and national resident training programs." *Pediatrics* 105, no. 3: 554–561.

Wymbs, Brian T., William E. Pelham Jr, Brooke SG Molina, Elizabeth M. Gnagy, Tracey K. Wilson, and Joel B. Greenhouse. 2008. "Rate and predictors of divorce among parents of youths with ADHD." *Journal of Consulting and Clinical Psychology* 76, no. 5: 735.

Children's Rights Council

When two parents choose to live apart and coparent, the transition may be challenging for children caught between the two parents' homes, rules, tensions, and beliefs. While children's needs should remain front and center, parents may be distracted or disengaged due to their own emotional experience of separating from their partner. The Children's Rights Council (CRC), founded in 1985, is a non-profit organization that aims to prevent unnecessary conflicts between parents during and after a separation. The common thread connecting all of the CRC's work is a commitment to ensuring that children have both parents in their life regardless of the parents' relationship status. In fact, the CRC's copyrighted slogan is "The Best Parent is Both Parents©."

While most of the direct services are based in Maryland, the CRC's website and training can provide information and guidance to anyone needing assistance during a family transition involving their child. According to their website, the mission of CRC includes (1) the need to protect the "Best Interests" and healthy development of children; (2) the need to advance social and legal justice; and (3) the need to provide community awareness and parental education (Children's Rights Council, n.d., a). This mission translates into five primary service goals that guide the work of the agency.

The first is the Maryland-based Mediation Program. This program offers a neutral third party to assist both coparents in coming to a resolution about a parenting plan that is often faster, cheaper, and less complicated than formal legal proceedings.

The second service goal is the Crossroads of Parenting and Divorce seminar. It aims to prevent situations where children might feel caught in the conflicts of their two parents. In fact, the term "divorce abuse" is introduced early in the curriculum. Divorce abuse can occur when the emotional experience of children is so compromised that the environment becomes emotionally abusive. Examples include when coparents refuse to value the other parent and extended family, interfere with the time spent with the other parent, or depend on the child for emotional support (Children's Rights Council, n.d., b).

The bulk of what the organization provides is the Supervised Parenting Time Training and Monitored Exchange for Maryland families. Family and friends who facilitate transitions until parents are able to safely and calmly exchangetheirchildrenareoftenappointed by the courts and benefit from this training.

The fourth service is another training that addresses basics in Child Personal Care and Skill Building for Parents. The class teaches the practical information needed for day-to-day childrearing. This course is offered for parents who may be sharing the duties of parenting for the first time, for those who may need more information about child development, or for those who may have been absent in their child's life for a significant period of time.

Finally, the fifth goal of the CRC is to provide Cooperative Parenting and Divorce: Shielding Children from Conflict, a psychoeducation program aiming to reduce parental conflict and address the risks that children might experience post-separation.

In a pilot survey, Levy (2009) offered promising results from the point of view of the parents involved with a select number of CRC centers. Yet, more research is needed to evaluate the efficacy of the programs listed above.

In summary, the Children's Rights Council is committed to providing an array of services and supports to families who have children being raised by coparents living apart.

Tara Katherine Hammar

See also: Child Abuse; Child Custody; Coparenting and Divorce; Parenting Plans and Custody Arrangements

Further Reading

Amato, Paul and Keith, Bruce. 1991. "Parental Divorce and the Well-being of Children: A Meta-analysis." *Psychological Bulletin*, 110: 26–46. https://doi .org/10.1037/0033-2909.110.1.26

Children's Rights Council (a). n.d. "Our Mission." Accessed July 30, 2019. https:// www.crckids.org/home/message/.

Children's Rights Council (b). n.d. "Crossroads of Parenting and Divorce." Accessed July 31, 2019. https://www .crckids.org/about-us/goals/crossroads -of-parenting-and-divorce/

Kelly, Joan. 2012. "Risk and Protective Factors Associated with Child and Adolescent Adjustment Following Separation and Divorce." In *Parenting Plan Evaluations: Applied Research for the Family Court*, edited by Kathryn Kuehnle and Leslie Drozd. New York: *Oxford University Press*, pp. 49–84.

Lally, Stephen and Higuchi, Shirley Ann. 2008. "The American Psychological Association Parenting Coordination Project: Development of the Project and Initial Review of the First Two Years." *Journal of Child Custody* 5(1/2): 101–121.

Levy, David L. 2009. "Lending a Hand One Child at a Time: The Children's Rights Council's Child Access and Transfer Centers." *The American Journal of Family Therapy*, 37(5), 396–413, DOI: 10.1080/01926180902942175

Pruett, Marsha Kline and Barker, Ryan. 2009. "Influencing Coparenting Effectiveness After Divorce: What Works and How It Works." In *Strengthening Couple Relationships for Optimal Child Development: Lessons from Research and Intervention*, edited by Marc Schulz, Marsha Kline Pruett, Patricia Kerig, and Ross Parke. Washington, D.C.: American Psychological Association, pp. 181–196.

Teubert, Daniela and Pinquart, Martin. 2010. "The Association between Coparenting and Child Adjustment: A Meta-Analysis." *Parenting: Science and Practice*, 10, 286–307. https://doi.org/10 .1080/15295192.2010.492040

Collaborative Divorce

Collaborative divorce is a relatively new kind of alternative dispute resolution (ADR), or way of resolving a divorce without involving the courts. In a traditional divorce, both spouses hire attorneys to represent them during court proceedings that can often be contentious. At the outset of a collaborative divorce, both spouses still hire their own attorneys but agree in writing to make every effort not to go to court to resolve issues related to their divorce. The parties and their attorneys then work together to reach agreements regarding the distribution of assets and debts, payment of alimony/spousal support, custody of children, child support, and any other issues related to dissolving their divorce. Collaborative divorce is different from other settlement methods such as mediation because the parties agree in a written contract that the attorneys must withdraw from the case if the parties are unable to reach an agreement through the collaborative process. This disqualification clause is supposed to provide an incentive for the parties to resolve their issues through the collaborative process; otherwise, they must expend additional time and money hiring new lawyers to litigate their case.

Family law attorney Stuart Webb is widely credited with creating the concept of collaborative divorce originated around 1990. Webb was discouraged by the siege-like mentality of divorce litigation and the toll that it took on both the parties and their attorneys. He decided that he would become a settlement specialist, and if he was unsuccessful in settling a case out of court, he would hand it over to another family law attorney to take the case to court. He recruited other attorneys to join the collaborative divorce movement (Webb and Ousky 2006, xv–xvi). The movement has grown from nine attorneys in 1989 to more than 5,000 members of the International Academy of Collaborative Professionals (IACP) today (International Academy of Collaborative Professionals, n.d.).

While the attorney disqualification clause is the defining feature of collaborative divorce, there are several other key aspects that distinguish it from other ADR methods. Mediation, for example, often occurs concurrently with litigation. After one of the parties files for divorce with a court, the judge may order the parties to participate in a specified number of mediation sessions with a neutral mediator before returning to court. In another ADR scenario, the parties and their attorneys might choose to engage in a four-way settlement negotiation without the help of a neutral mediator. This might occur before a party has filed for divorce, but it often occurs while litigation is ongoing. In a collaborative divorce, however, the parties agree at the outset that they want to avoid going to court. The parties agree to this in writing by signing a collaborative participation agreement that sets out the scope and terms of their participation and agreement to participate in good faith. The parties also agree to openly share relevant information, including financial data. Additionally, collaborative divorce is often interdisciplinary, meaning that financial and/or mental health professionals may also work with the parties. Financial professionals include accountants, financial planners, and real estate agents and appraisers. Mental health professionals may serve as divorce coaches, communication specialists, and/or parenting coaches. Rather than attempting to "win" particular assets or convince someone of the merits of their arguments, the parties and the professionals take a holistic approach, focusing on what arrangements will benefit the family as a whole. The professionals encourage the parties not to become entrenched in their positions and to focus on compromise.

Most attorneys and other professionals who are interested in handling collaborative divorce cases participate in extensive training to become certified by the IACP or state or local collaborative divorce associations. Some attorneys may only take collaborative divorce cases, while many continue to practice more traditional forms of divorce law in addition to handling collaborative divorce cases when appropriate.

Collaborative divorce proponents point to several advantages of the collaborative process over traditional divorce litigation or even other forms of settlement. In a traditional divorce, parties are often involved in a court process and settlement process concurrently. Thus, parties incur the cost of both litigation and settlement and must adhere to court-imposed deadlines. The threat of going to court always looms in the background; if they do not resolve their differences by the time their trial is scheduled, they must litigate their divorce. At that point, they forfeit all control over the resolution of their divorce and must allow a stranger (the judge) to make decisions about their children and their finances. In a collaborative divorce, however, the parties agree to focus solely on settlement and not pursue litigation unless the collaborative process ultimately fails. Proponents argue that the collaborative process allows divorcing spouses to control the divorce process, reach untraditional solutions that

a court might not have the authority to grant, communicate openly and honestly, and minimize adversity.

Critics of collaborative divorce argue that the collaborative process is often expensive, slow, and cumbersome. While the parties are not paying litigation costs, which include attorney's fees to file court papers, prepare for trial, and appear at trial, they are paying multiple professionals to assist with their case. Scheduling can be a distinct problem, as it is often difficult to find mutually agreeable meeting times for multiple busy professionals and their clients. Communication can also go slowly with so many people involved.

There are also ethical concerns. Skeptics of collaborative divorce often point to the attorney disqualification clause as problematic. If only one party wants to end the collaborative process, both spouses still have to find new attorneys. This means that one spouse can effectively force the other spouse to fire her lawyer and find another one. It is possible that an opposing party would do this simply to make things difficult for their spouse. Furthermore, clients who agree to the collaborative divorce process may not understand at the outset what a financial and emotional burden it can be to start over with a new attorney if the collaborative process ultimately fails. Additionally, in some cases, litigation may be the best option, and some divorce lawyers find it foolish to eliminate it as a possibility from the start (Apel 2004, 41–42).

Collaborative divorce may not be appropriate for all divorcing spouses. Domestic violence experts argue that it is inherently inequitable for an abused spouse to have to collaborate with her abuser. It may also not be appropriate when there are substance abuse issues. Spouses who are trying to hide assets are likely not good candidates for collaborative divorce. Because of the costs involved in collaborative divorce, it is often only available to more affluent parties.

Starting in 2009, states have begun officially recognizing collaborative divorce. In 2009, the Uniform Law Commission introduced the Uniform Collaborative Law Act ("UCLA"). A uniform act is a proposed law that state legislatures may choose to enact in their state. State laws regarding the same topic can vary widely, and the purpose of uniform laws is to provide consistency between state laws in certain areas. As of 2019, 18 states and the District of Columbia have enacted the UCLA. Several other states have enacted their own collaborative divorce laws. Most states view collaborative divorce favorably or neutrally. However, in 2007, the Colorado Bar Association Ethics Committee issued a formal opinion that a collaborative law participation agreement containing an attorney disqualification clause violates Colorado's ethics rules.

The future of collaborative divorce is uncertain. While collaborative divorce professionals are overwhelmingly positive about the process, the number of collaborative divorce cases does not seem to be growing. An attorney in Wisconsin found that less than 1% of divorce cases in his county in 2013 and 2014 were collaborative law cases. This was down from about 2% in 2008 (Herman 2015). The lack of growth may be due to the cost and length of the process or possibly because divorcing spouses prefer more established ADR options like mediation.

Shannon Roddy

See also: Divorce Coaching; Divorce Mediation

Further Reading

Apel, Susan B. 2004. "Collaborative Law: A Skeptic's View." *The Vermont Bar Journal* 30, no. 1 (Spring): 41–43.

Herman, Gregg M. 2015. "On Family Law: Collaborative Divorce Numbers Down, Why?" *Inside Track.* https://www.wisbar .org/NewsPublications/InsideTrack /Pages/Article.aspx?Volume=7&Issue =14&ArticleID=24212

International Academy of Collaborative Professionals. n.d. "IACP History." Accessed October 30, 2019. https://www .collaborativepractice.com/sites/ default /files/IACP%20%20History.pdf.

Webb, Stuart, and Ron Ousky. 2006. *The Collaborative Way to Divorce.* New York: Hudson Street Press.

Common Law Marriage

Common law marriage is a marriage valid in some states that dispenses of the usual formal requirements of a marriage license, wedding ceremony, and marriage certificate. Instead, other elements are required for a common law marriage, such as the agreement of a couple to live together as spouses and to hold themselves out as such to family and friends. In other words, common law marriage is viewed as marriage, but entered into a different way. The status of a common law marriage usually becomes an issue when one partner dies or the relationship ends, and the ownership of property is at stake.

People in a common law marriage have all the rights of a spouse, which include inheritance rights and property division at divorce. If two people living together are not recognized as a common law married couple, then they are considered to be cohabitants. Cohabitants have far fewer rights than a spouse. For example, cohabitants cannot inherit each other's property without a will and are usually not entitled to any legal remedies at separation, such as spousal support and property division.

Tracing back to informal marriage in Europe before the Reformation, common law marriage arose in the United States as a way to legally recognize the relationships of couples who lacked access to the clergy or a courthouse, such as those on the frontier. Common law marriage originally aimed to protect the more financially vulnerable partner at the dissolution of the relationship, allowing that person to have the same claims to the couple's property as a spouse would. As a result, formal divorce is required to dissolve a common law marriage.

Until the 20th century, nearly half of states recognized common law marriage. Since then, many states have abolished common law marriage either through state statutes or judicial case law. One of the reasons for abolishing common law marriage was the decreased need for common law marriage given that marriage formalities can easily be met in nearly all American locations today. Furthermore, the lack of formalities associated with common law marriage may facilitate fraudulent claims, such as false claims that a couple had agreed to a common law marriage. Finally, many states have historically discouraged cohabitation outside of formal marriage. Today, only a few states still allow common law marriage, and those are Colorado, District of Columbia, Iowa, Kansas, Montana, Rhode Island, Oklahoma, Utah, and Texas.

Most recently, in 2019, South Carolina joined the vast majority of U.S. states that no longer recognize common law marriage. In doing so, the South Carolina Supreme Court determined that common law marriage was outdated and could produce outcomes that were unpredictable and confusing. In that case, a couple had cohabitated for about two decades and shared two children, but never married. Following incidents of infidelity, the couple separated. The man claimed to have a common law marriage so that the couple's assets could be divided as if they were married. At trial, he testified that they had occasionally introduced themselves as husband and wife, but the woman presented evidence that she said she would never marry again. The South Carolina Supreme Court determined that their conduct did not demonstrate that they intended to be married. More broadly, the court held that common law marriage is too ambiguous of an institution to enforce, and no future common law marriages would be recognized.

Nonetheless, most states that do not recognize a common law marriage contracted within their own state borders will recognize a common law marriage that was validly contracted in another state. Thus, if a couple meets the criteria for common law marriage in a jurisdiction that recognizes the doctrine, and subsequently moves to a state that does not, the couple's common law marriage remains valid.

The few remaining states allowing common law marriage vary in the requirements to establish it. The elements of common law marriage generally include the capacity to marry, agreement to live together as spouses, and the presentation of the relationship as a marriage to the public. Couples can present themselves to the public as married by adopting the same surname, wearing a wedding band, or referring to each other as "husband" or "wife." A common misconception is that a couple who has been living together for a certain length of time is presumed to be common law married. However, mere cohabitation is not sufficient to establish a common law marriage.

Common law marriage is becoming less common today even in those states that still recognize it. Given the modern social acceptability of cohabitation, unmarried couples are less motivated to outwardly express their status as husband and wife. With fewer common law marriages and more cohabitations, some people have argued for other legal protections for long-term cohabitants.

In sum, a common law marriage does not require a formal ceremony and a marriage license. It is instead evidenced by cohabitation and an agreement to marry between two people legally capable of making a marriage contract. Most American states no longer recognize common law marriage today, which initially arose to legally recognize couples who could not access clergy or other marriage formalities in isolated geographic areas. Those American states that still allow common law marriages typically treat such marriages in the same way as formal marriages, which is particularly important when it comes to property division at death or the end of the relationship.

Margaret Ryznar

See also: Division of Assets; Unmarried Cohabitation

Further Reading

Brown, Cynthia Grant. 1996. "A Feminist Proposal to Bring Back Common Law Marriage." *Oregon Law Review* 75, no. 3: 709–780.

Primrose, Sarah. 2013. "The Decline of Common Law Marriage & the Unrecognized Cultural Effect." *Whittier Law Review* 34, no. 2: 187–214.

Stone v. Thompson, South Carolina Supreme Court, 2019.

Thomas, Jennifer. 2009. "Common Law Marriage." *Journal of the American Academy of Matrimonial Lawyers* 22, no. 1: 151–168.

Communication between Couples in Divorce

Although divorce brings an end to a marriage, the relationship and communication between the former couple may continue. There are various reasons for former spouses to continue to communicate following divorce, ranging from continued attachment to mutual children. Additional factors also contribute to the likelihood of former spouses communicating, such as the quality of the relationship between former partners and whether or not one or both partners have remarried. The ways in which former spouses communicate can vary by the frequency of communication, methods used to communicate, and topics of discussion. Better communication between former spouses is related to better outcomes for both adults and children.

Couples intentionally or unintentionally develop rules to determine the amount of information they share with one another and how they share this information. When the couple divorces, the privacy rules are changed as the relationship transforms. The communication boundaries determine when, with whom, and how private information is shared between former partners (Markham et al. 2017).

Divorced couples may lose contact altogether, purposefully end communication, connect infrequently, or communicate rather frequently. Overall, the frequency of communication between former spouses decreases with time (Fischer et al. 2005). Couples are more likely to have more frequent communication with one another when they were married for a longer period of time, had greater economic ties such as home ownership, and had liberal family values including the notion that individuals should remain friends following divorce (Fischer et al. 2005). When one or both of the former spouses has a new partner, communication between the former spouses tends to decrease. This can be for a number of reasons, including that one or both spouses have moved on and there is a decreased need to communicate, jealousy, or, in the case of parents, that the new partner serves as a third party for the other parent to communicate with rather than their former spouse (Markham et al. 2017).

The greatest predictor of former partner communication is whether or not they have mutual children. Couples without children are more likely than couples with children to lose contact following divorce. Fischer and colleagues (2005) found that 30% of couples without children were no longer in contact with each other the first year after divorce and 60% had lost contact after 10 years. In contrast, 70% of couples with children were still in contact with their former spouse 10 years after the divorce. For couples without children, divorce may be viewed as an opportunity to get a fresh start (Fischer et al. 2005).

For former partners who are parents, additional factors have been found to predict communication. Parents who had positive views of coparenting engaged in more frequent communication with their former partners than those who viewed coparenting negatively (Ganong et al. 2011). Additionally, mothers who believed they were encouraged by others to coparent and perceived they had control over their coparenting abilities communicated more frequently with their former partners. It may be that when mothers believe that cooperative coparenting is beneficial for themselves and their children and that others think they should coparent, they are more likely to communicate more frequently with their former spouse and have intentions to do so in the future (Ganong et al. 2011). Divorced parents who had informal custody arrangements where the parents determined the custody arrangement that worked for them tended to have more flexible communication boundaries with their former partners, often engaging in more frequent communication directly with their former partner than those with formal custody arrangements that were determined by the court and strictly adhered to (Markham et al. 2017).

When parents divorce, they must find new ways to communicate with one another as coparents rather than as spouses in order to raise their children (Graham 2003). Some parents have found that focusing on their children has helped them transition to the coparent role. In these cases, parents have decided to get along with their former partner for the sake of their children. Some have also found it helpful to have child-centered communication with their former partner, rather than on other topics, including relating to their former romantic relationship (Markham et al. 2017).

Divorced parents who are successful in being supportive of one another's parenting develop a cooperative coparenting style. Cooperative coparents communicate with one another to meet their children's needs, have infrequent disagreements, and do not undermine the other's parenting efforts (Beckmeyer et al. 2014). Not all parents, however, are able to effectively work together to raise their children; these couples may have conflictual relationships. Those who have high-conflict divorces engage in moderate to frequent conflict and may have high levels of anger, hostility, and distrust; incidences of abuse; high rate of custody disputes; and ongoing difficulty in communication and cooperation over childcare (Levite and Cohen 2011). Although divorced couples who have mutual children are more likely to remain in contact even years after the divorce (Fischer et al. 2005), this is not the case for all coparents. Some coparents have essentially stopped communicating with one another and make few, if any, attempts to communicate in regard to their child's care, resulting in a disengaged or dissolved coparenting relationship (Beckmeyer et al. 2014).

The quality of the former spousal relationship has been found to influence the rate of former spousal communication (Fischer et al. 2005). Fischer and colleagues (2005) determined that former spouses who engaged in antagonistic contact with their former partner were less likely than couples who had friendly contact to continue to communicate with their former spouse. Additionally, parents who had good relationships with their former spouse were more likely to communicate more frequently and openly share more information relating to their children than those who had poor relationships with their former partner (Markham and Coleman 2012; Markham et al. 2017).

The quality of the coparenting relationship is also related to the methods coparents use to communicate with one another. Currently, there are numerous methods available for coparents to utilize to remain in contact with one another, including in person, cell phone, texting, email, video calling, and social media. Coparents who had good relationships with their former partners were more likely to use technology to their benefit when communicating with their former partner (Ganong et al. 2012), and they were less likely to purposefully limit the methods of communication they utilized (Markham and Coleman 2012). Coparents with conflictual relationships, however, avoided communicating directly with their former partner by phone or in person (Markham and Coleman 2012) and used communication technology to limit their former partner's ability to provide input regarding decisions for their children and restrict their access to information (Ganong et al. 2012).

As coparents are no longer in a romantic relationship, they typically alter the topics they discuss with one another. A common topic of discussion for divorced parents is issues relating to their children, including logistics and the child's activities, academics, health, and behavior (Markham et al. 2017). Some divorced couples may continue to communicate about shared interests, including mutual friends, family, their relationship, and money. Many divorced couples establish a boundary that most aspects of their lives relating to new romantic partners is off limits (Miller 2009). Some parents have found that limiting their communication to information solely relating to their children has helped reduce interparental conflict (Markham et al. 2017).

The quality of divorced couples' communication can affect outcomes for the family members. Couples who are not able to effectively utilize conflict-management strategies tend to be less satisfied with their relationship. Additionally, when parents are conflictual, their children are more likely to be at risk for emotional and behavioral difficulties (Beckmeyer et al. 2014). Interparental conflict is especially harmful when children are caught in the middle of their parents' disagreements (Afifi and Hamrick 2006). This can happen in a variety of ways including having children send messages between the parents, speaking negatively about the other parent in front of the child, and probing the child for information about the former partner (Afifi and Schrodt 2003). Children who are caught in their parents' disputes are more likely to have externalizing and internalizing behaviors and problematic parent-child relations as adolescents and adults.

Melinda Stafford Markham
and Erin Guyette

See also: Communication between Parents and Children in Divorce; Coparenting and Divorce; Coparenting Typologies

Further Reading

Afifi, Tamara D., and Kellie Hamrick. 2006. "Communication Processes that Promote Risk and Resiliency in Postdivorce Families." In *Handbook of Divorce and Relationship Dissolution*, edited by Mark A. Fine and John H. Harvey. Mahweh, NJ: Lawrence Erlbaum Associates, pp. 435–456.

Afifi, Tamara D., and Paul Schrodt. 2003. "'Feeling Caught' as a Mediator of Adolescents' and Young Adults' Avoidance and Satisfaction with Their Parents in Divorced and Non-Divorced Households." *Communication Monographs*, no. 70: 142–173.

Beckmeyer, Jonathon J., Marilyn Coleman, and Lawrence H. Ganong. 2014. "Postdivorce Coparenting Typologies and Children's Adjustment." *Family Relations*, no. 63: 526–537.

Fischer, Tamar F. C., Paul M. De Graaf, and Matthijs Kalmijn. 2005. "Friendly and Antagonistic Contact between Former Spouses after Divorce Patterns and Determinants." *Journal of Family Issues*, no. 26: 1131–1163.

Ganong, L. H., M. Coleman, R. Feistman, T. Jamison, and M. S. Markham. 2012. "Communication Technology and Postdivorce Coparenting." *Family Relations* 61: 397–409. https://doi.org/10.1111/j.1741-3729.2012.00706.x

Ganong, L. H., M. Coleman, M. S. Markham, and T. Rothrauff. 2011. "Predicting Postdivorce Coparental Communication." *Journal of Divorce & Remarriage*, 52, no. 1: 1–18. https://doi.org/10.1080/10502556.2011.534391

Graham, Elizabeth E. 2003. "Dialectic Contradictions in Postmarital Relationships." *The Journal of Family Communication*, no. 3: 193–214.

Levite, Z., and O. Cohen. 2011. "The Tango of Loving Hate: Couple Dynamics in High-conflict Divorce." *Clinical Social Work Journal* 40: 45–55. https://doi.org/10.1007/s10615-011-0334-5

Markham, Melinda Stafford, and Marilyn Coleman. 2012. "The Good, the Bad, and the Ugly: Divorced Mothers' Experiences with Coparenting." *Family Relations*, no. 61: 586–600.

Markham, Melinda Stafford, Jaimee L. Hartenstein, Yolanda T. Mitchell, and Ghadir Aljayyousi-Khalil. 2017.

"Communication Among Parents Who Share Physical Custody After Divorce or Separation." *Journal of Family Issues*, no. 38: 1414–1442.

Miller, Aimee E. 2009. "Face Concerns and Facework: Strategies in Maintaining Postdivorce Coparenting and Dating Relationships." *Southern Communication Journal*, no. 74: 157–173.

Communication between Parents and Children in Divorce

"We're getting divorced." These are the words all parents hope they never have to say. However, the reality is that divorce is now so widespread that, according to data from the U.S. Organization for Economic Cooperation and Development (2018), it affects nearly half of all individuals who marry and roughly one million children per year.

When facing the hardships of divorce, one of the many casualties may be parents' open communication with their children. Divorce is typically a sensitive and emotional event, and it is common for parents to struggle with how to talk to their children about it. Parents may feel confused about what and how much to say or may fear upsetting their child. Other parents may be extremely vulnerable emotionally and worry about feeling overwhelmed when talking with their children. Children's short- and long-term reactions vary greatly, depending on how the parents respond to the child during and after the breakup. As difficult as it may be, more than ever, developing open and age-appropriate parent-child communication is very important to help children prepare, both cognitively and emotionally, for the changes in the moment and ahead.

Predictability is vital to children's security, as they feel more control over the enormous changes occurring in their lives. Therefore, letting children know what life will be like after the divorce is especially important. For example, children are entitled to know when the departing parent will move out (it's important that this does not happen right after disclosing the news), where they will live, and how much time they will have with each parent. One of the reasons that parents often refrain from engaging in such detailed conversations is the uncertainty about some aspects of life after divorce. The overall plan should be previously prepared by both parents before informing the child. In the case that parents are unsure about certain issues, children should know that they will be the first to know as soon as there is a decision.

Also, children will benefit from explanations for the divorce. When parents don't provide an explanation, children will create one of their own, which quite often includes blaming themselves. However, explanations should be age appropriate. That is, it is important to avoid providing children with specific details, for instance, adult infidelities or financial problems, in order to avoid drawing them into competing alliances with parents. Parents must communicate that this is a decision of both parents and that the child is in no way responsible or to blame for the divorce. Also, it must be clear that, as it is an adult decision, there is nothing they can do to fix it and that while parents may continue to communicate and interact, it is simply as a coparenting relationship. Children may fantasize about reconciliation, which may prevent them from coming to terms with the reality of their current lives and from successfully moving forward in their development.

Most often children will need reassurances that everything is going to work out fine and that everyone will get through these difficult times. Children also need to be repeatedly reassured and shown that they are loved and cared by both parents and that a permanent and continuing relationship with both parents is not only possible, but a priority for all involved. Being exposed to arguments, high conflict, and negative comments made by one parent about the other can directly impact children's long-term emotional and psychological health. Losing contact with a former present parent after the divorce is at the core of children's pain and one of the main protection factors for children of divorce is the parental ability to support the child's relationship with the other parent (especially the non-custodial parent). In fact, research has shown that one of the most important factors in parent-child relationships after divorce was the frequency of communication. The more frequent communication children had with their parents, the better their relationship was, regardless of the parent's relationship with each other (Beckmeyer, Markham, and Troilo 2018). When parents move apart, it is essential to provide the child with frequent, regularly scheduled contact that should begin immediately upon the parent's departure. Communication lines must remain open. Texting, social media, or other popular communication methods can be particularly important here as they help children, especially teens, to have more control and autonomy in keeping connected to their parents. On the other hand, if children refuse to communicate,

access to these technologies enables parents to continuously reassure the child of their love, presence, and interest in them.

Parents may repeatedly invite children to talk about the divorce, while respecting their own pace, by communicating their availability and interest to listen to whatever they may be thinking or feeling. In order to create a safe space for these conversations it is very important to avoid conveying, covertly or overtly, loyalty conflicts, in which children feel pressured to choose sides. Children want a relationship with both parents and feel profound sadness and anxiety when they believe that closeness with one parent can be experienced by the other as a disappointment or disloyalty.

In addition, it is very important that parents aren't afraid to show emotion and communicate their own feelings, but, at the same time, show the ability to regulate and communicate a sense of stability, calm, and control. Being overly emotional and sharing their adult-like problems with children, may make them feel responsible for their parent's emotional well-being and assume the role of supporters or caregivers. Children should never reverse roles with their parents and parents must show that they are in charge and that there are adult concerns and children concerns. It is very important that parents reinforce their social support system so that the child is not in the role of their confidant or emotional caretaker.

With all the challenges parents have to juggle after divorce (new living arrangements, financial worries, and their own personal losses), it is often hard to find enough time or emotional energy to respond to their children's heightened needs. Responding to their child's sadness and anger is one of the main challenges of parents in general. More importantly, among divorced parents where emotions usually run high between everyone in the family. First and foremost, it is important to acknowledge and accept the child's sad and angry feelings and avoid internalizing and taking hurtful behavior personally. Children adjust better when parents comfort them in their distress and offer genuine concern and affection. Also, children feel safer and more secure when parents are in control, set reasonable boundaries, and effectively discipline them. For example, it is important to enforce realistic rules and expectations, reward children's positive behavior and communicate clearly and directly what is expected of them. It is also essential that parents maintain an orderly household routine and model acceptable behavior.

Divorce is hard for everyone involved. Both parents and children grieve the loss of the family as they have known it. Nevertheless, children do not have to suffer long-term negative consequences of divorce. Parents' responsiveness to the child's needs and the quality of parenting after the divorce are the most important determinants of children's adjustment. Living apart does mean that opportunities for effective communication and bonding are more limited, but parents do have the chance to make the most of them and truly be emotionally present for their children.

Sara Albuquerque

See also: Child Custody; Divorce, Psychological Effects; Divorce Education; Parenting Plans and Custody Arrangements

Further Reading

Amato, Paul R. 2000. "The Consequences of Divorce for Adults and Children." *Journal of Marriage and the Family* 62, no. 4: 1269–1287.

Beckmeyer, Jonathon J., Markham, Melinda, and Troilo, Jessica. 2018. "Postdivorce Coparenting Relationships and Parent–Youth Relationships: Are Repartnership and Parent–Youth Contact Moderators?" *Journal of Family Issues* 40, no. 5: 613–636.

Emery, Robert E. 1999. *Marriage, Divorce, and Children's Adjustment.* Thousand Oaks: Sage Publications.

Kelly, Joan B. 2000. "Children's Adjustment in Conflicted Marriage and Divorce: A Decade Review of Research." *Journal of the American Academy of Child and Adolescent Psychiatry* 39, no. 8: 963–973.

OECD. 2018. *SF3.1: Marriage and Divorce Rates.* OECD Family Database.

Teyber, Edward. 1992. *Helping Children Cope with Divorce.* New York: Lexington Books.

Conflict Management

Conflict management has become a common topic of scientific examination due to its key role in romantic relationships, such as marriage, which have become central to individual well-being. For example, in comparison to never married or divorced individuals, those who are married generally experience better mental and physical health, greater levels of social support, and improved personal well-being (Lawrence et al. 2019). However, these benefits are most salient to marriages that are satisfying. Likely for this reason, scholars and practitioners (e.g., therapists, relationship educators) have studied factors that ease marital distress and promote marital adjustment. Communication skills, particularly conflict resolution behaviors, have been identified as key to developing and maintaining good marriages and other long-term close relationships (Fowers 2001, 104–107).

Despite the fact that most marriages and close relationships encounter some levels of disagreement, conflict has often been viewed as a negative construct that predicts dysfunction in a relationship. Some researchers, however, have challenged this view, suggesting that because conflict is inevitable in close relationships, it would be incorrect to presume that any source of conflict is a proxy for relationship discord (Cummings and Davies 2010, 8). Although avoiding conflict would first seem an ideal approach, interpersonal relationships can grow stronger when relational challenges are addressed and discussed. Some disagreements are necessary and even beneficial for marriage survival and optimal relationship functioning (Cummings and Davies 2010, 8). At the very least, engaging in conflict enables individuals to address interpersonal differences that otherwise might promote negative feelings with a potential to foster resentment in a relationship. Nonetheless, it is not the mere presence of conflict, but rather how the conflict is managed and expressed that has unique implications on relationship outcomes (Driver et al. 2012, 57). Based on common conflict management behaviors, scholars have broadly categorized conflict as either *destructive* or *constructive*, each of which is differentially linked to relationship functioning (Birditt et al. 2010).

Destructive conflict usually escalates beyond the issues of disagreement and includes typically cyclical negative reactions to relationship problems, such as open hostility, physical and verbal aggression, personal insults, coercion, and threats (Cummings and Davies 2010,

8). In an attempt to solve conflict, individuals using *destructive* strategies may yell, insult, criticize, belittle, blame, and manipulate the other person's actions. In comparison to these overt hostile behaviors, a less explored aspect of destructive conflict is covert withdrawn behaviors (Bradford et al. 2008). *Destructive* strategies may also include physical aggression, such as shoving or hitting (Cummings and Davies 2010, 63). Known as intimate partner violence, these behaviors have two major typologies (Kelly and Johnson 2008). Situational couple violence is the most common type of physical aggression among partners that is usually borne out of anger and frustration during disagreements, and is perpetrated by both partners. The second type is coercive controlling violence, which mostly includes power assertive, oppressive behavior designed to manipulate and control. It often includes non-physically abusive and demoralizing behaviors, such as blame, threats, intimidation, emotional manipulation, and isolation from family and friends. However, coercive controlling violence typically consists of severe physical violence (e.g., 88% of women who experience this type are injured). Less common than situational couple violence, it is most often perpetrated by men in heterosexual relationships.

It can be concluded that *destructive* conflict management behaviors include reactive and unregulated responses to interpersonal conflict (Cummings and Davies 2010, 8). Ultimately, these types of behaviors provoke hostility and deteriorate relationship quality. Indeed, couples who habitually argue destructively are likely to have less satisfying relationship putting them at an increased risk for divorce (Birditt et al.

2010) and relationship dissolution of non-marital unions (Kopystynska et al. 2017). *Destructive* conflict decreases the level of emotional closeness between spouses and is likely left unresolved. Moreover, these conflict behaviors have been linked to symptoms of depression (Johnson and Anderson 2015).

By contrast, *constructive* conflict is typically accompanied by mutual respect, regulated communication, positive affection, articulated reasons for disagreements, and progress toward resolution (Cummings and Davies 2010, 8). *Constructive* conflict is marked by focusing on the issue of disagreement and is carried out by negotiation and problem solving. Individuals engaging in *constructive* conflict management tend to have relatively positive reactions to problem-solving. This positivity is often rooted in both self-respect and respect for the other and is reflected in the ability to calmly discuss problems, engage in active and nondefensive listening, use repair attempts, compromise, provide support and affection, and use humor to alleviate any tension (Birditt et al. 2010). An important virtue (i.e., personal characteristic) that underpins *constructive* behaviors is being other-centered as opposed to self-centered (Fowers 2001, 104–105). As implied above, many behavioral characteristics of this conflict approach require a certain level of self-restraint or self-control, especially during heated disagreements. Because social science has historically been more interested in examining factors that predict psychopathology, as opposed to general well-being, relatively little is known about the implications of *constructive* conflict on marital outcomes, especially in comparison to that of *destructive* conflict. However,

existing evidence suggests that *constructive* conflict is related to lower rates of marital dissolution, but only when used by both spouses (Birditt et al. 2010). In other words, one spouse's attempts to handle disagreements with *constructive* behaviors may not save the marriage. It is both spouses' concerted efforts to treat each other with respect, affection, and understanding that ultimately predict favorable marital and relational outcomes.

Based on personal traits (e.g., temperament), it is likely that individuals lean toward specific behaviors during disagreements (Caspi et al. 2005). However, daily marital interactions typically include both positive and negative emotions, and it is unlikely that positive behaviors occur in the absence of negative ones and vice versa. Even spouses who are generally affectionate and attempt to solve their differences in *constructive* ways can get frustrated and impatient with each other sometimes, but the quality and the future of their relationships, tend not be the same as for spouses who are hostile toward one another on a consistent basis (Driver et al. 2012, 70–71). Regardless of individual inclination toward specific conflict management behaviors, couples can offset disagreements with positive interactions using a ratio of at least five positive behaviors to one negative behavior (5:1) as a successful formula for maintaining a healthy relationship (Driver et al. 2012, 63). Thus, for a satisfying relationship, couples need to focus on increasing positive affect and positive behaviors, and decrease those that are negative. Doing so can be particularly challenging for couples who primarily use *destructive* behaviors during disagreements because their relationship is tainted by high levels of negativity. In contrast, it is easier to repair a relationship from conflict in the atmosphere that continuously cultivates admiration and other-centeredness.

Given that many marriages involve the presence of children or youth, exposure to conflict has important implications on their development. Whereas *destructive* interparental conflict has shown to be related to a host of unfavorable developmental outcomes, such as behavior problems and academic underachievement, *constructive* type of marital conflict promotes social and emotional development of children (Cummings and Davies 2010, 59). When parents behave in an emotionally regulated manner and reason with each other in *constructive* ways during disagreements, children learn effective ways to handle interpersonal conflicts of their own. As such, children's exposure to *constructive* conflict management behaviors is not only beneficial, but even necessary to their social functioning because they learn useful strategies to solve problems, respectfully cooperate with others, and rationally cope with conflict outcomes. *Constructive* conflict is more effective in providing a child with a sense of security in the interparental relationship and family unity (Cummings and Davies 2010, 82). In other words, when parents solve their disputes constructively, children are less likely to feel threatened by the presence of conflict, feeling safe that challenges in the parents' relationship is not a cause for concern. Emerging evidence shows that children as young as three years of age are sensitive to interparental conflict and when exposed to parents' *constructive* management are likely to exhibit signs of healthy socioemotional development (Kopystynska et al. 2017).

As evidenced by the outcomes of some psychoeducational programs and couple therapy-based interventions, teaching and encouraging couples to engage in *constructive* conflict management has shown to be effective in improving marital processes, including marital satisfaction, parenting, and child well-being (Cummings and Davies 2010, 195–97). During sessions, couples learn techniques that help reduce and replace *destructive* conflict tactics, such as hostility and contempt, with *constructive* behaviors, such as respect, affection, compromise, and support. However, as stated before, these efforts are most fruitful when both spouses have mutual respect, are other-focused, and are committed to improving their relationship.

As illustrated throughout this summary, conflict is a natural aspect of any close relationship (Driver et al. 2012, 66). Successful relationships are not necessarily defined by the absence of conflict, but rather by the approach that individuals in the relationship take to manage their disagreements on a variety of topics (e.g., financial issues, housework, or intimacy). Conflict management is a vital skill for all human interactions. As such, learning and executing *constructive* behaviors is a suggested strategy for managing interpersonal conflict.

Olena Kopystynska and Kay Bradford

See also: Attachment Theory of Love; Love, Connection, and Intimacy; Triangular Theory of Love; Value Theory/Role Theory

Further Reading
Birditt, Kira S., Edna Brown, Terri L. Orbuch, and Jessica M. McIlvane. 2010. "Marital conflict behaviors and

implications for divorce over 16 years." *Journal of Marriage and Family* 72, no. 5: 1188–1204. Doi:10.1111/j.1741-3737 .2010.00758.x.

Bradford, Kay, LaToya Burns Vaughn, and Brian K. Barber. 2008. "When there is conflict: Interparental conflict, parent–child conflict, and youth problem behaviors." *Journal of Family Issues* 29, no. 6: 780–805. Doi:10.1177/0192513X07308043

Caspi, Avshalom, Brent W. Roberts, and Rebecca L. Shiner. 2005. "Personality development: Stability and change." *Annual Review of Psychology* 56: 453–484. Doi:10.1146/annurev.psych.55.090902 .141913.

Cummings, E. Mark, and Patrick T. Davies. 2010. *Marital Conflict and Children: An Emotional Security Perspective.* New York: The Guilford Press.

Driver, Janice, Amber Tabares, Alyson F. Shapiro, and John M. Gottman. 2012. "Couple interaction in happy and unhappy marriages: Gottman Laboratory studies." In *Normal Family Processes: Growing Diversity and Complexity*, 4th ed., edited by Froma Walsh. New York: The Guilford Press, pp. 57–77.

Fowers, Blaine J. 2001. *Beyond the Myth of Marital Happiness.* San Francisco: Jossey-Bass.

Johnson, Matthew D., and Jared R. Anderson. 2015. "Temporal ordering of intimate relationship efficacy and conflict." *Journal of Marriage and Family* 77, no. 4: 968–981. EBSCOhost, https://doi .org/10.1111/jomf.12198.

Kelly, Joan B., and Michael P. Johnson. 2008. "Differentiation among types of intimate partner violence: Research update and implications for interventions." *Family Court Review* 46, no. 3: 476–499.

Kopystynska, Olena, Katherine W. Paschall, Melissa A. Barnett, and Melissa A. Curran. 2017. "Patterns of interparental conflict, parenting, and children's emotional insecurity: A person-centered approach." *Journal of Family Psychology* 31, no. 7: 922–932. Doi:10.1037 /fam0000343.supp.

Lawrence, Elizabeth M., Richard G. Rogers, Anna Zajacova, and Tim Wadsworth. 2019. "Marital happiness, marital status, health, and longevity." *Journal of Happiness Studies* 20, no. 5: 1539–1561.

Contraception

Contraception has only been socially recognized and accepted in the last 50 years, more specifically starting in the 1960s when the first oral contraceptive was introduced. Since its contraceptive introduction is has been an essential and complicated area of modern life. The Centers for Disease Control and Prevention (CDC) reported that from 2015–2017, 72.2 million women in the United States aged 15–49 were using contraception. Additionally, the increased use of contraception increased with age. There was an increase from 37% among women aged 15–19 to 73% among women aged 40–49.

The history of contraception has been a long and embittered one in which women have struggled to gain control over their reproduction. Women's struggle to gain control is in relation to laws, regulations, and instruction by religious authorities, political authorities, and the medical profession. Contraceptive pills were an important landmark of the 20th century. Contraception was hailed as being a cure for controlling the world's rising population as well as social and political issues. Contraceptive pills continue to remain a revolutionary drug introduced in the 1960s; this "reshaped pharmacology, altered social perceptions of medication, and changed the regulatory process for new drugs during the second half of the twentieth century" (Marks 2001). Within six years of appearing in the United States, the contraceptive pill had become the most-sold pharmaceutical product worldwide.

The 20th century brought about a change in the birth control methods that couples used and relied on. If couples wanted to limit their family, they would use the following avoidance techniques: abstinence and withdrawal. Abstinence involved either delaying marriage or avoiding intercourse for certain periods; this has been shown to be the most effective form of birth control, though many find it unsatisfactory. The second birth control method is withdrawal. Withdrawal is when the male deliberately withdraws the penis from the vagina prior to ejaculation. The withdrawal method is seen as the least effective and reliant upon the male. Contraceptives can be used in a variety of ways, which include preventing sperm from getting to the eggs, keeping the woman's ovaries from releasing eggs that could be fertilized, and sterilization, which permanently prevents women from getting pregnant. Contraception is used by females that are of reproductive age and the available forms vary from intra-uterine devices (IUDs), vaginal rings, implants, injectables, oral contraception, and emergency contraception.

Oral contraceptives are pill-based contraceptives that are taken daily. There are two hormones that are included in oral contraceptives: estrogen and progestin. Both of these hormones are created naturally within a woman's body. Some oral contraceptives contain only contain progestin, which is sometimes called the "mini-pill." In recent years, IUDs have been more accepted in the United States. An IUD is a small piece of flexible plastic shaped like a T that prevents pregnancy by preventing sperm cells from reaching an egg. There are two types of IUDs: copper and hormonal. Vaginal rings are shaped like a doughnut and are designed to provide a controlled drug release. There are several advantages of using a vaginal ring: it doesn't require daily attention, it's easy to insert, it lacks adverse local effects, and it can be removed for up to two hours without compromising its pharmacological effect.

Contraceptive implants are comprised of one or more thin rods or tubes that contain a progestin hormone. Contraceptive implants are inserted under the skin of a female's arm and can provide at least three years of effective contraception. Since contraceptive implants are nonbiodegradable, it is suggested that women have the implant removed when the period of efficacy expires. Another option that can be used as an alternative to implants is an injectable contraception. The most studied and commonly used injectable contraceptive is Depo-Provera. Depo-Provera is an intramuscular injectable that is given every 12 weeks or 3 months. Depo-Provera prevents pregnancy through the inhibition of ovulation; it thickens and decreases the quality of cervical mucus, and the anti-estrogen prohibits sperm from penetrating.

Despite there being a wide range of available contraceptives, there are barriers to the effective use of contraception due to personal beliefs and values that have been shaped by culture and religion. When it comes to knowledge and attitudes regarding contraception and controlling fertility, there is a difference reflected among cultural and ethnic diversity. For instance, immigrants that migrate to the United States bring their tradition of folk medicine, which may not intermingle with medicine in general or contraception in the United States. The various contraception methods that are offered in the United States may not be known to immigrants. Additionally, the health care system within the United States may be drastically different, complicated, and inaccessible compared to the health care systems in their country of origin. For undocumented immigrants, it may difficulty to receive access to contraception due to their inability to use resources such as Medicaid. However, immigrants are not the only individuals that may have a difficult time with obtaining contraceptives. Some counties in the United States are known as *contraceptive deserts*, which are areas where the number of health centers offer the full range of methods; however, it is not enough to meet the needs of women eligible for publicly funded contraception. Lastly, when working with individuals who are culturally diverse, healthcare providers must be aware of the influence that culture and religion has on the couple's willingness to use contraception.

There are an abundance of reasons or factors that influence contraceptive use. Knowledge around contraception use and access to contraceptives, as well as personal and interpersonal factors, are influenced by the society at large. Contraceptives can be better understood in the context of political and economic structures, and social and cultural forms, among the individuals that use contraception. When the decision is made to begin using contraception it can be done in a social context; however, it can cause discouragement rather than promoting the use of contraception.

La Toya L Patterson

See also: Donor Insemination; Premarital Pregnancy; Unmarried Cohabitation; Unplanned Pregnancy

Further Reading

Birth Control Access. 2022. Retrieved from Birth Control Access 2022 | Power to Decide. https://powertodecide.org /contraceptive-deserts

Centers for Disease Control and Prevention. 2018. "Current Contraceptive Status among Women Aged 15–49: United States, 2015–2017." Retrieved from Products—Data Briefs—Number 327 – December 2018 (cdc.gov)

Cox-Gad, Shayne. 2008. *Pharmaceutical Manufacturing Handbook.* Hoboken: John Wiley & Sons.

Drucker, Donna J. 2020. *Contraception: A Concise History.* Cambridge: MIT Press.

Engelman, Peter C. 2011. *A History of the Birth Control Movement in America.* Santa Barbara: ABC-CLIO.

Hatcher, Robert, James Trussell, Anita L. Nelson, Willard Cates Jr., Felicia Stewart, and Deborah Kowal. 2009. *Contraceptive Technology.* New York: Ardent Media, Inc.

Marks, Lara V. 2001. *Sexual Chemistry: A History of the Contraceptive Pill.* New Haven: Yale University Press.

Sitruk-Ware, Regine, Nath, Anitha, and Mishell, Daniel R. 2013. "Contraception Technology: Past, Present, and Future." *Contraception*, 87, no. (3): 319–330.

Coparenting and Divorce

When couples with children divorce, their relationship changes from that of romantic partners who parent together to coparents living in separate households. Coparenting refers to ex-spouses interacting to coordinate their child's care, activities, and needs (Markham, Ganong, and

Coleman 2007). Families work with the legal system to file for divorce and sometimes will use legal services for custody arrangements. The nature of the divorce process and custody decisions have been shown to influence coparenting communication and satisfaction. Since the 1990s, courts have been granting parents joint custody versus favoring mothers' custody as evidence shows the importance of having both parents involved in a child's life.

Often following a divorce, an agreement on child custody and parenting arrangements, usually called a parenting plan, is made by the parents or a court service. This agreement creates the structure on how a divorcing couple's children are going to be raised. The coparents work on their own or with a legal service such as an attorney, mediator, or parenting consultant to formalize a parenting plan. Parenting plans consist of decisions about parenting time, holiday coordination, childcare, children's activities, medical care, etc. Each parent is expected to execute this plan as they parent their children.

Coparenting and divorce are adjustments for both parents and children in the family system. Following a divorce, the family members still exist as a family unit in regard to parents being responsible for their children and needing to create a foundation that supports their children's well-being (Amato, Kane, and James 2011). During the divorce process, families endure significant challenges as they establish new family roles, boundaries, and routines (Beckmeyer et al. 2021; Markham et al. 2017). For example, parents are adjusting to not seeing their children for periods of time as the children stay with their other parent and children are adjusting to going between separate households and lifestyles. Children

typically, however, go to one school, visit friends, and participate in activities and other obligations that the parents have to coordinate for their children.

Coparenting after divorce can be challenging for some parents because of the lasting conflict and tension from the divorce. After a divorce, conflict usually decreases with time, but about 8–12% of coparents stay highly conflictual for years following a divorce (Becher et al. 2019). Many individuals would not continue to communicate with an ex-spouse but interact with one another due to having a child together. Some former spouses limit the content of their discussions to relate to their children only; others talk about things unrelated to their children (Beckmeyer et al. 2021; Markham et al. 2017). As ex-spouses become coparents, they navigate and establish new boundaries due to the change to the family system.

Although children's reactions to divorce vary significantly, many studies have found an association between parental divorce and an increased risk of behavioral, psychological, and academic problems among children (Amato et al. 2011). Researchers have been interested in what factors increase the risk of adjustment problems and have found that parental conflict during the divorce process is a risk factor and can affect post-divorce family life (Becher et al. 2019). Children appear to suffer when parents argue frequently, have inconsistent structure, and undermine one another's parenting relationship with their child (Amato et al. 2011).

Poor coparenting relationships often have problematic behaviors that involve children, such as gatekeeping and triangulation. Gatekeeping exists when a parent either facilitates or restricts the other parent's access to a child or information about a child. In poor coparenting relationships, coparents are more likely to engage in restrictive gatekeeping in which they limit the other parent's access to their child (Markham, Gangong, and Coleman 2007). Triangulation occurs when a parent forms a coalition with the child and/or the child is caught between their parents' conflict (Teubert and Pinquart 2010). These problematic behaviors often cause children to be parentified, the process where a child takes on the role of a parent, which can be harmful to their well-being.

Often due to conflict or withdrawal of a parent communicating, some coparenting relationships are disengaged. Disengaged coparenting is when there is minimal contact between coparents and/or parents do not interact with one another, even on parenting matters (Beckmeyer et al. 2014). Some coparents who are disengaged practice parallel parenting, a method where each parent parents the child in their own way without working with the child's other parent (Amato et al. 2011). This can be challenging for children when parents are not communicating and practicing consistent parenting styles and routines for the children. Although having minimal conflict is better for children postdivorce, disengaged coparenting is still not the ideal post-divorce parenting practice. Children often still feel tension or become the communication method between parents.

Although conflict among coparents is common, there are some coparents that can maintain positive relationships and function in many respects like a healthy two-parent family (Amato et al. 2011). The best coparenting relationship for a child's healthy adjustment is cooperative coparenting. This occurs when two parents work together to make decisions and support each others' efforts in raising their children. Cooperation allows children to get their needs met, build relationships with both parents, and not deal with the outcomes of parental conflict. Emery and Dillon (1994) recommend establishing a "businesslike" relationship with the "business" being their child(ren). This would be communicating solely for the sake of the children and not making decisions based on personal agendas or emotions. Children can benefit from this approach as it reduces conflict by having constructive interactions. However, this can be challenging for recently separated couples as there are typically intense emotions surrounding a separation.

Cooperative coparenting is beneficial for parents and children because it reduces interparental conflict, improves coparents' satisfaction with each other, and creates space for coparents to continually work together (Beckmeyer et al. 2017). A stronger coparenting alliance and more positive parenting behaviors are protective factors for children experiencing parental divorce (Becher et al. 2019). During the divorce process and postdivorce, children benefit from parents who communicate regularly, when rules are consistent between households, and when both parents support each other's authority (Amato et al. 2011).

As for differences in outcomes between older and younger children, Beckmeyer and colleagues (in review), found that coparenting cooperation was related to more prosocial but less internalizing behavior in children (ages 4–9), but coparenting was not related to outcomes for older children (ages 10–18). This may indicate that cooperative coparenting with increased consistency between households and access to both parents may be particularly important for younger children as they are more reliant on their parents versus older children who can communicate their needs to their parents directly. Beckmeyer and colleagues (in review) also found that for both older and younger children, less boundary ambiguity between coparents was related to improved child well-being. The establishment of boundaries between coparents may facilitate child-centered interactions and move away from former relationship matters.

Positive postdivorce coparenting also results in parents having better relationships with their children, using more reasonable punishment with their children, and showing more parental support. Constructive interactions between coparents have a positive effect on parent-child relationships. Parents who provide parental warmth, support, and knowledge of their children's daily activity communicate to children that they are being cared for, and results in children experiencing less emotional distress and problem behaviors (Beckmeyer, Markham, and Trolio 2019).

Erin Guyette and
Melinda Stafford Markham

See also: Communication between Couples in Divorce; Coparenting Typologies

Further Reading

Amato, Paul R., Jennifer B. Kane, and Spencer James. 2011. "Reconsidering the 'Good Divorce.'" *Family Relations*, no. 60: 511–524.

Becher, Emily H., Hyunjun Kim, Sarah E. Cronin, Veronica Deenanath, Jenifer K. McGuire, Ellie M. McCann, and Sharon Powell. 2019. "Positive Parenting and Parental Conflict: Contributions to Resilient Coparenting during Divorce." *Family Relations*, no. 68: 150–164.

Beckmeyer, Jonathon J., Marilyn Coleman, and Lawrence H. Ganong. 2014. "Postdivorce Coparenting Typologies and Childrens Adjustment." *Family Relations*, no. 63: 526–537.

Beckmeyer, Jonathon J., Marilyn Coleman, Lawrence H. Ganong, and Melinda Stafford Markham. 2017. "Experiences with Coparenting Scale: A Semantic Differential Measure of Postdivorce Coparenting Satisfaction." *Journal of Family Issues*, no. 38: 1471–1490.

Beckmeyer, Jonathon J., Samantha J. Krejnick, Jasmin A. McCray, Jessica Troilo, and Melinda Stafford Markham. 2021. "A Multidimensional Perspective on Former Spouses' Ongoing Relationships: Associations with Children's Postdivorce Well-Being." *Family Relations* 70, no. 2 (2021): 467–482.

Beckmeyer, J. J., M. S. Markham, and J. Troilo. 2019. "Postdivorce Coparenting Relationships and Parent-Youth Relationships: Are Repartnership and Parent-Youth Contact Moderators?" *Journal of Family Issues* 40, no. 5: 613–636. https://doi.org/10.1177/0192513X18821395

Emery, Robert E., and Peter Dillon. 1994. "Conceptualizing the Divorce Process: Renegotiating Boundaries of Intimacy and Power in the Divorced Family System." *Family Relations*, no. 43: 374–379.

Markham, Melinda Stafford, Lawrence H. Ganong, and Marilyn Coleman. 2007. "Coparental Identity and Mothers: Cooperation in Coparental Relationships." *Family Relations*, no. 56: 369–377.

Markham, Melinda Stafford, Jaimee L. Hartenstein, Yolanda T. Mitchell, and Ghadir Aljayyousi-Khalil. 2017. "Communication Among Parents Who Share Physical Custody After Divorce or Separation." *Journal of Family Issues*, no. 38: 1414–1442.

Teubert, Daniela, and Martin Pinquart. 2010. "The Association Between Coparenting and Child Adjustment: A Meta-Analysis." *Parenting: Science and Practice*, no. 10: 286–307.

Coparenting Typologies

Coparenting typologies are classifications of diverse coparenting relationships. Coparenting typologies identify different types of coparents and are developed based on grouping certain characteristics demonstrated by former partners. Creating types that coparents can be assigned to allows researchers, facilitators, therapists, or judges, to provide services that are appropriate for their needs and their specific relationship. It also is helpful as different coparenting types are related to different outcomes for children and parents. It is important to note that although these typologies could be useful in many settings, they are not concrete. Coparenting types can change due to a number of reasons and are not limited by time.

The most widely known coparenting typology is one that was developed by Constance Ahrons, which was published in her 1994 book titled *The Good Divorce*. The five types of coparents Ahrons identified were perfect pals, cooperative colleagues, angry associates, fiery foes, and dissolved duos. Perfect pals were coparents that were quite friendly to one another post-divorce; their conversations included topics other than their shared children. Cooperative colleagues was the most common group of coparents; this group had high levels of communication and an average amount of conflict. Angry associates were coparents who communicated infrequently and often exhibited anger toward each other. Fiery

foes were identified as former partners who very seldom interacted or communicated and when they did, there was obvious conflict. Dissolved duos were former partners who had absolutely no communication or contact post-divorce. Ahrons' seminal coparenting typology opened doors for other researchers to explore the types of relationships that former partners can experience post-divorce.

Since Ahrons' work, numerous coparenting typologies have been developed based on quantitative and qualitative data. Coparenting typologies identified by researchers have typically utilized coparent communication, contact, and conflict to determine coparenting patterns. One distinct pattern that is found in many coparenting typologies is cooperation. This occurs when both coparents are involved in their child's life and the coparents engage in frequent discussion regarding their children's needs with low levels of conflict. Coparenting types relating to this pattern have been identified as "cooperative coparenting" (Amato, Kane, and James 2011; Maccoby, Depner, and Mnookin 1990), "cooperative and involved" (Beckmeyer, Coleman, and Ganong 2014), "cooperative" (Beckymeyer, Markham, and Troilo 2019), and "always amicable" (Markham and Coleman 2012). A second pattern involves coparenting conflict in which coparents have low to moderate levels of communication and high levels of conflict, with little coordination to provide care for their children. This pattern has been labeled "infrequent but conflictual coparenting" (Beckmeyer et al. 2014), "conflicted" (Maccoby et al. 1990), "continuously contentious" (Markham and Coleman 2012), and "conflictual and disengaged" (Beckmeyer et al. 2019). A final pattern consists of families in which one parent is no longer involved with the children and, therefore, is also not communicating with the other parent. This coparenting pattern has been called "single parenting" (Amato et al. 2011) and "disengaged" (Maccoby et al. 1990).

Although many of the identified coparenting types fall within these three general patterns, there are a few other distinct types to highlight. Amato and colleagues (2011) also identified a type called "parallel parenting," which was the most common coparenting type in their study. This type consisted of parents who parented independently, made contact every now and again but did not discuss parenting with one another often, and experienced slightly more conflict than the cooperative coparents. Maccoby and colleagues (1990) identified a type they labeled "mixed." Although this type had high levels of conflict, similar to the conflicted coparents, these coparents were distinct in that they also engaged in high levels of communication with their coparent. Finally, Markham and Coleman (2012) identified a coparenting type called "bad to better," which consisted of coparents that were conflictual in the beginning but worked overtime to improve their coparenting relationship. This type demonstrated that coparenting is dynamic and coparenting relationships can change with time. Some of these changes could stem from establishing boundaries, improved communication, and reduced conflict.

Identifying types of coparenting is important because "the style of interaction and communication a couple develops post-divorce affects all of their future relationships" (Ahrons 1994, 7). The relationship that is often affected the most is parent-child relationships. Parent-child

relationships can suffer from the marital dissolution, particularly father-child relationships when the father is removed from the child's home, which can affect the child's overall well-being. When coparents can work together to engage in effective discussion and reduce their conflict, not only does it have positive effects on the child, but it helps sustain a positive coparental relationship over time (Ahrons 2007). Professionals who work with families could utilize these typologies to provide them with skills to increase communication and reduce conflict, while educating them about the effect of their coparenting type on their children.

Researchers have found cooperative coparenting relationships to be beneficial to children because they allow them to sustain relationships with other members of their families, particularly their nonresidential father, better handle the stressors of divorce (Amato et al. 2011; Sobolewski and King 2005), and younger children have been found to have fewer behavior problems (Amato et al. 2011). Additionally, Beckmeyer and colleagues (2014) found that when parents engaged in less conflict and demonstrated higher communication, adjustment issues in children decreased, but regardless of their parents' coparenting type, the children still internalized and externalized their parents' divorce in similar ways. Similarly, differences have not been found based on coparenting type in parental warmth and support, parental knowledge, inconsistent discipline (Beckmeyer et al. 2019), or school grades (Amato et al. 2011)

Although most research focuses on parent-child relationships and child outcomes, the findings are mixed; additional research is needed to better understand how coparenting types affect relationships and child outcomes.

McKenzie L. Cox-Zimmermann and Melinda Stafford Markham

See also: Collaborative Divorce; Communication between Couples in Divorce; Coparenting and Divorce

Further Reading

Ahrons, Constance R. 1994. *The Good Divorce: Keeping Your Family Together When Your Marriage Comes Apart.* New York: HarperCollins.

Ahrons, Constance R. 2007. "Family Ties after Divorce: Long-Term Implications for Children." *Family Process,* no. 46: 53–65.

Amato, Paul R., Jennifer B. Kane, and Spencer James. 2011. "Reconsidering the 'Good Divorce.'" *Family Relations,* no. 60: 511–524.

Beckmeyer, Jonathon J., Marilyn Coleman, and Lawrence H. Ganong. 2014. "Postdivorce Coparenting Typologies and Children's Adjustment." *Family Relations,* no. 63: 526–537.

Beckmeyer, Jonathon J., Melinda Stafford Markham, and Jessica Troilo. 2019. "Postdivorce Coparenting Relationships and Parent-Youth Relationships: Are Repartnership and Parent-Youth Contact Moderators?" *Journal of Family Issues,* no. 40: 613–636.

Maccoby, Elanor E., Charlene E. Depner, and Robert H. Mnookin. 1990. "Coparenting in the Second Year after Divorce." *Journal of Marriage and the Family,* no. 52: 141–155.

Markham, Melinda Stafford, and Marilyn Coleman. 2012. "The Good, the Bad, and the Ugly: Divorced Mothers' Experiences with Coparenting." *Family Relations,* no. 61: 586–600.

Sobolewski, Juliana M., and Valerie King. 2005. "The Importance of the Coparental Relationships for Nonresident Fathers' Ties to Children." *Journal of Marriage and Family,* no. 67: 1196–1212.

Cycle of Violence

The term "cycle of violence" may be applied to several instances of violence within a family. Initially coined by Lenore Walker in 1979, she was attempting to explain the cycle of intimate partner violence (IPV). Walker developed the three phases in which IPV occurs: the phase of *tension building* between the partners, the *battery phase*, and lastly the *honeymoon phase*. These phases or segments of the abuse cycle will often repeat; thus, the cycle of violence continues. Walker established the phases based on the psychological explanation of learned helplessness (Daigle 2018, 283). Learned helplessness can be defined as a depressed state of an individual where they feel powerless and feel like a failure. Individuals suffering from learned helplessness will repeatedly reject chances to change the situation they are in, nor do they attempt to. This explanation reflects on the physical and emotional environment of the individual and giving up is the best response; thus, nothing the individual does will control the outcome.

Walker's IPV cycle of violence is centered around three distinct phases. Phase one of the cycle of violence is labeled as the *tension-building* phase. In this phase, the tension between partners continues to build. These incidents can and may seem small and meaningless yet add a layer of tension to the relationship. Often, pressures from outside of the relationship will harm the relationship, adding yet another negative stress layer. At first, this stage of the cycle of violence usually consists of verbal arguing; however, it can and has led to minor physical assaults on a partner. In most insistences, the woman is the victim and feels as if no matter what she does or says will result in a verbal or small physical assault. She often will feel as if she has to tread lightly with her partner to avoid conflict (Jerin and Moriarty 2010, 152).

The *tension-building* phase of the cycle of violence leads to the next stage, the battery phase. In the *battery* phase of the cycle of violence, the dominant partner engages in physical abuse, sexual abuse, psychological abuse, or the destruction of property of the other. This abuse can start as minor infractions such as pushing, shoving, or striking the other. In several instances, the abuse in this phase will become significantly more aggressive, which may include aggravated assault and aggravated battery (Daigle 2018, 283). In some occurrences, the violence will be severe, and the victim will require professional medical attention. When the victim seeks professional medical attention, medical professionals are required by law to report the event to law enforcement.

It is at this stage in the cycle of violence when law enforcement may be first made aware of the abuse in the relationship. In years past, law enforcement would take a report and most often leave it to the victim to press charges against their partner. Frequently, the victim did not elect to press charges, and the violence continued. Many victims declined to take legal action in fear for themselves or their children, believe they somehow deserved the abuse, or feel there are no other options as they feel they require

their partner for financial or other types of stability. Today, with changes to domestic violence laws, in general, if law enforcement can determine an aggressor, an arrest is made. The local prosecutor will then elect to bring charges upon the aggressor allowing the victim to remain out of the decision-making process to prosecute.

As the battery stage of the cycle of violence ends, the makeup or otherwise known as the *honeymoon* phase begins. The honeymoon phase may begin as early as the assault(s) against the partner have occurred but will also continue long after that. During this phase of the cycle of violence, the abuser becomes peaceful and gentle toward their partner. At this stage, the abuser will often ask for forgiveness, promising the victim the abuse will stop, and they will be happy together. The offender sees the opportunity as a way to regain the trust of the partner again. This attempts to repair the relationship by justifying the actions or blaming them on factors outside the relationship, such as stress caused at work. Many offenders will even consent to therapy or counseling sessions in attempts to convince the victim they have or are trying to change their violent ways (Jerin and Moriarty 2010, 152).

As the cycle of violence completes the last phase of the cycle, the cycle then begins again. The cycle returns to the tension-building phase at the end of the honeymoon phase due to an insignificant event, builds upon these minor events, shifts to the battery stage where the abuse returns, then become full circle to the honeymoon phase. Thus, the cycle of violence continues within a relationship.

In the attempt to discover the causes of the cycle of violence, studies have been conducted and reveal common traits among the abusers. These traits include but are not limited to: the abuse of alcohol, the abuser or victim was raised in a home where domestic violence experienced frequently, financial hardships, low self-esteem or low self-worth, mental illness, psychological issues, jealousy, the inability to process and handle stress, and difficulty in communicating feelings towards the partner. Just the fact that an individual has any of these traits does not make them engage in the cycle of violence; however, with these traits present, the chance of violence increases significantly. A combination of these traits leads to the propensity of being either the offender or the victim of the cycle of violence.

As with the indicators of susceptibility to the cycle of violence, there are several theories that attempt to explain the cycle of violence. Of the numerous theories, general systems theory (along with learned helplessness as discussed earlier) attempts to explain the cycle of violence via the use of eight propositions:

1. Violence has many causes and roots.
2. More violence occurs than reported.
3. Family or IPV violence is mostly ignored.
4. Violence is learned.
5. Violence is reaffirmed via social interactions.
6. Violence produces positive feedback when desired results are achieved.
7. Additional violence occurs when original violence is outside of family norms.
8. Labeling encourages violence.

These eight propositions reflect a deeper reflection of how the cycle of violence begins and continues (Jerin and Moriarty 2010, 148). Each phase of the cycle of violence reflects a series of events that influence the acts to occur.

Joseph R. Budd

See also: Economic Independence; Intimate Partner Violence

Further Reading
Daigle, Leah. 2018. *Victimology: A Text Reader.* Thousand Oaks: Sage Publications.

Gelles, Richard. "Family Violence." In Hampton, R. L., Gullotta, T. P., Adams, G. R., Potter, E. H., III, and Weissberg, R. P. (Eds.). 1993. *Family Violence: Prevention and Treatment.* Newbury Park: Sage Publications.

Jerin, Robert and Moriarty, Laura. 2010. *The Victims of Crime.* Upper Saddle River: Prentice Hall.

Walker, Lenore. 1979. *The Battered Woman.* New York: Harper and Row.

Walker, Lenore. 2000. *Battered Woman Syndrome* (2nd ed.). New York: Springer Publishing Company.

D

Dating, Paradigm Shifts

As a society, America has repeatedly been subject to major events that necessitated thorough adaptations and revisions in assumptions. Some of these shifts affected social structures such as partner selection, the maintenance of relationships, and family formation.

Paradigm Shifts

In essence, a paradigm shift refers to a fundamental change, which affects related areas and ideas. The reasons that act as catalysts to precipitate major changes are manifold and include scientific breakthroughs, medical advances, inventions, world events, wars, natural disasters, and more. These can combine to create a climate that is ripe for a revision in a worldview that will affect thinking and understanding. Key ideas are adapted, revised, and replaced by newer insights that better reflect and respond to a changed situation or worldview. The *systemic* change allows for fresh understanding and insight, making it impossible to revert to the previous mindset. The analogy would be what has been seen cannot be unseen. The technical term for this occurrence is a "paradigm shift," a concept borrowed from scientific theory. In terms of dating behavior and our thinking about dating, several major paradigm shifts have occurred. These include a greater openness and understanding of sexuality and gender, medical insights and advances related to controlling fertility, increased individualism and autonomy, access to information and social networks through the internet also affecting dating opportunities, and unique to the 2020s, the COVID endemic.

Talking about Sexuality

Dating is a way of actively searching for a long-term and permanent partner. During the 1800s, the societally sanctioned way of dating was sequential monogamy. The earlier paradigm shifts as the 1800s ended and the 1900s began laid the groundwork for change and can be partially linked to the *psychoanalytic movement*, which had influenced the thinking about the expression (and repression) of sexuality. Topics that had been hush-hush were examined in an increasingly uncensored manner. The strict conformity of the Victorian era shifted and relaxed to make way for greater freedom of expression, in civic as well as artistic contexts. This opening up was supported and probably accelerated by the *growth of psychology* and sociology as areas of expertise. Human behavior was studied, and self-reflection became an object of psychotherapeutic interventions.

Dating lost some parental control and was perceived as an exploration of identity, especially during emerging adulthood. This set the stage for partnering and ultimately family formation. Traditionally, dating was orchestrated by parents, well-meaning relatives, and matchmakers. Increasingly, the responsibility rested in the hands of individuals who had a say in their own choices. Social contexts that facilitated non-chaperoned dating behavior increased with the wide availability of cars (and the privacy they provided) and dating venues such as cinemas, dancing halls, eateries, and venues catering specifically to singles. Dating was an expression of individuality and autonomy and acknowledged the rite of passage that signaled emerging adulthood and the lifespan beyond.

From War to Web

The midpoint of the 20th century represented a turning point: the Second World War had ended several years earlier, and the Baby Boomer generation was being born against the backdrop of post-war optimism and hope. Large-scale war-related societal forces had given women responsibilities that initiated a paradigm shift in roles, and related educational, career, and economic opportunities. Leading up to that shift was a gradual but noticeable change that permeated most aspects of the dating game. Marketing and the blossoming advertising world hoped to channel and direct motivation toward increased consumerism, which in turn promised economic growth. In some ways that consumption included relationships in romantic contexts.

The decades spanning the second half of the 20th century, ushered in dramatic research in the sciences, accessibility to information, greater access to education, and importantly the advent of the world wide web. This ushered in modernity previously unthinkable. Medical advances offered reliable contraception, which allowed greater intentionality in planning a family. The risk of sexually transmitted infections was addressed until the AIDS epidemic changed the rules yet again.

Dating behavior varied on a continuum ranging from conservative to liberal. Overall attitudes toward sexuality and the taboos surrounding sex before marriage relaxed. These sociocultural events and movements, including the emancipation of women, increased gender equality, greater social empowerment, access to education and jobs, and freedom of speech also influenced dating options. Working women could contribute to the cost of the date, allowing for a more balanced power dynamic. Women made their voices heard in partner choices and became increasingly active in the dating process. The roles of men changed in tandem, allowing for dual parenting, dual-income families, emotional expression, and partnerships representing greater equality. These paradigm shifts importantly affected LGBTQ identity expression and partner choices and filtered through to law and social policy.

Communication and Accessibility

In a boundary-shattering paradigm shift starting in the early 1990s, the internet became the biggest socially acceptable matchmaker of them all. Communication was released from the confines of the landline, and mobile phones made their owners accessible anytime and anywhere. Texting messages included "sexting," and each new wave of innovation opened new dimensions. As the World Wide Web expanded, matchmaking and dating behaviors became subject to the algorithms of dedicated websites. Joining a matching website was open to anyone desiring access to this bigger world of partner selection. By 2020, more than half of all couples admitted that the internet had facilitated their match or had featured in their dating history. The norms and restrictions concerning permanence of relationships eased.

One approach does not fit all in a country as diverse as America. We find the entire continuum of behavior and ideology from the orthodox through to the liberal and unconventional, with many nuances in between. That same variety can be found in dating and partnering practices.

Over the decades leading up to the year 2000, dating with the end goal of marriage underwent shifts. Cohabitation before marriage as well as cohabitation instead of marriage, became commonplace. Many couples chose to reserve marriage for the permanence required to raise a family, but not a necessity for their expression of personal commitment. Breadwinners were likely to be responsible for child support, many being women. Lower incidence of marriage commitment translated to fewer divorces, and divorce in turn could be a no-fault divorce with joint custody. Single parenthood, parenthood through surrogacy, and various forms or artificial reproductive techniques opened options to same-sex couples and others for whom biological parenthood had been elusive.

An Endemic: The Big "C"
In the 2020s, the advent of the COVID-19 endemic and the accompanying widespread requirements of social distancing confronted dating and partnering with unusual and seemingly insurmountable challenges. The world was blanketed in uncertainty; there was no exact precedent and initially there were no clear and defined paths forward. As science raced to unravel the COVID-enigma, the populations affected by it experienced wide disparities of intensely human emotions. The dark sides of the human psyche had

an opportunity to resurface, including fear, denial, defiance, anger, frustration, depression, and mourning. Some of these accumulated frustrations were vented in compliance fatigue, as persons rebelled against health-related guidelines. On the other hand, there was the hopeful side: the empathy, social cohesiveness, mutual support, creativity, emotional adjustment and readjustment, reassessment, and recalibration of values and beliefs. In short, a deeply human vulnerability was recognized in ourselves and others. Numerous persons personally experienced COVID-related losses or knew someone affected. People were interconnected and part of a society deeply scarred by the ravages of the endemic. The acute loss concerned loss of life, but extended to health, wellbeing, homes, livelihoods, finances, and futures. Like a wildfire, the effects of COVID ravaged their way forward.

COVID affected every dimension of societal life. The endemic posed a unique and tough challenge to the dating and partnering environment and severely restricted the formation of new partnerships. Existing partnerships were also affected: engagements and marriages were put on hold; celebrations were subdued or nonexistent; people felt robbed of the rituals marking major social transitions. The predominant guidelines before vaccination were lockdown, social distancing, and wearing of masks. With these recommendations in place how was a single to meet and get to know partners? This renewed emphasis placed a new lease on communication and getting to know a person on a platonic level through socially distanced forms of communication. This became the prelude before committing to an intimate relationship, which in turn could prove to be risky if it spread COVID.

One significant occurrence was that individuals reignited relationships with previous partners. The partner with whom one had parted ways proved to be better than no partner at all. The choice of "friends with benefits," formerly platonic relationships that diversified into sexual partners, gained significance. The pandemic also magnified fault lines in relationships. Isolated within households and with restricted living arrangements, the challenges of juggling multiple roles became overwhelming. Relationship turbulence with all the accompanying stressors ensued. The overfamiliarity of a live-in partner could show up every minute irritation, that would otherwise have been forgiven. Just as major stressful life events can make or break a relationship, the COVID-reality forced relationships into either camp: they deepened and even flourished or unraveled as the stress mounted. Intimate partner violence increased as a threat, with the added risk that avenues for escape were very limited. The solace people find through civic engagement and in religious communities was absent as these activities had to find a new expression through online platforms. COVID-related effects have connected people across all divides, to the extent that people have acknowledged a changed reality, a profound reassessment of values and priorities. In short, a paradigm shift. The reality of COVID was unprecedented in its unique expression.

With each major paradigm shift, the expressions of partnering and related family life undergo new changes. In a bidirectional manner, these expressions of dating are the outcome of changing societies. In turn, they influence those same societies in profound ways.

Clara Gerhardt

See also: Dating and Courtship Pre-1950; Dating and Courtship 1950–2000; Dating and Courtship 2000–Present

Further Reading

Lupton, Deborah and Willis, Karen (Eds). 2021. *The Covid-19 crisis: Social perspectives.* New York: Routledge.

Scott, Christina L. and Blair, Sampson Lee (Eds.). 2017. *Intimate relationships and social change: The dynamic nature of dating, mating, and coupling.* Contemporary perspectives in family research Volume 11. Emerald Publishing.

Silton, Nava R. 2017. *Family dynamics and romantic relationships in a changing society.* IGI Global.

Wright, Michelle F. (Ed.). 2017. *Identity, sexuality, and relationships among emerging adults in the digital age.* IGI Global.

Dating, Technology and

Advances in technology have changed the landscape of how people interact with each other. This includes how individuals find, meet, and communicate with potential dating partners. The internet allows people access to communication with many people from around the world from one's own home. Social networking sites, chatrooms, online gaming platforms, online dating websites, and mobile web applications (apps) allow individuals to interact with friends and meet strangers in a virtual space. In fact, a nationally representative survey found that 39% of different-gender couples and 65% of same-gender couples described meeting online (Rosenfeld, Thomas, and Hausen 2019, 4). Online dating websites and mobile web applications are specifically designed for this purpose and promote dating by allowing users to create profiles to attract potential dating partners, and different websites have varying affordances for allowing users to communicate with each other. There are a large variety of online dating sites including free websites (Plenty of Fish); websites that attempt to utilize algorithms or other means to pair users based on compatibility (eHarmony and Chemistry); mobile web apps (Tinder and Bumble); websites for LGBTQ users (Grindr, Her, and LGBTQutie); websites for a specific race, ethnicity, religion, culture, etc. (Black People Meet, Christian Mingle, and Jdate); websites for casual sex (Adult Friend Finder and Be Naughty); and websites for people looking for other specific categories (Farmers Only for farmers, Bristlr for those with beards, and Cougar Life for older women interested in younger men).

The precursor to online dating were newspaper personal ads, which allowed individuals to advertise themselves to people who they may not interact with otherwise. These newspaper personals began to appear as early as the late 1600s; however, they were not particularly popular, and few people met romantic partners this way. The invention of the computer brought on attempts in the mid-1900s to use questionnaires to find matches for interested parties. In 1995, the availability of the internet allowed for online dating to begin to become commercially popular as websites such as match.com and kiss.com launched to help people meet. Later in the decade, the movie *You've Got Mail* provided a pop culture example of how the popularity of email and instant messaging altered how individuals communicated and dated online. In the early 2000s, social networking sites, such as Myspace and Facebook, became popular, and although not specifically designed for dating, did allow for easier connecting, re-connecting, and communicating between users. The most recent innovation is location-based dating apps such as Tinder and Bumble, which are most popular among adults aged 18–24 and tripled in popularity between 2013 and 2016 (Smith 2016).

Online dating has been growing in popularity since it began. Online dating was once seen as only for individuals who were desperate or would not be successful at dating in real life. However, surveys from Pew Research in 2016 have shown that this viewpoint has been steadily decreasing over time, and now only 23% of individuals believe online dating is for desperate people and 59% of people believe that online dating is a good way to meet people. This also corresponds to an increase use in online dating over time as 15% of adults in 2015 describe themselves as online dating users (up from 11% in 2013). For adults aged 18–24, the rate of participation in online dating increased most dramatically from 10% in 2013 to 27% in 2015 in part due to the emergence of dating apps and are now the age cohort that uses online dating most, passing the age group 25–34. Proportions of online daters are similar for individuals of different races and incomes, and online daters are more likely to be college-educated (Smith 2016) and be lower in dating related anxiety (Valkenburg and Peter 2007, 851).

There are a number of advantages to meeting potential romantic partners online compared to face-to-face. Most notably, online dating expands the dating pool for users beyond daily in-person interactions. This is especially helpful for individuals who may have smaller dating pools, such as sexual minority individuals in areas without a large LGBTQ community. Online dating also requires little effort and can be done from one's own home or mobile device. The combination of accessibility and simplicity of use makes online dating ideal for individuals who have time constraints, are new to a geographic area, or recently went through a relationship transition. The matching feature of some dating websites also allow for users to potentially be matched with someone they could be more compatible with than the average person. Users can also assess other users to find a more compatible match by browsing other users' profiles and set up their own profile in a way that would attract partners one would be interested in. Interested parties can then exchange messages online until they feel comfortable moving forward in the relationship (e.g., exchanging contact or personal information, meeting in person, defining the relationship). Messages that are positive, pro-social, and focus on the other person are more likely to be viewed positively and result in more messages (Finkel et al. 2012, 18). Communication that takes place online can also build intimacy and foster relationship development in a way that approximates face-to-face communication.

Despite these advantages, there are also negatives to online dating. Since interactions take place in a virtual space, it is common for online dating users to exaggerate or lie on their profiles. This is colloquially known as "catfishing," named after a documentary and subsequent TV show on MTV about people lying about their identity online. Men are more likely than women to lie in an online dating context and often exaggerate status, such as income, while women are more likely to exaggerate appearance (Guadagno, Okdie, and Kruse 2012, 642–646). Another risk to online dating is that because online communication can only approximate face-to-face interaction, individuals may overly idealize the people they meet online (Baym 2015, 145–146). These issues can lead to risks of dating a person whom one isn't as compatible with as one believed or becoming the victim of crimes such as identity theft, money scams, or violent crime.

Innovations with technology have continued to change what the dating process looks like today. The drive to find a compatible romantic partner creates a need for companies to create better, safer, and more streamlined ways to meet people. Dating sites and apps continue to work on ways to improve people's ability to find an ideal romantic partner.

Eric T. Goodcase and Denzel L. Jones

See also: Dating and Courtship 2000–Present; Relationships, Technology and

Further Reading

Ansari, Aziz and Eric Klinenburg. 2015. *Modern Romance.* Penguin Books.

Baym, Nancy K. 2015. *Personal Connections in the Digital Age.* John Wiley & Sons.

Finkel, Eli J., Paul W. Eastwick, Benjamin R. Karney, Harry T. Reis, and Susan Sprecher. 2012. "Online dating: A critical analysis from the perspective of psychological science." *Psychological Science in the Public Interest* 13, no. 1: 3–66.

Guadagno, Rosanna E., Bradley M. Okdie, and Sara A. Kruse. 2012. "Dating deception: Gender, online dating, and exaggerated self-presentation." *Computers in Human Behavior* 28, no. 2: 642–647.

Rosenfeld, Michael J., Reuben J. Thomas, and Sonia Hausen. 2019. "Disintermediating your friends: How online dating in the United States displaces other ways of meeting." *Proceedings of the National Academy of Sciences* 116, no. 36: 17753–17758.

Smith, Aaron. 2016. "15% of American adults have used online dating sites or mobile dating apps." Pew Research Center. Last modified February 11, 2016. http://www.Pewinternet.org.

Valkenburg, Patti M. and Jochen Peter. 2007. "Who visits online dating sites? Exploring some characteristics of online daters." *CyberPsychology & Behavior* 10, no. 6: 849–852.

Dating after Divorce

Though one relationship may be ending, divorce or filing for divorce typically does not end a person's desire for partnership. In fact, 30% of divorced individuals remarry within one year of divorce and additionally 50% of individuals will be married within five years from their divorce (Wilson and Clarke 1992, 123–141; Bramlett and Mosher 2002). Moreover, research indicates that more than half of individuals filing for divorce had already begun dating a new partner within sixty days (Anderson et al. 2004, 61–75). Additionally, 25% stated that their new relationship was already considered serious. Dating after divorce can take many forms ranging from casual evening events to engagements and even marriage, depending upon the circumstances and desires of the individuals. These relationships can either begin before the ending of the previous marriage or begin several years after the dissolution of the marriage.

Given the challenges associated with post-divorce adjustment, many experts believe it is better for adults to wait to date in order to adjust to their newly single life, while other experts state that the time a parent should wait is variable or inconsequential. The concern is related to the ruptured sense of personal identity that with time and reflection may assist in rebuilding a healthier and solid sense of self (Jones et al. 2019). Dating too soon may not afford ample opportunity to reflect on past mistakes, and the person may inadvertently enter into a new relationship based on the same sense of self. Other experts are concerned with the influence a dating relationship has on the children in terms of potential attachments that may be formed with new dating partners who may not work out and inadvertently expose children to subsequent divorce like experiences (Anderson et al. 2004, 61–75). Children may also feel like the dating relationship is a competition for their parents love and attention or their hopes for their parents' reconciliation may be dashed. As such, much consideration has been given by professionals in the divorce field on how specifically to introduce the topic of parent dating to their children with emphases on ensuring that parents don't introduce their dating partners to their children too soon (i.e., before the family system restabilizes) or that the dating relationship will lead to their family being whole again (Lansky 2009, 210).

Scholars have identified several relationship transitions that divorced parents may experience through the dating process. These relationships are not mutually exclusive, and one must not complete one stage to move on to the next. The first transition is dating initiation with approximately 80% of parents enter this stage within one year of filing for divorce (Anderson and Greene 2005, 47–62). Factors that may influence parent's decision to initiate dating include custody arrangements, cultural values, socioeconomic status, and gender and ethnicity of the parent. As parents initiate dating, the next stage involves introducing children to the new dating partner. This phase is both stressful for the parents, because of how the children might react to the partner, and for the children, because they recognize that their parent's relationship will influence their life. This phase can also be troubling for children as they may see their parents' dating partner as a replacement for their other parent. The basic recommendation is to "go slow" and create clear boundaries, introducing new dating partners to children as "friends" (Lansky 2009, 212) and even keeping the exposure to parent dating to a minimum (e.g., date when your children are with your coparent; Lansky 2009, 212). The next step in repartnering is termed serious involvement, when possible stepparents begin engaging in parent-child interactions on a more frequent basis. As the relationship continues to increase in seriousness, the next stages focus on the sleeping arrangements of the parents.

Many parenting plans/custody agreements include details related to what legal professionals call the "morality clause," which involves the limitation of overnight guests in the home while the children are present (see Parenting Plans and Custody Arrangements). Though not always practical to divorcing parents' plans for repartnering, the aim of this clause is to limit children's exposure to adult behavior. Nonetheless, across all economic backgrounds, the rate at which partners cohabitate before marriage has increased to be about 66% of remarriages (Bumpass, Raley, and Sweet 1995, 425–436).

It is very unlikely that an individual will date and marry the first person that they began dating after their initial divorce. Most individuals date between three to five partners, and in some cases more than ten, prior to recommitment (Anderson and Greene 2005, 47–62). These partnerships may have been in any one of the transitional states, but the break-up of a serious relationship has been associated with decreases in functioning in both children and adults mirroring decreases observed when the original marriage was dissolved. Research has begun to look at the ways in which repartnering influences both the parents and the children in order to better understand the negative effects experienced. It has been found that parents who date engage in less supervision and are more inconsistent in their discipline, which in turn influences children's externalizing behavior (Jones et al. 2019). Ultimately, parents may inadvertently be harming their children by beginning to repartner at a time when the children need the parents to be emotionally available to them.

The transition period between divorce and remarriage tends to be described as stressful and anxiety provoking. A time in which parents and children alike are confused and concerned for the future. Parents often times search out relationships in order to increase stability in their life with the hope to increase the stability in the child's life. However, at times, parents may get caught up in their new dating experience which can at times inadvertently impede their child's recovery.

Dating During the Divorce Process. Research suggests that approximately 40% of divorces involved infidelity (Marin, Christensen, and Atkins 2014), and an estimated 30% of individuals have moved into dating relationships even prior to the divorce being finalized (Worthy 2019). Though there are numerous overlaps with the aforementioned recommendations for going slow and protecting children from the normative challenges associated with the divorce process, there are additional factors to consider when dating during the divorce process.

As parents consider dating a new partner before the finalization of the divorce, they need to consider the potential systemic effects that their decisions might have. For one, children may see the new dating partner as the reason their parents are getting a divorce, experience a potential attachment injury, and align with one parent over the other. There is also the impact that a new dating relationship might have on immediate family, extended family, and friends, ultimately impacting the support system. The impact can be difficult especially if those individuals do not agree with the choices that particular parent is making. One must also think about the dissolving marriage and what the introduction of a new partner so soon might do to the coparenting relationship. New partners being introduced too quickly may lead to greater conflict within the coparenting relationship.

Not only are there relational systemic effects, but as one expands further there are even potential legal ramifications for beginning a dating relationship before the divorce has been finalized. In some states, dating before the divorce has been finalized

may be deemed "adultery" and could be seen as "fault" affecting custody decisions and child support. This can be cited as a reason for the dissolution of the marriage by the other parent and can then affect a judge's ruling for the division of the marital assets (e.g., the other parent awarded the home). There is also the potential for the new dating partner to be subpoenaed and asked to testify as a witness in a divorce hearing. The general legal counsel is to avoid dating until after the divorce is finalized in order to avoid these issues. In fact, some states even have a window of time following divorce where individuals are not allowed to cohabit or remarry.

It is important for each person to individually weigh the costs and benefits of beginning a new relationship at any time, but there are special considerations that should be taken when thinking about starting a relationship before the finalization of a divorce.

Ethan Jones, Todd Spencer,
and Matthew Brosi

See also: Remarriage; Stepfamilies; Stepfamilies, Developmental Stages; Stepfamily Education

Further Reading

Anderson, Edward R. and Shannon M. Greene. 2005. "Transitions in parental repartnering after divorce." *Journal of Divorce & Remarriage* 43, no. 3–4: 47–62.

Anderson, Edward R., Shannon M. Greene, Lisa Walker, Catherine A. Malerba, Marion S. Forgatch, and David S. DeGarmo. 2004. "Ready to take a chance again: Transitions into dating among divorced parents." *Journal of Divorce & Remarriage* 40, no. 3–4: 61–75.

Bramlett, Matthew D., and William D. Mosher. 2002. "Cohabitation, marriage, divorce, and remarriage in the United States."

Bumpass, Larry L., R. Kelly Raley, and James A. Sweet. 1995. "The changing character of stepfamilies: Implications of cohabitation and nonmarital childbearing." *Demography* 32, no. 3: 425–436.

Jones, Ethan R., Matthew Brosi, Todd Spencer, and Nathan Hardy. 2019. "The influence of divorcing parents' post-separation dating relationships on children's behavior" (Unpublished master's thesis). Stillwater, Oklahoma: Oklahoma State University.

Lansky, Vicki. 2009. *Divorce book for parents: Helping your children cope with divorce and its aftermath.* Minnetonka, MN: Book Peddlers.

Marín, Rebeca A., Andrew Christensen, and David C. Atkins. 2014. "Infidelity and behavioral couple therapy: Relationship outcomes over 5 years following therapy." *Couple and Family Psychology: Research and Practice* 3, no. 1: 1.

Wilson, Barbara Foley, and Sally Cuningham Clarke. 1992. "Remarriages: A demographic profile." *Journal of Family Issues* 13, no. 2: 123–141.

Worthy. 2019. "Jumping in: Dating after divorce in 2019." Retrieved on February 22, 2023 from: https://www.worthy .com/blog/knowledge-center/insights /study-on-dating-after-divorce-in-2019/

Dating and Courtship Pre-1950

An integral part of the traditional adult lifespan is devoted to partnering and relationship formation. In the pre-1950s public acknowledgment focused predominantly on heterosexual meeting and dating rituals, with marriages paving the way to family formation. Courtship and dating occurred in a clandestine manner in the LGBTQ community. The combination of the terms "dating" and "mating" often occur in publications, denoting the interrelatedness of these topics; the one paving the way for the other. This represents the overly simplified version of the "girl meets boy/boy meets girl" scenario, historically referred to as "courting." Courting represented formality and serious intent, and during the 1800s chaperones ensured respectability.

The intricacies of dating are complex and nuanced by cultural customs, education, socio-economic resources, time-related socio-cultural shifts relating especially to gender roles, women in the workforce, individual and financial autonomy, dual parenting, and more. Dating before the mid-1950s was strongly influenced by factors that included economic considerations, power and status within a community, families (and empires) seeking to be united through marriage; all playing out against an intricate backdrop of religion, customs, culture, authoritarianism within the family structure, and the like. In short, marriage was often a contract between families, and courting was a step toward the progression of a legal union.

Dating and Gender Roles

At the risk of stereotyping, central themes can be distinguished. Prior to the 1950s, society's perception of gender roles in a heterosexual context tended to place men in authoritative even authoritarian and leadership positions, while women balanced out the power hierarchies by being mostly subservient and acquiescent counterparts. This key gender role difference dictated that breadwinners were predominantly men, while full-time homemakers were likely women. Parenting was divided into roles of the nurturing homemaker-mother and the discipline enforcing head-of-the household father. The Industrial Revolution revealed alternative models of labor for wages, with women working both inside and outside the home, and taking their places in home industries as well as factories. Children were also drawn into the labor market and child labor was common in working classes, occurring at the expense of an education. If there were alternatives to the traditional male/female role configurations, these occurred in secretive contexts, as openly and in many instances legally, the society neither empathically approached nor sanctioned diversity in gender roles nor in sexual expression.

Romantic Love

Prior to the 1950s, romantic love was a bonus if it occurred, but was not considered a necessity for a marital match. It was not practical to follow one's heart when there were such serious considerations at stake as who was inheriting from whom, how family alliances could be strengthened, and the power base expanded. Ideally, a person wanted to "marry up," meaning finding a spouse who had a better or more respected position in society or had one or other attribute signaling higher societal status and assets. Romantic love was the domain for novels and poetry—a wonderful yet impractical indulgence. Of course, it occurred and was strived for, and the sense of longing and pining for fulfillment made excellent material for the arts. Even so the realities of matched unions with financial and other incentives meant that romantic love was readily assigned to pre- and extra-marital affairs, and it was not uncommon for romance to be sacrificed

for the communal good of the families. As individualism and related personal independence as cultural traits became more pronounced, personal wishes would compete with the collective desires of the families being united through a specific marriage.

Carnal Love

Sexual expressions of love are part of the chain of procreation. The taboos and barriers discouraging premarital sex were considerable, and thus virginity in women was valued. Double standards persisted, with men encouraged to "sow their wild oats" before settling down. Virginity became an asset in the transaction between partners, signaling exclusivity of sex within the stable parameters of marriage. Monogamy ensured that offspring were indeed direct genetic offspring of the marital pair.

Partnering as an Economic and Social Transaction

Unless a woman inherited wealth, she was dependent on her husband. Dating, for that same economic reason, might be seen as "making a good match" which had more to do with financial (including social status and power) than romantic expectations. The transaction had fiduciary implications and consequences, that spilled over into social roles. Frequently men had the final say over financial transactions, including those pertaining to their wife's assets. These customs further disempowered women. Marriage provided social acceptance and stability. Divorce was risky business as it had the potential of disrupting financial stability and social respectability. It was still several decades before the advent of the "no-fault divorce" and to exit a partnership meant finding and laying blame. The repercussions circled outward to alimony and child support arrangements. The first no-fault divorce bill in the United States was only signed in 1969, and yet as recently as 2010 all 50 states allowed this option in divorce proceedings.

Social Exchange Theory
This theory addresses transactions where assets such as power, position, affluence, beauty, youth, and innocence, are used to barter in the marriage stakes. The classic stereotype is the "spring/autumn marriage" where the older rich gentleman in his autumn years, marries the younger beautiful lady in the spring of her life. On the other hand, younger men have married older women motivated by the prospect of a considerable inheritance or a title.

Education and Career Opportunities
Women's vulnerability in terms of marriage choices and marital roles was linked to gender inequality and lack of societal rights, including voting rights. The right for women to vote was only ratified in 1920 and was the culmination of a lengthy struggle. Men tended to occupy the entire range of professions, women's education opened the doors predominantly to teaching and nursing. Education as an act of self-actualization was rare, and women were formally addressed by their husband's name.

Matching and Meeting
Many hours were spent trying to figure out who was available on the "marriage market," a term that hints at the transactional nature of the liaisons. Official matchmakers could be consulted, and these roles persist in very closed, and traditional contexts. Matched marriage arrangements

continue to this day in select cultural contexts, where immigrant grooms may return to their parental country of origin to be introduced to a culturally suitable marriage prospect. Often parents would meet first and decide if the match would be acceptable to them as parents, before making it an option for consideration by the couple. Even in post millennial America, some of these cultural customs persist in small niches of society.

Naturally, variations have always existed outside these stereotypical divisions and dating practices. History abounds with examples of strong women who raised families and followed personal destinies despite societal constraints. Couples who found each other against all odds and crossed religious, political, racial, gender, and ethnic divides to declare their love, whether publicly or in secret. For every generalization, there is an exception, as love has found a way to cross barriers and overcome obstacles.

Clara Gerhardt

See also: Dating and Courtship 1950–2000; Dating and Courtship 2000–Present

Further Reading
Demir, Melikşah and Sümer, Nebi. 2018. *Close relationships and happiness across cultures.* Springer.
Whyte, Martin King. 1990/2018. *Dating, mating and marriage.* Routledge.

Dating and Courtship 1950–2000

In the last half of the 20th century, courtship started to replace marriage as the primary context for young heterosexual Americans' first sexual experiences. This shift began in the 1950s and 1960s when sex outside of marriage could be justified by love and commitment. By the 1980s and 1990s, most young people expected to have sex with a boyfriend or girlfriend before getting married. Even though marriage declined in importance between 1950 and 2000, courtship played a constant and central role in the lives of young Americans.

In the 1950s, the decade following World War II, marriage was a stabilizing force, and "people saw marriage as the gateway to the good life" (Coontz 2005, 232). It was common for people to get married right after they graduated high school or college. Those who were still in school started forming relationships that offered the social security of marriage without the long-term commitment (LeMasters 1957, 123). In 1955, sociologist Robert Herman (1955, 36) repurposed the term "going steady" to describe these new courtship practices. Going steady referred to a relationship that lasted long enough for the couple to be acknowledged as an item by their peers (Herman 1955, 36). Previously, going steady had applied exclusively to couples on the path to marriage, but couples going steady in the 1950s "acted *as if* they were married," even when they did not "[expect] to marry each other" (Bailey 1988, 49).

Although going steady mimicked the structure of marriage-oriented relationships, it had very little to do with mate selection, especially among high school students (LeMasters 1957, 123). Going steady was crucial in the social lives of American youth because everything was built for couples (Bailey 1988, 53). Going steady meant always having a date, and so young people felt obligated to form a steady relationship whether or not they wanted one (LeMasters 1957, 122).

Couples in the 1950s spent a lot of time together, and as relationships progressed, so did the desire for sexual intimacy beyond necking (kissing) and petting (caressing) (LeMasters 1957, 139). This was nothing different for men, but it conflicted with the social expectation that a respectable woman would be a virgin when she got married. Going steady provided a framework for women to have sex and remain marriage material. "Being in love" justified sexual activity, whether or not emotion was actually involved or how long the "love" lasted (Littauer 2015, 133). In other words, a woman could have sex before marriage without risking her reputation if she was in love with and committed to her boyfriend.

By the mid-1960s, this practice of "permissiveness with affection" was widely accepted and practiced (Spurlock 2016, 109). Young women were able to exercise sexual agency within the parameters of committed relationships, regardless of how short-term and fleeting those relationships actually were (Littauer 2015, 125). This logic also set a precedent that allowed men to demand certain levels of sexual intimacy from their girlfriends (Littauer 2015, 129).

By the late-1960s and into the 1970s, marriage started to lose its social significance, and though the majority of people still got married, they did not marry as early as they did in the 1950s (Coontz 2005, 261). Relationships started developing earlier and they lasted longer, often extending beyond college (Spurlock 2016, 125). It became more common for couples to live together (cohabitate) before getting married, which made the period of courtship even longer.

By the 1970s, people stopped using the term going steady altogether. Although most sex still happened within the context of a relationship, premarital sex did not require the same level of justification. Sexual activity increased the most among young women, in part because of the growing availability of birth control (Spurlock 2016, 138). During the sexual revolution in the 1960s and 1970s, women fought against the sexual double standard, emphasized the importance of sexual pleasure, and criticized marriage as an institution. Relationships were no longer required to justify sex, but most sexual activity still took place within the context of a steady relationship. Even those in the counterculture who embraced "free love" and rejected traditional values often maintained a sexual relationship with a "primary partner" (Spurlock 2016, 113).

In the 1980s, on the heels of the sexual revolution, sex was a "rite of passage" for many teenagers (Spurlock 2016, 134). *Going out* and *dating* were the terms used to describe relationships, which started in the early teens and remained the context for many first sexual experiences. Unlike going steady, which had specific rules and expectations, the expectations for dating and going out were ambiguous and often confusing (Bailey 1988, 143). The introduction of the internet in the 1990s offered a new way for people to meet through online dating, which added to the complexity of the already-confusing dating scene. Still, couple culture was important for the sexual and social lives of young Americans in the 1980s through the 1990s (Spurlock 2016, 135).

The idea that sex is okay if two people are in love remained applicable through the 1990s, even without the concepts of "permissiveness with affection" and "going steady" from the 1950s. From 1950–2000, courtship was the source of sexual experience and the foundation of social status among young people in America. It remained a central component in young American lives, even as the overall significance of marriage declined.

In 2000, scholars started to discuss a hookup culture developing on college campuses, centering on sex specifically outside of love and commitment (Paul, McManus, and Hayes 2000, 76). It was possible that courtship norms were changing within the context of hookup culture, and scholars debated whether relationships and couple culture would lose importance in the 21st century.

Sam Kendrick

See also: Dating and Courtship Pre-1950; Dating and Courtship 2000–Present

Further Reading
Bailey, Beth L. 1988. *From Front Porch to Back Seat: Courtship in Twentieth-Century America.* Baltimore: Johns Hopkins University Press.

Coontz, Stephanie. 2005. *Marriage, a History: From Obedience to Intimacy, or How Love Conquered Marriage.* New York: Viking.

Herman, Robert D. 1955. "The 'Going Steady' Complex: A Re-Examination." *Marriage and Family Living* 17, no. 1: 36–40.

LeMasters, E. E. 1957. *Modern Courtship and Marriage.* New York: The Macmillan Company.

Littauer, Amanda H. 2015. *Bad Girls: Young Women, Sex, and Rebellion before the Sixties.* Chapel Hill, NC: University of North Carolina Press.

Paul, Elizabeth L., Brian McManus, and Allison Hayes. 2000. "'Hookups': Characteristics and Correlates of College Students' Spontaneous and Anonymous Sexual Experiences." *Journal of Sex Research* 37, no. 1: 76–88.

Spurlock, John. 2016. *Youth and Sexuality in the Twentieth-Century United States*. New York: Routledge.

Syrett, Nicholas L. 2009. *The Company He Keeps: A History of White Fraternities*. Chapel Hill, NC: The University of North Carolina Press.

Dating and Courtship 2000–Present

Alongside the ringing in of the new millennium came significant expansion and dependence upon technology. The increasing reliance and integration upon technology in our lives has had a significant impact in how we date and find mates. As people are increasingly communicating through Facebook updates, Instagram posts, Tweets, and Snaps, dating apps have also seen a significant increase of users. According to Ariana Abad (2015), traditional dating has become nearly obsolete, as technology has had a tremendous influence on the 21st century mode of thinking.

Abad goes on to say that while traditional courtship was considered something sacred, the current dating culture does not see such a gradual process. Courtship used to entail face-to-face meetings between potential mates, with the goal of getting to know one another more intimately to determine if they would be a suitable husband or wife. In the 1980s, self-advertising became a commonplace practice to meet friends and potential mates. According to Elizabeth Jagger in *Marketing Molly and Melville: Dating in a Postmodern, Consumer Society*, self-advertising was no longer considered "sad" and viewed negatively as indicative of failure in modern life circumstances which she claimed are mass-mediated, time-pressured, and work-centered. Jagger claims that self-advertisements are now deemed to be "relationally efficient" and "natural" responses to modern-life circumstances.

Now, with over 90% of the population using cell phone technology that fosters a sense of urgency and immediate gratification, we are seeing a further deviation away from courtship rituals. In a culture that is even more work-focused and short on excess time, people are not wanting to "waste time" on meeting face to face to see if a potential mate is "the one." Rather, people communicate with potential partners through dating apps and mobile technology to assess if they are worthy to meet in person.

Andrea J. Baker researches the differences in spaces, places, and settings online. Baker stated in 2008 that researchers of online relationships recognize that people online often feel as though they have gotten to know each other quite well after spending time communicating solely through their mobile devices. When individuals meet online, there is oftentimes a shared similarity or hobby of sorts. Whether that be what type of relationship they want, similar political beliefs, or how they spend their leisure time.

Are there differences between the sexes in their methods of online dating? Dinh et al. analyzed data compiled from eHarmony to assess how men and women differ in their approach to finding a potential mate. This study confirmed gender differences, such as women are prone to being more selective in their potential dating pool than men.

In *Computational Courtship: Understanding the Evolution of Online Dating through Large-scale Data Analysis*,

McWilliams and Barrett examine involvement in online dating with individual's ages 53–74. The aging population generally does not receive a lot of attention in regard to their romantic needs and dating options. In direct contrast to this stigma, many single and unmarried adults over 50 do in fact desire a romantic partner and companionship. eHarmony reports that between 2005 and 2019 online dating sites became the most common way for adults over the age of 50 to meet their marital partners. Finding a mate as an aging adult has particular challenges, such as not having bars or nightclubs as a dating pool option. One user in this study remarked that one is expected to find a mate in social clubs, church, bars . . . or through friends. They continued on to say that, other than that, there would be no other way to meet people. They claim that older people do not go to bars much and they do not have too many friends because their friends are dying out. They ask then, what's left? Social clubs and church. While this study did not examine the successful outcomes of online dating in this population, it did examine the motivation that drove them to use this method of meeting potential mates. These findings supported gendered views by claiming that men want to find physically attractive women and women look for men who could participate in active social lives and intelligent conversation.

When examining how successful online dating is considered, Ansari and Klineberg found that three quarters of singles in the United States have tried dating sites, and up to one third of newly married couples originally met online. It is important to consider the possibility of negative consequences that come with the freedom of filtering the pool of potential mates. Dinh et al. wrote in a Bloomberg report that dating apps such as Luxy and League are arguably negatively impacting income inequality, by making it easier for couples to match by their socioeconomic status.

More research must be done with same-sex and non-binary dyads, as they the fastest growing segment of online dating users. It is important to note that the studies referenced in this entry reflect heterosexual partnerships only. The evolution of courtship styles among the LGBTQI+ community and people of color should be researched thoroughly, as their experiences are undoubtedly different than heterosexual couples.

Sarah White

See also: Dating and Courtship Pre-1950; Dating and Courtship 1950–2000; On-Again, Off-Again Relationships

Further Reading

Abad, Ariana. 2015. "'I "5683" you': Dating and Relationships in the Technology Age." *Bergen Scholarly Journal*, 2: 8–17.

Baker, Andrea. 2008. "Down the Rabbit Hole: The Role of Place in the Initiation and Development of Online Relationships." In *Psychological Aspects of Cyberspace: Theory, Research, Applications,* edited by Andrea J. Baker. Cambridge: Cambridge University Press, pp. 163–184.

Dinh, Rachel, Patrick Gildersleve, and Taha Yasseri. 2018. "Computational Courtship: Understanding the Evolution of Online Dating through Large-scale Data Analysis." *ArXiv* : 1–19.

Jagger, Elizabeth. 2001. "Marketing Molly and Melville: Dating in a Postmodern, Consumer Society." *Sociology*, 35, no. 1: 39–57.

McWilliams, Summer, and Anne E. Barrett. 2014. "Online Dating in Middle and Later Life: Gendered Expectations and Experiences." *Journal of Family Issues*, 411–436.

Death of a Child

"Death of a child" and "Bereaved Parents" are terms that should not go together. The United Nations World Populations Prospects report indicated that the U.S. infant mortality rate in 2022 was 5.547 deaths per 1000 live births. Globally, UN Inter-agency Group for Child Mortality data shows that in 2021, 5 million children under 5 years of age (38 per 1,000 live births) and 2.1 million children ages 5–24 years (17 deaths per 1,000 children) died.

In the last decades, the world has made a notable improvement in terms of child survival. For example, according to UNICEF, the global under-five children mortality rate declined by 61%, from 93 deaths per 1,000 live births in 1990 to 37 in 2020. Nevertheless, those that go through the untimely and devastating ordeal of losing a child are affected in fundamental ways. The death of a child challenges the perceived natural order of life events and the individual's basic assumptions about safety, justice, predictability, and stability in the world. Losing a child is recognized as one of the most traumatic events in the context of human relations.

Parents are impacted in all aspects of human functioning, including the physical, psychological, and social. Research has shown that losing a child is associated with a higher risk for intense and prolonged emotional distress including suicidal behaviors (Murphy et al. 2003, 5–25), complicated grief—which is what occurs when grief persists at an intense level for an extended period—anxiety, posttraumatic stress, and depression. Intense emotions such as shock, disbelief, anger, blame, sadness, weariness, hopelessness, guilt, sorrow, shame, anger, hostility, and despair are common both shorter and longer after the loss. Bereaved parents also report higher rates of psychiatric hospitalizations, worse physical health, and increased early mortality rates (dying before average life expectancy) (e.g., Rogers et al. 2008, 203–211; Song et al. 2019). Bereaved parents also present increased alcohol-related (Christiansen et al. 2020, e038826) and heart failure-related mortality (Wei et al. 2021, 181–189).

Additionally, in losing a child, parents also lose what their child embodies, such as a joint future and descendants, unfulfilled dreams, expectations, and ambitions, as well as their role as caregivers and nurturers of that child. Life will never be as previously envisioned, and parents have a new role as bereaved parents. Nevertheless, attention to the positive aspects of the aftermath of trauma has increased over the past years. For example, there is evidence of the possibility of personal growth, perception of increased empathy for others, the need to adjust values or reprioritize goals, and the experience of competence and strength (Engelkemeyer and Marwit 2008).

In addition, when a child dies, parents are confronted with the need to address both the changes in themselves as individuals as well as in their relationship with their partners. Questions such as "How much can our relationship withstand?" or "Is our relationship going to survive after the loss of our child?" are present in many bereaved parents' minds after the death of their child. This is not surprising, as the death of a child inevitably poses special and complex challenges to their relationship. After all, it is a relationship between two people who share a very substantial loss and face their bereavement simultaneously.

According to the 2020 CDC/NCHS National Vital Statistics System, the national divorce rate in the United States of America was 2.3 per 1000 population. However, the statistics do not specify reasons for divorce such as the loss of a child. Nevertheless, studies have shown an increased risk of divorce for bereaved couples (e.g., Lyngstad 2013, 79–86). Also, research has shown that the risk of intimate partner violence initiation rises after the death of children under age 5 (Weitzman and Smith-Greenaway 2020, 347–371).

Having to cope physically and emotionally with the overwhelming effects of the death of a child can contribute to depriving parents of individual resources, which may place a significant strain on the couple's relationship. Parents' different coping styles might also add to their distress and lead to marital difficulties. To make this context even more complex, not only has the parent lost a child but also the one person the parent would usually turn to is likewise consumed in his/her grief and may be too distressed to help and provide support. Accordingly, a bereaved couple is faced with the dual stress of being simultaneously the recipients and providers of support (to each other and the family) (Rosenblatt 2000).

Couples can respond to and cope with the death of their child in different ways. Even though a child's death always has an extensive impact on the couple's relationship, this event may strengthen or weaken the marital bond. Hence, some partners may become distant and emotionally alienated from one another, with marital conflicts/disagreements, diminished marital satisfaction over time, and an overall strained relationship. However, a child's death can also have a cohesive impact on the marital relationship, such as higher closeness between parents and strengthening of the relationship. Variables that may account for these differences in marital outcomes include situational factors, such as the cause and type of death and the child's age at the time of death; dyad-level factors, such as surviving children, the pre-death characteristics of the relationship, communication, and incongruent grieving; and individual-level factors, such as the family of origin's processing of trauma, social support, religious affiliation, and finding meaning (Albuquerque, Pereira, and Narciso 2015, 30–53).

The process of parental grief is complex, nonlinear, intense, highly individualized, and enduring. Also, parents share the loss of their children and are confronted with each other's grief. Therefore, grief after the loss of a child is not only an individual but also an interpersonal phenomenon and both individual and relational processes should be considered when working with bereaved parents.

Sara Albuquerque

See also: Child and Illness; Death of a Spouse

Further Reading

Albuquerque, Sara, Pereira, Marco, and Narciso, Isabel. 2015. "Couple's relationship after the death of a child: A systematic review." *Journal of Child and Family Studies* 25, no. 1: 30–53.

Christiansen, Solveig G., Reneflot, Anne, Stene-Larsen, Kim, and Hauge, Lars J. 2020. "Alcohol-related mortality following the loss of a child: A register-based follow-up study from Norway." *BMJ Open* 10, no. 6: e038826.

Engelkemeyer, S. M., and Marwit, S. J. 2008. "Posttraumatic growth in bereaved parents." *Journal of Traumatic Stress* 21, no. 3: 344–346.

Gilbert, Kathleen R. 1997. "Couple coping with the death of a child." In *The series in trauma and loss. Death and trauma: The traumatology of grieving*, edited by Charles R. Figley, Brian E. Bride, and Nicholas Mazza. Philadelphia: Taylor & Francis, pp. 101–121.

Lyngstad, T. H. 2013. "Bereavement and divorce: Does the death of a child affect parents' marital stability?" *Family Science* 4, no. 1: 79–86.

Murphy, Shirley, Tapper, Viva, Johnson, Clark, and Lohan, Janet. 2003. "Suicide ideation among parents bereaved by the violent deaths of their children." *Issues Mental Health Nursing* 24, no. 1: 5–25.

Rogers, Catherine H., Floyd, Frank J., Seltzer, Marsha Mailick, Greenberg, Jan, and Hong, Jinkuk. 2008. "Long-term effects of the death of a child on parents' adjustment in midlife." *Journal of Family Psychology* 22, no. 2: 203–211.

Rosenblatt, Paul C. 2000. *Parent grief: Narratives of loss and relationship*. Philadelphia: Taylor & Francis.

Song, Jieun, Mailick, Marsha R., Greenberg, Jan S., and Floyd, Frank J. "Mortality in parents after the death of a child." *Social Science & Medicine* 239 (2019): 112522. https://doi.org/10.1016/j.socscimed.2019.112522.

Stroebe, Margaret, Schut, Henk, and Finkenauer, Catrin. 2013. "Parents coping with the death of their child: From individual to interpersonal to interactive perspectives." *Family Science* 4, no. 1: 28–36.

Wei, Dang, Li, Jiong, Janszky, Imre, Chen, Hua, Fang, Fang, Ljung, Rickard, and László, Krisztina D. 2021. "Death of a child and the risk of heart failure: A population-based cohort study from Denmark and Sweden." *European Journal of Heart Failure* 24, no. 1: 181–189.

Weitzman, Abigail and Smith-Greenaway, Emily. 2020. "The marital implications of bereavement: Child death and intimate partner violence in West and Central Africa." *Demography* 57, no. 1: 347–371.

Death of a Spouse

Partnered relationships are highly sought after and valued in American society. Therefore, the death of a spouse has long been considered one of the most difficult stressors of adult life. One of the reasons the death of a spouse is such a stressor is that the spousal relationship tends to deepen over time. Spouses learn about each other and share their lives in ways that are unique to all other forms of adult relationships. Since not all couples are legally married, the terms death of a partner or significant other will also be used.

For many people, the death of their spouse means that the first person they would turn to for comfort and solace is gone at the time they need them the most. Grieving the death of a spouse or significant other also challenges a person's identity. Many people question who they are if their partner is no longer present. The death of a spouse or significant other is a relational trauma, meaning a severe emotional wound to the relationship between partners that can often feel overwhelming. Death breaks the bond and disrupts the relationship; the bonds that are formed through partnership with a significant other usually means that spouses prioritize each other's needs. When a spouse dies it can feel like the surviving partner has been physically, emotionally, and or spiritually wounded.

While a spouse or partner can die at any age, most deaths are experienced by people 65 years or older (Neimeyer et al. 2011, 82–90). In this age group, most deaths are due to chronic illness; the four leading causes are heart disease, cancer, cerebrovascular disease, and chronic obstructive pulmonary disease (Federal Interagency Forum on Aging-Related Statistics 2016). Due to women having a longer life trajectory than men, women experience the death of a partner more than their male counterparts. Women are also more likely to have been caregivers to their partners before death. Yet men are more likely to remarry than women and often choose younger partners.

The nature of the relationship, the cause of death, social support, and personality all have a significant impact on how a partner will grieve. A critical component of the grief process is the relationship between the spouses. All relationships have fluctuations over time, however, the current state of the relationship at the time of the loss is important. The partnership may have been satisfying, complicated, healthy, problematic, or even abusive. Bereaved spouses grieve regardless of the satisfaction within their relationship. Partnerships with high conflict are no less likely to grieve than those identified as low conflict.

When the death of a spouse occurs, there are important factors that influence the process of bereavement. The first is the timing of death in the life cycle. The expectation and assumption are that we are born, age normally, and then die in our later years. When a partner or spouse dies young, it can be even more difficult to make sense of, because it goes against the assumed natural order of aging.

The cause of a spouse's death can have a dramatic impact on a partner's ability to heal. A death that is anticipated, such as death due to a chronic illness, may mean that a spouse has had a chance to talk with their partner about dying and offer comfort, support, and love through caregiving. Although this process can be difficult and often wears on the partner, many spouses also feel thankful for the opportunity to spend time together. Sudden and traumatic deaths, such as car accidents or homicide, are difficult due to the shock of the circumstances and the inability of spouses to prepare. One of the major differences between anticipated versus sudden and traumatic deaths is the opportunity for spouses to say goodbye.

Deaths that can have negative associations or shame attached to them such as self-harm, suicide, drug overdose, etc. often add additional stressors to the bereavement process. These losses may be stigmatized, meaning there is a societal mark of disgrace attached to the loss (Doka 2002). The bereaved partner may struggle with blame, shame, and guilt. Often, these types of losses make others uncomfortable and there can be less social support given. Resources and social support from family, friends, and loved ones play a significant role in the grieving process.

Additional considerations are timing and concurrent stressors, the health of the spousal relationship, and the resources available. Timing and concurrent stressors refer to the timing of the loss regarding the family life cycle. For example, the death of a spouse has different implications for a young widower in his 30s who may also have young children versus an elderly widow in her 70s with adult children. In addition to grieving, this young widower might also have the additional stressors of work, actively raising children, and responsibilities of caring for aging parents, whereas an elderly widow is at a point in the family life cycle where she is no longer working, may be on a fixed income, may or may not have the support of adult children, may have her own health challenges or limitations, and/or may have a smaller network of social support.

Finances are also a real source of concern related to the death of a significant other. For many couples, one person is in charge of the household finances and the death of a partner forever changes the financial landscape for the surviving partner. In addition, social class often impacts the types of rituals the bereaved can participate in. For example, there are often new expenses that are unanticipated such as costs from funeral services and hospital or hospice bills, in addition to the loss of an income or household contribution.

There are many assumptions about how men and women are supposed to grieve based on gender stereotypes. However, it is more helpful to think about different styles of grief that either women or men may display. The grieving process is more of a spectrum between an intuitive style, referring to emotional responses and sharing with others, and an instrumental or a cognitive style, with an emphasis on daily routine, behaviors, and activity (Doka and Martin 2011, 125–142).

The death of a spouse usually proceeds with other subsequent losses that the bereaved individual is often unprepared for and did not anticipate. There are losses associated with assumptions of the world that are shattered. For example,

many people assume they will die before their partner, so they do not think about or plan for dealing with grief. Another area of concern for the bereaved is their ability to grieve while coping with their life responsibilities.

After the death of a partner, the bereaved need support. However, many individuals do not require the professional help of a therapist. What bereaved spouses have stated is helpful is having social support. This support can take shape in many ways and may include family, friends, and loved ones recognizing that the bereaved need time and attention. They may not reach out for support even when they need it the most. It is helpful for loved ones to keep in mind that the bereaved are often the loneliest in the weeks and months immediately after services and ritual arrangements. This is usually the time when life goes back to normal for everyone else but the bereaved are struggling to adjust to the new normal. It is helpful when loved ones remember that holidays, anniversaries, and special occasions are often difficult.

When a bereaved partner is struggling, support groups and therapy can be very helpful. One of the powerful aspects of a support group is the ability to normalize grief responses; meaning, group members can share experiences and recognize that others are having similar thoughts and feelings. The group also provides an opportunity to learn new strategies for coping and healing.

When therapy is needed, it is often because the bereaved or a loved one has concerns about how the grief process is being adjusted to. However, therapy can help the bereaved manage expectations, de-bunk myths associated with grief, have a safe place to express difficult thoughts and feelings, and then develop a new life without the deceased.

A brief summary of the tasks for therapy includes four general goals. The first is to help the bereaved to understand the death, and the grief process, and make meaning of the loss. Second, therapists facilitate the grieving partner's ability to access and express thoughts and emotions in healthy and helpful ways. Next, therapy provides an opportunity to help the bereaved to develop ways to honor and remember their spouse. This is different and separate from the immediate rituals that happen soon after the death. Significant others often state that they were in a fog or feeling numb in the immediate days following the loss. This allows the bereaved to participate in something that may feel more personal and less prescribed. A ritual that reflects their current feelings once the initial shock has dissipated and healing has begun. Last, the goal is to support the bereaved in reinvesting in life and developing a new normal for the future.

Cadmona A. Hall

See also: Death of a Child

Further Reading

Doka, Kenneth J. 2002. "How we die: Stigmatized death and disenfranchised grief." In *Disenfranchised grief: New directions, challenges, and strategies for practice.* New York: Research Press.

Doka, Kenneth J. and Martin, Terry L. 2011. *Grieving beyond gender: Understanding the ways men and women mourn.* New York: Routledge.

Federal Interagency Forum on Aging-Related Statistics. 2016. *Older Americans update 2016: Key indicators of well-being.* Washington, DC: U.S.

Neimeyer, Robert, Haris, Darcy L, Winokuer, Howard R., and Thornton, Gordon F. 2011. *Grief and bereavement in contemporary society: Bridging research and practice.* New York: Routledge.

Deinstitutionalization of Marriage

First outlined by sociologist Andrew J. Cherlin in an influential research article from 2004, the "deinstitutionalization of marriage" refers to the idea that marriage has changed so significantly in recent decades that it may no longer be, or will soon no longer be, a social institution. In sociology, social institutions are macro-level systems that contain very stable statuses, roles, and norms. In his article, Cherlin argues that the norms of marriage have weakened so much that the social institution of marriage is now in decline. Specifically, Cherlin argues that marriage is declining in two ways. First, he argues that the norms *around* marriage have weakened, making marriage more optional than ever before. According to Cherlin, alternatives to traditional marriage have both become more common and acceptable over time. For example, whereas cohabitation outside of marriage was once stigmatized as "shacking up" or "living in sin," approximately two-thirds of all women have now been in a cohabiting relationship (Hemez and Manning 2017), and most of these relationships never become marriages (Guzzo 2014). Likewise, although marriage was once considered the only legitimate context within which a couple could have and raise children, non-marital births have become relatively common, especially for those with lower levels of education and income. For Cherlin, these trends, among others, suggest that marriage is now one option among many and that couples no longer feel the same pressure they once did to formalize their relationships through marriage.

Beyond this, Cherlin also argues that norms *within* marriage have weakened, making the marital relationship more open to interpretation than at any point in history. In particular, Cherlin argues that the norms that once organized marriages have fallen away, or are in the process of doing so, leaving married couples to decide for themselves how their relationships will be organized. On this point, Cherlin highlights the emergence of what he terms an "individualized" model of marriage in which couples get married because of the social and emotional benefits that it provides for them as individuals. Before industrialization, during the era of "institutional" marriages, people married not for love but rather to meet their basic survival needs, and they had limited control over who their spouses would be. By the end of World War II, this was replaced by the "companionate" model of marriage in which couples expected to love and cherish one another as "soulmates" (Burgess and Locke 1945). However, companionate marriages were built on a gendered division of labor, with husbands primarily assuming the role of breadwinning and wives primarily assuming the role of homemaking. With the cultural upheavals of the 1960s and 1970s, the companionate model of marriage was challenged, and people increasingly began to expect greater freedom or autonomy within their relationships. For example, as women entered the paid labor force in historically unprecedented numbers,

it became important for many to have more flexible roles within the marriage so that they could balance paid work with domestic responsibilities.

Under the "individualized" model of marriage, individuals and couples now expect their marital relationships to: (a) facilitate or at least allow for the personal and professional development of each spouse; (b) be flexible such that roles (i.e., who handles what) can be negotiated on an ongoing basis; and (c) involve a high degree of open and honest communication, in part to promote intimacy but also to facilitate the negotiation of marital roles (Cancian 1987). Although such individualization allows couples to break from longstanding and often repressive norms (e.g., the breadwinner-homemaker model of companionate marriage), it also forces couples to decide for themselves what their marriages will look like, and they must make such decisions, day in and day out, without the same degree of guidance from the larger institution of marriage.

Although he argues that marriage is deinstitutionalizing in both of these ways—first, that alternatives to marriage have become more common and acceptable, and second, that marital relationships are increasingly individualized—Cherlin also argues that marriage continues to be symbolically important. In other words, people continue to marry, although at a lower rate than in the past, because marriage is still constructed by the larger culture as the highest, most committed relationship form.

Still, the "deinstitutionalization of marriage" has been critiqued by scholars in several ways. Perhaps most notably, many claim that Cherlin provides insufficient and/or irrelevant evidence to support his argument. After all, institutions include explicit norms (e.g., laws, social expectations) but also taken-for-granted assumptions about how things are or should be. Even if there are fewer norms now explicitly regulating how couples organize their marriages, people still carry taken-for-granted ideas about what a marriage should look like (Lauer and Yodanis 2010). For example, laws and social expectations may no longer require that married couples share a home and pool their financial resources, but research suggests that nearly all married couples continue to do both in large part because they simply assume that sharing a home and a bank account are a part of what it means to be married (Yodanis and Lauer 2014).

Partly in response to these and other critiques, in 2020, Cherlin wrote a research article re-assessing the extent to which, in his view, marriage has become deinstitutionalized. In it, he argues that the deinstitutionalization of marriage thesis is only partially supported by evidence that has developed since 2004. Specifically, he suggests that marriage has become less common and therefore more optional, especially among individuals without a college degree, who are now considerably less likely to marry than those with a college degree. For example, one research study estimates that while 84% of those who earn a college degree will eventually marry, the same will be true for 72% of those who do not earn a degree (Martin, Astone, and Peters 2014). However, Cherlin concedes that evidence does not generally support his argument that marriage has become more open to interpretation given the ongoing prevalence of many marital norms, especially around the division of

labor. Thus, Cherlin himself concludes that marriage is indeed deinstitutionalizing in the first way he outlined, primarily for those with lower levels of education, but that marriage is not deinstitutionalizing in the second way, as many norms continue to shape how married couples organize their relationships.

Patrice Delevante

See also: Marriage, Financial Implications; Marriage and Divorce, White Americans

Further Reading
Burgess, Ernest W. and Harvey J. Locke. 1945. *The family: From institution to companionship.* New York: American Books.

Cancian, Francesca M. 1987. *Love in America: Gender and self-development.* Cambridge, UK: Cambridge University Press.

Cherlin, Andrew J. 2004. "The deinstitutionalization of American marriage." *Journal of Marriage and Family* 66, no. 4: 848–861.

Cherlin, Andrew J. 2020. "Degrees of change: An assessment of the deinstitutionalization of marriage thesis." *Journal of Marriage and Family* 82, no. 1: 62–80.

Guzzo, Karen Benjamin. 2014. "Trends in cohabitation outcomes: Compositional changes and engagement among never-married young adults." *Journal of Marriage and Family* 76, no. 4: 826–842.

Hemez, Paul and Wendy D. Manning. 2017. "Over twenty-five years of change in cohabitation experience in the U.S., 1987–2013." Bowling Green, OH: National Center for Family and Marriage Research.

Lauer, Sean and Carrie Yodanis. 2010. "The deinstitutionalization of marriage revisited: A new institutional approach to marriage." *Journal of Family Theory and Review* 2, no. 1: 58–72.

Martin, Steven P., Nan Marie Astone, and H. Elizabeth Peters. 2014. "Fewer marriages, more divergence: Marriage projections for millennials to age 40." Washington, D.C.: Urban Institute.

Yodanis, Carrie and Sean Lauer. 2014. "Is marriage individualized? What couples actually do." *Journal of Family Theory and Review* 6, no. 2: 184–197.

Delaying Marriage

Delaying marriage is one of the significant demographic changes in American marriage. In the last several decades, the average age at first marriage has risen by approximately seven years; from 1960–2018, the median age at first marriage increased from 22.8–29.8 for men and from 20.3–27.8 for women (U.S. Census Bureau 2018). Interestingly, the average age at which women give birth, however, has not risen as high as that of first marriage; the median age at first birth proceeds about one year before that of first marriage for women. This phenomenon, having a child before marriage, is called *the great crossover* (Hymowitz et al. 2013, 17–19).

With the weakening of the social norms related to marriage, alternatives to marriage, such as cohabitation, have become more acceptable (Cherlin 2004, 852). However, marriage provides benefits, and most people expect to marry sometime. For example, tying the knot has symbolic importance to individuals as a marker of prestige: becoming an adult. Marriage also helps form a solid union through a public commitment in front of significant others, such as parents, siblings, and extended family members, which enables each partner to invest his or her resources in the partnership with relatively less fear of breakup (Cherlin 2004, 854). Although an increasing number of people remain single their entire lives, nearly 90% of women are expected to marry at some point in life. Given these benefits of marriage and willingness to marry, people seem to delay marriage rather than remain unmarried (Goldstein and Kenney 2001, 511–512).

There are two main reasons why people postpone marriage: lack of economic resources and cultural shift in marriage value. First, young American adults need more time to become financially ready for marriage than those in the past. Compared to the mid-20th century, individuals tend to experience more struggles in finding decent jobs to help them be financially independent and to support their families. In response to this difficulty, a growing number of people pursue a higher degree, expecting that educational attainment may bring greater earnings. In fact, by 2011, a college graduate received an 84% higher salary on average than a high school graduate. As such, more and more young adults delay their marriage with more training and higher educational attainment (Hymowitz et al. 2013, 26–29). Second, as marriage has changed in the way of emphasizing personal choice and expanding self-development, more people, especially women, want to develop a career that brings personal meaning to them (e.g., gaining autonomy), thus postponing marriage. Therefore, marriage is considered a capstone rather than a cornerstone of adult life. In other words, marriage was once seen as the first step into adulthood, while it is now regarded as the last step (Cherlin 2004, 852).

In terms of the societal consequences of delaying marriage, there are benefits as well as costs. Delaying marriage brings benefits, such as elevating the socioeconomic status of individuals and lowering the divorce rate. First, by postponing marriage, young adults can have the opportunity to finish their education training and to develop their careers, which is related to having a higher income compared to those who marry earlier. For example, female college graduates can have an annual income premium of about $18,000 when delaying marriage to the age of 30 or later than getting married before 20 (Hymowitz et al. 2013, 15). Besides, a woman marrying at age 27 and having her first child at age 30 is expected to get nearly 75% higher hourly wages by age 36 than a woman marrying at age 21 and having her first child at age 25 when assuming they begin the same wage path (Loughran and Zissimopoulos 2004, 16–18). As such, young adults who finish college and delay marriage are more likely to have a better start in life compared to those who do not. Next, later marriage is considered to have helped to lower divorce rates in America because people who marry later are less likely to divorce than those who marry earlier; individuals who tie the knot later are more likely to be mature, careful to make a life decision, and financially stable than those who marry in their twenties or earlier. For instance, the National Survey of Family Growth 2006–2010 shows the estimates of divorce risk within five years of the first marriage were 32% for those who are under 20 years old and 14% for those who are between 30 and 34 years old (Wolfinger 2015).

Meanwhile, delaying marriage also may result in some costs, such as increasing non-marital births and various negative outcomes (Hymowitz et al. 2013, 20–22). First, an increasing number of

women give birth before they marry; nearly 50% of first births are to unmarried parents. For women, the median age at first birth is lower than that of the first marriage (i.e., the *great crossover*). It is reported that this *great crossover* has been more common among women who have a high-school degree or less, while college-educated women tend to experience childbearing about two years after being married; those who become parents out of wedlock among individuals with less educated and lower socioeconomic status are likely to depend on government assistance. As far as other negative consequences, unmarried adults in their 20s are more likely to feel depressed, have lower life satisfaction, and overdrink compared to those who are married (Glenn, Uecker, and Love Jr. 2010, 9). Also, children born to unmarried parents are more likely to experience emotional problems, lower academic achievement, and family instability than those born to married parents.

Given that childbirth results in suppressing the wage growth of women (Loughran and Zissimopoulos 2004, 16–18), less-educated and lower-income women with their children are more likely to pay the cost of postponing marriage compared to college-educated and higher-income married women in America. For this reason, it would be beneficial to synchronize marriage and childbirth to promote child well-being (Haskins and Sawhill 2009, 14–15). The *success sequence* of life events is as follows: completing education, getting a job, being married, and having children.

Delaying marriage has been observed in America with increasing age at first marriage. Lack of economic resources and cultural shifts in marriage value are addressed as the major reasons for delaying marriage, and a recent phenomenon called *the great crossover* has emerged along with an increasing number of individuals who postpone marriage. Delaying marriage seems to continue to characterize American families. Given the costs of delaying marriage, such as the increase in non-marital childbirth, following a sequence of life (e.g., getting married and then having children) may be beneficial for young adults.

Kwangman Ko and *Youngjin Kang*

See also: Marriage and Divorce, White Americans; Marriage and Education Level

Further Reading

Cherlin, Andrew J. 2004. "The deinstitutionalization of American marriage." *Journal of Marriage and Family* 66, no. 4: 848–861.

Glenn, Norval D., Jeremy E. Uecker, and Robert W. B. Love, Jr. 2010. "Later first marriage and marital success." *Social Science Research*, 39, no. 5: 787–800.

Goldstein, Joshua R., and Catherine T. Kenney. 2001. "Marriage delayed or marriage forgone? New cohort forecasts of first marriage for U.S. women." *American Sociological Review* 66, no. 4: 506–519.

Haskins, Ron, and Isabel V. Sawhill. 2009. *Creating an Opportunity Society.* Washington, D.C.: Brookings Institution Press.

Hymowitz, Kay S., Jason S. Carroll, W. Bradford Wilcox, and Kelleen Kaye. 2013. "Knot yet: The benefits and costs of delayed marriage in America." The National Marriage Project at the University of Virginia, The National Campaign to Prevent Teen and Unplanned Pregnancy, and The Relate Institute.

Loughran, David S., and Julie M. Zissimopoulos. 2004. "Are there gains to delaying marriage? The effect of age at first marriage on career development and wages." RAND Labor and Population.

U.S. Census Bureau. 2018. "Historical marital status tables: Estimated median age at first marriage, by sex: 1890 to the present." Accessed July 30, 2019. https://www.census.gov/data/tables/time-series/demo/families/marital.html

Wolfinger, Nicholas H. 2015. "Want to avoid divorce? Wait to get married, but not too long." Accessed August 4, 2019. https://ifstudies.org/blog/want-to-avoid-divorce-wait-to-get-married-but-not-too-long/

Destination Wedding

The traditions surrounding weddings have evolved over the centuries. From the placement of the bride and groom, the role of those participating in the ceremony, the color of the dress, and the departure to the honeymoon following the ceremony, weddings have been steeped in symbolism. While many of the traditions that we see in modern wedding ceremonies are carryovers from decades past, we are seeing an evolution in how couples are approaching formalizing their unions.

There has been plenty of news coverage highlighting how millennials are leading to the downfall of marriage, but the realities are more complex than that. Weddings are expensive, with the average cost of a wedding being $30,000–$45,000 and increasing every year (Park 2019). Add to that cost the potential for the burden of student debt or trying to purchase a house, and younger generations are not able to financially do as much as those before them. This has serious implications for how they opt to spend their money, especially when it comes to a wedding. While the DIY (do it yourself) wedding craze helped to cut down costs, destination weddings have become a great way to maximize your bang for your buck.

What Are Destination Weddings?

Just as the name suggests, destination weddings are those that take place in a specific location, which is often not near where the soon-to-be-married couple resides. Often, these locations have a particular meaning to the couple or serve as a means to travel to a place they want to honeymoon. Destination weddings are also distinguished from other out-of-the-area weddings by the noticeably smaller guest list. Due to the amount of travel and cost involved, these weddings are typically reserved for the couple's nearest and dearest friends and family members to attend.

By definition, some weddings become destination weddings due to the amount of travel involved, even if that was not the intention. This is a by-product of moving away from home and going to college. Friendships are formed at college that can last a lifetime and after graduation, most people move and start their lives in a new place. This means that attending a college friend's wedding could require traveling a good distance. This makes it a destination wedding for the guests, but not necessarily the couple. In 2017, 23% of weddings happened more than 200 miles from where the couple currently lived (Guzman and Perry n.d.).

The Guest List

The increased travel costs associated with a destination wedding often limit who can attend. Often, the guest list is intentionally kept small, such as immediate family only or a few friends to serve as witnesses. The smaller guest list evokes a more intimate feeling to the ceremony but also highlights whom the couple considers to be most important in their lives. While the guest list may be more intimate, some who may have been invited to a traditional wedding and reception may be excluded and those who do make the guest list may not be able to afford to go.

For destination weddings that do not require international travel, the guest list might be larger. Even though these weddings may still require some guests to travel a bit further, the locations and expenses for the wedding itself might not be as cost prohibitive for having a larger guest list. The weddings cost slightly more than international weddings at $38,000 (Guzman and Perry n.d.).

All in One–Cost

While traveling for a destination wedding may add a bit to the cost, being in a location that you might not otherwise be able to visit can make up for that. Especially since couples are maximizing their budget by combining the wedding and honeymoon. Since the average U.S. wedding costs $30,000–$45,000, spending $27,000–$28,000 on a destination wedding provides the opportunity to have it all with a smaller financial burden (Guzman and Perry n.d.). This means that the couple will have time with their friends and families, while still being able to extend their time at the destination for their honeymoon, which they might not have been able to do otherwise. Many couples focus on making memories for themselves and not orchestrating an expensive wedding. Expensive weddings can be so costly that couples sometimes cannot afford a honeymoon until they settle the debts accrued from the wedding.

Popular Locations

Beach and island destinations tend to be the most frequent locations for destination weddings, including Mexico, Jamaica, The Dominican Republic, The Bahamas, and Hawaii. There are often services and vendors already prepared to handle these events as they have become a staple of the local economy (The Knot n.d.). The appeal of a venue that is prepared for everything has its perks; however, that does not necessarily mean that this is the most desired form of tourism for a given destination. The overall impact of destination weddings on the location would need to be assessed on a case-by-case basis.

Since island destinations might not be everyone's choice, other local sites of interest also draw couples in. The allure of getting married at a castle, a historic site, or a place that holds history to the couple or their families are also popular places to hold a destination wedding. Like the more popular island destinations, some of these locations are set up to accommodate destination weddings and others may not. However, as the cornerstone of destination weddings tends to be their smaller scale in terms of venue and number of guests, it is possible to make any location a destination wedding. It is only a matter of finding vendors for the ceremony and reception.

Acceptance of Relationships

In addition to the rising cost of a traditional wedding or the appeal of a particular destination, part of the draw of a particular destination can also be the marriage laws. Countries or jurisdictions that have laws that are more inclusive to same-sex or polyamorous relationships might have appeal for those seeking those kinds of weddings and unions as often they are not legal in the couples' home country yet the symbolism and ability to have such a ceremony that validates their relationships is important to them. Before the legalization of same-sex marriage in the United States, many same-sex couples would go to Canada to be married. With the increasing number of countries that are legalizing same-sex marriage, this has also expanded the potential locations that couples may seek out for their destination wedding. To date, 29 countries recognize and perform both same and opposite-sex marriages (Pew Forum 2019).

Marriages that are performed abroad are legally recognized by state and federal governments as long as the couple would have been able to legally marry in the United States. If the marriage would not meet the legal requirements set forth by a state, then the marriage would only be legally binding in the country in which it was performed.

In addition to costing less than a traditional wedding, destination weddings provide the opportunity for couples to get married in some of the most scenic places around the world. These weddings provide the intimacy of a small wedding combined with a honeymoon experience that couples might not otherwise get to have.

Melanie L. Duncan

See also: Wedding Party; Wedding Venues

Further Reading

Guzman, Angela and Christin Perry. n.d. "This Is the Average Destination Wedding Cost." Accessed on September 2, 2019. https://www.theknot.com/content/average-destination-wedding-cost.

The Knot. n.d. "The Top 50 Destination Wedding Spots." Accessed on September 2, 2019. https://www.theknot.com/content/best-destination-wedding-locations.

Park, Andrea. 2019. "Here's How Much the Average Wedding in 2018 Cost—and Who Paid." Last modified January 13, 2019, https://www.brides.com/story/unction-wedding-study-how-much-average-wedding-2018-cost.

Pew Forum. 2019. "Same-Sex Marriage Around the World," last Modified May 17, 2019. https://www.pewforum.org/fact-sheet/gay-marriage-around-the-world/.

Disillusionment

What Are Romantic and Marital Disillusionment?

Romantic/marital disillusionment refers to one or both partners' perception of negative changes in a relationship over time, such as declining love and affection. The stronger the contrast between a person's initially favorable thoughts and happy feelings for one's partner and the less favorable thoughts and emotions, later on, the greater the disillusionment. Disillusionment most readily occurs when couples transition from dating to living together full-time (marriage or non-marital cohabitation). Once this happens, the daily grind of housework, disagreements, and other hassles may drive home to individuals the dramatic differences between the idealized partner they *thought* they were getting and the flawed human they are *actually with*.

How Is Romantic Disillusionment Different from Dissatisfaction, Disappointment, and Regret?

Social scientists use several terms to describe when a relationship is not going well, such as dissatisfaction, disappointment, and regret. Many scientists see romantic/marital disillusionment as distinct from these other terms, although there are some similarities. Dissatisfaction refers to a moderately negative or unpleasant assessment of one's partner or relationship at one moment in time. Events happen all the time to spur dissatisfaction in couples, such as one partner forgetting to do something or messing things up in the house. Unlike disillusionment, however, dissatisfaction does not reflect a feeling that the relationship has changed for the worse or that one's partner no longer meets one's expectations. Dissatisfaction also does not carry the sense of hopelessness and recrimination that disillusionment does. Furthermore, rather than distancing oneself from one's partner emotionally, as may occur with disillusionment, dissatisfied partners are often motivated to improve their relationship (see Niehuis, Reifman, Al-Khalil et al. 2019).

We experience disappointment when our decisions yield worse outcomes than we anticipated or desired. Disillusionment is worse than disappointment, however, because disillusionment includes the additional element of regret ("I wish I had acted differently"), as well as a sense of the relationship being irreparable. Indeed, some argue that disillusionment emerges only when a person's core beliefs and sense of meaning have been violated.

For example, a partner's infidelity may well shatter one's core beliefs about the nature of romantic/marital relationships.

History, Theory, and Research

According to 1930s sociologist Willard Waller, romantic partners typically idealize one another, thinking the other is the most wonderful person they have ever met. This experience feels great at the time, so partners try to maintain it by showing their best side and hiding their flaws. As a result, neither partner sees the other for who they really are. Idealization is a normal and, Waller argues, necessary part of dating and courtship. We might never marry our partner if we saw him or her entirely realistically, "warts and all." However, idealization may also be dangerous, leading us to marry someone who truly bears little resemblance to the seemingly perfect person we started dating. Once we and our partners are no longer willing or able to effectively hide our flaws, disillusionment can set in. Research studies in this area typically use questionnaires such as the Relationship Disillusionment Scale (RDS) by Sylvia Niehuis and her colleagues. The RDS contains 11 items such as "I'm beginning to see my relationship in a somewhat more negative light" and "I feel no longer quite as positively about my partner as I once did," to which individuals indicate their degree of agreement or disagreement.

What Predicts Disillusionment?

Relatively few researchers have addressed what leads to romantic disillusionment in the first place, but those who have suggest three domains may be important. First, certain *behavioral traits* of partners may signal disillusionment. Couples who exhibit signs of disillusionment (e.g., pronounced declines in marital satisfaction) are relatively emotionally unstable, angry, verbally or physically violent, prone to let out negative emotions, low in self-esteem, and reticent to express positive emotions (Lavner and Bradbury 2010). Second, certain *actions* likely produce disillusionment. According to one study, the more one's partner engaged in transgressions (e.g., failed to keep a promise, lied to the partner, cheated on the partner) during one month, the more disillusioned the person became with the partner in the next month (Niehuis, Reifman, and Oldham 2019). This finding suggests that transgressions—especially if multiple ones pile up—can produce long-lasting damage. Finally, characteristics of couples' *courtships* may lead to later disillusionment. In fact, two different courtship pathways may do so: quickly accelerating/highly passionate relationships (i.e., falling in love, engaging in sexual intercourse, and becoming committed to marriage very rapidly), and slowly progressing/dispassionate relationships Couples with moderately paced relationships—not too fast or too slow—were the least likely to exhibit signs of disillusionment. Couples in quickly accelerated/passionate relationships likely become disillusioned because they engage in much impression management, focus on their sexual relationship, and consequently fail to discover incompatibilities and test their conflict-resolution skills. Couples in slowly progressing/dispassionate relationships, on the other hand, likely become disillusioned because they see problems in the relationship, but discount them, perhaps hoping things will get better once married (see Niehuis et al. 2016).

Consequences of Disillusionment

Several researchers have examined the potential consequences of disillusionment in relationships. Specifically, in a national (U.S.) survey of cohabiting and married couples, Sylvia Niehuis and her colleagues showed that partners who scored highly on the RDS also reported higher estimates of how likely they were to break up with their partner. This link between disillusionment and break-up likelihood remained in effect, even when the authors accounted for relationship satisfaction, commitment, and duration. In addition, three longitudinal studies of married couples (in which partners continue to fill out surveys over periods of many years) showed that signs of disillusionment (e.g., loss of love and affection, decrease in one's perception that the partner was responsive, and increases in feelings of ambivalence) were associated with subsequent divorce (see Huston et al. 2001).

Outstanding Issues

Though we now have theories of disillusionment (and the features distinguishing it from related concepts), an established scale to measure it, and findings indicating some of the apparent causes and consequences of disillusionment, other issues remain to be addressed. For instance, it is unclear how best to help couples when one or both partners begin to feel disillusioned but want to rebuild their relationship. Future research will need to explore how best to apply current knowledge of disillusionment in clinical settings.

Sylvia Niehuis

See also: Infidelity; Marital Expectations; Marital Success

Further Reading

Birditt, Kira S., Susannah Hope, Edna Brown, and Terri Orbuch. 2012. "Developmental trajectories of marital happiness over 16 years." *Research in Human Development* 9: 126–144.

Huston, Ted L., John P. Caughlin, Shanna E. Smith, and Laurie J. George. 2001. "The connubial crucible: Newlywed years as predictors of marital delight, distress, and divorce." *Journal of Personality and Social Psychology* 80: 237–252.

Lavner, Justin A., and Thomas N. Bradbury. 2010. "Patterns of change in marital happiness over the newlywed years." *Journal of Marriage and Family* 75: 1171–1187.

Niehuis, Sylvia. 2007. "Convergent and discriminant validity of the Marital Disillusionment Scale." *Psychological Reports* 100: 203–207.

Niehuis, Sylvia, and Denise Bartell. 2006. "The Marital Disillusionment Scale: Development and psychometric properties." *North American Journal of Psychology* 8: 69–84.

Niehuis, Sylvia, Alan Reifman, Kareem Al-Khalil, Cary Rebecca Oldham, Dan Fang, Michael O'Boyle, and Tyler Davis. 2019. "Functional magnetic resonance imaging activation in response to prompts of romantically disillusioning events." *Personal Relationships* 26: 209–231.

Niehuis, Sylvia, Alan Reifman, Du Feng, and Ted L. Huston. 2016. "Courtship progression rate and declines in expressed affection early in marriage: A test of the disillusionment model." *Journal of Family Issues* 37: 1074–1100.

Niehuis, Sylvia, Alan Reifman, and Kyung-Hee Lee. 2015. "Disillusionment in cohabiting and married couples: A national study." *Journal of Family Issues* 36: 951–973.

Niehuis, Sylvia, Alan Reifman, and Cary Rebecca Oldham. 2019. "Effects of relationship transgressions on idealization of and disillusionment with one's romantic partner: A three-wave longitudinal study." *Personal Relationships* 26: 466–489.

Waller, Willard. 1938. *The family: A dynamic interpretation.* New York: Henry Holt.

Diversity in Marriage

Diversity in the context of marriage implies that different elements are represented; there is variety in the mix. Diversity in marriage can pertain to the variances *within* marriages. Diversity also bears relevance to the differences *between* marriages such as cultural, religious, and legal expressions.

Marriages cannot be discussed in isolation, as these unions also address attitudes, cultural constructs, social policies, legislation, and more. Marriage draws in and reflects reigning attitudes about gender, education, family roles, responsibilities, economics, socio-economic class, social pressures and expectations, personal versus family choices, and the like. The combinations of elements represented are virtually endless, and it depends on the marriage partners, embedded within the subculture of their families and societal contexts, how they would like to see the diversity of elements represented in their union. Each of the subsystems that envelop the couple will likely be influential in their choices, as well as the outcomes of those choices, as marital expectations, traditions, cultural norms, and other domains of influence exert direct and indirect influences.

Diversity plays a role in a particular marital relationship, as the marital partners will express their preferences overtly and covertly. Typically, diversity is associated with ethnicity, race, cultural background, gender, and sexual orientation. But the concept can reach wider to include education, socio-economic class, age, physical and mental abilities, economic potential, experience, and more. Traditionally, elaborate rules as well as legislation guided and attempted to enforce who could marry whom, e.g., the minimum age at the time of marriage. These rules in themselves can represent a form of diversity or a way of enforcing conformity in providing a suggested organization concerning the structure of communities. Most societies have explicit as well as implicit rules contributing to choices in marital partners. There can be complexity in these rules and guidelines to ensure kinship bonds and cultural, wealth, and power preservation, to mention a few.

Ideologies are typically among the leading factors in determining emotional compatibility. These ideologies can represent religious, political, or other worldviews. Relationships are solidified when the partners find an emotional and intellectual resonance in terms of values, attitudes, and beliefs. In marriages, partners decide and express what core values, characteristics, and values are sufficiently important to them, that they demand an agreement between partners concerning these dimensions. What is non-negotiable for one couple may be negotiable for another. This is an important consideration when it comes to diversity in partnerships, namely the recognition that no two couples follow the same rules. Couples are diverse in the expression of their needs and desires.

What is acceptable, even attractive to whom, provides endless variations as marriage partners strive for compatibility. Diversity within a marriage presumes that for the persons involved in that particular partnership, diversity facilitates harmonious outcomes. Where some couples seek out cultural differences, other couples value a similar cultural background. The dimensions with which they feel comfortable can vary and be very personal and individual. As an example, for a couple to whom religion is a cornerstone value, differences in religion will probably be a deal breaker. On the other hand, if religion does not rank high on the list of qualities a partner seeks in the other, an entirely different attitude towards religion and spirituality, in general, may be acceptable.

If marriage is seen as a partnership in which resources are pooled and shared, it makes sense to add diversity in some form or other to the mix. This is where the folk wisdom that "opposites attract" rings true. It adds to variety and complementarity. The extroverted talker in the relationship may find a good listener in the more introverted partner. Two extroverts might outdo one another in a competitive style. On the other hand, folk wisdom also tells us that "birds of a feather flock together." This takes us back to negotiable versus non-negotiable variables. If something is a core value, then it follows that the same level of involvement in a partner is important. The subtle pressures exerted by a specific subgroup within which one or both of the partners are embedded can further amplify these needs and expectations.

Marriage itself is diverse. Diversity can be expressed in the many forms and functions of marriage. Nanda (2019) explores a variety of contexts where marriage is an expression of unique cultural norms and traditions. What is acceptable in one context may seem unconventional in another. There may be differences in whether marriages are arranged or not, whether they represent a patriarchal form of bargaining to ensure wealth transmission and preservation, or a matriarchal way of preserving the lineage and providing stability of care. They may be driven by ideologies that seek homogeneity between partners and their ideological and cultural contexts. Sexuality may play a greater or lesser role, the pressure to have offspring could be a key concern, and the wealth and lineage of the partners could be relevant. In short, marriage becomes an expression of both the differences as well as the similarities between people (Nanda 2019).

The diversity between marriages colors the expressions of how pairing occurs in particular contexts. If marriage represents the legal union between two people, the realities preceding that formalized event are complex. Numerous precursors set the scene to contribute to who eventually marries whom. In almost all cultural contexts worldwide, ceremonies and rituals mark the pairing of persons, and these partnerships can be sanctioned by formal marriage ceremonies, which will also reflect the cultural, social, religious, and legal contexts within which these betrothals occur. In a culture-universal (*etic*) approach to marriage, we observe partnering being virtually universal, even if the cultural specifics mean that these unions are characterized by varied expressions. On the other hand, a culturally specific (*emic*) approach allows us an insider's view as it may occur within a specific cultural context.

Cultures can find themselves on a continuum ranging from extremely traditional, as in orthodox, through to liberal and unconventional; from being guarded and restrictive, to being open and permissive. In many traditional societies, partnering celebrations are often linked to family formation, especially if these are first-time marriages. Different cultures vary in their attitudes toward the expression of sexuality: chastity versus premarital sex, sexual orientation, expectations, and obligations surrounding partnerships, the choice of a partner, and the rituals surrounding the actual marriage ceremony may all be interpreted along the continuum of conformity/nonconformity. The polar opposites on the continuum influence and color everything surrounding the process of contemplating marriage to being contractually married. Cultural practices and tolerance of diversity color almost all facets of marriage, even if that marriage is based on mutual attraction and an expression of love.

These cultural enclaves can vary concerning the openness displayed and the availability of choice in sexual and marital matters. This greater societal context will contribute to whether the couple is accepted or criticized for the diversity displayed. Generally, couples need societal and family support, and this also applies to the diversity within their union. Diversity can provide an emotional barrier in that the societal and family support of that couple may not be as outspoken. Families may even display overt critical reactions that do not allow the in-law to be assimilated and welcomed into the larger family. Additionally, there is a generational difference in that younger persons may be more accepting of diversity than their grandparents' generation. Intercultural communication styles can contain many nuances of difference that lend themselves to miscommunication and misinterpretation, not only by the partners within the union but also by their extended family.

Traditionally, establishing a household through marriage provided a socially sanctioned manner to express sexuality in an exclusive relationship. Theories that seek to clarify diversity in marriage include the social exchange theory. Partners may each decide what attributes they are willing to exchange, and what they expect in return. It is a sophisticated yet covert form of bartering of assets, that keeps cost benefits in mind, each party hoping to be strengthened by or to gain from the union of seeming opposites. For instance, youth and beauty versus social and economic power have been a frequently occurring theme in the marital stakes. Diversity of assets, qualities, and characteristics lend themselves to a social exchange. This in turn implicates costs and rewards. It may not be surprising that even diversity can be a playing card in the complicated game of marriage.

Clara Gerhardt

See also: Interfaith Marriage; International Marriage; Interracial Marriage

Further Reading

Fincham, Frank D. and Steven R. H. Beach. 2010. "Marriage in the new millennium: A decade in review." *Journal of Marriage and the Family* 72, no. 3. https://doi.org/10.1111/j.1741-3737.2010.00722.x

Nanda, Serena. 2019. *Love and marriage: Cultural diversity in a changing world.* Long Grove, IL: Waveland Press.

Division of Assets

One of the consequences of divorce is property division, which generally proceeds in two stages. The first stage is determining the assets, while the second stage is dividing the assets by equitable distribution or community property principles. Both stages are governed by state law, but a couple may change the legal default with a prenuptial or postnuptial agreement. Couples can also agree to a particular division of assets in their divorce settlement agreement.

States differ on what types of assets and liabilities are subject to division during divorce. Some states, such as California, divide only property acquired during the marriage, while others, such as Indiana, also divide premarital property and that received by inheritance or gift.

Divisible assets can include the marital home and pensions, which are typically the most significant assets that couples own. In dividing the marital home, courts might examine who provided the money to buy the marital house, whether it was purchased before the marriage, or whether there was a commingling of the parties' assets to pay the mortgage or make improvements. However, the custodial parent might be able to continue living in the home under certain circumstances so that the children do not have to relocate.

In contrast, workers' compensation benefits intended to replace future wages, eventual proceeds from pending personal injury actions, certain disability pensions, and educational degrees may not be divisible in some states. Spousal maintenance, also known as alimony, is separate from property division because it divides future income instead of present property.

A spouse may try to hide assets by changing the title or transferring them to unknown accounts. The other spouse can uncover these assets through the discovery phase of the divorce proceedings by seeking financial information from employers and banks under court order.

Once the divisible property is identified, the property division proceeds according to common law or community property principles, depending on the state. Community property is that which is owned jointly by a married couple. The community property approach is the default approach in only a minority of states, which currently include Arizona, California, Idaho, Louisiana, Nevada, New Mexico, Texas, Washington, and Wisconsin. In a community property state, each spouse's earnings and the property bought with those earnings during marriage are owned equally by the spouses, although some states may exclude premarital property and property received by gift or inheritance. In the community property regime, marriage is treated as a partnership in which property and debts acquired during the marriage belong to both spouses in equal, undivided shares. Thus, during divorce, the spouses' property may be divided equally into community property states, but each community property state may differ in the exact approach.

The vast majority of American states, however, are common law states. In these states, the property belongs to the spouse who acquired it. There is no automatic sharing of earnings on account of the marriage. During marriage, the spouses own everything separately. In other words, the spouse who earned the money is the one who owns the money and everything that it buys.

At divorce in common law states, however, a judge has the discretion to divide the property between the spouses regardless of who earned or owned it during the marriage. The standard for the property division is "equitable distribution." This approach seeks an equitable, but not necessarily an equal division between the spouses. A few states might define equitable as requiring a 50/50 starting point for the divisible property, but in other states, a 95/5 property division can be equitable. The judge typically considers several factors when seeking an equitable property division between the spouses, such as the length of the marriage, the causes for the dissolution of the marriage, the age and health of the parties, and the amount and sources of income, as well as the vocational skills, liabilities, and needs of each party.

Equitable distribution has been likened to partnership dissolution: although the partners have a partnership stake, the stakes are not necessarily equal. At the dissolution, the partners receive shares equal to their contributions. In the marital context, however, contributions need not be financial and include childcare.

In common law states, the courts, therefore, have significant discretion in property division, and the resulting decisions are often fact specific. Due to its greyness, equitable distribution has triggered substantial litigation on the proper division of assets following a divorce. The debate regarding the meaning of equitable is particularly acute in divorce

cases involving wealthier couples. In these cases, property divisions are often greatly disproportionate to reflect one partner's significant financial contribution to the marriage, an outcome that has been challenged in the courts.

In sum, the first stage of property division at divorce is identifying the assets subject to division. The second stage is applying common law or community property principles to divide the property. Couples can change the relevant legal defaults through a prenuptial or postnuptial agreement or agree to a particular division of assets in their divorce settlement agreement.

Margaret Ryznar

See also: Divorce, Process of; Spousal Support; Unmarried Cohabitation

Further Reading

Garrison, Marsha. 2011. "What's Fair in Divorce Property Distribution: Cross-National Perspectives from Survey Evidence." *Louisiana Law Review* 72, no. 1: 57–88.

Jules, Adrienne Hunter and Fernanda G. Nicola. 2014. "The Contractualization of Family Law in the United States." *American Journal of Comparative Law* 62, no. 4: 151–184.

Mahoney, Margaret M. 2010. "The Equitable Distribution of Marital Debts." *UMKC Law Review* 79, no. 2: 445–476.

Musselman, James L. 2018. "Rights of Creditors to Collect Marital Debts after Divorce in Community Property Jurisdictions." *Pace Law Review* 39, no. 1: 309–360.

Ratner, James R. 2011. "Distribution of Marital Assets in Community Property Jurisdictions: Equitable Doesn't Equal." *Louisiana Law Review* 72, no. 1: 21–55.

Divorce, Alternatives to

Deciding whether to divorce or not is one of the most difficult and stressful decisions that a person may encounter during their life span (Allen and Hawkins 2017). Recent research among a nationally representative sample in the United States indicates that 25% of married Americans have had recent thoughts of divorce and that an additional 28% had previous thoughts of divorce but remained married (Hawkins et al. 2017). Such findings indicate that even beyond couples who have divorced, many individuals are in the process of deciding to end their relationship. Demographers estimate that approximately half of the marriages in the United States will end in divorce (Kennedy and Ruggles 2014). Furthermore, according to U.S. Census data, only 68% of children will spend their entire childhood in an intact family (Vespa, Lewis, and Kreider 2013) and that divorce affects more than 1 million children a year (National Center for Health Statistics 2008).

Reconciliation

Previous research has indicated that approximately 25% of divorcing individuals report a belief that their marriage could be saved (Doherty, Willoughby, and Peterson 2011). Specifically, 1/3 of couples had at least one partner reporting reconciliation beliefs, and 10% of both partners reporting beliefs that the marriage doesn't need to end in divorce (Doherty et al. 2011). The potential for reconciliation may be particularly true for low-conflict couples who are considering divorce.

Amato and Hohmann-Marriott (2007) identified two distinct clusters of divorcing couples. The first cluster was highly conflictual with reports of frequent arguments, physical violence, low commitment to marriage, and higher perceived number of problems. The second cluster consisted of low-conflict divorcing couples who reported moderate levels of marital happiness, little physical violence, and infrequent arguments. Furthermore, research suggests that both men and women typically report growing apart, lack of attention from their spouse, and communication difficulties as the most common reasons for divorce (Hawkings, Willoughby, and Doherty 2012). Moreover, there is evidence that divorced couples from low-conflict marriages typically report declines in overall well-being compared to individuals who divorced from high-conflict marriages (i.e., domestic violence) (Amato and Hohmann-Marriott 2007). Additionally, nearly half of divorced individuals report wishing they would have worked harder to resolve their marital differences (Hawkings et al. 2012).

The prevalence of reconciliation beliefs among divorcing populations has led researchers to posit that remains an opportunity to assist couples on the brink of divorce, even after divorce has been filed (Hawkins et al. 2012). Amato (2010) describes this ambiguous stage in the divorce process as "not quite married and not quite divorced" (p. 661).

When considering alternatives to divorce it is important to note that couples who once considered divorce yet remained together may or may not be working on improving relationship quality. Allen and Hawkins (2017) posit that the term *reconciliation* consists of all "non-divorce" options and may promote a false dichotomy between marriage and divorce. Research that approaches reconciliation with binary assumptions may not accurately capture couples' lived experiences of the divorce and reconciliation processes. Allen and Hawkins further argue that couples on the verge of divorce who decide to "reconcile" don't automatically engage in marital repair. Rather, many couples who do not divorce may stay married out of convenience, denial, and tolerance (Allen and Hawkins 2017).

Additional Alternatives

It is important to note that there are additional alternatives to divorce besides reconciliation. For example, Gadoua and Larson (2014) identified three specific alternatives to divorce where couples reconsider the boundaries and overall function of their marriage (e.g., they identified that couples may choose to "live apart together"). This occurs as couples live in separate residences but maintain a marital union. Such an arrangement may help balance a struggling couple's need to remain connected while gaining needed autonomy and independence. However, financially this may not be an option for many couples due to the cost of two separate residences.

An additional alternative to divorce is developing a "parenting marriage." A parenting marriage occurs as couples decide to shift toward a more platonic relationship that is rooted in coparenting together. In doing so, partners modify their expectations of the marriage meeting their emotional needs, and strive to experience fulfillment through coparenting without divorcing. In a "parenting marriage," couples avoid divorce or separation but at the cost of romantic marital fulfillment.

The last alternative to divorce that Gadoua and Larson (2014) propose is that couples may consider an "open marriage" in which both partners have consented to allow sexual and emotional needs to be met by other people outside the marriage. Couples in open marriages may open and close the marriage to outside partners as they see fit rather than divorce. While there is evidence of more couples participating in open-marriages limited research is available on the challenges and benefits of being in an open marriage.

While divorce remains an appropriate option for many couples who are experiencing significant marital distress there are viable alternatives to divorce. Specifically, low-conflict marriages may consider reconciliation before pursuing divorce. However, other couples have pursued separation, parent-centered marriages, and open unions as alternatives to divorce.

Todd Spencer, Matthew Brosi,
and Ethan Jones

See also: Divorce, Process of; Open Marriage; Parallel Parenting

Further Reading

Allen, Sarah, and Alan J. Hawkins. 2017. "Theorizing the decision-making process for divorce or reconciliation." *Journal of Family Theory & Review* 9, no. 1: 50–68.

Amato, Paul R. 2010. "Research on divorce: Continuing trends and new developments." *Journal of Marriage and Family* 72, no. 3: 650–666. https://doi .org/10.1111/j.1741-3737.2010.00723.x

Amato, Paul R., and Bryndl Hohmann-Marriott. 2007. "A comparison of high- and low-distress marriages that end in divorce." *Journal of Marriage and Family* 69, no. 3: 621–638.

Doherty, William J., Brian J. Willoughby, and Bruce Peterson. 2011. "Interest in marital reconciliation among divorcing parents." *Family Court Review* 49, no. 2: 313–321.

Gadoua, Susan Pease, and Vicki Larson. 2014. *The new I do: Reshaping marriage for skeptics, realists and rebels.* Seal Press.

Hawkins, A. J., A. M. Galovan, S. M. Harris, S. E. Allen, S. M. Allen, K. M. Roberts, and D. G. Schramm. 2017. "What Are They Thinking? A National Study of Stability and Change in Divorce Ideation." *Family Process* 56: 852–868. https://doi.org/10.1111/famp.12299

Hawkins, Alan J., Brian J. Willoughby, and William J. Doherty. 2012. "Reasons for divorce and openness to marital reconciliation." *Journal of Divorce & Remarriage* 53, no. 6: 453–463.

Kennedy, Sheela, and Steven Ruggles. 2014. "Breaking up is hard to count: The rise of divorce in the United States, 1980–2010." *Demography* 51, no. 2: 587–598.

National Center for Health Statistics. 2008. Marriage and divorce.

National Divorce Decision-Making Project. 2015. "What are they thinking? A national survey of married individuals who are thinking about divorce." doi:10.13140/RG.2.1.4905.6724

Vespa, Jonathan, Jamie M. Lewis, and Rose M. Kreider. 2013. "America's families and living arrangements: 2012." *Current Population Reports* 20, no. 2013: P570.

Divorce, Causes/Risk Factors of

Currently, the divorce rate in the United States is thought to be between 40–50% (Olson 2015). Despite indications that the divorce rate has actually been leveling off since the mid-1990s, the current divorce rate still stands at a level approximately 10 times higher than in the year 1950 (Olson 2015). High divorce rates, paired with the negative ramifications of divorce on divorcees, families, and children of divorce (Amato and Sobolewski 2001, 916–919) make it important to understand the risk factors and causes of marital dissolution.

First, it is important to consider the legal and cultural backdrop for the rise in divorce. Before the 18th century, marriages served a primarily pragmatic function: they were mainly sought for purposes of societal organization, which included childbearing, social connectivity, and in some cases, social and political advancement. This began to change during the late 18th century, however: "love" for one's partner replaced pragmatism as the primary motivator for marriage, shifting the way that people sought suitors and expectations for marriage. The extent to which partners were compatible was primarily dependent on how much love they felt for each other. This trend reached new heights in the mid-20th century when the sexual connection between partners became a key ingredient of love (Coontz 2006, 4–5). Predictably, when love—and sexual connection—became the non-negotiable elements of marriage, "falling out of love" became a highly cited reason for seeking divorce.

From a legal standpoint, divorces become much easier to obtain around this time. Before 1969, married couples could not typically obtain a divorce unless (a) both partners consented (followed by a lengthy period of separation before the divorce could be granted), and/or (b) one of the partners could establish fault (e.g., abuse, cruelty, abandonment). This changed in 1969, however, when

California was the first state to enact "no-fault" divorce laws, which for the first time allowed one partner to precipitate a divorce by citing "irreconcilable differences." The enactment of this law coincided with what was known as the "free love" era, where two ideas counter to the traditional view of marriage—ideas of women's self-sufficiency (i.e., women don't need men) and more free sexual expression—became more normalized. The combination of these three cultural changes—love as a prerequisite for marriage, no-fault divorce law, and the free love era—seems to have played a role in the spike in divorce rates; in 1960, there were 393,000 divorces, and in 1980—about a decade after the enactment of no-fault divorce laws—the number of divorces tripled to 1,184,175 (Olson 2015).

It is also important to consider the individual-level factors that increase one's risk of divorce—age, gender, socioeconomic status, educational attainment, and marital history appear to play a role: people who marry as a teenager (Amato 2010), are female (Amato and Previti 2003), who are poor and/unemployed, who report lower levels of education, or who have been previously married (Amato 2010) report higher levels of divorce than their older, male, wealthier and/or employed, highly educated, first-marriage counterparts. Additionally, people who report frequent drug and/or alcohol use are more likely to experience divorce (Collins, Ellickson, and Klein 2007). Certain childhood experiences, such as consistent exposure to high levels of parental conflict and/or experience of parental divorce, heighten children's risk of experiencing divorce themselves (Amato 1996); this is likely due in part to the transmission of negative communication/conflict resolution styles to their own marriages. With regard to family structure, living in a single-parent household has also been shown to be a risk factor (Amato 1996).

Once people are partnered, specific couple dynamics have been shown to predict/cause divorce. Certain couple-level behaviors that occur before getting married have been shown to predict marital problems. Premarital cohabitation—a living arrangement that has become increasingly prevalent—is significantly associated with a future divorce (Stanley, Rhoades, and Markman 2006). Regardless of premarital living arrangements, if a couple has a child before their wedding day, or if partners (one or both) bring one or more children from a previous relationship into his or her new relationship, they are also more likely to get divorced (Amato 2010).

After the wedding day, specific interpersonal behaviors have been cited as reasons for divorce. These behaviors include domestic violence (Kelly and Johnson 2008), communication issues, conflict, and infidelity (Amato and Previti 2003). With regard to communication and conflict resolution, John Gottman, the renowned couple therapist, identified six couple-level behaviors that put couples at a higher risk for divorce: (1) harsh start-up (beginning a conversation in a critical or attacking way); (2) the "Four Horsemen of the Apocalypse" (criticism, contempt, defensiveness, stonewalling); (3) flooding (psychological and emotional overwhelm); (4) negative body language; (5) failed repair (i.e., reconciliation) attempts; and (6) bad memories. Based on his observations of couples communicating, Gottman has been able to predict a couple's outcomes (divorce or no divorce) with 91% accuracy based on these six indicators (Gottman and Silver 2015). Regarding infidelity—an especially strong predictor of divorce—individuals who reported ever having had extramarital sex were more likely to report being divorced and remarried, divorced and not remarried, or separated (Allen and Atkins 2012, 1486). The advent of the technological age has spawned a new form of infidelity: internet betrayal. For example, in 2011, approximately 33% of divorce filings contained information about partner transgressions committed on Facebook (Lumpkin 2012). Other relational reasons cited by couples for divorce—which are vaguer but still reported often—include growing apart, incompatibility (Amato and Previti 2003), lack of commitment to each other (Scott et al. 2013), and "falling out of love," which was described as a loss of trust, intimacy, and feeling loved (Sailor 2013).

Researchers have identified numerous risk factors and causes of divorce, which include shifting cultural norms and factors at the individual and dyadic (couple) levels. While many risk factors exist, researchers' ability to identify these variables has been valuable—perhaps most notably, it has led to an increase in divorce prevention efforts, including relationship education for emerging adults, premarital education/counseling for engaged couples, and relationship enhancement programs for married couples.

Richard S. Dell'Isola

See also: Divorce Pre-1950; Divorce 1950–2000

Further Reading

Allen, Elizabeth S., and David C. Atkins. 2012. "The association of divorce and extramarital sex in a representative U.S. sample." *Journal of Family Issues* 33, no. 11: 1477–1493.

Amato, Paul R. 1996. "Explaining the intergenerational transmission of divorce." *Journal of Marriage and the Family* 58, no. 3: 628–640.

Amato, Paul R. 2010. "Research on divorce: Continuing trends and new developments." *Journal of Marriage and Family* 72, no. 3: 650–666.

Amato, Paul R., and Denise Previti. 2003. "People's reasons for divorcing: Gender, social class, the life course, and adjustment." *Journal of Family Issues* 24, no. 5: 602–626.

Amato, Paul R., and Juliana M. Sobolewski. 2001. "The effects of divorce and marital discord on adult children's psychological well-being." *American Sociological Review* 66, no. 6: 900–921.

Collins, Rebecca L., Phyllis L. Ellickson, and David J. Klein. 2007. "The role of substance use in young adult divorce." *Addiction* 102, no. 5: 786–794.

Coontz, Stephanie. 2006. *Marriage, a history: How love conquered marriage.* New York: Penguin.

Gottman, John Mordechai, and Nan Silver. 2015. *The seven principles for making marriage work: A practical guide from the country's foremost relationship expert.* Harmony.

Kelly, Joan B., and Michael P. Johnson. 2008. "Differentiation among types of intimate partner violence: Research update and implications for interventions." *Family Court Review* 46, no. 3: 476–499.

Lumpkin, Sydney. 2012. "Can facebook ruin your marriage?" *ABC News.* https://abcnews.go.com/Technology/facebook-relationship-status/story?id=16406245#.T8e02F9PE

Olson, Randal. 2015. "144 years of marriage and divorce in 1 chart." *Randal S. Olsen* 15.

Sailor, Joanni L. 2013. "A phenomenological study of falling out of romantic love." *Qualitative Report* 18: 1–22.

Scott, Shelby B., Galena K. Rhoades, Scott M. Stanley, Elizabeth S. Allen, and Howard J. Markman. 2013. "Reasons for divorce and recollections of premarital intervention: Implications for improving relationship education." *Couple and Family Psychology: Research and Practice* 2, no. 2: 131–145.

Stanley, Scott M., Galena Kline Rhoades, and Howard J. Markman. 2006. "Sliding versus deciding: Inertia and the premarital cohabitation effect." *Family Relations* 55, no. 4: 499–509.

Divorce, Economic Consequences (Personal)

When married couples separate and/or divorce, there are often numerous physical, emotional, and social consequences for both adults and children, if present. There are also economic consequences that usually affect all involved. Several decades of research have attempted to identify and quantify these personal costs of divorce. The results from these studies are often different, depending on the sample of divorced couples, the financial measures and surveys used, and whether the data come from a longitudinal data set, or collected from government agencies or divorced individuals. Additionally, the personal costs of divorce have changed over time as more women have entered the paid workforce over the past few decades. But most of the research concludes that both men, women, and any children tend to experience negative consequences financially immediately following a divorce, and this includes cohabiting relationships that end in separation. Beyond financial effects, divorce often results in health, life, and lifestyle changes for both adults and children,

which may affect their economic, social, and personal well-being.

Divorce often results in negative economic effects for divorcing individuals. However, there are mixed findings on how divorce affects men and women differently. Part of the reason is due to the different ways economic well-being is measured across studies. To better understand the personal economic consequences of divorce, it is important to explore the various aspects of finances and the measures used, such as annual personal earnings, household income, per capita income, income-to-needs ratio, and poverty rate.

Divorce nearly always affects both parties' annual personal earnings or income. Historically, men lost much smaller shares of their income and even experienced increases in their standard of living compared to women. A smaller percentage of men and women experienced increases in their income following divorce, often as a result of working more hours, finding employment, or seeking higher-paying work. Most agree that the gender gap related to post-divorce personal economic outcomes appears to be decreasing as a result of more women entering the paid workforce in recent decades.

Divorce nearly always results in a decrease in household income, which is the sum total of both partners' personal earnings. For many divorcing couples, both men and women are working outside of the home, and the removal of the other partner's income results in decreases in overall household income. While both partners experience a decline in combined household income, men, on average, are more likely to experience an economic recovery more quickly than women (Gadalla 2009, 56–57).

Much of the disagreement and differences in study findings about the economic consequences of divorce for men and women are due to family size. This is referred to as income per capita, which is the total household income divided by the number of household members. Some argue that this is not an accurate reflection of the costs of divorce because this method assumes that a family of four would cost twice as much as a family of two.

The income-to-needs ratio is another measure of the economic costs of divorce for couples. This method uses federal poverty level (FPL) thresholds, which takes into account family size by using annual total household income as the numerator and the annual federal poverty threshold that corresponds to the family's size as the denominator. A value of less than 1 indicates a family is living below the poverty line, and a value of 1 to 1.5 indicates a family is "near-poor" (Smock et al. 1999). This measure is believed to be a more accurate reflection of economic well-being and generally shows that men often experience an increase in their economic well-being compared to women, due to more children living with their mothers than their fathers.

Poverty is the fifth method of assessing the personal costs of divorce. The U.S. Census Bureau determines poverty status by comparing pre-tax cash income against a threshold that is updated annually for inflation and adjusted for family size, composition, and age of householder. Poverty is closely related to the income-to-needs ratio because both take into account income and family size. Women tend to experience poverty following divorce more often than men because, despite an increase in joint custody arrangements after divorce, women still tend to have the children for more of the time and have relatively smaller household incomes, on average, compared to men.

Numerous financial costs of divorce usually affect both adults. These include legal costs, divorce filing fees, mediation, and other court fees. Additional costs include child support, childcare, and costs associated with mediation and/or counseling. These costs sometimes result in difficult changes including bankruptcy, cashing out retirement, dropping insurance, or taking out high-interest short-term loans. Others struggle with medical bills and paying for their children's activities. For some divorced individuals, a change in employment or increase in the number of hours worked is needed, or even getting a second job. Additionally, most divorces result in one or both individuals moving with subsequent changes in travel costs, and costs associated with renting/buying, furnishings, and other household goods needed to live separately.

Divorce not only affects men's and women's income, but it also affects their overall financial situation, wealth, and net worth. Following divorce, both men and women typically have less money to save, and some men and/or women may lose their health insurance. Retirement benefits are also often influenced by divorce and many divorced individuals acquire new debts, including car loans, home loans, and credit card debt to maintain their standard of living or to simply survive. Some are even forced to file for bankruptcy. Given the changes in income, wealth, and other financial areas, some divorced men and women need financial assistance and/or material assistance and turn to family, friends, community and church organizations, and government programs. Divorce may also be related to other health and lifestyle changes, including decreases in physical and mental health that affects men, women, and their children.

Divorce often results in other personal costs that are lesser known. These include changing schools for children, and many parents spend less money on themselves and maintaining their previous lifestyle. This includes less money spent on food, clothing, entertainment, and even charitable contributions. Other activities and expenses that may be adjusted or eliminated following divorce include eating out, going out to movies, savings, going out with friends, haircuts, vacations, groceries, and even doctor and dentist visits. These adjustments, combined with other emotional and personal economic costs of divorce, contribute to the overall challenges for many adults and children following divorce.

David G. Schramm

See also: Divorce, Causes/Risk Factors of; Divorce, Economic Consequences (Taxpayers)

Further Reading

Gadalla, Tahany M. 2009. "Impact of marital dissolution on men's and women's incomes: A longitudinal study." *Journal of Divorce & Remarriage* 50: 55–65.

Scafidi, Benjamin. 2008. *The taxpayer costs of divorce and unwed childbearing: First-ever estimates for the nation and all fifty states.* New York, NY: Institute for American Values.

Schramm, David G. 2006. "Individual and social costs of divorce in Utah." *Journal of Family and Economic Issues* 21: 133–151.

Schramm, David G., Steven Harris, Jason Whiting, Alan Hawkins, Matt Brown, and Rob Porter. 2013. "Economic costs and policy implications associated with divorce: Texas as a case study." *Journal of Divorce & Remarriage* 54: 1–24.

Smock, Pamela J., Wendy D. Manning, and Sanjiv Gupta. 1999. "The effect of marriage and divorce on women's economic well-being." *American Sociological Review* 64: 794–812.

Divorce, Economic Consequences (Taxpayers)

When married individuals decide to end their relationship by divorcing, there are numerous consequences, both positive and negative, for men, women, their children, and even their extended family. In addition to the personal, physical, emotional, economic, and social consequences, there are economic consequences of divorce that are often absorbed by local communities and state and federal governments. Few studies have attempted to document the costs of divorce to state and federal governments (see Schramm 2006, 133–151 and Schramm et al. 2013, 1–24 for exceptions). The most comprehensive report on the costs of family fragmentation to date is by Scafidi (2008), where he documents the taxpayer costs of divorce and unwed childbearing for all 50 states.

Examining the economic consequences of divorce at a broader level is very complex. Studies have shown at least two primary reasons for the public economic consequences of divorce to taxpayers. First, when a divorce occurs, in many cases, the individuals involved (more often the mother with children, if present) may not be able to afford or provide the basic necessities to sustain their current level of living. As a result, some turn to a variety of sources for assistance, including family members, the broader community, and even state and federal programs. These are examples of direct public economic consequences of divorce. A second reason why exploring the economic consequences of divorce is difficult is the indirect costs of divorce. Many studies have shown that divorce is one of the most stressful and emotional experiences one can experience. As a result, many adults and children face unique challenges such as working multiple jobs, resulting in less monitoring from parents, and children moving between households, that ultimately relate to a greater likelihood of drug abuse, mental health struggles, parenting stress, incarceration, lost time at work, higher drop-out rates for teens, and physical and emotional abuse, among other challenges. These indirect challenges related to divorce and family break up often have taxpayer costs that are difficult to measure. Both direct and indirect public costs of divorce will be examined next.

Direct Costs of Divorce to Communities

When marriage ends in divorce, there are many direct costs related to the impact it often has on the local community where it occurs. It is common not only for immediate and extended family members to provide emotional and financial assistance, but various forms of assistance may also be offered from local food banks, schools, charities, religious organizations, family support centers, social service agencies,

and other nonprofit organizations. Collectively, these organizations are largely funded to assist families during times of crisis, including divorce.

Direct Costs of Divorce to State and Federal Governments

Divorce often results in a spill-over effect wherein the breakup of the family unit results in difficulties and numerous additional living costs associated with two separate families instead of one. That is, the effects of divorce spill over into other areas of the individuals' lives, particularly their financial situation. As a result, some families turn to state and federal government assistance for both temporary and long-term aid. There are over 70 welfare programs funded by the federal government to assist low-income Americans. Programs at the state level also assist primarily through matching federal welfare contributions. Many divorced individuals turn to these and other programs for assistance following divorce.

Some of the larger federal and state programs designed to assist needy families include programs to help with: providing food (e.g., Supplemental Nutrition Assistance Programs [SNAP], formerly known as food stamps), including Women, Infants, and Children (WIC), cash assistance (Temporary Assistance for Needy Families, TANF), utility and housing assistance (Low-Income Home Energy Assistance Programs, LIHEAP), child welfare programs, school lunch and breakfast programs, subsidized child care programs, and Head Start and Early Head Start. Other federal grants aimed at helping individuals in need include social security and community development block grants and jobs and job training (e.g., Workforce Investment Act, Job Corps). Various government-funded medical programs also may assist some divorced families. These include Medicaid and State Children's Health Insurance Programs (SCHIP). These and other government-funded programs assist divorced individuals and are viewed as an additional cost of divorce to taxpayers.

Divorce often results in other legal costs that are difficult to quantify but are nonetheless very real. These include costs associated with judges and commissioners to process the divorce cases, administrative and record expenses, costs to modify custody and parenting plan arrangements, and child support enforcement—it costs taxpayers when government agencies invest time and money to track down parents to pay child support owed.

Indirect Costs of Divorce to Society

The spill-over effects of divorce spread beyond direct costs associated with local organizations and larger government agencies to the broader society. These are even more difficult to quantify. While large bodies of research have shown that divorce contributes independently to a host of negative outcomes in society, several other factors combine to put divorced individuals and children from divorce at greater risk. Some of these negative outcomes include higher levels of crime and incarceration, mental health challenges, abuse and neglect, drug abuse, higher rates of school dropout, juvenile delinquency, and teenage pregnancy.

Summary

While the personal economic consequences related to divorce may be more familiar and easier to quantify, many direct and indirect public costs of divorce spill over for taxpayers and into the broader society. Numerous community, state, and federal tax-funded programs have been designed to assist individuals, families, and children when they experience challenges, including divorce. Some have attempted to quantify and explore these public economic consequences. Ultimately, however, the exact economic consequences of divorce to taxpayers will never be completely known.

David G. Schramm

See also: Divorce, Causes/Risk Factors of; Divorce, Economic Consequences (Personal)

Further Reading

Scafidi, Benjamin. 2008. *The taxpayer costs of divorce and unwed childbearing: First-ever estimates for the nation and all fifty states.* New York, NY: Institute for American Values.

Schramm, David G. 2006. "Individual and social costs of divorce in Utah." *Journal of Family and Economic Issues* 21, no. 1: 133–151.

Schramm, David G., Harris, Steven M., Whiting, Jason B., Hawkins, Alan J., Brown, Matt., and Porter, Rob. 2013. "Economic costs and policy implications associated with divorce: Texas as a case study." *Journal of Divorce & Remarriage* 54, no. 1: 1–24.

Divorce, Grandparents and

Although grandparents often play an important part in the lives of their grandchildren, recent demographic trends highlight the importance of intergenerational relationships more than ever before. More than 80% of older adults ages 65 and over are grandparents in the

United States (Krogstad 2015), indicating that multigenerational families are a growing population of the changing American family and that intergenerational solidarity is part of individual life courses and a shared experience in family life. Increasing life expectancy due to the improvements in medical conditions offers more years and opportunities to enjoy grandparent-grandchild ties as part of the life span among most individuals. In addition, when women have fewer children (Fry 2019), grandparents are likely to be able to invest more time and effort in raising and supporting their grandchildren. However, extended longevity also increases the likelihood of experiencing marital disruptions (e.g., separation, divorce) and repartnering (e.g., remarriage, cohabitation). Taken together, these demographic changes shape not only immediate family relationships (e.g., father-child tie) but also intergenerational relationships (e.g., grandparent-grandchild bond) in different ways.

Grandparents can be a great source of support by helping raise their grandchildren and promoting the children's well-being and healthy development. This is particularly true when the parents and their children are experiencing family transitions, such as divorce. Grandparents' assistance and support are invaluable, enabling them to overcome difficult times. For example, grandparents can help their grandchildren deal with grief and anger, have a positive view in the middle of uncertainty, and continue to focus on daily routines and school activities (Barth 2004, 41–44). In addition, grandparents can ensure that their grandchildren are loved and that parents and grandparents will continue to be there for them,

and maintain a positive grandparent-grandchild bond (Barth 2004, 41–44).

Grandparents, however, do not necessarily play a positive role in the lives of their grandchildren during their parents' divorce. Grandparents may be absent, regardless of their willingness to stay involved in their grandchildren, or they may negatively affect grandchildren by engaging in disputes during the divorce process. For example, in a study of the role of grandparents in post-divorce families by Jordan Soliz (2008), some adult grandchildren retrospectively reported that their grandparents disappeared or did not support them following their parents' divorce, talked badly about the divorce decision or their children's ex-spouse, could not provide help with aging, and/or avoid discussing the divorce with them (76–77).

It should be noted that grandparent-grandchild ties are significantly affected by the middle-generation divorced parents and their divorce and their coparenting arrangements to a great extent given that grandparents have no control over their adult children's divorce, as neither do children of the divorcing parents. For example, researchers found children of divorcees were more likely to maintain contact with the parents of the residential parent, which in turn affected grandparent-grandchild relationships (Jappens and Van Bavel 2016). Parental involvement of one parent (usually fathers) may decline over time, and this affects children's relationships with their fathers, as well as family ties with paternal grandparents (Ahrons 2007, 61).

The coparenting relationship between divorced parents also has implications for the quality of the grandparent-grandchild relationship. For example, family researcher Constance Ahrons (2007, 58) found that children of divorced parents who worked cooperatively in raising their children maintained positive relationships with their relatives (e.g., grandparents), as well as new stepfamily members (e.g., stepsiblings). Based on the research findings previously discussed, it seems that parental involvement of both parents in their children's lives, a cooperative and amicable coparenting relationship between divorced parents, and perhaps grandparents' attempts to maintain the already-established ties with their grandchildren are critical for positive and stable grandparent-grandchild relationships following the middle-generation parents' divorce.

To maintain grandparent-grandchild ties, some grandparents may request custody of their grandchildren if they believe that grandchildren staying with them would be better for their post-divorce adjustment. Regardless of the relationship quality and grandparents' willingness to obtain legal rights for custody of their grandchildren, whether or not grandparents obtain legal rights is likely to be primarily affected by the best interests of a child, parents' wishes, parental rights, and parents' agreement (Justia 2018). For example, if divorced parents are still alive or considered a good fit for parenting children without a major issue (e.g., substance abuse), the chance of getting custody of a child is low for grandparents (Justia 2018).

Grandparenting and grandparent-grandchild relationships can also be affected by the grandparents' divorce. For example, in a study of the consequences of grandparents' divorce on grandparenting and intergenerational ties, divorced grandparents reported less contact and fewer shared activities with their teen grandchildren, feeling less close to them, higher conflict in the relationship, and the less significant role that they played in the lives of their grandchildren, compared to never-divorced grandparents (King 2003). These associations were further explained by a few factors, such as geographic distance and the quality of grandparent-adult-child relationships (King 2003).

As grandparents can play a significant role in the lives of their grandchildren in times of the parents' divorce, grandchildren also can provide support and help that aging grandparents need. Adult grandchildren may feel strong obligations or responsibilities to their aging grandparents as their parents do. However, given that normative beliefs and attitudes toward family obligations and the exchanges of intergenerational support are contextual (Ganong and Coleman 1998, 288), divorce, either that of aging grandparents or the parents, may weaken intergenerational obligations and support of both adult children and grandchildren given to grandparents, which has implications for the aging society.

Youngjin Kang

See also: Coparenting and Divorce; Marital Separation; Remarriage

Further Reading

Ahrons, Constance R. 2007. "Family Ties After Divorce: Long-Term Implications for Children." *Family Process* 46, no. 1: 53–65. https://doi.org/10.1111/j.1545-5300.2006.00191.x.

Barth, Joan C. 2004. "Grandparents Dealing with the Divorce of Their Child: Tips for Grandparents and Therapists." *Contemporary Family Therapy* 26, no. 1: 41–44. https://doi.org/10.1023/B:COFT.0000016910.22865.5b.

Fry, Richard. 2019. "The Number of People in the Average U.S. Household Is Going Up for the First Time in over 160 Years." Accessed June 10, 2022. https://www.pewresearch.org/fact-tank/2019/10/01/the-number-of-people-in-the-average-u-s-household-is-going-up-for-the-first-time-in-over-160-years/

Ganong, Lawrence H., and Marilyn Coleman. 1998. "Attitudes Regarding Filial Responsibilities to Help Elderly Divorced Parents and Stepparents." *Journal of Aging Studies* 12, no. 3: 271–290. https://doi.org/10.1016/S0890-4065(98)90004-4.

Jappens, Maaike and Jan Van Bavel. 2016. "Parental Divorce, Residence Arrangements, and Contact between Grandchildren and Grandparents." *Journal of Marriage and Family* 78, no. 2: 451–467. https://doi.org/10.1111/jomf.12275.

Justia. 2018. "Grandparent Custody and Visitation." Accessed October 2, 2019. https://www.justia.com/family/child-custody-and-support/child-custody/grandparent-custody-and-visitation/

King, Valarie. 2003. "The Legacy of a Grandparent's Divorce: Consequences for Ties between Grandparents and Grandchildren." *Journal of Marriage and Family* 65, no. 1: 170–183.

Krogstad, Jens M. 2015. "5 Facts about American Grandparents." Accessed July 15, 2019. https://www.pewresearch.org/fact-tank/2015/09/13/5-facts-about-american-grandparents/

Pew Research Center. 2013. "Parents Who Live with Their Children While Children are Being Cared for Primarily by Grandparents." Accessed July 15, 2019. https://www.pewsocialtrends.org/2013/09/04/parents-who-live-with-their-children-while-children-are-being-cared-for-primarily-by-grandparents/

Soliz, Jordan. 2008. "Intergenerational Support and the Role of Grandparents in Post-Divorce Families: Retrospective Accounts of Young Adult Grandchildren." *Qualitative Research Reports in Communication* no. 9: 72–80. https://doi.org/10.1080/17459430802400373

Divorce, Intergenerational Transmission

Intergenerational transmission of divorce is the likelihood that individuals from divorced parents will also terminate their marriages in the same manner as their parents. Research into intergenerational transmission of divorce became popular in the 1970s when divorce became more acceptable. Unlike the previous dispensation of fault divorce where there must be a justification in terms of blaming either the husband or wife as a reason for the divorce, the new system of no-fault divorce did not require a justification or blame. It is enough to seek a divorce based on irreconcilable differences.

Some scholars believe that divorce runs in families, passed from one generation to another. Divorce tends to cause turmoil in the lives of the individuals involved as well as the children of the separating couple, who have the potential to suffer long-term psychological distress resulting from their parental divorce (Amato 2000, 1280). One of the long-term consequences of divorce is that individuals from divorced parents tend to imitate the patterns of their parents' marital situation. Many studies in the United States and many European countries have confirmed this tendency (Amato and Cheadle 2005, 202; Diekmann and Schmidheiny 2008, 1).

There has long been controversy over why divorce may run in families. A few researchers attribute intergenerational transmission of divorce to genes inherited from one's biological parents. They explained that like some diseases, divorce can be biologically passed from parents to their children. A study conducted in Sweden concluded that biological factors were a stronger reason for the intergenerational transmission of divorce than the environment in which children were raised (Salvatore et al. 2018). This study found that children who were adopted resembled their biological parents' divorce history rather than their adoptive parents in their decision to get divorced in adulthood.

The majority of researchers however believe that the intergenerational transmission of divorce is influenced by the environment in which children are raised. They argue that children of divorced parents are more likely to get divorced because they grew up watching their parents struggle to make their marriage work.

Family is the foundation of all human societies. The primary role of the family is to ensure the continuity of the society through procreation and socialization of children to ensure that they grow up to become productive members of society. An intimate relationship between two individuals known as marriage is generally seen as a lifelong commitment usually by two partners. When the partners in the marriage live in harmony, it is generally believed that this is the perfect atmosphere to raise children.

The role of parents includes teaching their children what is considered acceptable behavior in society. It is within the family setting that children learn social values which influence their attitudes in adulthood. One of the important ways by which children learn how to behave in the community is by observing the conduct and actions of their parents. Such observation tends to influence the behavior of children. During this period, children may see their parents as role models. The implication is that what children learn during their childhood years generally affects their behavior in adulthood.

Children need to grow up in an environment that includes a healthy parental relationship. Studies have shown that a stable relationship among parents has the biggest impact on the happiness of children and their emotional development. The higher the quality of the relationship among parents, the happier children tend to be. But when marital discord sets in, leading to divorce and separation, the children's emotional growth is impaired with lifelong consequences.

The main influence of divorce on children appears to be the interparental conflict that sometimes precedes separation by parents. Interparental conflict is unhealthy for the children's well-being. Children who witness the divorce or separation of their parents tend to be negatively affected by the experience, with long-term effects on their behavior in adulthood. Parental divorce has been known to cause behavioral problems in children, which may affect their psychological well-being into adulthood. Some individuals have been known to have a higher risk of depression and an inability to sustain social relationships (Amato and Cheadle 2008, 1139–1161).

It is said that nearly 876,000 divorces take place annually in the United States, which is nearly 2,400 divorces each day. Since the early 20th century, the divorce rate in the United States has risen astronomically. In 1890, the divorce rate was

3 couples per 1,000. By 1920, it rose to 8 couples being divorced out of every 1,000. In 2002, 29% of first marriages among women within the 15–44 age range ended in divorce within 10 years of marriage. In recent years, the divorce rate has gone up. It is estimated that 41–50% of all first marriages will end up in divorce, while 60–67% of all second marriages will meet with the same fate and 73–74% of third marriages will also lead to divorce (Divorce Statistics).

Some studies in Europe have reported that intergenerational transmission of divorce is more common among women than men (Feng et al. 1999, 451; Lyngstad and Engelhardt 2009, 173; Gähler and Härkönen 2014, 11). In one study covering 18 countries, it was found that women in 17 countries whose parents divorced during their childhood years are at higher risk of divorce (Dronkers and Härkönen 2008, 281).

One possible explanation for intergenerational transmission of divorce is that individuals who experienced parental divorce while growing up observe the experience as normal behavior. The experience affects such individuals' attitudes toward divorce and marriage as they tend to view marriage as a relationship that could potentially dissolve. They are likely to harbor skepticism in romantic relationships and expect separation and divorce during difficulties in intimate relationships. This can be compared to how family violence can run in a family from one generation to another when children who grew up in a violent family situation become perpetrators or victims of family violence as adults. Researchers have found that parental violence can affect the offspring of such parents and eventually end up either as victims or perpetrators of intimate partner violence.

Various studies have also suggested that individuals from divorced parents are more likely to exhibit a lack of faith in marriage by either staying unmarried or by choosing cohabitation (Valle and Tillman 2014, 5; Perelli-Harris et al. 2017, 323). Individuals from intact families are more likely to hold a positive opinion about marriage compared to those from divorced families and therefore more likely to fight harder to save their marriages. On the other hand, individuals from divorced families are more likely to have a favorable opinion of divorce than individuals from intact families (Cunningham and Thornton 2005, 119). Individuals from divorced families are also more likely to marry partners who similarly experienced parental divorce and such relationships have a higher risk of failing than if only one of the partners came from a divorced family (Wolfinger 2003, 14). Childhood exposure to constant conflict between parents is also more likely to lead to unstable romantic relationships among children from divorced families (Cui and Fincham 2010, 331). Individuals from divorced parents are also likely to lack the communication and problem-solving skills that are necessary to manage romance and marital relationships.

The pain of parental divorce may also affect the parent-child relationship. A study of 401 American college students, for example, revealed that students from divorced homes are less close to their parents. Their expectations of romantic relationships were also different compared to college students from non-divorced parents (Shimkowski et al. 2018, 1).

Abiodun Raufu

See also: Divorce, Psychological Effects; Marital Separation

Further Reading

Amato, Paul R. 2000. "The Consequences of Divorce for Adults and Children." *Journal of Marriage & Family* 62, no. 4: 1269–1287.

Amato, Paul R. and Jacob Cheadle. 2005. "The Long Reach of Divorce: Divorce and Child Well-Being across Three Generations." *Journal of Marriage and Family* 67, no. 1: 191–206.

Amato, Paul R. and Jacob E. Cheadle. 2008. "Parental Divorce, Marital Conflict and Children's Behavior Problems: A Comparison of Adopted and Biological Children." *Social Forces* 86, no. 3: 1139–1161.

Collardeau, Fanie, and Marion Ehrenberg. 2016. "Parental Divorce and Attitudes and Feelings toward Marriage and Divorce in Emerging Adulthood: New Insights from a Multiway-Frequency Analysis." *Journal of European Psychology Students* 7, no. 1: 24–33.

Cui, Ming Min, and Frank D. Fincham. 2010. "The Differential Effects of Parental Divorce and Marital Conflict on Young Adult Romantic Relationships." *Personal Relationships* 17, no. 3: 331–343.

Cunningham, Mick, and Arland Thornton. 2005. "The Influences of Parents' and Offsprings' Experience with Cohabitation, Marriage, and Divorce on Attitudes Toward Divorce in Young Adulthood." *Journal of Divorce & Remarriage* 44, no. 1–2: 119–144.

Diekmann, Andreas, and Kurt Schmidheiny. 2008. "The Intergenerational Transmission of Divorce: A Fifteen-Country Study with the Fertility and Family Survey." *ETH Zurich Sociology Working Paper no. 4*: 1–17.

Divorce Statistics. https://www.divorcestatistics.info/some-devastating-effects-of-divorce-in-the-usa.html

Dronkers, Jaap, and Juho Härkönen. 2008. "The Intergenerational Transmission of Divorce in Cross-national Perspective: Results from the Fertility and Family Surveys." *Population Studies* 62, no. 3: 273–288.

Feng, Du, Roseann Giarrusso, Vern L. Bengtson, and Nancy E. Frye. 1999. "Intergenerational Transmission of Marital Quality and Marital Instability." *Journal of Marriage and Family* 61, no. 2: 451–463.

Gähler, Michael, and Juho Härkönen. 2014. "Intergenerational Transmission of Divorce—the Swedish Trend." *Family and Societies Working Paper Series*, 1–27.

Harold, Gordon T., and Leslie D. Leve. 2018. "Parents as Partners: How the Parental Relationship affects Children's Psychological Development." In Andrew Balfour, Mary Morgan, and Christopher Vincent (Eds.), *How Couple Relationships Shape our World: Clinical Practice, Research, and Policy Perspectives*. London: Routledge.

Lyngstad, Torkild H. and Henriette Engelhardt. 2009. "The Influence of Offspring's Sex and Age at Parents' Divorce on the Intergenerational Transmission of Divorce, Norwegian First Marriages 1980–2003." *Population Studies* 63, no. 2: 173–185. DOI: 10.1080/00324720902896044

Perelli-Harris, Brienna, Ann Berrington, Nora Sánchez Gassen, Paulina Galezewska, and Jennifer A. Holland. 2017. "The Rise in Divorce and Cohabitation: Is There a Link?" *Population & Development Review* 43, no. 2: 303–329.

Salvatore, Jessica E., Sara Larsson Lönn, Jan Sundquist, Kristina Sundquist, and Kenneth S. Kendler. 2018. "Genetics, the Rearing Environment, and the Intergenerational Transmission of Divorce: A Swedish National Adoption Study." *Psychological Science* 29, no. 3: 370–378.

Shimkowski, Jenna R., Narissra Punyanunt-Carter, Malinda J. Colwell and Mary S. Norman. 2018. "Perceptions of Divorce, Closeness, Marital Attitudes, Romantic Beliefs, and Religiosity Among Emergent Adults from Divorced and Nondivorced Families." *Journal of Divorce & Remarriage* 59, no. 3: 1–15. DOI: 10.1080/10502556.2017.1403820

Valle, Giuseppina, and Kathryn H. Tillman. 2014. "Childhood Family Structure and Romantic Relationships During the Transition to Adulthood." *Journal of Family Issues* 35, no. 1: 97–124.

Wolfinger, Nicholas H. 2003. "Family Structure Homogamy: The Effects of Parental Divorce on Partner Selection and Marital Stability." *Social Science Research* 32, no. 1: 1–18. https://isiarticles.com/bundles/Article/pre/pdf/37100.pdf

Divorce, No-Fault and Fault-Based

When looking at the evolution of the grounds for which people could file for divorce within the United States, there have been some key changes over the decades. While some of these changes are centered on who could file for divorce, most are centered on the justification needed to even initiate divorce proceedings, let alone getting the divorce granted. The following is an overview of fault and no-fault divorce and the implications that it had on access to divorce.

Historically, divorce was not a widely available option to dissolve a marriage. As marriages were often contracts between families, to end a marriage would have far-reaching implications. Marital dissatisfaction would not have been viewed as a socially or legally acceptable reason to

petition for a divorce. In most instances, divorces could only be initiated by husbands and not wives. Men could file for divorce because their wives were not fulfilling their responsibilities to the marriage in terms of bearing children, yet there was no guarantee that children did not result from the union due to an infertility issue on the part of the wife. This gendered approach to divorce continued to persist up until the 1970s when divorce laws started to change.

As previously noted, before the 1970s, men were predominantly the ones who could initiate divorce proceedings. In only very rare circumstances would a woman be granted a similar courtesy. An abusive marriage was often not viewed as a justifiable reason to file for divorce at this time. This is due in large part to domestic and intimate partner violence being viewed as a family issue and not one that the law should be concerned with. It is important to note that social and legal perspectives on domestic and intimate partner violence started to shift in the 1970s at the same time that social and legal perspectives on divorce were evolving.

The system of divorce that was in place before 1970 was fault-based. This was exemplified by one of the parties in the marriage filing for divorce and specifically citing a reason why the marriage should be terminated. The justification for the termination of the marriage had to lay blame as to why the marriage had failed. This is why early divorce laws permitted husbands to file for divorce if their wives did not bear children. However, the most commonly cited reason for divorce under the fault-based system of divorce was adultery. The spouse filing for divorce had to submit proof that the cheating spouse was indeed cheating and at-fault for the marriage ending. Proof often came in the form of photographic evidence of the adultery.

While the fault-based divorce system fit the social norms for the time in which it was created, where marriages were mostly viewed as contractual and not so strongly based on emotions like love and affection, it became apparent that the burden of proving fault left many couples without an option to end a marriage that was unhappy or even abusive. This led to a restructuring of the laws in 1970 on a state-by-state basis.

California became the first state to implement a no-fault divorce system in 1970 after it had passed the Family Law Act of 1969. Under the new method for filing for divorce, couples were no longer required to lay blame and prove that someone was at-fault for the marriage ending. Instead, couples could file for divorce and simply state that it was due to irreconcilable differences or irretrievably broken. This did not necessarily mean that divorce proceedings went any smoother; however, it opened up doors for couples to divorce who had previously been unable to do so. Fault was still something that could be used in terms of divorce settlements, especially in terms of adultery or abuse, which was starting to be viewed as a social and legal problem that could be prosecuted.

Over the next 15 years, every state but New York passed some form of the no-fault-based divorce system. While some states only have no-fault divorces, some of them have it as an option in addition to being able to apply under the fault-based system. Modern fault-based divorce laws permitted couples to file for divorce on the grounds of abuse

(the most commonly cited reason today), dissertation, imprisonment, adultery, or an inability to have sexual intercourse (not known before marriage). New York became the 50th and final state to enact no-fault divorce in August 2010. This meant that couples were now able actively to seek a divorce without having to resort to collusion. Before 2010, couples in New York had to file for divorce under the fault-based system and collude with one another to fabricate evidence that one of the spouses was cheating to end their marriage.

Today, all 50 states have some form of no-fault divorce available. While some states are exclusively using a no-fault divorce system, some have the option to identify fault or not. Either way, the no-fault divorce system created the opportunity for more inclusive reasons for filing for divorce and ending a marriage.

Melanie L. Duncan

See also: Divorce, Causes/Risk Factors of; Divorce, Process of; Divorce Pre-1950; Divorce 1950–2000

Further Reading
Doskow, Emily. 2020. *Nolo's Essential Guide to Divorce*, 8th ed. Bang Printing.

FindLaw. "Fault and No-Fault Divorce: An Overview." Last Updated September 28, 2018. https://www.findlaw.com/family/divorce/an-overview-of-no-fault-and-fault-divorce-law.html

NOLO. "No Fault Divorce Vs. Fault Divorce FAQ." Accessed on April 26, 2021. https://www.nolo.com/legal-encyclopedia/no-fault-divorce-vs-fault-divorce-faq.html

Steinbock, Delmar David, Jr. "The Case for No Fault Divorce." *Tulsa Law Review.* Accessed on April 26, 2021. https://core.ac.uk/download/pdf/232679828.pdf

Weisberg, D. Kelly. 2020. *Modern Family Law: Cases and Materials.* New York: Wolters Kluwer.

Divorce, Process of

Divorce is a process of legal marriage dissolution. When a married couple wishes to legally end their state-sanctioned marriage, the process is called divorce. Nearly 90% of people in the United States enter a marriage at some point in their lives. The rate of divorce for first marriages is between 40 and 50%, increasing for subsequent marriages as of 2020.

Divorce history: In early colonial history there were no divorce provisions. By the mid-1800s, divorce laws were common in the United States. Before the 1970s, couples were required to produce evidence to a judge that there were sufficient grounds for a divorce, a divorce with fault. In the 1970s, no-fault divorce laws were passed, removing the requirement to prove fault. This was a significant improvement for women's rights, as many women had been denied the ability to leave unhealthy and unhappy marriages up until this point. The result of no-fault divorce laws was a rapid increase in divorce rates. Divorce rates are said to have increased for several other reasons, including women being less financially dependent upon men, divorce becoming more socially acceptable, and changes in divorce laws that have made the process easier (Grow, Schnor, and Van Bavel 2017, 16).

Reasons for divorce are complex and vary depending on the parties involved. Some common reasons for divorce include: conflict, infidelity, lack of commitment, physical or emotional distancing, communication problems, parenting

inconsistency, domestic violence, financial problems, impotence, and/or addictions. Some studies suggest pornography use is a factor related to a higher likelihood of divorce (Perry and Schleifer 2018, 284).

The process of divorce varies by state, municipality, and/or local jurisdiction. Divorce can be complex depending on the family structure. For example, for families with children, divorce will often include the need to establish parenting plans (court-mandated time-sharing). Divorces can be contested and stretch on for years, or some parties reach agreements quickly. Some issues decided in divorce decrees include equitable division of property, alimony, child time-sharing, and/or child support. However, divorce processes vary depending on the needs and desires of individual families. Many courts require family law mediation before dissolution. Family law mediation is an alternative dispute resolution process whereby a neutral third party is used to assist parties in reaching an agreement (see Further Reading). Some parties hire private attorneys and work on agreements largely outside of the courts and bring the agreement to be finalized by a judge.

A typical divorce in the United States follows the process of:

1. Filing a divorce petition.
2. Asking for any temporary orders that may be needed (example-temporary spousal support, child support, and/or child custody).
3. The spouse that did not file the petition must be served and a response is often given.
4. Settlement negotiation.
5. Finalize the judgment.

Filing a divorce petition: The divorce petition is a legal request for the dissolution of marriage. The petition includes a statement that the party filing meets the residency requirements to file in that court, the grounds for divorce, and any other statutory information required by that particular state.

Temporary orders: For some divorcing parties, the length of time it takes to see a judge may be longer than they can wait for some decisions to be made. Therefore, a temporary order can be requested. Temporary orders will be processed more quickly than the final divorce and will typically be ordered until the final judgment is processed. Some items that may be decided temporarily are child support, child custody, spousal support or alimony, debt payments, restraining orders or orders of protection, protection from a spouse selling or getting rid of marital properties, medical decision-making authority, travel arrangements, and other issues that may be necessary to have a quick court order.

Service of paperwork: The non-filing spouse must receive a copy of the divorce petition and acknowledge receipt of the paperwork. Some spouses may be unwilling or unable to accept the paperwork and then the paperwork may be delivered by a service processor (see service processor) which provides proof of delivery.

Response: The party that receives the petition paperwork (typically referred to as the respondent or defendant) must file a response to the petitioner's attorney or the court within a certain period as indicated on the petition. The responding party may contest the reasons listed in the petition for divorce or the requests for temporary orders in their response.

Settlement negotiation: Parties may choose to hire attorneys, which is required in most states. Parties may be required, or choose to enter the process of family law mediation. Issues like parenting time, equitable distribution of property, alimony or spousal support, child support, and other issues will be negotiated during this time. The negotiation period can be quick or can take many meetings and be contentious or not. Divorce attorneys who specialize in family law work with parties to reach a negotiated settlement. Should parties fail to reach a settlement a divorce trial will be held, where the courts will aid in reaching an agreement. A trial takes much of the power and control away from the parties and puts it in the hands of the courts.

Final judgment: After a settlement is reached, whether through mediation, divorce settlement with attorneys, or a divorce trial, a judge will sign the final divorce settlement or "order of dissolution" with the courts outlining the agreed-upon stipulations.

Changes to divorce documents: Once a final order is filed with the courts, a party may alter or change the divorce guidelines by filing a petition to alter the settlement with the courts. This often requires the same process outlined above: the party is served with the petition, they can offer a response, a settlement is reached, and a final judgment is ordered.

Gender and social inequalities impact access to, and experiences with divorce. Access to divorce is an important issue for gender equity (Yefet 2020, 794). Divorce remains a process that is easier to access for those in higher income brackets. The average cost of divorce is estimated to be around $15,000. There are calls for a reimagining of marriage as an institution to recognize the variation in desires and wishes for couples in the modern era (Carroll 2020, 478).

Elaina K. Behounek

See also: Child Custody; Parenting Plans and Custody Arrangements

Further Reading

Carroll, Mary Charlotte Y. 2020. "When Marriage Is Too Much: Reviving the Registered Partnership in a Diverse Society." *Yale Law Journal* no. 2: 478. https://search.ebscohost.com/login .aspx?direct=true&AuthType=ip,shib& db=edsgov&AN=edsgcl.649536411&site =eds-live&scope=site.

Centers for Disease Control. 2019. "Marriage, Divorce." https://www.cdc.gov /nchs/fastats/marriage-divorce.htm.

Grow, André, Christine Schnor, and Jan Van Bavel. 2017. "The Reversal of the Gender Gap in Education and Relative Divorce Risks: A Matter of Alternatives in Partner Choice?" *Population Studies* 71 (March): 15–34. doi:10.1080/00324728.2017.1371477.

Perry, Samuel L, and Cyrus Schleifer. 2018. "Till Porn Do Us Part? A Longitudinal Examination of Pornography Use and Divorce." *Journal of Sex Research* 55, no. 3: 284–296. doi:10.1080/00224499 .2017.1317709.

Potter, Marina Haddock. 2021. "Social Support and Divorce among American Couples." *Journal of Family Issues* 42, no. 1: 88–109. https://search.ebscohost .com/login.aspx?direct=true&AuthType =ip,shib&db=edb&AN=147312916&site =eds-live&scope=site.

Yefet, Karin, Carmit. 2020. "Divorce as a Formal Gender-Equality Right." *Journal of Constitutional Law* 22, no. 3: 793–834.

Divorce, Psychological Effects

Divorce can be defined as the termination of marriage through a legal procedure. The divorce rate in the United States is high. Specifically, 40–50% of all first marriages end in divorce and the divorce rate for second marriages is even higher (Stewart 2006). Divorce affects the psychological well-being of women, men, and children.

Depending on people's experiences, the divorce process can be a long and very stressful legal procedure. This process includes determining the distribution of property, division of debt, and child custody. Among other divorce procedures, those married with children experience a more complicated set of procedures.

Divorce is related to several emotional, behavioral, and social problems including anger, fear, worry, economic hardship, and loneliness (Pedro-Carroll 2005). These issues lead to psychological distress including depression, anxiety, hopelessness, feelings of isolation, lower life satisfaction, a weaker sense of personal control, and greater use of mental health services (Amato and Sobolewski 2001). Some of the reasons for experiencing poor psychological health can be losing social support, handling and the stressful divorce process, and financial concerns after divorce.

Marriage has several benefits for married couples and their children. Most research shows that married individuals are happier and healthier than unmarried people (Waite and Gallagher 2000). Married people, especially married women, often identify themselves as spouses or parents of their children. This situation is common among those with traditional values which promote marriage and family. When divorce happens, people change their marital identity (e.g., divorcee and single parent). These changes may have a big impact on people's perception of themselves and make the divorce process stressful. In some cases, women—especially economically-advantaged women—show better psychological outcomes than men. Specifically, if women experience greater marital dissatisfaction, they feel relieved after divorce. Moreover, women typically have more social ties than men so they can get more support and help from their friends and relatives. If women find new roles and engage in social activities after divorce, they may more readily cope with divorce stress and increase their self-esteem.

Furthermore, intact families typically have more household income than other family unions (e.g., single-parent households). Since two-parent families are in an economically advantaged position, their children demonstrate better social, economic, academic, and health outcomes (Amato and Sobolewski 2001). In contrast, many experience economic hardship after divorce, which leads to psychological distress.

Moreover, intact families provide strong social and emotional support to family members. Conversely, disruption of two-parent families can lead to poor family relationships (Demir-Dagdas et al. 2018). Thus, children who live in single-parent households through divorce or separation may have less parental support and less supervision. Recent research on parental divorce and social engagement demonstrates that parental divorce is associated with a decrease in attending social meetings

and religious services (Demir-Dagdas 2019). Thus, divorce has negative effects on both formal (e.g., meetings, religious attendance) and informal (e.g., family) social relationships. Because single parents are often more resource-poor (e.g., time and money), and they may not have social support from a spouse, they may have more negative psychological outcomes. However, many individuals balance their post-divorce lives by sharing a home with another family member, using grandparents (and especially grandmothers as an "other mother,") and/or still sharing economic responsibility with their ex-spouse for the children. In these cases, some of the stress of single parenthood is alleviated, and the children can benefit from more economic stability and a constant presence in the household. Continued contact with grandparents is a factor in psychological well-being post-divorce. For some children, the relationship between the paternal grandparents becomes less frequent and strong (Drentea 2019).

Previous research examining marital quality suggests that if married couples live with high marital problems and feel less satisfaction from their marriages, divorce has a less negative impact on their psychological well-being (Kalmijn and Monden 2006). Some marriages involve physical and verbal abuse, and people from poor marriages feel less distressed after marital dissolution. This is true, especially for women.

Classical divorce studies focus on the negative psychological effects of divorce on children. However, emerging research suggests that children suffer mental health issues including stress, depression, anxiety, and loneliness due to parental conflict pre-divorce. Family researchers view parental conflict and parental marital problems instead of divorce as the most critical mechanisms which determine children's adjustment after divorce (Kalmijn and Monden 2006). When divorced parents continue parental support and involvement, including effective communication with their children following divorce, their children do better after divorce and exhibit positive psychological well-being. Specifically, children's mental health in the divorce process depends on three factors: the quality of family relationships with both mothers and fathers before divorce or separation, the length of parental marital problems and conflict before divorce, and the quality of communication and parent-child relationships (e.g., support, contact) after divorce.

Boys and girls show different emotional reactions to their parent's divorce. Boys exhibit behavioral symptoms including anger, disappointment, and hurt so they may face problems in their social and personal lives. For example, they may fight with their friends. However, girls show psychological symptoms including depression, lack of sleep, and eating disorders. These mental health issues may lead to poor grades in school (Amato 2001).

Even in the United States, the context of divorce and marriage varies among different cultures. In traditional cultures, divorce is still unacceptable, and being a divorcee is considered embarrassing and disgraceful. This situation may affect the divorcee's social and psychological status in the long term. Moreover, some people think that divorce occurs between two married individuals. However, like marriage, divorce happens in people's communities, including friends and families. Thus, sometimes people who decide

to divorce have a difficult time sharing the news with their loved ones. Telling others may be beneficial to get support from the communities and overcome the negative psychological effects of divorce.

Taken together, divorce has negative effects on the psychological well-being of women, men, and children. However, if there is an unhappy marriage or high conflict between married couples, divorce may have a positive impact on mental health. It is important to account for some factors while examining the psychological effects of divorce, including gender, socioeconomic status, and cultural backgrounds of people who are involved.

Tuba Demir-Dagdas and Patricia Drentea

See also: Divorce, Causes/Risk Factors of; Divorce, Economic Consequences (Personal); Divorce, Economic Consequences (Taxpayers)

Further Reading

Amato, Paul R. 2001. "Children of divorce in the 1990s: An update of the Amato and Keith (1991) meta-analysis." *Journal of Family Psychology* 15, no. 3: 355–370.

Amato, Paul R., and Juliana M. Sobolewski. 2001. "The effects of divorce and marital discord on adult children's psychological well-being." *American Sociological Review* 66, no. 6: 900–921.

Demir-Dagdas, Tuba. 2019. "Parental divorce or separation during childhood and adult smoking: A mediation effects of social engagement." *Vulnerable Children and Youth Studies* 14, no. 3: 248–258.

Demir-Dagdas, Tuba, Zeynep Isik-Ercan, Seyma Intepe-Tingir, and Yasemin Cava-Tadik. 2018. "Parental divorce and children from diverse backgrounds: Multidisciplinary perspectives on mental health, parent–child relationships, and educational experiences." *Journal of Divorce & Remarriage* 59, no. 6: 469–485.

Drentea, Patricia. 2019. *Families and Aging*. Rowman & Littlefield.

Kalmijn, Matthijs, and Christiaan W. S. Monden. 2006. "Are the negative effects of divorce on well-being dependent on marital quality?" *Journal of Marriage and Family* 68, no. 5: 1197–1213.

Pedro-Carroll, JoAnne L. 2005. "Fostering resilience in the aftermath of divorce: The role of evidence-based programs for children." *Family Court Review* 43, no. 1: 52–64.

Stewart, Susan D. 2006. *Brave new stepfamilies: Diverse paths toward stepfamily living*. Sage Publications.

Waite, Linda J., and Maggie Gallagher. 2000. *The case for marriage: Why married people are happier, healthier, and better off financially*. New York: Doubleday.

Divorce, Stigma

Stigma is shame or embarrassment based on a perceived characteristic(s). Erving Goffman, a sociologist and social psychologist, transformed how scholars studied stigma. Drawing on Erving Goffman's (1922–1982) theory of stigma, stigmatization can be defined as "the condition of being denied full social acceptance" (Goffman 1963, 4). In 2013, Robert Emery, a professor of psychology and director of the Center for Children, Families, and the Law at the University of Virginia argued that most researchers use the dictionary definition, a "mark of disgrace" when describing stigma. However, there is no consensus regarding the definition of stigma, even though it remains to be a powerful negative attribute in social contexts.

There are many ways in which the stigma of divorce is seen (i.e., economical, legal, social, and emotional) as well as many studies that have examined its complexities. In the 20th century, sociologists began to speculate that divorce was the result of economic and social conditions and psychologists suggested it was the result of psychological problems (Clarke-Stewart and Brentano 2006). Due to its multidimensional nature, divorce can be described as more stressful in comparison to other life changes such as unemployment, chronic illness, and job change (Demo and Fine 2010). When examining the process of divorce, it needs to be viewed as separate from examining social groups. There are many contextual differences between individuals and families. Divorce is better understood as a complex and multidimensional process that unfolds over several years (Demo and Fine 2010). Regardless of the reason for divorce, individuals are susceptible to stigmatization and blame following the termination of the relationship (Gerstel 1987). In American culture, it is common for the institution of marriage to take place with the use of vows. These vows will typically involve a verbal and legal commitment to one another. When the decision is made to divorce a partner, this is often viewed as a failure to meet that commitment. In turn, the couple will be subject to social stigma for the perceived failure. In the United States, marriage is highly valued. Statistically, almost 90% of Americans eventually marry at some point in their lives (Demo and Fine 2010). Marriage is not only a commitment but an investment that comes with costs and rewards. Couples are more motivated to remain married when the rewards are higher than the costs and when a partner is contemplating divorce, one of the costs they must consider is a social stigma (Previtit and Amato 2003).

The circumstances of the divorce, rather than the divorce itself, are now most often the subject of disapproval (Gerstel 1987). It is important to note that families are dynamic and change over time and there has been a paradigm shift in the nuclear family. The variation in family life has increased significantly in the United States (Gerstel 1987). More couples are accomplishing certain life transitions such as having children and establishing careers before they are married. Historically, marriage was a decision made within a religious context, and divorce was considered an immoral act against that commitment. Divorce is now a personal decision based on societal, familial, and cultural influences rather than one influenced by religious affiliation, the legislature, or the spouse. In more recent generations, the idea of marriage has evolved to include approaches of personal choice and fulfillment rather than religious affiliation. This, in turn, has shifted the stigma of divorce. In the last decade, stigma has been understood more within the context of psychological, social, and emotional contexts. There is also a set of gender-based beliefs when it comes to the divorce process. Specific disapproval is associated with gender and the stigma attached to divorce. One study that has explored the experiences of divorce-related stigma has identified five ways in which young adult women experience stigma following divorce: (1) self-stigma versus public stigma; (2) failure, embarrassment, and perceptions of blame; (3) religion and stigma; (4) nondisclosure and impression management; and (5) contextual considerations (Konstam et al. 2016, 173). For men who engaged in an affair before divorce and for women who had children before the divorce, they were more likely to receive disapproval (Gerstel 1987). Those in the process of getting a divorce or those who were divorced also found themselves alienated from part or all of mutual friend groups. They were no longer respected as a person but rather viewed through the lens of what they were working through in their personal life. For both men and women, many people in their current and former friend groups felt threatened by the fact they were newly single and sexually available. Individuals who are divorced are also more likely to lose other coupled or married friends for fear that the divorce will act as a disease by influencing their spouse to cheat or to leave them for other reasons like personal dissatisfaction with the relationship (Gerstel 1987). However, women are still more likely to be subject to stigmatization following divorce due to cultural influences such as patriarchy (Sievens 2004). Patriarchy is directed by men's central power and their control of property and has significantly shifted attitudes toward the sexes following divorce (Moghadam 2004). During a divorce, a woman can be described as the property of her husband. The patriarchal culture emphasizes a woman's virginity as well as her role in being a mother within the family (i.e., having children, caregiving) and a beneficiary of property. When a woman cannot meet societal qualifications, such as procreating, she is more likely to be socially stigmatized. These characteristics of a patriarchal society then formulate further disapproving attitudes towards women following divorce (Boostani, Abdinia, and Anaraki 2013).

Even though divorce is more accepted than in previous decades, it continues to be stigmatized. Research on stigma shows that individuals will work to hide the negative attributes to protect themselves from negative effects (Emery 2013). However, individuals eventually develop resiliency skills to cope with the impact of stigmatization. Although individuals develop resiliency skills, it is unclear whether the impacts of stigmatization related to divorce persist (Konstam et al. 2016).

Audrey Besch and Kwangman Ko

See also: Divorce, Causes/Risk Factors of; Divorce, No-Fault and Fault-Based; Divorce Pre-1950; Divorce 1950–2000

Further Reading

Boostani, Dariush, Abdinia, Shokofeh, and Anaraki, Nahid. 2013. "Women victims of self-immolation: A 'Grounded Theory' study in Iran. Quality & Quantity." *International Journal of Methodology* 47, no. 6: 3153–3165.

Clarke-Stewart, Alison, and Brentano, Cornelia. 2006. *Divorce causes and consequences.* New Haven and London: Yale University Press, pp. 1–28.

Demo, David and Fine, Mark. 2010. *Beyond the average divorce.* Thousand Oaks, CA: Sage Publications.

Emery, Robert. 2013. *Cultural Sociology of Divorce: An Encyclopedia.* Thousand Oaks, CA: Sage Publications.

Gerstel, Naomi. 1987. "Divorce and Stigma." *Social Problems* 172–186.

Goffman, Erving. 1963. *Stigma: Notes on theIt of spoiled identity.* New York, NY: Simon & Schuster.

Konstam, Varda, Karwin, Samantha, Curran, Teyana, Lyons, Meaghan, and Celen-Demirtas, Selda. 2016. "Stigma and Divorce: A relevent lens for emerging and young adult women?" *Journal of Divorce & Remarriage* 57, no. 3: 173–194. http://dx.doi.org/10.1080/10502556.2016.1150149.

Moghadam, V. 2004. "Patriarchy in transition: Women and the changing family in the Middle East." *Journal of Comparative Family Studies* 35, no. 2: 137–162.

Previtit, Denise and Amato, Paul. 2003. "Why stay married? Rewards, barriers, and marital stability." *Journal of Marriage and Family* 561–573. https://doi.org/10.1111/j.1741-3737.2003.00561.x.

Sievens, Mary. 2004. "Divorce, patriarchal authority, and masculinity: A case from early national Vermont." *Journal of Social History* 37, no. 3: 651–661.

Divorce, Types of

Marriage and divorce are both common experiences. Marriage is a relationship affected by various influences at different times. Some marriages end abruptly, others linger, contingent on the prior nature of the relationship, emotional volatility and tumultuous dealings within the marriage, potential for reconciliation, situational constraints, or prolonged legal battles to end the marriage (Fine and Harvey 2006). Generally, divorce is treated as a dichotomous event in which the marriage is either still intact or terminated. Yet, the progression from encountering an unsatisfactory marriage to divorce is neither uniform across couples nor totally idiosyncratic. Divorce is a dynamic, and complex array of experiences that are as diverse as those that lead to marriage.). Marital dissolution is characterized by many physiological responses, cognitive appraisals, mood states, various life changes, and personal adjustments.

Many consider divorce a single event; the outcome of sequential, orderly stages or phases spouses go through as they terminate their relationships. For example, Bohannon (1971) suggested one of the earliest models with six stages of divorce, beginning with the *emotional* and moving through the *legal, economic, coparental, community*, and finally *psychic* stations. Another significant model is proposed by Kessler (1975) in seven stages—*disillusionment, erosion, detachment, physical separation, mourning, second adolescence*, and *hard work*—model. Kessler's model differs from Bohannan in that it begins its analysis at an earlier point in the process of marital dissolution. Another five-stage model developed by Knapp (1978) consists of *differentiating, circumscribing, stagnating, avoiding*, and *terminating*.

While a legal event occurs when a decree of marital dissolution is signed, the divorce process commences earlier when one or both spouses begin to experience thoughts and feelings which may include disillusionment and dissatisfaction with the marital relationship. Kaslow and Schwartz (1987) developed a dialectic model with seven stages. The first or *emotional* stage begins when either one or both spouses recognize significant discontent with the marital relationship. During stage two (or *legal* stage), either one or both spouses instigates legal action and consults an attorney/mediator. Either one or both spouses may be unable to leave an unhappy and unfulfilling marriage during the *economic*, or third, stage due to financial insecurity and instability. Child custody, *coparenting*, and issues related to contact with children comprise stage four. As with the economic and coparenting stages, the *social* and community

stage starts early and continues beyond the legal divorce. Individuals find the support and empathy given by those concerned family and friends extremely helpful. Stage six (or *religious* divorce) includes specified rituals and ceremonies that adherents of certain religious groups are obliged to undergo in addition to a civil divorce. The final stage involves *psychic* divorce in which former spouses endeavor to reestablish their lives in new and more meaningful ways.

The topography of the divorce process was developed by Duck (1982). Marital dissolution adhered to a four-phase—*intrapsychic, dyadic, social*, and *grave-dressing*—structure. During the *intrapsychic* phase, spouses grapple with significant marital dissatisfaction that jeopardizes the continuity of the relationship. Spouses negotiate the possibility of dissolution with the partner during the second (or *dyadic*) phase. The third (or *social)* phase involves public awareness of the imminent divorce. Finally, *grave dressing* focuses on retrospection about, and recovery from the termination of the marriage. The postulation of steps or stages of divorce offers a useful conceptualization. Although previous efforts to conceptualize stages have provided some theoretically compelling ideas, sequential stage models fail to fully comprehend the complexity of the divorce process.

The view of the divorce process as unidimensional by suggesting stages is overly simplistic. Current systematic accounts of the divorce process have stressed a multidimensional process. A sound understanding of the divorce process must attend to the nature and course in which individual, dyadic, social, and circumstantial factors may all be involved. Yet, little attention is given to what takes place between individuals or couples during the divorce process.

Several typologies support divorce as a multifaceted process that unfolds over time. Kressel, Jaffee, Tuchman, Watson, and Deutsch (1980) recorded mediation sessions and post-divorce interviews with both former spouses. Four distinct patterns—*enmeshed, autocratic, direct-conflict*, and *disengaged*—separated divorcing couples by communication patterns, ambivalence, and conflict. Hagestad and Smyer (1982) derived patterns in an exploratory study of divorce in long-term marriages. The former husbands and wives provided marked contrasts in describing their divorce experiences. These divorces were characterized as orderly or disorderly based on the spouse's attachment to either marital roles, former spouses, or shared marital routines, the amount of personal control over the process, and the time available to adjust to the marital termination. Both studies employed primarily intuitive rather than empirical methods to derive their typologies. Given the description and small sample size, findings can only be suggestive of what takes place as spouses move toward divorce.

Systematic empirical evidence of the patterned differences is limited. Little is known about the patterned differences between spouses or couples as they move toward divorce. Lee (1984) combined stages and process views in a five-scenario model. Scenarios were specified by the stage, actor(s), content of issues/terms, and time between stages. Four types based on spouses moving through five stages—*Discovery of Dissatisfaction, Exposure, Negotiation, Resolution*, and *Transformation*—were noted. The

simple type was defined in that all stages occurred. *Omission* types were those in which some stages were skipped. The *Extension* type occurred when different features are exposed gradually and discussed over an extended period or when one decision is enacted and then a different one replaces it before terminating. Finally, *Mixed* types include combinations of the above types and usually produce a tortuous ending.

Most past research focused on individual factors associated with divorce. Vannoy (1996) created a paradigm that combines various roles to identify four types of divorce circumstances (the abandonment, the set-up, the escape, and the release). Eight divorce trajectories described by Baxter (1984) based on six features: (1) sudden/gradual onset; (2) unilateral/bilateral; (3) direct/indirect; (4) rapid/ extended; (5) presence/absence of repair attempts; and (6) termination/continuation. *Persevering Indirectness* was the most common dissolution trajectory. It was unilateral and indirect, with no attempted relationship repairs during an extended trajectory. Two additional types followed. *Ambivalent Indirectness* was unilateral, indirect, and delayed with attempted repair, before termination. The other, *Swift Explicit Mutuality*, was bilateral and direct, rapid with no attempted repairs with termination achieved on the first attempt. The next two types were labeled *Swift Indirectness* and *Swift Implicit Mutuality*. Swift Indirectness was unilateral and indirect, with no attempted repair and termination with the first disengagement action. Swift Implicit Mutuality had no attempted repairs, with termination through bilateral indirect action. The last two were *Ambivalent Directness* and

Swift Directness. Ambivalent Directness moved to termination after unilateral and direct actions were offset with an unsuccessful repair attempt and further disengagement action. *Swift Directness* involved unilateral and direct which readily accomplished termination.

The intercouple variations in the experience of divorce are amenable to the grouping into a limited number of distinct types. Various types of divorce capture the underlying coherence with the variety of couple dimensions. Ponzetti and Cate (2008) empirically identified three types of trajectories to marital dissolution. Rapid, gradual, and extended pattern types were discerned by the distinct properties evident in trajectories to marital termination. The rapid type proceeded to divorce quickly and deliberately. Extended types exhibited a longer time frame and more indecision about divorce characterized by several reconciliations before the final dissolution. Gradual types were moderate relative to the other two types. Select relationship dimensions changed as individuals progressed through the divorce process. Types were differentiated by the attributions of turning points that occurred during the divorce process. Interestingly, types did not differ from one another on select relationship dimensions—love, conflict, maintenance, ambivalence, trust, marital satisfaction, and perception of alternatives to the relationship—which were the basis for other typologies.

Although divorce can be an experience of growth and positive change for some, it is a time of stress, disruption, and uncertainty for others. However, an escalation of negative emotions and interactions need not transpire without an understanding of the powerful dynamics of the divorce process. Divorce is not a dichotomous event, rather it is characterized by distinct types as a multidimensional process. Various types of divorce are indicative of the inherent diversity in the process of ending marital relationships. The path or progression to divorce is distinguished by individual, dyadic, social, circumstantial, and the combination of these factors.

James J. Ponzetti, Jr.

See also: Divorce, Process of; Divorce Coaching; Divorce Education

Further Reading

Baxter, Leslie. 1984. "Trajectories of Relationship Disengagement." *Journal of Social and Personal Relationship*, 1, no. 1 (March): 29–48. https://doi.org/10.1177/0265407584011003

Bohannon, Paul (Ed.). 1971. *Divorce and After*. New York: Doubleday.

Duck, Steve. 1982. "A Topography of Relationship Disengagement and Dissolution." In Steve Duck (Ed.), *Personal Relationships, vol. 4: Dissolving Personal Relationships*. London: Academic Press, pp. 1–29.

Fine, Mark, and Harvey, John (Eds.). 2006. *Handbook of Divorce and Relationship Dissolution*. Mahwah, NJ: Lawrence Erlbaum Associates.

Hagestad, Gunhild, and Smyer, Michael. 1982. "Dissolving Long-term Relationships: Patterns of Divorcing in Middle Age." In Steve Duck (Ed.), *Personal Relationships, vol. 4: Dissolving Personal Relationships*. London: Academic Press, pp. 155–188.

Kaslow, Florence, and Schwartz, Lita. 1987. *The Dynamics of Divorce: A Life Cycle Perspective*. Philadelphia: Brunner/Mazel.

Kessler, Sheila. 1975. *The American Way of Divorce: Prescriptions for Change*. Chicago: Nelson Hall.

Knapp, Mark. 1978. *Social Intercourse: From Greeting to Goodbye*. Boston: Allyn and Bacon.

Kressel, Kenneth, Jaffee, Nancy, Tuchman, Bruce, Watson, Carol, and Deutsch, Morton. 1980. "A Typology of Divorcing Couples: Implications for Mediation and the Divorce Process." *Family Process*, 19, no. 2(June): 101–116. https://doi.org/10.1111/j.1545-5300.1980.00101.x

Lee, L. 1984. "Sequences in Separation: A Framework for Investigating Endings of the Personal (Romantic) Relationship." *Journal of Social and Personal Relationships*, 1, no. 1 (March): 49–73. https://doi.org/10.1177/0265407584011004

Ponzetti, James, and Cate, Rodney. 2008. "The Divorce Process: Toward a Typology of Marital Dissolution." *Journal of Divorce*, 11, no. 3 (October): 1–20. https://doi.org/10.1300/J279v11n03_01

Vannoy, Dana. 1996. "A Paradigm of Roles in the Divorce Process." *Journal of Divorce & Remarriage*, 24, no. 3: 71–88. https://doi: 10.1300/J087v24n03_05

Divorce and Incarceration

There are several ways to look at the topic of incarceration and divorce. From one perspective, someone may go through a bitter divorce and, ultimately, make a poor decision that results in incarceration. Another may watch their marriage fall apart as a result of their or their spouse's incarceration. The fact that a growing number of people in prisons are afflicted with some form of mental illness—either before or as a result of incarceration—can also influence marital decisions and outcomes. Also, the old cliché of "out of sight, out of mind" plays a significant role in failed marriages due to incarceration. If one spouse is placed at a prison several hours from home, it

may cause such a burden on the other spouse to visit, that the couple grows apart. Telephone calls are quite expensive, and it is generally accepted that many people with criminal records come from lower socioeconomic backgrounds, so even telephone calls can be an economic hardship. House finances, particularly if there are children involved, fall on the unincarcerated spouse completely, which is sometimes impossible for one person to handle alone. Finally, many things impact the success of a marriage, including, but not limited to, socioeconomic background, criminal friends, and age of the offender/marriage partner.

Research shows that incarceration and divorce are positively related, meaning that when one spouse is incarcerated, the likelihood of divorce increases. That likelihood increases with each year of incarceration and does not disappear when that person is released. In fact, the marriage can still fail after release, possibly due to the strain put upon the marriage during the incarceration and how much the two partners grow and change during that period (Siennick, Stewart, and Staff 2014, 4–5). Conversely, people are less likely to become incarcerated if they are already married since married couples tend to spend less time with unattached young people engaged in impulsive, and sometimes criminogenic, behaviors.

It is possible to not only get married while incarcerated but also to get divorced. Pursuing a divorce may be a little harder if the person seeking the divorce is incarcerated due to a lack of financial resources and power to appear in divorce court, but it is possible. Ease will vary with state laws governing the procedures for divorce. For example, some states have no-fault divorces where no verifiable reason must be stated for the divorce to be finalized. Others may require at least a statement of irreconcilable differences. In some states, though, incarceration is grounds for divorce regardless of other factors.

Massoglia, Remster, and King (2011, 147) compared marriages of military personnel to marriages of incarcerated individuals in an attempt to determine if the stigma of incarceration was to blame for the failure of the marriages. Their findings indicate, however, that stigma is less influential on marital outcomes than simple physical separation, though it does still exert influence on the marriage. The stigma variable seems to exert more influence through other contextual issues, though, including the difficulty of finding employment after incarceration putting financial strain on the marriage, more so than the idea of being married to an "excon" (Massoglia, Remster, and King 2011, 148). To add to the stress of separation and stigma, others have found, "that incarcerations occurring during marriage are associated with less love between spouses, more marital violence, and greater odds of extramarital sex . . ." (Siennick, Steward, and Staff 2014, 390). This seems to imply the possibility that those who are prone to criminogenic behavior are also prone to poorly planned marriages, though that is unclear from the extant research.

Another factor that could add to the financial strain discussed above is children. Incarcerated parents cannot financially provide for their children due to a lack of income (Turney, Schnittker, and Wildeman 2012, 1161). Also, women who had children with recently incarcerated men have reported less financial support from the men, resulting in greater strain on the mother as sole provider (Turney,

Schnittker, and Wildeman 2012, 1159). These men, in either case, may have a difficult time forming emotional bonds with those children as well, due to lingering psychological effects of incarceration or due to not being around the children during important developmental stages.

Further, those who do not marry before incarceration may face a completely different set of issues. Criminology literature supports that marriage helps prevent criminogenic behaviors, and, thus, incarceration. Once someone has been incarcerated and released, though, they may not have access to the same pool of marriage partners as someone without a prison record. This can result in marriage to someone who is equally at risk for incarceration as the released felon, which can lead to several things: incarceration/reincarceration of one or both spouses causing strain on the marriage, financial strain as discussed above, and simply different lifestyle choices and behaviors in one or both partners (Apel et al. 2010, 290–291).

Also of note is the impact that incarceration has on marriage and divorce in the Black American community. Increasing incarceration rates over the last several decades, particularly of Black males due to sentencing enhancements and institutional racism, has led to an increase in single-parent, female-headed households in many urban, Black American communities (Lopoo and Western 2005, 731–732). It is hard to distinguish, though, whether divorce rates are increased due largely in part to incarceration or backgrounds in low socioeconomic areas, because both groups tend to marry less and for shorter periods, regardless of race.

It is exceedingly difficult to give a definitive reason for marriages failing in conjunction with incarceration because there are so many influencing variables that picking out just one reason is nearly impossible. There are some things that research clearly lays out, though, regarding the connection between divorce and incarceration. The stigma attached to the "ex-con" is, perhaps, the most negligible, while financial strain and physical separation appear to influence the decision to divorce more heavily. Also, trajectory along the life course leads to the idea that marriage can help prevent incarceration or vice versa, and the social contexts in which people find themselves before or after incarceration may not be conducive to securing a healthy marriage. As with most social sciences, the answer is that many things may connect divorce and incarceration.

Jennifer M. Miller

See also: Child Custody; Coparenting and Divorce; Incarceration, Coparenting and; Marriage and Incarceration

Further Reading
Apel, Robert, Arjan A. J. Blokland, Paul Nieuwbeerta, and Marieke van Schellen. 2010. "The Impact of Imprisonment on Marriage and Divorce: A Risk Set Matching Approach." *Journal of Quantitative Criminology* 26: 269–300.

Lopoo, Leonard M. and Bruce Western. 2005. "Incarceration and the Formation and Stability of Marital Unions." *Journal of Marriage and Family* 67, no. 3: 721–734.

Massoglia, Michael, Brianna Remster, and Ryan D. King. 2011. "Stigma or Separation? Understanding the Incarceration-Divorce Relationship." *Social Forces* 90, no. 1: 133–156.

Siennick, Sonja E., Eric A. Stewart, and Jeremy Staff. 2014. "Explaining the Association between Incarceration and Divorce." *Criminology* 52, no. 3: 371–398.

Turney, Kristin, Jason Schnittker, and Christopher Wildeman. 2012. "Those They Leave Behind: Paternal Incarceration and Maternal Instrumental Support." *Journal of Marriage and Family* 74, no. 5: 1149–1165.

Divorce and Legal Planning

Although difficult and often painful, divorce may be the best possible action for many situations. Divorcing couples who can intentionally plan for post-divorce logistics may reduce the potential negative impacts of divorce on families. Legal end-of-marriage planning topics include child custody, child support, alimony, and property division. These topics and other relevant matters are included in the divorce decree, a document that both spouses sign and become a legally binding agreement. Lawyers can be hired to assist spouses with the complexities of paperwork and litigation. However, a divorce action does not require expensive legal counsel when divorcing couples can negotiate the legal terrain on their own. A collaborative divorce involves some measure of legal counsel but without an expensive and often adversarial (petitioner vs. respondent) arrangement (Van Oorschot 2008). Mediation is also an option that involves a third party who assists both parties in exploring options and discovering resolutions. Monetary and sentimental value issues often make the end of marriage difficult to navigate. The goal is to grant each spouse an equitable division of child access, financial support, and shared property.

Spousal Maintenance

Alimony, or spousal support, is monetary support awarded to supplement or assist in creating a similar lifestyle that was experienced in marriage (Murray 2014). Alimony also serves to compensate for the contributions in time, effort, and money the supported spouse gave to their partner in the course of their union. Alimony can be paid in large sums at the beginning of a divorce or distributed over many years (Murray 2014). This support is often terminated in the event the supported spouse remarries, the youngest child turns 18 years old, or for a variety of other reasons that can be defined in the divorce decree.

Property Distribution

Property distribution does not necessarily involve a 50/50 split. A judge may define what is equitable based on factors such as a spouse's financial contribution to the union, their current economic situation, how long the marriage endured, and the pre-marital economics of each party (Van Oorschot 2008).

Property to be divided includes pensions, retirement benefits, stocks, 401(k)s, equity in any business operated together, equipment, inventory, accounts receivable, professional degrees (in some states), real estate property, household items, financial accounts, vehicles, animals, firearms, etc. The retainment of a variety of legal counsel and other professional service providers may include, real estate, pension, business, and accounting legal counselors, as well as a family law expert.

Child Custody

In terms of child custody issues, the two major factors are physical custody and legal custody. Physical custody defines where the child lives and how the time between parents is to be shared. These details in the divorce decree extend to how parents are to handle weekends, evenings, and holidays. Legal custody refers to education, medical decisions, and other important issues (Van Oorschot 2008). In high-conflict divorces, custody plans are often made by the services of the court. Child custody evaluators (or mediators) are sometimes required to examine the plethora of considerations involved and even make recommendations to the judge as to the fitness of parents and/or their living arrangements and how those details will affect the children involved (Kushner 2008).

Physical custody and legal custody can be individual ("sole") or shared ("joint"). Custody is determined by looking at the best interest of the children. It is recommended that each party keep calendars of time spent with children. This may become helpful to avoid "he said, she said" dynamics. It is also important that communication between parties happen through e-mail for any legal purpose in the future (Van Oorschot 2008).

Child Support

Child support intends to divide the costs of caring for children and their physical needs. Child support is the financial support that is usually paid by the noncustodial parent. These payments are usually paid monthly and a schedule of parent time, and how many overnights, are calculated to determine the amount of support that is owed. Each state has an online child support calculator that determines how much a parent is owed or owes. If a parent is unwilling to voluntarily fulfill their fiduciary responsibilities inherent to the raising of their offspring, many states offer a formal recovery service to assist the parent that is receiving support. This may include the garnishment of wages, tax returns, etc. (Vogel 2020).

Planning for divorce can be instrumental in protecting the financial and emotional future of children and couples affected by divorce. It is important to understand that a divorce decree can be modified post-divorce as needed. This is usually done 6 months to 3 years after the divorce (state timelines are different). One party or both may contact the court and submit modification petitions. States require certain changes to have been met before they will grant the case to be modified. The petitions can be submitted as often as circumstances change or arise, and this does not guarantee that the judge will grant the change. Issues that may need to be revisited are changes in income, earning potential, etc., and some of the issues that the parties were facing at the time of the divorce may no longer be relevant. If either person in the divorce party wishes to modify a judgment, and they are successful, a new agreement through a court order will be issued (Schrodt et al. 2006).

Melissa Barton, Michael Anderson, and Todd Spencer

See also: Division of Assets; Spousal Support

Further Reading

Amendt, G. 2017. "Hidden perspectives in the discourse of divorce." *New Male Studies*, 6, no. (2): 90–108.

Cohen, O., Dattner, N., and Luxenburg, A. 1996. "Planning parenthood in the divorce transition—through mediation." *American Journal of Family Therapy*, 24, no. (2): 181–188.

Kushner, M. A. 2008. "Contextual slippage: A detriment to child custody planning." *Journal of Child Custody*, 5, no. (3/4): 276–298.

Murray, M. 2014. "Alimony as an equalizing force in divorce." *Journal of Contemporary Legal Issues*, 22: 3–9.

Quinn, T. S., and Dancer, W. T. 1998. "Poor divorce planning can be costly." *Journal of Accountancy*, 185, no. (5): 83.

Schrodt, P., Baxter, L. A., McBride, M. C., Braithwaite, D. O., and Fine, M. A. 2006. "The divorce decree, communication, and the structuration of coparenting relationships in stepfamilies." *Journal of Social & Personal Relationships*, 23, no. (5): 741–759.

Van Oorschot, M. 2008. "Planning for your divorce . . . and your next marriage." *GPSolo*, 25, no. (7): 34–39.

Vogel, L. K. 2020. "Help me help you: Identifying and addressing barriers to child support compliance." *Children and Youth Services Review*, 110.

Divorce Coaching

During a divorce, families are often in a vulnerable state and have fears and anxiety about their unknown future (Herman 2007, 273). Some of these fears may include the fear of losing financial stability, having less time with their children, or losing cherished possessions such as family homes. These worries can make it difficult to communicate effectively and make clear judgments that will dictate future arrangements. A growing trend for families experiencing divorce or family law modifications is to hire a divorce coach. Divorce coaches work with clients to help them reach client-identified goals and are one of the many coaching subgroups that fall under the umbrella of family life coaching. The field of family life coaching is solution-focused, and likewise, a divorce coach facilitates a solution-focused environment for learning, growth, and helping the client plan and create positive change. Divorce coaching emerged in the early 1990s as a field that helps families successfully transition from one household to two, and it promotes healthy relationship habits that the families can take with them once the divorce is complete.

While a standard training system for all coaches is not yet available, most divorce coaches bring a unique set of skills that allows them to work with clients to help them communicate effectively and create arrangements that meet the needs of the whole family. The unique set of skills that divorce coaches acquire through their training include standard coaching skills as well as communication and family law-specific skills. Coaching skills include active listening, asking powerful questions, paraphrasing and summarizing, and giving and receiving feedback (Oti 2017, 350–351). In addition to their coach-specific knowledge, divorce coaches are expected to know and even have prior experience in industries such as family science, mental health, family law, and finance, among others (Dalton 2017, 32–33). The coach's additional expertise

can add extra value for their clients as they navigate specific issues such as their children's developmental needs, splitting assets, and financial planning.

There is no standard divorce coaching session as divorce coaches work directly with the clients, they serve to help them meet unique goals set by the client and are often dictated by external factors such as property, location, number of children, etc. Even though the topics and issues may vary, the process for coaching is specific. During each session, the divorce coach will use their expertise to aid the client in setting goals, encouraging deeper thinking and problem solving by asking open-ended questions. It is not within the parameters of the divorce coaches' role to give their clients general advice. Instead, divorce coaches ask powerful questions in a way that will help their clients create solutions that best suit his or her familial needs. There is, however, an exception to the "no advice" rule. If a divorce coach is also an expert in a relevant field such as family science or finance, the coach may ask the client if they would be interested in hearing about research or best practices that relate to the client's particular situation. The coach may share insights if and when the client asks or gives permission. This process ensures that the client is seen as the expert in their family life, but that the coach can also bring content expertise.

Divorce coaching most commonly occurs in two settings, collaborative law, and litigation. Collaborative law is a process in which divorce negotiations occur outside of the court while attorneys lead the negotiations. This process involves a team of additional specialists including divorce coaches, a financial neutral, and a child specialist. The process relies on full transparency and collaboration from all parties (Alba-Fisch 2016). Different from collaborative law, traditional litigation involves the court system, and family law attorneys, and may at times include divorce coaches and financial and child specialists to support the clients. Less common but also a growing industry is the use of divorce coaches in mediation; divorce coaches do support clients that are going through mediation, a process facilitated by a neutral mediator.

Clients may find divorce coaches through a referral from an attorney or another professional, or clients may decide to seek support from a divorce coach on their own (Robinson 2016, 196–197). Attorneys often become more involved in emotionally stabilizing their clients than makes sense for the parameters of their work, and because of this, it may be more effective to have a specialist support the client in this capacity. Once the client receives support from a divorce coach, attorneys can better focus their attention on the legal aspects of the divorce, creating an overall smoother process.

As with any process, there are advantages to hiring a divorce coach. One of the advantages that appeal to many clients is that coaching has less of a stigma than therapy (Robinson 2016, 444–457). Some clients view going to therapy as meaning something is wrong whereas coaching is more often seen as a positive process of goal setting and growth opportunity. Another advantage of divorce coaching is that the cost of hiring a divorce coach per hour is often less than what one would pay an attorney per hour. By appropriately utilizing a divorce coach's time as well as an attorney's time, clients could see an overall decrease in the amount they are billed.

Within the divorce coaching process, disadvantages are also present. While there are several training programs for coaching and divorce coaching, it is not a requirement that an individual is trained in the coaching process to call themselves a "divorce coach." It can be difficult for clients who are seeking support from a coach to differentiate between qualified and unqualified coaches. This also creates concern for attorneys who are looking to add divorce coaches to their team as they want to ensure whomever they add does not take away but adds to the effectiveness of the team. Some coaches do belong to a governing agency such as the International Coaching Federation and Center for Credentialing and Education, and each of these agencies has ethical guidelines that their coaches are expected to abide by. If the coach works within Collaborative Law, they will also be expected to abide by the ethical guidelines created by the International Academy of Collaborative Professionals.

Amber Harkey and Kimberly Allen

See also: Divorce, Process of; Divorce, Types of; Divorce Education

Further Reading

Alba-Fisch, Maria. 2016. "Collaborative Divorce: An Effort to Reduce the Damage of Divorce." *Journal of Clinical Psychology* 72, no. (5): 444–457.

Dalton, Elizabeth A. 2017. "Divorce and Co-Parent Coaching." *Utah Bar Journal* 30, no. (5): 32–33.

Herman, Gregg M. 2007. "Coaching, Not Therapy." *American Journal of Family Law* 21, no. (1): 273–274.

Oti, Janet. 2017. "An Introduction to Coaching Skills: A Practical Guide— Book Review." *International Journal of Mentoring and Coaching in Education* 6, no. (4): 350–351.

Robinson, Tamara Harris. 2016. "Understanding Divorce Coaches." *American Journal of Family Law* 29, no. (4): 193–197.

Divorce Education

Divorce education has become a common element in divorce proceedings for parents who have minor children and are seeking to dissolve their marital union. In a majority of states, participation in these programs has become court-mandated to receive an official divorce decree. The overarching goals of most divorce education programs include informing parents of the divorce process, sensitizing divorcing parties to the impact divorce can have on children, reducing negative conflict, promoting cooperative coparenting where possible, and helping parents and children make healthy adjustments throughout the separation and divorce process (Douglas 2006, 170–171).

In general, divorce education programs have been successful in meeting their short-term objectives, which pertain to increasing parental knowledge and awareness of divorce-related issues. The increase in court-mandated divorce education programs has resulted in widespread implementation that is characterized by a lack of standardization in terms of length, delivery methods, goals and objectives, content priorities, and cost for those participating. For instance, program frequency and length can vary from one session that may last as little as one hour, to multiple sessions lasting up to 12 hours. Delivery methods can also vary depending on the requirements of the state or municipality in which the divorce petition has been filed. Some states or municipalities may require traditional, face-to-face participation, while others may provide online or other interactive options. Costs also vary, both within and between states. While some programs are offered free of charge, others require relatively expensive fees, which may include the purchase of course materials.

The Divorce Education Intervention Model (Blaisure and Geasler 2000, 506–510) has accounted for the varying factors involved in divorce education in its three-level categorization of divorce education programs. With Level 1 programs, participation is more passive and programs are typically shorter in length. Level 2 programs are more focused on skill-building and often require multiple sessions. Families with special needs are commonly referred to as Level 3 programs, which may employ the services of trained professionals to address issues such as domestic violence.

With more states requiring divorce education, the courts that mandate participation in these programs have tended to favor shorter (or brief) divorce education programs. These brief programs, which tend to last four hours or less, account for the majority of all court-mandated divorce education programs (Fackrell, Hawkins, and Kay 2011, 115). The adoption of brief, court-mandated programs has coincided with the increased offering of online formats for divorce education. Advocates of online divorce education have highlighted the benefits of such a format for those required to participate, which include more convenient participation for parents living in remote areas and a more flexible schedule for program completion for parents dealing with childcare arrangements and rigid work schedules.

Research related to online divorce education programs has provided evidence of their effectiveness. For example, 2,584 parents who participated in an online divorce education program reported an improved understanding of divorce-related issues and intentions to practice positive coparenting (Turner et al. 2021, 179). Further, studies have shown that online divorce education programs are often as effective as traditional face-to-face programs (Schramm and McCaulley 2012, 602). Despite these findings, some remain skeptical of the ability of both brief and online divorce education programs to adequately cover the most crucial divorce-related issues that families typically face.

The most pressing issue related to the adoption of brief divorce education programs is the establishment of content priorities that remain consistent with the original goals of divorce education, which involves sensitizing parents to the ways divorce can impact children and the pivotal role that coparenting plays during family reorganization. In establishing content priorities, practitioners have applied the divorce-stress-adjustment model (Amato 2000, 1271–1273) to identify the topic areas most in need of attention for a divorce education program to achieve its intended outcomes (Schramm et al. 2018, 203–213). Through this theory driven-approach, child-centered topics, adult-centered topics, and supplemental and special topics, such as domestic abuse, were identified as the most critical primary, secondary, and tertiary topics to be covered in a typical divorce education program for parents.

With divorce rates remaining steady and the further adoption of brief divorce education programming, the reinforcement of research-based content priorities will be critical for the continued success of divorce education programs. Other priorities include the development of measures to gauge the long-term impacts of divorce education programming for participants and their families. It will also be important to gather feedback from participants as a way to assess participant utilization and program helpfulness, and inform practitioners and courts on ways divorce education programs can be strengthened.

Joshua Turner, Brian J. Higginbotham, and David G. Schramm

See also: Coparenting Typologies; Divorce, Process of; Divorce Coaching; Parent Education Programs

Further Reading

Amato, Paul R. 2000. "Consequences of divorce for adults and children." *Journal of Marriage and the Family* 62, no. 4: 1269–1287.

Blaisure, Karen R., and Margie J. Geasler. 2000. "The divorce education intervention model." *Family Court Review* 38, no. 4: 501–513.

Blaisure, Karen R., and Margie J. Geasler. 2006. "Educational interventions for separating and divorcing parents and their children." In *Handbook of Divorce and Relationship Dissolution*, edited by Mark A. Fine and John H. Harvey. Mahwah, NJ: Lawrence Erlbaum Associates, Inc., pp. 575–604.

Bowers, Jill R., Elissa Thomann Mitchell, Jennifer L. Hardesty, and Robert Hughes, Jr. 2011. "A review of online divorce education programs." *Family Court Review* 49, no. 4: 776–787.

Douglas, Emily M. 2006. *Mending broken families: Social policies for divorced families: How effective are they?* Lanham, MD: Rowman & Littlefield.

Fackrell, Tamera A., Alan J. Hawkins, and Nicole M. Kay. 2011. "How effective are court-affiliated divorcing parents education programs? A meta-analytic study." *Family Court Review* 49, no. 1: 107–119.

Mulroy, Maureen T., Jane Riffe, Denise Brandon, Yi-An Lo, and Harini Vaidyanath. 2013. "Serving the needs of separating and divorcing families: A national survey of Extension parenting education programs and resources." *Journal of Extension* 51, no. 2: Article 2FEA4.

Schramm, David G., Jeremy B. Kanter, Sean E. Brotherson, and Brooke Kranzler. 2018. "An empirically based framework for content selection and management in divorce education programs." *Journal of Divorce & Remarriage* 59, no. 3: 195–221.

Schramm, David G., and Graham McCaulley. 2012. "Divorce education for parents: A comparison of online and in-person delivery methods." *Journal of Divorce & Remarriage* 53, no. 3: 602–617.

Turner, Joshua, Olena Kopystynska, Kay Bradford, David G. Schramm, and Brian Higginbotham. 2021. "Evaluating perceived impact of Utah's online divorce education program." *Journal of Divorce and Remarriage* 62, no. 3: 179–198.

Divorce Initiation

The topic of divorce initiation is a growing area of interest among the general public as evidenced by recent publications in sources of popular media (e.g., *New York Times*, Huffington Post, *Men's Health*). Clinicians and researchers involved in issues related to marriage and divorce highlight the important implications of one's divorce initiation status (i.e., initiator versus non-initiator) for psychological well-being throughout the divorce process. Much of the existing research identifies divorce initiator status as a dichotomous classification (e.g., "leaver" versus "left") (Braver, Whitley, and Ng 1993). However, it is important to understand that divorce initiation is a complex, multifaceted construct.

Divorce is a twofold process typically preceded by a long period of marital deterioration in which both partners contribute to and experience distress. Therefore, it would follow that divorce initiator status is a complex psychological, social, and legal variable. Bohannon (1970) identified several categories, including subjective (e.g., emotional) and objective (e.g., legal) aspects of divorce initiation, and their effect on how divorcing couples identify. That is, a spouse may take the physical and legal steps toward ending the marriage (e.g., obtain a new residence and seek legal counsel), yet not perceive him or herself as responsible for the marital dissolution. As an example, a spouse who experiences physical abuse and manipulation by the other spouse may consequently believe there is no choice but to take the physical and legal steps toward ending the marriage. This spouse may take the physical steps toward divorce as a means of self-protection by moving out of their shared residence and hiring an attorney to assist with drafting and filing the necessary paperwork to initiate divorce proceedings. However, the subjective aspects of divorce that suggest *responsibility* for the deterioration of the marriage would likely be attributed to the abusive spouse.

This is only a single example that underscores the multifaceted nature of divorce initiation. It is a concept that extends beyond a clear "either/or" distinction and, as such, should be considered when reviewing the influence of initiator status on the divorce process in the extant literature.

Researchers have examined factors associated with initiator status as it relates to one's emotional well-being, psychological states, and post-divorce adjustment. Divorce occurs following some degree of planning by the spouse that can be classified as the *initiator* based on perceived provocation by the other spouse and/or a personal desire to dissolve the marriage. This spouse generally begins emotionally disengaging from his or her partner while he/she is still physically present. Contemplation about marital dissolution and the process of disengagement can begin for the initiator long before their partner is made aware. That is, the spouse that would typically be considered the *non-initiator* is characterized by having a reduced influence on the decision to dissolve the marriage. Furthermore, emotional disengagement generally does not begin for this partner until physical disengagement is initiated by his/her spouse. With these differing roles, it has been demonstrated that the spouse classified as the initiator generally has more feelings of control over the divorce process and a higher level of post-divorce adjustment. By contrast, the non-initiator often experiences higher levels of emotional and psychological distress and lower post-divorce adjustment. These trends tend to be the strongest in the first few years after separation. The available research has also demonstrated a greater likelihood for women to be divorce initiators. Research suggests this gender influence exists in part due to women having a greater role as the emotional barometer of the relationship. That is, women tend to be more aware of marital problems and, consequently, experience lower levels of relationship satisfaction as compared to their male counterparts (Baum 2003). However, a multidimensional assessment of divorce initiation contextualizes the above findings, making important contributions to ongoing research and clinical practice.

When considering how to assess this multifaceted construct in research and/ or clinical practice one should consider utilizing a measure that addresses the complex nature of divorce initiation. The Divorce Initiation Inventory (DII; Diamond and Parker 2018) is a five-item, continuous instrument developed to synthesize the various aspects of divorce initiation that have been highlighted throughout the literature. This is an alternative to relying on a single question to determine one's initiator status. In research, the DII can allow for a more thorough assessment of the various facets contributing to divorce initiation, and, in clinical practice, items can be used for a clinical assessment of the client's subjective experience of the dissolution process (Diamond and Parker 2018). Ultimately, the factors leading to martial dissolution, the decision to separate and legal actions are all aspects of the divorce process shown to influence post-divorce outcomes and should be considered in terms of divorce initiation.

Rachel M. Diamond and M.L. Parker

See also: Divorce, Process of; Divorce, Types of; Divorce Education

Further Reading

Baum, Nehami. 2003. "Divorce process variables and the co-parental relationship and parental role fulfillment of divorced parents." *Family Process* 42, no. (1): 117. DOI: 10.1111/j.1545-5300.2003.00117.x

Bohannon, Paul. 1970. "The six stations of divorce." In *Divorce and after: An analysis of the emotional and social problems of divorce.* New York: Doubleday, pp. 29–55.

Braver, Sanford L., Marnie Whitley, and Christine Ng. 1993. "Who divorced whom? Methodological and theoretical issues." *Journal of Divorce & Remarriage* 20, no. (1/2): 1–19.

Diamond, Rachel M. and M. L. Parker. 2018. "Development of the divorce initiation inventory." *Contemporary Family Therapy* 40, no. (4): 346–356. DOI: 10.1007/s10591-018-9463-0

Divorce Later in Life

Divorce among older adults (ages 50 and older) who have been married for a long time is referred to as divorce later in life or gray divorce. Although such divorce is not a new phenomenon, it has gained a great deal of attention due to its rapidly increasing rate. According to a recent report by the Pew Research Center (2017), the number of individuals who end up with divorce later in life per every 1,000 married individuals has doubled since the 1990s. Within the group, the divorce rate among individuals ages 65 and older has even more rapidly increased; it is about three times as high as that of the 1990s (Stepler 2017). The sharp rise in gray divorce clearly shows a different pattern than the divorce rates among younger adults: the divorce rate for adults aged 40–49 years has increased only 14% since 1990, whereas its rate for younger adults aged 25–39 years has decreased 21% since 1990 (Stepler 2017). Given that people live longer, marital dissolution among older adults will continue to be observed.

It has been known that various factors lead to divorce among older adults. In a qualitative investigation of marital disruptions, researchers found several reasons for gray divorce reported by study participants, such as flawed reasoning in the decision to marry, personal or spousal "baggage" brought to the marriage (e.g., emotional issues that preexisted before marriage), physical and emotional abuse, communication issues (e.g., dysfunctional communication), increase in perceived inequity in role and responsibility in the marital dyad, postponed divorce decision for various reasons (e.g., childrearing), and changes in spouse or self, and/or change in interests (Canham et al. 2014, 596). Health and caregiving issues that emerge later in life are also contributing factors to divorce (Penning and Wu 2019). In addition, some demographic characteristics are associated with gray divorce, such as minority status, less education, poorer health, and remarriage status (Brown, Lin, and Hammersmith 2015, 446).

Although divorce at any stage of life is stressful, gray divorce affects older adults in a particular way. Economic disadvantages are one of the consequences of divorce among these individuals. For example, marital dissolution among older adults was found to be associated with a significant loss of total wealth, defined as wealth components summed up less any debt (Sharma 2015, 301), which was worse for female divorcees than men and older divorcees than younger divorcees within the group. Loss of social support is also a significant consequence of divorce later in life. For example, researchers found that older adult divorcees reported they perceived decreased weekly contact with friends, as well as less social support from adult children and relatives (Glaser et al. 2006). The middle-generation parents and grandchildren often are actively involved in the process of grandparents' divorce and repartnering, feeling resentment towards the one who initiates or is responsible for the divorce (Chapman et al. 2018). In this case, divorced or divorcing grandparents are less likely to receive support from their offspring than those who remain married. Given that older adults are limited by their social networks and social activities, losing support from family members is particularly concerning. Finally, later-life divorce involves issues of inheritances, social security, pension and insurance plans, and caregiving (Dillon 2019), which may not be relevant to younger divorcees.

Although some older adults may remain single following divorce, the majority of them start dating relationships. Seeking dating partners among senior divorcees is different from younger adults or those who lost their spouse through widowhood. For example, the dating pool for older divorcees is much more limited than that of younger adults; social clubs, church, and online dating sites are where they conventionally meet their romantic partners due to their shrinking social networks (McWilliams and Barrett 2014, 421–423). Divorced older adults also seem more skeptical and critical about mate selection due to their past relationships and are possibly perceived as less desirable than those who have remained single or widows/widowers, which also means a smaller dating pool (McWilliams and Barrett 2014, 419). The dating pool for older female divorcees is even more limited by

gendered expectations and preferences. For example, men try to meet those who are younger and are eager to remarry sooner than women, while women seek companionship rather than potential partners for remarriage, not wanting to play a caregiver role that has burdened their lives once they were married and are more sensitive to their physical appearance than men (McWilliams and Barrett 2014, 422–428).

Dating relationships following gray divorce may prompt older adults to develop a stable union. Remarriage is one of the conventional ways of recoupling among them; the remarriage rate for divorcees aged between 55 and 64 was approximately 20% in 2015 (Huijing Wu 2017). Other older adults who previously married may choose alternatives to remarriage, such as cohabiting and Living Apart Together (LAT) relationships. Those who opt to engage in LAT relationships avoid possible negative consequences of remarriage or cohabitation (e.g., complexity in making a decision on pensions, inheritances, or other legal issues, less receipt of support from children), while taking advantage of this type of relationships (e.g., enjoying independence and companionship, less social stigma; Benson and Coleman 2016).

The rise of gray divorce is one of the most significant demographic changes in the United States. Older adults who divorce later in life face unique challenges and attribute their divorce to somewhat different factors compared to younger divorcees. Given that intergenerational ties and solidarity are more emphasized than ever before, how this phenomenon affects family relationships and intergenerational obligations are of great interest to policymakers and family researchers. As older adults experience multiple transitions in their romantic relationships (e.g., dating, cohabiting, LAT, remarriage) following gray divorce, intergenerational relationships and obligations may also be transformed.

Youngjin Kang

See also: Remarriage

Further Reading

Benson, Jacquelyn and Marilyn Coleman. 2016. "Older Adults Developing a Preference for Living Apart Together." *Journal of Marriage and Family*, 78, no. 3: 797–812. https://doi.org/ 10.1111/jomf.12292.

Brown, Susan, I-Feb Lin, and Anna M. Hammersmith. 2015. "Antecedents of Divorce in Later Life." *The Gerontologist*, 55, no. Suppl_2: 446–46. https://doi.org/10.1093/geront/gnv191.10.

Canham, Sarah, Atiya Mahmood, Sarah Stott, Judith Sixsmith, and Norm O'Rourke. 2014. "'Til Divorce Do Us Part: Marriage Dissolution in Later Life." *Journal of Divorce and Remarriage*, 55, no. 8: 591–612. https://doi.org/10.1080/10502556.2014.959097.

Chapman, Ashton, Youngjin Kang, Lawrence Ganong, Caroline Sanner, and Marilyn Coleman. 2018. "A Comparison of Stepgrandchildren's Perceptions of Long-Term and Later-Life Stepgrandparents." *Journal of Aging Studies*, 47: 104–113. doi:10.1016/j.jaging.2018.03.005.

Dillon, Joe. 2019. "Facing a Gray Divorce? Watch Out for These 7 Critical Issues." Accessed October 5, 2019. https://www.equitablemediation.com/blog/gray-divorce

Glaser, Karen, Cecilia Tomassini, Filomena Racioppi, and Rachel Stuchbury. 2006. "Marital Disruptions and Loss of Support in Later Life: A Longitudinal Study of the United Kingdom." *European Journal of Ageing: Social, Behavioral and Health Perspectives* 3, no. 4: 207–216. https://doi.org/10.1007/s10433-006-0036-y.

Huijing Wu. 2017. "Age Variation in the Remarriage Rate, 1990–2015." Family Profiles, FP-17-21. Bowling Green, OH: National Center for Family & Marriage Research. Accessed July 7, 2019. https://www.bgsu.edu/ncfmr/resources/data/family-profiles/wu-age-variation-remarriage-rate-1990-2015-fp-17-21.html

McWilliams, Summer and Anne E. Barrett. 2014. "Online Dating in Middle and Later Life: Gendered Expectations and Experiences." *Journal of Family Issues*, 35, no. 3: 411–436. doi:10.1177/0192513X12468437.

Penning, Margaret J. and Zheng Wu. 2019. "Caregiving and Union Instability in Middle and Later Life." *Journal of Marriage and Family*, 81, no. 1: 79–98. https://doi.org/10.1111/jomf.12534.

Sharma, Andy. 2015. "Divorce/Separation in Later-Life: A Fixed Effects Analysis of Economic Well-Being by Gender." *Journal of Family and Economic Issues*, 36, no. 2: 299–306. https://doi.org/10.1007/s10834-014-9432-1.

Stepler, Renee. 2017. "Led by Baby Boomers, Divorce Rates Climb for America's 50+ Population." Accessed July 5, 2019. https://www.pewresearch.org/fact-tank/2017/03/09/led-by-baby-boomers-divorce-rates-climb-for-americas-50-population/

Divorce Mediation

Mediation is the process by which divorce separation decisions are made between the two spouses and a neutral third party, as opposed to going through the court to settle a dispute. Most court systems have a mandated mediation process before the couple can go before a family court judge, as the dockets for family court are full. Generally, mediation covers topics such as the distribution of assets or distributions of liabilities, child custody, parenting time, child support, alimony, retirement, or taxes.

Mediation is a private process that allows the spouses to make decisions about their separation, unlike the process of divorce court, which is a public domain and where the judge makes the ultimate decision of how the couples' property, children, assets, and/or retirement are divided. The divorcing spouses may choose to see a mediator with or without a lawyer, but generally, no other parties are allowed in the room. Mediation is voluntary, where parties must agree to mediation and progress through the process willingly.

Eligibility

Some couples are not well suited for mediation. Couples who have a history of domestic violence, or the threat of violence, may not be well suited for mediation. Power differentials in the room may make the mediation more coerced. Some studies have found that the threat of violence or generalized fear is more detrimental to settling, whereas those with actual domestic violence have more success settling (Johnson and Leone 2005). Mediation with these couples can be successful, but careful screening and precautions by the mediator are necessary. For example, the couple may need to be seen in separate rooms, with the mediator going back and forth between the rooms when one side is exhibiting power over the other and may be stopped if someone is being coerced or abused in the room. Couples typically successful in mediation are those who know what they want to keep, have

some agreement already, or are willing to negotiate.

The Process

The mediation process begins when the couple or a family court judge finds a mediator. The mediator is generally someone who is neutral and has no ties to either spouse or their attorneys. Generally, the parties meet all together in one room. Occasionally, the mediator will caucus or meet with each spouse privately to ascertain the power in the room, comfort level, individual goals or priorities, or because the lawyers are being difficult. The first step the mediator usually takes is to eliminate those items which can simply be decided. For example, each spouse is most likely keeping their cars, and children may be staying in the same school or the same activities. This allows the couple to see that there is already agreement on some issues and decreases the time that is needed to negotiate more difficult issues. Next, each spouse usually gets an opportunity to state their priorities for mediation. Once the mediator has heard the list of things each spouse feels needs to be discussed, they can decide which item to discuss first. Each item is discussed, and the couple decides how that item will be handled. The spouses may or may not agree on the item. When they cannot reach an agreement, the mediator will negotiate then with the couple, help brainstorm solutions, or move on to another item. The couple may have home/property, child custody, or retirement account decisions that require more time and be governed by laws surrounding how they are handled. The mediator must have some knowledge of these issues, but often lawyers are present to discuss any laws that govern mediated decisions. The mediator may have agreement on all, some, or just a few items that the couple wanted to have mediated. At the end of the mediation session, if all the issues have not been decided upon, the spouses may choose to have another attempt or to be done with the mediation. If no decisions are made, the mediator may call an impasse. All parties usually sign a note that documents the agreements determined. The mediator, or one of the lawyers, then will write up a more formal agreement that is then signed and submitted to the judge. The judge usually accepts the mediated agreement, but still holds ultimate authority if necessary.

Mediation can be much less expensive than court costs. Usually, the mediator requires a retainer ($200–250), that may apply toward the first hour, and then a $150 per hour average, every additional hour. Mediation allows the spouses to have some control over the decisions made about the division of property. Participants in mediation find that they save money on attorney's fees, missed work, and the stress of having a judge decide for them. Mediation tends to be less contentious than a court case and helps to create a starting point for the newly separated couple to make future decisions for themselves that may come up. In a study of the value of mediation beyond the settlement, Barton (year) found that even couples who did not reach an agreement within their mediation, went to court better prepared to defend their case, and with a better understanding of their own and the other person's position. Mediation is a growing field; the Bureau of Labor and Statistics in 2017 noted that the mediation field has an 11% growth rate. Most court systems now actively use mediation as a tool for pre-trial settlements, often mandating a required mediation for each case before they receive a court date on the docket. Outside of the court system, many people often seek mediation on their own when seeking a divorce. They may want to maintain a good relationship with their partner and have already made decisions about the separation of their marriage.

Julia M. Bernard

See also: Association of Family and Conciliation Courts; Child-Inclusive Mediation

Further Reading

Bernard, Julia M., Nicole Manick, and Maike Klein. 2016. "Ethical, Legal, and Professional Issues in Mediation and Parent Coordination." *Ethics and Professional Issues in Couple and Family Therapy* 215–232.

James, Brian. 2007. "What Is Divorce Mediation?" Mediate.com. Accessed August 2 2019.

Johnson, Michael P., and Janel M. Leone. 2005. "The Differential Effects of Intimate Terrorism and Situational Couple Violence: Findings From the National Violence Against Women Survey." *Journal of family issues* 26, no. 3: 322–349.

Raines, Susan S. 2018. "Building a Knowledge-Based Foundation for Mediation Practice & Program Administration." *ACResolution* 18, no. 1: 8.

Raines, Susan, Yeju Choi, Joshua Johnson, and Katrina Coker. 2016. "Safety, Satisfaction, and Settlement in Domestic Relations Mediations: New Findings." Family Court Review 54, no. 4: 603–619.

Divorce Mill

As divorce in the United States is governed at the state level, there are distinct differences between states regarding the processes surrounding the legal dissolution of marriage. For religious reasons, among others, some states have historically sought to make this process easier than others. These states have been dubbed "divorce mill states." While there are no specific criteria for defining a state as a divorce mill, states such as Indiana, Nevada, North Dakota, South Dakota, and Utah have historically received reputations for having access to easily obtainable divorces. Married individuals seeking a divorce have options for obtaining one in other states, as determined by the U.S. Supreme Court ruling in *Williams v. North Carolina* (317 U.S. 287, 1942), which decided that states have to recognize divorces issued in other states based on the United States Constitution's "full faith and credit" clause.

Trends in the attraction of an easily obtainable divorce, however, are not recent. By 1887, the prevalence of divorce created enough national concern or moral panic that Congress ordered statistics to be collected on divorce rates. The high traffic reported by divorce mill states led to the 1903 Inter-Church Conference on Marriage and Divorce, which took a religious approach to attempt to reduce divorce rates in the United States. Despite these efforts, divorce rates as well as traffic to divorce mill states continued to increase at drastic rates. In 1909, for instance, Reno, Nevada, was given the title of "the divorce capital of the world." Nevada embraced this title and their appearance as a divorce mill state because of its economic value as divorce seekers spend money in-state on accommodations, food, and general cost of living, supporting the state's hospitality industry. In Nevada, since 1931, divorce seekers only have to demonstrate six weeks of residency and provide an uncorroborated statement regarding grounds for divorce. In response to some of the divorce mill states, other states took opposite approaches in the 1900s. South Carolina, for instance, responded to some states moving to improve access to divorce by abolishing all divorces. These restrictive practices in some states, however, only drove divorce seekers toward divorce mill states.

By 1916, the United States had the highest divorce rate in the world, which only supported the growing industry of assisting individuals in obtaining divorces. At this time, roughly one of every seven marriages was dissolved by divorce. Much of this, and the associated growth of divorce mill states, is attributed to social changes, including the women's movement, industrialization, and the First World War. By the 1920s, the divorce rate reached 15%. Bergerson's *The Divorce Mill Advertises* (1935) expresses concern regarding the migration surrounding the growing industry of migration for divorce. These efforts also led to numerous deceptive practices to obtain a divorce within the "fault system," which then led to the "no-fault divorce" option in the late 1960s. With the emergence of laws across the nation that made access to divorces easier, including the development of the Family Court system, migration to divorce mill states is no longer necessary.

Candace Forbes Bright

See also: Association of Family and Conciliation Courts; Divorce, No-Fault and Fault-Based; Divorce, Types of; Divorce Initiation

Further Reading

Bergeson, Rollo. 1935. "The divorce mill advertises." *Law & Contemporary Problems* 2: 348.

Friedman, Lawrence M. 1985. "Rights of passage: Divorce law in historical perspective." *Oregon Law Review* 63: 649.

Nakonezny, Paul A., Robert D. Shull, and Joseph Lee Rodgers. 1995. "The effect of no-fault divorce law on the divorce rate across the 50 states and its relation to income, education, and religiosity." *Journal of Marriage and the Family* 477–488.

Stetson, Dorothy M., and Gerald C. Wright Jr. 1975. "The effects of laws on divorce in American states." *Journal of Marriage and the Family* 537–547.

Divorce Pre-1950

Divorce has been a part of American history since colonial days. Although divorce was not common early on, the standing of marriage as a civil contract allowed for the possibility of divorce in many jurisdictions (Kitchin 1912, 211). However, the rigidity or existence of divorce law was highly variant across colonies with Southern colonies generally disallowing divorce completely, consistent with the canon law of England, and more northern states having progressively less restrictive laws, the farther north the less restrictive (Amato and Irving 2006, 43). Regardless, relief from marriage could be granted but only under extreme conditions. This was reflected in early divorces that required gubernatorial approval, or in less restrictive cases by state legislatures; in fact, divorce was so rare that before the Revolutionary War there are only four documented divorces that occurred in New York (Kitchin 1912, 212).

Part of the reason for the low divorce rates in early America was the restrictive nature of how one could obtain a divorce. For a divorce to be granted, fault had to be established under specific grounds that were deemed acceptable by jurisdictions. Fault-based divorces require that one party is attributed with blame for the dissolution of the marriage. The most common ground for divorce was adultery, although other common fault-based grounds included cruelty, abandonment, bigamy, and failure to provide, with harsh consequences for the individual found to be at fault including fines, incarceration, and even an inability to remarry (Amato and Irving 2006, 43).

When one was found to be at fault, this would oftentimes set the stage for the custody determinations of children. Initially, custody of children following divorce would be granted almost exclusively to fathers, which followed the presumption from English law that fathers were the natural guardians of their children (noteworthy is that children were actually viewed as property of their fathers in early American history), a presumption that would be cited in custody determinations following a divorce even into the early 1900s (Einhorn 1986, 120–123). However, emerging during the 1800s were new ideas about the determination of child custody, with courts often citing "tender years" as a rationale to award mothers custody following divorce. In many cases, taking into account the fault for the cause of divorce in the determination of custody, and then ultimately by the early 1900s an emergence of focus on what was in the "best interests of the child" (Einhorn 1986, 125–130).

The cultural push toward the best interests of the child standard, less restrictive, fault-based rationales, and a recognition of women and children as independent Americans (i.e., not the property of their husbands or fathers) was a staple of the early 1900s. Freedom from encumbering or dissatisfying marriages became an important aspect of the feminist movement. As women began to see their worth within society, they began to demand civil, sexual, financial, and marital rights that were not directly tied to their husbands (Hilfer 2003, 594–595). Once again, cultural influence from England drove much of this emphasis in America, with higher-ranking officials and members of the British monarchy seeking divorces during this time (Hilfer 2003, 594–595). Although there was a shift toward the best interests of the child standard and the independence of women and children from men the following divorce, judicial decision-making in the United States took some time to evolve. There was a great deal of inconsistency in custody determinations and it was in rare cases that judges would make concentrated efforts toward the geographic proximity of parents following divorce and shared parenting time (Einhorn 1986, 133–134). This inconsistency would continue past into the latter half of the century.

According to the National Center on Health Statistics (NCHS 1973, 9–10), at the turn of the 20th century, divorce rates gradually increased year after year with few exceptions (1913, 1918, 1921–1922, 1930–1932, and 1946–1950 were the only years where there was a decline in the crude divorce rate). The social consciousness surrounding divorce became ever-present in the early 1900s as well, with divorce rates rising to the point where one in ten marriages would end in divorce, which sparked a renewed emphasis on social welfare and education (Clarke-Stewart and Brentano 2006, 5). This social change would continue to promote marriage, but it did not functionally deter divorce, and as such divorce rates continued to rise. The trends in divorce aligned with trends in marriage rates at the time, with gradual increases experienced and peaks that surrounded World War I and World War II. In addition, marriage rates saw a drastic decline in the early 1930s following the Great Depression, which was reflected in a brief decline in divorce rates over that time as well. By 1950, divorce rates had begun a multiyear decline but that would all change in the years to come, with the introduction of no-fault divorce legislation just on the horizon (NCHS 1973, 9–10).

Anthony J. Ferraro and
McKenzie L. Cox-Zimmermann

See also: Divorce, Causes/Risk Factors of; Divorce, No-Fault and Fault-Based; Divorce, Process of; Divorce, Stigma; Divorce Pre-1950; Divorce 1950–2000

Further Reading

Amato, Paul R., and Shelley Irving. 2006. "Historical Trends in Divorce in the United States." In *Handbook of Divorce and Relationship Dissolution*, edited by Mark A. Fine and John H. Harvey, 41–58. Mahwah, NJ: Lawrence Erlbaum Associates.

Clarke-Stewart, Alison, and Cornelia Brentano. 2006. *Divorce: Causes and Consequences*. New Haven, CT: Yale University Press.

Einhorn, Jay. 1986. "Child Custody in Historical Perspective: A Study of Changing Social Perceptions of Divorce and Child Custody in Anglo-American Law." *Behavioral Sciences and the Law* 4, no. 2: 119–135.

Hilfer, Tony, 2003. "Marriage and Divorce in America." *American Literary History* 15, no. 3: 592–602.

Kitchin, S. B. 1912. *A History of Divorce.* London, England: Chapman and Hall.

National Center for Health Statistics (NCHS). 1973. *100 Years of Marriage and Divorce Statistics: United States, 1867–1967* (no. HRA 74-1902). Rockville, MD: United States Department of Health, Education, and Welfare.

Divorce 1950–2000

The principal event in the history of divorce in the latter portion of the 20th century was the adoption of no-fault provisions to existing divorce grounds by some states and the adoption of exclusively no-fault grounds by others. No-fault divorce provides a method by which divorcing spouses can go through the legal divorce process without the added adversarial conditions of assigning blame to one party or the other for the failings of a marriage. No-fault divorce is the current standard in the United States; however, this was not always the case. Before the no-fault divorce, common grounds for divorce included acts such as adultery, insanity, cruelty, and abandonment, and for a fault-based judgment to be granted would require a finding of fault based on one of these conditions. However, beginning with Oklahoma in 1953, states progressively began adding no-fault grounds for divorce, with five states adding provisions to existing divorce laws before 1970 (Vlosky and Monroe 2002, 319–320). The next major milestone for no-fault divorce was the California Family Law Act of 1969, which went into effect in January 1970, and in effect made irreconcilable differences the only grounds for divorce in the state. By 1991, every state in the country included at least a provision for no-fault divorce. However, as of 2000, still more than half of the states in the United States allow for divorce on fault-based grounds (i.e., are not exclusively no-fault).

Changes reflected in the legislation of the late 1900s were closely aligned with changing values and social expectations surrounding marriage and divorce. For example, media portrayals of single-family households and single parenting were often the result of widowhood rather than divorce (despite the growing number of marriages that ended in divorce over this time), with the first depictions of divorce on television occurring in the early-to-mid 1960s (Moore 1992, 52–53). It was not until the 1970s that realistic depictions of parental roles began to emerge in mainstream media, particularly realistic depictions of fathering. Up until this time, fathers had been emphasized as providers with little interest in or incompetence in caregiving for children (LaRossa et al. 1991, 987–988). This gradual shift in the culture surrounding divorce post-1950 saw families being represented and discussed in more expansive and unconventional roles and contexts. However, this change was gradual and often divorce was still treated with a tone of humor, most likely because of the notion that divorce was still largely considered a taboo topic among the public at large (Moore 1992, 57–58).

Trends in the frequency of divorce during this time would follow the alignment of changing cultural norms, with the divorce rate reaching a peak around the early 1980s before gradually decreasing over the subsequent decades. By 2000, refined divorce rates (divorces per 1,000 married women ages 15 and older) had become fairly static. although a new pattern began to emerge, with decreases in the overall number of divorces per year continuing but accompanying decreases in the number of marriages per year (Kreider and Ellis 2011, 12–14). This is to say, the number of divorces continued to decrease at the turn of the 21st century, but when taken within the context of a decreasing number of marriages, the proportion of marriages that end in divorce has remained fairly stable.

Research on divorce also grew drastically during this time, with a peak in the volume of research occurring in the 1980s (see review by Ferraro et al. 2016), following a recognition of the multifaceted experience of divorce and its impacts on life post-divorce. Six primary stations of divorce that underscored this process were identified and guided this burgeoning focus of family scholars on the impacts of divorce on both adults and children: (1) the emotional divorce; (2) the legal divorce; (3) the economic divorce; (4) the coparental divorce; (5) the community divorce; and (6) the psychic divorce (Bohannan 1970, 34). By the end of the 20th century, it was recognized that divorce was a far-reaching, long-term process that involved a renegotiation of roles for both parents and children, economic decline, the decline in contact and emotional support, and strains that could last decades after the divorce occurred. An emphasis on meaning-making, coping skills, interpersonal networks, and community services was present (Amato 2000, 1271–1272), as was an emphasis on mitigating interparental conflict and building supportive coparental relationships following divorce (Pollet and Lombreglia 2008, 377). By the late 1980s and early 1990s there became an emphasis on divorce education as a means to prepare parents for this process, with a proliferation of programs accompanying a growing number of states that began requiring parent education before the granting of a divorce decree (Pollet and Lombreglia 2008, 376).

Anthony J. Ferraro and
McKenzie L. Cox-Zimmermann

See also: Divorce, Causes/Risk Factors of; Divorce, Process of; Divorce, Stigma; Divorce Pre-1950; Divorce 1950–2000

Further Reading

Amato, Paul R. 2000. "The consequences of divorce for adults and children." *Journal of Marriage and Family* 62, no. 4: 1269–1287.

Bohannan, Paul. 1970. *Divorce and After: An Analysis of the Emotional and Social Problems of Divorce.* New York: Doubleday & Company.

Ferraro, Anthony J., Taylor R. Davis, Raymond E. Petren, and Kay Pasley. 2016. "Postdivorce parenting: A study of recently divorced mothers and fathers." *Journal of Divorce and Remarriage* 57, no. 7: 485–503.

Kreider, Rose M., and Renee Ellis. 2011. *Number, Timing, and Duration of Marriages and Divorce: 2009.* Washington, DC: United States Census Bureau, pp. 470–125.

LaRossa, Ralph, Betty Anne Gordon, Ronald Jay Wilson, Annette Bairan, and Charles Jaret. 1991. "The fluctuating image of the 20th century American father." *Journal of Marriage and Family* 53, no. 4: 987–997.

Moore, Marvin L. 1992. "The family as portrayed on prime-time television, 1947–1990: Structure and characteristics." *Sex Roles* 26: 41–61.

Pollet, Susan L., and Melissa Lombreglia. 2008. "A nationwide survey of mandatory parent education." *Family Court Review* 46, no. 2: 375–394.

Vlosky, Denese A., and Pamela A. Monroe. 2002. "The effective dates of no-fault divorce laws in the 50 states." *Family Relations* 51, no. 4: 317–324.

Divorce Support Groups

Divorce is a common experience in the United States and Western societies and can be a source of stressors for everyone involved (Demo and Fine 2010). Post-divorce stressors adults may face are having the responsibility as the sole parent, loss of custody of children, lack of emotional support, conflict with an ex-spouse, and an economic decline (Amato 2000). Children's stressors may include a lack of parental support, lack of effective control, loss of contact with a parent, conflict among parents, and an economic decline (Amato 2000). One resource to help parents and children deal with these stressors are divorce support groups. In the United States, in-person adult divorce support groups include Divorce Care, Divorce Support Meetup Groups, and Parents Without Partners. Other groups, such as Divorce Separation and Singles Support, Divorced Moms on a Mission, Divorce Force, and Jason Levoy with Your Divorce Resource Community, can be found online. An individual can join a divorce support group by going to womansdivorce.com and searching for support groups near them.

Research has shown parents and children's participation in divorce support groups can help with the adjustment to divorce (Farmer and Galaris 1993; Øygard 2001). Adults who participated in divorce support groups had less depression and anxiety, higher self-esteem, higher self-confidence, and had an enhanced trust of others (Graff, Whitehead, and LeCompte 1986; Øygard 2001). Another benefit of support groups for adults is having a sense of belonging (Lee and Hett 1990). Loneliness and isolation are common feelings after a divorce (Lee and Hett 1990). Divorce support groups are also a safe environment for adults to discuss their thoughts and feelings with individuals who are going through similar situations.

Divorce support groups can also be beneficial for children. Parents of divorce working with therapists at the Marriage Council of Philadelphia expressed concerns regarding their children not having the emotional support they needed during their parent's divorce. Divorce support groups allow children to express and process their thoughts and feelings regarding their parents' divorce. Parents reported discussions about separation and divorce were easier and more frequent with their children after the support groups. Parents also said children were able to discuss their feelings about separation and divorce with peers and adults after participating in the group (Farmer and Galaris 1993).

Divorce is a common experience that may cause stressors for parents and children. Divorce support groups can help parents and children with stressors and help with the adjustment to separation and divorce. Participation in support groups can help adults and children process their thoughts and feelings toward the divorce.

Elizabeth Laughlin

See also: Father Support Groups; Parent Education Programs

Further Reading

Amato, Paul R. 2000. "The Consequences of Divorce for Adults and Children." *Journal of Marriage and Family* 62, no. 4: 1269–1287. https://doi.org/10.1111/j.1741-3737.2000.01269.x.

Demo, David H. and Mark A. Fine. 2010. *Beyond the Average Divorce*. Los Angeles: SAGE.

Farmer, Sherry and Diana Galaris. 1993. "Support Groups for Children of Divorce." *American Journal of Family Therapy* 21, no. 1: 40–50. https://doi.org/10.1080/01926189308250994.

Graff, Robert W., George I. Whitehead and Michael Lecompte. 1986. "Group Treatment with Divorced Women Using Cognitive-Behavioral and Supportive-Insight Methods." *Journal of Counseling Psychology* 33, no. 3: 276–281. https://doi.org/10.1037//0022-0167.33.3.276.

Lee, James M. and Geoffrey G. Hett. 1990. "Post-Divorce Adjustment: An Assessment of a Group Intervention." *Canadian Journal of Counselling and Psychotherapy* 24, no. 3.

Øygard, Lisbet. 2001. "Therapeutic Factors in Divorce Support Groups." *Journal of Divorce & Remarriage* 36, no. 1–2: 141–158. https://doi.org/10.1300/j087v36n01_08.

Donor Insemination

In vitro fertilization (IVF) is an increasingly common, but physically invasive, somewhat controversial, and potentially expensive assisted reproductive technology (ART) used to help conceive a child. IVF is often referred to Louise Brown, born on July 25, 1978, is considered the first baby conceived with IVF. People choose to use IVF for various reasons. Among them are the inability to independently conceive a child in the context of their relationship due to the specific partnership, the desire to conceive a child without a partner, and infertility, which can involve female factors (e.g., birth abnormalities, ovulation disorder, blocked fallopian tubes, and endometriosis) and male factors (e.g., genetic disease or having no, few, or malformed sperm). According to the Centers for Disease Control and Prevention, approximately 12% of women aged 15–44 struggle to get or stay pregnant. IVF may involve one's own fresh or frozen eggs and/or sperm or a donor's fresh or frozen egg and/or sperm or embryo. The ability to freeze eggs, sperm, and embryos through cryopreservation has allowed individuals to extend childbearing years, simplify future rounds of infertility treatments, and conceive biologically related children after cancer treatment via IVF.

IVF is a medical procedure performed by fertility specialists that involves combining egg and sperm outside the body. A typical IVF cycle involves multiple steps including (a) egg stimulation via fertility drugs, (b) egg removal from the body, (c) fertilization of egg(s) with sperm to create one or more embryo(s), (d) embryo transfer to the uterus, and (e) pregnancy testing. Transferring more than one embryo to the uterus may lead to multiple births, such as twins and triplets. IVF may result in the production of more embryos than the number transferred back to the uterus. Individuals may choose to freeze extra embryos for a later cycle or place them for adoption. Additional and sometimes controversial procedures that may be associated with IVF include Preimplantation Genetic Diagnosis (PGD), Comprehensive Chromosomal Screening (CCS), and gender selection. Side effects of IVF may include emotional and financial strain as well as physical ailments such as bleeding and infection. IVF success rates differ due to a variety of factors, which include patient age and health, procedure options, and medical provider. Success rates are typically calculated by either (a) dividing the number of positive pregnancies by the number of procedures or (b) dividing the number of live births by the number of procedures. The live birth per IVF cycle rate in the United States decreases with maternal age and ranges from approximately 42% for women under 30 to approximately 15.5% for women over 40 (American Pregnancy Association 2019). Success rates often increase with multiple cycles.

For a variety of reasons, including health-related factors, relationship-related factors, or the decision to be a solo parent, an individual may choose to use donor sperm, egg (oocyte), or embryo. This is often referred to as third party reproduction. Sperm donor insemination is the most frequent and least physically invasive form of the three. Although sperm donor insemination can occur naturally and without medical assistance, many individuals will utilize fertility specialists and ARTs, such as IVF or intrauterine insemination (IUI), in their attempt to establish a pregnancy. IUI is considered less intrusive than IVF and involves the use of a syringe to eject a partner or donor's semen into a woman's vagina in the attempt to achieve pregnancy. Donors may be known to the recipient or anonymous.

The use of anonymous donors is often considered controversial because it prevents donor-conceived offspring from accessing their complete medical history and identity-related information. Countries and states differ on regulations when it comes to third-party reproduction, including whether or not sperm donors are protected from paying child support and/or whether donor-related information is shared with donor-conceived offspring. For example, in the United Kingdom, children conceived using anonymous donor insemination are now able to determine the identity of their donors once they turn 18. Individuals may choose donors based on certain physical or social characteristics such as the degree of physical resemblance to a biological or non-biological parent (e.g., height, hair color), medical history, and/or interests or qualities (e.g., artistic, athletic, intellectual). The use of donors, especially sperm donors, may result in offspring having donor siblings, which are half sibling who share a donor. Many donor-conceived offspring seek to identify their donors and/or donor siblings and use various online resources to do so. For example, as of August 14, 2019, the Donor Sibling Registry reports that their website has helped connect over 17,000 donor families.

Historically, donor insemination was taboo, and many non-biological parents chose to pass for biological parents. Today, people are more accepting of third-party reproduction and open with their children about it. Donor-conceived families may receive professional advice for how to talk about donor insemination with their children. Many religions accept the use of IVF, but the acceptance is not as widespread when a third party is involved, as is the case with donor insemination. Roman Catholicism is often described as the most resistant to the use of ARTs, including IVF and donor insemination.

Affordability is a factor that may influence a person's decision to use IVF and a donor. IVF is costly with the average cost for one cycle of IVF to be $23,000 in the United States (Center for Human Reproduction 2019). Some health insurance plans cover portions of the cost and/or some individuals may be eligible for participation in discount programs or opt to engage in crowdfunding, but many expenses remain with the individual or couple. Using donor sperm, egg, or embryo may add to that cost in significant ways. The payment to and for egg donors is much higher than the payment to and for sperm donors because of the physical invasiveness of egg donation. Frozen embryos may be adopted from couples, but often still with an expense.

Meredith Marko Harrigan

See also: Parenting Plans and Custody Arrangements; Planned Parenthood

Further Reading

American Pregnancy Association. 2019. "In Vitro Fertilization: IVF." Last modified July 1, 2019. https://americanpregnancy .org/infertility/in-vitro-fertilization/.

Cahn, Naomi R. 2013. *The New Kinship.* New York: NYU Press.

Center for Human Reproduction. 2019. "IVF Cost: Affordable Fertility Treatments." Accessed August 29, 2019. https://www.centerforhumanreprod .com/services/discountprograms/ivfl/.

Centers for Disease Control and Prevention. 2019. "Infertility FAQs." Last modified January 16, 2019. https://www.cdc.gov /reproductivehealth/infertility/index.htm.

Donor Sibling Registry. n.d. "Educating, Connecting, and Supporting Donor Families." Accessed August 14, 2019. https://www.donorsiblingregistry.com/.

Ginsburg, Elizabeth S. and Catherine Racowsky. 2012. *In Vitro Fertilization: A Comprehensive Guide.* New York: Springer eBook.

Dowries

Dowry, often referred to as the bride price in some cultures, has been a system in place in several cultures to ensure economic safety and prosperity for generations. It is an exchange of currency or valued goods in a particular society to validate a marriage. In fact, for many cultures, marriages that exist without the dowry being paid are considered invalid in the culture even if they are considered valid in the terms of the law (Anyogu and Ibekwe 2021, 137).

For those not familiar with the process, meaning, and ritual surrounding dowries, the concept seems as though the groom is paying for ownership of the wife— which, at face value, he is. However, the dowry system can take place in several forms. In cultures where the woman leaves their home to join their husband's home, the dowry is often considered payment a husband owes to a bride's parents for the right to her labor and reproductive capabilities (Anderson 2007, 155). In some cases, the father of the bride pays the husband to secure the financial stability of the wife and the children she might bore (Rashkow 2022, 148). For centuries, dowry payment has been seen as the first step in ensuring a happy, wealthy, and prosperous marriage.

In Western societies such as the United States, most people encounter dowries by knowing or marrying someone from a culture that participates in the dowry tradition. There is a lot of exposure to the tradition that dates back centuries in history and the delicate ways in which they have evolved depending on the culture they are marrying into. Each culture places meaning and expectations on the practice (Anyogu and Ibekwe 2021, 136).

Dowries were once commonplace but as countries developed and societal expectations changed, they became less common, especially in Western developed nations. Dowries still occur in the Western world, but mostly by immigrants who feel attached to the practice. This practice is still very much alive in several developing nations but is not documented very thoroughly beyond South Asian and South African cultures. Even still, the statistics are still unknown because this practice is not required to be documented in ways that would provide a clear picture of the frequency at which it occurs (Makino 2019, 770).

This practice of dowries has been in place since ancient Mesopotamia (Anderson 2000, 152) when it was primarily referred to as the bride price. Currently, most African and Southern Asian countries still practice this tradition. In India, this tradition became illegal in 1961 through The Dowry Prohibition Act of 1961, which defines a dowry as a demand for property or valuable security from the side of the bride's parents or relatives to the groom or his parents and/or guardian for the agreement to wed the bride. However, despite this law and many like that that have outlawed this practice, dowries are still very much a commonplace tradition in India, in particular the rural areas (Makino 2019, 771).

There are two distinct dowries to be paid: the "stridhan," which is the parent's gift to the bride, and the modern-day version of payment from the bride's parents to the groom and his parents (Anderson 2007, 152). The size of the payment typically depends on how desirable the groom is. The effects of this tradition have made headlines in India in recent years (Lolayekar et al. 2020; Rajkhowa et al. 2022); interpersonal violence against women has increased so rapidly that "dowry deaths" became a term used when a bride was murdered by her husband and/or his family due to the stressors of the dowry (Srinivasan and Bedi 2007, 1–4).

In Pakistan, it has been noted that the dowry has three distinct purposes: (1) a transfer of wealth to the groom's household to pay for a high-quality groom; (2) a compensation payment to the groom's household for receiving a bride who is an economic liability; and (3) a pre-mortem inheritance given to the bride (Anderson 2000, 2–4).

Dowries are most common in Africa, with one study claiming that dowries are given in 90% of sub-Saharan countries (Anderson 2007, 158). For most African cultures, the dowry is seen as appreciation to the bride's family for raising the bride, a demonstration of respect and acknowledgment to the bride's family. The size of the dowry depends on how much the father values his daughter and this depends on birth order, whether the daughter is an only child or other inquiries for marriage

Among southern African tribes such as the Shona, Bantu, and Zulu, the practice is called *labola* (Anyogu and Ibekwe 2021, 3). The labola is paid to the bride's parents, usually in the form of cash or livestock, to show gratitude for raising the bride (Anderson 2007). Among the Shona, the labola is so deeply entrenched in the culture that few people refuse to participate due to a superstition that the marriage will be doomed to fail without the price being paid. In fact, a survey conducted in Harare, the capital of Zimbabwe, in the 1980s, showed that only 5%

of marriages were performed without the labola being paid (Ansell 2001).

As society begins to change, so does the practice of dowry. In recent years, the average dowry payments have increased in some countries by as much as 6x the per capita annual household income (Srinivasan and Bedi 2007), and this has put lives at risk. The economic pressures of the dowry system have been shown to increase power and control issues within the relationship and inspire dowry deaths, which are so prevalent that it is now a classification of murder in Indian law. Instances of domestic violence due to dowry have been commonplace because of these traditions (Lolayekar et al. 2020; Rajkhowa et al. 2022).

Eunice Makunzva

See also: Intimate Partner Violence; Mail-Order Brides

Further Reading

Anderson, Siwan. 2000. "The Economics of Dowry Payments in Pakistan." *SSRN Electronic Journal* 35, no. 5 (August): 1–43. https://doi.org/10.2139/ssrn.244659.

Anderson, Siwan. 2007. "The Economics of Dowry and Brideprice." *Journal of Economic Perspectives* 21, no. 4 (Fall): 151–174. https://doi.org/10.1257/jpeg.21.4.151

Ansell, Nicola. 2001. "Because Its Our Culture! (Re)Negotiating the Meaning of Lobola in Southern African Secondary Schools." *Journal of Southern African Studies* 27, no. 4 (December): 697–716. https://doi.org/10.1080/03057070120090691.

Anyogu, F., and C. S. Ibekwe. 2021. "A Comparative Exposition of Customary Law Marriages in Nigeria and South Africa." *International Journal of Comparative Law and Legal Philosophy* 2 (2), 1–4.

Belur, Jyoti, Nick Tilley, Nayreen Daruwalla, Meena Kumar, Vinay Tiwari, and David Osrin. 2014. "The Social Construction of 'Dowry Deaths.'" *Social Science & Medicine* 119 (October): 1–9. https://doi.org/10.1016/j.socscimed.2014.07.044.

Lolayekar, A. P., S. Desouza, and P. Mukhopadhyay. 2020. "Crimes Against Women in India: A District-Level Analysis (1991–2011)." *Journal of Interpersonal Violence* 37 (9–10). https://doi.org/10.1177/0886260520967147

Makino, Momoe. 2019. "Marriage, Dowry, and Women's Status in Rural Punjab, Pakistan." *Journal of Population Economics* 32. 10.1007/s00148-018-0713-0.

Rajkhowa, A., S. Dhanji, and S. Kotnala. 2022. "Perspectives on Mediatised Discourses About and State Intervention into Dowry-Related Abuse and Intimate-Partner Violence Among Indian Migrants in Australia: Implications for Health and Human Services." *Journal of Progressive Human Services* 33, no. 2: 205–221. https://doi.org/10.1080/10428232.2022.2042928

Rashkow, I. 2022. "'How Much Is She Worth?' A Comparison of Six Ancient Near East Laws Relating to Bride-Price, Dowry, Inhetitance, and Divorce." *Jewish Bible Quarterly* 50, no. 3: 143–159.

Srinivasan, Sharada, and Arjun S. Bedi. 2007. "Domestic Violence and Dowry: Evidence from a South Indian Village." *World Development* 35, no. 5 (May): 857–880. https://doi.org/10.1016/j.worlddev.2006.08.005.

E

Economic Independence

Economic independence is the minimum subsistence level a person or family needs to survive and is an increasingly important consideration for men and women in choosing when and whom to marry. Historically, male economic viability has been a hallmark of marriage, and men with more potential to obtain higher incomes have been more likely to marry younger. Today, people are more considerate of both partners' economic stability before marriage. Although the 2010 U.S. Census indicates that husbands continue to out earn their wives despite attaining a lower or similar education, the trend is not the same for cohabiting couples. As gender and racial economic inequity gaps close, cohabiting couples are more likely to have similar incomes and educational attainment, and they often cite finances as a significant reason not to marry or to delay marriage.

Traditionally, marriage has benefited couples by reducing financial strain, especially in households where two partners are working. Married couples have more access to financial cost-sharing, time off to care for family needs, and tax benefits that increase financial security. However, increases in the cost of living and decreased earning potential have shifted martial benefits and expectations. Scholars and policy analysts cite changes in property laws and access to college prompted several social shifts. Women

and people of color began obtaining higher education degrees, increasing their access to economic independence and more potential partners.

Although marriage is an indicator of the transition to adulthood around the world and often serves as the basis for childrearing and continuing the family life cycle, there is a strong trend globally toward a unique developmental period, "emerging adulthood." This period is indicated as the time between adolescence and adulthood when young adults focus on themselves, often choosing to pursue an education and financial independence before marriage and childrearing. This also allows young adults to find a compatible partner and opens the marriage market. This may be beneficial as those who wait longer to marry and those who are college-educated are less likely to divorce and have more economic stability as individuals. According to the U.S. Census in 2010, 34% of women and 33% of men over age 20 who had ever been married had also been divorced, which was lower than in 2008. By 2014, over half of men and women in their first marriage (married from 1970 to 1984) had reached their 25th anniversary.

The modern economic independence movement is deeply rooted in the women's and civil rights movements. Pioneers in these movements from 1776 to the present day, such as Abigail Adams, Sojourner Truth, Susan B. Anthony, and Rosa Parks, paved the way for significant social and political change through the 1960s. Policies such as the Equal Pay Act of 1963, the Civil Rights Act of 1964, and the Lilly Ledbetter Fair Pay Act of 2009 increased the potential for economic freedom for women and people of color. This was an important shift for freedom, safety, and economic sustainability. Women's attitudes shifted over time, increasing their attention to the independence and selectiveness of their partners, rather than focusing solely on the economic viability of a partner. This shift improves marriage sustainability and reduces the likelihood of domestic violence.

Men's attitudes have shifted as well. Male college students who reported feeling comfortable with their female partners outearning them increased from 41% in 1980 to 60% in 1990. Through the past decade, men around the world consistently report increased comfort in their partners outearning them. Today, growing attention to economic independence before and during marriage and divorce is evident on social media platforms and podcasts. Encouragement from many financial advisors, awareness of economic conditions, later marriages, and being children of divorced parents, millennials are obtaining prenuptial agreements more often than previous generations. Couples also indicate cohabitation, rather than marriage, is a more viable relationship due to outstanding debts and the financial stress of marriage.

Economic independence is a significant factor in determining whether to divorce as well. When economic factors are not a stressor or when the costs of the divorce are low, couples may be more likely to get divorced. Financial strain may increase the likelihood of divorce or may deter a couple from divorce should they not have the financial stability to live separately or to pay for the divorce. Women's economic independence increases the likelihood of divorce in long-term marriages as well. It may be that financial strain in divorce is more impactful on women. In 2016, women who were divorced were more likely to live in poverty than men in the year following the divorce. Further, divorce may put additional pressure on single mothers. Economically independent women may feel stable on their own, increasing the likelihood of initiating divorce.

In longer marriages, children leaving the home and economic factors are common factors in considering divorce. Following a divorce, single mothers with more than two children are less responsive and available to their children. Many mothers have to shift their priority from parenting to rebuilding intimate relationships and aiming to achieve economic independence. As mothers aim to shift priorities, their adolescents are more likely to engage in delinquent behavior and truancy, which increases parental stress and decreases the likelihood of economic stability.

Although this entry primarily focuses on economic independence in the United States, it is also important to note that a shift in perspectives on economic independence is shifting globally. Studies in Kenya, China, Argentina, France, and other countries around the world indicate similar trends.

Megan L. Chapman

See also: Divorce, Economic Consequences (Personal); Marriage, Financial Implications

Further Reading

Cancian, Maria, and Daniel R. Meyer. 2014. "Testing the economic independence hypothesis: The effect of an exogenous increase in child support on subsequent marriage and cohabitation." *Demography* 51: 857–880.

Hiedemann, Bridget, Olga Suhomlinova, and Angela M. O'Rand. 1998. "Economic independence, economic status, and empty nest in midlife marital disruption." *Journal of Marriage and the Family* 60: 219–231.

Lloyd, Kim M. 2006. "Latinas' transition to first marriage: An examination of four theoretical perspectives." *Journal of Marriage and Family* 68: 993–1014.

Mayol-Garcia, Yeris, Benjamin Gurrentz, and Rose M. Kreider. 2021. "Number, timing, and duration of marriages and divorces: 2016." U.S. Census.

Wallerstein, Judith, Julia Lewis, and Sherrin Rosenthal. 2013. "Mothers and their children after divorce: Report from a 25-year longitudinal study." *Psychoanalytic Psychology* 30: 167. 10.1037/a0032511.

Elopement

In the past, elopement was considered more of a secret endeavor, especially when there were parents involved that disapproved of the union. Modern elopements are more often associated with those who want to avoid the pressures and stressors that accompany a more traditional wedding. Elopement usually means avoiding the heavy costs associated with weddings, as well as potential familial and social problems that are common with the planning and execution of a wedding ceremony, reception, etc. There are no penalties in the United States for choosing elopement, so couples often find it a simple option (Solernou 2016). The process of a couple eloping is generally very minimal; there are not normally announcements or registries, the ceremony is small with very few or no relatives or friends in attendance, it is not usually followed by any kind of reception and does not always have a formal honeymoon.

Research indicates there may be differences between "healthy elopement," and "escape elopement" (Reynolds 2015). The key factor between both forms of elopement is the motivation of the couple for choosing elopement as their marriage option. Couples who choose elopement to avoid the high costs of weddings, or who have previously had marriage ceremonies and weren't concerned with the theatrics of the experience, were those who fell under the healthy elopement description. Their motivations were focused on what the couple needed and what would be right for them both. Some factors of an escape elopement include couples who choose to elope to avoid family dysfunction that may arise from the wedding, or chose to elope under the influence of substances or when decision-making is otherwise impaired (Reynolds 2015).

The motivations for couples who choose to elope can shift over the years. Some couples that have already been married previously may take elopement into greater account, or couples who feel more non-traditional may simply want to avoid the norm. Some couples elope and then decide to have a formal wedding later. While there are many ways couples can go about eloping, many states still have a lengthy process for obtaining a marriage certificate. The most commonly known state for elopement is Nevada, which often has Hollywood portrayals of people getting married on a whim during a stay in the city. Other states, such as Louisiana, Florida, New Jersey, and others, have adjusted their marriage laws that make elopement an easier option. States like California have created specific venues for elopement ceremonies that can cater specifically to the interests of the couple (Associated Press 2012).

For those couples who end up choosing a wedding ceremony over an elopement, key factors generally include the desire to have wider support in their decision to be married. Wedding ceremonies provide a wide array of witnesses to a marriage that can create a greater sense of validity. Some feel a greater reality in their marriage due to having a formal ceremony that sets the experience apart (Reynolds 2015). These factors, like the decision to elope, however, all vary depending on the couple themselves, and again, on what their motivations are for choosing either an elopement or more traditional options. It does not imply that those who choose to elope have any less valid marriages than those who have a wedding ceremony, nor is elopement a predictor of the subsequent strength of a marriage. Some feel the most important factor is simply the act of being married to each other, and all other factors seem trivial. That alone may not justify the choice to elope but is a common starting point for a couple to begin exploring if the decision to elope is right for them.

In 2020, the impact of the COVID-19 pandemic seemed to spike the commonality of elopement. Nationwide mandates to avoid large groups and gatherings in small venues created difficulties for any wedding planning. Many couples who were anxious to be wed that previously desired a more traditional wedding ceremony were bypassing this option and choosing the path of elopement due to the uncertainties of how long they would have to wait before the state of the pandemic would ease enough for their previously imagined wedding. Many potentially large wedding events were minimized to a few guests and small locales.

Brendan Ewell, Whitney Sanchez, and Todd Spencer

See also: Annulment; Arranged Marriage; Common Law Marriage; Deinstitutionalization of Marriage; Destination Wedding; Honeymoon; Interfaith Marriage; Marriage, Financial Implications; Marriage Certificate/License; *90 Day Fiancé*; Open Marriage; Unmarried Cohabitation

Further Reading

The Associated Press. 2012. "A Look at the States Entering the Elopement Biz." *The San Diego Union-Tribune.*

Reyes, Nina. 2020. "An Elopement Closer to Home." *The New York Times.* https://www.nytimes.com/2020/04/18/fashion/weddings/an-elopement-closer-to-home.html.

Reynolds, Jessica. 2015. "Elope: Pros and Cons of Skipping the Wedding." *Chicago Tribune.*

Solernou, Daniel J. 2016. "Elopement." *Encyclopedia of Family Studies,* 1–2. https://doi.org/10.1002/9781119085621.wbefs279.

Endogamy

The first use of the term *endogamy* and the related term *exogamy* are attributed to John Ferguson McLennan in 1865 in his book *Primitive Marriage* (*Oxford Dictionary of English*, "Endogamy noun" 2010). The prefix *endo–*, meaning "inside, within, internal," is a derivative of the Greek word *endon* (*Oxford Dictionary of English*, "Endo" 2019); the suffix *–gamy*, also with Greek roots, means *marriage* when referring to anthropological topics (Online Etymology Dictionary, "Gamy" 2019). *Endogamy* is a term describing the social customs or laws which require or expect marriage within one's own group.

Common groups associated with endogamy are race, religion, education, age, and social class, and individuals are expected to marry within one or more of these groups. For example, in 1967, the United States Supreme Court struck down Virginia's Racial Integrity Act of 1924 in *Loving v. Virginia*. According to Natalie de Guzman and Adrienne Nishina (2017), before that time, anti-miscegenation laws, laws which outlawed marriage between whites and non-whites, were, at one point, common in almost all states (557). These laws would be considered endogamous laws because they required marriage within one's own group. In this case, the group is race.

However, one's own group changes depending on the issue. For instance, one's own group may be social class or age. In India, for example, the divisions between inherited social classes, or castes, is well documented. According to Pralip Kumar Narzary and Laishram Ladusingh (2019), the long-held societal norm that one should marry within one's own caste can cause community resentment, or worse, if violated (588). The societal custom to marry within the same caste is an example of an endogamous rule.

Endogamy can be explicitly mandated by law or by long-held societal customs, but endogamous mate selection expectations may be communicated more implicitly. For instance, a father might forbid his high school daughter from marrying a man who is 20 years her senior. In this example, the societal expectation is that the two people entering into a marriage should be in a similar age group. Or, a Jewish grandmother may announce that she hopes her granddaughter can find a nice Jewish young man while at college. The message communicated is that marriage should be between two people with the same religious beliefs, another example of an endogamous rule.

As in the case of interracial marriage, the law may change, but societal customs and opinions may take longer to evolve. Although the Supreme Court paved the way for interracial marriages in 1967, it was 1990 before a majority of Americans approved (de Guzman and Nishina 2017, 558). Only 3% of newly married couples were interracial in 1967. By 2015, that number increased to 17% according to a Pew Research Center analysis representing a steady incline of societal acceptance (Geiger and Livingston 2019). Whether by law or by societal custom, the belief that it is in the best interest of society to marry someone within the same group is the definition of endogamy.

Kristie Chandler

See also: Exogamy; Interfaith Marriage; International Marriage; Interracial Marriage

Further Reading

de Guzman, Natalie S. and Nishina, Adrienne. 2017. "50 Years of Loving: Interracial Romantic Relationships and Recommendations for Future Research." *Journal of Family Theory & Review* 9, no. 4: 557. Accessed September 1, 2019, https://doi.org/10.1111/jftr.12215

Geiger, A. W. and Livingston, Gretchen. "8 Facts about Love and Marriage in America." Pew Research Center. Last modified February 13, 2019. https://www .pewresearch.org/fact-tank/2019/02/13 /8-facts-about-love-and-marriage/.

Narzary, Pralip Kumar and Ladusingh, Laishram. 2019. "Discovering the Saga of Inter-Caste Marriage." *Journal of Asian and African Studies* 54, no. 4: 588–599.

Online Etymology Dictionary. 2019. "Endo-." Accessed November 22, 2019, https://www.etymonline.com/word/endo -#etymonline_v_8656.

Online Etymology Dictionary. 2019. "Gamy-." Accessed November 22, 2019, https://www.etymonline.com/word/-gamy #etymonline_v_40907.

Oxford Dictionary of English. 2010. "Endogamy Noun." Oxford University Press. doi:10.1093/acref/9780199571123.013 .m-en_gb-msdict-00002-0265250.

Oxford Dictionary of English. 2010. "Exogamy Noun." Oxford University Press. doi:10.1093/acref/9780199571123.013 .m-en_gb-msdict-00002-0280530.

Engagements

An engagement is a period that begins when two people agree to marry and ends when they get married or otherwise end the engagement. During this time, the couple is referred to as engaged. A man who is engaged to be married is referred to as the fiancé, while a woman who is engaged to be married is referred to as the fiancée.

In the United States today, the average engagement age is mid- to late-20s. The typical duration of an engagement is approximately one year, but engagements may be indefinite or very short, depending on the couple's age, finances, culture, readiness, and eagerness to marry.

The only requirement for an engagement is an agreement to marry. While many couples plan their wedding during their engagement, engagements can vary based on the period, culture, and the couple's preferences. For example, the couple's family and friends may be involved leading up to or at the time of the engagement, or a subsequent engagement party may celebrate the couple. New engagements may be announced in newspapers or on social media. Couples may hire a photographer for engagement photos or lawyers for prenuptial agreements. In some religious traditions, engaged couples must undergo premarital counseling or other marriage preparation programs before getting married.

In the United States today, there is no legal status associated with an engagement. Thus, if an engagement ends between two people, there is usually no legal remedy. However, a few states may still recognize the breach of promise to marry. People may choose to sue for a breach of promise to marry at the breakup of their engagement, particularly if they incur financial costs in planning the wedding.

For example, in Georgia a few years ago, a court awarded a woman $43,500 for breach of promise to marry and fraud, in addition to attorney fees of $6,500. In Illinois, when a cattle rancher separated from his fiancée attorney, a jury returned her a $178,000 verdict, but the appellate court later reversed this decision. North Carolina even allows an award of punitive damages to punish a particularly outrageous breach of contract to marry.

Nonetheless, today only a few states allow claims for breach of promise to marry. A woman legislator from Indiana successfully sponsored a bill in 1935 that outlawed such suits in the state. Many other states followed Indiana in the 1930s and additional states followed in the 1960s when sexual attitudes became more permissive.

While less common in other parts of the world, many couples in the United States today become engaged with an engagement ring worn on the left hand, signaling to other suitors an exit from the dating market. After the wedding ceremony, those with an engagement ring often wear it alongside a wedding band.

One of the earliest diamond engagement rings was given by Archduke Maximilian of Austria in 1477 to Mary of Burgundy. However, the majority of Americans did not start wearing engagement rings until the 1930s, when the De Beers diamond company started to advertise engagement rings after the company experienced decreased jewelry sales around the time of the Great Depression. The De Beers campaign included the slogan "A Diamond is Forever" and promoted a guideline that the cost of an engagement ring should equal a man's monthly salary. Since then, some Americans have followed an informal rule that an engagement ring should cost 2–3 times the salary of the person proposing marriage.

Today, jewelry companies advertise engagement rings for men, but these are less popular than those for women. There also has been more attention paid to the ethical sourcing of diamonds in engagement rings following concerns that foreign civil wars were being funded by blood diamonds.

If an engagement ends without marriage, the question may arise of who should receive the engagement ring. Couples often simply agree, with nothing preventing them from reaching their own arrangements. In the absence of an agreement, couples may litigate the issue, especially if the engagement ring was expensive.

In most states, the default rule is that the engagement ring is a conditional gift given in contemplation of marriage and therefore it is conditioned on the occurrence of the marriage. Thus, the person who bought the engagement ring should receive the ring back if the engagement ends without marriage. In some states, if both parties contributed to the purchase of the ring, they each may receive the value of their contribution. Other states, however, consider who is at fault for the breakup when determining who receives the ring, making the decision less predictable and increasing the chance of litigation over the ring.

In sum, there are no standard rules concerning engagements. The engagement ring is the most common symbol of an engagement in the United States, and each state has a different approach to who receives the engagement ring if the engagement does not end in marriage. Furthermore, while the relationship of an engaged couple is not a legally recognized status, a few states allow recovery of financial damages for the breach of promise to marry.

Margaret Ryznar

See also: Marriage and Legal Planning; Marriage Certificate/License

Further Reading

Brinig, Margaret F. 1990. "Rings and Promises." *Journal of Law, Economics, and Organization* 6, no. 1: 203–215.

Frazier, Barbara. 2001. "'But I Can't Marry You': Who Is Entitled to the Engagement Ring When the Conditional Performance Falls Short of the Altar?" *Journal of the American Academy of Matrimonial Lawyers* 17, no: 2: 419–440.

Grant, Alan and Emily Grant. 2007. "The Bride, the Groom, and the Court: A One-Ring Circus." *Capital University Law Review* 35, no. 3: 743–760.

Exhibitionism

Exhibitionism is an atypical sexual behavior in which an individual exposes him or herself to another individual without their consent. Historically, exhibitionists tend to be heterosexual males, and the victims tend to be females. However, existing data may reflect this due to underreporting. The American Psychiatric Association defines the criteria for exhibitionism as, "lasting over a period of at least 6 months, recurrent, intense sexual arousal from the exposure of one's genitals to an unsuspecting person, as manifested by fantasies, urges, or behaviors" (Hopkins et al. 2016). The behaviors of exhibitionists have evolved, from flashing victims on the street, to obscene phone calls, and now with increasing dependence on technology, sending unsolicited "dick pics" (DPs).

Statistics regarding exhibitionism are hard to collect, due to suspected underreporting both from perpetrators and victims. Traditionally and culturally, exhibitionism has not been treated as a serious sexual offense; rather, it's been treated as a public nuisance. Existing research shows that victims of exhibitionists are overwhelmingly female-identified, and perpetrators are largely male-identified. Research written by Clark et al. show that rates of victimization of females working in large medical centers in the United States and Guatemala reflect that 52% of American women and 45% of Guatemalan women have reported being victims of exhibitionism at some point in their lives.

Exhibitionism is not a victimless atypical sexual behavior, even though there is no unwanted physical touch. Not only can this behavior be pathological and disrupt the daily life of the exhibitionist, but those who face the unwanted exposure have reported can be subject to severe distress after the incident. Hopkins et al. discuss a frightening statistic that states an estimated average of 1.6 million children are exposed to each year. There is an obvious danger in making light of unwanted sexual exposure.

With the rise of social media and dating apps has come the new practice of sending unsolicited DPs. DPs have become a cultural phenomenon and have brought forth a feminist movement, and even art installations. In *Unsolicited dick pics: erotica, exhibitionism or entitlement?* Hayes and Dragiewicz define DPs as the colloquial term for men sending images of their own penises via email, messaging application, or text. The conversational spaces surrounding dating apps, Reddit, Instagram, and Twitter are laden with anecdotes of females pushing back against an onslaught of unsolicited DPs. While there has been established research and literature published on the topics of online nonconsensual pornography and revenge porn, there is a void of research that specifically addresses unsolicited DPs. Hayes and Dragiewicz note, "the omission of dick pics from emerging research on image-based sexual abuse is surprising given that offline forms of genital exposure to non-consenting parties (i.e., "flashing") have long been criminalized as a non-consensual sexual offense" (Hayes and Dragiewicz 2018).

With the lack of current research on unsolicited DPs, specifically, many scholars are asking the question: Why? What is the motivation to send DPs to women via text, e-mail, or messenger app? In their article, Waling and Pym discuss an interview with a clinical psychologist who attributes DPs to heterosexual men seeking pictures from women in return; enjoying the "shock value," and being excited by negative attention.

An exhibitionist is defined as an individual that has persistent desires and behaviors that sexually arouse them, which are comprised of exposing their genitalia to often unwilling bystanders, usually women. There are multiple modes of treatment that therapists can use for patients diagnosed with exhibitionism. The common goal is to bring the behavior to extinction, and this can be done through Cognitive Behavioral Treatment, role-playing, covert sensitization, and minimal arousal conditioning. Note that this list is not exhaustive.

According to Beech, "a number of CBT [Cognitive Behavioral Therapy] approaches are used with exhibitionists including working with intimacy deficits and boundaries and identifying and meeting emotional needs" (Beech 2012). Role play (RP) is also used in treatment, with empathy training a major component of this modality. According to Beech, RP focuses on improving the management of deviant urges and impulses. Clients are asked to identify the events, feelings, and thoughts that lead them to expose themselves. Exhibitionists are less likely than other offenders to recognize the

harm they have caused others because they have not made physical contact with the other person. Accordingly, it is of utmost importance to attempt to get the patients to see how their behavior impacts the victim.

Cognitive Behavioral Therapy (CBT) and role-play have both shown impressive results as methods of treatment for exhibitionism. Beech notes that "(Alexander) found positive treatment effects in a meta-analysis of sex offender treatment in that no exhibitionists who attended a CBT/RP program had recidivated, compared to 21% of those who attended another program and 57% of untreated samples" (Beech 2012).

In a follow-up of several group treatment studies, outcomes of behavioral procedures showed that there was no self-reported recidivism of exhibitionist behaviors at the 6-month through 4-year follow-ups. Beech (2012) reported that there were 7 group treatment studies, ranging from 10–45 participants examining the efficacy of treatment and concluded that CBT was the most effective form of therapy for exhibitionism.

It is important to draw attention to the fact that existing research is largely male-to-female in nature. One of the only studies done to research male-to-male exhibition and frotteurism was done by Clark et al., who states, "although the number of males reporting victimization is small, especially when compared with the rates of female victimization, all victims reported negative feelings toward the event, indicating that males do consider the act to be a violation. And yet, no males in this sample reported the crime to authorities" (Clark et al. 2016). A question is raised if this indicates an existing stigma that males feel about being victimized.

Further research should be done to investigate the gap between "in real life" sexual harassment and online sexual harassment. As mentioned previously, flashing someone in a public space has been a criminal offense for quite some time. Why are DPs being treated as a nuisance? Waling believes it is to articulate the idea of DPs as harassment, and that some feminist approaches reframe them as an unwelcome intrusion into the receiver's offline personal space. However, Waling asserts that such approaches draw attention to the disconnect between digital and offline norms, inviting recognition of such behavior as harassment. There is a need to include unsolicited DPs in the research and discussion of image-based sexual abuse. While there is an acknowledged void in research and literature on the evolution of dick pics as a form of exhibitionism, what published works available are bringing the discussion to the forefront of online sexual harassment.

Sarah White

See also: Love, Connection, and Intimacy; Styles of Love

Further Reading

Beech, Anthony R. 2012. "DSM-IV paraphilia: Descriptions, demographics and treatment interventions." *Aggression and Violent Behavior* 527–539.

Clark, Stephanie K., Elizabeth L. Jeglic, Cynthia Calkins, and Joseph R. Tatar. 2016. "More than a nuisance: The prevalence and consequences of frotteurism and exhibitionism." *Sexual Abuse: A Journal of Research and Treatment* 3–19.

Hayes, Rebecca M., and Molly Dragiewicz. 2018. "Unsolicited dick pics: Erotica, exhibitionism or entitlement?" *Women's Studies International Forum* 114–120.

Hopkins, Tiffany A., Bradley A. Green, Patrick J. Carnes, and Susan Campling. 2016. "Varieties of intrusion: Exhibitionism and voyeurism." *Sexual Addiction & Compulsivity* 4–33.

Swindell, Sam, Sandra S. Stroebel, Stephen L. O'keefe, Keith W. Beard, Sheila R. Robinett, and Martin Kommor. 2011. "Correlates of exhibition-like experiences in childhood and adolescence: A model for development of exhibitionsim in heterosexual males." *Sexual Addiction & Compulsivity* 135–156.

Vitis, Laura, and Fairleigh Gilmour. 2017. "Dick pics on blast: A women's resistance to online sexual harassment using humour, art and Instagram." *Crime Media Culture* 335–355.

Waling, Andrea, and Tinonee Pym. 2019. "C'mon, no one wants a dick pic: Exploring the cultural framings of the 'Dick Pic' in contemporary online publics." *Journal of Gender Studies* 70–85.

Exogamy

The first use of the term *exogamy* and the related term *endogamy* are attributed to John Ferguson McLennan in 1865 in his book *Primitive Marriage* (Simpson and Weiner 1989). Both of Greek origin, the prefix *exo–* means "outer, outside, other part" (Online Etymology Dictionary, "Exo" 2019) and the suffix *–gamy* implies *marriage* when referring to anthropological topics (Online Etymology Dictionary, "Gamy" 2019). *Exogamy* is a term describing the social customs or laws which require or expect marriage outside one's own group.

Common groups associated with exogamy are kinship and gender, and individuals are expected or mandated to marry outside of these groups. For instance, the incest taboo, one of the oldest and most universal exogamous rules, mandates that sexual relations be outside the kinship group. In other words, sexual relations between close relatives such as brother and sister, or father and daughter, are not allowed (Benokraitis 2015).

Marrying outside one's gender is another example of an exogamous rule or law. In the United States, this law was first tested in 1970 when a same-sex couple was denied a marriage license. Although the lower courts upheld the decision to deny the marriage license, the Supreme Court refused to hear the case which, instead, left the decision to each state for several decades. Maryland was the first state to pass a law stating that marriage had to be between a man and a woman, thus requiring marriage outside one's gender group which was an exogamous law ("Gay Marriage" 2019).

However, laws and societal norms can change over time, which is the case with same-sex marriage. In June 2015, the Supreme Court ruled in *Obergefell v. Rogers* that same-sex marriage was legal across the country ("Gay Marriage" 2019). Social norms have also been evolving regarding the exogamous expectation that marriage had to be outside of one's own gender group. According to the Pew Research Center, in just one decade, Americans' opinions about same-sex marriage went from 54% opposed to legalizing same-sex marriage in 2007 to 62% in favor of legalization in 2017 (Geiger and Livingston 2019).

While laws and societal norms have shaped marriage for centuries, whether one must marry within (endogamy) or outside one's own group (exogamy) will continue to change as societal laws and expectations change.

Kristie Chandler

See also: Endogamy; Incest; LGBTQ Marriages and Unions

Further Reading

Benokraitis, Nijole V. 2015. *Marriages & Families Changes, Choices, and Constraints*. Pearson.

"Gay Marriage." History.com. Accessed December 3, 2019. https://www.history.com/topics/gay-rights/gay-marriage#section_1.

Geiger, A. W. and Livingston, Gretchen. "8 Facts about Love and Marriage in America." Pew Research Center. Last modified February 13, 2019, https://www.pewresearch.org/fact-tank/2019/02/13/8-facts-about-love-and-marriage/.

Online Etymology Dictionary. "Endo." Accessed November 22, 2019. https://www.etymonline.com/word/endo-

Online Etymology Dictionary. "Exo-." Accessed November 22, 2019. https://www.etymonline.com/search?q=exo-

Online Etymology Dictionary. "Gamy-." Accessed November 22, 2019. https://www.etymonline.com/word/-gamy#etymonline_v_40907.

Simpson, J. A. and Weiner, E. S. C. 1989. *The Oxford English Dictionary*. Oxford: Clarendon Press.

F

Father Support Groups

Between 1960 and 1970, the Father's Rights Movement (FRM) emerged in an attempt to support parental interest relating to family law (i.e., child support settlements, alimony, and assumption of maternal custody). According to The Father's Rights Movement National Organization, before FRM, custody battles were not as common in the United States and virtually unheard of. In the late 1980s, those who were interested in studying families concluded that fathers had a lack of engagement with their families. Some research suggests that the more effective the father feels, the more likely they are to be engaged in fathering (Stone 2008, 16). Moving into the 1990s, the United States started seeing more initiatives and large organizations being developed to support fathers such as the American Coalition for Fathers and Children and Dads Against Discrimination (DADS). These initiatives at the grassroots level were also subject to criticism and controversy by women's groups, who stated that they aimed to restructure child support and custody policy in ways that deprived mothers (Crowley 2008, 101). To explore the various contexts in which fathers seek and utilize these groups, Crowley (2008) conducted a study to see beyond the characterizations and accusations made by women's groups. Jocelyn Crowley, a social researcher, conducted 158 in-depth interviews with fathers in 2008 and found that 17% of fathers sought out the groups for emotional support, and 49% mentioned that personal case management was the most defining factor. The groups not only helped with emotional support but also gave fathers the resources needed to help in their cases following divorce.

Father support groups are not all court or divorce case related (i.e., married, step, single, widowed, or gay fathers). Types of other father support groups offer guidance, inspiration, counseling, and educational opportunities for father-child relationship building. These groups help fathers to feel empowered and understand the positive impact they can have on their children. Special activities that include fathers, especially father support groups further assist fathers in being engaged. For example, *City Dads*, a group with 13,000 members across 37 cities, is designed to help expecting and new fathers adjust to their parental role through outings and sharing resources (Shrayber 2019). There are other examples, such as father support groups designed to give fathers of children with special needs a comfortable place to discuss parenting issues (Crowell and Leeper 1994, chap. 1).

Even with the increase in advocacy for fathers in the United States over the last 50 years, the disparity is evident when comparing the resources available to the number of support groups and programs for new mothers. With an increase in the amount of time fathers spend with children due to certain circumstances (i.e., maternal employment, variability in work schedules, and home-based work) there is also an increase in the demand for parental involvement within the family (Cabrera et al. 2000). As the United States has seen a shift in the cultural perspective about a fathers' role within the family, providing values and emotional support rather than breadwinner, the need for these groups is vital to the well-being of the family.

Audrey Besch and Kwangman Ko

See also: Absent Father; Divorce Support Groups; Nonresidential Fathers; Parent Education Programs

Further Reading

Cabrera, Natasha, Catherine S. Tamis-LeMonda, Robert H. Bradley, Sandra L. Hofferth, and Michael E. Lamb. 2000. "Fatherhood in the twenty-first century." *Child Development* 71, no. 1: 127–136.

Crowell, Nancy, and Ethel Leeper, eds. 1994. *America's fathers and public policy.* Washington: National Academy Press. https://www.nap.edu/read/9193/chapter/1

Crowley, J. 2008. "Organizational responses to the fatherhood crisis." *Marriage & Family Review* 39, no. 1: 99–120.

The Fathers' Rights Movement National Organization. 2018. "About Us." Accessed September 21, 2019. https://fathersrightsmovement.us/about/.

Shrayber, M. 2019. "These men created a support groups for fathers. They're changing what it means to be a dad." *Upworthy.* https://www.upworthy.com/these-men-created-a-support-group-for-fathers-they-re-changing-what-it-means-to-be-a-dad

Stone, G. 2008. "An exploration of factors influencing the quality of children's relationships with their father following divorce." *Journal of Divorce and Marriage* 46, no. 1–2: 13–28.

Five Love Languages

The "Five Love Languages," created by Dr. Gary Chapman in 1995, can be used as a communication tool within the context of relationships or families. According to Chapman, the five love languages are *words of affirmation* (using encouraging and affirming language when communicating, sending unexpected notes or texts, and recognizing efforts); *acts of service* (doing chores together or helping out with a task, and having follow-through); *receiving gifts* (thoughtfulness, gratitude and receiving small meaningful gifts); *quality time* (uninterrupted conversations and one-on-one time); and *physical touch* (making intimacy a priority, hugs, kisses, and holding hands). Each individual has a primary love language and a secondary love language which represent an avenue change of emotional connection. A person can have high scores on more than one primary love language, however, relationships are complex and fundamental to what it means to be human. To understand the complexity of relationships, one must understand the complexity of individuals. Our perceptions, thoughts, and beliefs about the world cannot be the same as someone else. This is what makes a person an individual and determines how information is interpreted. In turn, information processing determines the conflict that one might have with their partner. In a relationship, partners must work constantly to construct and interpret information. This in turn creates meaning in their experiences with each other (Bradbury and Karney 2014). Couples must understand a complex set of experiences for each partner. Here is an example of information processing using the five love languages.

Riley, whose primary love language is "acts of service," is in a relationship with Sam, whose love language is "words of affirmation." Sam notices that Riley has been very busy with work lately and that they have not had a chance to clean the car or get a full tank of gas. Knowing that Riley's love language is acts of service, Sam decides to offer help and surprise Riley. Now, Sam could have approached this information differently. Sam could have seen the dirty car and unfilled tank and assumed that Riley was lazy, but Sam interpreted it differently and decided to use Riley's love language as a tool. When Riley realizes what Sam has done, they are very happy and decided to express Sam's love language—words of affirmation—by bragging about what a great partner Sam is the next time they are around friends.

Over time, specific perceptions will change about the partner's behavior; the five love languages are a relationship-building tool in which to navigate these perceptions and a better understanding of how love is expressed and received. Couples can take *The 5 Love Languages*® test online as well as find other resources (i.e., podcasts, conferences, books, videos, apps, and stories).

In one exploratory study, researchers examined the outcomes of a relationship education program using the five love languages described by Chapman. Two groups were compared concerning relationship functioning. One group in the program received a book, tips, and reminders to practice the five love languages. Results indicated that the group receiving information on the five love languages gained confidence in using their partner's language, communication tools, and skills in expressing

love, increased empathy, and learned to meet their partner's needs (Nichols et al. 2018). Some authors argue that the five love languages influence co-dependence within relationships and hinder growth (Biancalana 2013). The idea of using love languages as the main tool for communication is thought to create a sense of codependence between partners. So, if partners use love languages without having other areas of growth, they create codependence. However, evidence-based literature has found benefits in relationship functioning through using the five love languages (Nichols et al. 2018; The Gottman Institute 2019). Partners are about to use love languages as a way of identifying needs and meeting those needs for the other person. By using this tool, couples can find healthy ways of communicating, meeting each other's needs, and overall strengthening their relationship.

Audrey Besch

See also: Attachment Theory of Love; Gottman Institute; Love, Connection, and Intimacy; Marital Expectations

Further Reading

Biancalana, Roy. 2013. *The hidden danger of the five love languages.* https://coaching withroy.com/the-hidden-danger-of-the -five-love-languages/.

Bradbury, Thomas and Benjamin Karney. 2014. *Intimate Relationships.* New York: W. W. Norton & Company, Inc.

The Gottman Institute. 2018. "Learn to speak your partner's love language." *The Gottman Institute: A Research-based approach to relationships.* https:// www.gottman.com/blog/learn-speak -partners-love-languages/.

The Gottman Institute. 2019. "Build strong family connections by speaking love languages." *The Gottman Institute: A Research-Based Approach to Relationships.* https://www.gottman.com/blog /build-stronger-family-connections -speaking-love-languages/.

Miller, Susie. 2019. "How to speak your spouse's love language chart." *Susie Miller International.* http://www.susiemiller.com /5ll-chart/#.

Nichols, Allison, Jane Riffe, Cheryl Kaczor, Ami Cook, Gwen Crum, Andrea Hoover, Terrill Peck, and Rebecca Smith. 2018. "The five love languages program: An exploratory investigation points to improvements in relationship functioning." *Journal of Human Sciences and Extension* 40–58.

Focus on the Family

Focus on the Family is a Christian organization founded by American psychologist James Dobson in 1977. It has the stated goal of helping people build and maintain happy and healthy families. Focus on the Family promotes conservative viewpoints regarding homosexuality, divorce, abortion, some birth control methods, and other social issues. The association has gained international prominence, branching out from its original radio broadcast to a variety of ministries, and taking in a reported $98 million USD in 2018. Dale Buss, Dobson's biographer, refers to the founder as "the most influential Christian in America," although Dobson states that not all of his opinions are reflective of Focus on the Family's official positions. Since 2005, Jim Daly has served as president. His tenure has seen the organization more open to dialog with other viewpoints while maintaining its core beliefs.

Dobson's initial outreach came through his weekly "Let's Get Acquainted" radio broadcast, which offered advice to families. By 1980, Dobson was hosting the daily radio show "Focus on the Family" for 100 stations. In 2008, the program was inducted into the National Radio Hall of Fame. The organization also included magazines, Dobson's book, educational packages, and conferences to spread its views and to counsel couples in their marriages and child raising. In 1993, Focus on the Family had grown so large that it built a new headquarters on a 45-acre property in Colorado Springs, Colorado.

Focus on the Family offers a wide variety of articles and resources for married couples. They provide advice related to such issues as infidelity, intimacy concerns, financial struggles, and difficulties surrounding pregnancy and raising children. Support is offered through conferences, retreats, and counseling.

The organization was also part of the increasing prominence of evangelical Christianity, which gained momentum through the late 1970s and 1980s and endorses socially conservative positions. The group opposes sex outside of heterosexual marriage and has offered training materials to families to assist them in teaching their children that God's plan for marriage is between one man and one woman. It also opposes divorce and remarriage, offering support to couples who are struggling in their relationship. From 1998–2009, it also ran the Love Won Out ministry, which hosted conferences to steer people away from their gay lifestyle and provide support to people who chose to renounce homosexuality.

Focus on the Family has a strong pro-life agenda, which includes a desire to overturn the 1973 Supreme Court decision *Roe v. Wade* that legalized abortion in the United States. It endorses political candidates supportive of this view, and it has paid to install ultrasound machines in crisis pregnancy centers. These machines are intended to show the fetus to expecting mothers and form an emotional attachment that dissuades them from obtaining abortions. The pro-life stance also includes any contraceptives that prevent pregnancy after the point of fertilization, including some birth control pills.

In recent years, Jim Daly has spoken about the need for more positive conversations with people holding opposing viewpoints, as he recognized the futility of winning new supporters through condemnation. Focus on the Family has branched out around the world and now has offices in a dozen countries.

Kevin Hogg

See also: Marriage Counseling; Marriage Retreats

Further Reading

Bailey, Sarah Pulliam. 2011. "Refocusing on the family." *Christianity Today* 55, no. 7: 20–26.

Buss, Dale. 2005. *Family Man: The Biography of Dr. James Dobson*. Wheaton, IL: Tyndale House.

Dobson, James. 1970. *Dare to Discipline*. Wheaton, IL: Tyndale House.

Focus on the Family. 2002. *Focus on the Family: Celebrating 25 Years of God's Faithfulness*. San Diego, CA: Tehabi.

Friendship and Divorce

Divorce affects many aspects of life, including friendships. Friendship is often characterized by trust and companionship and varies across individuals and cultures. Considering that couples tend to share friendship networks, a loss of friends after a divorce may occur. It is estimated that individuals will lose 10% of their social networks within the first 12 years after divorce (Terhell et al. 2004, 733). Individuals may also find themselves having different social schedules and interests than their married friends and may even be viewed as a source of strain in their friends' relationships. A recently divorced friend may be viewed as someone whom a spouse could have an affair with. Moreover, a couple is more likely to divorce if individuals in their friend group are currently in the process of divorce. Additionally, friends may disapprove of a divorce, creating further strife in the friendship.

Along with loss, a divorce may also provide an opportunity for an individual to grow their friendship network in new ways. Divorced individuals may find themselves having more time to cultivate their friendships. As divorce may be viewed as a crisis, friends may be able to provide much-needed support after the loss of a marriage. Those who have close friends whom they can talk to tend to fare better in the adjustment period after divorce. With regard to friendship experiences after a divorce, the time frame of a divorce, whether early or later in a marriage, along with the spouses' gender are necessary to consider.

Gender

In heterosexual marriages, the gender of both spouses may mean that individuals have different experiences among their friendship networks after divorce. Women's friendships tend to be defined as "face-to-face" whereas men's friendships tend to be defined as "side-by-side"

(Wright 1982, 1–20). For example, women tend to take part in friendships that are characterized by intimacy and communion whereas men's friendships tend to be characterized by activities. Even searching "women's friendships" and "men's friendships" on the internet yields different results, with photos stereotypically depicting women talking to one another and men engaging in activities such as video games. Married men tend to have smaller friendship networks compared to married women. This pattern continues after divorce. Among both men and women, friendship networks tend to be less satisfying among the divorced compared to the married (McLaughlin et al. 2010, 675).

Less is known about friendship experiences after a divorce in same-sex marriages. Family of choice, which often includes friends, is much more common among lesbian and gay individuals compared to those who identify as heterosexual (Dewaele et al. 2011, 320–321). Lesbian and gay friendship networks tend to be denser, meaning their social networks are characterized by individuals who know one another (i.e., greater overlap). Therefore, divorce may potentially mean less friendship change after divorce among same-sex couples due to higher network density and endorsement of friends as a family of choice. More work needs to be done to learn about the friendship networks of LGBTQ partners post-divorce.

Timing Divorce

The timing of divorce may also play a role in how friendship patterns manifest post-divorce. Divorce often occurs within the first few years of marriage, however, divorce after marriages of longer durations, including "grey divorce" which entails divorcing later in life, is on the rise. When divorce occurs after a lengthy marriage, the individual may face extensive changes in how they navigate their social network compared to those who divorce earlier on in a marriage.

Friendship definitions change over the life course as well as the meaning of and interactions with social networks. Compared to younger adults, older adults tend to have smaller social networks characterized by greater quality. Therefore, a divorce earlier on in life may afford individuals the ability to sift through a larger social network for friendships after a divorce. In contrast, a divorce later in life may mean that individuals have fewer friends to rely on for emotional support.

Friendship with a Spouse after Divorce

After a divorce, an individual may continue to be friends with a former spouse. This more commonly occurs for those with children as the preference for shared custody of children requires ex-spouses to communicate with one another. In one classification, post-divorce parents can range from perfect pals (i.e., very friendly) to dissolved duos (i.e., ceasing contact entirely; Ahrons 2007, 58). As time went on, several parents moved into the category of perfect pals with their ex-spouse (Ahrons 2007, 58). For children, the conflict between parents can be stressful and is associated with poorer outcomes in the post-divorce period, especially since children tend to fare better after a divorce if contact is maintained with both parents.

An individual becoming friends with their former spouse may be best characterized as a process. This may especially be the case as it is still often viewed as taboo to be friends with an ex, with judgment stemming from others. For those who do become friends with a former spouse, an alternation between stability and change, and intimacy and detachment may occur (Masheter and Harris 1986, 177). Ex-spouses must navigate these relational dialectics all while moving from a relationship previously characterized by romance to a relationship that merely entails friendship (Schneller and Arditti 2004, 18–19). The former spouses also must move forward in a friendship knowing that a loss had previously occurred in the relationship. It should also be noted that friendships between exes can be problematic for some. This may especially be the case if the marriage was characterized by abuse. Moreover, those who have relationships with their ex-spouse characterized by low preoccupation (e.g., fewer thoughts about the ex-spouse, the marriage) tend to have the best well-being post-divorce (Masheter 1997, 471).

There is much to be learned about divorce and friendship. Two fruitful avenues for future research involve the experience of divorce and friendship among same-sex couples due to the recent legalization of same-sex marriage and among older adults due to the increase in "grey divorce" (i.e., increasing divorce rates among older adults). Divorce may affect friendship networks differently for individuals. For some, divorce enables the opportunity to further create and grow friendships. For others, divorce may result in the loss of friendships.

Ashley E. Ermer

See also: Communication between Couples in Divorce; Divorce, Process of; Divorce, Psychological Effects

Further Reading

Ahrons, Constance. 2007. "Family Ties After Divorce: Long-Term Implications for Children." *Family Process* 46, no. 1: 53–65.

Dewaele, Alexis, Nele Cox, Wim Van den Berghe and John Vincke. 2011. "Families of Choice? Exploring the Supportive Networks of Lesbians, Gay Men, and Bisexuals." *Journal of Applied Social Psychology* 41, no. 2: 312–331.

Masheter, Carol. 1997. "Healthy and Unhealthy Friendship and Hostility Between Ex-Spouses." *Journal of Marriage and the Family* 59, no. 2: 463–475.

Masheter, Carol and Linda Harris. 1986. "From Divorce to Friendship: A Study of Dialectic Relationship Development." *Journal of Social and Personal Relationships* 3, no. 2: 177–189.

McLaughlin, Diedre, Dimitrios Vagenas, Nancy Pachana, Nelufa Begum, and Annette Dobson. 2010. "Gender Differences in Social Network Size and Satisfaction in Adults in Their 70s." *Journal of Health Psychology* 15, no. 5: 671–679.

Schneller, Debora and Joyce Arditti. 2004. "After the Breakup: Interpreting Divorce and Rethinking Intimacy." *Journal of Divorce & Remarriage* 42, no. 1–2: 1–37.

Terhell, Elisabeth, Marjolein Broese van Groenou, and Theo van Tilburg. 2004. "Network Dynamics in the Long-Term Period After Divorce." *Journal of Social and Personal Relationships* 21, no. 6: 719–738.

Wright, Paul. 1982. "Men's Friendships, Women's Friendships and the Alleged Inferiority of the Latter." *Sex Roles* 8, no. 1: 1–20.

G

Gender Roles

Gender roles impact decision-making and interactions between couples, as well as overall relationship satisfaction. The term "gender roles" refers to the accepted behavior of a person based on their sex. Gender roles are categorized on a continuum between traditional and egalitarian. A person with traditional gender roles supports the division of behaviors and jobs based on sex. For example, people who hold traditional gender roles may believe that women should be homemakers and men should be financial providers. A person with egalitarian gender roles supports an equal distribution of household and work responsibilities regardless of sex.

Experts suggest that gender roles encourage sexism. Sexism has two components, hostile sexism and benevolent sexism. Hostile sexism represents hostility and blatant prejudice toward women. Benevolent sexism represents stereotypical behaviors and attitudes toward women but is positive in tone. These benevolent sexist behaviors and attitudes are often interpreted as intimate and chivalrous, such as society thinking women need to be protected and taken care of by men. Though benevolent sexism is often perceived as positive, the undertone is rooted in masculine dominance. Both forms of sexism reinforce and uphold traditional gender roles (Glick and Fiske 1996, 491).

People learn gender roles through their family dynamics and from messages conveyed by broader society. Typically, men tend to hold stronger traditional gender roles compared to females. Additionally, people who have lower education levels, are more religious and live in rural areas usually have stronger traditional gender role attitudes. Strict gender expectations exist across all racial and ethnic groups. However, research suggests that Black/African American and Caucasian individuals have more egalitarian gender role attitudes compared to Hispanic/Latino individuals. These trends are due to various cultural, historical, and political factors (Boehnke 2011, 60).

Attitudes toward gender roles are influenced by evolutionary and societal development over time. Traditionally in the United States, men were viewed as the powerful, assertive, and financial providers in the relationship, while women were viewed as submissive and supportive homemakers. In selecting a mate for marriage, men were historically drawn to partners who were obedient, attractive, and able to bare children for reproduction purposes. Women were drawn to partners who were intelligent and could provide for them financially due to their limited economic opportunities (Chen, Fiske, and Lee 2009, 767). Due to the husband's financial advantage in the marriage, men were viewed as the decision-makers, while the woman remained dependent upon him. Because women's primary roles were to raise children and take care of the housekeeping tasks, there was less expectation for men to participate in these tasks. As a result, men were able to devote more energy to career pursuits and earning income, which reestablished their dominance and power in marital relationships.

Over the last several decades in the United States, there has been a gradual shift in gender expectations. Modern feminist movements have encouraged people to question traditional gender roles and their consequences on families and society. Today, women have an increasing amount of financial and decision-making power in their relationships, largely due to increased education levels and career pursuits. Additionally, modern financial circumstances require most families to have multiple sources of income per household, and thus, women's work outside the home is more valued in current times compared to previous decades. Women are also waiting until later in life to get married and have children, compared to previous generations, giving them an opportunity to advance their careers and earning potential. In the United States today, the majority of both men and women work outside the home.

Today, women often experience stress and conflict as opportunities and freedom are progressing quicker in their employment, compared to in their relationships and home life. When today's relationships are formed, most women are working in their careers and in an environment where they have independence and more freedom. Yet, relationships are still formed and maintained largely through more traditional gender dynamics. For example, men ask women out on dates, often pay for dates,

and propose to women before marriage. Then, when marriage occurs, women still take on more of the household and child-rearing responsibilities. These contradictions cause women to have to navigate and negotiate these intersecting work and family life realms (Lamont 2014, 190). In fact, more women today choose to maintain their independence and freedom over getting married, where they may have to compromise their freedom. Moreover, sexual expectations for men and women are driven by gender roles. Society typically promotes the idea that men are sexual beings, whereas women are encouraged to suppress their sexual desires. As a result, men and women often enter into marriage with different beliefs and experiences regarding sex, which can lead to conflict and stress (Elliott and Umberson 2008, 191–192).

In both male and female same-sex relationships, expectations for couples are more egalitarian. The division of roles and labor is divided more evenly, based on time, availability, and personal preferences (Kelly and Hauck 2015, 438–439). However, the expected division of work based on gender pervades the lives of same-sex couples, who are often presumed to have one of the partners assuming the "male" role and the other assuming the "female" role.

Although traditional gender roles can be interpreted as positive at times, they can be problematic and have negative consequences for both men and women. Strict gender roles prevent us from seeing the unique traits of a person and cause us to have rigid expectations for behaviors and attitudes. When men or women choose different paths that contradict traditional gender expectations, they may be judged, which may cause them to be self-conscious. These expectations then trickle down from parents to children, which can limit opportunities and areas for growth based on what is deemed appropriate for gender.

For families with members who have different views toward gender roles, they often experience stress, tension, and confusion in day-to-day behaviors, as well as with long-term pursuits. Additionally, research shows that individuals with stronger traditional gender roles are more likely to have supportive attitudes toward intimate partner violence and are more likely to be involved in abusive relationships (Reyes et al. 2016, 350). Due to recent shifting gender roles, conflict is more likely to arise in relationships. Experts argue that as women gain more social and economic status, men are more likely to exert violence in their relationships as a way to uphold their power (Overall et al. 2016, 26).

Overall, gender roles create and translate to power within families and society. Gender roles have shifted from traditional to more egalitarian over time, which for some, has contributed to stress and tension. Gender roles will continue to evolve, which will cause relationships and families to renegotiate dynamics and behaviors.

Sarah Taylor and Katya Ruiz

See also: Economic Independence; Individualized Marriages

Further Reading

Boehnke, Mandy. 2011. "Gender role attitudes around the globe: Egalitarian vs. traditional views." *Asian Journal of Social Science*: 57–74.

Chen, Zhixia, Susan T. Fiske, and Tiane L. Lee. 2009. "Ambivalent sexism and power-related gender-role ideology in marriage." *Sex Roles* 60, no. 11–12: 765–778.

Elliott, Sinikka, and Debra Umberson. 2008. "The performance of desire: Gender and sexual negotiation in long-term marriages." *Journal of Marriage and Family* 70, no. 2: 391–406.

Glick, Peter, and Susan T. Fiske. 1996. "The ambivalent sexism inventory: Differentiating hostile and benevolent sexism." *Journal of Personality and Social Psychology* 70, no. 3: 491–512.

Kelly, Maura, and Elizabeth Hauck. 2015. "Doing housework, redoing gender: Queer couples negotiate the household division of labor." *Journal of GLBT Family Studies* 11, no. 5: 438–464.

Lamont, Ellen. 2014. "Negotiating courtship: Reconciling egalitarian ideals with traditional gender norms." *Gender & Society* 28, no. 2: 189–211.

Overall, Nickola C., Matthew D. Hammond, James K. McNulty, and Eli J. Finkel. 2016. "When power shapes interpersonal behavior: Low relationship power predicts men's aggressive responses to low situational power." *Journal of Personality and Social Psychology* 111, no. 2: 195.

Reyes, H. Luz McNaughton, Vangie A. Foshee, Phyllis Holditch Niolon, Dennis E. Reidy, and Jeffrey E. Hall. 2016. "Gender role attitudes and male adolescent dating violence perpetration: Normative beliefs as moderators." *Journal of Youth and Adolescence* 45, no. 2: 350–360.

Genealogy

The interest in family genealogy research has grown by leaps and bounds over the past two decades. This popularity can be attributed to the ease and accessibility provided by genealogy websites and affordable at-home and mail-away DNA kits. As with any cultural phenomenon, however, it is important to understand the impact such interest has on society.

Depending on the level of engagement amateur genealogists desire, genealogy research can take a considerable amount of time and energy. It is not uncommon to hear hobby genealogists discuss how they "go down rabbit holes" through their family data and become consumed with finding answers about their ancestry (Smith 2012). Within the amateur genealogy community, there is a shared language system with common terminology that researchers use to communicate with one another.

It is useful to have an understanding of some of the shared terminology when thinking of the impact of family genealogy research. Genealogy expert Jackie Arnold discusses the "beginnings of kinship," offering reasons for ancestral research such as kinship (genetic and otherwise) and shared traits. She reviews the concept of monogamy, which she believes is responsible for the shift between maternal (cave people) and paternal (Neolithic era) kinship lines. In paternal kinship, clans are formed and then blend into tribes. Breeding within the social group (endogamy) was commonplace under this system, but as tribes expanded it became more common for breeding outside of the social group (exogamy) to be the norm. It became more desirable to bring new blood to the family line (outbreeding) than to breed within the same familial DNA (Arnold 1990).

Much like there is a shared language system amongst genealogists, there are also common problems one might encounter when collecting genealogical data. Many marriage, divorce, birth,

and death records before the rise of civil registration are non-existent or lost. Census data, a common tool for genealogy researchers, can be unreliable if the family member wasn't recorded, experienced a marital name change, or the records can't be located for any given decade. Similarly, court documents may be challenging when the records room or entire courthouse encounters catastrophic damage. Genealogy expert Marsha Rising lists ten mistakes to avoid when conducting family research: only using one or two good sources exclusively; getting locked into an idea or theory you have developed; justifying reasons for conflict within the data; trying to link oneself to "desirable" ancestors; only examining one piece of data at a time; looking for "magic" documents that will answer all your questions; hopscotching across decades; only looking at surnames; giving documents significance based on age; and, putting off assembling, organizing, and publishing your work (2019). Mistakes are inevitable but being familiar with common issues can save genealogists time and energy otherwise spent going down the wrong path.

Beyond common mistakes researchers may encounter, difficulties tracing family historical data may be more challenging for different types or groups of people. Female ancestors may be difficult to locate or follow due to marital name changes and laws excluding women from particular aspects of social life: before 1840 women could not own land in their name, before 1850 women were excluded from the U.S. Census, and before 1920 women were not allowed to vote. Genealogy researchers may need to rely more heavily upon alternate data sources, such as newspapers, city directories, church records, and private journals when searching for female ancestors. Val Greenwood (2017) provides a timeline of women's property and ownership rights over time, which may offer readers better insight into how and where to search for their ancestors, as well as how to read particular documents. Given the lack of information about the lives of women during different historical periods, researcher Sharon Carmack recommends looking to family bibles, personal letters, and diaries for insight into female ancestors and suggests that family genealogists not only document the significant dates, but also include the social history of women over time, including topics such as sexuality, women's work, childbearing, and the moral reform movement (2013).

In the United States record system, non-white people often encounter similar challenges when tracing genealogical information. When seeking data for Native-American ancestors it is important to research tribal traditions and naming practices within the tribes being researched. Understanding practical solutions for locating tribe names and resources, overcoming challenges surrounding given/tribal names versus assigned English names, and methods for communicating with the Bureau of Indian Affairs are often necessary for these searches.

Locating genealogical data for African-American ancestors may result in similar challenges due to the forced entry of many people of African descent into the United States as slaves. Sources such as Freedman's Savings and Trust Company, the National Union Catalog of Manuscript Collections (NUCMC), and the Bureau of Refugees, as well as reviewing chattel, manumission, and emancipation records may be necessary to follow family lineage. In many cases, it is often useful to seek records of the slaveholders for additional information on ancestors who were forced into slavery.

The current proliferation of user-friendly DNA kits and services makes using DNA results to trace family genealogical data easier than ever before. People taking these DNA tests should be aware of their limitations around accuracy, as well as possible safety risks. Most kits come with warnings about the possibility of learning information about your family that may be unexpected, incomplete, or inaccurate, such as racial/ethnic data or inconclusive health information. DNA results may also be used in ways the person did not expect or give permission for, such as criminal procedures or familial custody disputes. Users should understand these risks before using a DNA testing service.

Genealogical data, which is often centered on canonical family events such as births, marriages, divorces, and deaths, is only part of the story, however. Individual narratives and "existential turning points" (Jorgenson and Bochner 2004, 527), or stories outside the record books, are often excluded because they are not universal experiences. This is especially true when the stories belong to marginalized people, such as women and persons of color. When excluded, the impact of these stories remains unexplained, obscuring how the family identity was developed. The current increase in community membership and ease of data access in the field of family genealogy offers a unique opportunity to address this lack and create space for these voices to be heard.

Amy M. Smith

See also: Adoption; Blended Families

Further Reading

Arnold, Jackie Smith. 1990. *Kinship: It's all relative*. Baltimore, MD: Genealogical Publishing Co., Inc.

Carmack, Sharon D. 2013. *Finding female ancestors*. Genealogy at a Glance. Baltimore, MD: Genealogical Publishing Company.

Greenwood, Val D. 2017. *The researcher's guide to American genealogy* (4th ed.). Baltimore, MD: Genealogical Publishing Company.

Jorgenson, Jane, and Bochner, Arthur P. 2004. "Imagining families through stories and rituals." In *Handbook of family communication*, edited by Anita L. Vangelisti. Mahwah, NJ: Lawrence Erlbaum Associates, Publishers, pp. 513–539.

Rising, Marsha H. 2019. *The family tree problem solver: Tried-and-true tactics for tracing elusive ancestors* (3rd ed.). Cincinnati, OH: Family Tree Books.

Smith, Amy M. 2012. *Tracing family lines: The impact of women's genealogy research on family communication*. Lanham, MD: Lexington Books.

Gottman Institute

Dr. John Gottman and Dr. Julie Schwartz Gottman founded the Gottman Institute to provide services for marital relationship health through the advancement of research on types of relationships (The Gottman Institute). It researches the dynamics of marriage but does not limit itself to research on heterosexual couples or couples of a certain age or the marital issue type (Aycock 2002, 34; Gottman and Gottman 2015). For example, the Gottman Institute has studied homosexual couples, heterosexual couples of retirement age, and violent couples (Gottman and Gottman 2015). The Institute researches the influence of family life on marriage and child-rearing. The Gottman Institute's extensive research on marital relationships can provide help for people in a broad range of circumstances (Aycock 2002, 34).

Dr. John Gottman's goal for the Gottman Institute has been to create a math-based theory for understanding marital relationships (Young 2005, 223). Before his research and research done by the Gottman Institute, there were a few different approaches to treating relationship problems, but few looked at how the problems were arising within the relationship and their consequences (Gottman and Gottman 2015). Dr. Gottman began his research by studying university couples while they discussed a problem in their relationship for fifteen minutes. With the data he collected from this study, he and his graduate student went on to create the Couples Interaction Scoring System (Gottman and Gottman 2015). The Couple's Interaction Scoring System is a coding system used to identify problem-solving behaviors.

The Gottman Institute is home to the Family Research Lab, where research on marital stability is conducted. The lab is set up to mimic a bed-in-breakfast setting, however, cameras are recording the couples to collect data on how the couples interact with each other. It is set up in this way to make couples feel more comfortable and interact normally with each other (Gottman and Gottman 2015).

Over time, other researchers have added methods to observation techniques used by the Gottman Institute. For example, researcher Robert

Levenson began to incorporate psycho-physiological measures within research on relationships. Three years after Levenson's initial observations, couples were asked to return to the lab and the observations were repeated. The data collected helped Gottman and Levenson develop a powerful predictor of relationship trajectory, which has been accurate 90% of the time (Gottman and Gottman 2015). The Gottman Institute provides a list of articles the research center has published on subjects related to marital relationships, which allows people interested in the subject from a research or clinical perspective access to the information gathered in the lab (Anon 2015).

Makena Nail

See also: Ackerman Institute for Family Therapy; Focus on the Family

Further Reading

Anon. 2015. "The Gottman Institute." *The Gottman Institute*. Retrieved February 9, 2023. https://www.gottman.com.

Aycock, Anthony. 2002. "The Gottman Institute / Smart Marriages." *Library Journal* 127, no. 2: 34.

Gottman, Julie Schwartz, and John Gottman. 2015. "Lessons from the Love Lab." *Psychotherapy Networker* 39, no. 6.

Liebovitch, Larry S., Paul R. Peluso, Michael D. Norman, Jessica Su, and John M. Gottman. 2011. "Mathematical Model of the Dynamics of Psychotherapy." *Cognitive Neurodynamics* 5, no. 3: 265–275. https://doi.org/10.1007/s11571-011-9157-x.

Young, Mark A. 2005. "Creating a Confluence: An Interview with Susan Johnson and John Gottman." *The Family Journal* 13, no. 2: 219–225. https://doi.org/10.1177/1066480704272597

H

Half-Siblings and Stepsiblings

There are many sibling types represented in modern families today, ranging from full biological siblings to adoptive or foster siblings. Two sibling types on the rise in current family structures are half-siblings and stepsiblings resulting from a divorce and remarriage. It is estimated that 40% of households in the United States include stepchildren (Wiemers et al. 2019), and an estimated two-thirds of all stepfamilies go on to produce half-siblings within the first four years of stepfamily formation (Bumpass 1984). Although the prevalence of both half- and stepsiblings after divorce and remarriage is on the rise, these sibling types have distinct characteristics.

The term *half-sibling* refers to brothers or sisters who share only one biological parent. Half-siblings have either the same biological mother or father and thus share 25% genetic relatedness. Although half-siblings may result from the death of a biological parent or an extramarital affair, half-siblings are most likely to be part of a post-divorce, remarried blended family dynamic (Coleman et al. 2001). Seventy-eight percent of the United States population report living with a sibling, with 14% reporting living with at least one half-sibling (Krieder and Ellis 2011). Indeed, a large portion of half-siblings (as opposed to stepsiblings) will live within the same residence, especially during their childhood.

Research has reported that living with a half-sibling can be associated with lower well-being. Interestingly, stepchildren who live in a household that includes half-siblings are further impacted, with research reporting decreased academic performance and more behavior problems in comparison to stepchildren living in a household that does not include half-siblings (Wood Strow and Strow 2008). Half-sibling relationships are expected to be negatively impacted by the stress and grief of losing a biological parent due to divorce; having to share resources and the attention of the shared biological parent; potentially lowered socioeconomic status due to the divorce and remarriage; and increased uncertainty about appropriate family roles in their blended family.

Stepsiblings are brothers or sisters who are related only through the marital ties of their parents. Stepsiblings share no biological relations and thus are 0% genetically related. Stepsiblings may or may not live in the same residence across their lifetime and unlike the permanency of half-biologically related siblings, stepsibling relationships may be terminated if the individuals' parents divorce. Stepsiblings experience similar stressors due to divorce and remarriage as half-siblings; however, research argues stepparents may withdraw attention from their stepchildren after producing a biological half-sibling themselves, transferring their emotional and relational resources into the new biological offspring instead. As a result, the various sibling relationships in a blended family may suffer due to this perceived parental favoring behavior. Additionally, stepsiblings are expected to provide and receive less support from one another in comparison to biologically related siblings (including half-siblings) (Mikkelson, Floyd, and Pauley 2011).

Stepsiblings have been heavily researched since the 1980s due to the increase in divorce and remarriage rates. However, although a common dyad within prevalent modern family structures, half-siblings are largely left out of present-day family research. Moreover, when half-siblings are studied or discussed in the research, they are often combined into the same group as stepsiblings. This combination obscures the differences between these two unique sibling types, especially since one includes shared biology and the other does not. When step and half-sibling relationships are researched, much data also reflects the hardships typical to these sibling types resulting from restructuring a family after divorce. Less research focuses on how half- and stepsiblings can overcome these hardships due to restructuration and instead cultivate positive or resilient sibling bonds.

Current researchers such as Tamara D. Golish (2003) have called on present and upcoming family researchers to study resilient half- and stepfamily relationships. Authors who have answered this call note forgiveness, prosocial actions, and spending quality time together help stepfamily bonding (Waldron et al. 2018). Additionally, authors who have studied resilient half-sibling relationships note that not using the word "half" when referring to a half-sibling; having joint activities; being positive and open with one another; and having the stepparents and biological parents positively intervene and encourage communication between half-siblings can all help lessen some of the challenges due to divorce and remarriage (Oliver 2018).

Bailey M. Oliver-Blackburn

See also: Coparenting and Divorce; Divorce, Psychological Effects; Remarriage; Stepfamilies

Further Reading

Bumpass, Larry L. 1984. "Children and marital disruption: A replication and update." *Demography* 21, no. 1: 71–82.

Coleman, Marilyn, Mark A. Fine, Lawrence H. Ganong, Kimberly J. M. Downs, and Nicole Pauk. 2001. "When you're not the *Brady Bunch*: Identifying perceived conflicts and resolution strategies in stepfamilies." *Personal Relationships* 8, no. 1: 55–73.

Golish, Tamara D. 2003. "Stepfamily communication strengths: Understanding the ties that bind." *Human Communication Research* 29, no. 1: 41–80.

Guzzo, Karen Benjamin. 2014. "New partners, more kids: Multiple-partner fertility in the United States." *The ANNALS of the American Academy of Political and Social Science* 654, no. 1: 66–86.

Kreider, Rose M. and Renee Ellis. 2011. "Living arrangements of children: 2009." *Current Population Reports*. Washington, DC: U.S. Census Bureau, pp. 70–126.

Mikkelson, Alan C., Kory Floyd, and Perry M. Pauley. 2011. "Differential solicitude of social support in different types of adult sibling relationships." *Journal of Family Communication* 11, no. 4: 220–236.

Oliver, Bailey M. 2018. "Blended family resilience: Communication practices in positive adult half sibling relationships." PhD Diss. Arizona State University.

Waldron, Vincent R., Dawn O. Braithwaite, Bailey M. Oliver, Dayna N. Kloeber, and Jaclyn Marsh. 2018. "Discourses of forgiveness and resilience in stepchild–stepparent relationships." *Journal of Applied Communication Research* 46, no. 5: 561–582.

Wiemers, Emily E., Judith A. Seltzer, Robert F. Schoeni, V. Joseph Hotz, and Suzanne M. Bianchi. 2019. "Stepfamily structure and transfers between generations in U.S. families." *Demography* 56, no. 1: 229–260.

Wood Strow, Claudia, and Brian Kent Strow. 2008. "Evidence that the presence of a half sibling negatively impacts a child's personal development." *American Journal of Economics and Sociology* 67, no. 2: 177–206.

Halo Effect

The halo effect is a cognitive bias in which people overestimate the overall qualities they perceive in others on the rating of one positive or negative attribute, i.e., when a person perceives another as having a desirable trait or quality (such as being attractive), they are more likely to perceive them as having other desirable traits or qualities (such as also being intelligent and a hard worker). For example, on the first date with a potential romantic partner, one might have little information about a person; however, if they perceive their date as physically attractive, the halo effect contends that they are likely to attribute other positive qualities to their date, such as being intelligent, kind, or a suitable romantic partner.

The American psychologist Edward L. Thorndike (1874–1949) first referred to the term *halo* in his study published in 1920 on military officers. Thorndike found that when military officers were asked to rank their subordinates on a list of qualities such as physical traits, leadership ability, character traits, and intelligence, he found that if an officer rated a subordinate as high in one quality or trait, they were more likely to rate the subordinate high in other qualities or traits. For example, if an officer rated a subordinate high on physical traits, such as physique or level of energy, they were likely to rate them as having high intellectual abilities or leadership skills. However, if officers rated subordinates as negative on one quality, they were also likely to rate the subordinate as negative in other qualities. Thorndike, therefore, concluded that the overall evaluation of qualities cannot be determined on an individual basis; in other words, a positive rating on one trait biases perceptions of ratings on other traits.

A later study by Solomon Asch (1946) on first impressions of personality characteristics concluded that when participants were read a series of adjectives that described a person, the first adjective describing the individual, whether it was positive or negative, influenced their overall perception of the participant. Asch's participants listened to one list of adjectives that began with positive traits and ended with negative traits and another list of adjectives that started with negative traits and ended with positive traits. If the participant heard the list that began with positive traits first, they were more likely to rate the people they observed as positive; conversely, if a participant heard the list that began with negative traits first, they were more likely to rate people they observed negatively. For example, if a person was initially described as being intelligent, the participant's further and overall evaluations of people were positive, and therefore the order of the list of adjectives colored their perceptions of the individuals they were rating. Initial impressions, or information regarding a person's characteristics or traits, ultimately influenced the participant's overall global assessment of others.

The halo effect is ultimately one of the most observable influences within social life. Following these initial studies by Thorndike and Asch, many contemporary researchers have observed the halo effect in a variety of situations and circumstances. For example, Keeley et al. (2013) found that the halo effect can directly influence students' ratings of professors' performances. Efrain and Patterson (1974) found the halo to influence voting preferences in national elections with voters being more likely to elect candidates they rated as physically attractive. Kozłowski (2018) found that the halo effect may also influence how consumers perceive and evaluate institutions, such as the case with the tendency for clients to positively rate local banking institutions that resemble and have similar characteristics to other banks that are doing well financially.

Alexander L. Smith

See also: Love, Connection, and Intimacy; Love at First Sight

Further Reading

Asch, Solomon E. 1946. "Forming Impressions of Personality." *The Journal of Abnormal and Social Psychology* 41, no. 3: 258–90. Doi:10.1037/h0055756.

Efran, Michael G., and E. W. J. Patterson. 1974. "Voters Vote Beautiful: The Effect of Physical Appearance on a National Election." *Canadian Journal of Behavioural Science/Revue Canadienne Des Sciences Du Comportement.* 6, no. 4: 352–356

Keeley, Jared W., Taylor English, Jessica Irons, and Amber M. Henslee. 2013. "Investigating Halo and Ceiling Effects in Student Evaluations of Instruction." *Educational and Psychological Measurement* 73, no. 3: 440–457.

Kozłowski, Łukasz. 2018. "The Halo Effect in Banking: Evidence from Local Markets." *Finance a Uver* 68, no. 5: 416–441. http://search.proquest.com/docview/2137103320/.

Thorndike, Edward L. 1920. "A Constant Error in Psychological Ratings." *Journal of Applied Psychology* 4, no. 1: 25–29.

Homogamy

Social status shapes family habits and rituals, relationships with extended family and others, appearance and genetic traits, and access to resources and support. The theory of homogamy suggests that individuals marry partners with similar characteristics which helps individuals pass on their genetic traits and values (*"birds of a feather flock together"*). Although the theory most commonly refers to people from similar socioeconomic backgrounds, researchers have also examined racial, ethnic, and religious homogamy. People in homogamous marriages report higher family cohesion, marital satisfaction and stability, and lower divorce rates than those in intermarriages. However, homogamous marriages can also increase the risk of passing on genetic mutations and abnormalities and increase social division.

These factors are important when considering a partner, building extended family networks, and making parenting and family decisions.

As of 2010, the U.S. Census reports homogamous marriages are the most common family types in the United States. Approximately 80% of couples have obtained the same level of education, and more than 90% of couples are of the same race. In religious couples, those with a higher education are more likely to report religion as a significant factor in mate selection. This preference for similarities may be explained by *phenotype matching,* which suggests individuals may have an unconscious biological drive to marry those who look, act, or even smell like their parents. This is important as individuals consider passing on preferred genetic traits and personality characteristics through their children, as well as accessing appropriate and sustainable resources.

While biological factors may be influential, social factors may be even more evident in mate selection, which can explain why siblings have a sexual aversion to one another despite their biological connection and why children who were adopted prefer characteristics of their adoptive family over their birth family. Further, social circumstances such as birth order contribute to mate selection. Older male children, for example, are more likely to be sexually attracted to pregnant or lactating women than their younger siblings, possibly due to witnessing their mothers caring for siblings. Daughters whose fathers are alcoholics are three times more likely to marry an alcoholic than those whose fathers aren't alcoholics, and daughters whose fathers are older are more likely to

be attracted to men with older facial features. Religion is also deeply connected to partner choice, the number, and timing of children, career preferences, and other significant life decisions. This social connection to mate preference is called *sexual imprinting.*

The developmental timing of the sensitive zone of sexual imprinting is unknown, but mate selection may also be influenced by social change. For example, according to the Pew Research Center, interracial marriages nearly tripled from 1980–2010, especially among college-educated individuals. Developmental psychologists suggest one explanation for this change may be that college is a distinct time for cognitive and social development for those who have access and attend. College increases proximity to individuals with similar interests from various cultural backgrounds and connects them through a common university cultural experience. Religious students, for example, often have religious services and events on college campuses, which help solidify a sense of group cohesion d a core identity. As such+, higher education increases the likelihood of religion being a factor in individuals' partner choices. As individuals build new social connections and learn more advanced cognitive skills, their mate preference often shifts away from biological or familial phenotypes toward a preference for shared values and complementarity.

The social shift in partner preference may be beneficial for long-term human survival, as "extreme" homogamy increases the likelihood of inbreeding. Having children with people who are very genetically similar increases genetic abnormalities and the likelihood of passing on genetic mutations. Genetic diversity, or "outbreeding," increases the chances of species survival by reducing the chances of passing on autosomal recessive genetic disorders. Scientists suggest genetic diversity is making children smarter and taller than previous generations and is increasing life longevity.

Despite the risks of genetic homogamy, couples who establish a strong family identity have higher self-esteem, increased family and group cohesion, and more positive life outcomes. Homogamy can promote a clear shared cultural understanding of family identity, which increases relationship satisfaction and lowers conflict and divorce rates. These factors establish a sense of comfort, security, and predictability in homogamous marriages that increases the likelihood of passing on favorable genetic and character traits, increases the longevity of the marriage, and promotes healthy family and individual development.

Megan L. Chapman

See also: Hypomogamy and Hypermogamy; Socioeconomic Status and Marriage

Further Reading

Kalmijn, Matthijs. 1998. "Intermarriage and homogamy: Causes, patterns, and trends." *Annual Review of Sociology* 24, 395–421.

Lareau, Annette. 2011. *Unequal Childhoods: Class, Race, and Family Life.* Berkeley: University of California Press.

McDowell, Teresa, Melendez-Rhodes, Tatiana, Althusius, Erin, Hergic, Sara, Sleeman, Gillian, Kieu My Ton, Nicky, Zimpfer-Bak, A. J. 2013. "Exploring social class: Voices of inter-class couples." *Journal of Marital and Family Therapy* 39, no. 29: 59–71.

Sigalow, Emily, Shain, Michelle, and Bergey, Meredith R. "Religion and decisions about marriage, residence, occupation, and children." *Journal for the Scientific Study of Religion,* 51, no. 2: 304–323.

Sterbova, Zuzana, and Valentova, Jaroslava. 2013. "Influence of homogamy, complementarity, and sexual imprinting on mate choice." *Anthropologie* 50, no. 1: 47–60.

Honeymoon

The original term "honeymoon" can be traced to the 16th century, which is derived from the Scandinavian culture. The time for "honey" (or sweetness) in a marriage is much older than the poet John Heywood, and his eloquent use of the phrase "it was yet but the hony moone" to be free to express joyful feelings within a marriage. It also refers to the period of a full-moon cycle, which has supposedly promoted conception in some cultures.

The custom of travel evolved in 19th-century Britain, i.e., that newlywed couples visit families and friends who were unable to attend the ceremony. The term is derived from Western tradition to enhance bonding, relaxation, and plans for the future. In other countries, a couple may take a day or a week for the wedding ceremony, in addition to the honeymoon: its modern definition is a holiday for newlywed couples to relax after the ceremony. This practice continues across different cultures, with romantic love as a prominent feature of marriage.

Honeymoon is also a term "to warn newlyweds about waning love," as Liz Susong (2020), editor of Catalyst Wedding Company, highlights on her website. The phrase promotes the romantic notion that marriage is filled with love, romance, and travel. Honeymoons revolve around a "coming of age tradition," i.e., in which two people become adults and will soon be creating a family. According to Lee, Fakfare, and Han (2020), this tradition dates back to the 1800s as a time for celebration (Susong 2020) and a time for the couple to explore themselves with a post-wedding trip.

The honeymoon is now a choice for newlywed couples, regardless of how societal expectations have changed, and despite their cost becoming exorbitant. Tourism adds to their dynamic nature, as it refers to a trip taken only by the new couple or may coincide with a destination wedding, which is a couple's trip to celebrate with family and friends. The length of the honeymoon varies between cultures, but a couple mutually agrees on how it will be handled.

A honeymoon honors a new beginning, the Idea of "two-becoming-one," fulfilling couples in their physical and emotional needs, as well as having their own time (Susong 2020). The term "honeymoon" may remind the reader of a moon cycle—and how it simulates life patterns, focusing on the satisfaction inherent in married life.

Seungyeon Lee

See also: Wedding Party; Wedding Reception.

Further Reading

Heywood, John. 1562. *The Proverbs and Epigrams of John Heywood*.

Lee, Jin-Soo, Fakfare, Pipatpong, and Han, HeeSup. 2020. "Honeymoon tourism: Exploring must-be, Hybrid and value-added quality attributes." *Tourism Management*, 76: 103938.

Susong, Liz. 2020. "Everything you need to know about the honeymoon tradition." *Bride*. https://www.brides.com/story/the -gloomy-history-behind-honeymoons.

Hypomogamy and Hypermogamy

Hypomogomy is marrying someone of a lower social or economic class, and hypermogamy is marrying someone of an equal or higher social class. Social class is generally defined as a combination of a person's education and income, which contribute to a person's social connections and opportunities. These factors influence family habits and rituals, relationships with extended family and others, and access to resources and support. For example, children from poor and working-class families tend to spend more time with family and neighbors, and middle-class children are more likely to spend time with their parents or in extracurricular activities. In intermarried couples, partners must negotiate these and other values and practices to resolve conflict and establish a distinct family system, identity, and sense of belongingness.

Socioeconomic factors have long been known to be a decisive feature in mate selection and have been deeply influenced by gender norms. Historically, social trends indicate men in the United States have obtained higher educations than their wives. These social trends originate in patriarchal norms, which expected men to obtain an education to improve their odds in both the labor and marriage markets. An increase in education would increase financial and social potential, which improves the odds of marrying a more desirable partner. These gender-related trends in hypergamy continued through much of U.S. history to the extent that before the 1980s, marriages in which women obtained higher educations were more likely to result in divorce.

Today, trends have shifted significantly. In most countries around the world, women obtain almost equal numbers of higher education degrees as men. In some regions, such as Western Europe and the United States, women have reversed the educational attainment gap and are obtaining higher education degrees more frequently than men. This shift has had an impact on relationship attitudes and marital trends as well. From 1980–1990, men who reported feeling comfortable with their partners making more money than they increased from 41% in 1980 to 60% in 1990 (Pew Research Center 2017). Since then, women's educational attainment has not had a statistically significant impact on divorce rates. Further, according to the 2012 U.S. Census, most couples tend to have the same education. Of partners with differences in educational attainment, 12% of married heterosexual men and 10% of married heterosexual women had obtained a higher education than their partners.

Cultural beliefs and values, women's roles and status, macroeconomics, and social inequity contribute to changes in marital patterns over time. Despite educational shifts, men are still more likely to be the breadwinners of the family. Among heterosexual married couples in 2012, 20% earned within $5000 of each other, and 55% of men made at least $5000 more per year than their wives compared to 20% of women making more than their husbands (Pew Research

Center 2017). Several theories have emerged to understand hypergamy, especially as it relates to gender.

One common theory suggests that as women gain increased access to education and financial independence, the need for marriage decreases, and standards for minimally acceptable partners increase. Women, then, may be more likely to match with a partner with lower educational attainment but more similar or increased potential for earning. This aligns with statistics from Pew Research Center (2017), which suggest homogonous marriages are declining for most social groups, especially those with higher educational attainment and those who live in metropolitan areas. This aligns with other statistics which suggest that women who marry after age 30 are more likely to marry men with less educational attainment than younger women. Younger women are more likely to match with partners based on their expected education or earning potential rather than their actual education or earning attainment. This may contribute to generational changes and trends, including an increase in divorce rates for partners who marry at a younger age.

There is a clear connection between socioeconomic position and family functioning. Despite this understanding of changing trends and social awareness of cultural differences in marriage, little research highlights the importance of socioeconomic status in marital decision-making, child-rearing, and other important aspects of marriage. Research that does exist has primarily been conducted in countries in which a stratification system is in place. That is, in which upward class mobility is possible. This may influence couples to see themselves as coming from different socioeconomic backgrounds but as the same socioeconomic status as a couple, which may sway the importance of class culture in research results and attention to socioeconomic status in practice. Although little is known about the relational effect of socioeconomic differences in couples, there is a clear impact on family decision-making, child-rearing, and family functioning.

Megan L. Chapman

See also: Economic Independence; Homogamy

Further Reading

Kalmijn, Matthijs. 1998. "Intermarriage and homogamy: Causes, patterns, and trends." *Annual Review of Sociology* 24, 395–421.

Lareau, Annette. 2011. *Unequal Childhoods: Class, Race, and Family Life.* Berkeley: University of California Press.

McDowell, Teresa, Melendez-Rhodes, Tatiana, Althusius, Erin, Hergic, Sara, Sleeman, Gillian, Kieu My Ton, Nicky, Zimpfer-Bak, A. J. 2013. "Exploring social class: Voices of inter-class couples." *Journal of Marital and Family Therapy* 39, no. 29: 59–71.

Pew Research Center. 2017, May 18. "Intermarriage in the U.S. 50 years after Loving v. Virginia," by Gretchen Livingston and Anna Brown.

Sterbova, Zuzana, and Valentova, Jaroslava. 2013. "Influence of homogamy, complementarity, and sexual imprinting on mate choice." *Anthropologie* 50, no. 1: 47–60. https://www.ojp.gov/ncjrs/virtual -library/abstracts/parents-prison-and -their-minor-children

I

Incarceration, Coparenting and

Incarcerated coparenting is a relationship that negotiates roles, rules, responsibilities, and contributions between individuals to provide nurturance to a shared child while at least one of the caregivers is in the custody of the criminal justice system. This working definition incorporates the most significant and interactive aspects of incarcerated and coparenting populations using a Tadros Theory lens to account for the various complexities within the family system.

Incarceration is the holding of an individual in a prison or jail for an extended period, often years, and can occur before and following a trial. The individual and family of the incarcerated commonly face a variety of intended or unintended consequences, including interference in family cohesion and function, social stigma, physical and mental health problems, and financial burdens, in addition to many others. By the end of 2016, there were 2,162,400 individual adults incarcerated in the United States (Kaeble and Cowhig 2018). Fifty-two percent of state offenders and 63% of federal offenders are parents to an estimated 1.7 million minor children; these children are 2.3% of the U.S. population under the age of 18 (Glaze and Maruschak 2008; Sexton 2016, 62).

Coparenting is defined as the relationship through which parents negotiate roles, rules, responsibilities, and contributions to their shared child (Margolin, Gordis, and John 2001, 10). Coparenting can be undertaken by biological or adoptive parents, legal guardians or caregivers, relatives, or anyone in a parental role, regardless of marital status. There is an abundance of research on both incarceration and coparenting, however, there is very limited research on their intersection.

Incarceration poses many challenges to coparenting. Practical barriers to contact exist when a loved one is incarcerated, such as physical separation, which incurs financial and time costs of transportation for meetings and phone calls or letters for communication (Tadros and Finney 2018, 257). This severance from the rest of the family can impede parenting interventions and leave the unincarcerated parent essentially unsupported, even when attempting to enact agreed-upon parenting measures.

The effects of incarceration on the individual can also affect the family bond negatively. Incarceration can result in significant decreases in mental and physical health through exposure to violence, lack of proper medical care, and emotional trauma, which can act as stressors or barriers to communication or satisfaction in the coparenting or parent-child relationship from all involved members of the family (Barretti and Beitin 2009, 40–41; McKay et al. 2018, 69). Furthermore, involuntary separation from a parent is often associated with behavioral and emotional disturbance in children and can have long-term negative effects on development in these areas if not properly addressed. Among other subjects, coparents must negotiate how they will speak to the child about the incarceration of one of their caregivers.

Relationship turmoil can arise most easily during transition phases in family structure, including initial incarceration and reentry. Research has documented negative feelings and consequences experienced by partners of an incarcerated individual such as shame and anger make them typically less willing to compromise during disagreements after feeling as if they have compromised enough (Barretti and Beitin 2009, 40). The reluctance of a partner to surrender newly established independence or the stubbornness of the released partner to fixate on seeking employment over attending to family matters are two such examples. Similar feelings can arise when the relationship is with a non-romantic coparent.

The endeavor to coparent while incarcerated can have many motivators. Quality family relationships consist of both supportive communication patterns between children and parents and positive communication and partnerships between coparents (Loper et al. 2014, 225). The research shows that it may be beneficial to address necessary parenting and communication skills as well as issues between coparents before release when there is a temporary state of stability that can allow for proactive measures. Studies have found instances of couples rating relationship happiness and intimacy as higher during incarceration compared to post-release. Strengthening the coparenting alliance is associated with more positive moods, such as being attentive, active, alert, excited, enthusiastic, determined, inspired, proud,

interested, and strong, among children. This can potentially increase the likelihood of more positive interactions between family members.

Given the ever-increasing prevalence of families coparenting with an incarcerated parent and the unique challenges and opportunities faced by this population, special consideration by individuals and institutions can provide significant improvements in such families' mental health outcomes and overall functioning. Although there is sufficient evidence that concludes how incarcerated parents, significant others, and coparenting partners continue to be adversely affected by traumatizing risk factors associated with incarceration, there continues to be a need for further research that provides the tools to navigate the incarcerated experience for offenders and their coparents, both pre- and post-release.

Eman Tadros and Taylor Ogden

See also: Coparenting and Divorce; Coparenting Typologies; Marriage and Incarceration

Further Reading

Barretti, Louis M. and Beitin, Ben K. 2009. "Creating Internships in Marriage and Family Therapy: A Collaboration Between a Training Program and an Offender Reentry Facility." *Contemporary Family Therapy: An International Journal* 32, no. 1: 39–51. doi:10.1007/s10591-009-9109-3.

Glaze, Lauren E. and Maruschak, Laura M. 2008. "Parents in Prison and Their Minor Children." Bureau of Justice Statistics (BJS). Accessed June 28, 2019. https://www.bjs.gov/index.cfm?ty=pbdetail&iid=823.

Kaeble, Danielle and Cowhig, Mary. 2018. "Correctional Populations in the United

States, 2016." *Bureau of Justice Statistics (BJS)*. Accessed June 28, 2019. https://www.bjs.gov/index.cfm?ty=pbdetail&iid=6226.

Loper, Ann Booker, Victoria Phillips, Emily Bever Nichols, and Danielle H. Dallaire. 2014. "Characteristics and Effects of the Coparenting Alliance between Incarcerated Parents and Child Caregivers." *Journal of Child and Family Studies* 23, no. 2: 225–41. doi: 10.1007/s10826-012-9709-7.

Margolin, Gayla, Elana B. Gordis, and Richard S. John. 2001. "Coparenting: A Link between Marital Conflict and Parenting in Two-Parent Families." *Journal of Family Psychology* 15, no. 1: 3–21. doi: 10.1037/0893-3200.15.1.3.

McKay, Tasseli, Megan Comfort, Lexie Grove, Anupa Bir, and Christine Lindquist. 2018. "Whose Punishment, Whose Crime: Understanding Parenting and Partnership in a Time of Mass Incarceration." *Journal of Offender Rehabilitation,* 57, no. 2: 69–82. doi:10.1080/10509674.2017.1294640.

Sexton, Thomas L. 2016. "Incarceration as a Family Affair: Thinking Beyond the Individual." *Couple and Family Psychology: Research and Practice* 5, no. 2: 61–64. doi: 10.1037/cfp0000062.

Tadros, Eman and Natasha Finney. 2018. "Structural Family Therapy with Incarcerated Families." *Family Journal* 26, no. 2: 253–261. doi: 10.1177/1066480718777409.

Incarceration, Couples Therapy and

Rates of incarceration have risen dramatically since the 1990s. The U.S. Department of Justice Bureau of Statistics has reported that there were 2,162,400 adult individuals incarcerated by the end of 2016 (Kaeble and Cowhig 2018). The extremely high number of incarcerated individuals has led to many partners not having their significant others present in their everyday lives. Incarcerated individuals are an exceptionally underserved population, specifically in the realm of mental health and marriage and family therapy. Historically, the focus of mental health services has been individual treatment; however, partners and family members are significantly impacted by their loved one's absence during incarceration. Incorporating partners and family members into the therapeutic process can aid in improving reentry into the family system and building relationships.

Studies have revealed that conflict within the family system can have a strong and negative effect on the reentry process. Research has shown that visitation by family members and people with close ties to an offender can decrease reoffending. In fact, research shows that conflict with a partner was the second most common impact on reoffending (Zamble and Quinsey 1997). Due to the severely negative experience documented by individuals who are or have been incarcerated, it is typical for offenders to tend to socially withdraw and remain detached from relationships leading to dysfunction in their relationships with partners, family members, and others (Haney 2001). However, offenders are not alone in the process of incarceration—they still maintain their roles as fathers, mothers, husbands, and wives.

According to the American Association for Marriage and Family Therapy's (AAMFT) website, "In marriage and family therapy, the unit of treatment isn't just the person—even if only a single person is interviewed—it is the set of relationships in which the person is imbedded." Marriage and family therapy is brief, solution-focused, and specific, with attainable therapeutic goals. Clients that have participated in treatment have reported improvements in their couple relationship. In couples therapy, clients are observed within the context of these everyday relationships to gain insight into their interactional cycle.

Marriage and family therapists (MFTs) work in a variety of settings and contexts (agencies, clinics, universities, consultants, government, private practice, hospitals, schools, in-home, etc.). MFTs are trained on how to help families restructure, open up lines of communication, gain insight, create boundaries, reframe stories, generate solutions to problems, etc. MFTs can help families become aware of the process occurring in their relationships rather than placing their emphasis on the content of their issues. Further, employing a systemic approach to therapy enables presenting problems to be seen in relational terms. This is particularly helpful as MFTs can share insight into how parents who return from periods of incarceration may still be dependent on institutional structures and routines, therefore, it may be difficult for them to effectively organize the lives of their children or engage in any initiative or autonomous decision-making that parenting involves without first engaging in family therapy (Tadros and Finney 2018). Consequently, impacting the lives of various members simultaneously, particularly significant others.

A major benefit of having MFTs in incarcerated facilities is that therapy can create a safe environment allowing for growth. MFTs must focus on empowering and encouraging their clients as well as challenging them to produce change.

Couples therapy is designed to prevent marital distress and divorce by teaching skills and principles to couples to maintain healthy and lasting relationships. Couples therapy offers offenders and their families an opportunity to learn and develop tools to create a stable and supportive environment, such as increasing connection, communication skills, conflict resolution skills, validation, empathy, and acceptance (Tadros et al. 2019).

Unfortunately, there are very few MFTs working within the incarcerated system. The system as it currently stands is not always conducive to therapeutic services due to financial constraints as well as present policy. For MFTs who do work in these systems, they (1) must represent MFTs well by advocating for the unique services they provide and (2) apply systemic principles to the distinctive and complex issues faced by both individuals and families when a loved one is incarcerated. Future directions include the incorporation of MFTs into incarcerated facilities to assist couples in repairing and/or maintaining relationships.

Eman Tadros

See also: Divorce and Incarceration; Marriage and Incarceration; Marriage Counseling

Further Reading

American Association for Marriage and Family Therapy (AAMFT). 2018. https://www.aamft.org/About_AAMFT/About_Marriage_and_Family_Therapists.aspx

Barretti, Louis M. and Ben K. Beitin. 2009. "Creating Internships in Marriage and Family Therapy: A Collaboration Between a Training Program and an Offender Reentry Facility."

Contemporary Family Therapy: An International Journal 32, no. 1: 39–51. doi:10.1007/s10591-009-9109-3.

Haney, Craig. 2001. "The Psychological Impact of Incarceration: Implications for Post-Prison Adjustment." In *From Prison to Home: The Effect of Incarceration and Reentry on Children, Families, and Communities*. U.S. Department of Health & Human Services.

Kaeble, Danielle and Mary Cowhig. 2018. "Correctional Populations in the United States, 2016." *Bureau of Justice Statistics (BJS)*. Accessed June 28, 2019. https://www.bjs.gov/index.cfm?ty=pbdetail&iid=6226.

Tadros, Eman and Natasha Finney. 2018. "Structural Family Therapy with Incarcerated Families." *Family Journal* 26, no. 2: 253–261. doi: 10.1177/1066480718777409.

Tadros, Eman, Janelle M. Fye, Christine L. McCrone, and Natasha Finney. 2019. "Incorporating Multicultural Couple and Family Therapy into Incarcerated Settings." *International Journal of Offender Therapy and Comparative Criminology* 63, no. 4: 641–658. doi: 10.1177/0306624x18823442.

Zamble, Edward, and Vernon L. Quinsey. 1997. *The Criminal Recidivism Process*. Cambridge Studies in Criminology. Cambridge: Cambridge University Press. doi:10.1017/CBO9780511527579.

Incest

Incest, biologically defined, refers to the reproduction between two closely related parents. Individuals produced by incest run a much greater risk of birth defects than those produced by two parents that are not closely related. Incest taboos exist in every culture. But cultures define incest for social as well as biological reasons. For instance, in some cultures, first-cousin marriage is considered to be legitimate, even ideal, while in other cultures first-cousin marriage is defined as incest. First-cousin marriage is legal in some U.S. states, while illegal in others. Societal reaction to incest also varies greatly by culture, from death and imprisonment to a much milder sanction such as ridicule.

Various theories have attempted to explain the incest taboo. Sigmund Freud, a psychologist, believed that people are sexually attracted to family members but that those urges need to be contained. In discussing the Oedipus complex, Freud believed that during a person's psychosexual stages of development that a child would desire his/her opposite-sex parent and feel jealous toward his/her same-sex parent.

Edvard Westermarck, a sociologist, also believed that family members could be sexually attracted to each other. Westermarck, however, believed that family members who have regular contact from an early age will not become sexually attracted to one another.

Another anthropologist, Bronislaw Malinowski, believed that family members were naturally attracted to each other, but that, sexual competition within a family would disrupt relationships and the structure of the family. The family relationships necessary for the healthy operation of a family do not allow room for sexual competition within the family. Malinowski's theory could explain why cultures have incest taboos even when the family members are not biologically related. For instance, two parents may live with their biological child and then adopt another who is not biologically related. Both children could grow up together but not be allowed to marry, culturally or legally. According to Malinowski, an incest taboo would be necessary to promote healthy family dynamics, not to protect against birth defects.

Still, others believe that incest promotes exogamy, or marriage outside of one's group, which help integrates members of society. Successful societies need to integrate their members. Successful societies, then, need to make sure that individuals are interconnected. One way to do this is by having people from one family marry into another. Marriages have been arranged between members of two families to stop inter-family feuds.

Incest may be divided into two main types: *consensual* and *forcible*, or rape. The concept of "consensual incest" may be an oxymoron due to the power differentials involved in families. In other words, the question is whether or not two people in a family can consent to sex given the familial relationships that they have. There are cases, however, in which two adults, closely related, have apparently engaged in a consensual sexual relationship.

These have involved typically half-siblings or even parent-child relationships who have not lived with each other while the child(ren) involved were growing up. This would support Westermarck's theory that relatives are attracted to each other but develop an aversion to each other as they grow up. As relatively uncommon as these cases are, it is extremely rare for them to be prosecuted. One example of consensual incest is the case of Patrick Stuebing and Susan Karolewiski.

They are a German couple, who are brother and sister that were separated at a young age and later reunited. In 2001, they began an incestuous relationship and fought for their right to raise a family together. Patrick was ultimately sent to prison due to his sexual relationship with his sister. Patrick's incarceration, however, was not a deterrent.

Forcible incest, or rape of a family member, is more common than consensual incest. Approximately 25% of girls and 16% of boys have had an adult family member or non-family member, rape or molest them before their 18th birthday. Children who are sexually abused by family members are doubly injured. These children are hurt by the sexual assault but also by the betrayal of those who should provide comfort and support. Children need to have their physical needs (e.g., food, shelter) met but also their emotional needs; children need to feel safe to grow into healthy adults. When children are sexually abused by a family member, they risk developing post-traumatic stress disorder (PTSD) which can lead to a variety of maladaptive interpersonal traits and behaviors. PTSD is characterized by flashbacks, hyperarousal, avoidance of people and situations that remind a person of the trauma, poor self-esteem, lack of trust in self or others, emotional regulation, and dissociation. Children who have been sexually abused by family members may develop eating disorders, problems with relationships, and even be vengeful to their abuser. In addition, children sexually abused by a family member may feel that they have nowhere to turn to for comfort and support. Only about 30% of all incest is reported. Victims may underreport incest for a variety of reasons: shame; belief that they, the victim, are responsible; a family that wants to hide the abuse; and/or a belief that no one will believe them. An example of forcible incest is the case that involves Josef Fitzel. Josef Fitzel is an Austrian man who kidnapped his own daughter, Elisabeth, imprisoned her in a dungeon that he created and raped her for 25 years. Holding her captive in his home annex, Elisabeth was raped several times per day during her abduction which happened when Elisabeth was 11 years old.

Survivors of incest can be helped through counseling. One of the biggest hurdles to overcome, however, is that survivors often do not trust their therapist. This lack of trust may cause survivors seeking treatment to move from counselor to counselor. According to Cook et al. (2005), counselors need to focus on helping the client (1) feel safe—survivors who do not have an adequate sense of safety will not be able to thrive, only survive; (2) enhance self-regulation—survivors often have not developed the ability to deal with their emotional state; (3) improve self-reflective information processing—help survivor to develop a coherent view of their life; (4) integrate traumatic experiences—survivors need to be able to process their experiences; (5) improve relational engagement—therapists can help the survivor develop a healthy attachment to others; and (6) positive affect enhancement—develop better self-worth and self-esteem.

Incest is taboo for various reasons. Incest can cause birth defects, disrupts family relationships, and can leave victims with PTSD. Also, marrying outside the family improves social cohesion; when people marry people from another family it increases the connection between more people in society.

Daniel W. Phillips III and Brooks Evans

See also: Cycle of Violence; Endogamy; Exogamy; Intimate Partner Violence; Toxic Relationships

Further Reading

Ballantine, Margaret. 2012. "Sibling sexual abuse—Uncovering the secret." *Social Work Today* 12, no. 6: 18.

Cook, Alexandria, Joseph Spinazzola, Julian Ford, Cheryle Lanktree, Margaret Blaustein, Marylene Cloitre, Ruth DeRosa, Rebecca Hubbard, Richard Kagan, Joan Liautaud, Karen Mallah, Erna Olafson, and Bessel van der Kolk. 2005. "Complex trauma in children and adolescents." *Psychiatric Annals* 35: 390–398.

Tener, Dafna and Michal Silberstein. 2019. "Therapeutic interventions with child survivors of sibling sexual abuse: The professionals' perspective." *Child Abuse & Neglect* 89: 192–202.

Individualized Marriages

Individualization theory, conceived by Andrew Cherlin (2004, 2020), describes the types of marriages where the roles of partners become more adaptative and open to discussion. Couples in the United States, similar to other highly individualized societies, are more likely to form these types of marriages. One of the big challenges of this research is that the term *individualized* is used in different ways but rarely defined. Individualized marriages can fall under two categories. *Individualized* may mean that there are few norms or scripts for how to build and maintain a marriage, so couples must establish their own. Alternatively, individualized marriages can represent the assumptions people make about relationships and what they should look like by emphasizing the individuals within them and their well-being and happiness, perhaps at the expense of the couple as a unit. This first aspect of individualized marriages is known as self-development, where the individuals in a marriage put their own well-being front and center. In addition, individualized marriages examine the aspects of how roles within a marriage are negotiable and flexible. Lastly, individualized marriages prioritize communication and openness in tackling conflict as essential for maintaining these ever-changing romantic relationships.

When the norms or cultural scripts that define people's behavior in social institutions such as marriage are weakened, it creates a process known as deinstitutionalization (Cherlin 2004). Couples integrate most resources and tasks but maintain some autonomy. For these reasons, scholars who study individualized marriages within the United States look at three major categories: child-rearing, division of labor, and finances. Examination of these three categories among married couples allows scholars to follow the transition from companionate relationship models to individualized partnerships that began in the 1960s (Amato 2012; Cherlin 2004). Emerging laws that were granted for child-rearing outside of marriage posed significant changes to traditional ways of being wed. This meant, for example, more women who had children out of marriage were granted the same economic support and financial protection as mothers who bore children within a marriage. These rights were coupled with more husbands sharing more childcare and household duties. As a result, more women entered the labor market by choice and the age of marriage rose among young adults. In addition, before the *Oregon v. Rideout*

decision, that criminalized spousal (marital) rape, women were at the mercy of their husband's desires even if it diminished their own. Moreover, women have more financial freedom and autonomy within marriage than ever before.

Individualization research has several limitations that should be taken into consideration. It is worth emphasizing that, in general, this research found that most marriages in this category are partially individualized (Lauer and Yodanis 2011). For example, more than eight in ten spouses combine all their finances or simultaneously maintain separate and joint accounts (Sutherland 2014). Exclusively managing separate bills and expenses within marriage is still rare among spouses.

Moreover, there is limited available evidence of individualized marriages. For instance, more than nine in ten women still take their husbands' last names when they marry, a marker of traditional male leadership in marriages (Sutherland 2014). Moreover, only 3% (excluding separation) of married people live in a different household than their partner (Sutherland 2014). Individualization research also suggests that young people with low socio-economic status and people of color, in particular, appear more likely to hold individualized understandings of marriage (Cherlin 2020). Furthermore, millennials (those born between 1981 and 1996) are more divided on their views of gender norms and expectations and more individualized in relationships than previous generations (Amato 2012; Risman 2018). Although many people are more individualized in their perspectives of marriage, most couples spend more time together in joint activities than apart (Sutherland 2014). Lastly, most research on individualized marriages is limited to heterosexual participants.

Before individualized marriages, marriage was based on economic survival and arrangement for familial gain. For instance, women and children conceived within a relationship were limited from being property owners outside of the confines of marriage. Following the establishment of individualized marriages, marriages are based primarily on intimacy and love versus the merging of assets. For example, more couples are opting to keep a portion or all of their money apart from their spouses. In turn, more couples in individualized marriages are focused on mental well-being, compatibility, and happiness. Furthermore, cohabiting often carries some or even all of the same rights that come with marriage. This reduces the idea that marriage is a necessary step for romantic relationships. Marriage has increasingly become more of a symbolic expression of a relationship milestone.

Couples in individualized marriages provide a range of reasons for doing so. Most people in individualized marriages cite three primary incentives. The first and most common is more freedom in choosing a partner. Previously, families were more heavily involved in the courting process to the benefit or detriment of an individual's dating preferences. The second motivating factor for choosing an individualized marriage is it makes the process of divorcing slightly easier than in past decades. For example, it is more socially acceptable to leave a marriage when you want for varying circumstances. The third reason is individualized marriages appear to have significant benefits for couples. The core of individualized relationships is where

both partners' individual achievements come first. Therefore, the goal would be for each person to negotiate flexible roles so that both can achieve their goals. In turn, both parties' careers and personal goals are prioritized. In theory, there is more shared household work, child-rearing, and paid labor. This may significantly reduce strain or dependency on the traditional roles of one spouse being the sole provider or homemaker.

Chelsea-Alexis Jackson

See also: Economic Independence; Marriage, Financial Implications

Further Reading

Amato, Paul, ed. 2012. "Institutional, Companionate, and Individualistic Marriages." In *Marriage at the Crossroads; Law, Policy, and the Brave New World of Twenty-First Century Families.* Cambridge, England: Cambridge University Press, pp. 107–112.

Amato, Paul, Alan Booth, David R. Johnson and Stacy J. Rogers. 2007. *Alone Together: How Marriage in America is Changing.* Cambridge, MA: Harvard University Press.

Cherlin, Andrew J. 2004. "The Deinstitutionalization of American Marriage." *Journal of Marriage and Family* 66, no. 4: 848–861.

Cherlin, Andrew J. 2020. "Degrees of Change: An Assessment of the Deinstitutionalization of Marriage Thesis." *Journal of Marriage and Family* 82, no. 1: 62–80.

Giddens, Anthony, ed. 1992. *The Transformation of Intimacy: Sexuality, Love, and Eroticism in Modern Societies.* Cambridge, England: Cambridge Polity.

Lauer, R. Sean., and Carrie Yodanis. 2011. "Individualized Marriage and the Integration of Resources." *Journal of Marriage and Family* 73, no. 2: 669–683.

Risman, Barbara A., ed. 2018. *Where the Millennials Will Take Us: A New Generation Wrestles with the Gender Structure.* New York: Oxford University Press.

Sutherland, Anna. 2014. "Modern Marriage: Individualistic or Interdependent?" Institute for Family Studies. Retrieved from (https://ifstudies.org/blog/modern-marriage-individualisti-interdependent)

Infidelity

Infidelity refers to events where individuals in a relationship with monogamy as an expectation violate the romantic and/or sexual expectations of an outside party. Infidelity differs significantly from Consensual Non-Monogamy (CNM) in that those participating in the former lack an agreement with their partner that either party can engage in outside sexual and romantic relationships, which is present among individuals participating in the latter. Defining the specific acts that constitute infidelity proves challenging as definitions of infidelity are highly individualized. So much so that two individuals in the same relationship may hold differing opinions regarding what "counts" as cheating. While one partner may consider only sexual intercourse as infidelity, the other may include a host of other acts, e.g., kissing, flirting, oral sex, etc. Further complicating the issue, many couples never explicitly define what monogamy means to them, instead leaving it as an unspoken expectation. As a result, partners may unintentionally commit acts their partner considers infidelity. Infidelity stands as the most commonly reported reason for seeking therapy and the most difficult issue to resolve (Bravo and Lumpkin 2010; Fife,

Weeks, and Gambescia 2008; Gordon, Baucom, and Snyder 2005; Heintzelman et al. 2014). Some therapists report a couple's survival rate from a physical affair is around 50% (Solomon and Teagno 2016). Other research shows that at the five-year mark after therapy, couples enjoyed good outcomes (Atkins et al. 2010; Marin, Christensen, and Atkins 2014).

In the United States, a stigma exists around infidelity. Polls consistently show that citizens disapprove of participation in infidelity for any reason. Despite this, research shows a gap between what people claim to value and their behavior. No one wants to discover their partner cheated. Rarely do individuals admit past incidents of their own indiscretions. Infidelity functions as a yardstick for evaluating relationship quality, as evidenced by statements such as, "At least he doesn't cheat on me." Individuals may rationalize negative aspects of their relationship (e.g., selfishness, not spending enough time with you) with an assertion of their certainty of their partner's (assumed) monogamy. These murky definitions complicate the study of infidelity as well. Generally, researchers allow participants to define infidelity for themselves.

The incidence of infidelity cannot be determined with any certainty. The reported rates vary, in part due to the manner researchers pose the question. Asking about the lifetime incidence of infidelity results in higher reported rates than asking about the last year or the last six months. Additionally, people tend to edit their sexual histories. They omit partners from their count for a host of reasons, including shame and unpleasant memories. Some people fail to include incidents absent their own orgasm or about which they feel guilty. Thus, reliable measures of infidelity prove difficult to find, and existing measures employ methods that have been called into question (Atkins, Baucom, and Johnson 2001) because most draw from the General Social Survey (GSS), which relies upon in-person interviews. Research suggests participants are less likely to report their infidelity when asked by researchers in-person (Whisman and Snyder 2007). Research estimating the lifetime incidence of sexual infidelity ranges from 20% to 37.5% (Atkins et al. 2001). However, this rate is likely low. While pinpointing the exact incidence proves challenging, the data suggests that at least some people struggle with monogamy. Although people give lip service to their value of monogamy, for some this value exists more in theory than in practice.

With the increase in technology, the incidence of cyber affairs is increasing as well. In the past, contact with affair partners came with risk due to shared landline phones, but the proliferation of mobile phones grants both the freedom to hunt for potential partners online and the privacy to make frequent contact. Never before "has it been so easy to enjoy both the stability of a marriage and the thrills of the dating scene at the same time" (Mileham 2007, 11). Social media sites make connecting with an ex or a former classmate easier than ever. Stories abound of high school sweethearts making contact online and picking up where they left off romantically. But even without the aid of social media, an internet search allows someone to locate any ex-lover—permitting people to find and initiate an affair with virtually anyone. While most dating sites target singles, married individuals use them as well. Several sites now exist catering to the market of marital affairs. While some people question whether online relationships count as infidelity, research shows that the impact can be "almost as severe as sexual intercourse" (Whitty and Quigley 2008, 463), and a correlation exists between online affairs and in-person affairs (Wysocki and Childers 2011).

The causes of infidelity vary. While some research attempts to locate the cause within the individual, relationship quality and participation in infidelity correlate. Sexual incompatibility between spouses also stands as a risk for infidelity. However, research shows that for at least some, the mere presentation of an opportunity to participate in infidelity can be enough to induce the initiation of an affair. Meaning, if an individual finds themselves with an opportunity to participate in sexual/romantic association with someone outside of their marriage, they are more likely to act on it. Given the increase of women in the workplace and the shrinking of the world via the internet, many more opportunities for extra-relational sexual/romantic contact now exist.

Monogamy is often embraced as *the* ideal, however, the decision to stray needs only the presentation of an opportunity. Further, research shows that infidelity with coworkers does not signal dissatisfaction with the primary relationship (Atkins et al. 2001; Treas and Giesen 2000). Some participants reported higher levels of marital satisfaction than those engaged in affairs with non-coworker partners. The data certainly suggests that most people are capable of participating in infidelity and that cheating does not necessarily indicate an individual's moral failing. However, the idea that a partner could be happy at home, but still cheat because of an opportunity can be unsettling.

The discovery of infidelity damages relationships and inflicts emotional and psychological suffering on the cheated-upon partner. The cheater may suffer with guilt and confusion as they grapple with knowing the level of pain they inflicted on their partner. Individuals who discover their partner's cheating experience greater vulnerability to depression, lowered self-esteem, and trust issues. Additionally, infidelity is often cited as the reason for intimate partner violence. After the discovery of a partner's infidelity, some individuals struggle to trust anyone they meet and carry that hurt into future relationships.

To guard against experiencing the pain of having been cheated on, many people resort to monitoring their partner's online activity, emails, bank accounts, and texts. Others keep tabs on their partner's comings and goings. Men who perceive themselves at risk to be cheated on spend more time performing oral sex and do so with more frequency (Pham, Shackelford, and Sela 2013). By contrast, women fail to utilize the provision of oral sex as a preventative measure.

Infidelity persists as a cited factor in reports of marital distress as well as decisions to end marriages (Fincham and May 2017). The most commonly reported reason cited for seeking out couple's therapy is infidelity and therapists deem it as the most difficult issue to resolve (Heintzelman et al. 2014). The social narrative that "cheaters never change" likely helps to make repairing a marriage broken by infidelity more challenging. A couple's

survival rate after a physical affair hovers around 50% (Solomon and Teagno 2016).

At present, expectations of marriage are higher than in any previous cultural moment, in part because people now tend to marry for love. At the same time, bloated to-do lists and a breakneck pace of life make finding time to invest in romantic relationships challenging. A cultural sense of entitlement to personal fulfillment and happiness makes people believe they *deserve* to have their expectations met. When marriages fail to meet a partner's high expectations, infidelity stands as an attractive bandage.

Alicia M. Walker

See also: Polyamory; Polygamy

Further Reading

Atkins, David C., Donald H. Baucom, and Neil S. Jacobson. 2001. "Understanding Infidelity: Correlates in a National Random Sample." *Journal of Family Psychology* 15, no. 4: 735–749.

Atkins, David C., Rebeca A. Marín, Tracy T. Y. Lo, Notker Klann, and Kurt Hahlweg. 2010. "Outcomes of Couples with Infidelity in a Community-Based Sample of Couple Therapy." *Journal of Family Psychology* 24, no. 2: 212–216.

Bravo, Irene M., and Peyton White Lumpkin. 2010. "The Complex Case of Marital Infidelity: An Explanatory Model of Contributory Processes to Facilitate Psychotherapy." *The American Journal of Family Therapy* 38, no. 5: 421–432.

Fife, Stephen T., Gerald R. Weeks, and Nancy Gambescia. 2008. "Treating Infidelity: An Integrative Approach." *The Family Journal: Counseling and Therapy For Couples And Families* 16: 316–323.

Fincham, Frank D., and Ross May. 2017. "Infidelity in Romantic Relationships." *Current Opinion in Psychology* 13: 70–74.

Gordon, Kristen C., Donald H. Baucom, and Douglas K. Snyder. 2005. "Treating Couples Recovering from Infidelity: An Integrative Approach." *Journal of Clinical Psychology* 61: 1393–1405.

Heintzelman, Ahsley, Nancy L. Murdock, Romana C. Krycak, and Larissa Seay. 2014. "Recovery from Infidelity: Differentiation of Self, Trauma, Forgiveness, and Posttraumatic Growth among Couples in Continuing Relationships." *Couple and Family Psychology: Research and Practice* 3, no. 1: 13–29.

Marín, Rebeca A., Andrew Christensen, and David C. Atkins. 2014. "Infidelity and Behavioral Couple Therapy: Relationship Outcomes over 5 Years Following Therapy." *Couple and Family Psychology: Research and Practice* 3, no. 1: 1–12.

Mileham, Beatriz Lia Avila. 2007. "Online Infidelity in Internet Chat Rooms: An Ethnographic Exploration." *Computers in Human Behavior* 23, no. 1: 11–31.

Pham, Michael N., Todd K. Shackelford, and Yael Sela. 2013. "Women's Oral Sex Behaviors and Risk of Partner Infidelity." *Personality and Individual Differences* 55, no. 4: 446–449.

Solomon, Steven D., and Lorie J. Teagno. 2016. "'Making up Is Hard to Do'— Couples Therapy after Infidelity." Edited by ContinuingEdCourses.Net: The Relationship Institute. http://www.continuingedcourses.net/active/courses/course089.php.

Treas, Judith, and Deidre Giesen. 2000. "Sexual Infidelity among Married and Cohabiting Americans." *Journal of Marriage and the Family* 62, no. 1: 48–60.

Whisman, Mark A., and Douglas K. Snyder. 2007. "Sexual Infidelity in a National Survey of American Women: Differences in Prevalence and Correlates as a Function of Method of Assessment." *Journal of Family Psychology* 21, no. 2: 147–154.

Whitty, Monica T., and Laura-Lee Quigley. 2008. "Emotional and Sexual Infidelity Offline and in Cyberspace." *Journal of Marital and Family Therapy* 34, no. 4: 461–468.

Wysocki, Diane Kholos, and Cheryl D. Childers. 2011. "'Let My Fingers Do the Talking': Sexting and Infidelity in Cyberspace." *Sexuality & Culture* 16, no. 3: 217–239.

In-Laws

In-laws are the parents of a person's partner, such as mother-in-law, father-in-law, stepmother-in-law, and stepfather-in-law. In-laws can impact marital relationships in both positive and perplexing ways. In both current society and past research, the relationship between in-laws and their children/children-in-law is one full of challenges. Television shows such as *Modern Family* and *Everybody Loves Raymond* poke fun at parents-in-law (Fowler and Rittenour 2017, 254–272). Even though relationships between in-laws are often viewed as challenging, they can also be positive. Scholars have argued there are times in-laws can share positive and frustrated feelings simultaneously. In-laws and the relationship they have with their children can impact the child's overall well-being (Fowler and Rittenour 2017, 254–272; Goetting 1990, 67–90; Merrill 2007). Furthermore, if the relationship the in-law has with their child(ren) is problematic or filled with hurtful sentiments it can negatively impact their relationship, but also the family as a whole.

For the in-law relationship to thrive, there needs to be a mutual understanding about disclosure, as each person needs to make choices about what they want to tell each other and what they want to keep to themselves. Disclosure is one of the most essential parts of any close relationship and this is especially true for in-laws with their child(ren) and children-in-law. The more positive the disclosure (e.g., acceptance) is shared between in-laws, the more the children feel satisfied that the relationship is overall positive (Morr Serewicz and Canary 2008, 333–357).

In 1954, Evelyn Duvall first encouraged more research to be done in the study of in-law relationships. Since 1954, family communication scholars have been studying in-law relationships and noting their many challenges. In-law relationships are often met with a lot of unknowns and uncertainty from each other, making the relationship difficult to negotiate. Some researchers have studied how the length of the marriage predicts the child(ren)-in-law's perception of the behavior exhibited by their parent-in-law (Fowler and Rittenour 2017, 254–272). Meaning that over time child(ren)-in-law could better understand the motives behind why their parent-in-law said or did something, improving their relationship. One aspect of the in-law relationship is how the relationship changes with the addition of grandchildren. (Grand)children can create some tension in the relationship between parent and child(ren)-in-laws, as it adds another layer of discussion that was not previously present in their relationship. When these tensions arise child(ren)-in-laws assess the situation and investigate their privacy rules and then decide if they need to formulate a new boundary. The context of the situation, having children, dictates how the child(ren)-in-laws

formulated privacy rules with their parent-in-law.

In-laws often have doubts when they try to integrate their new child(ren)-in-law into their family because merging families is not an easy task. In-laws might be strategic in establishing boundaries with the new child(ren)-in-law entering the family or the boundaries might be less clear (Mikucki-Enyart 2011, 237–263). For example, the in-laws might decide what they will and will not share with the child (in-law-law ahead of time and set clear boundaries on off-limit topics. But in-laws may not share the boundaries with the rest of the family and risk these boundaries being crossed by new family members (i.e., their children-in-law). It is important to note that it is not only the in-laws making decisions about what information to share and what to keep to themselves about the family's private information. There might be members of the extended family who are willing to share this information with the new child(ren)-in-laws, which might cause some problems if the boundaries were not clear to that family member.

On the other hand, it is not always easy for the child(ren)-in-law to enter into a new family that might share different family norms to which they are not accustomed (Prentice 2009, 67–89) regarding family membership, behaviors, and communication. In-law disclosures can also have an influence over the child(ren)-in-law's marital relationship and the child(ren)-in-law's feelings of family in-group status (Mikucki-Enyart 2011, 237–263; Morr Serewicz and Canary 2008, 333–357). The child(ren)-in-laws, similar to the in-laws, have the same decisions to make regarding what they want to reveal and what they want to keep between them and their spouse. However, it is important to understand what factors are involved in making these decisions. Children-in-law bring their own perspectives into their new families and knowing these boundaries helps in-laws to better understand how to incorporate their child(ren)-in-law into the family (Mikucki-Enyart 2011, 237–263; Morr Serewicz and Canary 2008, 333–357).

For a successful in-law relationship to develop, it is important to have attainable boundaries in place (Wenzel Egan and Hesse 2018). As scholars have found, when privacy rules are not followed, it can lead to boundary turbulence and conflict can enter the relationship (Miller 2009). One way to avoid boundary turbulence is to explicitly negotiate privacy rules, though even then there is no guarantee that boundary turbulence will not creep in. However, having explicit privacy rules agreed upon does help to lessen the confusion surrounding boundaries and therefore aids in hopefully less boundary turbulence within the relationship.

Scholars have found that navigating the in-law relationship is challenging, but supportive communication is related to the child (in-law'saw's feeling of satisfaction with their in-laws and a stronger family identity. Rittenour (2012) examined the role of supportive communication and family self-disclosure standards between the mother-in-law and daughter-in-law relationship by looking specifically at two outcomes of relational quality: relational satisfaction and shared family identity. Meaning, that the daughters-in-law felt happier with their mothers-in-law and held an identity closer to that of their in-law family when supportive communication was practiced. These findings show that families who engage in supportive communication had higher satisfaction in their relationships with their in-laws than those who received negative communication from their in-laws. Goetting (1990) documented that supportive relationships among couples and their in-laws happen when their in-laws provide support of some type (e.g., financial assistance and childcare) for their adult children in the early years of their marriage. In addition, other scholars have found that within in-law relationships, families who engage in supportive communication have higher satisfaction than if there is negative communication (e.g., gossiping about family members) between family members (Morr Serewicz and Canary 2008, 333–357). Additionally, rejection by the in-law family negatively impacts the relationship, but acceptance strengthens the bond. It is important to note that having a positive relationship with one's in-laws can provide stability and increase the quality of one's marriage in addition to making the relationship stronger between the child(ren)-in-law and the in-laws.

Jaclyn S. Marsh

See also: Childcare and Eldercare; Divorce, Grandparents and

Further Reading

Duvall, Evelyn. 1954. *In-laws: Pros and cons.* New York: Association Press.

Fowler, Craig and Christine Rittenour. 2017. "A life-span approach to children-in-law's perceptions of parent-in-law communication." *Journal of Family Communication* 17, no. 3: 254–272.

Goetting, Ann. 1990. "Patterns of support among in-laws in the United States." *Journal of Family Issues* 11: 67–90.

Merrill, Deborah. 2007. *Mothers-in-law and daughters-in-law: Understanding the relationship and what makes them friends or foe.* Westport: Praeger.

Mikucki-Enyart, Sylvia. 2011. "Parent-in-law privacy management: An examination of the links among relational uncertainty, topic avoidance, in-group status, and in-law satisfaction." *Journal of Family Communication* 11, no. 4: 237–263.

Miller, A. E. 2009. "Revealing and concealing postmarital dating information: Divorced coparents' privacy rule development and boundary coordination processes." *Journal of Family Communication* 9, no. 3: 135–149. doi: 10.1080/15267430902773287

Morr Serewicz, Mary Claire, and Daniel J. Canary. 2008. "Assessments of disclosure from the in-laws: Links among disclosure topics, family privacy orientations, and relational quality." *Journal of Social and Personal Relationships* 25, no. 2: 333–357.

Prentice, Carolyn. 2009. "Relational dialectics among in-laws." *Journal of Family Communication* 9, no. 2: 67–89.

Rittenour, Christin. 2012. "Daughter-in-law standards for mother-in-law communication: Associations with daughter-in-law perceptions of relational satisfaction and shared family identity." *Journal of Family Communication* 12, no. 2: 93–110.

Wenzel Egan, Kristina A., and Colin Hess. 2018. "'Tell me so that I can help you': Private information and privacy coordination issues in the context of eldercare." *Journal of Family Communication* 18, no. 3: 217–232.

Interfaith Marriage

Interfaith marriage has increased significantly since the 1960s. This increase is related to the change in public attitudes and the change in marriage laws. Interfaith marriage rates vary significantly by specific religion and denomination and by age. Interfaith marriage refers to a marriage between people of separate faiths such as when a Jewish person marries a Muslim person (separate religions). An interfaith marriage could even occur when there is a marriage between a person who belongs to one religion and another person who has no religious affiliation (religion and no religion). Interdenominational marriage refers to the marriage between two people of different denominations within one faith as is the case when a Baptist marries a Lutheran (separate Christian denominations). In this work, the term "interfaith marriage" is broadly defined to include "interdenominational marriage" as well.

Until the 1960s, marrying outside of one's faith was considered taboo, similar to interracial marriage. Across all faith groups, interfaith marriage is becoming more common in the United States. This is partially due to the broad acceptance of interracial marriage beginning in the Civil Rights era and a decreasing faithfulness to organized religions in the last decades. Interfaith marriages are often intertwined with interethnic marriages. In 1967, the Supreme Court of the United States (SCOTUS) decriminalized interracial marriage in the case of *Loving v. Virginia*. Until SCOTUS ruled in that case, states still had laws on the books that allowed a lawfully married couple of two different races to be prosecuted and even imprisoned simply for being married to one another.

According to Murphy who discusses a YouGov survey, in the United States, approximately 20% of marriages before the 1960s were interfaith marriages. Since the 1960s, interfaith marriages have doubled. The percentage of interfaith marriages has reached approximately 45%. Although interfaith marriages have been increasing, interfaith marriage varies by different religions and denominations: 27% of Jews, 23% of Catholics, 39% of Buddhists, 18% of Baptists, and 21% of Muslims. Today, studies have shown with recent marriages, having a spouse who shares and practices the same faith is of less importance to many Americans. A majority of interfaith marriages consist of those who identify as Christian and those who have no religious affiliation. The percentage of Americans who are unaffiliated with religion has more than quadrupled since 1990. A polling firm, YouGov, conducted a national survey in 2010 of more than 2,000 American couples in interfaith marriages. The survey found interfaith marriages are becoming more common, regardless of geography, education, or economic level. But age is one demographic factor that can predict the likelihood of interfaith marriages. The older a person is when he/she gets married, the more likely he/she is to marry outside of his/her faith. According to the YouGov survey, 48% of those who married before the age of 25 were in interfaith marriages, compared with 58% of those who married between the age range of 26–35, and 67% of those who entered into a marriage between the ages of 36–45.

As the world becomes more open and globalized, interfaith, and interethnic relationships are more common. Due to digital technology, people have more opportunities to find a partner of a different religion, race, and culture. Attitudes toward interfaith marriages are becoming more liberal in the developed world, removing the once powerful stigma that may prevent these types of marriages in the past. Many see intermarriage as a good opportunity for diversity and a way to shatter barriers and bring harmony between different faith communities.

Lisa A. Singleton and
Daniel W. Phillips III

See also: Interfaith Marriage; International Marriage; Interracial Marriage

Further Reading

Chouhoud, Y. 2021. *To Have and to Hold.* Institute for Social Policy and Understanding. Available at: https://www.ispu.org/to-have-and-to-hold-interfaith-marriage-just-as-common-among-muslim-americans-as-christians/. Accessed March 19, 2021.

Encyclopedia.com. 2021. *Interfaith Marriage.* Available at: https://www.encyclopedia.com/reference/encyclopedias-almanacs-transcripts-and-maps/interfaith-marriage. Accessed February 19, 2021.

Focus on the Family. 2021. *Marriage in the Melting Pot—Focus on the Family.* Available at: https://www.focusonthefamily.com/marriage/marriage-in-the-melting-pot/. Accessed March 20, 2021.

Lia, S. 2020. *Mapping Faith: Theologies of Migration and Community.* London; Philadelphia: Jessica Kingsley Publishers, pp. 49–56.

"Loving v. Virginia." *Oyez.* Available at: https://www.oyez.org/cases/1966/395. Accessed March 31, 2021.

Mehrotra, M., Zemba, S. and Hoffman, K. 2021. "Students' Attitudes Toward Interfaith Relationships: The Impact of Parents, Religiosity, and Christian Privilege." *Journal of College and Character* 22, no. 1: 31–45.

Murphy, C. M. 2021. "Interfaith Marriage is Common in U.S., Particularly Among the Recently Wed." Pew Research Center. Available at: https://www.pewresearch.org/fact-tank/2015/06/02/interfaith-marriage/. Accessed March 20, 2021.

New World Encyclopedia contributors. "Intermarriage." *New World Encyclopedia,* https://www.newworldencyclopedia.org/p/index.php?title=Intermarriage&oldid=1009501. Accessed March 22, 2021.

Pirola, F. and Pirola, B. 2021. *Interfaith Marriages.* Marriage Resource Centre. Available at: https://marriageresourcecentre.org/interfaith-marriages/. Accessed March 20, 2021.

Selina, M. 2021. *Spouses' Common Religion Helps in Intercultural Marriage.* Available at: https://iq.hse.ru/en/news/416624411.html. Accessed March 21, 2021.

International Association for Relationship Research

The International Association for Relationship Research (IARR) is an international interdisciplinary organization dedicated to the study of personal and social relationships (IARR, n.d., "About IARR"). IARR members are individuals from areas of study including anthropology, child/lifespan development, clinical work, communication, education, family studies, gerontology, philosophy, psychology, sociology, and more. IARR officers (e.g., president, treasurer, secretary) represent a similar range of disciplines, nationalities, and backgrounds. The organization offers several membership category options with different associated fees and subscription periods, including regular member and student/reduced fee/emeritus member. Members enjoy benefits such as newsletters, announcements, discounted conference registration fees, and mentoring or networking opportunities.

IARR encourages scholarly collaboration among its members, in large part by hosting conferences and sponsoring journals, a book series, and a newsletter. IARR organizes an international conference every other year, as well as numerous workshops and focused mini-conferences (IARR, n.d., "Conferences"). For example, the biennial conference took place in Fort Collins, Colorado, United States, in 2018 and in Toronto, Ontario, Canada, in 2016. Specialty conferences included two in 2015: one focused on relationships, health, and wellness at Rutgers University in New Brunswick, New Jersey, United States, and another on self-regulation and close relationships in Amsterdam, The Netherlands. IARR typically holds conferences in June or July. IARR also sponsors two peer-reviewed journals that publish scholarship that examines social and personal relationships: *Personal Relationships* and *Journal of Social and Personal Relationships.* The nature and form of relationships of interest vary greatly including (but not limited to) married couples, romantic or intimate partners, parent-child dyads, siblings, and co-workers, and topics of study are similarly varied (e.g., attachment, conflict, trust, online relationships, long-distance relationships). In addition to these journals, IARR sponsors a book series called *Advances in Personal Relationships,* which publishes edited collections of innovative research and theoretical contributions in the scholarship of relationships (Cambridge University Press, n.d.). For example, a recent edition focused on research that explored associations between relationships and health (Theiss and Greene

2018). Finally, IARR sponsors a newsletter entitled *Relationship Research News* that integrates research-based content, organizational updates, teaching advice, reports from IARR officers, and other submissions (e.g., humorous pieces).

Patricia E. Gettings

See also: Ackerman Institute for Family Therapy; American Association for Marriage and Family Therapy; Gottman Institute

Further Reading

Cambridge University Press. n.d. "Advances in personal relationships." Accessed July 1, 2020. https://www.cambridge.org /us/academic/subjects/psychology/series /advances-personal-relationships

International Association for Relationship Research. n.d. "About IARR." Accessed July 1, 2020. https://iarr.org/about.html

International Association for Relationship Research. n.d. "Conferences." Accessed July 1, 2020. https://iarr.org/conferences .html

Journal of Social and Personal Relationships. n.d. "About this journal." Accessed July 1, 2020. https://journals .sagepub.com/home/spr

Personal Relationships. n.d. "About this journal." Accessed July 1, 2020. https:// onlinelibrary.wiley.com/journal/14756811

Theiss, Jennifer A., and Greene, Kathryn, eds. 2018. *Contemporary Studies on Relationships, Health, and Wellness.* New York: Cambridge University Press.

International Marriage

The term *international marriage* is generally applied when a person marries someone in another country—a union in an international context. An alternative, lesser-used term is *transnational marriage*. There are numerous reasons for marrying across borders, ranging from genuine commitment and attraction, to potentially problematic variations of international matchmaking and human bartering for economic gain. Accordingly, the outcomes can be varied, depending on how well the person knew their prospective partner, their circumstances before the liaison, and what was expected from the ensuing marriage.

The reasons which lead to an international marriage can be straightforward and constructive, such as international education and work opportunities, which allow the person to meet a prospective spouse in the host country. In these instances, there is already an understanding of the host culture, and the partner may be known as a fellow student or co-worker. The motivation to be permanently united and to be living in the host country is genuine, as opposed to breaking up the relationship because one person is returning to their country of origin. Family reunification can be a strong motive for migration, although economic opportunities seem to have an even stronger drawing card (Brettell 2017). The prospect of attaining permanent and legal residence in a country such as the United States can be a strong incentive, especially if opportunities in the country of origin are limited by comparison. This phenomenon is called "marital citizenship" (Fresnoza-Flot and Ricordeau 2017).

In many cases of international marriage, it can become a transaction for gain, whereby each party, as well as the matchmakers, have profit motives in mind. The prospective spouses hope to gain in terms of social assets. A person may be actively seeking a partner but has not been successful in their own environment. The persons leaving their own country for marriage are predominantly women, who do so to improve their social and economic circumstances. They enter these relationships knowing that it is an exchange of sorts and that there will be social and sexual demands made on them as marriage partners, in addition to the possibility of raising a family. The theoretical construct that most closely describes these scenarios is the *social exchange theory*, which states that prospective partners can metaphorically trade or barter their assets, in return for what they hope the marriage may bring them.

Historically, World War II caused a great number of prospective brides to follow the American and Canadian soldiers they had met in Europe. British and German brides, especially, found new homes in the Americas, when the tremendous loss of life during the war made it virtually impossible to find suitable marriage partners in their countries of origin. The Vietnam War is another example of the unintended facilitation of international liaisons. Children from these unions faced social implications. Forming relationships with allies is one thing, but marriages across perceived enemy lines can be challenging, as divided loyalties fuel prejudice and stereotypes.

In some Asian countries, population growth has been declining. Within legal parameters, some families tried to exert a choice concerning the gender of their offspring. This occurred during the years of the one-child policy in China. It resulted in macrosystemic gender imbalances, with young men facing difficulties in procuring marital partners. Asian nations such as Japan and South Korea have encouraged international marriage by offering lucrative opportunities for young women from neighboring Asian countries (Fresnoza-Flot and Ricordeau 2017).

The potential yet the realistic danger of international marriages is that they can serve as a front for illegal transactions, where human lives are brokered. This international procurement of what is indirectly called "love" masks the sinister realities of human trafficking (Quek 2018). If international marriage is commercialized, it can be accompanied by power inequities such as false information, spousal abuse, economic insecurity, prejudice, disrespect, disempowerment, and more. In many of these cases, the women are expected to work and are trapped in inescapable situations. Some become indentured laborers, with little or no hope of escape or of improving their circumstances. The lure and the promise of an international marriage may disguise the possibility that these women are unknowingly being recruited as sex workers (Yakushko and Rajan 2017). Additionally, there is a very real problem of transnational marriage abandonment. Women with limited resources are left in the lurch in hostile environments having to fend for themselves. These women, who often identify as minorities, may lose custody of their offspring. Because of the mixed status of the spouses, domestic violence finds a breeding ground (Brettell 2017).

As the lifespan progresses, the reasons and motivations for marital partnerships can be increasingly individual, ranging from traditional to nontraditional. Partners who choose to marry across cultures, tend to be less traditional and more flexible in embracing cultural values other than their own. If the marriage was a transaction of opportunity, the emotional price may be higher. For the spouse who has not mastered the language of the host country, social isolation is a serious threat. Depending on personal circumstances in the country of origin, prospective spouses may be willing to pay that price. On the other hand, if the couple shares a language, values, and a genuine sense of attraction, they can create a flexible cultural context for their offspring.

International marriages display the entire range of cultural possibilities reflecting traditions, moral values, ideology, political, and other values and dimensions developed within a societal context. When two persons commit to an international or transnational marriage, they have to find ways of constructively blending their differing cultural backgrounds. Awareness of the darker side of international marriage is important, to prevent the abuse of marriage as a front for human rights violations.

On the optimistic side, people have sacrificed for what they thought was true love. They have left behind familiar roots to seek new opportunities and fuel their hopes for a better future, shared with a spouse from another land. International marriage, under ideal circumstances, can be the vehicle that builds cultural bridges.

Clara Gerhardt

See also: Diversity in Marriage; Interfaith Marriage; Interracial Marriage; Mail-Order Brides

Further Reading

Brettell, Caroline B. 2017. "Marriage and Migration." *Annual Review of Anthropology* 46, no. 1: 81–97.

Fresnoza-Flot, A., and Ricordeau, G., eds. 2017. *International Marriages and Marital Citizenship: Southeast Asian Women on the Move*. New York: Routledge. DOI: 10.1177/0117196817753766

Quek, Kaye. 2018. *Marriage Trafficking: Women in Forced Wedlock*. New York: Routledge. DOI: 10.1201/9781315620138

Yakushko, Oksana and Rajan, Indhushree. 2017. "Global love for sale: Divergence and convergence of human trafficking with 'mail order brides' and international arranged marriage phenomena." *Women & Therapy*, 40, 1–2: 190–206. DOI: 10.1080/02703149.2016.1213605

Interracial Marriage

There has been a color line shift in America from a predominately white-majority and Black minority society to a society with diverse racial and ethnic groups. With increasing social contacts among racial and ethnic groups, there has been a rise in interracial and interethnic marriages. According to the U.S. Census Bureau data, the rate of interracial and interethnic marriages has increased from 3% in 1967—the year interracial marriage was legalized in the United States to 17% in 2015. Among the interracial and interethnic marriages, non-Hispanic white and Hispanic couples are the largest groups, making up for 42% of all interracial and interethnic couple populations. Non-Hispanic white and non-Hispanic Black couples represent 11%. Among those in racial and ethnic minority groups, Asian Americans are the most likely to marry someone from another racial/ethnic group (29%), followed by Hispanics (27%). There are also gender differences in interracial and interethnic marriages, as Black men (24%) are more likely to intermarry than Black women (12%) whereas Asian women (36%) are more likely to intermarry than Asian men (21%).

Even after Barack Obama was elected as America's first president of color, some interracial couples were still not allowed to legally marry at some locales within the United States (which violates the federal law as determined by *Loving v. Virginia)*. With the growing number of interracial and interethnic marriages, colorism, which describes the allocation of privilege and disadvantage according to the color of one's skin, has brought awareness among relationship researchers. Some consider interracial and interethnic marriages as "inherently dysfunctional" and regard the studies of them as "irrelevant" (Gaines 1997, 353–355). Therefore, it carries significant public health and policy relevance to investigate the difficulties and challenges interracial and interethnic couples face, identify possible resilience factors, and inform marriage education programs to be culturally sensitive.

Couples in interracial and interethnic marriages face challenges associated with social discrimination, such as differential treatment and disapproval of family and community, which could become sources of conflict, dissolution, and stress. Further, from a cultural-ecological perspective, behavioral interactions in relationships should be understood through the couple's cultural backgrounds. Compared with monoracial and monoethnic couples who share similar cultural backgrounds, interracial and interethnic couples may experience more cultural differences (e.g., racial/ethnic identity, cultural orientation) which could potentially be reflected in many areas of marital interactions, such as communication styles. These factors could lead to challenges among interracial and interethnic couples, such as more conflict and violence.

There is limited research that compares interracial/interethnic and monoracial/monoethnic couples. Findings on couple conflict and violence suggested that rates of violence were higher in interracial and interethnic relationships compared to white-white and ethnic minority monoracial relationships. However, the results are not always consistent with some suggesting no differences in relationship violence and conflict between interracial/interethnic and monoracial/monoethnic marriages. Interracial and interethnic marriages also have implications for couples' mental and behavioral health outcomes. Findings on psychological well-being suggested higher rates of distress among couples in interracial/interethnic marriages than those in monoracial/monoethnic marriages.

Despite some studies suggesting the benefits of interracial and interethnic marriages (e.g., higher relationship satisfaction reported by one study), the literature on interracial and interethnic marriages has mostly focused on and reported negative aspects. Indeed, given the increasing prevalence and potential challenges, it is imperative to identify factors that could promote resilience among interracial and interethnic couples. The cultural-ecological perspective attends to culture by recognizing the different experiences of couples in interracial and interethnic marriages within a mainstream society of monoracial/monoethnic marriages. Combined with a resilience framework, these theories suggest that a culturally sensitive environment can provide a protective foundation that interracial/interethnic couples can draw upon in times of distress. From such perspectives, previous experiences and exposure to interracial/interethnic social contexts may play a critical role in their relationship and health, such as exposure to a racially/ethnically diverse environment (e.g., neighborhood heterogeneity) and experience of interracial peer relations and friendships.

While investigating the relationship and health of couples in interracial and interethnic marriages, the difficulties and challenges they face, and possible resilience factors, several other aspects should be considered in future research in this area. First, most studies have focused exclusively on Black and white racial group comparison and did not consider other racial or ethnic groups. In particular, while Asian Americans have the highest rate of marrying someone of a different race and ethnicity, they have been described as "conspicuously absent from" relational and health studies.

Second, gender and social economic status could play an important role in interracial and interethnic marriages. Compared to men, women in marriages are more likely to be adversely affected because of role stresses, perceived disapproval, and reduced social support. Depending on which partner in an interracial marriage comes from a more socially dominant group, gender may play a different role in interracial marriages. Further, with most marriage research focused on heterosexual marriages but same-sex marriage is now legal in all 50 U.S. states, future research should include same-sex interracial and interethnic couples when studying interracial and interethnic marriages.

Finally, studies on interracial and interethnic marriages should expand to examine interracial and interethnic relationships in general. The number of interracial/interethnic relationships has seen an even greater increase in the last several decades. Many interracial relationships do not end in marriages. One study suggested that, for those in interracial relationships, the preference for marriage was lower than for other types of relationships (e.g., dating, cohabitation). Further, the differences among married, cohabiting, and dating individuals in interracial/interethnic relationships regarding relationship processes and health are largely unknown.

Research on interracial and interethnic marriages (and relationships in general) will highlight the importance of recognizing the diverse racial/ethnic backgrounds of individuals in intimate relationships and the unique challenges and difficulties those in interracial/interethnic relationships face. Such research efforts will help identify specific resilience factors that could promote relationships and health among interracial couples. Specifically, these findings could inform marriage and relationship education (MRE) by incorporating cultural differences and unique challenges in interracial and interethnic relationships into the curriculum (e.g., conflict resolution, violence prevention, communication skills) of the current major MRE programs (e.g., RELATE, ePREP) to respond respectfully and effectively to the needs of couples from diverse backgrounds.

Ming Cui

See also: Interfaith Marriage; International Marriage

Further Reading

Bratter, Jenifer L, and Eschbach, Karl. 2006. "'What about the couple?' Interracial marriage and psychical distress." *Social Science Research* 35, no. 4: 1025–1047.

Burton, Linda M., Bonilla-Silva, Eduardo, Ray, Victor, Buckelew, Rose, and Freeman, Elizabeth H. 2010. "Critical race theories, colorism, and the decade's research on families of color." *Journal of Marriage and Family* 72, no. 3: 440–459.

Fincham, Frank D., Stanley, Scott M., and Rhodes, Galena K. 2011. "Relationship education in emerging adulthood: Problems and prospects." In F. D. Fincham and M. Cui (Eds.), *Romantic relationships in emerging adulthood* (pp. 293–316). New York: Cambridge University Press.

Fusco, Rachel A. 2010. "Intimate partner violence in interracial couples: A comparison to white and ethnic minority monoracial couples." *Journal of Interpersonal Violence* 25, no. 10: 1785–1800.

Gaines, Stanley O., Jr. 1997. "Communalism and the reciprocity of affection and respect among interracial married couples." *Journal of Black Studies* 27, no. 3: 352–364.

Garcia Coll, Cynthia, Lamberty, Gontran, Jenkins, Renee, McAdoo, Harriet Pipes, Crnic, Keith, Wasik, Barbara Hanna, Garcia, Heidie Vázquez. 1996. "An integrative model for the study of developmental competencies in minority children." *Child Development* 67, no. 5: 1891–1914.

Martin, Brittny, Cui, Ming, Ueno, Koji, and Fincham, Frank D. 2013. "Intimate partner violence in interracial and monoracial couples." *Family Relations* 62, no.1: 202–211.

The Pew Research Center. 2017. *Intermarriage in the U.S. 50 years after Loving v. Virginia.* https://www.pewresearch.org/social-trends/2017/05/18/intermarriage-in-the-u-s-50-years-after-loving-v-virginia/

Qian, Zhenchao, and Lichter, Daniel T. 2011. "Changing patterns of interracial marriage in a multiracial society." *Journal of Marriage and Family* 73, no. 5: 1065–1084.

Troy, Adam, B., Lewis-Smith, Jamie, and Laurenceau, Jean-Philippe. 2006. "Interracial and intraracial romantic relationships: The search for differences in satisfaction, conflict, and attachment style." *Journal of Social and Personal Relationships* 23, no. 1: 65–80.

Intimate Partner Violence

Intimate partner violence is a public health concern that occurs in current and former dating, cohabiting, and marital relationships. The term "intimate partner violence" encompasses a variety of violent and aggressive behaviors, including physical violence, sexual violence, psychological aggression, stalking, social isolation, intimidation, and economic deprivation. Types of intimate partner violence may be perpetrated together, and the severity and frequency of behaviors vary. Additionally, intimate partner violence spans all gender, ages, sexualorientationsn, races, cultures, and economic groups.

Various terms are oftentimes interchanged with intimate partner violence. Some of these terms include domestic violence, domestic abuse, and interpersonal violence. Historically, intimate partner violence has been understood with a gendered perspective, where males were understood to be the perpetrators and females the victims. However, understanding the context surrounding intimate partner violence has been emphasized in recent years. Experts now recognize that intimate partner violence occurs in different circumstances and is not just unidirectional from males perpetrated to females. Intimate partner violence can also be perpetrated by a victim as a form of resistance toward a violent perpetrator, both pre-meditated or unintentional. Additionally, some intimate partner violence occurs in the context of conflict, perpetrated by both partners, starting with verbal aggression and escalating to physical abuse (Johnson 2011, 290).

There are a variety of factors that place an individual at risk for intimate partner violence. Risk factors are not consistent across all victims and perpetrators. However, it is likely for individuals involved in intimate partner violence to experience a range of risk factors. Common risk factors for intimate partner violence include drug and alcohol use, lack of problem-solving skills, attitudes accepting violent behaviors, economic stress, social isolation, low self-esteem, and exposure to violence in their family of origin (Capaldi et al. 2012, 7–15). It is important to recognize that not everyone who experiences risk factors becomes involved in intimate partner violence. Additionally, these factors are not direct causes of intimate partner violence; they merely increase an individual's likelihood of experiencing abuse. Common protective factors from intimate partner violence include social and financial support from friends and family, access to community services and resources, and previous education on healthy relationships.

The consequences of intimate partner violence are extensive and can severely impact individual and family well-being. Common physical consequences to victims include migraines, chronic pain, broken bones, difficulties hearing and seeing, hypertension, and sexually transmitted infections (Coker et al. 2000, 454). In addition to physical consequences, victims often experience extensive psychological outcomes, including sleep disorders, anxiety, depression, suicidal thoughts, and long-term stress. As a result of physical and psychological outcomes, many victims engage in risky behaviors as a coping mechanism, such as illicit drug use and risky sexual behaviors (Caldwell, Swan, and Woodbrown 2012, 44–49). It is important to note, however, that survivors of intimate partner violence also have many strengths that aid in their resiliency, such as perseverance and willingness to seek out formal and informal support (Anderson, Renner, and Danis 2012, 1291–1292).

Though many victims experience physical and psychological consequences, immigrant victims face additional unique challenges compared to non-immigrant victims. Immigrant victims are frequently isolated due to language barriers in the United States, lack of family and friends in their community, and fear of deportation. Many are also unaware of their legal rights, depending upon their residency status (Vidales 2010, 536–539). These factors can perpetuate violence in immigrant relationships. Understandings of intimate partner violence continue to expand to include cultural and social impacts on experiences.

According to the National Domestic Violence Hotline, a survivor will leave their partner an average of seven times before they can leave them for good. Experts suggest that there are various reasons why people stay in abusive relationships. Many survivors stay with an abusive partner out of fear for their safety and what their future will hold if they leave. Financial dependence on an abuser is another common reason survivors stay in their relationship. Many abusers have control over their partner's finances, leaving them with no choice but to stay in the relationship. For survivors who have children with their abuser, they can be hesitant to leave. Many oftentimes believe their children need a father in their life or fear that their partner will be granted custody of their children.

Intimate partner violence prevention targets factors that place individuals at risk and aims to stop abuse before it occurs. Intimate partner violence often starts early in life, suggesting the importance of healthy relationship education and dating violence prevention programs for youth. These prevention programs aim to change attitudes toward intimate partner violence to prevent perpetration. Prevention programs encourage positive communication, conflict resolution skills, and healthy relationship behaviors. Example prevention programs include Safe Dates and Shifting Boundaries, which are mainly used in youth programming (Foshee et al. 1996; Taylor et al. 2013). Additionally, early intervention targets parents, couples, and families deemed at risk for abuse with skill development and enrichment programs.

Intervention for intimate partner violence aims to prevent further danger and offer support to those involved. Experts emphasize comprehensive services for survivors, where social services, health care, the criminal justice system, and other community agencies work together to provide support. This approach recognizes that survivors typically have a range of needs that can be best met through the collaboration of advocacy and intervention services. Many survivors seek out support from intimate partner violence shelters that offer a temporary place for survivors to live, but also additional resources that support and empower survivors. These services help to increase decision-making, self-efficacy, coping skills, and feelings of safety (Bennett et al. 2004, 826). Intervention for perpetrators focuses on providing skills-based education and guidance for alternatives to violence, such as education on communication skills, relaxation techniques, and anger management (Stover, Meadows, and Kaufman 2009, 224). Today, many intervention programs for perpetrators aim to change attitudes toward power and control in relationships. However, there is a lack of research evidence on the effectiveness of perpetrator intervention programs.

Sarah Taylor and Katya Ruiz

See also: Cycle of Violence; Economic Independence

Further Reading

Anderson, Kim M., Lynette M. Renner, and Fran S. Danis. 2012. "Recovery: Resilience and growth in the aftermath of domestic violence." *Violence Against Women* 18, no. 11: 1279–1299.

Bennett, Larry, Stephanie Riger, Paul Schewe, April Howard, and Sharon Wasco. 2004. "Effectiveness of hotline, advocacy, counseling, and shelter services for victims of domestic violence: A statewide evaluation." *Journal of Interpersonal Violence* 19, no. 7: 815–829.

Caldwell, Jennifer E., Suzanne C. Swan, and V. Diane Woodbrown. 2012. "Gender differences in intimate partner violence outcomes." *Psychology of Violence* 2, no. 1: 42.

Capaldi, Deborah M., Naomi B. Knoble, Joann Wu Shortt, and Hyoun K. Kim. 2012. "A systematic review of risk factors for intimate partner violence." *Partner Abuse* 3, no. 2: 231–280.

Coker, Ann L., Paige H. Smith, Lesa Bethea, Melissa R. King, and Robert E. McKeown. 2000. "Physical health consequences of physical and psychological intimate partner violence." *Archives of Family Medicine* 9, no. 5: 451–457.

Foshee, Vangie A., G. Fletcher Linder, Karl E. Bauman, Stacey A. Langwick, Ximena B. Arriaga, Janet L. Heath, Pamela M. McMahon, and Shrikant Bangdiwala. 1996. "The Safe Dates Project: Theoretical basis, evaluation design, and selected baseline findings." *American Journal of Preventive Medicine* 12, no. 5: 39–47.

Johnson, Michael P. 2011. "Gender and types of intimate partner violence: A response to an anti-feminist literature review." *Aggression and Violent Behavior* 16, no. 4: 289–296.

Stover, Carla Smith, Amy Lynn Meadows, and Joan Kaufman. 2009. "Interventions for intimate partner violence: Review and implications for evidence-based practice." *Professional Psychology: Research and Practice* 40, no. 3: 223–233.

Taylor, Bruce G., Nan D. Stein, Elizabeth A. Mumford, and Daniel Woods. 2013. "Shifting boundaries: An experimental evaluation of a dating violence prevention program in middle schools." *Prevention Science* 14, no. 1: 64–76.

Vidales, Guadalupe T. 2010. "Arrested justice: The multifaceted plight of immigrant Latinas who faced domestic violence." *Journal of Family Violence* 25, no. 6: 533–544.

L

LGBTQ Divorces and Separations

Divorce and relationship separation among lesbian, gay, bisexual, transgender, and queer (LGBTQ) people is a topic about which researchers know relatively little. Researching this topic has been difficult, partly because LGBTQ people and their relationships are stigmatized throughout society. Such stigma has made researchers reluctant to examine divorce and separation among LGBTQ people and LGBTQ people themselves reluctant to participate in research. Furthermore, what research does exist has several limitations that should be taken into consideration. For instance, much of this research is decades old and thus may not apply to the present day, especially given how much the lives of LGBTQ people have changed in recent years. In addition, much of the existing research relies on non-random, or convenience, samples, which limits researchers' ability to generalize from the data. Finally, research on this topic tends to rely on samples that are not fully representative of the LGBTQ population. In particular, these samples often include mostly white, well-educated, and affluent LGBTQ people who live in urban areas and are more "out," or open about their sexual identities, than most. Readers should consider these limitations when interpreting the research discussed below.

Same-sex couples throughout the United States were only recently granted the legal right to marry, so most of the existing research on relationship separation among LGBTQ people focuses specifically on their separation from nonmarital relationships. Before the legalization of same-sex marriage, researchers compared unmarried same-sex couples to married heterosexual couples to observe differences in their stability. In general, this research found that same-sex couples were less stable, or more likely to separate, than heterosexual couples. For example, in their pioneering research conducted in the 1980s, Phillip Blumstein and Pepper Schwartz (1983) followed a sample of married heterosexual couples, cohabiting gay male couples, and cohabiting lesbian couples over eighteen months and found that the heterosexual couples were the least likely to break up followed by the gay male couples, then the lesbian couples. It is worth emphasizing, however, that because this research compared unmarried same-sex couples to married different-sex couples, it could not rule out the likelihood that marriage itself played a significant role in making different-sex couples more stable.

Despite separating at a higher rate than married heterosexual couples, this body of research suggests that same-sex couples tend to separate for the same reasons that heterosexual couples do. For instance, Lawrence Kurdek (1991, 1997) found that the two most common reasons LGBTQ people give for ending a relationship are a lack of communication and problems with one's former partner, such as an addiction to drugs or alcohol; these are very similar to the reasons that heterosexual people give for ending their relationships. Similarly, Phillip Blumstein and Pepper Schwartz (1983) found that same-sex and different-sex couples alike are prone to end their relationships when they argue about money matters, when their work responsibilities intrude on their relationships, and when they feel sexually unsatisfied. Although same-sex and different-sex couples are generally quite similar in the reasons they give for separating, gay male couples do stand out concerning extramarital sex: whereas extramarital sex is likely to cause a separation for different-sex and lesbian couples, gay males couples who report engaging in extramarital sex are not more likely to separate as a result.

Same-sex couples across the United States gained access to divorce on June 26, 2015, when the Supreme Court issued its landmark decision in *Obergefell v. Hodges.* Celebrated mostly for making marriage equality the law nationwide, the *Obergefell* decision also granted all same-sex couples the right to end a legal marriage through divorce. Although it may not seem so, the right to divorce is crucial, as it allows couples to rely on the court system to make impartial decisions about how they will divide their assets and responsibilities upon ending the marriage. In addition, the court system can enforce this decision. Before *Obergefell*, same-sex couples were forced to make such decisions themselves and had little legal recourse if one individual chose not to adhere to the decisions

made. For these reasons, scholars and activists like Ellen Ann Andersen (2009) advocated for marriage equality in part because they believed in the importance of the right to divorce.

Since LGBTQ people have had the right to marry (either in particular states or nationwide), scholars have been able to examine the same-sex divorce rate and how it compares to the rate for different-sex couples. In general, this research suggests that same-sex couples end legal marriages at a rate that is quite similar to, if perhaps slightly lower than, the rate for different-sex couples. For instance, research conducted by The Williams Institute uses administrative data from New Hampshire and Vermont, two states that were among the first to legalize same-sex marriage, and reports that in those states, approximately 1.1% of same-sex couples end their marriage each year (Badgett and Mallory 2014, 1). This is slightly lower than the annual divorce rate for different-sex couples. However, Michael Rosenfeld (2014), who uses nationally representative data, finds that there is no significant difference in the divorce or dissolution rate when same-sex and different-sex couples are compared. Specifically, he finds that same-sex couples who are married or in marriage-like relationships are no more likely to end their relationship than married heterosexual couples. In any case, the preliminary research suggests that same-sex couples do not divorce more often than different-sex couples.

Scholars have yet to examine the ways that getting divorced impacts LGBTQ people. Although considerable research details how heterosexual people benefit and suffer following the dissolution of a marriage, research that addresses the consequences of divorce for LGBTQ people is still needed. One of the only studies on this topic is a small-scale, qualitative study conducted by Aaron Hoy (2018), which shows that some divorced LGBTQ people feel as though their experiences with divorce are invisible to others. Because same-sex marriage is so new, most people continue to assume that marriage and divorce are experiences only heterosexual people have. As a result, same-sex divorces are invisible to these individuals. In addition, some divorced LGBTQ people report feeling stigmatized not only because of their sexual identity but because of their status as divorced. Still, far more research is needed to fully understand how LGBTQ people are impacted by divorce.

Aaron Hoy

See also: LGBTQ Marriages and Unions; LGBTQ Parenthood

Further Reading

Andersen, Ellen Ann. 2009. "The gay divorcee: The case of the missing argument." In *Queer mobilizations: LGBT activists confront the law*, edited by Scott Barclay, Mary Bernstein, and Anna-Maria Marshall, 281–302. New York: New York University Press.

Badgett, M. V. Lee and Christy Mallory. 2014. *Patterns of relationship recognition for same-sex couples: Divorce and terminations*. Los Angeles: The Williams Institute.

Blumstein, Phillip and Pepper Schwartz. 1983. *American couples: Money, work, sex*. New York: William Morrow and Company.

Hoy, Aaron. 2018. "Invisibility, illegibility, and stigma: The citizenship experiences of divorced gays and lesbians." *Journal of Divorce and Remarriage* 59, no. 2: 69–91.

Kurdek, Lawrence A. 1991. "The dissolution of gay and lesbians couples." *Journal of Social and Personal Relationships* 8, no. 2: 265–278.

Kurdek, Lawrence A. 1997. "Adjustment to relationship dissolution in gay, lesbian, and heterosexual partners." *Personal Relationships* 4, no. 2: 145–161.

Rosenfeld, Michael J. 2014. "Couple longevity in the era of same-sex marriage in the United States." *Journal of Marriage and Family* 76, no. 5: 905–918.

LGBTQ Marriages and Unions

Lesbian, gay, bisexual, transgender, and queer (LGBTQ) people throughout the United States have the legal right to marry, equal to the rights of heterosexuals. The right to marry was granted to LGBTQ people nationwide as a result of the Supreme Court's *Obergefell v. Hodges* decision, which was announced on June 26, 2015. At the time of the *Obergefell* decision, some states allowed LGBTQ people to marry, but many did not. Furthermore, LGBTQ marriages that were contracted before the *Obergefell* decision were not recognized by all states, which posed significant challenges for married LGBTQ people who traveled or moved from states in which their marriages were recognized to those in which they were not. For example, a lesbian couple who married in Massachusetts but traveled to Mississippi may have worried that their rights as a married couple would not be respected while traveling, given that Mississippi did not recognize same-sex marriages at the time. As a result, the *Obergefell* decision is widely considered a major victory for LGBTQ rights as it extended equal marriage rights to all LGBTQ people and ensured that their marriages would be equally recognized by all states.

Before the *Obergefell* decision, many states across the country began offering LGBTQ people various ways of having their relationships legally recognized, and these often carried some or even all of the same rights that come with marriage. For instance, many states offered same-sex couples domestic partnerships or civil unions, and the specific rights attached to these varied from state to state, with some offering few rights at all and others offering nearly the same rights as marriage. However, the federal government has only ever recognized heterosexual marriages, and as a result, any rights specifically conferred by the federal government were inaccessible to same-sex couples who entered into either a domestic partnership or civil union. This meant, for example, that same-sex couples were unable to file joint federal income taxes or receive a spouse's Social Security after they died. Furthermore, same-sex relationships were not legally recognized by all states nationwide. Following the *Obergefell* decision, some states have continued to grant these alternative forms of relationship recognition, while others have begun recognizing only marriages.

Immediately following the *Obergefell* decision, the number of same-sex marriages in the United States increased significantly. According to research conducted by The Williams Institute, in June 2015, when the decision was announced, there were approximately 390,000 married same-sex couples across the country (Gates and Brown 2015, 1). However, by June 2017, just two years later, that number had increased to 547,000 (Romero 2017, 1). Today, of the nearly 1.1 million American adults who identify as lesbian, gay, bisexual, and/or transgender, approximately 10.2% are married to someone of the same sex (Jones 2017, 1). However, it is important to note that LGBTQ people are still more likely to marry someone of a different sex given that approximately half of all LGBTQ people identify as bisexual (Jones 2017, 2). It is also important to note that there is some sociodemographic variation among those who marry a same-sex spouse. For instance, marrying a same-sex spouse is slightly more common among LGBTQ men than women. Specifically, 11.4% of LGBTQ men are married to another man compared to 9.3% of LGBTQ women who are married to another woman (Jones 2017, 2). In addition, older LGBTQ people are more likely than those who are younger to marry a same-sex spouse. Research conducted at The Williams Institute also shows that among LGBTQ people ages 18–25, only 6% are currently married, compared to 48% among LGBTQ people ages 52–59 (Meyer and Krueger 2019, 1).

LGBTQ people who marry cite diverse reasons for doing so. For example, in her study of those who married in California in 2004 during the so-called Winter of Love, Katrina Kimport (2014) found that LGBTQ people tend to give three primary reasons for marrying. The first and most common is simply that they are in love and want to spend the rest of their lives together. The second is that they want or need one or more of the rights that come with marriage. For example, LGBTQ couples with children often cite the need for both spouses to have equal parenting rights. The third reason is that they want to make a political statement about the equality of same-sex and different-sex couples. For example, holding a traditional wedding to celebrate a same-sex marriage or using marital language like "husband" or "wife" sends the message that same-sex couples are the same as and therefore equal to different-sex couples. Of course, not all LGBTQ people want to marry, and some are even critical of marriage, which they see as an institution that oppresses LGBTQ people and women.

Upon getting married, LGBTQ people often find that their relationships change. For example, Adam Isaiah Green (2010) found that marriage makes LGBTQ people feel more committed to and settled within their relationships. Marriage can also legitimize LGBTQ people's relationships. Research shows that married couples, including married same-sex couples, are often seen as more serious and respectable. In turn, this helps married LGBTQ people build stronger relationships with others, including family members. This can be especially meaningful given that on average, LGBTQ people have weaker family relationships. However, Abigail Ocobock's (2013) research shows that in some cases, getting married can have little impact on or even weaken family relationships for LGBTQ people. Family members who are intolerant of diverse sexualities or oppose same-sex marriage sometimes cause stress for married LGBTQ people within their families.

Still, getting married appears to have significant benefits for LGBTQ people. A considerable amount of research shows that getting married tends to improve LGBTQ people's health and well-being. For instance, those who marry tend to feel more comfortable with their sexual identity and more accepted by others. This, in turn, reduces their stress and anxiety levels. In fact, a study conducted by Wight, LeBlanc, and Badgett (2013) found that although there are significant disparities between heterosexuals and LGBTQ people in terms of psychological distress, such disparities do not exist among those who are married. That is, married heterosexual and LGBTQ people report similar levels of psychological distress, suggesting that marriage can help eliminate inequalities in terms of mental health.

Aaron Hoy

See also: LGBTQ Divorces and Separations; LGBTQ Parenthood

Further Reading

Gates, Gary J. and Taylor N. T. Brown. 2015. "Marriage and same-sex couples after *Obergefell.*" Los Angeles: The Williams Institute.

Green, Adam Isaiah. 2010. "Queer unions: Same-sex spouses marrying tradition and innovation." *Canadian Journal of Sociology* 35, no. 3: 399–436.

Jones, Jeffrey M. 2017. "In U.S., 10.2% of LGBT adults now married to same-sex spouse." Washington, D.C.: Gallup Daily. Available at https://news.gallup.com/poll/212702/lgbt-adults-married-sex-spouse.aspx

Kimport, Katrina. 2014. *Queering Marriage: Challenging Family Formation in the United States.* New Brunswick: Rutgers University Press.

Meyer, Ilan H. and Evan A. Krueger. 2019. "Legally married LGB people in the United States." Los Angeles: The Williams Institute.

Ocobock, Abigail. 2013. "The power and limits of marriage: Married gay men's family relationships." *Journal of Marriage and Family* 75, no. 1: 191–205.

Romero, Adam P. 2017. "1.1 million LGBT adults are married to someone of the same sex at the two year anniversary of *Obergefell v. Hodges*." Los Angeles: The Williams Institute.

Wight, Richard G., Allen J. LeBlanc, and M. V. Lee Badgett. 2013. "Same-sex legal marriage and psychological well-being: Findings from the California Health Interview Survey." *American Journal of Public Health* 103, no. 2: 339–346.

LGBTQ Parenthood

LGBTQ (lesbian, gay, bisexual, transgender, queer) individuals in the United States have historically faced barriers to growing their families through parenthood and have had to fight for equal parenting rights. Both social stigmatization and denied opportunities such as adoption and legal custody have prevented sexual-minority individuals from forming families through parenthood. With changing social climates, there is now greater support and opportunity for LGBTQ individuals to become parents. Notably, however, most research focuses on lesbian women and gay men, and as such, little is yet known about bisexual and transgender parents. For this reason, this entry focuses primarily on parenthood among those who identify as gay or lesbian.

Despite increased social acceptance and the reduction of legal barriers, gay men and lesbian women are less likely than their heterosexual peers to be parents. The 2017 American Community Survey (ACS) estimated that there were 935,229 same-sex couples (approximately 48% male-male; 52% female-female) in the United States. Approximately 16.4% of same-sex couples are estimated to have children in their households compared to 38.8% of opposite-sex couples. This includes biological children (including children from former heterosexual marriages), stepchildren, adopted children, and nonrelative children. Rates of parenthood are higher among female-female couples (23.8%) compared to male-male couples (8.5%) (U.S. Census Bureau 2018). This survey may underestimate the number of same-sex couples and same-sex parents if responders did not wish to disclose their sexual orientation, and it notably does not include information on single parents. Still, it is clear that parenthood is less common among gay men and lesbian women compared to heterosexuals. Trends suggest that the rate of parenthood among same-sex couples is not increasing—the percentages of both same-sex and opposite-sex couples with children have decreased slightly since 2005, and the gap between parenthood in same-sex and opposite couples has remained consistent (U.S. Census Bureau 2018).

There may be several reasons that lesbian and gay couples are less likely to become parents, including greater logistical barriers to parenthood and simply a lack of desire to become parents (Patterson and Riskind 2010, 328). For example, lesbian women and gay men are importantly less likely than their heterosexual counterparts to experience an unplanned pregnancy, and the decision to become parents through opportunities such as adoption or surrogacy can take much time, resources, and planning. Lack of desire to become parents may also partially explain the lower rates of parenting among gay and lesbian couples. A 2002 survey found that many gay and lesbian individuals do wish to become parents, with 52%

of childless gay men and 41% of childless lesbian women expressing a desire to have a child (Gates et al. 2007, 5). In the same survey, 67% of childless heterosexual men and 53% of childless heterosexual women expressed a desire to have a child. Though research has not explored *why* the desire for parenthood is lower among gay men and lesbian women, it is possible that logistical/financial barriers and fear of social stigmatization could play a role. Though planning, logistics, and financial concerns are also challenges that heterosexual parents face, these are likely more pronounced for lesbian and gay parents.

For the many lesbian and gay individuals who do wish to become parents, there are several possible pathways to parenthood, and these opportunities have increased over time. The earliest research on lesbian and gay parents focused on individuals who had come out later in life, after having children with an opposite-sex, heterosexual partner, and it was assumed this was the primary pathway to parenthood. With reduced legal barriers and increased social support, lesbian and gay individuals now have multiple options to pursue parenthood, and some researchers suggest there may be a "generational shift" in the routes to parenthood for non-heterosexual individuals (Patterson and Riskind 2010, 335). For example, women may choose donor insemination from either known or unknown donors, and men may choose surrogacy, in which a woman carries a child that will later be reared by another individual or couple. Both men and women may become parents through adoption or foster care arrangements. LGBTQ individuals can now legally adopt in all 50 U.S. states,

though individual agencies may be more or less LGBTQ-friendly. Despite the reduction of legal barriers, LGBTQ couples looking to adopt have historically faced barriers such as homophobia, and sometimes these families are scrutinized in terms of parenting ability and mental health. However, LGBTQ parents who adopt may also be an important resource for children as they are particularly likely to adopt older and special-needs children (Brodzinsky 2011, 35). While this may be due to personal preference, it may also be due to bias in that agencies choose to place higher-need children with LGBTQ parents (Brodzinsky and Pertman 2012).

Research has also begun to focus on the outcomes of children raised by lesbian and gay parents. In the past, it was simply assumed that children would be harmed if they were raised outside of a "traditional" heterosexual family context, and this view was a primary source for social and legal discrimination against gay and lesbian parents. However, recent studies have made it clear that parents' sexual orientation has no negative impact on children's development. Studies comparing outcomes of adopted children in both heterosexual and lesbian/gay families found no differences in child adjustment based on parents' sexual orientation (Farr 2017). Both early and modern research finds that children raised by gay or lesbian parents fare no differently than children raised by heterosexual parents in terms of social, behavioral, and academic outcomes (Patterson 2017). The earliest studies compared children of gay or lesbian parents after a divorce to post-divorce children of heterosexual parents also found no differences in adjustment.

Contemporary research has studied child outcomes among a more diverse variety of family structures including lesbian or gay couples who have adopted children and more ethnically, geographically, and socioeconomically diverse families. Across all studies, children from households headed by gay or lesbian couples are indistinguishable from children from households headed by heterosexual couples in terms of outcomes.

In sum, children of LGBTQ parents are just as likely as children of heterosexual parents to grow up socially, emotionally, and behaviorally well-adjusted. There are also unique positive features of LGBTQ parenthood that may serve as positive influences on child outcomes. LGBTQ couples tend to be more egalitarian in that they split household chores and childcare more evenly, and socialization practices suggest that LGBTQ parents often promote their children's awareness of the importance of diversity by celebrating LGBTQ culture and gender equality (Oakley, Farr, and Scherer 2017, 66–67; Patterson 2017, 47).

Jordan E. Greenburg and Adam Winsler

See also: LGBTQ Divorces and Separations; LGBTQ Marriages and Unions

Further Reading

Brodzinsky, David M. 2011. *Expanding Resources for Children III: Research-Based Best Practices in Adoption by Gays and Lesbians*. Accessed September 3, 2019. https://www.adoptioninstitute.org/wp-content/uploads/2013/12/2011_10_Expanding_Resources_BestPractices.pdf

Brodzinsky, David M., and Adam Pertman. 2012. *Adoption by Lesbians and Gay Men: A New Dimension in Family Diversity*. New York: Oxford University Press.

Farr, Rachel H. 2017. "Does Parental Sexual Orientation Matter? A Longitudinal Follow-up of Adoptive Families with School-Age Children." *Developmental Psychology* 53, no. 2: 252–264.

Gates, Gary J., M. V. Lee Badgett, Jennifer Ehrle Macomber, and Kate Chambers. 2007. "Adoption and Foster Care by Gay and Lesbian Parents in the United States." https://williamsinstitute.law.ucla.edu/wp-content/uploads/Gates-Badgett-Macomber-Chambers-Final-Adoption-Report-Mar-2007.pdf

Goldberg, Abbie E., and Katherine R. Allen, eds. 2013. *LGBT-Parent Families: Innovations in Research and Implications for Practice*. New York: Springer-Verlag.

Oakley, Marykate, Rachel H. Farr, and David G. Scherer. 2017. "Same-Sex Parent Socialization: Understanding Gay and Lesbian Parenting Practices as Social Culturalization." *Journal of GLBT Family Studies* 13, no. 1: 56–75.

Patterson, Charlotte J. 2017. "Parents' Sexual Orientation and Children's Development." *Child Development Perspectives* 11, no. 1: 45–49.

Patterson, Charlotte J., and Rachel G. Riskind. 2010. "To Be a Parent: Issues in Family Formation among Gay and Lesbian Adults." *Journal of GLBT Family Studies* 6, no. 3: 326–340.

U.S. Census Bureau. 2018. "Characteristics of Same-Sex Couple Households: 2005 to Present." Accessed August 30, 2019. https://www.census.gov/data/tables/time-series/demo/same-sex-couples/ssc-house-characteristics.html

U.S. Census Bureau. n.d. "Household Characteristics of Opposite-Sex and Same-Sex Couple Households: 2017 American Community Survey." Accessed August 16, 2019. https://www.census.gov/data/tbles/time-series/demo/same-sex-couples/ssc-house-characteristics.html

Living Apart Together

Living apart together is when couples choose not to share a home and instead live at different addresses. Living apart together is a type of relationship, but such couples do not have any particular legal rights or obligations. More couples are choosing living apart together, with some research estimating that nearly 10% of couples do so today.

Living apart together particularly appeals to older people in new relationships because they are already established in their homes. People in dual-career couples may also find it more convenient to each live near their jobs, or to move alone to take a job without uprooting the partner. During an economic slowdown, one member of a couple may have to take a job elsewhere, resulting in a period of living apart together. In addition, some creative people may find living separately helpful because they can work uninterrupted and on their own schedules. Finally, a new couple with children from previous relationships may be living apart together as they begin the process of joining their families together. However, all types of people are choosing living apart together when they do not want to compromise their space and independence in their relationship.

There are no requirements to living apart together other than residing at different addresses. Couples living apart together may have different commitment levels, visit each other in differing amounts, spend different amounts of overnights together, and have various distances between them. They may vacation and spend the holidays together or do so separately. People's backgrounds, ages, and preferences can cause such variations among couples living apart together. Nonetheless, couples living apart together often have many of the emotional, social, and other commitments of couples who live together.

Couples report certain benefits to living apart together. For example, they have more personal time and do not need to adapt to someone else's lifestyle. There are fewer opportunities for couples living apart together to argue or to establish routines that put them into a rut. Couples living apart may be more excited to see each other when they do, and modern technology can connect them between visits.

However, there are also challenges to living apart together. For example, suspicions may arise when couples do not trust each other. Without overlapping routines and schedules, it may be more difficult to communicate, the relationship may become more strained, and the couple may grow apart. From a practical perspective, it is more expensive to maintain two homes instead of only one. In fact, one of the biggest financial advantages to living together as a couple is saving on living costs, which does not benefit couples living apart together. Finally, friends and family may disapprove of or misunderstand such relationships.

In sum, living apart together is a relatively recent type of relationship arrangement that allows people to maintain separate homes. As relationship ideals continue to change, more couples are choosing to live together apart.

Margaret Ryznar

See also: Unmarried Cohabitation

Further Reading

Bowman, Cynthia Grant. 2017. "Living Apart Together, Women, and Family

Law." *Cardozo Journal of Equal Rights and Social Justice* 24, no. 1: 47–80.

Bowman, Cynthia Grant. 2018. "Living Apart Together as a 'Family Form' Among Persons of Retirement Age: The Appropriate Family Law Response." *Family Law Quarterly* 52, no. 1: 1–26.

Love, Connection, and Intimacy

Within relationships, an individual's perception of love, connection, attraction, and safety can be understood through several patterns as well as through an understanding of attachment theory. Attachment theory describes how our learned attachment style impacts relationships, communication, vulnerability, and intimacy. Furthermore, attachment shapes the internal working model of the individual—in other words, how individuals view themselves, others, and relationships. However, love, connection, and intimacy come through the communication of love often displayed through both sexual and emotional intimacy as well as congruent behaviors.

When couples come to therapy, it is common to ask what brought the couple together. A common response is attraction. Often physical and sexual attraction are the first explorations of getting to know someone intimately. During this "honeymoon" period, the excitement of getting to know each other is a large part of the attraction. Once the sexual or physical attraction is sustained, the relationship turns to gain a deeper understanding of the partner. This is where communication, sharing thoughts and feelings, opens the doors to another avenue of intimacy. One where each partner knows the other in ways no one else knows.

There is a level of intimacy with friendships and family, shared experiences, and vulnerability that create memories and bonds. Within those relationships, we share ourselves intentionally or unintentionally, and our families and siblings know us—what we like, dislike, and behaviors that we display that communicate those thoughts or feelings. We also see demonstrated, and practice, how to communicate love. The *Five Love Languages* by Gary Chapman talks about how we understand and receive love. The way we receive love, and the way we communicate love and affection, those styles differ. Chapman (2008) identified five styles: words of affirmation, quality time, receiving gifts, acts of service, and physical touch. The theme is understanding our style of communicating love and affection, as well as how we communicate this to our loved ones. Often, these patterns are learned through our family of origin and in observing our caregiver interactions. This is practiced in how we develop and maintain friendships. This is then practiced again in adolescents as teens are working through identity development and again later in early adulthood as we understand identity development through intimate relationships.

During these pivotal times in development, over the course of our interactions growing up, we practice intimacy in getting to know friends or family. Depending on the health of those relationships, this means practicing vulnerability or self-preservation. In relationships where both individuals feel emotionally and physically safe, vulnerability (e.g., sharing thoughts or feelings to be better understood) is a core of that intimacy in the relationship. In relationships where an individual does not feel emotionally or physically safe, self-preservation can take hold; meaning withholding information to feel more protected. Our interactions with people over the course of our lifetime shape *what* and *how* we share information about ourselves.

Two phenomena occur in relationships: transactional or relational interactions. In transactional relationships or interactions, an exchange occurs; meaning that to receive affection, an act must occur. This is akin to credits and debits, with relational interactions being a transaction to meet an individual's needs or demands. Another is a relational interaction; one where unconditional positive regard (e.g., consistently showing care) is at the root of the interaction and the interaction is reciprocal. These are two different styles of interaction, with roots in how we relate, communicate, and share thoughts or feelings. Reciprocal relationships require compromise.

Virginia Satir (1991) talked about congruent stances and that our behavior demonstrates a congruent or incongruent stance. In an incongruent stance, we can take a few roles: Placating, Blaming, Irrelevance, and Super-Rational (Satir 1991). These stances can come as a form of self-protection, one where context, self, or others are or are not acknowledged. Meaning that context acknowledges the background information that is relevant to an experience; the self is acknowledging our needs; and others are acknowledging the needs of others. In the congruent stance, we acknowledge ourselves, balanced with others, while taking context into account. In incongruent stances, there is an imbalance. For example, in the blaming stance a person often displays tyrannical, domineering, loud, and/or violent behavior

to ward off a perceived threat; self and context are acknowledged, but others are not (Gehart and Tuttle 2003). According to Satir (1991), when we take the placating stance "when we placate, we disregard our own feelings of worth, hand our power to someone else, and say yes to everything," context and others are acknowledged, while the self is not. Super-reasonable is rigid, only considering context; and irrelevance demonstrates distracting behaviors, acknowledging neither self, others, nor context. To connect and love, it requires a congruent stance where context, self, and others are considered in communication, behaviors, and interactions.

The love that is shared within a romantic relationship requires the foundation of communicating love and affection, an understanding of our partner's thoughts and feelings, as well as having the desire and sexual attraction. When couples have communication concerns, it is common that they are withholding communication or withdraw. In what Gottman calls the Pursuer/Distancer, this relates to attachment and often, our family of origin. However, when we acknowledge ourselves and our needs, accept our partner and their needs, and understand the context behind their behaviors (e.g., if they are stressed, they may not talk as much), then we are better able to understand and connect.

Individuals with a secure attachment style have an internal working model of themselves as confident and others as relatively trustworthy and well-intentioned. They often find satisfaction, trust, commitment, and dependence in relationships. For example, an individual with a secure attachment may be more prone to allow themselves to be vulnerable with a partner, opening and sharing thoughts and feelings. On the contrary, those with an anxious-ambivalent style view themselves as unsure and misunderstood but well-intentioned, and others as unreliable or unwilling to commit. They find themselves less able to trust in relationships, experience less satisfaction, and therefore they have an imbalance of dependence in those relationships. For example, they may open up to a partner but then pull away not reciprocated. Lastly, those with an anxious-avoidant style have an internal working model of themselves as unworthy, skeptical, and aloof and others as unreliable or over-eager to commit. This attachment style tends to be more reserved and distant in relationships, experiencing less trust, commitment, and dependence. For example, in communication this may reflect a partner that is not as easy to understand, that may withhold thoughts or feelings to avoid being dismissed or seen as unworthy.

Another aspect of love and connection involves caretaking. According to Kunce and Shaver (1994), adult caregiving behaviors include four characteristics: proximity, sensitivity, control, and compulsive caregiving. These patterns of reactivity to stress persist from childhood, whether it is in our caregiving response or our internal response to anxiety and fear. In breaking down these characteristics, proximity speaks to physical and emotional distance or closeness. How we allow ourselves to be seen and known, as well as sharing activities and doing things together. Sensitivity is demonstrated in showing care and compassion when something vulnerable is shared or when our partner is in a vulnerable state. Like in attachment theory, a partner that is sensitive to their partner's

needs demonstrates that they care. Control can be presented in overly dominating or controlling behaviors. Control in relationships can be one-sided, with needs often focused on the individual that requires control. This phenomenon can be found in relationships with intimate partner violence. Another example of a one-sided relationship is compulsive caregiving, with partners overcompensating for one another, and the focus is directed outward.

Love necessitates intimacy. Intimacy can take two forms: emotional and sexual. Within relationships, the latter can often be confused with lust. However, in relationships, the balance between emotional and sexual intimacy is the key to a deeper and long-lasting relationship. Philosophers have long tried to understand love; one such response expresses love as *"devotion that renders vulnerable and expresses liking"* (Shpall 2018, 91). Shpall (2018) continues that love "is the most meaning-generating psychological condition with which we are familiar" (92). This understanding of love speaks to another important aspect of intimacy: vulnerability. Brene Brown, a researcher looking at connection, found that empathy and vulnerability are important in all relationships. In relationships that were unsafe, either emotionally or physically, or in our early childhood with insecure attachment, we develop emotional "wounds," a term that describes a pain that we protect or ignore. If the initial wound was from an inconsistent or unsafe relationship or environment, we then develop a pattern in future relationships to protect the self, and therein vulnerability is not easily explored. In taking risks in intimacy and vulnerability, individuals develop new meaning and a new working model of themselves within relationships.

As the adult attachment patterns soften, and the partner learns to communicate their feelings and vulnerability, the relationship deepens and so does the level of intimacy experienced by both partners, both sexually and emotionally. The key is continual maintenance of this model (both internal and external) to shift and change. As partners communicate, they develop a better sense of what the other needs and therein change their caregiving response. As our working model changes, it alters how we see ourselves, ourselves within a relationship, how we view relationships, and how to respond to others' needs.

Bita Ashouri Rivas

See also: Attachment Theory of Love; Five Love Languages; Love at First Sight; Styles of Love; Triangular Theory of Love

Further Reading

Chapman, Gary. 2008. *The five love languages of children.* Northfield Publishing: Chicago,

Crowell, Judith A., and Everett Waters. 1994. "Bowlby's Theory Grown Up: The Role of Attachment in Adult Love Relationships." *Psychological Inquiry* 5, no. 1: 31–34.

Dillow, Megan R., Alan K. Goodboy, and San Bolkan. 2014. "Attachment and the Expression of Affection in Romantic Relationships: The Mediating Role of Romantic Love." *Communication Reports* 27, no. 2: 102–115.

Galinha, Iolanda, Costa Oishi, Shigehiro Pereira, Cicero Wirtz, and Roberto Esteves. 2014. "Adult Attachment, Love Styles, Relationship Experiences and Subjective Well-Being: Cross-Cultural and Gender Comparison between Americans, Portuguese, and Mozambicans." *Social Indicators Research* 119, no. 2: 823–852.

Gehart, D. R. and Tuttle, A. R. 2003. *Theory Based Treatment Planning for Marriage and Family Therapists.* 1st ed. Cengage Learning.

Gladding, S. T. 2019. *Family Therapy: History, Theory, and Practice.* 7th ed. The Merrill Counseling Series, Pearson Inc.

Kunce, Linda J., and Phillip R. Shaver. 1994. "An Attachment-theoretical Approach to Caregiving in Romantic Relationships." In K. Bartholomew and D. Perlman (Eds.), *Attachment Processes in Adulthood*, pp. 205–237. Jessica Kingsley Publishers.

Naar, Hichem. 2013. "A Dispositional Theory of Love." *Pacific Philosophical Quarterly* 94, no. 3: 342–357.

Péloquin, Katherine, Audrey Brassard, Marie-France Lafontaine, and Phillip R. Shaver. 2014. "Sexuality Examined Through the Lens of Attachment Theory: Attachment, Caregiving, and Sexual Satisfaction." *The Journal of Sex Research* 51, no. 5: 561–576.

Ringel, Shoshana, and Jerrold R. Brandell. 2012. *Trauma: Contemporary Directions in Theory, Practice, and Research.* Cengage.

Satir, Virginia, John Banmen, Maria Gomori, and Jane Gerber. 1991. *The Satir model: Family Therapy and Beyond.* Palo Alto, Calif.: Science and Behavior Books.

Shaver, Phillip R., and Cindy Hazan. 1988. "A Biased Overview of the Study of Love." *Journal of Social and Personal Relationships* 5, no. 4: 473–501.

Shpall, Sam. 2018. "A Tripartite Theory of Love." *Journal of Ethics & Social Philosophy* 13, no. 2: 91.

Simpson, Jeffry A. 1990. "Influence of Attachment Styles on Romantic Relationships." (Interpersonal Relations and Group Processes). *Journal of Personality and Social Psychology* 59, no. 5: 971–980.

Simpson, J. A., and W. Steven Rholes. 2017. "Adult Attachment, Stress, and Romantic Relationships." *Current Opinion in Psychology* 13: 19–24. doi:10.1016/j.copsyc.2016.04.006

Love at First Sight

Love at first sight refers to an experience of instant romantic attraction that occurs when an individual first sees or meets someone else. Often referred to in hindsight (e.g., "it was love at first sight"), this phenomenon can occur in romantic pairings of any gender composition (e.g., heterosexual, gay, lesbian), and can be experienced as mutual attraction or (more typically) as a one-sided immediate romantic interest. People of all genders report love at first sight, with men potentially reporting more love-at-first-sight experiences. Love at first sight can mark the beginning of a short-term affair, a long-term relationship, or no relationship at all; in all cases, however, a hallmark feature of love at first sight is the *desire* for a relationship.

Scholars and lay people alike have questioned whether love at first sight occurs in real time or whether it is a false memory constructed through the lens of an existing or desired relationship. This debate over whether love at first sight is "real" balances people's anecdotal recollections of having experienced love at first sight against evidence that couples in high-quality relationships maintain biased positive beliefs about their romantic partners and their relationships. In other words, individuals' love-at-first-sight memories may be unconsciously constructed illusions that give added meaning to a relationship, promote romantic ideals of relationship uniqueness, and are consistent with current positive feelings toward a romantic partner. Retrospective reports of love at first sight, therefore, may provide more insight into the current health of a couple's relationship than what happened when the couple first met.

Complicating the debate over whether love at first sight exists is how people conceptualize love at first sight. Skeptics, for instance, may doubt the possibility of love at first sight because they define the term quite literally as instant *love*. Love reflects a high degree of interdependence and is generally characterized by such qualities as intimacy, closeness, trust, passion, emotional investment, and commitment. The depth involved in traditional definitions of love makes the instantaneous appearance of love unlikely. However, relationship scientists conceptualize love at first sight not as instant love, but rather as instant *attraction*, or a strong pull toward a stranger, accompanied by openness to begin a relationship. This distinction allows for the possibility of love at first sight.

A definitive feature of love at first sight is that an individual's attention is captured by another person quickly, at the very moment of an initial interpersonal encounter. For this to occur, people's attentional processes would need the ability to rapidly discriminate between stimuli (i.e., unknown people) and to quickly anchor to a specific stimulus (i.e., the target person in a love-at-first-sight encounter). Further, individuals would need the ability to form social judgments (i.e., impressions of another person) with access to only minimal information, often only visual information tied to a person's physical experience. Support for these social-cognitive abilities, and thus for the possible existence of love at first sight, comes in the form of evidence showing that individuals process new faces quickly and that such processing has immediate effects on attention and higher-order social judgments.

In terms of attention, people appear to exhibit early-stage attentional biases toward some faces over others. For example, laboratory research involving a visual task shows that both men and women have difficulty disengaging their attention from highly attractive female faces (Maner, Gailliot, and DeWall 2007, 28–36). Such an attentional bias toward physically attractive faces may have evolved to promote men's reproductive success by anchoring their interest to women who are healthy and fertile, for which physical attractiveness is a fairly reliable cue (for women, such bias could alert them to potential romantic competition). The attentional pull of attractive faces could provide a foundation for love at first sight, encouraging individuals to look for an extended time at potentially desirable romantic partners.

As for higher-order social judgments, individuals require little time to form these impressions. Research has found that people make rapid personality inferences about strangers after mere milliseconds of exposure to their faces (Willis and Todorov 2006, 592–598). To make these speedy first impressions, humans rely on an implicit processing system, an automatic and unconsciously-activated means of making decisions in contexts of minimal information. Among other traits, research has shown that people judge strangers' trustworthiness, competence, and likeability after only brief exposure to their faces. These judgments can be positive (e.g., high trustworthiness) or negative (e.g., low trustworthiness) and because they can include traits valued in a romantic partner, these inferences are relevant to love at first sight, regardless of their accuracy. Positive implicit judgments of a stranger could favorably shape expectations about that stranger and favorably affect future interpretations of that stranger's behavior, setting the stage for a romantic relationship.

Empirical evidence further supports the idea that people experience real-time love-at-first-sight encounters. Participants were asked whether or not they were experiencing love at first sight directly after they first met someone new, and, while it was rare, some people did report love at first sight (Zsok et al. 2017, 869–885). These reports were more often made by men than women and generally targeted highly physically attractive strangers. This preference for physically attractive others is consistent with the attentional bias that humans show toward physically attractive faces. It also corresponds with evidence showing that people with more beautiful faces are perceived as having more positive internal traits, a phenomenon called the halo effect. Whether these recorded love-at-first-sight encounters developed into actual relationships is unknown; presumably, some did, and some did not. This suggests that as much as retrospective reports of love at first sight identify a relationship as a singular and extraordinarily romantic connection, people may feel the strong pull that defines love at first sight multiple times over the course of their lives, only remembering those instances in which it results in a relationship.

Theresa E. DiDonato

See also: Attachment Theory of Love; Halo Effect; Love, Connection, and

Intimacy; Love, Styles of; Triangular Theory of Love

Further Reading

Maner, Jon K., Matthew T. Gailliot, and C. Nathan DeWall. 2007. "Adaptive attentional attunement: Evidence for mating-related perceptual bias." *Evolution and Human Behavior* 28, no. 1: 28–36.

Willis, Janine, and Alexander Todorov. 2006. "First impressions: Making up your mind after a 100-ms exposure to a face." *Psychological Science* 17, no. 7: 592–598.

Zsok, Florian, Matthias Haucke, Cornelia Y. De Wit, and Dick P. H. Barelds. 2017. "What kind of love is love at first sight? An empirical investigation." *Personal Relationships* 24, no. 4: 869–885.

M

Mail-Order Brides

Brokered marriage services, also known as "mail-order bride services," are businesses that provide databases of prospective, international partners and allow consumers to browse and contact potential mates for a fee. Online dating sites and brokered marriage services may seem similar, but there is an important distinction between them. All parties who use dating services can search for and initiate contact with potential mates without limitations. However, brokered marriage services consist strictly of third-party liaisons that only allow one-way communication. Only the consumers, often men from the United States and Western Europe, are allowed to choose the women with whom they will communicate. The women who list themselves with the services are unable to initiate contact.

The United States uses more mail-order bride services to find wives abroad than any other Western country (Yehl 2001). Today, mail-order brides are women mainly from mid-level developing countries such as Ukraine or Thailand. Yet, where they originated from has changed over the course of U.S. history and can be traced back to the colonial period (Pearce, Clifford, and Tandon 2011). The first mail-order service, known as Tobacco Brides, were women sent from England to Jamestown, Virginia, in 1619. Often, they were sent against their will and once in North America were auctioned off to male settlers for 150 pounds of tobacco. The number of mail-order brides was fairly small until the 1840s, because of long gaps in correspondence and travel times. However, the invention of the steam engine and photography increased the number of mail-order marriages in the United States. For example, in the early 20th century, many Japanese men who settled in the United States for work married women from their homeland called Picture Brides (Lee 2003). These marriages were arranged between the settlers and the brides' families through the exchange of photographs and money. Later, with the fall of the Soviet Union, Russian and Eastern European women entering the U.S. mail-order marriage market rapidly increased as well. To this day, the mail-order marriage market continues to grow thanks to the expansion of the internet and related technologies.

Research has documented why some U.S. men chose to marry mail-order brides rather than seek spouses through domestic dating sites. Largely, these men prefer a patriarchal family form, which is defined as a legally married couple consisting of a man who is the primary breadwinner and head of the household and a woman who is subordinate to her husband and is the caretaker for him, the household, and their biological children. In these studies, many U.S. men often blame feminism for their inability to find romantic partners. For example, some report that they feel that American women no longer seem to care about traditional family or traditional values because they are either too feminist or career-driven (Collins, Eng, and Yeoh 2013; Constable 2003; Palriwala and Uberoi 2008). Many of the male respondents imagine that non-Western women are both old-fashioned and sexually exotic, which makes them ideal partners for traditional marriages (Collins, Eng, and Yeoh 2013; Palriwala and Uberoi 2008). To generate business, mail-order bride services promote these patriarchal ideas of love, romance, and marriage to encourage men to bring foreign women into the U.S. nuclear family to save it from seemingly unfit U.S. women.

Some scholars and policymakers alike have argued that brokered marriage services create unequal gendered power dynamics that disadvantage women. There are no mail-order husbands (Constable 2003). Although the brokered marriage process requires women to voluntarily list their profiles with an agency, the authority over the process lies with the male consumers. According to Suzanne Jackson (2007), male consumers hold a majority of the power as they choose whom they will communicate with and decide whether to facilitate marriage and the immigration process with a particular partner. Further, women who participate in these services often come from economically depressed areas in Eastern Europe, East Asia, and Latin America (Constable 2003; Ehrenreich and Hochschild 2003). This can increase their vulnerability to potential exploitation.

Mail-order brides may also experience gendered violence at the hands of their partners. For example, two mail-order brides, Susanna Blackwell in 1995 and Anastasia King in 2000, were both abused and murdered by U.S. citizen men whom they had married through brokered arrangements. In the King case, the husband had already physically abused a previous foreign bride before he murdered King. As a result, the U.S. Congress created the 2005 International Marriage Broker Regulation Act which requires U.S. citizen men who marry through brokerage sites to submit to criminal background checks and potentially additional investigation before their partners can be issued visas to the United States.

In conclusion, mail-order marriages have a long history in the United States. Mail-order brides have many debates among scholars, politicians, and marriage partners alike.

Gina Marie Longo

See also: Dowries; Gender Roles

Further Reading

Collins, Francis L., Lai Ah Eng, and Brenda S. A. Yeoh. 2013. "Introduction: Approaching migration and diversity in Asian contexts." In *Migration and diversity in Asian contexts*, edited by Lai Ah Eng, Francis L. Collins, and Brenda S. A. Yeoh. Singapore: Institute of Southeast Asian Studies.

Constable, Nicole. 2003. *Romance on a global stage: Pen pals, virtual ethnography, and mail-order marriages.* Berkeley, CA: University of California Press.

Ehrenreich, Barbara, and Arlie Hochschild. 2003. "Introduction." In *Global woman: Nannies, maids, and sex workers in the new economy*, edited by Barbara Ehrenreich and Arlie Hochschild. New York: Macmillan.

Jackson, Suzanne. 2007. "Marriages of convenience: International marriage brokers, mail-order brides, and domestic servitude." *University of Toledo Law Review* 38, no. 3: 895–922.

Lee, Catherine. 2003. "Prostitutes and picture brides: Chinese and Japanese immigration, settlement, and American nation-building, 1870–1920." *Center for Comparative Immigration Studies*: 23.

Palriwala, Rajni and Patricia Uberoi. 2008. "Exploring the links: Gender issues in marriage and migration." In *Marriage, migration and gender,* edited by Rajni Palriwala and Patricia Uberoi. Thousand Oaks, CA: Sage Publications.

Pearce, Susan, Elizabeth Clifford, and Reena Tandon. 2011. *Immigration and women: Understanding the American experience.* New York: New York University Press

Yehl, Daniel. 2001. "The Mail-order bride industry: Globalized legal prostitution and the U.S. response." *Immigration & Nationality Law Review* 22: 681.

Marital Expectations

Marriage is a common experience among adults in the United States. Individuals' expectations about marriage influence their decision to get married, marital timing, marital standards and interactions, satisfaction, and divorce. Marital expectations have changed over time, shifting from a social and economic necessity to standard for what it means to be in a committed relationship. People enter marriages with different backgrounds, framed through gender, race/ethnicity, socioeconomic standing, and religion, and these experiences can influence marital expectations.

Marital expectations pertain to marital values and aspirations (Willoughby and Carroll 2016). These expectations include individuals' and couples' beliefs about getting and being married, which can affect the timing of marriage, satisfaction, stability, and dissolution. Today, many young adults are choosing to delay their marriage (Pew 2019), opting instead to cohabit with a partner (U.S. Census 2018; Mernitz 2018, 2082; Nugent and Daugherty 2018). Couples today have different expectations of marriage as a result of increased life expectancy, changes in the economy, and shifts in the social meaning attached to marriage. Marriage is seen less as an obligation or necessity, and more as a milestone to be achieved (Cherlin 2004, 856–857) and, as a result, people are taking time to invest in themselves and their future through obtaining additional years of schooling (see Iyigun and Lafortune 2016). Additionally, they are seeking out marriages that are satisfying and conducive to personal well-being (Finkel et al. 2014, 5–6). Sociologists Boxer, Noonan, and Whelan (2015) compared how heterosexual men and women ranked mate traits in 1939–2008 and found that "mutual attraction-love" rose to become the number one quality for both men and women to have in a spouse, with the characteristics "dependable character" and "emotional stability, maturity" ranking second and third (172).

People enter marriages with beliefs about how marriages should be (Vangelisti and Daly 1997, 203–204), and those expectations can have implications for the outcomes of the marriage. These beliefs reflect commonly held societal norms or represent individual expectations (McDonald 1981, 826–827). Expectations about marriage are linked to marital satisfaction (Alexander 2008, 740–743), conflict and instability (Larson and Holman 1994, 232), and divorce (Birditt et al. 2017, 13). Low marital standards are more likely to yield negative consequences (Baucom et al. 1997, 82–86; McNulty and Karney 2002, 771–772), such as infidelity, neglect, or abuse.

Marital expectations are formed before (Sager 1976) or during the relationship (Murray et al. 2011) and are influenced by a variety of factors including parental relationships, culture (see Juvva and Bhatti 2006), previous relationship experiences (see Rhoades and Stanely 2014), and exposure to romantic television (Osborn 2012, 740; Segrin and Nabi 2002, 255). Some scholars have found that couples are at increased risk for dissatisfaction and divorce when expectations of marriage are too high (Eidelson and Epstein 1982, 20–21; McNulty and Karney 2004, 735; Sharp and Ganong 2000, 74–75; Sullivan and Schwebel 1995, 303). Others have found that couples with high standards are more satisfied because they get more out of the marriage (Baucom et al. 1996, 82–86; McNulty and Karney 2004, 737–738; Vangelisti and Daly 1997, 214).

Research has examined many factors that can influence marital expectations, including gender, race/ethnicity, socioeconomic status, and religion.

Gender

Men and women in heterosexual couples share similar marital expectations, but these expectations are linked to different outcomes. Men tend to report greater satisfaction in relationships (Carr et al. 2014, 938–941) and, as a result, their expectations are more linked to marriage (Brown 2000, 840–843). Women, on the other hand, report more issues in their romantic relationships (Rubin, Peplau, and Hill 1981, 827), and are therefore more likely to initiate divorce (Rosenfeld 2017, 15–16). This may be because marriage is seen as a gendered institution that reproduces and reifies traditional gender roles, where men's needs are placed over

the needs of women (see Berk 1985; Hochschild and Machung 1989). Although men and women place equal emphasis on standards in relationships, women tend to have their standards met or fulfilled less frequently than men (Vangelisti and Daly 1997, 210–214). The women's role as caretakers, the intimate manner in which they interact, and their communication skills create relational contexts where the standards of men are more likely to be met than women's standards.

Race/Ethnicity

Overall, white Americans and Hispanics have higher marital expectations relative to Black Americans (Manning and Smock 2002, 1080; Plotnick 2007, 953). Sociologists Bulanda and Brown examined dimensions of marital quality and marital dissolution in 2007 for white Americans, Mexican Americans, and Black Americans and found that Mexican Americans and white Americans reported better marital quality relative to Black Americans (961). White Americans and Mexican Americans report greater marital happiness, more positive marital interactions, fewer marital disagreements, fewer marital problems, and perceived less instability than Black Americans. Processes underlying these patterns are differences in life circumstances and cultural norms among Black Americans (Bryant 2010). Unique factors known to negatively influence marital quality among Black Americans include financial strain, family obligations, children, racial discrimination, and minority stress. For instance, Black Americans have fewer socioeconomic circumstances, which is conducive to a lower socioeconomic status, meaning more exposure to a variety of stressors (Williams et al. 2010, 70) that lead to marital dissatisfaction and dissolution (Tucker 2000, 183).

Socioeconomic Status

The relationship between financial resources, family formation, and marital dissolution is well documented (see Conger et al. 1990; Falconier and Epstein 2011; Williamson, Karney, and Bradbury 2013). Individuals and couples with more resources hold greater desires to get married (Cherlin 2010, 404) and expect to marry sooner (Arocho and Dush 2018, 7). Literature from nearly a decade (2000–2010) shows that more financial resources increase the levels of marital satisfaction and happiness, thereby reducing the risk of separation and divorce (Conger, Conger, and Martin 2010, 5; Heaton 2002, 398; Karney and Bradbury 2005, 172). According to the Conger Family Stress Model, economic strain lowers overall marital quality through its influence on marital interactions (Conger et al. 1999, 55). Indeed, numerous studies have elucidated the mediating role of communication, affection, and love in documenting the effects of socioeconomic status on marital satisfaction and dissolution (see Conger, Reuter, and Elder 1999; Conger et al. 1993; Matthews, Conger, and Wickrama 1996; Robila and Krishnakumar 2005; White and Rogers 2000). For example, Psychologists Barton, Futris, and Nielsen analyzed survey data from married couples in 2015 and found that financial distress influenced marital quality indirectly, through its negative effects on communication styles and gratitude expression (541–546). In the past, the wife's income was positively associated with marital dissolution, however, this does not seem to be the case for couples who wed after the 1990s (Schwartz and Gonalons-Pons 2016, 227).

Religion

Religious involvement is positively associated with the timing of the first marriage (Xu, Hudspeth, and Bartkowski 2005, 606–612), as well as marital stability and success (Heaton and Pratt 1990, 198–204). That is, individuals who are affiliated with a religion, frequently attend church, and adhere to religious beliefs tend to get married earlier and report higher levels of marital satisfaction, which reduces the likelihood of divorce. Prior research suggests that distinctive theological perspectives, degree of personal religious commitment, and organizational religious involvement all contribute to marital expectations (see Bartkowski 2001; Gallagher 2003; Hegy and Martos 2000; Mullins 2016). The connection between religion and marital satisfaction is complicated by mediating factors. Psychologist Gary Hansen analyzed data on married couples in 1987 and found that women develop gender- and religious-based values of obedience, humility, compassion, and self-sacrifice. These attributes result in lower expectations of rewards from marriage while still being satisfied (265–268). Interviews with married couples indicate that faith is instrumental in the maintenance and growth of their relationship (Mullins 2016, 4–8; Robinson 1994, 210–214). Religious orientation and adherence affect marital relationships by providing a social context that gives sacred meaning to their marriage, which influences marital stability through moral guidance and social, emotional, and spiritual support. Denominational affiliation homogamy is most critical in terms of marital satisfaction, with church attendance homogamy contributing slightly to marital success (Heaton and Pratt 1990, 202–203).

Opportunity for Further Inquiry

Same-sex marriage in the United States expanded from one state in 2004 to all 50 states and Washington, D.C., in 2015, and as a result, little is known about marital expectations among individuals in same-sex marriages. Interviews with individuals in same-sex couples across the United States indicate that same-sex couples perceive marriage as important (Haas and Whitton 2015, 12–13), even though same-sex couples (both male and female) have higher relationship dissolution rates relative to different-sex couples (Lau 2012, 984). These findings are consistent with the minority stress perspective, which argues that unique challenges faced by same-sex couples contribute to stresses in the relationship which amount to the dissolution of the partnership (Frost and Gola 2015, 390). Although current research on sexuality and same-sex marital expectations is scarce, recent changes in marital laws and shifts in social perceptions of same-sex relationships warrant additional research on same-sex marital expectations.

Ismail Nooraddini and Shannon N. Davis

See also: Gender Roles; Interfaith Marriages; Interracial Marriages; LGBTQ Marriages and Unions; Living Apart Together

Further Reading

Alexander, Alicia L. 2008. "Relationship Resources for Coping with Unfulfilled Standards in Dating Relationships: Commitment, Satisfaction, and Closeness." *Journal of Social and Personal Relationships*, no. 25: 72–747. https://doi.org/10.1177/0265407508093783

Arocho, Rachel and Claire M. Kamp Dush. 2018. "Distant Horizons: Marital Expectations May Be Dampened by Economic Circumstances." *Couple and Family Psychology: Research and Practice* 7, no. 1: 1–11. https://doi.org/10.1037/cfp0000095.

Bartkowski, John P. 2001. *Remaking the Godly Marriage: Gender Negotiation in Evangelical Families*. New Brunswick: Rutgers University Press.

Barton, Allen W., Ted G. Futris, and Robert B. Nielsen. 2015. "Linking Financial Distress to Marital Quality: The Intermediary Roles of Demand/Withdraw and Spousal Gratitude Expressions." *Personal Relationships* 22, no. 3: 536–549. https://doi.org/10.1111/pere.12094.

Baucom, Donald H., Norman Epstein, Lynn A. Rankin, and Charles K. Burnett. 1996. "Assessing Relationship Standards: The Inventory of Specific Relationship Standards." *Journal of Family Psychology* 10, no. 1: 72. https://doi.org/10.1037/0893-3200.10.1.72.

Berk, Sarah Fenstermaker. 1985. *The Gender Factory: The Apportionment of Work in American Households*. New York: Plenum.

Birditt, Kira S., Wylie H. Wan, Terri L. Orbuch, and Toni C Antonucci. 2017. "The Development of Marital Tension: Implications for Divorce among Married Couples." *Developmental Psychology 53*, no. 10: 1995–2006. https://doi.org/10.1037/dev0000379

Boxer, Christie F., Mary C. Noonan, and Christine B. Whelan. 2015. "Measuring Mate Preferences: A Replication and Extension." *Journal of Family Issues* 36, no. 2: 163–187. https://doi.org/10.1177/0192513X13490404.

Brown, Susan L. 2000. "Union Transitions Among Cohabitors: The Significance of Relationship Assessments and Expectations." *Journal of Marriage and Family* 62, no. 3: 833–46. https://doi.org/10.1111/j.1741-3737.2000.00833.x.

Bryant. 2010. "Understanding the Intersection of Race and Marriage: Does One

Model Fit All?" Apa.org. Accessed August 8, 2019. https://www.apa.org/science/about/psa/2010/10/race-marriage.

Bulanda, Jennifer Roebuck, and Susan L. Brown. 2007. "Race-Ethnic Differences in Marital Quality and Divorce." *Social Science Research* 36, no. 3: 945–967. https://doi.org/10.1016/j.ssresearch.2006.04.001.

Carr, Deborah, Vicki A. Freedman, Jennifer C. Cornman, and Norbert Schwarz. 2014. "Happy Marriage, Happy Life? Marital Quality and Subjective Well-Being in Later Life." *Journal of Marriage and Family* 76, no. 5: 930–48. doi: 10.1111/jomf.12133

Cherlin, Andrew J. 2004. "The Deinstitutionalization of American Marriage." *Journal of Marriage and Family* 66, no. 4: 848–61. https://doi.org/10.1111/j.0022-2445.2004.00058.x

Cherlin, Andrew J. 2010. "Demographic Trends in the United States: A Review of Research in the 2000s." *Journal of Marriage and Family* 72, no. 3: 403–419. https://doi.org/10.1111/j.1741-3737.2010.00710.x.

Conger, Rand D., Katherine J. Conger, and Monica J. Martin. 2010. "Socioeconomic Status, Family Processes, and Individual Development." *Journal of Marriage and the Family* 72, no. 3: 685–704. https://doi.org/10.1111/j.1741-3737.2010.00725.x.

Conger, Rand D., Glen H. Elder, Frederick O. Lorenz, Katherine J. Conger, Ronald L. Simons, Les B. Whitbeck, Shirley Huck, Janet N. Melby. 1990. "Linking Economic Hardship to Marital Quality and Instability." *Journal of Marriage and the Family* 52, no. 3: 643. https://doi.org/10.2307/352931

Conger, Rand D., Frederick O. Lorenz, Glen H. Elder, Ronald L. Simons, and Xiaojia Ge. 1993. "Husband and Wife Differences in Response to Undesirable Life Events." *Journal of Health and Social Behavior* 34, no. 1: 71. https://doi.org/10.2307/2137305

Conger, Rand D., Martha A. Rueter, and Glen H. Elder. 1999. "Couple Resilience to Economic Pressure." *Journal of Personality and Social Psychology* 76, no. 1: 54–71. https://doi.org/10.1037/0022-3514.76.1.54

Eidelson, Roy J. and Norman Epstein. 1982. "Cognition and Relationship Maladjustment: Development of a Measure of Dysfunctional Relationship Beliefs." *Journal of Consulting and Clinical Psychology* 50, no. 5: 715–20.

Falconier, Mariana K. and Norman B. Epstein. 2011. "Couples Experiencing Financial Strain: What We Know and What We Can Do." *Family Relations* 60, no. 3: 303–17. https://doi.org/10.1111/j.1741-3729.2011.00650.x

Finkel, Eli J., Chin M. Hui, Kathleen L. Carswell, and Grace M. Larson. 2014. "The Suffocation of Marriage: Climbing Mount Maslow without Enough Oxygen." *Psychological Inquiry* 25, no. 1: 1–41. https://doi.org/10.1080/1047840X.2014.863723

Frost, David M. and Kelly A. Gola. 2015. "Meanings of Intimacy: A Comparison of Members of Heterosexual and Same-Sex Couples." *Analyses of Social Issues and Public Policy* 15, no. 1: 382–400. https://doi.org/10.1111/asap.12072

Gallagher, Sally K. 2003. *Evangelical Identity and Gendered Family Life.* New Brunswick, NJ: Rutgers University Press.

Haas, Stephen M. and Sarah W. Whitton. 2015. "The Significance of Living Together and Importance of Marriage in Same-Sex Couples." *Journal of Homosexuality* 62, no. 9: 1241–63. https://doi.org/10.1080/00918369.2015.1037137.

Hansen, Gary L. 1987. "The Effect of Religiosity on Factors Predicting Marital Adjustment." *Social Psychology Quarterly* 50, no. 3: 264–269. https://doi.org/10.2307/2786827.

Heaton, Tim B. 2002. "Factors Contributing to Increasing Marital Stability in the

United States." *Journal of Family Issues* 23, no. 3: 392–409. https://doi.org/10.1177/0192513X02023003004

Heaton, Tim B. and Edith L. Pratt. 1990. "The Effects of Religious Homogamy on Marital Satisfaction and Stability." *Journal of Family Issues* 11, no. 2: 191–207. https://doi.org/10.1177/019251390011002005.

Hegy, Pierre and Joseph Martos (Eds.). 2000. *Catholic Divorce: The Deception of Annulments.* Dulles, VA: Continuum.

Hochschild, Arlie R. and Anne Machung. 1989. *The Second Shift: Working Parents and the Revolution at Home.* New York, NY: Viking.

Iyigun, Murat F. and Jeanne Lafortune. 2016. "Why Wait? A Century of Education, Marriage Timing and Gender Roles." IZA Discussion Paper No. 9671, Available at SSRN: https://ssrn.com/abstract=2725032 or http://dx.doi.org/10.2139/ssrn.2725032

Juvva, Srilatha and Ranbir Bhatti. 2006. "Epigenetic Model of Marital Expectations." *Contemporary Family Therapy: An International Journal* 28, no. 1. DOI: 10.1007/s10591-006-9695-2

Karney, Benjamin R. and Thomas N. Bradbury. 2005. "Contextual Influences on Marriage: Implications for Policy and Intervention." *Current Directions in Psychological Science* 14, no. 4: 171–174. https://doi.org/10.1111/j.0963-7214.2005.00358.x

Larson, Jeffery H. and Thomas B. Holman. 1994. "Premarital Predictors of Marital Quality and Stability." *Family Relations: An Interdisciplinary Journal of Applied Family Studies* 43, no. 2: 228–237. https://doi.org/10.2307/585327

Lau, C.Q. 2012. "The Stability of Same-Sex Cohabitation, Different-Sex Cohabitation, and Marriage." *Journal of Marriage and Family* 74, no. 5: 973–988. doi:10.1111/j. 1741-3737.2012.01000.x.

Manning, Wendy D. and Pamela J. Smock. 2002. "First Comes Cohabitation Then Comes Marriage? A Research Note." *Journal of Family Issues* 23, no. 8: 1095–1087. https://doi.org/10.1177/019251302237303

Matthews, Lisa S., Rand D. Conger, and K. A. Wickrama. 1996. "Work-family Conflict and Marital Quality: Mediating Processes." *Social Psychology Quarterly* 59, no. 1: 62. https://doi.org/10.2307/2787119

McDonald, Gerald M. 1981. "Structural Exchange and Marital Satisfaction." *Journal of Marriage and the Family*, no. 43: 825–839. https://doi.org/10.2307/351340

McNulty, James K. and Benjamin R. Karney. 2002. "Expectancy Confirmation in Appraisals of Marital Interactions." *Personality and Social Psychology Bulletin* 28: 767–775. https://doi.org/10.1177/0146167202289006

McNulty, James K. and Benjamin R. Karney. 2004. "Positive Expectations in the Early Years of Marriage: Should Couples Expect the Best or Brace for the Worst?" *Journal of Personality and Social Psychology* 86, no. 5: 729–743. https://doi.org/10.1037/0022-3514.86.5.729

Mernitz, Sara. 2018. "A Cohort Comparison of Trends in First Cohabitation Duration in the United States." *Demographic Research* 38 (June): 2073–86. https://doi.org/10.4054/DemRes.2018.38.66.

Mullins, David. 2016. "The Effects of Religion on Enduring Marriages." *Social Sciences* 5, no. 2: 24. https://doi.org/10.3390/socsci5020024.

Murray, Sandra L., Dale W. Griffen, Jaye L. Derrick, Brianna Harris, Maya Aloni, and Sadie Leder. 2011. "Tempting Fate or Inviting Happiness?" *Psychological Science* 22, no. 5: 619–26. doi: 10.1177/0956797611403155

Nugent, Colleen and Jill Daugherty. 2018. "A Demographic, Attitudinal, and Behavioral Profile of Cohabiting Adults in the United States, 2011–2015." National Health Statistics Reports; no 111. Hyattsville, MD: National Center for Health Statistics. 2018

Osborn, Jeremy L. 2012. "When TV and Marriage Meet: A Social Exchange Analysis of the Impact of Television Viewing on Marital Satisfaction and Commitment." *Mass Communication and Society* 15, no. 5: 739–57. https://doi.org/10.1080/15205436.2011.618900

Pew Research Center. 2019. "Marriage and Cohabitation in the U.S." Retrieved From https://www.pewresearch.org/social-trends/2019/11/06/marriage-and-cohabitation-in-the-u-s/#:~:text=As%20more%20U.S.%20adults%20are,new%20Pew%20Research%20Center%20survey.

Plotnick, Robert D. 2007. "Adolescent Expectations and Desires about Marriage and Parenthood." *Journal of Adolescence* 30, no. 6: 943–63. https://doi.org/10.1016/j.adolescence.2007.01.003.

Rhoades, Galena K. and Scott M. Stanley. 2014. "Before 'I Do': What Do Premarital Experiences Have to Do with Marital Quality Among Today's Young Adults?' *The National Marriage Project at the University of Virginia*. Retrieved from https://www.nationalmarriageproject.org/wordpress/wp-content/uploads/2014/08/NMP-BeforeIDoReport-Final.pdf

Robila, Mihaela and Ambika Krishnakumar. 2005. "Effects of Economic Pressure on Marital Conflict in Romania." *Journal of Family Psychology* 19, no. 2: 246–51. https://doi.org/10.1037/0893-3200.19.2.246

Robinson, Linda. 1994. "Religious Orientation in Enduring Marriage: An Exploratory Study." *Review of Religious Research* 207–218. https://doi.org/10.2307/3511889

Rosenfeld, Michael J. 2017. "Who Wants the Breakup? Gender and Breakup in Heterosexual Couples." [White paper]. Retrieved from https://web.stanford.edu/~mrosenfe/Rosenfeld_gender_of_breakup.pdf

Rubin, Zick, Letitia Anne Peplau, and Charles T. Hill. 1981. "Loving and Leaving: Sex Differences in Romantic Attachments." *Sex Roles* 7, no. 8: 821–35.

Sager, Clifford J. 1976. *Marriage Contracts and Couple Therapy*. New York: Brunner/Mazel.

Schwartz, Christine R., and Pilar Gonalons-Pons. 2016. "Trends in Relative Earnings and Marital Dissolution: Are Wives Who Outearn Their Husbands Still More Likely to Divorce?" *The Russell Sage Foundation Journal of the Social Sciences: RSF* 2, 4: 218–236. doi:10.7758/rsf.2016.2.4.08

Segrin, Chris and Robin L. Nabi. 2002. "Does Television Viewing Cultivate Unrealistic Expectations about Marriage?" *Journal of Communication* 52, no. 2: 247–63. https://doi.org/10.1111/j.1460-2466.2002.tb02543.x

Sharp, Elizabeth A. and Lawrence H. Ganong. 2000. "Raising Awareness about Marital Expectations: Are Unrealistic Beliefs Changed by Integrative Teaching?" *Family Relations* 49, no. 1: 71–76. https://doi.org/10.1111/j.1741-3729.2000.00071.x

Sullivan, Bryce F. and Andrew I. Schwebel. 1995. "Relationship Beliefs and Expectations of Satisfaction in Marital Relationships: Implications for Family Practitioners." *The Family Journal* 3, no. 4: 298–305. https://doi.org/10.1177/1066480795034003

Tucker, M. Belinda. 2000. "Marital Values and Expectations in Context: Results from a 21 City Survey." In L. Waite, C. Bacharach, M. Hindin, E. Thomson, and A. Thornton (Eds.), *The Ties the Bind: Perspectives on Marriage and Cohabitation*. New York: Aldine de Gruyter. pp. 166–187.

U.S. Census Bureau. 2018. "U.S. Census Bureau Releases. 2018. Families and Living Arrangements Tables." Retrieved from https://www.census.gov/newsroom/press-releases/2018/families.html.

Vangelisti, Anita L. and John A. Daly. 1997. "Gender Differences in Standards for Romantic Relationships." *Personal Relationships* 4, no. 3: 203–219. https://doi .org/10.1111/j.1475-6811.1997.tb00140.x.

White, Lynn and Stacy J. Rogers. 2000. "Economic Circumstances and Family Outcomes: A Review of the 1990s." *Journal of Marriage and Family* 62, no. 4: 1035–51. https://doi.org/10.1111/j.1741-3737 .2000.01035.x

Williams, David R., Selina A. Mohammed, Jacinta Leavell, and Chiquita Collins. 2010. "Race, Socioeconomic Status, and Health: Complexities, Ongoing Challenges, and Research Opportunities." *Annals of the New York Academy of Sciences* 1186, no. 1: 69–101. doi:10.1111 /j.1749-6632.2009.05339.x.

Williamson, Hannah C., Benjamin R. Karney, and Thomas N. Bradbury. 2013. "Financial Strain and Stressful Events Predict Newlyweds' Negative Communication Independent of Relationship Satisfaction." *Journal of Family Psychology* 27, no. 1: 65–75. https://doi.org/10.1037 /a0031104

Willoughby, Brian J. and Jason S. Carroll. 2016. "On the Horizon: Marriage Timing, Beliefs, and Consequences in Emerging Adulthood." In J. J. Arnett (Ed.), *The Oxford Handbook of Emerging Adulthood* (pp. 280–295). Oxford University Press.

Xu, Xiaohe, Clark D. Hudspeth, and John P. Bartkowski. 2005. "The Timing of First Marriage." *Journal of Family Issues* 26, no. 5: 584–618. https://doi.org/10.1177 /0192513X04272398

Marital Separation

Marital separation is an often legally and relationally ambiguous status—not quite married not quite divorced. Although there is extensive research on marriage and divorce independently, there seems to be a lack of research on the interim period. A key reason is that the majority of marital separations end rather quickly, due to either reconciliation or divorce (Amato 2010, 650–666). Furthermore, past researchers have understood the idea of separation as closely synonymous with divorce, leaving little room for the idea or act of reconciliation. This speaks to the need for more attention and contemporary research to be paid to this nuanced phenomenon so we can have more clarity about what separation *really* is.

One way to consider separation is through legal status and involvement. Legally, separation can denote an action that has been taken by either one or both members of the couple. In this sense, each of the partners is still legally married, but, as issued by the court, living apart. Conversely, depending on the context of the separation as well as the relationship between the two partners, separation may be an action (e.g., a trial separation) that is decided by one or both spouses without legal involvement. In both instances, however, there is a lack of legal finality to the dissolution of the marriage. Thus, a certain amount of relational ambiguity exists.

In addition to legal considerations, clinicians must consider the complex relational aspects of this phenomenon, as one's perceived relational status can vary even within couples. Consider the following example, a couple enters therapy after one spouse (Casey) suggested a trial separation. Casey began subletting an apartment and moved out. The other spouse (Eli) was devastated, which led Eli to seek therapy. In the first session, Eli reports being "desperate to reconcile the relationship." Casey shrugs at this statement. Clearly, each spouse is in a different place relationally—Eli is "leaning in" while Casey is "leaning out" of the marriage (Doherty and Harris 2017). To move forward effectively, the therapist must identify and acknowledge the perceived relational status of each spouse at the onset and throughout therapy. Specific treatment frameworks have been developed when working with "last chance couples" (Fraenkel 2019, 569–594) or "mixed agenda couples" (Doherty and Harris 2017) when one or both members of the couple are considering ending the relationship, which can be particularly beneficial in cases of separation.

Whether a separation leads to marital dissolution or reconciliation, when children are involved, their coparents have been, are currently in, and will continue to be in a relationship with one another. There are not only historical intimate ties that link the spouses together, but there are current and future familial ties that link the parents to their children. During the separation process, children are also experiencing an ambiguous state within their families. Children may experience confusion, anger, and sadness during the separation process due to the lack of clarity. It can be difficult for children to trust when this ambiguous period will end, or *if* it will end. Evidence has shown that couples with children are more likely to seek professional counseling than couples without children and are more likely to remain together or reconcile in hopes of preventing potential harm caused by divorce. In therapy, an important point of emphasis when working with coparents is to try and keep children's life as consistent as before the separation (e.g., same or similar surroundings within home life, remaining at same school, etc.). This will help children feel more normalcy and

security within the ambiguous separation period. Moving forward, additional research focusing on children's social-emotional experiences throughout the process of parental separation is needed.

Rachel M. Diamond and Stevi Gould

See also: Divorce and Legal Planning; Living Apart Together; Marriage Counseling

Further Reading

Amato, Paul R. 2010. "Research on Divorce: Continuing Trends and New Developments." *Journal of Marriage and Family* 72, no. 3: 650–666. https://doi.org/10.1111/j.1741-3737.2010.00723.x.

Crabtree, Sarah A., and Steven M. Harris. 2019. "The Lived Experience of Ambiguous Marital Separation: A Phenomenological Study." *Journal of Marital and Family Therapy* 46, no. 3: 385–398. https://doi.org/10.1111/jmft.12419.

Doherty, William J., and Steven M. Harris. 2017. *Helping Couples on the Brink of Divorce: Discernment Counseling for Troubled Relationships*. Washington, DC: American Psychological Association.

Fraenkel, Peter. 2019. "Love in Action: An Integrative Approach to Last Chance Couple Therapy." *Family Process* 58, no. 3: 569–594. https://doi.org/10.1111/famp.12474.

Tumin, Dmitry, Siqi Han, and Zhenchao Qian. 2015. "Estimates and Meanings of Marital Separation." *Journal of Marriage and Family* 77, no. 1: 312–322. https://doi.org/10.1111/jomf.12149.

Marital Success

Contemporary U.S. marriage occurs amidst a changing landscape, with greater cultural diversity, legal status for LGBTQ unions, socioeconomic disparity, and a varied and expanded family lifecycle. Psychologist Froma Walsh (2015) writes that it is more common for today's couples to have 2–3 long-term committed relationships interspersed with periods of cohabitation and single living. Couples are marrying later—at an average of 30.4 years old for men and 28.6 years old for women, cohabitating before or in place of marriage (2020 U.S. Census) and experimenting with various forms of intimacy within marriage such as serial monogamy, polyamory, and living apart together (LAT).

Just as the form and function of the institution of marriage have evolved over time, so too has the definition of marital success. Often used interchangeably with satisfaction, happiness, and well-being, several criteria for success emerge consistently. In general, a successful marriage brings satisfaction and happiness to the partners. In their attempt to create a predictive model for marital satisfaction, Abreu-Afonso et al. (2021) found intrinsic motivation to be the strongest predictor. Therapists point out that criteria based on longevity may be misleading, citing that marriages that persist despite partner discontent and conflict should not be considered successful or satisfactory. Overall, the most robust determinants of whether people stay married are money and education. People with greater economic and other resources that support marital quality marry in greater numbers and stay married at higher rates (Finkle 2017).

Since the 1930s, scholars have investigated marriage to identify specific criteria that constitute success, guided by the idea that these criteria would inform premarital and marriage enrichment programs and influence marital treatment.

These criteria are also valuable in efforts to explain the linkage between successful marriages and better health outcomes, particularly for men and among the elderly (Lawrence et al. 2019). However, marital quality has been declining among recent cohorts, and the doubling of the divorce rate among persons over the age of 50 years foretells poorer quality marriages for today's midlife adults than a generation ago (Wright, Brown, and Manning 2021).

Studies of long-term marriages conducted between 1953 and 2004 identified commitment, love, sex, personality compatibility, decision-making ability, and religion as key components to success (Billengsley et al. 2005), and with some variation in emphasis, those factors continue to be important. Maintaining the initial closeness of early marriage over the long arc of the lifespan requires attention, flexibility, emotional agility, and an open, resilient mindset. Studies of marital satisfaction over time indicate a decline once children are born, one that doesn't recover until the "empty nest" phase. Contemporary marriage is pressured by societal expectations to find a love match (soulmate), unrealistic beliefs about the effort required for success, and the notion that one's partner will be a source of personal healing and psychological completion. Contemporary marriages are forged in a context of declining social networks, increased family mobility, high dual-demand work lives, and practices of time-intensive parenting-all of which leave partners little daily time to address relational needs. So, at the same time marriage has become more important, it has also become more fragile (Coontz 2006).

One of the most well-known researchers of marital success is the psychologist

John Gottman, who together with his wife psychologist, Julie Schwartz Gottman, has been overseeing the "Love Lab" in Seattle (Lawrence et al. 2019). For over 40 years, they have studied thousands of couples and have uncovered the elements of what they call the "Masters and Disasters" of marriage. Their formula for success consists of the following. First and foremost, successful partners treat each other like good friends. They pay attention, speak respectfully and with kindness and spend time together. They take one another's concerns seriously. Second, partners actively engage with each other; they allow themselves to be affected by the other's interests and wishes and seek to understand differences. Successful couples emphasize and cultivate their mutual admiration and fondness and regularly express gratitude. They have a relational (we) mindset, taking the attitude that they are facing life as a team. They turn toward one another's bids for emotional connection, learning to recognize the unique signals their partner sends to indicate both distress and affection. Third, the masters of marriage handle conflict in gentle and positive ways. They learn to control their reactivity and use humor to deflect tensions. Finally, and most critically, they can repair following negative interactions. They realize that conflict is inevitable, management is key, and they use skills that prioritize repair and healing.

Research and clinical work by psychologists Jefferson Singer and Karen Skerrett (2014) have refined the quality of we-ness and linked it to the development of mutuality and resilience. Viewing the relationship as a valuable entity to which both partners commit and invest time and attention allows for healthy dialogue and enduring trust. The cultivation of such a we-consciousness makes it more likely for partners to recognize that the choices they make will have consequences for their partner as well as the relationship, thus enhancing mutual awareness of what the marriage requires for success. Similarly, the work of psychologist Susan Johnson (2014), the developer of emotion-focused therapy, has illustrated that a capacity for empathy and compassion for each partner's vulnerability enables couples to move through conflict and reaffirm a loving commitment.

Karen Skerrett and Jefferson Alan Singer

See also: Love, Connection, and Intimacy; Styles of Love; Triangular Theory of Love

Further Reading

Abreu-Afonso, J., Ramos, M. M., Queiroz-Garcia, I., and Leal, I. 2021. "How couple's relationship lasts over time? A model for marital satisfaction." *Psychological Reports*, 00332941211000651.

Billengsley, Sam, Lim, M.-G., Caron, J., Harris, A. and Canada, R. 2005. "Historical overview of criteria for marital and family success." *Family Therapy* 32, no.1: 1–14.

Coontz, Stephanie. 2006. *Marriage, a history: How love conquered marriage.* New York: Penguin Books.

Finkle, Eli J. 2017. *The all or nothing marriage.* New York: Dutton Press.

Gottman, John. 2015. *The 7 Practices for making marriage work: A practitioner's guide from the country's foremost relationship expert.* New York: Harmony Press.

Lawrence, E., Rogers, R., Zajocova, A., and Wadsworth, T. 2019. "Marital happiness, marital status, health and longevity." *Journal of Happiness Studies* 20, no. 5: 1539–1561.

Singer, J. A. and Skerrett, K. 2014. *Positive couple therapy: Using we-stories to enhance resilience.* New York: Taylor & Francis Press.

Walsh, F. 2015. "A family developmental framework: Challenges and resilience across the life cycle." In *The handbook of family therapy: The science and practice of working with families and couples.* New York: Routledge Press.

Wiebe, Stephanie and Johnson, Susan. 2016. "A review of the research in Emotionally Focused Therapy for couples." *Family Process* 55, no. 3: 390–407.

Wright, M. R., Brown, S. L., and Manning, W. D. 2021. "A cohort comparison of midlife marital quality: A quarter century of change." *Journal of Family Issues,* 0192513X211054466.

Marriage, Financial Implications

Although the current perception of marriage is a pair bond between two people chosen out of love, it is in reality a legally sanctioned union regulated by tradition, family, culture, religion, and law. A central part of this contract is the provision and use of resources by both spouses as well as a means to pass along wealth to others in the family. In other words, marriage is a financial institution with implications for who marries and when; the control of such unions by legal and policy means reflective of dominant discourses and ideologies; and marriage's benefits and costs for individuals, couples, and society.

The timing and likelihood of marriage are related to factors such as income and education level, employment, and accumulated wealth. While in the past couples would marry first and then look for security in wages and employment, today that pattern is reversed. No longer is marriage the first step into adulthood; it comes after education, job training, employment, and even cohabitation and having children (Cherlin 2009). Marriage rates in the United States are at all-time lows. In 2020, there were 5.1 marriages per 1,000 people compared to the peak in 1946 of 16.4 (CDC/NCHS National Vital Statistics System; Curtin and Sutton 2020). The median age at first marriage for both men and women has also risen since 1900, with a dip in the years after World War II when economic conditions were favorable for some and government policies enabled early marriage. Further, since 1970, the number of adults remaining single has increased. Most recent numbers available indicate that 30.5% of women and 36.7% of men have never married, in contrast to 1970 percentages of 22 and 28 (U.S. Census Bureau 2021) Reduced economic prospects and increased risk of incarceration for men over 1969–2013 partially explain the decline in first marriage rates (Schneider et al. 2018, 805–806). Rising economic inequality is another explanation given for the reduced likelihood of marriage before birth for both men and women with this link is partially explained by the lack of middle-skilled jobs paying a living wage (Cherlin, Ribar, and Yasutake 2016, 759–766). The increase in percentages of adults remaining single over the past three decades has been higher for those with lower education and income levels.

These trends have also been explained by the *theory of marital timing* whereas young adults delay marriage until they feel financially stable through employment and savings. While other variables are involved in the decision to marry, several large-scale studies have found links between men's propensity to marry and financial variables, whereas findings for women have been mixed (Dew and Price 2011, 425). Higher-income men are more likely to marry and remarry, less likely to divorce, and more likely to have children than men with lower incomes; for women, income was not associated with the likelihood of marrying but was related to divorce and being less likely to remarry (Hopcroft 2021, 411–415). College graduates are more likely to marry than those with some college/no degree. Hours worked and job prestige is also linked to marriage likelihood as are visible financial markers (e.g., car, home ownership; Dew and Price 2011, 434). It may be that individuals with greater resources benefit more materially than those with lower who benefit less from marital legal protections (Cherlin 2009, 178–179). However, the value of marriage between individuals of various economic standings does not differ, rather, it is the perception that if one meets certain criteria enabling one to be able to marry then it opens the door to marriage

The link between higher rates of marriage for men with more resources has been explained as such men having higher value as long-term partners. Financial standing and future prospects of a potential spouse may be more important for women than men across multiple cultures (Walter et al. 2020, 418–420), with those offering this argument citing findings discussed previously. Although both members of a couple are now often employed outside the home for pay as affording life necessities requires two incomes, the husband as breadwinner ideology in heterosexual marriages persists.

The control of marital unions by formal laws reflects dominant discourses. The emphasis on men, and in particular white men, as providers and heads of household have been present throughout U.S. history. During colonial times, enslaved peoples did not have the right to marry and family relationships were destroyed and exploited as means to manipulate and control. Common law governing marriage was influenced by the coverture doctrine that arose in the Middle Ages, was codified into European laws, and then of other nations under the rule of these countries. This doctrine held that a husband and wife became one legal entity after marriage; laws then prescribed the wife's identity was subsumed by her husband's making her a nonperson legally with no independent rights. Any property or assets of hers became her husband's. She could not sue or sign legal documents without his approval. By the end of the U.S. Civil War (1861–1865), a majority of states had modified laws to allow women to own property and take some legal actions; but even after policy changes during the latter 20th century, traces of coverture remain. Multiple laws reflect these vestiges, but of particular importance here include: (1) *1935 Social Security Act*—based on the assumption that most adults marry with men as providers. Men receive support upon retirement and temporary unemployment assistance when needed. Women's support was only upon their husband's death through the Aid to Dependent Children program and later a small portion of their husband's SS benefits. (2) *The Servicemen's Readjustment Act (GI Bill) 1944* provided veterans benefits such as low-interest mortgage loans, education and job training subsidies, civil service job hiring preference, and unemployment compensation. It was also based upon the idea of men as responsible for the financial support of spouses and children. (3) *1948 Tax Law* lowered men's tax burden when wives earned little.

(4) *Equal Credit Opportunity Act in 1974* prohibited creditors from discriminating against applicants based on race, religion, national origin, sex, and marital status. Before this, women were not allowed to apply for credit or control their own bank accounts without permission/approval of their husbands. (5) *Personal Responsibility and Work Opportunity Act (Welfare Reform) 1996, Bush Administration's Healthy Marriage Initiative 2002* included provisions for encouraging and strengthening marriages with the view that this setting was best for children, mothers, AND fathers fill important roles, and support of children is a responsibility by parents, not society. Also influenced by findings that married parents have higher incomes and household wealth than single parents, so to reduce single-parent families among poorer communities, marriage was encouraged. As discussed above, individuals with higher incomes tend to marry, a point opponents of these programs stressed as the reason for these family structure differences, not that marriage increases wealth. These programs also sought to increase father involvement.

Being married also has financial benefits and costs. While marital status cannot be used as official criteria for benefits, married couples often are seen as less risk and receive better credit ratings and loan terms, breaks for insurance through possible increased options and discounts for carrying multiple policies, and higher wages and pay for married men to name a few. While the perception is that there is a marriage tax penalty, more people benefit on their taxes from being married (especially when differences in income levels exist) than are penalized. A credit rating of a spouse can also help or hurt one's own depending on the level of theirs

and married couples tend to have greater wealth and savings than single individuals. Part of this is due to the greater likelihood to marry with higher incomes, but also the couple's habits. Married young adults, more so than cohabiting and single, see greater importance in saving as a financial goal and are more likely to have individual retirement accounts and to participate in defined contribution pension plans (Knoll, Tamborini, and Whilnan 2012, 86–100).

Shannon E. Weaver

See also: Delaying Marriage; Economic Independence

Further Reading

Centers for Disease Control. 2022. "FAST-STATS—Marriage and divorce." Centers for Disease Control and Prevention, March 25, 2022. https://www.cdc.gov/nchs/fastats/marriage-divorce.htm

Cherlin, Andrew. 2009. *The Marriage-go-round: The State of Marriage and the Family in America Today.* New York: Knopf/Random House.

Cherlin, Andrew J., David C. Ribar, and Suzumi Yasutake. 2016. "Nonmarital first births, marriage, and income inequality." *American Sociological Review* 81, no. 4: 749–770.

Curtin, Sally and Paul Sutton. 2020. "Marriage rates in the United States, 1900–2018." *NCHS Health E-Stat.* April 2020. https://www.cdc.gov/nchs/data/hestat/marriage_rate_2018/marriage_rate_2018.htm

Dew, Jeffrey and Joseph Price. 2011. "Beyond employment and income: The association between young adults' finances and marital timing." *Journal of Family and Economic Issues* 32: 424–436.

Hopcroft, Rosemary L. 2021. "High income men have high value as long-term mates in the U.S.: Personal income and the probability of marriage, divorce, and childbearing." *Evolution and Human Behavior.* Available online at https://doi .org/10.1016/j.evolhumbehav.2021.03.004

Knoll, Melissa A., Christopher Tamborini, and Kevin Whilnan. 2012. "I do . . . want to save: Marriage and retirement savings in young households." *Journal of Marriage and Family* 74, no. 1: 86–100.

Schneider, Daniel, Kristen Harknett, and Matthew Stimpson. 2018. "What explains the decline in first marriage in the United States? Evidence from the panel study of income dynamics, 1969 to 2013." *Journal of Marriage and Family,* 80: 791–811.

U.S. Census Bureau. 2021. "Historical marital status tables." Census.gov, November 22, 2021. https://www.census.gov /data/tables/time-series/demo/families /marital.html.

Walter, Kathryn V., Daniel Conroy-Beam, David M. Buss, Kelly Asao et al. 2020. "Sex differences in mate preferences across 45 countries: A large-scale replication." *Psychological Science* 31 no. 4: 408–423.

Zagorsky, Jay L. 2005. "Marriage and divorce's impact on wealth." *Journal of Sociology* 41, no. 4: 406–424.

Marriage, Five Types of

Characteristics of marriage vary by couple and are influenced by various cultures that couples belong to. John and Julie Gottman are researchers based out of Seattle, WA, and are the most significant contributors to research dedicated to divorce prediction by creating the Love Lab (Gottman, Gottman, and Declaire 2006, 12). The dual relationships between two people have been observed and studied. John and Julie Gottman identified common interactional patterns produced by couples based on their observations in The Love Lab. They categorized them into five types: Conflict-Avoiding, Validating, Volatile, Hostile, and Hostile-Detached (Gottman and DeClaire 2001, 36).

Conflict-avoiding couples focus on their strengths and commonalities to navigate tension in their relationship and avoid conflict (Gottman and Silver 1999, 45). Couples who can avoid conflict also seem to have a healthy balance between their ability to self-regulate and the need for interdependence. Most often, emotion is not expressed. These couples prefer to manage their own emotions and keep conflict low.

On the other hand, *volatile couples* present with a lot of intense emotion. These couples generally tend to be passionate about winning an argument, and they love to debate with each other. Unlike the conflict-avoidant couple, volatile couples can express a range of emotions that include humor, sarcasm, and playful kindness, without disparaging remarks toward each other.

Couples who engage in empathetic interactions and show concern and appreciation for each other are known as *validating couples* (Gottman and Silver 1999, 120). Even amid conflict and despair, couples who are prone to validate each other keep their composure and search for understanding. Validating couples reserve their emotional energy to focus on connection and support. Their soft, mild emotions help to soothe each other, and so they address conflict with a calm approach.

Hostile couples function much like validating couples do. When there are no arguments, these types of couples interact calmly, and with little intensity. Most of the time, these couples are quite reasonable; the catch is what happens during disagreements. Hostile couples tend to comprise one partner functioning in the validator role and the other in the avoider role. When disagreements happen, both partners have the propensity to become defensive during a conflict and disputes. Because both partners engage the disagreements through a defensive lens, there is a tendency for these couples to criticize each other. Hostile couples can often be heard saying things to each other such as, "I'm the only one who" and "you always do." These disagreements are often one-sided, with a lot of focus and attention on their own point of view with no consideration or openness to understand or consider their partners' point of view. These couples often express significant levels of distress, but according to John Gottman, rarely get a divorce, despite their unhappiness (Gottman 1996, 189). Though these couples experience anger and contentment, they are still able to recognize their feelings while also having the emotional capacity to self-regulate. These couples do attempt to repair their relationship when too much damage has been done.

The *hostile-detached couples* are among the loneliest of the five types of marriages because they are in a mutual battle with each other with no clear winner. These couples experience emotional detachment from one another and often give up on their relationship. They often have feelings of frustration at their partner and attempts at repairing the relationship often result in stonewalling and contentment. Their communication style is to criticize each other while detaching from the relationship and compared to the other types of marriages that have honest (though sometimes displaced) expressions of emotions. With a hostile-detached couple, one partner typically tries to stop the arguing by withdrawing or backing down as an anxiety response. But, unlike hostile couples, the hostile-detached couples'

fight doesn't end when one partner withdraws. The other partner will typically not allow the fighting to stop and pursue the distancing partner with so much intensity, disengagement is no longer a viable option. According to John Gottman, these couples are the most dissatisfied, the most dysfunctional, and the most likely to divorce (Gottman and Silver 1999, 35).

Carrie Hatch and Rashida Ingram

See also: Diversity in Marriage; Individualized Marriages; Interfaith Marriage; International Marriage; Interracial Marriage

Further Reading

Gottman, John. 1994. *Why Marriages Succeed or Fail.* New York: Simon and Schuster.

Gottman, John. 1996. *What Predicts Divorce: The Measures.* New York: Lawrence Erlbaum Associates.

Gottman, John. 1999. *The Marriage Clinic.* New York: Norton.

Gottman, John and DeClaire, Joan. 2001. *The Relationship Cure.* New York: Crown Publishing.

Gottman, John, Gottman, Julie, and Declaire, Joan. 2006. *Ten Lessons to Transform Your Marriage: America's Love Lab Experts Share Their Strategies for Strengthening Your Relationship.* New York: Crown Publishing.

Gottman, John and Silver, Nan. 1999. *The Seven Principles for Making Marriage Work.* New York: Crown Publishing.

Johnson, Susan. 2008. *Hold Me Tight: Seven Conversations for a Lifetime of Love.* New York: Little Brown & Co.

Marriage, Sleep and

Married couples share their lives, and this partnership often includes sharing an evening routine and a bed. Even when couples fall asleep and wake up appears to be similar 60–90% of the time (Gunn et al. 2015). This considerable overlap suggests that the marital relationship is an important context in which sleep occurs. While aspects of sleep and relationships have been studied over time, research focusing on how marital quality and sleep affect each other has been gaining momentum more recently. Such a focus is critical, as sleep is a key factor in maintaining optimal health and well-being across the life course (CDC 2018) and approximately one-third of adults report getting less than the recommended 7 hours of sleep per night. There are many reasons for getting less sleep than recommended including individuals thinking they do not need much sleep, distractions, worries, work schedules, family life conflicts, and so forth.

Multiple sleep indicators are linked with marital outcomes, including sleep quality, sleep disturbances, sleep disorders, and even the correspondence of spousal sleep patterns. To explain these links the dynamic association model was developed, which suggests a bidirectional or two-way connection between relationship functioning and sleep that operates through a combination of chronobiological, behavioral, psychological, and physiological pathways. Consistent with this bidirectional relationship, Hasler and Troxel (2010) found that variations in objective and subjective sleep efficiency measures were linked with positive and negative partner interactions on the following day (sleep predicting marital functioning) in a sample of 29 heterosexual couples studied daily over a week. Moreover, those partner interactions in turn predicted individual reports of sleep quality on the following day (marital functioning predicting sleep).

Further evidence of the bidirectional nature of sleep and marital interactions comes from recent research demonstrating that spouses' use of destructive conflict is associated with poorer sleep quality over time (El-Sheikh et al. 2015). Unfortunately, there is evidence to also suggest that sleep problems are associated with higher levels of aggression (CDC 2018). Although such a destructive cycle is concerning, positive relationship interactions and sleep are also associated. For example, perceived partner responsiveness is associated with fewer sleep problems through its links with lower anxiety and depression and greater sleep efficiency (Selcuk et al. 2017). Yorgason and colleagues (2016) found that sleep in older couples was linked to daily marital interactions through its influence on individual mood. Thus, positive marital interactions can improve individual well-being which in turn aids sleep. Likewise, sleeping well can improve mood which can in turn improve marital quality. Together, these findings show that marital interactions and sleep are strongly predictive of each other—for better and, sometimes, unfortunately, for worse.

The relationship between marital quality and sleep remains important over the course of a marriage. For example, at the beginning of marriage, Maranges and McNulty (2017) used a weekly daily diary design to reveal that newlyweds' marital quality was higher on days after which they had slept for a longer period. Among middle-aged adults, decreases in marital quality over six months were associated with greater sleep disturbances (Brown et al. 2019). Finally, evidence from 138 more established, older couples showed that spouses were angrier in the morning when they woke up on days when their sleep was not as refreshing as usual (Marini et al. 2018).

Although the association appears consistent across the life course, developmentally unique aspects of life may differentially affect marriage and sleep quality. From night-time infant feedings, illnesses, and bad dreams in childhood to late-night activities of teenagers keeping worried parents awake, family obligations and stressors often cut into sleep time (Brown et al. 2019). Strikingly, even worries about grown children who have long since left the home can negatively affect middle-aged parents' sleep (Seidel et al. 2017). Other work has shown that later-life spousal assistance with medical/nursing tasks such as wound care is linked to greater sleep disturbances, particularly for those with serious illnesses such as dementia (Polenick et al. 2018). Beyond these stressors, even positive couple activities, such as going on dates or sexual intimacy, may enhance the marital relationship but could further cut into limited sleep time.

In addition to the aforementioned family factors, individual factors also may contribute to the overall quantity and quality of couples' sleep. For example, roughly 50 to 70 million adults have a chronic sleep disorder such as insomnia or obstructive sleep apnea (OSA; CDC 2018). Given the dyadic nature of sleep, a sleep disorder in one spouse likely increases the partner's risk for sleep disturbances. Spillover may also happen whereby daily stressors from one partner's work or other responsibilities outside the home may lead to sleep problems for that individual, which can potentially extend to one's spouse (Brown et al. 2019). Furthermore, spouses may have conflicting preferences (e.g., room temperature, bedding) that ultimately hinder the sleep patterns of one or both partners.

It is likely, however, that nearly all couples would benefit from enhancing their sleep. The National Sleep Foundation suggests establishing a regular, relaxing bedtime routine (e.g., consistent bedtime), engaging in regular exercise during the day, limiting daytime naps to 20–30 minutes, and avoiding stimulants (e.g., caffeine, nicotine) and indigestion-causing foods (e.g., heavy foods, carbonated drinks) close to bedtime. Couples also are encouraged to set up a sleep-conducive environment, which includes a cool, dark room (between 60 and 67 degrees is optimal, with minimal lights from lamps and devices such as TVs and cell phones) and a comfortable mattress and pillows. Although maintaining sleep hygiene can seem challenging at times, the rewards are present for both partners in terms of their health and relationship.

In conclusion, research indicates consistent links between how well couples sleep and the quality of their marriage. Couples and their clinicians should be aware of the bidirectional effects of typical sleep interruptions as well as sleep disorders on individual and marital health. Efforts to improve sleep may thus prove to be a cost-effective and more malleable way for couples to improve their marriage and their overall well-being.

Amber J. Seidel, Jeremy B. Yorgason, Amy J. Rauer, and Courtney A. Polenick

Acknowledgments
Courtney A. Polenick was supported by grant K01AG059829 from the National Institute on Aging.

See also: Marriage, Financial Implications; Marriage Squeeze; Neurodiversity and Marriage; Spousal Support

Further Reading

Brown, Braden J., Dave Robinson, Jakob F. Jensen, Ryan B. Seedall, Jennifer Hodgson, and Maria C. Norton. 2019. "Will improving my marriage improve my sleep?" *Journal of Couple & Relationship Therapy* 18, no. 2: 85–103. https://doi.org/10.1080/15332691.2017.1417938.

CDC. 2018. "Sleep and sleep disorders." National Center for Chronic Disease Prevention and Health Promotion, Division of Population Health. https://www.cdc.gov/sleep/index.html.

El-Sheikh, Mona, Ryan J. Kelly, Kalsea J. Koss, and Amy J. Rauer. 2015. "Longitudinal relations between constructive and destructive conflict and couples' sleep." *Journal of Family Psychology* 29, no. 3: 349–359. https://doi.org/10.1037/fam0000083.

Gunn, Heather E., Daniel J. Buysse, Brant P. Hasler, Amy Begley, and Wendy M. Troxel. 2015. "Sleep concordance in couples is associated with relationship characteristics." *Sleep* 38, no. 6: 933–939. https://doi.org/10.5665/sleep.4744.

Hasler, Brant P., and Wendy M. Troxel. 2010. "Couples' nighttime sleep efficiency and concordance: Evidence for bidirectional associations with daytime relationship functioning." *Psychosomatic Medicine* 72, no. 8: 794–801. https://doi.org/10.1097/PSY.0b013e3181ecd08a.

Maranges, Heather M. and James K. McNulty. 2017. "The rested relationship: Sleep benefits marital evaluations." *Journal of Family Psychology* 31, no. 1: 117–122. https://doi.org/10.1037/fam0000225.

Marini, Christina M., Lynn M. Martire, Dusti R. Jones, Ruixue Zhaoyang, and Orfeu M. Buxton. 2018. "Daily links between sleep and anger among spouses of chronic pain patients." *The Journals of Gerontology: Series B* 75, no. 5: 927–936. https://doi.org/10.1093/geronb/gby111

Polenick, Courtney A., Steffany J. Fredman, Kira S. Birditt, and Steven H. Zarit. 2018. "Relationship quality with parents: Implications for own and partner well-being in middle-aged couples." *Family Process* 57 (1): 253–268. https://doi.org/10.1111/famp.12275.

Seidel, Amber J., Jeremy B. Yorgason, Courtney A. Polenick, Steven H. Zarit, and Karen L. Fingerman. 2017. "Are you sleeping? Dyadic associations of support, stress, and worries regarding adult children on sleep." *The Gerontologist* 58, 2: 341–352. https://doi.org/10.1093/geront/gnw149.

Selcuk, Emre, Sarah C. E. Stanton, Richard B. Slatcher, and Anthony D. Ong. 2017. "Perceived partner responsiveness predicts better sleep quality through lower anxiety." *Social Psychological and Personality Science* 8 (1): 83–92. https://doi.org/10.1177/1948550616662128.

Yorgason, Jeremy B., Wesley B. Godfrey, Vaughn R. A. Call, Lance D. Erickson, Kathryn B. Gustafson, and Ariana H. Bond. 2016. "Daily sleep predicting marital interactions as mediated through mood." *The Journals of Gerontology Series B: Psychological Sciences and Social Sciences*, August, gbw093. https://doi.org/10.1093/geronb/gbw093.

Marriage and Divorce, African Americans

Married individuals regardless of race and ethnicity receive several psychosocial and economic benefits from these committed, heterosexual unions. Married individuals are happier and healthier, experience an increased life span, and have more financial stability (Wilcox et al. 2011). For African Americans, some research indicates that marriage serves as a protective factor for individual psychological well-being when comparing married and unmarried African Americans. Furthermore, marriage has been associated with several social and economic benefits. For example, Lincoln and Chae (2010) reported that marital quality was a key predictor of positive mental health status for African Americans and positive marital status served as a protector from the effects of financial burdens and psychological distress. Despite these benefits, marital rates have declined since the latter half of the 20th century with individuals choosing to delay marriage or not marry at all. In 2020, there are 41.6 million African Americans in the United States representing 13.6% of the U.S. population. Approximately 51% of African American men and 48% of African American women have never been married. Research indicates when African Americans do marry, they are less likely to remain married compared to white Americans. Additionally, African Americans report lower rates of marital satisfaction within their unions. Compared to other communities of color, African-American marital unions are less likely to persist compared to other ethnic minority groups including Latinos and Asians (Kreider and Ellis 2011).

Marriage instability among African American families is not just a contemporary issue but dates back to at least the 1800s and arguably is a lasting vestige from the institution of slavery. Under slavery, it was against the law for African Americans to marry. As a result, African Americans adapted and had to create a different norm regarding family formation because of this law

(Johnson and Staples 2004). Although enslaved Africans were in committed relationships, bore and raised children, and some married although not legally, families were routinely separated which further underscores instability and disruption as features in the experiences of African American families. It is critical to emphasize the impact of slavery on familial roots (spouse to spouse, parent to child) and social structures within the African American family.

From a contemporary standpoint, a variety of individual/ interpersonal and structural factors impact marital well-being for African Americans. These factors provide a lens to understand phenomena that impact marital satisfaction, marital well-being, and marriage longevity (Dixon 2009; Phillips, Wilmoth, and Marks 2012). Research indicated that individual factors may be shaped by motivation or attitudes toward marriage, religiosity, social support, and spousal alignment or similarity around core issues such as a desire to have children. The desire to marry, characteristics that partners look for in a potential partner, and motivation to commit also impact marriage rates for African Americans (Dixon 2009). Furthermore, research suggested that African Americans agree that remaining single is more advantageous than being unhappily married (Curran, Utley, and Muraco 2010). Couples who experience more dissimilarity are at higher risk for marital dissolution. For example, according to Clarkwest (2007) misalignment around areas such as church attendance, support for maternal employment, sexual attitudes, and beliefs resulted in a 50% increase in marital dissolution. Moreover, the researcher noted that African

American couples were more dissimilar at the time the couple match occurred and this dissimilarity created a greater risk for marital dissolution. Religious practice also impacts marital well-being. African Americans who are religious and engage in religious practices are more likely to marry and have more stable unions (Brown, Orbuch, and Bauermeister 2008; Clarkwest 2008). Religious beliefs and belonging to a faith community can provide social support during times of marital challenge which may provide some insight into well-being and longevity.

Structural factors are also indicators that influence marital satisfaction, well-being, and longevity. Researchers have suggested that trends in education, employment, and incarceration rates for African American men are examples of structural factors that have had a significant impact on marital rates and marital well-being. For example, Smith-Bynum (2013) suggested these trends have undermined couples' ability to fit into the broader cultural gender roles in the marriage of males serving as the breadwinner. These disruptions and gaps create marital strain as conflicts arise about failure to fit within these norms. Moreover, gaps in educational attainment and income may produce feelings of inadequacy which in turn creates a reluctance to marry African American males (Dixon 2009) because of their perceived or actual inability to meet these cultural standards. On the other hand, barriers to economic opportunities and inequality have created family systems that require more role flexibility in terms of household responsibility and division of labor including child-care responsibilities.

African American couples have faced unique challenges historically and still must confront issues that other white and non-white communities do not confront. Despite these challenges, several strengths have been noted in the research. Although role flexibility and equalitarianism with the division of labor occurred most likely in response to economics and practical needs, this practice is regarded as a key strength with African American couples. Additional areas of strength noted in the research included strong kinship bonds and strong religious orientation (Vaterlaus et al. 2017).

Felicia Law Murray

See also: Interracial Marriages; Marriage and Divorce, Latino Americans; Marriage and Divorce, White Americans

Further Reading

Brown, Edna, Terri L. Orbuch, and Jose A. Bauermeister. 2008. "Religiosity and marital stability among Black American and White American couples." *Family Relations* 57, no. 2: 186–197.

Clarkwest, A. 2006. "Premarital characteristics, selection into marriage, and African American marital disruption." *Journal of Comparative Family Studies* 37, no. 3: 361–380.

Clarkwest, Andrew. 2007. "Spousal dissimilarity, race, and marital dissolution." *Journal of Marriage and Family* 69, no. 3: 639–653.

Clarkwest, Andrew. 2008. "Neo-materialist theory and the temporal relationship between income inequality and longevity change." *Social Science & Medicine* 66, no. 9: 1871–1881.

Curran, Melissa A., Ebony A. Utley, and Joel A. Muraco. 2010. "An exploratory study of the meaning of marriage for African Americans." *Marriage & Family Review* 46, no. 5: 346–365.

Dixon, P. 2009. "Marriage among African Americans: What does the research reveal?" *Journal of African American Studies*, 13, no. 1: 29–46.

Johnson, L. B. and R. Staples. 2004. *Black families at the crossroads: Challenges and prospects.* Jossey-Bass.

Krieder, R. M. and R. Ellis. 2011. *Number, timing, and duration of marriages and divorce.* Current Populations Reports. Washington, DC: U.S. Census Bureau, pp. 70–125.

Lincoln, K. D. and D. H. Chae. 2010. "Stress, marital satisfaction, and psychological distress among African Americans." *Journal of Family Issues*, 31, 1081–1105.

Phillips, Tommy M., Joe D. Wilmoth, and Loren D. Marks. 2012. "Challenges and conflicts . . . strengths and supports: A study of enduring African American marriages." *Journal of Black Studies* 43, no. 8: 936–952.

Smith-Bynum, M. A. 2013. "African American families: Research progress and potential in the age of Obama." *Handbook of Marriage and the Family*, 683–704.

Vaterlaus, J. M., L. Skogrand, C. Chaney, and K. Gahagan. 2017. "Marital expectations in strong African American marriages." *Family Process*, 56, no. 4: 883–899.

Wilcox, W. B., E. Marquardt, D. Popenoe, and B. D. Whitehead. 2011. "When baby makes three: How parenthood makes life meaningful and how marriage makes parenthood bearable." The State of Our Unions: Marriage in America. Charlottesville, VA: University of Virginia. Retrieved from http://www.stateofourunions.org/2011/SOOU2011.pdf

Marriage and Divorce, American Indians

Data from 2020 show there are over 570 federally recognized American Indian tribes in the United States. According to the U.S. Census Bureau, the American Indian and Alaska Native alone population (3.7 million) accounted for 1.1 percent of all people living in the United States (Jones et al., 2021). There is great diversity in the language, customs, family structure, economic systems, and spiritual beliefs across tribes. American Indians, the official U.S. government term used in all treaties, policies, and laws, have a unique place in America in that they are both a distinct racial/ethnic group and have an official political status and relationship with the United States government. For example, laws like the Indian Child Welfare Act are specific to American Indians and require states and child welfare agencies to follow specified protocols in adoption and foster care proceedings involving Native Americans. So, while there is great diversity in the number of Native people, often there is consistency in how they are treated by government agencies.

Thus, when discussing American Indian families, and specifically marriage and divorce, one must understand the historical context of those relationships. War, conquest (including government genocide policies), assimilation, etc., all have had profound impacts on every aspect of Native life and culture. From a cultural perspective, many American Indian families and marriage relationships were matrilineal while others were egalitarian. In these cases, it was not until the *assimilation* period that the dominant culture's patriarchal relationships begin to have a negative influence and impact. Here, several government policies were instituted to disrupt the Native family structure that has impacted and continues to impact familial relationships, of which marriage definitions and divorce proceedings are important components.

Data on American Indian marriage and family formation are important but only tell part of the Native story. American Indian families often include extended family members, clans, and selected community members and are part of Native definitions of family, often reducing the expectations on nuclear family members who are expected to have primary responsibility, so common in Western societies and culture (Day, 2014).

American Indians, including Alaska Natives, are less likely to be married than the general population. Only 37% of American Indians are married, compared to 48% of the general population and 60% of whites (National Healthy Marriage Resource Center, 2012). American Indians have higher divorce rates than nearly all other racial/ethnic groups. Single-parent families account for 52% of American Indian households, compared to 24% of whites. While these last two statistics are typically seen as problematic in the predominant culture, when divorce occurs, the expectation for most Native parents is that they are still part of the family system. Similarly, with single parents, the broader Native family definition allows for multiple people to be involved in the parent-child relationship.

Another important statistic is that more than half (56%) of American Indians are married to individuals from other racial or ethnic groups. Given that many tribes require a blood quantum for tribal membership, with one-quarter blood being the most common, if a tribal member marries outside the tribe or to a non-Native, posterity will not be eligible for membership after only two generations. These figures show that American Indians face unique challenges in family formation and maintaining successful marriages and why tribes have a vested interest in marriage and divorce among their members.

Due to multi-generational trauma and lost parenting relationships resulting from boarding schools and systematic government child separation policies, American Indians also have high rates of victimization at 13.8 per 1000 children compared to 9.2 per 1000 for all children (United States Department of Health & Human Services, 2015). This results in additional challenges in child-parent and marriage relationships. Thus, even before having children, American Indians face many challenges in forming and sustaining healthy marriages. One of the greatest challenges is poverty. While poverty is not specific to Native people, the proportion of American Indians living below the poverty line is more than twice the national average. Similarly, American Indian children are twice as likely to live in poverty as their non-Native counterparts and almost twice as likely to be in a home in which neither parent is employed (National Healthy Marriage Resource Center, 2012). As a result, American Indians are more likely to be divorced, separated, or to have never married than the general population, all of which are impacted by the challenges of poverty and historic trauma, much of which can be attributed to government-imposed policies.

Regarding historical trauma, forced relocation and assimilation led to several negative outcomes as American Indian children grew up and eventually married. In addition to poverty, family violence, and trauma, American Indians are also at greater risk of substance abuse, which can also have debilitating effects on marriage and divorce. The rates of substance abuse among American Indians are generally much higher than those of the general U.S. population. Data indicate that Native Americans have the highest rates of alcohol, marijuana, cocaine, inhalant, and hallucinogen use disorders compared to other ethnic groups (Young and Joe, 2009). Tribal communities and service providers are working hard to help those impacted overcome historical experiences that have left deep scars and susceptible to these and other risk factors.

As we consider the negative outcomes and risk factors American Indian families face, Native children who live with their own married parents have better physical health than children in other family formations (Radel et al., 2016). On the other hand, Native children whose parents divorce have higher rates of psychological distress and mental illness (Kenney and Singh, 2016). In most cases, marriage is associated with better health and lower rates of injury, illness, and disability for both American Indian men and women and is seen as a stabilizing factor for couples and families (ACF, n.d.; Goins et al., 2018). Additionally, marriage increases the likelihood that American Indian fathers have good relationships with their children and married Native women appear to have a lower risk of experiencing domestic violence than do cohabiting or dating women (Sapra et al., 2014).

Many tribal communities have found that counteracting these negative risk factors through the reinstitution and understanding of cultural sovereignty, native language, religion, and other practices have been particularly helpful. Further, talking openly about the impact of multigenerational or historical trauma on the Native family and community can provide opportunities for compassion and healing. Sharing stories of ancestors and mourning their cultural losses help the healing process. Here, several tribes, including the Navajo Nation and the Lakota, have implemented parenting curricula designed to improve marital interventions and parenting practices. Thus, while there are still many challenges facing American Indian families and those who marry, there is hope for a brighter future as many relationship-strengthening interventions are developed and implemented.

Gordon Limb

See also: Diversity in Marriage; Interracial Marriage; Marriage and Divorce, African Americans; Marriage and Divorce, Latino Americans

Further Reading

Administration for Children and Families-Healthy Marriage Initiative, U.S. Health and Human Services. n.d. *Native American healthy marriage initiative: Fast facts.* Retrieved from http://web.archive.org/web/20060926154142/http://www2.acf.hhs.gov/programs/ana/documents/NAHMI_fast_facts.pdf

Day, P. A. 2014. "Raising healthy American Indian children: An indigenous perspective." In H. Weaver (Ed.), *Social issues in contemporary Native America: Reflections from Turtle Island* (pp. 93–112). Williston, VT: Ashgate.

Goins, R. T., Schure, M., Jensen, P. N., Suchy-Dicey, A., Nelson, L., Verney, S. P., Howard, B. V., and Buchwald, D. 2018. "Lower body functioning and correlates among older American Indians: The cerebrovascular disease and its consequences in American Indians study." *BMC Geriatrics*, 18(6), 1–9.

Jones, N., Marks, R., Ramirez, R., and Rios-Vargas, M. 2021. "2020 census illuminates racial and ethnic composition of the country." Retrieved from https://www.census.gov/library/stories/2021/08/improved-race-ethnicity-measures-reveal-united-states-population-much-more-multiracial.html

Kenney, M. K., and Singh, G. K. 2016. "Adverse childhood experiences among American Indian/Alaska Native children: The 2011–2012 National Survey of Children's Health." *Scientifica*, 2016, 1–14.

National Healthy Marriage Resource Center. 2012. "Native Americans." Retrieved from https://www.healthymarriageinfo.org/research-policy/marriage-facts-and-research/marriage-and-divorce-statistics-by-culture/native-americans/

Radel, L., Bramlett, M., Chow, K., and Waters, A. 2016. "Children living apart from their parents: Highlights from the National Survey of Children in Nonparental Care." Retrieved from https://aspe.hhs.gov/system/files/pdf/203352/NSCNC.pdf

Sapra, K. J., Jubinski, S. M., Tanaka, M. F., and Gershon, R. 2014. "Family and partner interpersonal violence among American Indians/Alaska Natives." *Injury Epidemiology*, 1(7), 1–14.

United States Department of Health & Human Services. 2015. "Child maltreatment." Retrieved from https://www.acf.hhs.gov/cb/report/child-maltreatment-2015

Young, R. S., and Joe, J. R. 2009. "Some thoughts about the epidemiology of alcohol and drug use among American Indian/Alaska Native populations." *Journal of Ethnicity in Substance Abuse*, 8(3), 223–241.

Marriage and Divorce, Latino Americans

According to the U.S. Census Bureau (2020), over 60 million Latinos accounted for 18.5% of the United States population. Latino refers to persons of Mexican, Puerto Rican, Cuban, Central American, South American, or other Spanish culture of origin (national healthy marriage resource center). Currently, Latinos are the largest ethnic or racial minority in the United States. The largest Latino subgroup in the United States is from the Mexican culture of origin at approximately 63% (U.S. Census Bureau 2020). It is projected by 2050 that 1 in 3 individuals in the United States will be of Latin descent. The notable growth of the Latino population in the United States has created increasing interest in understanding their familial structures and practices. Much of the research literature notes a void in understanding the unique characteristics and practices of Latino families. This is partially a result of the vast internal diversity among the individuals that are part of the Latin diaspora and the slow rate of the development of research that disaggregates the experiences of the Latino population by national origin. Additionally, the rate of acculturation or assimilation to the United States may impact the cultural viewpoints of second and third-generation Latinos which requires pivoting from potentially outdated ways of understanding their lived experiences. Within this context and as seen in other communities of color, profound demographic shifts have resulted in changes in family formation practices and behaviors. While there has been a rise in nonmarital childbearing, female-headed households, and cohabitating relationships, rates of marriage remain steady across the Latino community compared to other communities of color (e.g., African American). There are a few sociocultural underpinnings that may account for this higher rate of marriage trend.

Although we should take great care to avoid characterizing Latinos as a homogenous group, there are certain shared beliefs, values, or norms that may provide some insight into marital practices. Generally speaking, the role of religiosity in marriage formation in the Latino community is noteworthy. Numerous studies highlight the significant role religion has in Latino culture. In fact, some ethnographic studies on Latinos indicate that religion is one of the main contributing factors that lead to individuals' focus on familial relationships, particularly through the marriage union. Historically, Latinos have followed the traditions of the Roman Catholic Church; yet many are increasingly followers of the Protestant faith as well. In both traditions, marriage is viewed as a lifelong relationship. Additionally, clergy provide theological justification for marriage and for maintaining these unions, especially for individuals who desire to become parents (Wilcox 2004). Moreover, these institutions create opportunities and social experiences for adults to receive peer and emotional support that reinforces marriage as the norm (Wolfinger, Wilcox, and Hernandez 2010) and promotes healthy relationships.

Along with religious values and beliefs, the family is a major cornerstone in Latino culture. Traditional cultural values and beliefs related to the family in existing literature highlight the values of "familismo," "machismo," and "mariansmo" and "hembrismo" (McLoyd et al. 2000; Vega, 1990). *Familismo* is a term that describes a set of values that support the creation of familial relationships within the immediate and extended family system. Additionally, this value highlights the importance of marriage,

strong family bonds, mutual assistance, and placing the needs of the family over the needs of the individual (Vega 1990). Family relationships are held in even higher regard than marital relationships. This is a common belief among Latinos particularly those born outside of the United States (Oropesa and Landale 2004). Moreover, research on pro-marriage practices in the Latino community underscores early ages at first marriage, particularly for Latina women who may be socialized to believe that marriage is an essential life objective and part of a divine plan (Oropesa and Landale 2004). Additionally, Latinos tend to marry at younger ages.

Often considered in concert with "familismo," "mariansmo," and "machismo" are values that describe gender roles and expectations in Latino culture. Marianismo is based on the Catholic ideal of the Virgin Mary which emphasizes the role of women as wives, mothers, and caretakers. She is submissive, humble, and modest. On the other hand, the value "hembrismo" refers to the female as strong, courageous, and responsible for preserving tradition and enforcing religious values. Women are viewed as self-sacrificing as they place children and family first over self. On the other hand, machismo underscores the notion of the father and husband as the head of the household, thus underscoring the patriarchal family structure. While "familismo" is viewed as a strength in Latino families, literature also described these gender role characterizations as exaggerated or stereotypes as these values to dot consider the evolving family structure of the Latino family. For example, the number of female-headed households is steadily rising as well as women increasingly transitioning from the traditional mother role to the role of working mother. Additionally, socioeconomic factors have necessitated a shift from strict traditional gender roles to more shared responsibilities among married couples (Cruz et al. 2014).

While there are strong sociocultural traditions that value marriage, current demographic changes, and shifting cultural practices have led to a decline in the overall marriage rate in the Latino community. Over the past several decades, marriage rates have steeply declined. From 1960–2010, rates of marriage for Latinos decreased from 72% to 47%, compared to non-Hispanic whites where rates decreased from 74% to 55% (Pew Research Center 2013). Latinos also have higher rates of never marrying compared with the population at large: 38% of Latino men and 30% of Latino women have never married (vs. 30% of men and 24% of women in the U.S. population overall; Pew Research Center 2013). These statistics further suggest the need for further exploration to understand the values, beliefs, and practices of the Latino community.

Felicia Law Murray

See also: Marriage and Divorce, African Americans; Marriage and Divorce, White Americans

Further Reading

Cruz, Rick A., Nancy A. Gonzales, Marissa Corona, Kevin M. King, Ana Mari Cauce, Richard W. Robins, Keith F. Widaman, and Rand D. Conger. 2014. "Cultural dynamics and marital relationship quality in Mexican-Origin families." *Journal of Family Psychology* 28, no. 6: 844–854. doi: 10.1037/a0038123.

McLoyd, Vonnie C., Ana Mari Cauce, David Takeuchi, and Leon Wilson. 2000. "Marital processes and parental socialization in families of color: A decade review of research." *Journal of Marriage and Family* 62, no. 4: 1070–1093.

Oropesa, R. S. and Nancy S. Landale. 2004. "The future of marriage and Hispanics." *Journal of Marriage and Family* 66, no. 4: 901–920.

Pew Research Center. 2013. "Chapter 3: Demographic & economic data, by race." Pew Research Center's Social & Demographic Trends Project. https://www.pewresearch.org/social-trends/2013/08/22/chapter-3-demographic-economic-data-by-race/.

U.S. Census Bureau. 2020. "Race and ethnicity in the United States: 2010 Census and 2020 Census." Census.gov, August 18, 2022. https://www.census.gov/library/visualizations/interactive/race-and-ethnicity-in-the-united-state-2010-and-2020-census.html.

Vega, William A. 1990. "Hispanic families in the 1980s: A decade of research." *Journal of Marriage and Family* 52, no. 4: 1015–1024. doi: 10.2307/353316.

Wilcox, W. Bradford. 2004. *Soft patriarchs, new men: How Christianity shapes fathers and husbands.* Vol. 880. University of Chicago Press.

Wolfinger, Nicholas H., W. Bradford Wilcox, and Edwin I. Hernandez. 2009. "'Bendito Amor ('Blessed Love'): Religion and relationships among married and unmarried Latinos in urban America." *Journal of Latino-Latin American Studies* 3, no. 4: 171–188.

Marriage and Divorce, White Americans

Throughout the history of the United States, marriage has been a foundational institution. It remains so today, as most Americans report a desire to marry at some point in their lifetime, and about 87% of women do end up marrying (Schoen 2016), although this number is only 50% for adults under 44 (Horowitz et al. 2019). Even so, the state of marriage in America has dramatically changed since the 1960s. Changes in social attitudes and unequal social lives among the white population have shifted the landscape of who gets married when they marry, and why they marry. Additionally, white Americans have enjoyed a privileged position in research, as most studies of marriage are related to predominantly white samples, and this is assumed to be the norm. Although white Americans tend to have more privileges and advantages than ethnic minorities in the United States, there is significant variability in the experience of marriage within the white population.

Socioeconomic status has significant implications for marriage. Rates of marriage vary drastically along class lines, with college graduates far more likely to marry than those with a high school diploma or less (Horowitz et al. 2019). Although the likelihood of marriage is declining for all white people, it is declining more rapidly for those from low-income families (Bloome and Ang 2020), and many cohabitors report delaying marriage for financial reasons (Horowitz et al. 2019). Because of this, different family forms (e.g., married, cohabiting) are often reflective of socioeconomic inequalities. Furthermore, because marriage tends to incur economic benefits, the trend in who gets married might widen economic disparities, as the affluent marry and reap the benefits of marriage, whereas those from low-income backgrounds do not.

Although many white Americans seek to marry, there is variation in terms of when they do marry. The number of white adults living with a spouse has been declining for decades—in 1960, this number was about 79%; today, it is about 56% (U.S. Census Bureau 2020). At the same time, many white Americans are delaying marriage. In 1960, the median age at first marriage was about 24 years for men and 20.5 years for women; today, it is 30.4 for men and 28 for women (U.S. Census Bureau 2020). This increase is largely due to the prioritization of education, as many college-educated white Americans are delaying marriage until they have completed higher education and established their careers (Cherlin 2010). Furthermore, many white Americans are substituting marriage with nonmarital cohabitation; even so, many are remaining single throughout their twenties (Bloome and Ang 2020). Thus, educational attainment is contributing to the postponement of marriage, if an individual ever chooses to marry.

Interestingly, white Americans are less likely than other ethnicities to believe that marriage is becoming obsolete, and they report greater optimism about "traditional" marriage than other ethnic groups (Pew Research Center 2010). These attitudes, combined with socioeconomic advantage, may contribute to the higher rate of marriage among white Americans.

Those who marry do so for a variety of reasons. For instance, most people say that having a lifelong commitment, love, and companionship are important reasons for getting married (Horowitz et al. 2019). Psychologist Eli Finkel and his colleagues (2014) argue that since the mid-1960s, the meaning and purpose of marriage have shifted from a practical institution intended to meet economic, political, and pragmatic goals, to a means of personal growth, autonomy, and self-expression. Accordingly, individuals place greater pressure on their marriages to meet these goals. This leads to delays in marriage, as individuals are motivated to cohabitate before marriage to test a partner's ability to fulfill their self-expressive needs. Some scholars argue that this phenomenon is unique to affluent white people, further demonstrating the disparities surrounding the institution of marriage (Pietromonaco and Perry-Jenkins 2014). Thus, changes in expectations for marriage might also be contributing to delays in young white Americans' marital timing.

As current cohorts age, demographers will continue to examine patterns in marital timing and rates. Given structural inequalities between racial and socioeconomic groups, it is likely that future marital patterns will continue to diverge, as white, affluent individuals are more likely to marry than Black and/or low-income individuals. Additionally, researchers are seeking to diversify the study of marriage to include non-white individuals, broadening understanding of marriage in diverse populations so that it can be generalized across racial and ethnic groups. Because marital status is consequential for well-being (Hsu and Barrett 2020), changes in marital patterns along demographic characteristics are likely to intensify racial and economic inequalities.

Matthew A. Ogan

See also: Marriage and Divorce, Latino Americans

Further Reading

Bloome, Deirdre and Shannon Ang. 2020. "Marriage and union formation in the United States: Recent trends across racial groups and economic backgrounds." *Demography* 57, no. 5: 1753–1786. https://doi.org/10.1007/s13524-020-00910-7.

Cherlin, Andrew J. 2010. "Demographic trends in the United States: A review of research in the 2000s." *Journal of Marriage and Family* 72, no. 3: 403–419. https://doi.org/10.1111/j.1741-3737.2010.00710.x.

Finkel, Eli J., Chin Ming Hui, Kathleen L. Carswell, and Grace M. Larson. 2014. "The suffocation of marriage: Climbing Mount Maslow without enough oxygen." *Psychological Inquiry* 25, no. 1: 1–41. https://doi.org/10.1080/1047840X.2014.863723.

Horowitz, J. M., N. Graf, and G. Livingston. 2019. *Marriage and Cohabitation in the U.S.* Retrieved from Pew Research Center website: https://www.pewsocialtrends.org/2019/11/06/marriage-and-cohabitation-in-the-u-s/

Hsu, Tze-Li, and Anne E. Barrett. 2020. "The association between marital status and psychological well-being: Variation across negative and positive dimensions." *Journal of Family Issues* 41, no. 11: 2179–2202. https://doi.org/10.1177/0192513X20910184.

Pew Research Center. 2010. "The decline of marriage and rise of new families." https://www.pewresearch.org/social-trends/2010/11/18/the-decline-of-marriage-and-rise-of-new-families/

Pietromonaco, Paula R. and Maureen Perry-Jenkins. 2014. "Marriage in whose America? What the suffocation model misses." *Psychological Inquiry* 25, no. 1: 108–113. https://doi.org/10.1080/1047840X.2014.876909.

Schoen, Robert. 2016. "The continuing retreat of marriage: Figures from marital status life tables for United States females, 2000–2005 and 2005–2010." In *Dynamic Demographic Analysis*, edited by Robert Schoen, 203–215. The

Springer Series on Demographic Methods and Population Analysis. Cham: Springer International Publishing. https://doi.org/10.1007/978-3-319-26603-9_10.

U.S. Census Bureau. 2020. "Historical marital status tables." The United States Census Bureau. Accessed March 1, 2021. https://www.census.gov/data/tables/time-series/demo/families/marital.html.

Marriage and Education Level

The common American narrative is that some marry young and start families and those who go to school. That narrative was embellished by the legend of the old "hag" or the "old maid" who was characteristically portrayed in American literature as the librarian, the teacher, the principal, and another educated unmarried woman. There is another narrative, that of the MRS degree, in which a woman only attends college to meet eligible prospects. Statistically, we know that these are false narratives. Since the 1960s, the demographics of those that are married in the United States have changed drastically. In 1950, 70% of 30–44-year-old female college graduates and 80% of female high school graduates were currently married. In 2010, rates of married college-educated women remained consistent at 69%, but only 56% of those women with high school diplomas were married. For men in 1950, 85% of men aged 30–44 were married at all levels of education. By 2010, 70% of college-educated men were married, compared to 53% of those with a high school diploma. Those with some college but no degree have similar rates of marriage to those who have a high school diploma. The researchers of the family structure suggest that the reasons for these decreased rates are economic, as men who do not have an education may not be able to support a family as well as those with a college degree. In addition, researchers have found that those with college degrees are thought to marry because their commitment enables joint investment in their future and their children, whereas those with a high school diploma may not need to make this long-term commitment because that investment is not feasible (Lundberg, Pollak, and Stearns 2016).

Contrary to the original narrative of the "old maid," the educated woman has always had the same marriage prospects, as is shown in the consistent percentage married from 1950 to 2010, although she may choose to delay marriage until later. According to the Pew Research Center, college-educated women are also more likely to have long-lasting marriages, with an almost 8-in-10 chance of still being married after 20 years. Their review of data from the National Survey of Family Growth suggests that future heterosexual marriage patterns will be similar to what we are seeing today. Education tends to make a person both more likely to marry and also more likely to remain married.

Some researchers have noted that investment in education leads to a better marriage market, in addition to the labor market. Other researchers have suggested that the debt incurred by those who pursue education delays marriage until they pay down some student loans. There is no denying that college is an introduction to many new people, especially future partners.

Race and ethnicity differences in rates of marriage have also been noted in the literature. Black men and women have the highest median ages at the first marriage at 32 for men, and 30.4 for women, according to the American Community Survey in 2019. Hispanics have the lowest median age at first marriage at 27.5. The proportion of all marriages of Black women has declined more than those of whites. Race and ethnicity may also have an impact on the effects of education on marriage. Black men, according to Autor and Wasserman, have lower educational attainment rates than Black women and account for some of the decline in marriage rates.

Marriage, like any other social construct, is continuing to evolve in our country. The legalization of same-sex marriage, the recognition of people who are gender non-conforming or non-binary, and younger generations who are less religious may all contribute to changes in how marriage prospects are seen, and how a person's education may change, as well. Much like we saw changes to the dating realm when technology and the internet came along, we may also see a change in the marriage/education connection as education goes more and more online.

Julia M. Bernard

See also: Marital Success; Marriage and Education Level; Unmarried Cohabitation

Further Reading

Chiappori, Pierre-André, Monica Costa Dias, and Costas Meghir. 2018. "The marriage market, labor supply, and education choice." *Journal of Political Economy* 126, no. S1: S26–S72.

Lundberg, Shelly, Robert A. Pollak, and Jenna Stearns. 2016. "Family inequality: Diverging patterns in marriage, cohabitation, and childbearing." *Journal of Economic Perspectives* 30, no. 2: 79–102.

Wang, Wendy. 2015. "The link between a college education and a lasting marriage." *Pew Research Center Fact Tank.* http://www.pewresearch.org/fact-tank /2015/12/04/education-and-marriage/

Marriage and Immigration

Immigration represents a cultural as well as a physical journey. Typically, it requires moving to another country with the accompanying adaptation that has to occur in the new context. The word *immigration* denotes entering a new country or context; it is moving toward or entering. By contrast, the term *emigration* represents leaving one place for another; it is the moving from or the exiting. The term *immigrant* is also loosely applied in other contexts which denote entering a new or unknown domain, such as being a "digital immigrant," when a person (usually later in life) has to familiarize themselves with technology for the first time.

When both marriage partners make the immigration journey together, they may find solidarity in their shared culture of origin, and they can face the challenges of the welcoming cultural context as a team. Contrast this with the couple where one partner leaves the familiar cultural home base to join a spouse who identifies with and is embedded in the new or host cultural setting. Clearly, both scenarios contain challenges for the particular marriage. An allegiance is being formed with the spouse, while also finding and exploring another cultural context. Because cultural representations involve symbols, values, attitudes, and beliefs, it can be either disorienting or refreshing to familiarize oneself with the cultural landscape of the host country. Successful immigration also requires a degree of assimilation, emotional investment, and commitment to the host culture. The ease with which this process occurs depends on several factors including language skills pertaining to the host culture, the attitude, encouragement, and support of the peers and family one leaves behind in the country of origin, as well as the influences from a similar group of people in the country to which one has moved.

If both spouses are going through the same immigration journey, they can support each other by maintaining familiar rituals and cultural customs within the home that remind them of their own roots. If only one member of the couple transitions, that person finds support because their partner acts as a cultural translator, and supports them in the acculturation process. Once children are born, the cultural heritage of the country of origin is diluted as the children are predominantly exposed to the culture of the host country and because they are being socialized and educated in this new environment. The experience of the children will be vastly different from that of their parents. For the children, the ancestral culture of origin will eventually become a remote memory, especially if the language of that culture is not maintained. With each subsequent generation, family members become more integrated into mainstream cultural values and identify what was once a host culture for their parents and grandparents as their true home where their loyalties, hopes, and aspirations are anchored.

Considering the statistic from the 2020 U.S. Census that about 14% of the population claim to be born internationally (not in the U.S.), it follows that many families have experienced the immigration firsthand. This in turn affects marriage and family life. Another datapoint from the same 2020 Census is that pertaining to the foreign born group, about a fifth were aged 18 or under. This younger group may display greater flexibility in adapting to the challenges of the host culture. The immigration journey may offer unique challenges in terms of language, social integration, and economic survival. Each one of these dimensions affects marriage and family life significantly. Undoubtedly social change is all-pervasive, in that it affects many related areas including education, interconnectedness, the generation and maintenance of economic and financial outcomes, as well as technology (Greenfield 2016). Immigration attracts and motivates these large-scale social movements because of the promise of growth and improved outcomes, and parents consider the future of their children when making these decisions.

The immigration journey is always challenging, even if the outcomes are desired and constructive. These challenges are accompanied by stressors that test and tax the relationship. The stressors interact with the internal resources of the marital couple as well as the external support systems available to them. These interactions can lead to varied outcomes where the scenarios will be on a continuum, ranging from improved outcomes as a result of immigration right through to less desirable outcomes and accompanying hardship. It is a multidimensional factorial mix, consisting of the inner emotional resources of the couple as they interact with opportunities and challenges to display resilience, coping, and adaptation (Gerhardt 2020). The statement in folklore that an event can "make or break" a couple pertains to marriage and immigration in particular. The stressors involved are sufficient that weaker relationships are at risk of breaking up. Strong relationships, on the other hand, appear to be strengthened further because the couple shared the adversity and overcame it as a partnership. This in itself provides a very deep and meaningful bond.

Immigrant communities support and strengthen their members by providing a familiar cultural, spiritual, and social context. Additionally, the community can provide social and spiritual support to strengthen individual marriages and family life. Customs and expectations in the host country may vary from the norms in the country of origin. For instance, gender equality may make it possible for women to work outside the home, and get an extended education and childcare facilities can provide the necessary support to allow both adults in a family unit to work to meet the needs of their family in a new home country. These changes can be far-reaching for the family and affect all the members systemically. Migratory patterns influence individualism/independence as they play out within families and the workplace. According to Greenfield (2016), data from around the world reveals that large-scale shifts accompany immigration, and the subsequent effects are felt on a global economic scale, but the ripple effects extend to marriages and families.

In the United States, many families can connect to an immigration story in their distant or even recent past. If these events occurred two or more generations ago, it is a valuable part of one's own heritage to pause and reflect on the sacrifices made by the generation undertaking the immigration process. They left familiar ground with hope in their hearts, just as current-day immigrants and refugees hope for improved outcomes by migrating.

Clara Gerhardt

See also: International Marriage; Mail-Order Brides

Further Reading
Dauvergne, Catherine. 2016. *The new politics of immigration and the end of settler societies.* New York: Cambridge University Press.

Gerhardt, Clara. 2020. "Dynamics of culture and change." In *Families in motion: Dynamics in diverse contexts.* Chapter 14. Thousand Oaks, CA: SAGE, pp. 311–334.

Greenfield, Patricia. 2016. "Social change, cultural evolution, and human development." *Current Opinion in Psychology.* 8: 84–92. Elsevier. doi.org/10.1016/j.copsyc.2015.10.012

Marriage and Incarceration

As of 2016, there were 6.6 million people under the supervision of the adult correctional system in the United States (Kaeble and Cowhig 2018, 1). Since the 1970s, the rate of individuals coming into contact with the penal system has increased by 700%, despite violent and property crime rates falling since the 1990s, with one in every 38 adults under some form of correctional supervision. The increase has been attributed to the "tough on crime" and "war on drugs" policies that have resulted in mandatory minimum sentences, harsh and racially disparate penalties for minor drug offenses, and a significant increase in life sentences without the possibility of release (parole). The effects of incarceration are far-reaching beyond the imprisonment itself, including social disorganization of communities, reduced employment opportunities for ex-prisoners, financial hardships on families, and loss of social, parental, and marital relationships. Scholars have linked an increase in incarceration with low marriage rates, specifically among urban Black Americans, and an increase in the odds of divorce among married couples. Mass incarceration removes eligible individuals from the pool of potential romantic partners, thereby affecting marriage rates overall. Being in prison physically separates the inmate from their spouses and families, distancing them geographically and socially, and preventing them from engaging in prosocial roles such as spouse and parent. For every year behind bars, the odds that an inmate's marriage will end in divorce increases by 32% (Massoglia, Remster, and King 2011, 144). Maintaining relational ties between spouses while one is incarcerated has substantial benefits for the incarcerated individual and marriage overall yet can be highly challenging due to the restrictive policies of prison and the time spent separated.

Benefits of Marital Relationships during Incarceration

Maintaining spousal ties while one partner is incarcerated has positive benefits for the individuals and the marriage as a whole. For the incarcerated individual, frequent visitation from spouses and family has been attributed to positive rehabilitation while in prison and preventing future arrests after release from prison. Specifically, scholars have found consistent reports of a reduction in depressive symptoms and rule-breaking behavior by the incarcerated individual as a result of frequent visits (De Claire and Dixon 2017, 188–197). Frequent spousal visits were also found to reduce the probability of the individual being arrested after release from prison, reducing recidivism by as much as 30% (Bales and Mears 2008, 304–306). The argument is that inmates who continue to interact with and receive support from close loved ones are protected by the belief that they are cared for and are therefore better able to cope with the many challenges associated with imprisonment and reentry into society.

Despite the many restrictions that hinder contact between loved ones in prison, marital partners enact numerous strategic behaviors in order to ensure the continuation of their marriage and feelings of intimacy. Letter writing, phone calls, and face-to-face visits are the most reported means to maintain contact while an incarcerated spouse. With physical touch and intimacy not possible, incarceration forces committed partners to find alternatives to fulfilling intimacy needs by relying on an openness in communication and emotional intimate connections. The reliance on communication to maintain the marriage has the potential to cultivate stronger emotional connections and improve the quality of the relationship. For inmates that exhibit exceptionally good behavior while in prison and are legally married, some correctional departments have special Family Reunion Programs (FRPs) available in which the spouses (and immediate family members) can have extended overnight visits in private home-like settings on the correctional facility grounds. These overnight visits are also referred to as conjugal or extended family visits. As of 2015, only four states offer FRP or conjugal visits, including California, Connecticut, New York, and Washington.

Each state varies on eligibility for FRPs and locations in which they are available. For example, New York State lists 22 maximum-security prisons that provide FRPs. Studies have shown inmates and their spouses report stronger feelings of closeness after their FRP visits (Carlson and Cervera 1991, 325–327).

Negative Effects of Incarceration

Although the positive benefits of maintaining relational ties with spouses and family members is well known among scholars and prison reform advocates, strict regulations within the correctional institutions and policies in place can make it difficult for maintaining contact between inmates and their families. Of the most restrictive are policies for visitations. Individual correctional facilities vary on the number of visits inmates are allowed each month, the length of time families are allowed to visit, and specific days within the week in which visitors are allowed at the prison. The conditions under which visits occur also vary; some facilities house spousal and family visits in cafeteria settings, where loved ones can briefly hug and hold hands, whereas other facilities separate the inmates from their loved ones with a glass or plastic partition and the families speak over a telephone. Visitors coming into the prison are subject to strict policies regarding dress code, background checks, pat downs, or in some extreme cases strip searches and drug testing with ion scanners. Loved ones of inmates experiencing these policies have often reported feeling treated as criminals themselves, unwelcome guests, or humiliated and intimidated by corrections staff. This experience for non-incarcerated loved ones has been referred to as

secondary prisonization (Comfort 2003), in which the prison policies invisibly shackle legally innocent people, forcing them to alter their behavior, reorient their relational expectations, feel stigmatized, and personally experience the effects of disciplinary confinement, surveillance, and control. Further, the secondary prisonization and stigma affiliated with loving an inmate may reduce the perception of familial connection, thereby increasing feelings of isolation, judgment, depression, and shame. Feelings of loneliness and shame are felt not only by the non-incarcerated individua, but by the inmate as well (Segrin and Flora 2001, 163–168). Specifically, inmates experience loneliness in the separation from their families and the loss of outside relationships can be considered one of the most painful aspects of prison for inmates.

The stress of incarceration can carry over into the marriage, negatively impacting the satisfaction and sustainability of the marriage. Divorce rates during incarceration are substantially high, with incarcerated men being twice as likely to divorce compared to non-incarcerated men. Multiple reasons have been proposed for why incarceration often leads to divorce. First, incarceration itself causes a disturbance within the marital and familial unit, with the period of transition immediately following prison intake as the most jarring for families, both practically and emotionally, making families most vulnerable to dissolution during this period (Chui 2016, 7). Secondly, physical separation reduces the chances of forming relationships and engaging in frequent interactions with significant others. With 60% of inmates imprisoned more than 100 miles away from their families, face-to-face visits can be difficult and costly. This physical separation decreases the interaction between spouses, including opportunities for emotional connection and time spent engaging in shared activities. The length of time spouses are separated can also increase the likelihood of divorce, as research has found that every year in prison doubles the likelihood of divorce (Massoglia, Remster, and King 2011, 144). The risk of divorce does not end after the individual is released from prison, Cooke (2005) found that although formerly incarcerated men want to reunite with their wives and children, they describe great difficulty in the process and often experience shame and sadness. The stigma associated with being a convict continues after release from prison as ex-inmates face judgment regarding their criminal history and may be perceived as less desirable compared to individuals who have never served time in prison.

Bonnie M. Nickels

See also: Divorce and Incarceration; Incarceration, Coparenting and

Further Reading

Bales, William D. and Daniel P. Mears. 2008. "Inmate social ties and the transition to society: Does visitation reduce recidivism?" *Journal of Research in Crime and Delinquency* 45, no. 3: 287–321. doi: 10.1177/0022427808317574

Carlson, Bonnie E. and Neil Cervera. 1991. "Inmates and their families: Conjugal visits, family contact, and family functioning." *Criminal Justice and Behavior* 18, no. 3: 318–331.

Chui, Wing Hong. 2016. "Incarceration and family stress as understood through the Family Process Theory: Evidence from Hong Kong." *Frontiers in Psychology* 7: 881. doi: 10.3389/fpsyg.2016.00881

Comfort, Megan L. 2003. "In the tube at San Quentin: The 'secondary prisonization' of women visiting inmates." *Journal of Contemporary Ethnography* 32, no. 1: 77–107. doi: https://doi.org/10.1177/0891241602238939

Cooke, Cheryl L. 2005. "Going home: Formerly incarcerated African American men return to families and communities." *Journal of Family Nursing* 11, no. 4: 388–404. doi:10.1177/1074840705281753.

De Claire, Karen, and Louise Dixon. 2017. "The effects of prison visits from family members on prisoners' well-being, prison rule-breaking, and recidivism: A review of research since 1991." *Trauma, Violence, & Abuse* 18, no. 2: 185–199. doi:10.1177/1524838015603209.

Kaeble, Danielle, and Mary Cowhig. 2018. "Correctional populations in the United States, 2016." Bureau of Justice Statistics. http://www.bjs.gov/index.cfm?ty=pbdetail&iid=6226

Massoglia, Michael, Brianna Remster, and Ryan D. King. 2011. "Stigma or separation? Understanding the incarceration-divorce relationship." *Social Forces* 90, no. 1: 133–155. Doi: doi: 10.1093/sf/90.1.133

Segrin, Chris and Jeanne Flora. 2001. "Perceptions of relational histories, marital quality, and loneliness when communication is limited: An examination of married prison inmates." *The Journal of Family Communication* 1, no. 3: 151–173. doi: 10.1207/S15327698JFC0103_01

Marriage and Legal Planning

As the economic, legal, and societal landscape surrounding the idea of marriage has shifted over recent generations, the literature suggests that the meaning that society has placed behind the concept of marriage has shifted from a traditional "division of labor" perspective to a more modernistic emphasis on individualism, independence, and self-fulfillment. Given this cultural shift, greater consideration has been given to the validity and necessity of premarital agreements, often referred to as prenuptial agreements (Collier 2019).

A premarital agreement, in its simplest form, is a legal contract voluntarily entered into by both partners of a romantic relationship before they are officially wed. This contract establishes the division of financial resources of the couple, including assets and earnings, should the couple decide to divorce, or should one of the partners die (Knight and Knight 2013).

Prenuptial agreements have largely been frowned upon, generally considered to be for the heartless and the greedy. The "prenup," as it has commonly been nicknamed, has also been largely viewed as an indication of a lack of trust within the relationship (Marston 1997).

However, research has shown the potential that prenuptial agreements can decrease the likelihood of divorce. In the landmark Florida supreme court case regarding prenuptial agreements, *Posner v Posner,* it was concluded that the process of determining property rights for each partner in a marriage, as well as advocating for the individual's financial security, actually serves to encourage the health of the marriage, rather than its decline (Collier 2019).

Due to the media's focus on celebrities entering into prenuptial agreements, such contracts are oftentimes seen as necessary only for the rich in society. Importantly, though, experts have proposed other scenarios in which a prenuptial agreement may prove to be useful. These scenarios include couples with partners who have previously been divorced, couples with partners who own businesses or substantial amounts of wealth, couples with dual incomes, couples in which one partner has accrued significant debt, and couples who purchase a house before they are married (Marston, 1997).

Throughout history, the enforcement and interpretation of prenuptial agreements have been varied and inconsistent. In many cases, prenuptial agreements have favored the economically advantaged partner in the relationship, leaving the more vulnerable partner to bear the brunt of the financial burden in the unfortunate incident of divorce (Collucci 2017).

Despite this inconsistency, many courts across the United States have been reluctant to interfere with prenuptial agreements due to the opinion that these contracts made divorce too easy. In the early 1970s, this attitude toward premarital agreements transitioned as every state granted prospective spouses the ability to establish their individual rights to property in the form of a premarital agreement. In 1983, while courts wrestled with how to establish the validity of these agreements, The Uniform Law Commission (ULC) approved what was to be known as the Uniform Premarital Agreements Act (Ravdin 2017).

The Uniform Premarital Agreements Act (UPPA) served as a preliminary attempt to provide structure and governance for premarital agreements. While the UPPA did establish greater legal credibility for premarital agreements, it could not ensure that legal negotiations were conducted fairly during the construction of the agreement. Over the decades, the UPPA has undergone significant changes and modifications, although such changes have been met with varying amounts of acceptance from state to state. Ultimately, every state in the nation has adopted its own laws and regulations concerning the enforcement of premarital agreements, some of which are separate from the provisions found in the UPPA (Ravdin 2017).

Interestingly, a crucial part of drafting the prenuptial agreement is carefully piecing together a record in the unfortunate instance of future litigation (Stansbury and Drayton 2019), further enforcing the commonly held belief that prenuptial agreements are cold and loveless. Despite this perspective, and despite the uncertainty swirling around their enforcement, many argue that prenuptial agreements have no negative effect on image. Rather than being a symbol of distrust in a relationship, supporters argue that prenuptial agreements are, in fact, a symbol of deep trust between the couple, demonstrating that there are no secrets within the relationship (Marston 1997).

Additional research is required to understand the relationship more fully between prenuptial agreements and overall marriage quality. Ultimately, each couple must weigh their list of pros and cons and decide what legal planning before marriage is best for their own financial and relational goals.

Michael Anderson, Melissa Barton, and Todd Spencer

See also: Marriage Certificate/License; Postnuptial Agreement; Prenuptial Agreement

Further Reading

Collier, Rachel. 2019. "Tightening the Knot: Relational Contracting for a Better Future." *Houston Law Review* 56, no. 5: 1113–1150

Colucci, Jenna Christine. 2017. "The P Word: Ohio Should Adopt the Uniform Premarital Agreements Act to Achieve Consistency and Uniformity in the Treatment of Prenuptial Agreements." *Cleveland State Law Review* 66, no. 1: 215–[ii]

Knight, Lee G. and Ray A. Knight. 2013. "The Benefits and Limitations of Prenuptial Agreements." *CPA Journal* 83, no. 9: 62–66.

Margulies, Sam. 2003. "The Psychology of Prenuptial Agreements." *Journal of Psychiatry and Law* 31, no. 4: 415–432

Marston, Allison A. 1997. "Planning for Love: The Politics of Prenuptial Agreements." *Stanford Law Review* 49, no. 4: 887–916. Stanford University School of Law.

Oldham, J. Thomas. 2012. "Would Enactment of the Uniform Premarital and Marital Agreements Act in All Fifty States Change U.S. Law Regarding Premarital Agreements." *Family Law Quarterly* 46, no. 3: 367–384.

Ravdin, Linda J. 2017. "Premarital Agreements and the Uniform Acts." *Family Advocate* 39, no. 4: 34–37.

Stansbury, Carlton D. and Colin A. Drayton. 2019. "Increasing the Likelihood of Enforcing a Prenup." *American Journal of Family Law* 33, no. 1: 221–226.

Marriage and Military Families

Military marriage is similar in many ways to other marriage arrangements yet differs significantly in the consideration of marital status by the military profession. While other professions and employers do not discuss marital status, the military has deliberately established processes in place that impact a family's finances, living arrangements, and social networks. In some cases, the marriage precedes entry into military service, while in others a servicemember will marry and build a family while serving. As the definition of *family* and *marriage* have changed, so too has the integration of both with military service—changing support programs, financial agreements, and job locations based on the family structure.

The military lifestyle is one characterized by both security and uncertainty, and this extends to the military family. Since 1973, the United States has maintained an all-volunteer force rather than the previous combination of drafted and voluntary members. Though the maximum age of enlistment has varied over the years, generally new members are between 18 and 34 years of age. Recruitment continues to target this younger age for the physical requirements of service as well as the opportunity to develop experience and promotion within the military system. Employment is contingent on good performance and steady progress through the ranks but is far more secure than other professions and industries.

Conversely, employment location changes regularly and can occur with little notice, providing uncertainty as to how long a servicemember will be in a particular location. Servicemembers are routinely reassigned, or moved to a new unit and location, every few years at a minimum. These reassignments do not include deployments, short-term military education, and temporary duty assignments at another location. The uncertainty associated with the movement from one community to the next is a marked difference from civilian institutions.

As the average age for a servicemember coincides with the national average for marriage, married servicemembers are as much the norm as not. As the military does recognize marital status, it does not recognize cohabitants, girl/boyfriends, or other forms of couples for the purpose of financial support or relocation considerations. Servicemembers must provide a marriage license as part of their personnel file in order to gain additional benefits, such as a housing stipend and health care, for the spouse. This legal requirement, coupled with financial compensation, is credited as one of the factors keeping the average age of military marriage below the national average (Hogan and Furst Seifert 2010, 434). Some of these marriages can be considered marriages of convenience, where benefits such as access to health care, on base resources, and financial compensation for housing are part of the decision process for marriage over cohabitation. Military marriages of pure convenience are still rare, but it is not uncommon for couples to progress to marriage at a faster rate due to the legal requirements for relationship recognition within the military community.

Relocation of married servicemembers is similar to those who are not married, and marriage does not preclude reassignment to a location where the family cannot go. These restricted tours are similar to deployments and require the servicemember to make arrangements for family members in another location—whether their current residence or potentially closer to extended family. For family members, moving is part of the lifestyle and comes with its own advantages and disadvantages. Though moving from one community to another is difficult and requires a certain skill set for establishing a support network, there is often a ready network of other military families in a similar situation. The knowledge of others in a similar situation oftentimes creates a ready-made community at the next assignment but can also encourage the isolation of military families from non-military communities.

Military bases, both overseas and within the United States, have several programs specifically designed for family members, ranging from social clubs and support groups for adults to daycare centers, schools, and recreation programs for children. The military provides housing or a housing stipend to rent a home off-base as part of a compensation package that varies based on marital or parental status. Additionally, health care is provided for the servicemember and their families through either on-base hospitals or medical practices off-base. This attractive compensation package, particularly for an entry-level job, is both a recruitment tool for those servicemembers who already have families and a retention tool for those who marry after enlisting in the service (Bourg and Segal 1999, 644). However, for military families in more isolated assignments without a military base and its resources nearby, the integration into local communities and schools requires some understanding of the different stressors these families face.

The military as an institution has a culture that supports marriage and families, as these in turn provide support for military servicemembers. The stress of the military profession requires support and, similar to police and firefighter families, deals with unique stresses from professional dangers. Deployments to areas of conflict and natural disasters cause stress and strain on the individual and the family is often the first support network. Though in many professions a spouse may be a confidant at the end of the day, secrecy associated with work may prevent a servicemember from releasing stress by discussing their work with a spouse. Yet, the spouse often is responsible for creating a support system for these long days, difficult deployments, and separation from extended family (Lundquist and Xu 2014, 1066). Therefore, the military often provides support to these families as they in turn provide support for its servicemembers.

With an increase in multiple deployments and training during the 21st century, the military has changed how it supports spouses because of what is required of these families. Increased time apart due to deployments means the primary support network the military relies on—families—must remain steady in order to limit additional stressors in dangerous environments. To this end, education in self-reliance and resiliency has joined other programs provided to military spouses. This expectation of a supportive role means that the spouse often feels as if they are also serving and, in many cases, they are, as married servicemembers often serve longer and adjust to military life better (Karney and Crown 2011, 39). These benefits encourage the military to support marriages as a strategy for the retention and long-term service of individual members.

Marriage within the military is not always a first-time arrangement but oftentimes includes remarriage for one or both spouses. These marriages also may include a changed relationship for children, introducing stepchildren to the military as well as to a new parent. Just as relocation of a traditional military family is complicated, remarriages that include stepchildren must also consider legal custody agreements that may prevent moving children to a different state or country due to the servicemember's new assignment. As the definition of family expands to include this blended family scenario, the military has also navigated changes to benefits, compensation, and programs designed to support military families.

The changing definition of family and marriage within the United States has also changed the dynamic of a military marriage. Though the majority of military marriages are between a male servicemember and a civilian wife, the Defense Manpower Data Center reported in 2019 that women now comprise 17% of the armed forces and bring civilian husbands into the community. Though the military officially treats civilian spouses the same regardless of gender, the social and community programs and interactions are slower to change. One example is the shift from such "Officer's Wives Club" to a more inclusive "Spouses Group." The identity of both partners in this arrangement is still subject to societal role expectations but is continuing to adjust as military marriages vary.

Additionally, servicemembers who marry each other, referred to as *dual-military* households, are also redefining the term *military spouse*. With two sets of assignments and relocations to navigate, dual military servicemembers deal with many of the same stressors as other married military couples with the added tension of two sources of uncertainty. The advancement of women in non-military professions has also impacted the military's support of families, as many more spouses are in professions of their own

and are less flexible for movements. Ancillary organizations that strive to use spousal networks and lobby for cross-state boundary acceptance of credentials for military spouses are one way that the official and unofficial military community continues to support marriage. Spouses with teaching credentials, real estate licenses, and law practices make use of the same military support network in order to maintain their careers while supporting their servicemember and maintaining a joint household.

One of the most recent changes to military marriage was the Supreme Court's ruling on the 2015 Marriage Equality Act, recognizing same-sex marriage in all 50 states. Though still a relatively small population, same-sex military spouses are also part of the military community. The increase in cohabitation, separation agreements, and extended family members within the household has changed the military support network from a *spouse support club* to a *family readiness group* in an effort to recognize the changing face of the military family beyond the traditional definition. Though the regulatory requirements for a legal marriage and legal dependency of children still exist, socially the definition and the military's interaction and expectations of families has shifted to include what the servicemember declares as family.

Katie E. Matthew

See also: Marriage and Relocation; Marriage Certificate/License; Remarriage; Work Wives and Work Husbands

Further Reading

Bourg, Chris and Mady W. Segal. 1999. "The impact of family supportive policies and practices on organizational commitment to the Army." *Armed Forces & Society,* 25: 633–652.

Hogan, Paul F. and Rita Furst Seifert. 2010. "Marriage and the military: Evidence that those who serve marry earlier and divorce earlier." *Armed Forces & Society* 36: 420–438.

Karney, Benjamin R. and John S. Crown. 2011. "Does deployment keep military marriages together or break them apart? Evidence from Afghanistan and Iraq." In *Risk and Resilience in U.S. Military Families*, edited by Shelley M. Wadsworth and David Riggs. New York: Springer, pp. 23–45.

Lundquist, Jennifer and Zhun Xu. 2014. "Reinstitutionalizing families: Life course policy and marriage in the military." *Journal of Marriage and Family* 76, no. 5 (October): 1063–1081.

Marriage and Popular Culture

Our meaning, values, rituals, and legislation surrounding marriage, are strongly influenced by cultural content. That explains why the expression of this intensely personal human bond has so many varied nuances, depending on context.

Culture

Culture affects and shapes our beliefs, conduct, attitudes, values, traditions, and more. Culture provides us with a symbolic form of communication that provides shortcuts to meaning for those who can decode the message. Culture is reflected in expressions such as the visual arts, music, language, social customs, and rituals. These and many more bear the imprint of what is best understood within the unique original context.

Members with access to the specific cultural subgroup or identity can unlock that meaning and intent in a very direct and immediate way. It can occur without a verbal transcript; the code of cultural expression can be read by the insiders of that identified group, and it strengthens their cultural identity (Gerhardt 2020).

Culture has several characteristics. Importantly, it is *learned* behavior, which allows it to change and adapt. As it is acquired by learning and imitation, we pick it up from our ancestral heritage and peer cultural role models. We then pass it forward to subsequent generations. Hence, the insight that prejudice and judgmental behavior is learned behavior, largely imitated from cultural role models.

It is *bidirectional,* in that group members are influenced by their culture, but they in turn exert a counter influence, whereby culture becomes an expression of that group. In stable settings, culture has been linked to environment (geography), language, ethnicity, and more. But with increased globalization and virtually instant communication, these invisible boundaries have become permeable as they are subject to a greater array of influence.

Popular Culture

Popular culture, or pop culture, literally relates to the culture of the *population* or the people. It distinguishes itself from the traditional culture in that its turnover time is shorter. It tends to respond to the immediate, to what happens to be the currency of the moment. It is characterized by *trends,* with a relatively short lifespan. It can include any practices that are prevalent in each time context, including popular music with lyrics that express current values, media and web-based products, clothing and appearance (hairstyles, makeup), comics, language use (slang), sporting events, fast fashion (quick turnover, often disposable), trendy toys representing action heroes or celebrities, and the like. These products and expressions can be harnessed to make public statements, such as the slogans on T-shirts, the lyrics of music, the themes of media products, the style of dances. Popular culture has escalated with the advent of so-called *"influencers,"* who can push values, likes, dislikes, and opinions that are in vogue, by serving as highly visible role models shaping and directing behavior. Culture is accompanied by attitudes and beliefs, and these expressions form and influence value judgments. These can range from positive to negative and serve as a vehicle for protest. Pressure can also be exerted. The so-called "cancel culture" turns a cold shoulder to behavior and content which opposes current societal norms of what is regarded as acceptable and appropriate.

Popular culture as depicted in media products and on the internet has crept into virtually all aspects of family life. Social media, our involvement, and choices as consumers; all these and more are prey to forces trying to affect our behavior. The web influences how we find partners, how dating and courtship rituals play out, where we seek advice and solace, who our role models are, including the example of high-profile celebrities, and whom we may or may not wish to emulate. Unless we actively and intently protect our privacy, all things web-related can follow us and access the remotest corners of our existence, including the subtle and often subliminal shaping of our opinions and values.

Advocacy and Legislative Changes

Cultural values are complex; a phenomenon that can permeate through all layers of society in open and overt, as well as covert or hidden ways. Popular culture has left a distinct mark on our values, beliefs, and attitudes surrounding marriage. This in turn sets advocacy in motion which paves the way for social and ultimately legislative reform. Considering that culture is bidirectional, the changes in popular attitudes concerning marriage can ripple through several cornerstone concerns. Depending on where an individual identifies on the conservative/orthodox through to the liberal/unorthodox continuum, they will support or oppose some of the content precipitated by popular cultural movements. Religious, ethical, legal, and cultural values factor in strongly. A key concern in recent decades focused on the gender of participants in a marriage agreement. In countries supporting westernized cultural norms, marriage reform initiatives paved the way for legislative changes. With each reform, a subsequent long-held belief or attitude may have to be re-examined. This is a clear example of how culture changes and reinvents itself while responding to altered social, legal, and attitudinal realities.

Subcultures

Within popular culture, we find subgroups. These can be smaller pockets with distinct identifying features. Using fashion as an example, a subculture may subscribe to a fashion trend, and its unique expression serves as an identifier. Think of Goths, or by contrast Japanese Harajuku. The first group tends to dress in black with somber overtones. The second group is known for playful influences from comics and fantasy figures. Individuals choose to express themselves with the clothing and identifiers of a specific subgroup because the group's values resonate with their own; it becomes a *visible identifier*. It also allows for group membership and social cohesion. Apply these same qualities observed in popular subgroups into the realm of marriage, and it explains why popular culture links to *identity expression* and that in turn influences choices related to partnering and marriage (Gerhardt 2020).

Because popular culture influences values, beliefs, and attitudes in general, this influence also encompasses marriage and partnering practices. Global views on gender equality, diversity, family life, and the importance of religion are all topics heavily impacted by popular culture. Findings by the Pew Research Center (2019) gathered in 27 countries, indicated that most respondents felt that over the past two decades, several societal shifts had occurred: their countries displayed greater diversity, and increased gender equality. Over half thought that family ties had weakened. If audiences observe the diversity and entire spectrum of changing family life on screen and hear about lifestyles other than their own in popular songs, these often-subliminal messages conveyed by pop culture tend to normalize attitudes and dismantle prejudice. Popular cultural products, especially movies, are seen globally and are an integral part of entertainment. These products carry invisible messengers with them in the form of depictions of a variety of lifestyles about family form and function. Normalizing these in dramatic contexts fosters greater acceptance and awareness of a changing world.

A core characteristic of pop culture is its tendency to alter and reinvent itself. Popular culture tends to exert greater influence on those susceptible to its message; often the younger generation responds to the currency anchored in the present tense. Older persons tend to hold onto the beliefs they solidified during their own youth and early adulthood and may be less likely to change their opinions as life progresses. Hence there is a self-perpetuating renewal process within a society, as popular cultural values continually morph to reflect their context and, in turn, exert influence on persons witnessing a particular moment in history.

Clara Gerhardt

See also: Dating and Courtship 2000–Present

Further Reading

Gerhardt, Clara. 2020. "Dynamics of culture and change." In Gerhardt, C. (ed.), *Families in motion: dynamics in diverse contexts*. Thousand Oaks, CA: Sage, pp. 311–334.

Poushter, J. and J. Fetterolf. 2019. "A changing world: Global views on diversity, gender equality, family life and the importance of religion." Pew Research Center.

Marriage and Religion

There are many approaches to religion and its practice, acknowledging its complexity. How it is understood, whatever it is believed to represent, is intimately woven into the lives of the devotees. Religious beliefs and practices influence choices related to partnering, marriage, family creation, family roles, divorce, and more. Psychology and psychotherapy have approached religion from several viewpoints, especially where it intersects with therapeutic outcomes, acknowledging both the positive and the negative. Nevertheless "religiousness is too rich and too complex to be captured by easy formulas or simple summaries" (Pargament 2009).

Stereotypes, oversimplifications, and generalizations concerning religion fail to address the complexity of faith in relation to the human condition. "Religion refers to such a diverse and multifaceted constellation of beliefs and behaviors that it is highly unlikely to be the product of a unitary adaptation with a single identifiable function" (Kirkpatrick 1999, 926). Religion is an intimate and central part of self-identity and self-expression for persons who have internalized a reverence for a greater truth and a relationship to the transcendent. For this demographic, their religion co-defines who they are, what they stand for, where they are spiritually anchored, and how they see the meaning of life. It touches on values, hopes, rites, and rituals and on how they choose to shape their lives. In short, something beyond themselves and their immediate world.

Religion is embedded in cultural contexts. The expression of associated doctrine, rites, and rituals are heavily influenced by culture. There is a bidirectional influence as culture responds to and is shaped by religious traditions. The same major world religion may be uniform in its core teachings but depending on the cultural context there will be variations in for example how sacred spaces are created and presented, what cultural rituals are incorporated, and how faith is expressed during gatherings. Persons who do not identify as being religious

are influenced by select religious content as well because it is integral to cultural heritage and has shaped many rituals and events adopted in secular society. An example can be found in major holidays celebrated by most, although individual value attached to these events varies. In turn, culture has adapted and grown around religion, to the extent that it can be difficult to distinguish where religion ends and culture begins, or vice versa. Religion also represents sociological and psychological domains. Faith communities provide spaces for fellowship and ideally provide a reliable community network for support.

Frequently, religious communities celebrate shared developmental transitions and milestones which, in turn, enhance their meaning. Religion accompanies persons as major life events occur; births, physical maturation, transition into adulthood, partnering and marriage, commitment to the faith, support, and meaning during life's challenges, and ultimately the rites surrounding death and dying. Many religious communities address these lifespan transitions by incorporating and providing faith-based social services. Childcare, counseling and medical services, schools, respite, and elder care—all these display the interconnectedness between faith and community.

Partner choice and commitment in the form of marriage, are important life transitions that can signal the forming of nuclear families. Before modern reproductive technology, long-term partnering and the commitment represented by marriage were the predominant socially sanctioned avenues for the creation of children. Marriages have many roles and functions, but in religious communities they feature strongly as the couples' mutual commitment within the context of their faith expression. The seriousness of intent is reflected by vows, intended to be permanent, and couples may refer to one another as "soul mates." In turn, the religious community strengthens that marriage by providing communal support and reaffirmation. Persons may seek out a religious context that reflects their personal preferences concerning the interpretation and implementation of the core doctrines of a particular religion. The interpretation of any choice of identity within a religious group may be an expression of personal life views. These can range on a continuum from ultra-orthodox and conservative, through to unorthodox and liberal.

Marriage has been understood in a variety of ways, nuanced by societal, cultural, legal, and religious emphases. Some core topics of agreement/disagreement have focused on: who can marry whom, the gender of the participants, ending a marriage in divorce, as well as the faith-status of the participating parties. Partner choice can be influenced by religious expectations. Studies of interfaith or religiously heterogeneous marriages reveal no convenient answer. Instead, it hinges on the importance of the religious component in a marriage, and the participants' ability to focus on the unifying elements. Strong identification with the religion of choice, may suggest marrying someone like-minded. In a study of pre-marital religious influences, higher marital quality was anticipated if persons for whom religion was a core value could choose religiously committed spouses; in other words, the couple agreed on their fundamental religious outlook and its anticipated role in

their marriage (Perry 2015). Internalized and intrinsically motivated religion can be positively correlated to well-being if it is well integrated into the individual's life (Pargament 2009). Being in a stable, supportive partnership or marriage is also beneficial to long-term well-being. Shared spiritual values and/or religion have been identified as one of several pillars that support the house of marriage. Greater similarities for central concerns promise increased harmony and agreement, combined with a willingness to compromise, and respect for the individuality of the partner. Religious families believe moral development in their children to be associated with family faith and practice. In choosing faith-based values to pass on to children, it is advantageous if the parents display a united front. Vastly differing viewpoints may resurface during times of stress, loss, disability, and death when finding support, meaning, and hope take on greater relevance.

Research across the major world religions studied how three dimensions of religion influence marriages in supportive as well as challenging ways. These dimensions focused on faith communities, religious practices, and spiritual beliefs. Several themes emerged where religion and marriage intersect: influence of the clergy, involvement in the faith community, prayer, family rituals, marital fidelity, pro-marriage/anti-divorce beliefs, homogamy of religious beliefs, and faith as marital support (Marks 2005). For couples identifying as being similarly religious, their faith provides a framework that guides the commitment to the spouse, and several dimensions of social and communal life, including prayer and rituals within the home. Religion-based marriage decisions influence marital quality. But there is a cautionary note, namely that the influence of religion may not always be supportive and positive. Hurtful, controlling, intolerant, prescriptive, and gender-biased behavior, even spousal abuse, can and has occurred under cover of religious convictions. Coercion into marriage and arranged marriages against the will of typically the prospective bride may ignore the autonomy and well-being of the individuals committing to the state of matrimony. Research has revealed what family scientists have suspected: namely, that religious beliefs can unite *or* divide marriages. Religious practices can do the same and religious communities are prone to similar pitfalls: all these factors can make but also break partnerships and marriages. In short, religion in the context of marriage can be "both helpful and harmful" (Kelley, Marks, and Dollahite 2020). This can depend on whether religion is weaponized in the interest of personal motives, including power and control. For as many unifying forces shared religion in partnerships can represent, they can also yield divisive elements, underlining the multifactorial complexity of these concerns.

For many, the desire to practice the religion of their choice, or that of their ancestors, represents an intimate need, as well as a cultural identity. Because religion is so intensely personal, the current cultural climate emphasizes tolerance toward variance in faith expression, especially as communities display greater diversity. Research has also acknowledged the individual interpretation of religious doctrine: ". . . how individuals, marriages and families interpret and apply the teachings of their respective religion may have more to do with the influence of their religion than their particular denomination of religious attendance" (Leavitt et al. 2021). Mutual respect underlies differing points of view. Individual rights may extend to the right to differ, with the proviso that humankind can display appropriate tolerance, respect, and civility.

Clara Gerhardt

Acknowledgment

The insightful comments by Dr. Dale Wisely, Clinical Psychologist, are greatly valued.

See also: Interfaith Marriages; Wedding Officiant; Wedding Rituals

Further Reading

Kelley, H. H., Marks, L. D., and Dollahite, D. C. 2020. "Uniting and dividing influences of religion in marriage among highly religious couples." *Psychology of Religion and Spirituality* 12, no. 2: 167–177. https://doi.org/10.1037/rel0000262

Kirkpatrick, Lee. 1999. "Toward an evolutionary psychology of religion and personality." *Journal of Personality* 67, 921–952.

Leavitt, C. E., Allsop, D. B., Clarke, R. W. et al. 2021. "Sanctified sexual relationships in marriage: Reflections from religious wives and husbands." *Review of Religious Research* 63: 161–182. https://doi.org/10.1007/s13644-020-00440-z

Marks, Loren 2005. "How does religion influence marriage? Christian, Jewish, Mormon, and Muslim perspectives." *Marriage & Family Review* 38, no. 1: 85–111. DOI: 10.1300/J002v38n01_07

Pargament, Kenneth I. 2009. "The bitter and the sweet: An evaluation of the costs and benefits of religiousness." *Psychological Inquiry* 13, no. 3: 168–181. DOI: 10.1207/S15327965PLI1303_02

Perry, S. L. 2015. "A match made in heaven? Religion-based marriage decisions, marital quality, and the moderating effects of spouse's religious commitment." *Social Indicators Research* 123: 203–225. https://doi.org/10.1007/s11205-014-0730-7

Starkey, Caroline and Tomalin, Emma 2022. *The Routledge Handbook of Religion, Gender and Society.* Routledge. https://doi.org/10.4324/9780429466953

Marriage and Relocation

The reasons for geographical relocation in marriage and committed partnerships contain complex elements including push and pull motivators. Pushing these decisions can be the negatives; the realization that several vital dimensions of life are less than satisfactory and could be improved through mobilization. The pull is represented by the positives—the promise of a better life, which can include proximity to support networks, employment opportunities, and a desirable lifestyle matching individual interests and values. The push and pull motivators are so intertwined that it can be difficult to tease out the complexity of decisions. Add the mind games played, in terms of attribution bias and polarization in an individual's thinking. Another location may be idealized, which can be a strong impetus to deal with the frustrations of the actual move. At the same time, an individual may start finding fault with the present circumstances so that the decisions polarize, strengthening the push and pull effect. There is an interplay between factors that play into voluntary as well as involuntary decisions to relocate; some factors are within the control of a couple or family, whereas others are not.

Displacement and relocation rank among life's major disruptors. People form extended ecological contexts, and like trees, lay down intricate root systems when they settle (Rhodes 2018). Being uprooted can be disorienting, bewildering, even traumatic, and heralds a period of readjustment. For families affected by *housing insecurity*, frequent relocations may be destabilizing agents. A major relocation has the potential of exacerbating the fault lines in a relationship, exposing the points of weakness where relationships could fracture under stress. Major life transitions can strengthen or weaken the bonds, depending on the foundation and context in which these events occur. If couples manage to deal with major transitions in a unified and mutually supportive manner, that shared experience can strengthen relationships and represent an investment in well-being. Deciding which partner's priorities will determine major life decisions, can influence the quality of the partnership, and require mutual investment, respect, compromise, negotiation, and partner equality. Complexity occurs when two partners are not in agreement about proposed plans. One partner may be the catalyst precipitating mobilization. The other partner may feel as if they are making the greater sacrifice. Commuting and relationship sustainability is a recurrent theme in the literature. Couples who maintain long-distance relationships over a significant period may struggle to find feasible solutions, or factors beyond their control dictate possible resolution (e.g., extended higher education). The decision to relocate may also parallel the level of emotional commitment to the partnership. The ability to integrate major changes in the lifespan is influenced by long-term outcomes.

We relocate from personal living arrangements to neighborhoods, cities, and even countries and continents. A couple facing migration, even the extreme of refugee displacement, may focus on the hopeful rewards of the outcome, despite accompanying losses. It is a difficult journey with the desired end goal as the motivator and sustainer. Couples in the military, in international diplomacy, and in international trade, may expect to relocate frequently. In these cases, the employer typically provides an umbrella of benefits, facilitating the relocation. Some of these couples will be known as *ex-pats* in their new environments, and ties to their country of origin are maintained. The negative aspects of financially lucrative job-related relocations have been described using the term *golden handcuffs*, hinting at some of the challenges that accompany these decisions. Much has been written about the different dynamics of the family, in a short, limited timespan, and long-term relocations. Each scenario brings with it its own considerations.

Relocation of one person in a partnership has major implications for families with children; the term *relocation stress* is well documented. This can be precipitated by separation and divorce. Even if these decisions are amicable, they can strain children who feel that they move between the poles—and the geographical locations—of the two parents. The lead breadwinner can be the determining factor in whether a family moves or stays. Relocation can also have legal implications affecting custody arrangements. For children, this can have far-reaching

implications on emotional adjustment and social integration (Garboden, Leventhal, and Newman 2017). Children in late adolescence and emerging adulthood may be determined to launch into life independently rather than follow the family to a disrupting relocation far from their circle of familiarity (Firmin 2019). It can become a major dispute whether to give in to the wishes of early-adult children, especially if these decisions may not seem wise in the long run. An example would be emigration where one of the older children decides to stay in the country of origin. In years to come, these decisions may have lasting ramifications and affect the possibility of family reunification.

Residential relocation among the elderly may be voluntary or involuntary. Aging in place is an increasingly popular option with good outcomes. Other factors driving decisions are proximity to support systems including family, mental and physical health, cost of living, housing, and familiarity with a neighborhood. Retirement reduces the pressure of being an income-producing family unit. Persons with favorable financial retirement prospects can afford the luxury of picking locations based on overall desirability. Other decisions are not voluntary and are determined by declining income and health concerns, including cognitive impairment, that may necessitate relocation to assisted living. In the latter cases, the financial and caregiving support of family may be the dominant consideration for relocation.

During the COVID pandemic, couples explored the possibilities of working remotely. In the tech sector especially, this became a common choice. Instantly, this option opened new prospects, as the location the of domicile was not linked to the physical workplace. This allowed greater choice, often motivated by cost and quality of living providing options from urban to rural settings. As societies and ways of working evolve and diversify, individuals may have to rethink the reasons for relocation—although quality of life, especially family life, remains a strong motivator.

Clara Gerhardt

See also: International Marriage; Marriage and Military Families

Further Reading

Cochrane, William, Cameron, Michael P., and Alimi, Omoniyi (Eds.). 2021. *Labor Markets, Migration, and Mobility.* Singapore: Springer. DOI: 10.1007/978-981 -15-9275-1

Firmin, Carlene. 2019. "Relocation, relocation, relocation: Home and school-moves for children affected extra-familial risks during adolescence." *Children's Geographies* 523–535. DOI: 10.1080 /14733285.2019.1598545

Garboden, Philip M. E., Leventhal, Tama, and Newman, Sandra. 2017. "Estimating the effects of residential mobility: A methodological note." *Journal of Social Service Research* 43, no. 2: 246–261. DOI: 10.1080/01488376.2017.1282392

Rhodes, Anna. 2018. "Age of belonging: Friendship formation after residential mobility." *OUP Academic.* Oxford University Press. https://academic.oup.com /sf/article-abstract/97/2/583/5045215 https://doi.org/10.1093/sf/soy062

Marriage Certificate/License

To get married, couples must apply for a marriage license, which will ultimately convert to a marriage certificate once they are legally married. Marriage licenses are meant to track when and where a marriage occurs, but it is also legally binding in terms of who officiates the marriage and who is getting married. While each state sets its own legal requirements for who can and cannot marry, the requirements tend to center around age, marital status, relationship to one another, waiting periods, and other legal considerations.

Age

Age is probably one of the biggest factors that determine whether or not someone can marry. By law, individuals must be at least 18 years of age (legal adults) to get married. This is true in every state except for Nebraska, where the minimum age is 19 years, which is their marker for legally being considered an adult. While this is the age requirement that most individuals follow, it is possible in most states to get married as young as 16 years old. This requires parental permission to do so. In very rare cases, we have seen those as young as 14 get married, but that requires both parental permission and the permission of a judge to occur.

Marital Status

It is expected that at the time of filing for a marriage application that both parties are legally single. This means that if they were previously married that they need to have been divorced or widowed. This also means that you can only legally be married to only one person at a time. Bigamy and polygamy are not legal in any state.

Relationship to One Another

In addition to being legally single, it is also a legal requirement that couples are not related to one another. This means that children, parents, grandparents, etc.

are not able to apply for marriage certificates to get married. Essentially, anyone who is related by blood, marriage, or adoption is typically ineligible to get married. This is rooted in concerns about incest and individuals being genetically too similar to one another. The exception to this is first cousins. In some states, first cousins (your parent's sibling's children) can marry. This often requires that both parties are over a particular age (typically 55+ years of age) or at least one of the parties is unable to reproduce. This is meant to address any concerns about the couple having children who have parents who are too closely related. One state also prohibits double first cousins from marrying, which means that the parents of both sets of parents are siblings.

Waiting Periods

Once a couple is ready to apply for their marriage license, after ensuring that they meet the aforementioned requirements, they will need to take into consideration whether or not there are waiting periods for marriage licenses to be granted in the state that they are looking to get married in. The majority of states (29) have no waiting periods, while other states have waiting periods that range from 24 hours up to 6 days to have their license issued. Florida has no waiting period for residents, but it does require the completion of a marriage preparation course. Residency may also impact waiting periods.

Other Legal Considerations

In applying for marriage licenses, couples need to make sure that they have identified someone who is legally ordained to perform their ceremony. This varies from state to state and someone is often licensed to perform marriages in particular states.

Additionally, couples can get married in states that are not their state of residency, but they are bound by the laws of that state about obtaining a marriage license and certificate. Due to the Fair Faith and Credit Clause and Marriage Equality, if a couple marries in one state, it is legally recognized by all 50 states.

As of 2015, both opposite and same-sex couples can apply for marriage licenses to get married. There is no denying couples the right to marry based on sex or gender as long as they meet all of the aforementioned requirements.

Historically, blood tests have also been a requirement to get married. This was meant to screen for any health issues that may not be known or disclosed. This requirement has been eliminated in every state, except for Montana. Exemptions from having to submit a blood test can be requested.

While states have a large degree of flexibility in determining the criteria that couples must meet in order to apply for a marriage license, they are all relatively similar. Over the decades the requirements have become less rigid; however, it is unlikely that the requirements of age, marital status, and relationship to one another are likely to change much more.

Melanie L. Duncan

See also: Marriage and Legal Planning; Postnuptial Agreement; Prenuptial Agreement; Wedding Officiant

Further Reading

Brides. "Marriage Certificates and Licenses: Everything You Need to Know." Accessed on April 26, 2021. https://www

.brides.com/story/who-needs-to-sign-marriage-license

The Knot. "How to Get a Marriage License." Access on April 26, 2021. https://www.theknot.com/content/marriage-license-basics

NOLO. "Chart: State Marriage License and Blood Test Requirements." Accessed on April 26, 2021. https://www.nolo.com/legal-encyclopedia/chart-state-marriage-license-blood-29019.html

NOLO. "Marriage Law & Marriage Licenses." Accessed on April 26, 2021. https://www.nolo.com/legal-encyclopedia/marriage-license

Weisberg, D. Kelly. 2020. *Modern Family Law: Cases and Materials*. New York: Wolters Kluwer.

Marriage Counseling

Marriage counseling, also known as relationship or couples counseling, is a form of counseling designed to help couples communicate better, prepare for marriage resolve conflict, improve the condition of their relationship overall, or simply navigate better understandings within the relationship (Mudd and Preston 1950). This form of counseling dates back to the 1900s (Mudd and Preston 1950) and has evolved to include non-traditional couple types. In couples-based counseling, couples work primarily on issues affecting their relationship. While many seek marriage counseling after their union, relationship counseling is also utilized for premarital counseling of those seeking to get married or live together long-term as well. Additionally, though many think of marriage counseling as a form of counseling for opposite-sex couples, this form of counseling is open to all couple types regardless of sexual orientation (Ossana 2000), gender identity, or relationship type (i.e., monogamous, monogamish, polyamorous and polyfidelity polyandrous, polyandry polygamy).

Counseling is a service provided by those with specialized training (Mudd and Preston 1950). Those providing counseling services to couples are licensed professionals both certified in Marriage and Family Therapy and those counseling professionals that are practicing more general therapy as well. While many do not typically seek counseling on a long-term basis, counseling can last anywhere from a few sessions to several months or years depending on the issues or distress experienced in the relationship. It is safe to say that all couples experience issues and conflict within their relationship. Relationships are not easy and couples often learn this quickly after getting together. Hard work and commitment are necessary for relationships to succeed. While every relationship experiences the honeymoon phase, questions regarding compatibility, agreement, and long-term harmony often begin to arise for many soon after commitment. Varying issues are addressed in couples counseling. Among them are issues with communication, value judgments, conflicts regarding parenting, interpersonal family relations, the difficulties of joining families (blended families), sexual difficulties, infidelity, financial issues, anger management, and lifestyle choices among other challenges.

Marriage counseling is not solely reserved for those who have distress in their relationship. This form of counseling works with couples to develop stronger communication skills, understand the importance of vulnerability and intimacy, rebuilding the relationship after relationship trauma has occurred, or helping couples decide when it is time for their relationship to end. Couples counseling is also utilized for couples seeking to grow their level of intimacy, make the bond in their relationship stronger, set the important expectation, explore hopes for the relationship, process implications of the decision made within the union, and explore differences in opinion and how to resolve them respectfully. This can be done through learning new ways or levels of communication and learning new or improving upon relationship skills (i.e., communication skills, interpersonal skills, and problem-solving skills).

Another reason couples counseling can be helpful is to help partners gain a more realistic view of their partner, rather than viewing them as whom they want them to be. Frequently, misunderstandings arise when we look for people to be what we want rather than accepting them as they are and working together to be better individuals overall. Couples counseling can also aid in better understanding the origins of conflict within a relationship. Many things can test the strength or solidity of a relationship. Things once found to be cute, sweet, or lovable in a relationship, may become annoying or exasperating the longer couples are together. Further, infidelity, loss of physical or sexual attraction, or generally growing apart can lead to the breakdown of a relationship. Regardless of the cause, feelings of sadness, tension, and fear among others can increase with distress in a relationship. While many believe if they ignore the problems in their relationship, they will simply go away, this is often not the case. Frequently, this

makes the situation worse and other problems, such and physical violence or emotional abuse ensue. This can lead to more widespread issues in another aspect of life for those experiencing distress within their relationship.

While disclosing challenges within the relationship to a stranger can be difficult, having an unbiased party help to navigate some of the challenges faced is often beneficial. Finding common ground and avoiding miscommunication is much easier when partners understand and respect each other's views and desires. Counseling can also hold couples accountable for their actions, habits, and the choices that lead them to counseling to begin with.

Jahaan R. Abdullah

See also: Divorce, Process of; Premarital Counseling; Remarriage

Further Reading

Cuber, J. F. 1945. "Functions of the marriage counselor." *Marriage and Family Living* 7, no. 1: 3–5.

Johnson, D. 1961. *Marriage counseling: Theory and practice.* Prentice-Hall.

Mace, D. R. 1954. "What is a marriage counselor?" *Marriage and Family Living* 16, no. 2: 135–138.

Mudd, E. H. and Preston, M. G. 1950. "The contemporary status of marriage counseling." *The ANNALS of the American Academy of Political and Social Science* 272, no. 1: 102–109.

Ossana, S. M. 2000. "Relationship and couples counseling." In R. M. Perez, K. A. DeBord, and K. J. Bieschke (Eds.), *Handbook of counseling and psychotherapy with lesbian, gay, and bisexual clients.* American Psychological Association, pp. 275–302. https://doi.org/10.1037/10339-012

Reiter, M. D. 2017. "Couples counseling." In Michael D. Reiter and Ronald J. Chenail (Eds.), *Behavioral, humanistic-existential, and psychodynamic approaches to couples counseling.* New York: Routledge, pp. 1–8.

Marriage Retreats

Marriage retreats are events developed for groups of couples as opposed to just one couple. The length of the retreat varies. They are typically voluntary events couples participate in with the primary goal of strengthening the marriage relationship. Marriage retreats often are offered by religious groups or denominations, whether locally, regionally, or nationally. Most research suggests the retreats are not designed to address a marital relationship that is on the fringe of ending. However, the retreats may bring to the surface areas in a marriage that need to be addressed further through marital counseling.

The typical purpose of a marriage retreat is to strengthen and develop the marital relationship. The desired outcome might be to help couples remain committed to each other throughout their lives. However, many retreats seek to address short-range goals such as communication, intimacy, verbalizing expectations, or strategies for the ongoing health of the marriage.

Marriage retreats may occur over one afternoon, a weekend, or longer, though a weekend or 2–3-day setting seems to be the norm. Activities include keynote speaker, workshops, and personal and couple reflection time. Other activities may be included and are typically determined by the individual or group leading the retreat.

The setting for marriage retreats varies as much as the length of the retreat. Retreats may take place in a park or resort setting, on cruises, or in a simple building. There are typical costs involved and these are determined by the retreat organizer. For example, a weekend marriage retreat held in a local setting organized by a small group could be free or cost up to a few hundred dollars. If the marriage retreat is a large event to which people from different geographical locations are invited, costs could run as much as several hundred dollars.

Marriage retreats often involve couples who already know each other, such as a church or religious group. Retreats can also involve couples who have never met.

There is little to no research on the effectiveness of marriage retreats. Defining effectiveness related to the results of a marriage retreat would prove a challenge because effectiveness, in this case, is subjective. Available research is often related to a particular institution's research, which gives little attention to the effectiveness of retreats by other groups or institutions. That is not to say, though, that retreats are not effective. Some research suggests that the effectiveness of a marriage retreat differs between husband and wife. Research has also been focused on marital counseling with a focused topic.

As with any type of intentional effort to improve one's health or skills, success is determined to a great extent by, in the case of marriage retreats, the couple's willingness to commit to the disciplines, practices, and strategies necessary for ongoing improvement.

Marriage retreats are attended by couples of all ages and varied years of marriage. Couples may choose to attend a marriage retreat yearly or regularly, or they may attend only once. Marriage retreats differ from marital counseling which seeks to address a specific problem(s).

S. Thomas Valentine

See also: Focus on the Family; Marriage Counseling

Further Reading

Gottman, John, Julie Schwartz Gottman, Ronald Abrams, and Rachel Carllton Abrams. 2019. *Eight Dates: Essential Conversations for a Lifetime of Love.* New York: Workman Publishing, Inc.

Gottman, John, Nan Silver. 2015. *Seven Principles for Making Marriage Work: A Practical Guide from the Country's Foremost Relationship Expert.* New York: Harmony Books.

Lester, Andrew D. and Judith L. Lester. 1998. *It Takes Two: The Joys of Intimate Marriage.* Louisville, KY: Westminster John Knox Press.

Orbuch, Terri L. 2015. *5 Simple Steps to Take Your Marriage from Good to Great.* Austin, TX: River Grove Books.

Marriage Squeeze

A marriage squeeze occurs when people wanting to marry cannot do so due to a demographic imbalance in which the number of marriageable women is roughly unequal to the number of marriageable men. Marriage is a market, where eligible men pair up with eligible women. In a marriage squeeze, some people are squeezed out of the marriage market and must remain unmarried against their wishes.

A marriage squeeze creates competitive conditions for marriage. In such a market, those able to marry might have to be particularly charming, good-looking, educated, or wealthy. Professor Grossbard (1985) has written that women who face a marriage squeeze will often cohabitate more and participate in the labor market at a higher rate to financially support themselves.

Marriage markets change over time, creating marriage squeezes in different parts of the world and at different times. Several marriage squeezes recently occurred in some parts of Asia because of unbalanced sex ratios. For example, due to the one-child policy in China, some parents preferred having a son to having a daughter. When these children grew up and became adults, men outnumbered women and thus not all men could get married.

Marriage squeezes can also occur from the interaction between changing demographics and the common custom of men marrying younger women. For example, when birth rates fell in the 1930s, men soon faced a marriage squeeze because they outnumbered younger women. In contrast, women of the early Baby-Boomer generation faced a marriage squeeze because they outnumbered eligible men born right before them. Thus, both genders have suffered from marriage squeezes in the United States at different times in history.

Today, there continue to be several examples of marriage squeezes in the United States. For example, some women prefer to marry men who are equally or more educated than they are, but more women are now college-educated than men. Thus, not all college-educated women are able to marry a college-educated man and some are squeezed out of the marriage market.

In sum, a marriage squeeze prevents people from succeeding in the marriage market due to demographic patterns and shifts. Some marriage squeezes are manufactured, such as a parental preference for sons, while other marriage squeezes are naturally occurring, such as changes in birth rates. Regardless of the cause of the marriage squeeze, the result is that not everyone who wants to get married can do so.

Margaret Ryznar

See also: Homogamy; Marriage and Education; Unmarried Cohabitation

Further Reading

Banks, R. Richard and Su Jin Gatlin. 2005. "African American Intimacy: The Racial Gap in Marriage." *Michigan Journal of Race & Law* 11, no. 1: 115–132.

Billig, Michael S. 1991. "The Marriage Squeeze on High-Caste Rajasthani Women." *Journal of Asian Studies* 50, no. 2: 341–360.

Grossbard, Shoshana Amyra. 1985. "Marriage Squeezes and the Marriage Market." In Kingsley Davis (ed.), *Contemporary Marriage*. New York: Russell Sage Foundation.

Maternal Gatekeeping

Children and families benefit when fathers are more involved in child-rearing and family work. Since the late 1980s, researchers indicated that children with fathers who are actively involved in parenting experience positive outcomes such as better academic performance and higher levels of self-esteem. Moreover, past research revealed that the interpersonal relationship between the mother and the father influences the level and quality of fathers' involvement with their children. Maternal gatekeeping is one term used to describe these relationship dynamics between mothers and fathers that impact parental contributions to childcare responsibilities. These dynamics can exist in multiple family formations including intact families, families of divorce, and families with non-resident fathers.

Early researchers examined maternal gatekeeping via the perspective of mothers' influence on the father-child relationship; thus, definitions of maternal gatekeeping reflected this perspective. For example, De Luccie (1995) discussed maternal gatekeeping in relation to mothers' satisfaction with paternal involvement. De Luccie found that mothers' attitudes and level of satisfaction with fathers' involvement influenced gatekeeping behaviors and the frequency of father involvement (128). Allen and Hawkins (1999) were the first to attempt to measure maternal gatekeeping. They defined maternal gatekeeping as a collection of behaviors and beliefs that disrupt the ability of men and women to collaborate in family work by limiting men's opportunity to learn and grow through the practice of parenting (Allen and Hawkins 1999, 200). The researchers identified components to measure gatekeeping: amount of time spent on family work (e.g., division of labor), control over family work (e.g., how work is done), setting high standards for childcare and household responsibilities, and adherence to traditional gender-based family roles where mothers provide the majority of the household and childcare labor. Three dimensions of gatekeeping emerged: active gatekeepers, intermediaries, and collaborators. Gate-keepers limited fathers' opportunities in day-to-day family work or completely excluded fathers entirely. Intermediaries managed the level of family work performed by fathers in a way that was collaborative yet restrictive. Collaborators incorporated equitable parenting practices ensuring shared responsibility for family work. Twenty-one percent of mothers were active gatekeepers engaging in five more hours of household responsibilities compared to mothers who served as intermediaries and collaborators. In these instances, mothers were more likely to restrict or limit fathers' contributions to childcare responsibilities.

Another model defined maternal gatekeeping as a set of maternal attitudes about the role of fathers in the family, mothers' satisfaction with fathers' role performance, and the relationship between maternal attitudes and father involvement. For example, Fagan and Barnett (2003) explored mothers' preferences for managing childcare responsibilities versus sharing these responsibilities with fathers in families with resident and nonresident fathers. They hypothesized that mothers' attitudes were linked to the level of father involvement, but maternal gatekeeping mediates these attitudes, thus, impacting father involvement. The researchers noted a relationship between mothers' perceptions of fathers' ability to care for their children or parenting competence and the amount of father's involvement with his children. Moreover, the researchers indicated that mothers engaged in more gatekeeping behaviors with fathers not residing in the home due to concerns about fathers' parenting competence (1036).

While maternal gatekeeping was initially characterized as a prohibitive parenting strategy, some scholars suggested that gatekeeping occurs on a continuum with restrictive and supportive dimensions. Thus, maternal gatekeeping behaviors could hinder father-child relationships (gate close) or encourage (gate open) father involvement. For example, Austin, Fieldstone, and Pruett (2013, 4) suggested a range of gatekeeping attitudes and behaviors (very facilitative, cooperative, disengaged, restrictive, and very restrictive). Facilitative gatekeeping is defined as attitudes and behaviors that support the other parent-child relationship (5). Conversely, restrictive gatekeeping are attitudes and behaviors that hamper the other parent's involvement with the child and the quality of the parent-child relationship (5). Using child custody as an example, facilitative behaviors may include urging the child to phone the other parent, sharing pertinent information about the child's activities, and praising the other parent to the child. Restrictive behaviors could include withholding information about the child or ignoring phone calls. The researchers posited that restrictive behaviors create the most barriers to establishing and maintaining positive parent-child relationships. Other researchers have examined maternal gate opening and gate closing with findings supporting gate closing or restrictive behaviors negatively impacting father involvement and father-child relationships while gate-opening influences positive father involvement in childcare activities.

In certain instances, maternal gatekeeping is a protective or proactive strategy against the perceptions of problematic parenting behaviors of fathers.

In these instances, mothers limit or halt father involvement or attempt to redirect fathers' parenting styles. For example, Pederson (2012) examined mothers' and fathers' perceptions of good parenting with the context of cultural expectations and values. Mothers in the study disclosed that they served as intermediaries when fathers discipline too harshly or use tones that made mothers feel uncomfortable (235). In another study, mothers reported a level of mistrust with the non-residential father of their child due to concerns about their child's physical and emotional safety while under their fathers' care (Sano, Richards, and Zvonkovic 2008, 1714). This mistrust centered about their child's physical safety, reports of the fathers' inability to nurture, and fathers' practice of leaving the child with other relatives during scheduled visitation time. Another study examining the behaviors of mothers of children of incarcerated fathers noted that mothers limited displayed gate-closing behaviors after fathers' release from prison due to issues like paternal substance abuse or a history of violence.

Although scholars of maternal gatekeeping acknowledge that this phenomenon occurs with both mothers and fathers, research primarily focuses on mothers' influence, attitudes, and behaviors. Perhaps this is a result of traditional role expectations where mothers are primarily responsible for childcare responsibilities (Yavorsky, Kamp Dush, and Schoppe-Sullivan 2015, 673). Moreover, data illustrates that mothers have a greater influence on fathers' parenting than the reverse (Belsky 1979, 781) and that mothers' overall satisfaction with the level of fathers' parenting would mediate fathers' level of involvement (De Luccie 1995, 128). Other factors that may predict maternal gatekeeping include parental psychological functioning, traditional gender role attitudes and expectations, maternal expectations (e.g., mothers' assessment of fathers' fitness for parenting), father characteristics (e.g., fathers' ability to parent), and maternal religiosity (Schoppe-Sullivan et al. 2015, 179–181).

Felicia Law Murray

See also: Absent Father; National Father Initiative; Nonresidential Fathers

Further Reading

Allen, Sarah M., and Alan J. Hawkins. 1999. "Maternal gatekeeping: Mothers' beliefs and behaviors that inhibit greater father involvement in family work." *Journal of Marriage and Family* 51, no. 1: 199–212.

Austin, William G., Linda Fieldstone, and Marsha Klein Pruitt. 2013. "Bench book for assessing gatekeeping in parenting disputes: Understanding the dynamics of gate-closing and opening in the best interests of children." *Journal of Child Custody: Research Issues, and Practices* 3, no. 3/4: 1–16.

Belsky, Jay. 1979. "The interrelation of parental and spousal behavior during infancy in traditional nuclear families: An exploratory analysis." *Journal of Marriage and Family* 4, no. 4: 501–519.

De Luccie, Mary F. 1995. "Mothers as gatekeepers: A model of maternal mediators of father involvement." *The Journal of Genetic Psychology* 156, no. 1: 115–131.

Fagan, Jay and Marina Barnett. 2003. "The relationship between maternal gatekeeping, paternal competence, mothers' attitudes about the father role, and father involvement." *Journal of Family Issues* 24, no. 8: 1020–1043.

Pedersen, Daphne E. 2012. "The good mother, the good father, the good parent: Gendered definitions of parenting." *Journal of Feminist Family Therapy* 24, no. 3: 230–246.

Sano, Yoshie, Leslie N. Richards, and Anisa M. Zvonkovic. 2008. "Are mothers really 'gatekeepers' of children? Rural mothers' perceptions of nonresident father involvement in low-income families." *Journal of Family Issues* 29, no. 12: 1701–1723.

Schoppe-Sullivan, Sarah J., Lauren E. Altenburger, Meghan A. Lee, Daniel J. Bower, and Claire M. Kamp Dush. 2015. "Who are the gatekeepers? Predictors of maternal gatekeeping." *Parenting: Science and Practice* 15, no. 3: 166–186.

Yavorsky, Jill E., Claire M. Kamp Dush, and Sarah J. Schoppe-Sullivan. 2015. "The production of inequality: The gender division of labor across the transition to parenthood." *Journal of Marriage and Family* 77, no. 3: 662–679.

Monogamy

Monogamy is having only one romantic partner at a time. Scientists estimate that less than 5% of species form lifelong, monogamous bonds. Monogamous mammals include humans, beavers, wolves, swans, and snowy owls.

The evolution of monogamy in humans may have resulted from the need for fathers to help care for their children. Human children have a prolonged developmental period and a delayed maturity compared to other species, making them vulnerable for a longer time.

Monogamy may also be a social construct in humans. Some religions and countries permit multiple romantic partners, but the cultural norms in the United States strongly favor monogamy. The American narrative of having a "soul mate" or finding "the one" is strong. This narrative precludes having more than one romantic partner in life and favors marriage and a lifetime of devotion to one person.

Laws in the United States also reinforce monogamy. For example, all states have bigamy laws that invalidate subsequent marriages if a previous marriage exists and is still valid. Furthermore, states have historically criminalized adultery. The justifications offered for such laws include the protection of women and children. Finally, some states continue to allow lawsuits against people who have ruined a marriage. For example, alienation of affection laws, also known as "homewrecker" laws, permit a spouse to sue for monetary damages to another person for purposefully interfering with the marriage.

Thus, American society still prefers monogamous relationships. Monogamy is considered virtuous, and a commitment to faithfulness appears in some people's wedding vows. However, marital monogamy does not necessarily mean sexual monogamy. Many married people have extramarital affairs, and some people have open marriages that allow for additional sexual partners.

With the broadening of sexual mores over the years, more people of both genders are willing to consider nonmonogamous relationships. As a result, some couples choose to discuss their expectations for monogamy in their relationship, often as early as possible.

There are certain advantages to monogamy. These include the potential for increased stability and security for both partners. There is also a smaller risk of emotional complexities in monogamy, such as jealousy resulting from simultaneous romantic relationships. A monogamous relationship can be simpler not only emotionally, but also financially and logistically. Finally, monogamy helps avoid sexually transmitted diseases and paternity issues.

The disadvantages of monogamy include potential boredom with having the same partner for an extended period. Furthermore, people may become incompatible or sexually frustrated with each other, or even completely grow apart, but they stay in their monogamous relationship due to a commitment to monogamy.

Margaret Ryznar

See also: Polyamory; Polygamy; Swingers

Further Reading

Emens, Elizabeth F. 2004. "Monogamy's Law: Compulsory Monogamy and Polyamorous Existence." *New York University Review of Law & Social Change* 29, no. 2: 277–376.

French, Jeffrey A., Jon Cavanaugh, Aaryn C. Mustoe, Sarah B. Carp, and Stephanie L. Womack. 2018. "Social Monogamy in Nonhuman Primates: Phylogeny, Phenotype, and Physiology." *Journal of Sex Research* 55, no. 4: 410–434.

Miller, Alyssa. 2018. "Punishing Passion: A Comparative Analysis of Adultery Laws in the United States of America and Taiwan and Their Effects on Women." *Fordham International Law Journal* 41, no. 2: 425–472.

N

Name Changes

Name changes are the practice of changing one's surname following the formation or dissolution of a marital union. In the United States, the most common form of name change observed occurs in heterogamous unions where a woman takes her husband's surname following marriage. This patronymic type of name change is derived from state laws, which at one time required married women to take their husbands' surnames to participate in basic civic activities such as driving or voting (Emens 2007, 772). While these laws are no longer enforced, the effects of them are still evident, exemplified by the fact that in all 50 states women have the statutory right to either change their name upon the signing of the marriage certificate, use the name of their spouse, or the right to retain their maiden name. In contrast, only nine states allowed men to do the same as of the mid-2010s. Men who wish to change their surname to that of their wives are usually required to obtain a court order which may be costly and time-consuming (Slade 2015, 337).

While the majority of women in the United States use their husband's surname after marriage there is a small percentage of women who continue to use their maiden name after marriage (Gooding and Kreider 2010, 683). This practice is rising among younger Americans, though. A 2015 study conducted by the *New York Times* through a Google Consumer Survey found that 20% of women who were married in recent years kept their maiden names (Miller and Willis 2015). Other types of name changes observed after marriage include one or both spouses hyphenating their surnames, using both surnames without a hyphen, using a maiden name as a middle name, or combining surnames to create a new family name (Scheuble and Johnson 2016, 203–205). From a demographic perspective, women who chose "unconventional" name changes after marriage tend to have higher levels of education, have fewer children, and are more likely to be women of color or immigrant women (Scheuble and Johnson 2016, 205–206).

Name changes following divorce are exemplified by spouses petitioning to reuse their maiden names on the dissolution of the union. There is limited empirical research on this topic but evidence suggests that this reversion to maiden names post-divorce is impacted in part by age, educational level, the length of the marriage, and the presence of children in the union (Hoffnung and Williams 2016, 29–30). Younger women and those with more years of education are more likely to resume their maiden names post-divorce. In addition, women with fewer years of marriage and fewer children are more likely to resume using their maiden names post-divorce.

Names are integral to identity and provide a unique way to advertise gender, kinship, and familial connections (e.g., Obasi 2016; Obasi et al. 2019). Names are also a powerful way to indicate the formation or dissolution of a union. While name changes at the formation and dissolution of heterogamous unions are reasonably well-documented there is a need for empirical research examining name changes associated with the formation and dissolution of homogamous unions, especially with the legalization of same-sex marriage in the United States.

Sharon N. Obasi

See also: Focus on the Family

Further Reading

Emens, E. F. 2007. "Changing name changing: framing rules and the future of marital names." *The University of Chicago Law Review* 74: 761–863.

Gooding, Gretchen E. and Kreider, Rose M. 2010. "Women's marital naming choices in a nationally representative sample." *Journal of Family Issues* 31, no. 5: 681–701.

Hoffnung, Michelle and Williams, Michelle A. 2016. "When Mr. Right becomes Mr. Wrong: Women's postdivorce name choice." *Journal of Divorce & Remarriage* 57, no. 1: 12–35, DOI: 10.1080/10502556.2015.1113814

Miller, Claire Cain and Willis, Derek. 2015. "Maiden names, on the rise again." *New York Times* "Upshot" blog, June 27. https://www.nytimes.com/2015/06/28/upshot/maiden-names-on-the-rise-again.html

Obasi, S. 2016. "Naming patterns in rural South Central Nebraska." *Names: A Journal of Onomastics* 64, no. 3: 158–165. http://dx.doi.org/10.1080/00277738.2016.1197644

Obasi, Sharon N., Mocarski, Richard, Holt, Natalie, Hope, Debra A., and Woodruff, Nathan. 2019. "Renaming me: Assessing the influence of gender identity on name selection." *Names: A Journal of Onomastics* 67, no. 4: 199–211 DOI: 10.1080/00277738.2018.1536188

Scheuble, Laurie K. and Johnson, David R. 2016. "Keeping her surname as a middle name at marriage: what predicts this practice among married women who take their husband's last name?" *Names: A Journal of Onomastics* 64, no. 4: 202–216.

Slade, Michael 2015. "Who wears the pants: The difficulties men face when trying to take their spouse's surname after marriage." *Family Court Review* 53, no. 2: 336–354.

National Council on Family Relations

The National Council on Family Relations (NCFR) is a professional organization with members whose focus is on family research, practice, and education. The headquarters of NCFR is in St. Paul, Minnesota. The roughly 2700 members of NCFR (M. Hansen, personal communication, February 25, 2021) come from all 50 states and over 35 countries, according to the organization's website (National Council on Family Relations, n.d.). The National Council on Family Relations was founded in 1938, and the primary objective of the organization is to understand and strengthen families. More specifically, NCFR's mission is ". . . to provide an educational forum for family researchers, educators, and practitioners to share in the development and dissemination of knowledge about families and family relationships, establish professional standards, and work to promote family well-being" (National Council on Family Relations, n.d.).

Professionals and students who join the National Council on Family Relations come from a variety of backgrounds: Human Development, Marriage and Family Therapy, Sociology, Family Science, Family Life Education, Psychology, Social Work, Health, Anthropology, and more. Relatedly, members of NCFR work in a wide variety of professional settings. The settings include family services, social services, education, faith-based organizations, healthcare, early childhood education, and government agencies (Family Science, n.d.).

One important contribution made by the National Council on Family Relations is the platform it creates for the field of Family Science. Family Science is the scientific study of families and close interpersonal relationships. Family Science is focused on the relationships that exist within families (e.g., partner and couple, children and parents, siblings, etc.) across the lifespan. Family Science is evidenced-based and applied; that is, although research guides the discipline, Family Science is meant to be useful in the "real world." The field of Family Science is also a strengths-oriented profession. This means that professionals in the field believe that all families have positive features and attributes that make them resilient. Finally, practitioners of Family Science are preventative in nature. This means, as a discipline, Family Science professionals are committed to emphasizing the education of clients to prevent problems from occurring.

NCFR establishes professional standards that guide the work of Family Science practitioners while also providing more visibility for the important work being done by these professionals. More specifically, the National Council on Family Relations is the governing body for professionals who hold the Certified Family Life Educator (CFLE) credential. This credential provides validation of the knowledge and work experience of those who identify as a CFLE. According to their website, there are approximately 125 college and university Family Science degree programs in the United States and Canada using the curriculum standards proposed by NCFR's Family Life Education curriculum (National Council on Family Relations, n.d.).

A second important contribution made by the National Council on Family Relations is the three scholarly journals published by the organization. The first, the *Journal of Marriage and Family,* was established in 1939 under the name *Living* and was renamed to its current title in 1964 and leads the professional conversation on Family Science. The second journal, *Family Relations: Interdisciplinary Journal of Applied Family Science*, is useful to practitioners in the field for its emphasis on exploring a wide variety of issues that those in direct practice often face. The third publication, the *Journal of Family Theory and Review*, offers readers who are interested in family theory a variety of original contributions. Taken together, these three journals offer research, theory, and practice from authors around the world that helps scholars and practitioners to better understand families and family life.

A third important contribution made by the National Council on Family Relations is the organization of an annual conference. This event brings together professionals from across the United States and around the globe who care about, study, and support families in their professional roles. The conference creates opportunities for students and professionals in the field to simultaneously learn from one another and build their professional networks.

One final contribution made by the National Council on Family Relations is the organization's efforts to increase the visibility of issues that impact families by strengthening the connections among the community of family scholars and practitioners. NCFR facilitates ongoing professional dialogue through webinars and discussion groups (offered in various forms at the state, regional, and local levels) and disseminates various publications such as the NCFR Report (a member magazine) and Certified Family Life Education Network Newsletter. This ongoing dialogue and discourse are also offered to policymakers through research and policy briefs on a variety of family topics to help support ongoing legislative and policymaking efforts.

In summary, the National Council on Family Relations is a vibrant organization that takes a holistic approach to strengthening families by providing a variety of professional support to those who work directly with and on behalf of all families.

Tara Katherine Hammar

See also: Ackerman Institute for Family Therapy; American Association for Marriage and Family Therapy; Focus on the Family; Gottman Institute

Further Reading

Family Science. n.d. "Family Scientists Work in Many Professions to Understand & Strengthen Families." Accessed February 25, 2021. https://family.science/where-we-work

National Council on Family Relations. n.d. "National Council on Family Relations: About Us." Accessed February 1, 2021. https://www.ncfr.org/about

National Father Initiative

The National Fatherhood Initiative (NFI) is an independent, private, non-profit organization that aims to promote father involvement to improve the well-being of children. NFI was established in March 1994 by Don Eberly, and the headquarters are in Germantown, Maryland. NFI identifies the lack of fathers' involvement in their children's lives as the underlying cause of many challenges in society such as poverty, substance use, and incarceration (National Father Initiative, n.d.). From the early 1960s to the early 1990s, the proportion of children living in father-absent homes had risen to nearly 40% and it has leveled off to about 33%. In response to this father-absence, NFI has highlighted an involved, responsible, and committed father as one of the most important keys to a child's well-being. NFI also aims to (1) inform society of fathers' important contributions, (2) help organizations with resources and training by equipping them to support fathers, and (3) work in partnerships with various sectors of society to promote engaged fatherhood (National Father Initiative, n.d.). Additionally, as the attention to children's wellbeing and father involvement has risen, administrative support has been provided to responsible fatherhood programs, which includes Congress appropriated $3 million as well as an additional $500,000 for NFI (Solomon-Fears 2015, 17).

To meet its goals, NFI has worked with individuals, communities, military organizations, and government agencies. NFI is the largest provider of a variety of resources, programs, and training in terms of responsible fatherhood in the country, and it has distributed over 8 million resources to date. The major core programs include *24/7 Dad®*, *InsideOut Dad*, *Understanding Dad*, and *Fathering in 15*. Among them, *24/7 Dad* is the most widely used fatherhood program in the United States providing fundamental fathering principles, and *InsideOut Dad* is specially designed evidence-based program for incarcerated fathers. *Understanding Dad* helps mothers improve the relationship with fathers for the sake of children and *Fathering in 15* also offers fathers 15 interactive topics such as being a man and dad, work-family balance, and child development.

While many programs facilitating father involvement with their children are working to document their successes (Concha et al. 2016), NFI has reported its program evaluation results (Gordon et al. 2012). For example, *24/7 Dad®* was proven to be effective in increasing instrumental father involvement (e.g., supporting mom) and improving the quality of the relationship with the child (Lewin-Bizan 2015). As for *InsideOut Dad®*, program, an evaluation study demonstrated that there were statistically significant changes among program participants in terms of fathering confidence, knowledge, attitude, and contact with children compared to the control group (Steven et al. 2014).

Additionally, NFI has other programs such as *FatherTopics Booster Sessions* (e.g., non-custodial dads, maternal gatekeeping, communications, and domestic violence). Moreover, NFI provides online certificate programs that are affordable and accessible on-demand such as *Father Engagement Certificate* and *Effective Facilitation Certificate*. For instance, *Father Engagement Certificate* includes the five core elements of how fathers effectively engage their children's lives: foundational, program design, recruitment and retention, involving moms, and fundraising. NFI also offers other resources such as posters, pocket guides brochures, and tip cards (National Father Initiative, n.d.).

Kwangman Ko

See also: Absent Father; Father Support Groups; Nonresidential Father

Further Reading

Concha, Maritza, Maria Elena Villar, Rocio Tafur-Salgado, Sandra Ibanez, and Lauren Azevedo. 2016. "Fatherhood Education from a Cultural Perspective: Evolving Roles and Identities after a Fatherhood Intervention for Latinos in South Florida." *Journal of Latinos and Education* 15, no. 3: 170–179. http://dx.doi.org/10.1080/15348431.2015.1099532

Gordon, Derrick M., Arazais Oliveros, Samuel W. Hawes, Derek K. Iwamoto, and Brett S. Rayford. 2012. "Engaging Fathers in Child Protection Services: A Review of Factors and Strategies across Ecological Systems." *Children and Youth Services Review* 34, no. 8: 1399–1417. https://doi.org/10.1016/j.childyouth.2012.03.021.

Lewin-Bizan, Selva. 2015. *24/7Dad® Program in Hawaii: Sample, Design, and Preliminary Results*. Honolulu, HI: University of Hawaii at Mānoa.

National Father Initiative. n.d. "Educating and Equipping Communities to Engage Fathers." Accessed September 1, 2019. https://www.fatherhood.org

Solomon-Fears, C. 2015. *Fatherhood Initiatives: Connecting Fathers to Their*

Children. Washington, DC: Congressional Research Service.

Steven, Block, Christopher A. Brown, Louis M. Barretti, Erin Walker, Michael Yudt, and Ralph Fretz. 2014. "A Mixed-Method Assessment of a Parenting Program for Incarcerated Fathers." *Journal of Correctional Education* 65, no. 1: 50–67.

Neurodiversity and Marriage

A neurodiverse marriage or mixed neurological marriage is a relationship between a normally developing person and a person diagnosed with a diverse neurobiology, such as being on the autism spectrum, which is just one example of neurodiversity. The exact number of neurodiverse couples is unknown, as many people are diagnosed in adulthood, after they are already married. Those who have high-functioning autism (autism without intellectual or language impairment) suffer from a neurodevelopmental disorder that affects the person's communication and, hence, their social interactions (Janai and Arad 2018). Attention Deficit Hyperactivity Disorder (ADHD) may be another form of neurodiversity, with the person also having issues with communication or social interactions. When the couple has different ways of thinking, communicating, and socializing, it may lead to problems in a marriage. Diagnosis and treatment may help with the understanding of the disorder, and may facilitate empathy, compassion, and understanding in the normally developing person. Often, no diagnosis is ever made, which makes it even more difficult to find understanding or resources, such as therapy (Janai and Arad 2018). Adding to the complexity, marriages can be mixed or have two neurodiverse partners.

There is no clear consensus on when neurologically based human behavior goes from normal to pathological. For 20 years, the scientific community has found that many disorders of the brain or mind are not just weaknesses, but also strengths (Armstrong 2015). In the last few decades, the United States has moved to recognize neurological differences as diversity rather than a defect in the brain's make up. This paradigm shifts from a "disability" perspective to a "diversity" perspective that takes into account strengths and weaknesses, along with the notion that this diversity can be positive, brought forth the term *neurodiversity* from the autism rights community. This complemented the use of biodiversity and cultural diversity movements, already in use in their respective scientific communities (Armstrong 2015). There is still a lack of evidence-based information focusing on how persons who are neurodiverse can be best supported, especially through mating and marriage. Any person who is helping a neurodiverse couple should do so with the understanding that any approach should be rooted in the knowledge that neurodiverse youth may have very complex gender narratives and need affirmation and support. For example, a male may be very set on what a man is supposed to do in a relationship; it is part of his story to be a certain way as that is what he has seen/read/been explained.

There are barriers in mixed neurological relationship, such as lack of flexibility toward their partner, awareness of communication, and understanding the needs of others (Janai and Arad 2018; Pearlman-Avnion, Cohen, Eldan 2017). Couples in mixed-neurological relationships often struggle with communication issues. From a theoretical perspective, communication barriers in mixed neurological relationships can be understood through Expectancy Violation Theory, a theory of communication that evaluates how individuals respond to unexpected violations of social norms. In these mixed neurological relationships, couples face many communication incompatibilities related to the differences in their brains and become more vulnerable to domestic abuse with both partners being vulnerable to trauma (Janai and Arad 2018). Being vulnerable to abuse, especially psychological is often very dangerous for couples in mixed neurological relationships which increases the need for therapy services.

Individuals with high-functioning autism, or other forms of neurodiversity, often marry without their partner's knowledge of their autism (Janai and Arad 2018). For those who do know their partner has autism, this can create feelings of compatibility in the beginning of the relationship. The couple will often find a sense of balance in the differences between them. Typically, developing partners may feel their skills (i.e., social and communication) are of value and may enjoy helping their partners with autism in this area (Janai and Arad 2018). Partners with autism may feel comfortable with typically developing people as relationship tutor capacity. The typically developing partner may have a heightened awareness of others' perspectives and needs that can help the partner with autism to navigate relationships. They may initially feel their partner seems to understand and accept them in ways others cannot (Janai and Arad 2018). The most commonly used marriage therapy techniques are not feasible with neurodiverse partners or a mixed-neurological marriage (Lorant 2012). Because such techniques are based on emotion-focused, reciprocal communication about feelings, they often are not appropriate for someone who has trouble with these pieces of social interaction. While the functioning of marital relationships has been widely studied, there is a lack of evidence-based research for how to work with neurologically mixed couples. Cognitive behavioral approaches that focus on changing thoughts, behaviors through practice, may be a better fit for these couples.

Julia M. Bernard and Audrey Besch

See also: Divorce, Causes/Risk Factors of

Further Reading

Armstrong, Thomas. 2015. "The myth of the normal brain: Embracing neurodiversity." *AMA Journal of Ethics* 17, no. 4: 348–352.

Austin, Robert D. and Gary P. Pisano. 2017. "Neurodiversity as a competitive advantage." *Harvard Business Review* 95, no. 3: 96–103.

Ben-Naim, Shiri, Inbal Marom, Michal Krashin, Beatris Gifter, and Keren Arad. 2017. "Life with a partner with ADHD: The moderating role of intimacy." *Journal of Child and Family Studies* 26, no. 5: 1365–1373.

Ersoy, Mehmet A., and Hatice Topçu Ersoy. 2019. "Gender-role attitudes mediate the effects of adult ADHD on marriage and relationships." *Journal of Attention Disorders* 23, no. 1: 40–50.

Hode, Marlo Goldstein. 2014. "Just another Aspie/NT love story: A narrative inquiry into neurologically-mixed romantic relationships." *Interpersona: An International Journal on Personal Relationships* 8, no. 1: 70–84.

Irvine, Karen. 2019. "Facing neurotypical normativity: An ethical call for therapeutic sensitivity to neurodiversity." Lesley University.

Janai, Anne and Pnina Arad. 2018. "An introduction to mixed-neurological marriage." http://mixedneurological.com/wp-content/uploads/2019/07/Beginners-Guide-for-ASD-Partner.pdf

Lorant, Jennifer B. 2012. "Impact on emotional connectivity in couples in which one partner has Asperger's syndrome." Alliant International University.

Pearlman-Avnion, Shiri, Noa Cohen, and Anat Eldan. 2017. "Sexual well-being and quality of life among high-functioning adults with autism." *Sexuality and Disability* 35, no. 3: 279–293.

Strunz, Sandra, Constanze Schermuck, Sarah Ballerstein, Christoph J. Ahlers, Isabel Dziobek, and Stefan Roepke. 2017. "Romantic relationships and relationship satisfaction among adults with Asperger syndrome and high-functioning autism." *Journal of Clinical Psychology* 73, no. 1: 113–125.

van Schalkwyk, Gerrit Ian. 2018. "At the intersection of neurodiversity and gender diversity." *Journal of Autism and Developmental Disorders* 48: 3973.

90 Day Fiancé

90 Day Fiancé is a reality television dating "docu-series" that first aired on TLC on January 12, 2014. The show documents couples going through the K-1 visa process, which is a route for foreign nationals to marry American citizens. According to the K-1 visa process, the couples have 90 days to marry in the United States before the visa expires and the foreign fiancé must leave the country. The show began, as reported in the *Reality Life* podcast, when reality TV producer Matt Sharp came across an article in a magazine on Americans going abroad to find marriage partners. He then pitched the idea to TLC, which picked up the show. Although the show first aired in 2014, the K-1 visa dates back to the 1970 Public Law 91-225 amendment to the Immigration and National Act of 1952.

As of August 2019, seven seasons with a total of 70 episodes have aired on American television. Across these seasons, viewers witness culture shock, rejection and skepticism from family and friends of the couple. *90 Day Fiancé* is classified as a reality "living" show. Although focused on relationships, it shares less in common with reality "dating" shows because the show is not designed to introduce couples or play matchmaker in a game format, but rather to document the lives of individuals already in a romantic relationship. The couples met, either online or in-person, prior to applying to be on the show, so they are not introduced by casting directors. The couples on the show apply through the *90 Day Fiancé* Website and. if interested, the show reaches out to them. The show is also unique in its exhibition of the complexities of international romance, while showing the differences between couples. Like many other reality shows, couples receive payments per episode, with reported payments being between $500 and $1,500 per episode.

The cultural importance of *90 Day Fiancé* is that it introduced audiences to the many different obstacles, both cultural and legal, faced by people in cross-national relationships. Culturally, there are many language and social barriers that the couples face on the show. In many instances, the international partner is stigmatized as a mail order bride or characterized as solely focused on pursuing marriage to obtain a green card. Additionally, there are several partners who are depicted as "gold diggers." The motives of both partners are continuously discussed and challenged across the seasons and situations presented. Additionally, the program documents challenges of long-distance relationships and the logistics of communicating and moving across the world. Romantically, the show ultimately reveals whether the 90-day period leads to marriage. Legally, the show often highlights challenges related to legal status of the non-American partner.

As a reality television series, the program also presents scenes that are staged for audiences or that couples may not feel accurately display their relationships. For instance, Mark Shoemaker, an American partner on the show, sued Sharp Production and TLC's parent company, Discovery Communications, for what he felt like was an unfair depiction of him and his relationship. The court ruled that the couples signed contracts that allowed the show editing rights.

Despite these challenges, executive producer Matt Sharp notes that the divorce rate of couples on the show is lower than the current divorce rate in the United States. This may, however, also be attributed to legal factors surrounding the K-1 visa process. More specifically, the couples have to marry within 90 days to receive their green cards or risk deportation and once married, they have to stay married at least two years to not lose their green card. The green card obtained through the K-1 visa process comes with conditions and does not equate to citizenship. After three years as a green card holder, individuals can apply for naturalization if they can demonstrate they have been living in marital union with an American partner. There are ample websites dedicated to updating fans on the relationship status of past stars.

The show has also led to several spin-off shows to provide fans with updates on past couples and to introduce new couples in similar situations, albeit sometimes at different relationship stages: *90 Day Fiancé: Happily Ever After?*; *90 Day Fiancé: Before the 90 Days*; *90 Day Fiancé: What Now?*; *90 Day Fiancé: Pillow Talk*; *90 Day Fiancé: The Other Way*; and *The Family Chantel. 90 Day Fiancé: Happily Ever After?* first aired September 11, 2016 and followed select *90 Day Fiancé* couples to document their post-marriage struggles. As the name suggests, this docu-series, which has aired for four seasons from 2016–2019, follows five or six couples each season.

Additionally, eight couples are featured on a single season of *90 Day Fiancé: Happily Ever After?*. The second spin-off series, *90 Day Fiancé: Before the 90 Days*, first aired in August 2017. Whereas the original *90 Day Fiancé* followed couples going through the K-1 visa process focusing on the 90 days leading to marriage (or not) in the United States and *90 Day Fiancé: Happily Ever After?* focused on marriage after the K-1 visa process, *90 Day Fiancé: Before the 90 Days* is a docu-series focuses on relationships prior to the start of the K-1 visa process. The third spin-off series, *90 Day Fiancé: What Now?*, was announced in March 2017 by TLCgo, uploaded online July 30, 2017, and aired September 17 and 24th, 2017 as combined segments. A second and third series aired in 2018 and 2019, respectively. The *What Now?* Series provided updates on couples from other *90 Day Fiancé* and spin-off shows. In April 2019, TLC aired *90 Day Fiancé: Pillow Talk*, which featured previous cast members commenting on and reacting to Season 6 of *90 Day Fiancé*. On June 3, 2019, TLC aired *90 Day Fiancé: The Other Way*, which followed Americans moving abroad to be engaged. Finally, the Family Chantel, which aired July 22, 2019 is the only *90 Day Fiancé* spin-off to focus on a single couple, Season 4's Pedro and Chantel.

Candace Forbes Bright

See also: Dating and Courtship 2000–Present; International Marriage; Mail-Order Brides

Further Reading

"About 90 Day Fiancé." TLC 90 Day Fiancé. Accessed at https://www.tlc.com/tv-shows/90-day-fiance/about

Bennett, Margaret E. 2015. "How Real is Reality?: An Examination of Perceived Realism and Permissive Sexual Attitudes in Relation to Reality Dating Shows." *Theses* 56. https://irl.umsl.edu/thesis/56

Meszaros, Julia. 2018. "Race, Space, and Agency in the International Introduction Industry: How American Men Perceive Women's Agency in Colombia, Ukraine and the Philippines." *Gender, Place & Culture* 25.2: 268–287.

Nonresidential Fathers

Contemporary custody agreements typically grant one parent more physical custody, or time spent co-residing, of their children than the other parent and outline a visitation schedule for the parent with less physical custody. This parent, also called the "nonresidential parent," may have visitation with their children every weekend or other weekend and one evening during the week. Specifics of visitation agreements can vary widely; however, a common thread these parents experience is not living with their children all or most of the time (Braithwaite and Baxter 2006). In this case, these nonresidential parents have less physical time with their children than the residential parent or caregiver.

While it is common for the terms *nonresidential* and *noncustodial* to be used interchangeably in conversation, these are two very different parental statuses. A nonresidential parent has less physical, co-residential time with their children; however, they could still retain their full custodial rights over their children, whereas *noncustodial* refers to parents that no longer have legal rights over their children. A noncustodial parent may or may not have regular visitation with their child, but either way, they do not possess the legal authority to make decisions about and for their children regarding things like healthcare and education. A nonresidential parent, on the other hand, maintains their legal, custodial rights to participate in parental decision-making processes. Therefore, it is not accurate to use the terms *nonresidential* and *noncustodial* interchangeably and the rest of this entry will address the experiences of nonresidential fathers.

Both popular press representations of nonresidential parents and the social scientific research on nonresidential parents, normalize and emphasize the experiences of nonresidential fathers. Historically, legal precedent more often than not granted residential parenting status to mothers, which, by default, created a larger population of nonresidential fathers than nonresidential mothers. According to the U.S. Census Bureau, in 2009 82% of nonresidential parents were nonresidential fathers. While nonresidential mothering has become more and more common since the 1980s, fathers still make up the vast majority of this parenting group. This majority, paired with more commonly seen representations of nonresidential parents as fathers in popular media and even within one's own social circle, mean nonresidential fathers are more socially accepted than nonresidential mothers; however, these fathers can still be stereotyped. These stereotypes of nonresidential fathers are likely the consequence of traditional or institutionalized views of parents that claim fathers "should" live with their children as well as stigma attached to "Deadbeat Dads"; however, a Deadbeat Dad actually refers to the father that does not pay court-mandated child support. Just because a father is nonresidential, that does not mean he has been court-ordered to pay child support and even if he has, it does not mean he is in default of those payments.

The most pervasive stereotype of nonresidential fathers is that of the "Disneyland Dad" (Stewart 1999). Disneyland Dads are nonresidential fathers who emphasize fun at the expense of real-world tasks, like homework and chores. Instead of engaging in common daily parenting practices such as enforcing the rules, assisting with homework, and requiring their children to do chores around the house, Disneyland Dads spend their visitation time engaged in entertainment and other fun activities. While not all of these dads are taking their children to Disneyland, a father could still be considered a "Disneyland Dad" if he is taking his children to the movie theater, go-carting, sporting events, shopping, and other activities that are of entertainment value. This stereotype negatively impacts perceptions of nonresidential fathers because they are seen as the "fun parent" who is not really engaged in many of the parenting practices society deems as instrumental in the raising of children. This means that while dads get to be the "fun parents," residential mothers are then required to be the "real parents" by engaging in the parenting behaviors these fathers are skipping out on at the expense of engaging in entertainment over real-life. The Disneyland Dad stereotype is problematic for several reasons. First, not all nonresidential fathers engage in entertainment-based activities at the expense of other activities. In these cases, the Disneyland Dad stereotype does not actually apply. In other cases, this stereotype oversimplifies the motivation of nonresidential fathers who engage in entertainment-based activities during visitation time. These fathers are not necessarily using entertainment as a way to curtail their parental responsibility but are engaging in these activities because they want to make the most of the limited time they get to spend with their children. These fathers report only seeing their children a few days out of the month and therefore want to pack in as much activity and fun as they can during this time. In these cases, fathers are trying to make the most of their limited time because they want to be able to enjoy their children, not because they don't want to do the work being a parent requires. This illustrates how their nonresidential status can impact the way fathers spend time with their children.

Another common nonresidential fathering experience is paying child support. In American culture, traditional gender roles identify men as the primary breadwinners or providers. Historically, this gendered expectation has influenced how society views the paternal role. While mothers are seen as nurturers, fathers are largely seen as financial providers. Child support is a primary means through which society believes nonresidential fathers should still engage with this fatherly responsibility. As a result, much of the research on nonresidential fathers has focused on various aspects of child support from how fathers make sense of this duty to statistical studies of the percentage of fathers that consistently pay their child support payments on time (Natalier and Hewitt 2010). While child support is one important means for nonresidential fathers to show ongoing responsibility for their children, and it could be indicative of paternal involvement, looking at child support payments alone often does not provide much information into the quality of their relationships with their children nor the variety of other ways in which these fathers participate as parents such as spending time with their children, providing them with emotional support, and being involved in their children's education and extracurricular activities to name a few (Kartch 2013).

Not all nonresidential parents stay actively involved in their children's lives for a variety of different reasons. The most common reasons for lack of nonresidential father involvement are: fathers' negative relationships with the residential mothers of their children (Dudley 1991; Kartch 2013), personal difficulties such as substance abuse (Dudley 1991), a large geographical distance between them and their children (Dudley 1991), children wanting to spend more time with friends and not as much time with their nonresidential fathers (Dudley 1991), and challenges utilizing technology to stay in contact with their children (Kartch and Timmerman 2015).

Falon Kartch

See also: Child Custody; Parenting Plans and Custody Arrangements; Nonresidential Mothers; Shared Custody

Further Reading

Braithwaite, Dawn O. and Leslie A. Baxter. 2006. "'You're My Parent but You're Not': Dialectical Tensions in Stepchildren's Perceptions about Communicating with the Nonresidential Parent." *Journal of Applied Communication Research* 34, no. 1: 30–48.

Braithwaite, Dawn O., Chad M. McBride, and Paul Schrodt. 2006. "'Parent Teams' and the Everyday Interactions of Co-Parenting in Stepfamilies." *Communication Reports* 16, no. 2: 93–111. https://doi.org/10.1080/08934210309384493

Dudley, James R. 1991. "Increasing Our Understanding of Divorced Fathers Who Have Infrequent Contact with Their Children." *Family Relations* 40, no. 3: 279–285.

Kartch, Falon. 2013. "Nonresidential Parenting: Parental Roles and Parent/Child Relationships." Phd diss., University of Wisconsin-Milwaukee.

Kartch, Falon and Lindsay M. Timmerman. 2015. "Nonresidential Parenting and New Media Technologies: A Double-Edged Sword." In *Family Communication in the Age of Digital and Social Media*, edited by Carol Bruess. New York: Peter Lang, pp. 447–468.

Natalier, Kristin and Belinda Hewitt. 2010. "'It's Not Just About Money:' Nonresidential Fathers' Perspectives on

Paying Child Support." *Sociology* 44, no. 3: 489–505. https://doi.org/10.1177/0038038510362470

Stewart, Susan D. 1999. "Disneyland Dads, Disneyland Moms? How Nonresidential Parents Spend Time with Absent Children." *Journal of Family Issues* 20, no 4: 539–556. https://doi.org/10.1177/019251399020004006

Nonresidential Mothers

In contemporary custody agreements, it is common for one parent to receive more physical custody of their children than the other parent. Physical custody refers to the time a child spends living under the same roof as their parent. These custody agreements typically determine a visitation schedule for parents to follow. It is common for the parent with less physical custody, who is referred to as the nonresidential parent, to have visitation with their children every other weekend, or sometimes every other weekend and Wednesday evenings. While the specifics of visitation agreements can vary widely, the common thread these parents experience is not living with their children all or most of the time (Braithwaite and Baxter 2006). In this case, these nonresidential parents have less physical time with their children than the residential parent or caregiver.

While it is common for the terms *nonresidential* and *noncustodial* to be used interchangeably in conversation, these are two very different parental statuses. A nonresidential parent has less physical, co-residential time with their children; however, they could still retain their full custodial rights over their children, whereas *noncustodial* refers to parents that no longer have legal rights over their children. A noncustodial parent may or may not have regular visitation with their child, but either way, they do not possess the legal authority to make decisions about and for their children regarding things like healthcare and education. A nonresidential parent, on the other hand, maintains their legal, custodial rights to participate in parental decision-making processes. Therefore, it is not accurate to use the terms *nonresidential* and *noncustodial* interchangeably and the rest of this entry will address the experiences of nonresidential mothers.

While cultural perceptions suggest that mothers receive more physical custody of their children that is not always the case. In the past, it was common legal practice for residential status to fall to the mother following divorce, but that trend has been slowly shifting since the 1980s as paternal involvement started to become more emphasized. According to the U.S. Census Bureau, in 2009 18% of nonresidential parents were nonresidential mothers. While fathers still make up the largest population of nonresidential parents, these nonresidential mothers make up an important subset of nonresidential parents.

One can become a nonresidential mother in a variety of ways (Kielty 2008). Some mothers become nonresidential parents voluntarily for several reasons. First, some mothers feel that becoming a nonresidential parent will create less disruption in the day-to-day lives of their children. Second, some mothers report having ex-spouses with greater financial resources and are therefore better able to provide for their children. Other mothers become nonresidential parents involuntarily. For these women, their nonresidential status was a decision determined by the courts.

Being both a mother and nonresidential parent creates a unique experience for these women. In American culture, perceptions of femininity are tied to the appropriate display of gendered roles. While these gender roles include much more than parenting practices, parenting is one aspect of a woman's life in which gender roles outline expectations for the successful completion of the parental, or in this case, motherly, role. First off, "good women" according to these social norms, want to be mothers. Scholars have labeled this as the "mommy myth" (Douglas and Michaels 2004). According to the mommy myth, all women desire to be mothers and the role of mother is the most important role a woman will have in her lifetime. Mothering is elevated to the status of one's deepest calling in life. Since society has ascribed to this mommy myth, the expectation is to be a "good woman" one must desire to and eventually become a mother, but simply becoming a mother is not enough. Society also has expectations for how women will enact their mothering and these expectations include the notion that mothers should be with their children. Nonresidential mothers are, by definition, mothering outside of these established norms as these mothers are not with their children all or even most of the time. This creates a parenting experience for nonresidential mothers that differs from those of nonresidential fathers who are not presumed by society to want or need to be with their children all the time. Due to these societal expectations, nonresidential mothers have reported feeling shame, guilt, and isolation as a result of either direct judgment from family, friends, and others, or a perception that if people knew of their nonresidential status they would be judged. For these reasons, nonresidential mothers may perceive they lack access to social support resources. Nonresidential mothers also report a lack of understanding from others regarding their parenting status and being questioned by others as to what they "did wrong" to not be the residential parent.

There are other ways in which research shows the perspectives and experiences of nonresidential mothers and nonresidential fathers are not so different. When asked to describe their roles as parents, nonresidential mothers said while their roles can be limited, they see themselves as active participants, nurturers, providers, coparents, and sole parents (Kartch 2013). Nonresidential fathers, in the same sample, all reported these roles (Kartch 2013). While nonresidential mothers may face stigma, at least some nonresidential mothers and fathers have similar understandings of what their roles are as nonresidential parents. In the same study, nonresidential mothers were asked to describe their parenting practices. These mothers described the following parenting behaviors: involvement in their children's schooling, spending time with their children, keeping in touch with their children, financially providing, assuring their children, showing physical affection, providing emotional support, disciplining, teaching, coparenting, and involvement in their children's physical well-being. No differences emerged between nonresidential mothers and nonresidential fathers regarding these parenting practices. Research also indicates that both nonresidential mothers' and nonresidential fathers' ability to maintain relationships with their children is limited because of their periods of absence from one another, which impacts the content and quality of their parent/child interactions (Rollie Rodriguez 2014). These parents spend more conversational time catching up on what they missed in their children's lives during periods of separation. They also have to work harder to "extract" information from their children about what is going on in their lives and they report receiving more "highlights" from their children as opposed to detailed information about their lives (Rollie Rodriguez 2014). Nonresidential mothers and fathers also report the same challenges when using technology to communicate with their children (Kartch and Timmerman 2015).

Falon Kartch

See also: Child Custody; Parenting Plans and Custody Arrangements; Nonresidential Fathers; Shared Custody

Further Reading

Braithwaite, Dawn O., and Leslie A. Baxter. "'You're My Parent but You're Not': Dialectical Tensions in Stepchildren's Perceptions about Communicating with the Nonresidential Parent." *Journal of Applied Communication Research* 34, no. 1 (2006): 30–48.

Braithwaite, Dawn O., Chad M. McBride, and Paul Schrodt. 2006. "'Parent Teams' and the Everyday Interactions of Co-Parenting in Stepfamilies." *Communication Reports* 16, no. 2: 93–111. https://doi.org/10.1080/08934210309384493

Douglas, Susan J. and Meredith W. Michaels. 2004. *The Mommy Myth: The Idealization of Motherhood and How it has Undermined Women.* New York: Free Press.

Kartch, Falon. 2013. "Nonresidential Parenting: Parental Roles and Parent/Child Relationships." PhD diss., University of Wisconsin-Milwaukee.

Kartch, Falon and Lindsay M. Timmerman. 2015. "Nonresidential Parenting and New Media Technologies: A Double-Edged Sword." In *Family Communication in the Age of Digital and Social Media*, edited by Carol Bruess. New York: Peter Lang, pp. 447–468.

Kielty, Sandra. 2008. "Non-resident Motherhood: Managing a Threatened Identity." *Child and Family Social Work* 13, no. 1: 32–40. https://doi.org/10.1111/j.1365-2206.2007.00512.x

Rollie Rodriguez, Stephanie. 2014. "'We'll Only See Parts of Each Other's Lives': The Role of Mundane Talk in Maintaining Nonresidential Parent-Child Relationships." *Journal of Social and Personal Relationships* 31, no. 8: 1134–1152. https://doi.org/10.1177/0265407514522898

O

On-Again, Off-Again Relationships

On-again, off-again (on-off) relationships are characterized by romantic partners breaking-up and getting back together (Dailey et al. 2009). At least one breakup and renewal in a relationship are known as a "cycle," and some researchers reference on-off relationship patterns as *cyclical* or *relationship churning* (Halpern-Meekin et al. 2013a, 166). On-off relationships are very prevalent, with about 65% of people having experienced an on-off relationship at some point in their dating history (Dailey et al. 2009; Halpern-Meekin et al. 2013a), and between 30–45% of people's most recent or current relationship is cyclical in nature (Halpern-Meekin et al. 2013a). Partners in on-off relationships tend to break up and get back together at least 2.5 times, on average, ranging anywhere between one and ten times, with less than 1/3 of on-off partners reporting only one renewal (e.g., Dailey et al. 2009). People who are married or living together are less likely to break up and get back together than those in dating relationships, and those living together (but not married) are more likely to be in an on-off relationship than married couples (Halpern-Meekin and Tach 2013; Vennum, Lindstrom et al. 2014). Breaking up and getting back together in the early stages of a dating relationship increases the chances for subsequent breakups and renewals in the relationship (Vennum, Lindstrom et al. 2014),

including during marriage (Vennum and Johnson 2014). Similarly, partners are more likely to have sex with their ex if there have been previous breakups and renewals in the relationship (Halpern-Meekin et al. 2013a).

Partners in on-off relationships are significantly more likely to report psychological and physical aggression than partners in relationships who have not cycled (Halpern-Meekin et al. 2013b). On-off partners are more likely to report verbal abuse (64%) than those who have never broken up and renewed (42%) or who never got back together with their ex after a breakup (45%) (Halpern-Meekin et al. 2013b). Also, an average of 57% of on-off partners report physical conflict in their relationships, as compared to 27% of those who have never cycled in and out of their relationship (Halpern-Meekin et al. 2013b). On-off cycling is also associated with increased psychological distress, including anxiety and depressive symptoms (Monk, Ogolsky, and Oswald 2018).

Although little research has addressed whether certain types of people are more likely to engage in on-off relationships, it does not appear that on-off and noncyclical partners differ in their relationship dispositions (e.g, attachment orientations, implicit beliefs about relationships; Dailey, Zhong, Pett, Scott, and Krawietz, 2020). Having a disadvantaged background (e.g., minority race, lower education, experiencing financial hardship) is associated with cycling (Halpern-Meekin et al. 2013a; Vennum, Lindstrom et al. 2014), and partners in cyclical relationships are also more likely to cite childcare as a reason for living together (Vennum, Lindstrom et al. 2014).

Inertia theory (Stanley, Rhoades, and Markman 2006) is commonly used to understand what keeps partners stuck in this on-off dynamic by describing how partners can "slide" into the next steps in their relationship (e.g., cohabitation, renewals) rather than consciously and explicitly deciding to make relationship transitions. Anxiety tends to build when the current or future status of relationships are unclear, making it harder to talk about the relationship for fear one's partner will say something contrary to one's own expectations (Knobloch and Theiss 2011; Owen et al. 2014).

Partners in on-off relationships tend to avoid explicit discussion and decision-making (sliding) regarding their relationship more often than partners without an on-off history (Vennum, Lindstrom et al. 2014). Unfortunately, this sliding can result in relationships progressing with lower quality (due to less intentionality used in communication tactics, more uncertainty, more avoidance, etc.) while constraints to permanently ending the relationship continue to build over time, such as shared living space and friend groups, time invested, or even children (Stanley, Rhoades, and Markman 2006). If partners return to a relationship without clarifying how dedicated they are to improve the union, this may increase the chances that a lower quality relationship continues out of familiarity or constraints, rather than commitment.

Although on-off relationships come with a set of unique risks, there are positive components that should be noted.

On-off partners who are more explicit in discussing their relationship (e.g., relationship status, reasons for breaking up or getting back together) have similar levels of relationship quality when compared to non-cyclical partners. Some partners can use breakups and renewals as opportunities to improve their relationship or themselves (Dailey et al. 2013). On-off relationship cycling might also have certain benefits regarding parenting. For example, mothers having on-off relationships with their children's father is associated with greater father involvement as compared to when mothers form new relationships with other partners (Turney and Halpern-Meekin 2017). Accumulating evidence also suggests partners in on-off relationships are not as distressed by fluctuations in their relationships (e.g., fluctuating satisfaction) as partners without an on-off history, and it may be that people in on-off relationships expect or desire a certain level of instability in their partnership (Dailey et al. 2017).

There are a variety of recommendations for helping professionals (e.g., therapists, counselors, relationship educators) working to reduce the risks of on-off cycling (Washburn-Busk 2018). First, helping professionals can focus on interrupting on-off cycles by working with individuals in unstable unions to identify personal values and goals (short- and long-term) that will assist in intentional decision-making through relationship transitions. Additionally, assessing for why partners are committed (or feel obligated to stay) can elicit useful information and discussions to steer couples toward a more solidified dedication to one another and working on the relationship or to a finalized dissolution. For example, it is important to assess the degree to which partners' self-esteem hinges on their partner or their relationship, in addition to other external and internal constraints (such as a shared social network or apartment lease) that make a permanent breakup more difficult. Helping professionals can educate on-off partners about constraints and discuss alternative sources of support that can help facilitate clear, deliberate decision-making (Washburn-Busk 2018).

When working with on-off couples who are trying to improve the relationship, helping professionals should be attuned to communication styles and pursue-withdraw patterns that involve chronic avoidance of discussing relationship status or important relationship transitions. Helping professionals can assess for and educate individuals about how power imbalances between partners can impair healthy relationship behaviors and productive communication which can perpetuate sliding behaviors (Washburn-Busk 2018).

For partners who decide to permanently end the relationship, helping partners differentiate between "hard" and "soft" breakups is key in reducing the likelihood of another on-off cycle from taking place. Hard breakups are clear and direct, and soft breakups leave the relationship status more ambiguous and invite sliding behaviors into the relationship (Stanley 2013). Helping professionals might consider assessing for continued contact with exes and educating clients about how continued contact is a risk factor for sliding back into an on-off relationship (Halpern-Meekin et al. 2013a). Clinicians can also explore with clientele what core motivations (e.g., intrinsic vs. external) are driving breakups and

renewals to facilitate insight that promotes decision-making grounded in core values.

Michelle Washburn-Busk, Amber Vennum, René Dailey, and J. Kale Monk

See also: Dating, Technology and; Dating and Courtship 2000–Present; Relationships, Technology and; Unmarried Cohabitation

Further Reading

Dailey, René M., Brittani Crook, Nicholas Brody, and Leah LeFebvre. 2017. "Fluctuations in On-Again/Off-Again Romantic Relationships: Foreboding or Functional?" *Personal Relationships* 24: 748–767.

Dailey, René M., Andrea A. Mccracken, Borae Jin, Kelly R. Rossetto, and Erik W. Green. 2013. "Negotiating Breakups and Renewals: Types of On-Again/Off-Again Dating Relationships." *Western Journal of Communication* 77, no. 4: 382–410. doi: 10.1080/10570314.2013.775325.

Dailey, René M., Abigail Pfiester, Borae Jin, Gary Beck, and Gretchen Clark. 2009. "On-Again/Off-Again Dating Relationships: How Are They Different from Other Dating Relationships?" *Personal Relationships* 16, no. 1: 23–47. doi:10.1111/j.1475-6811.2009.01208.x

Dailey, René M., Lingzi Zhong, Rudy Pett, Darby Scott, and Colton Krawietz. 2020. "Investigating Relationship Dispositions as Explanations for On-again/off-again Relationships." *Journal of Social and Personal Relationships* 37, no. 1: 201–211.

Halpern-Meekin, S., Wendy D. Manning, Peggy C. Giordano, and Monica A. Longmore. 2013a. "Relationship Churning in Emerging Adulthood: On/Off Relationships and Sex with an Ex." *Journal of Adolescent Research* 28, no. 2: 166–188. doi:10.1177/074355841246452-4.

Halpern-Meekin, S., Wendy D. Manning, Peggy C. Giordano, and Monica A. Longmore. 2013b. "Relationship Churning, Physical Violence, and Verbal Abuse in Young Adult Relationships." *Journal of Marriage and Family* 75, No. 1: 2–12. doi: 10.1111/j.1741-3737.2012.01029.x.

Halpern-Meekin, Sarah, and Laura Tach. 2013. "Discordance in Couples' Reporting of Courtship Stages: Implications for Measurement and Marital Quality." *Social Science Research* 42, no. 4: 1143–1155.

Knobloch, Leanne K. and Jennifer A. Theiss. 2011. "Relational Uncertainty and Relationship Talk Within Courtship: A Longitudinal Actor-Partner Interdependence Model." *Communication Monographs,* 78, no. 1: 3–26.

Monk, J. Kale, Brian G. Ogolsky, and Ramona F. Oswald. 2018. "Coming Out and Getting Back In: Relationship Cycling and Distress in Same- and Different-Sex Relationships." *Family Relations* 67, no. 4: 523–538. Advanced online publication. https://onlinelibrary.wiley.com/doi/full/10.1111/fare.12336.

Owen, Jesse, Galena Rhoades, Brad Shuck, Frank D. Fincham, Scott Stanley, Howard Markman, and Kayla Knopp. 2014. "Commitment Uncertainty: A Theoretical Overview." *Couple and Family Psychology: Research and Practice* 3, no. 4: 207–219.

Rhoades, Galena K., Scott M. Stanley, and Howard J. Markman. 2010. "Should I Stay or Should I Go? Predicting Dating Relationship Stability from Four Aspects of Commitment." *Journal of Family Psychology* 24, no. 5: 543–550.

Stanley, S. 2013. "The Soft Breakup." *Sliding vs. Deciding: Scott Stanley's Blog,* August 7, 2013. Retrieved from http://slidingvsdeciding.blogspot.com/2013/08/the-soft-break-up.html.

Stanley, Scott M., Galena K. Rhoades, and Howard J. Markman. 2006. "Sliding Versus Deciding: Inertia and the Premarital Cohabitation Effect." *Family Relations* 55, no. 4: 499–509. doi: 10.1111/j.1741-3729.2006.00418.x.

Turney, K. and Sarah Halpern-Meekin. 2017. "Parenting in On/Off Relationships: The Link Between Relationship Churning and Father Involvement." *Demography* 54, no. 3: 861–886.

Vennum, Amber, Nathan Hardy, D. Scott Sibley, and Frank D. Fincham. 2015. "Dedication and Sliding in Emerging Adult Cyclical and Non-Cyclical Romantic Relationships." *Family Relations* 64, no. 3: 407–419.

Vennum, Amber, and Matthew D. Johnson. 2014. "The Impact of Premarital Cycling on Early Marriage." *Family Relations* 63, no. 4: 439–452. DOI:10.1111/fare.12082.

Vennum, Amber, Rachel Lindstrom, J. Kale Monk, and Rebekah Adams. 2014. "'It's Complicated': The Continuity and Correlates of Cycling in Cohabitating and Marital Relationships." *Journal of Social and Personal Relationships* 31, no. 3: 410–430. doi: 10.1177/0265407513501987.

Washburn-Busk, Michelle. 2018. "An Exploratory Study of Change Mechanisms for Ambivalence Reduction in Young Adult Cyclical Relationships." MS thesis, Kansas State University.

Open Marriage

Open marriage is a form of ethical, consensual non-monogamy. The term *open marriage* is varied enough to be under the umbrella of consensual non-monogamy based upon the primary couple opening their primary relationship to sexual contact with others. Couples choose to open their marriage for a variety of reasons, including sex, relationship orientation, and additional romantic pursuits. The most common form of open marriage is when a married couple takes on one or more additional partners, which always remain secondary to the primary married couple. The couple can take on an additional partner together, or the couple can separately choose additional partners. Multiple configuration options are available, completely dependent upon the needs and terms of the married couple. There is no one way to open a marriage. That said, for a marriage to open up requires a significant amount of communication and negotiations in advance of taking on a new partner(s). While no couple completely accounts for every possible scenario in advance, a foundation of agreements needs to be in place. Decisions around time, money, coming out to others or not, sharing information about other partners, and safe sex practices are a few examples of decisions made before taking on new partners. More questions exist to establish the initial foundation of expectations; even more, negotiations occur as situations arise over time. The couple revisits and renegotiates their agreements multiple times. How the agreement exists between the couple ranges.

Open marriage is often mistakenly conflated with infidelity (Conley et al. 2013, 2). Open marriages are constructed on a carefully created and communicated set of boundaries and understandings between the primary couple and the additional partners. Infidelity is a nonconsensual non-monogamy, as not all parties involved are aware of and agree to additional partners (Kleinplatz and Diamond 2014, 253).

Open marriage is also known as monogamish, a term coined by famous author and podcast host Dan Savage (The Ezra Klein Show 2023). Monogamish, like open marriage, begins with an established primary couple that is mostly monogamous with varying degrees of sexual contact with other partners based upon boundaries determined by the primary couple. Other related, but not synonymous, relationship terms are swinging, polyamorous, polyfidelitous, and anarchist relationships (Sheff 2013; Levine et al. 2018, 2). Polyamory is a form of consensual non-monogamy in which a person establishes emotionally and/or sexually intimate relationships with multiple persons simultaneously (Sheff 2013). Polyfidelity is a group of three or more individuals participating in an egalitarian, closed relationship (Easton and Hardy 2017). The term anarchist relationship is a throwback to early 19th-century free lovers; those who practiced free love were seen as destroyers of the social and moral order due to their disregard for monogamy and traditional marriage (Koenig 2004, 200). These terms also fall within the umbrella of consensual non-monogamy, and sometimes include primary married couples participating in these alternative relationship configurations.

Anthropologists George and Nena O'Neill (1972) proposed that open marriages are relationships in which the partners commit to their own and each other's growth, flexible in allowing for change, constantly negotiating for changing needs, have a consensus in decision making, a tolerance for individual growth, and openness to new possibilities. Open marriages are a departure from conformity of established marital roles. Open marriages can often be undertaken for sexual release and not intended to be an ongoing emotional relationship outside of the marital relationship. Alternately, Sari van Anders (2015) constructed the Sexual Configurations Theory. Sexual Configurations

Theory posits that a person can receive primary sexual or emotional needs from one primary partner (the spouse) while being oriented to having multiple sexual or nurturance partners outside of the marriage. This relationship orientation is not unlike a person's sexual orientation, as it is a piece of their identity.

Open marriages are not a new construct. Consensually nonmonogamous marriages have a long history, dating back to ancient Greece, Italy, China, Africa, Rome and England (Kleinplatz and Diamond 2014, 253). Open marriages also have a wide presence in various non-Western and indigenous cultures (Coontz 2005, 10, 20, 26). While the idea of an open marriage is not new, more attention is being paid to the construct as more people are willing to share their relationship configuration publicly.

Some critics equate open marriages, both historically and currently, with a lack of personal and sexual morality. There are ongoing political debates that open marriages and other forms of consensual non-monogamy are about promiscuity and classifies nonmonogamous relationships as sexually immature (Conley et al. 2013, 4). Marriage provided economic stability to the female and the offspring (Perel 2007, 175). With economic stability and procreation no longer requiring marriage, the focus of marriage has shifted to the equitable satisfaction of its partners (Green et al. 2016, 416; Perel 2007, 178–179).

Hard data on how many marriages identify as open is hard to find. Current research suggests that anywhere between 4 and 20% of the U.S. population identifies as consensually nonmonogamous; 1.7% of that identifies as an open marriage (Conley et al. 2012, 126; Levine et al. 2018, 3). Another article currently shows up to 4% of the U.S. population identify as an open marriage (Conley et al. 2012). However, those percentages come with limitations. One limitation is that due to social stigma and political debate, a couple may be reticent to identify as an open marriage. Fear of loss of support, judgment, and potential job loss are a few reasons why a couple may keep their relationship status quiet. Another limitation is that the couple could identify more as a swinger or a polyamorous couple and be married, thus not identifying with the relationship status of open marriage for data purposes. Research on consensual non-monogamy tends to focus mostly on polyamory as a whole, sometimes to the detriment of empirical data regarding open marriages specifically. Polyamorous persons in data are typically white and affluent, which does not account for people of color or those that are not middle and upper-middle class. Another consideration is that not all open marriages remain open for the duration of the marital relationship. Based upon needs of the marital couple, needs of other partners, or lifespan stages, the marriage can vacillate between an open and closed status over its lifetime.

Anthropologists George and Nena O'Neill (1972) state that open marriages teach and reinforce living for the now, having realistic expectations within relationships, a sense of privacy, role flexibility, open and honest communication, open companionship, a sense of equality, personal identity, and trust for those involved. Research conducted by Conley et al. (2012) shows that open marriages have overall higher relational satisfaction and higher levels of communication. Couples participating in open marriages tend to have reflexive, more plastic views of marriage (Green et al. 2016, 422–424). Reflexive views on marriage means that the couple is open to finding what works for their specific relationship needs rather than adhering to strict monogamy guidelines due to external expectations (Green et al. 2016, 422). Plastic views on marriage refers to the malleability of addressing each individual's needs within the relationship (Green et al. 2016, 424). While open marriages are sometimes viewed externally as less healthy by some critics, there is no proven truth to that belief. Further, open marriages tend to their sexual health better, exercise more condom use, and seek out more frequent STI testing (Conley et al. 2012, 127–129).

There can be some disadvantages to opening a marriage. If the couple is not in agreement about pursuing an open marriage, or if one partner is not fully invested in the process, negative consequences could occur for the marital relationship and their potential partners. Opening a marriage requires communication, trust, and honesty between the primary couple; if there is a lack of trust or transparency, the primary and secondary relationships will suffer. As in all relationships, there is the potential for breakups and subsequent heartbreak. Social stigma and negative attitudes pervading society about nonmonogamous relationships cause negative feelings, prevent the couple from being open and honest about their situation for fear of consequence or retribution. Bias against nonmonogamous persons exist on many societal levels. People fear losing friends or jobs. Doctors are not educated on being socially sensitive to nonmonogamous persons; implicit and explicit bias occur around sexual health with multiple partners or who is present if one of the partners is ill. While not all potential disadvantages lie within the marital couple, all factors play a role in the success or failure of opening the marriage.

Karen Washington

See also: Infidelity; Monogamy; Polyamory; Polygamy

Further Reading

Conley, T. D., Moors, A. C., Matsick, J. L., and Ziegler, A. 2013. "The Fewer the Merrier?: Assessing Stigma Surrounding Consensually Non-Monogamous Romantic Relationships." *Analyses of Social Issues and Public Policy* 13, no. 1: 1–30. Doi: 10.1111/j.1530-2415.2012.01286.x

Conley, T. D., Ziegler, A., Moors, A. C., Matsick, J. L., and Valentine, B. 2012. "A Critical Examination of Popular Assumptions about the Benefits and Outcomes of Monogamous Relationships." *Personality and Social Psychology Review* 17, no. 2: 124–141. Doi: 10.1177/1088868312467087

Coontz, S. 2005. *Marriage, a History.* New York: Penguin Books.

The Ezra Klein Show. 2023. "Opinion | Dan Savage on Polyamory, Chosen Family and Better Sex." *The New York Times*, January 10, 2023, sec. Opinion. https://www.nytimes.com/2023/01/10/opinion/ezra-klein-podcast-dan-savage.html.

Green, A. I., Valleriani, J., and Adam, B. 2016. "Marital Monogamy as Ideal and Practice: The Detraditionalization Thesis in Contemporary Marriages." *Journal of Marriage and Family* 78: 416–430. Doi: 10.1111/jomf.12277

Hardy, J. W. and Easton, D. 2017. *The Ethical Slut, Third Edition: A Practical Guide to Polyamory, Open Relationships, and Other Freedoms in Sex and Love.* Berkeley: Ten Speed Press.

Kleinplatz, P. J. and Diamond, L. M. 2014. "Sexual Diversity." *APA Handbook of Sexuality and Psychology*, edited by D. L. Tolman and L. M. Diamond, 487–522. American Psychological Association.

Koenig, B. 2004. "Law and Disorder at Home: Free Love, Free Speech, and the Search for an Anarchist Utopia." *Labor History* 45, no. 2: 199–223. DOI: 10.1080/0023656042000217255

Levine, E. C., Herbenick, D., Martinez, O., Fu, T-C., and Dodge, B. 2018. "Open Relationships, Nonconsensual Nonmonogamy, and Monogamy Among U.S. Adults: Findings from the 2012 National Survey of Sexual Health and Behavior." *Archives of Sexual Behavior* 47, no. 5: 1439–1450. doi: 10.1007/s10508-018-1178-7

O'Neill, N. and O'Neill, G. 1972. "Open Marriage: A Synergic Model." *The Family Coordinator* 403–409.

Perel, E. 2007. *Mating in Captivity*. New York: Harper Publishing.

Savage, D. 2011. *Monogamish*. Savage Love. July 20, 2011. https://savage.love/savagelove/2011/07/20/monogamish/

Sheff, E. 2013. "What Polyamory Is—and What It Is Not." Retrieved from: https://www.psychologytoday.com/us/blog/the-polyamorists-next-door/201309/what-polyamory-is-and-what-it-is-not

van Anders, S. M. 2015. "Beyond Sexual Orientation: Integrating Gender/Sex and Diverse Sexualities via Sexual Configurations Theory." *Archives of Sexual Behavior* 44, no. 5: 1177–1213.

P

Parallel Parenting

Coparenting after a divorce or separation is common in America and is built upon a foundation of collaboration, mutual support, and respectful communication to make shared decisions regarding a child's upbringing. However, coparenting is difficult under circumstances involving post-divorce parental conflict (e.g., one parent exhibits narcissistic or borderline personality disorders, power and control issues, or other forms of toxic behavior). When domestic violence has been clearly established, courts usually intervene. However, in the majority of families struggling with continued post-divorce conflict, many courts do not factor in toxic behavior when deciding legal and physical custody. Instead, courts opt for shared custody and coparenting after divorce, allowing conflict to continue often resulting in the toxic parent abusing the coparenting relationship to harass, threaten, or sabotage the coparent.

Toxic parents exhibit many forms of hostile communication ranging from belittling comments (e.g., daily emails criticizing the coparent's lifestyle) to intimation (e.g., continual texts to the coparent threatening to file for full custody) to using triangulation or a third party who acts as a proxy to carry out harassment (e.g., spreading rumors, or contacting Child Protective Services with false allegations).

Given that it is more difficult for children to navigate and cope with negative emotions of anger, fear, and sadness, previous researchers have consistently demonstrated that post-divorce parental conflict adversely affects the children's well-being and self-esteem, resulting in increased rates of depression and aggressive behavior. Moreover, children who grow up witnessing interparental conflict are more likely to exhibit or tolerate abuse in their own subsequent dating relationships.

While the recommended approach for a victim of hostile communication is to follow a "no contact" order thereby removing any possible physical or emotional control from the abuser, in a shared custody situation requiring coparenting "no contact" is impossible. In order to navigate shared custody and disengage from repeated harassment with a toxic parent, and protect the children, parallel parenting is the recommended approach.

Parallel parenting is a relatively recent parenting strategy, first introduced in the 1980s, whereby the parents maintain not only separate households but separate parenting as they raise their children in parallel and disengage in physical contact and communication as much as possible (Furstenberg 1988). In parallel parenting, only the fundamentals (e.g., exchanges, medical information, and educational information) are communicated between the parents, and any information regarding personal life, parenting philosophies, and home life is eliminated. As courts are favoring shared custody more and more each year, the need to parallel parent may also increase with each court ruling.

While coparenting a child requires shared communication and a flexible approach to navigating children's educational, physical, emotional, and social development, toxic individuals thrive on creating disruptive environments. When one parent seeks to actively sabotage the other, firm boundaries rather than flexible strategies must be consistently employed. Parallel parenting requires a detail-oriented custody order to prevent any potential for miscommunication or sabotage. For example, the specific days of the visits or exchanges complete with times, locations, who is responsible for transportation, and specific provisions for holidays, school closures, and illness must all be outlined.

Triangulation is when one or both parents involved in conflict involve a third party. Since triangulation of using a new partner to harass the coparent is a common tactic among toxic parents, additional clauses regarding no third-party interference in making major decisions or attending parent-teacher or school meetings may also be needed. Further clauses are often recommended to include the nature of communication regarding children sleeping over at non parental homes. Moreover, procedures must be outlined in the event of a dispute between the parents over medical, educational, or religious decisions. These procedures generally involve attending coparenting counseling or legal mediation to help resolve conflicts and avoid repeated lengthy and costly returns to court.

As many toxic parents lack empathy, violate boundaries, and seek power and control over the coparent (American Psychiatric Association 2013), once they lose control over the coparent they often attempt to control the coparent's emotions. Therefore, their initial response to parallel parenting may be an increase in harassment, triangulation, and false threats to produce an emotional reaction from the coparent. While rare, violent threats to physically harm or kill should be immediately reported to the police. However, the majority of toxic parents use psychological manipulation tactics that, while abusive, are permitted within the parameters of the legal system. Common tactics employed by toxic parents may include gaslighting, which is distorting reality in an attempt to cause the coparent self-doubt, and projection, which is accusing the coparent of their own misbehavior. Since conflict is gratifying to toxic parents, additional strategies aid in the continued success of parallel parenting which include Justify, Argue, Defend, or Explain (JADE) and the Gray Rock Method.

First introduced by Al-Anon, a support program for family members impacted by alcoholism, JADE is a technique employed to disengage in conflict and minimize arguments. To create conflict, toxic parents routinely falsely accuse coparents of poor parenting, irresponsible behavior, and child abuse via email or text. If the coparent responds to these allegations, the conflict continues, and the toxic parent will likely then continue that harassment. To prevent this cycle and succeed in parallel parenting, coparenting should not justify actions, disengage in arguing, not defend behavior, and not explain the truth. While these types of harassment and insults from the toxic parent must be ignored, the communication should be documented for any future court evidence.

The Gray Rock Method ("Gray rock method" n.d.), first introduced in dealing with individuals with personality disorders, is a form of communication to eliminate stalking and harassment by removing any emotional response. Gray Rock employs minimal responses that are boring and monotonous. Within parallel parenting, Gray Rock limits communication to facts and dates regarding fundamental information while everything else is eliminated (e.g., no sharing information of personal life, successes, or small talk, no asking any questions, and no discussion of the past). Given that toxic parents thrive on conflict, repeated use of Gray Rock can result in the reduction of repeated attempts of unwanted communication.

In a high conflict post-divorce relationship, researchers have consistently shown that parallel parenting results in an improvement in adjustment for children in comparison to coparenting (Whiteside 1998). By minimizing physical contact and communication, parenting separately in independent households, parallel parenting is a recommended technique to reduce ongoing conflict.

Gayle T. Dow

See also: Child Custody; Coparenting and Divorce; Intimate Partner Violence

Further Reading

American Psychiatric Association. 2013. *Diagnostic and statistical manual of mental disorders (DSM-5®)*. American Psychiatric Pub.

Dowell, Marilyn R. 2011. *Compassion for Annie: A healthy response to mental disorders*. Hillcrest Publishing Group.

Furstenberg, Frank F., Jr. 1988. "Child care after divorce and remarriage." In E. M. Hetherington and J. D. Arasteh (Eds.), *Impact of divorce, single parenting, and stepparenting on children* (pp. 245–261). Lawrence Erlbaum Associates, Inc.

"Grey rock method: What it is and how to use it effectively." n.d. Medical News Today. MediLexicon International. Accessed June 8, 2023. https://www.medicalnewstoday.com/articles/grey-rock.

Katz, Lynn Fainsilber, and John M. Gottman. 1996. "Spillover effects of marital conflict: In search of parenting and coparenting mechanisms." *New Directions for Child and Adolescent Development* 74: 57–76.

Kinsfogel, Kristen M., and John H. Grych. 2004. "Interparental conflict and adolescent dating relationships: Integrating cognitive, emotional, and peer influences." *Journal of Family Psychology* 18: 505–15.

Kreger, Randi, and Bill Eddy. 2011. *Splitting: Protecting yourself while divorcing someone with borderline or narcissistic personality disorder*. New Harbinger Publications.

Whiteside, Mary. 1998. "The parental alliance following divorce: An overview." *Journal of Marital and Family Therapy* 24: 3–24.

Parent Education Programs

Many child-rearing practices have evolved over the 20th century, as various disciplines such as pedagogy, psychology, and counseling have found more distinct professional identities. Parenting programs exist not only with parents and their children in mind, but also any relationship involving responsible adults overseeing children of various ages. Coparents, educators, foster parents, social workers, and other family-oriented professionals who carry the best interests of families at heart can benefit greatly from formal guidelines concerning these vital mentoring relationships between adults and children (birth through adolescence to young adulthood).

In an effort to systematize and implement these practices and provide guidelines for constructive parenting interactions, parenting programs mushroomed. In the English language alone, there are thousands ranging from the exemplary to the outright harmful. Various efforts have been initiated to introduce standards of best practice and outcome-based points of accountability, based on research. Parenting programs can target special population groups, for instance children with vulnerabilities, disruptive and destructive behavior patterns, addictive disorders, attachment challenges, teens in conflict with the law, adolescent parents, and many more.

The parenting programs lean heavily on the major theoretical approaches represented within counseling and psychology. Programs evolve to reflect current best practices, bearing ethical principles in mind when interacting with underage and vulnerable demographic groups. The following broad theoretical approaches pertain, although in reality several approaches have been integrated successfully: Cognitive behavioral, Social learning, Relationship-based, and Multimodal approaches.

In the late 1990s, the Pew Charitable Trusts published a report summarizing major federal initiatives and educational programs pertaining to parenting practices (Carter and Kahn 1996). Post millennium, the efforts were on a larger scale and focused on comprehensive registries. For example, the *National Registry of Evidence-based Programs and Practices* (NREPP), established by the U.S. Department of Health and Human Services in 1997, was dismantled 20 years later.

There are about a dozen major registries, often linked to research centers. Programs typically have to meet several criteria including evidence-based practices based on quality research, and readiness for dissemination. SAMHSA (Substance Abuse and Mental Health Services Administration), serves as a resource center for evidence-based practices in a variety of contexts, especially mental illness. The University of Colorado Boulder houses *Blueprints for Healthy Youth Development*. The University of Wisconsin-Madison publishes *What Works: Effective Prevention Programs for Children, Youth and Families*. The U.S. Department of Health and Human Services provides extensive information at their *Child Welfare Information Gateway*. These are but three examples from an extensive list, which can be accessed in an entry on Family-based Prevention Programs (Small and Huser 2016), published in the Encyclopedia of Adolescence. Increasingly exemplary parenting programs are offered in other languages, including Spanish. Websites dedicated to general principles and research promoting good parenting practices are also helpful. One such site is *Center on the Developing Child* by Harvard University. Additionally, a selection of ten highly ranked evidence-based parenting programs is presented in a book titled, *Evidence-based Parenting Education* edited by James Ponzetti (2016).

As this is a constantly evolving field, family-related professionals need to be aware that newer developments may be in the offering, and that the resources mentioned in this entry may be neither definitive nor exhaustive.

Clara Gerhardt

Further Reading

Bigner, Jerry J. and Gerhardt, Clara. 2019. "Parenting approaches." In *Parent-child Relations: An Introduction to Parenting.* 10th ed. New York: Pearson.

Carter, N. and Kahn, L. 1996. *See How We Grow: A Report on the Status of Parenting Education in the U.S.* Philadelphia, PA: Pew Charitable Trusts.

Ponzetti, James J., Jr., ed. 2016. *Evidence-based Parenting Education: A Global Perspective.* New York: Routledge.

Small, Stephen A. and Huser, Mary. 2016. "Family-based prevention programs." In Levesque, Roger J. R. (ed.), *Encyclopedia of Adolescence.* New York: Springer. DOI: https://doi.org/10.1007/978-3-319 -32132-5_161–2.

See also: Ackerman Institute for Family Therapy; Coparenting Typologies; Divorce Education

Parental Alienation

Parental alienation is the common catch-all name for various phenomena where a child who has formerly had an adequate relationship with a parent begins to resist or refuse to spend time with that parent without an identifiable or rational cause. These phenomena are seen as a rare result of ongoing family dysfunction following separation or divorce, and they differ from estrangement, where there are real reasons for a child resisting contact with a parent. These two phenomena (alienation and estrangement) are not always categorically distinct, as with children who display disproportionate or unreasonable responses to a flawed parent.

A unifying thread encountered in cases involving alienation dynamics, also referred to as resist/refuse dynamics, is that the non-resisted parent (often referred to as the favored parent or preferred parent) conveys negative emotional information regarding the resisted parent to the child, setting up a dynamic where the child's resistance is encouraged and reinforced. Such action by the preferred parent is not always intentional. Lack of awareness on the part of the preferred parent about their own negative impact on the child's relationships may inadvertently lead the preferred parent to blame the resisted parent for increased family conflict, further cementing the negative emotional information the preferred parent communicates to the child. In other cases, such action by the preferred parent is intended to disrupt the child's relationship with the resisted parent, alienating the child's affection for that parent (hence the name for the phenomenon).

Historically alienation came to light in the treatment community through these latter types of cases, where children's resistance to contact was seen clinically as the result of a malicious parent with poorly managed emotions. While such extreme examples were useful in initially identifying and exploring this phenomenon, in the broader society there is a significant amount of nuance seen from case to case and extremely divergent conceptualizations of the process of and treatment for alienation.

Warshak (2015) offered one of the most succinct and overarching descriptions of the characteristics of parental alienation when he noted, "The children's treatment of the rejected parents is disproportionate to those parents' behavior and is inconsistent with the prior history of their affectionate and close relationships" (p. 118). In evaluating issues of alienation, the aspects of disproportionality and history are critical. In the half-century, since the concept was proposed, there has been significant professional debate over the conceptual validity and even the very existence of parental alienation. Much of this stems from researchers and practitioners in the fields of domestic violence and child abuse, who routinely saw abusive parents claim that their children's fear of them and resistance to contact with them was not due to their physical or psychological violence, but rather due to alienation by the parent who had been their victim. On the face of it, such claims by abusive parents clearly reverse cause and effect; however, it is often profoundly difficult to distinguish competing allegations during the course of contentious divorce and child custody disputes. At the same time, claims of interpersonal violence may be a tool of alienation, indoctrinating a child to make false outcries against a responsible and genuinely caring parent. Indeed, even the leading child maltreatment prevention group in the western hemisphere, the American Professional Society on the Abuse of Children, notes "one possible explanation for the false allegation may be an attempt to alienate the child from a parent. Significant evidence of intentional indoctrination by a parent should be considered in determining the best interest. Such indoctrination is a form of psychological maltreatment" (p. 5).

Intervention and treatment for cases of parental alienation remains controversial even as understanding and acceptance of such behaviors continue. This is partially due to the issue being both a legal and behavioral health problem. On the legal side of the issue is the compliance of parents with orders for the contact between

the child and both parents, contact which, by definition, the court has found to be in the best interests of the child or children in question. Children may arguably dislike having to transition from one parent's home to their other parent's home for a variety of developmental reasons (e.g., one parent being more geographically isolated from the child's peer group, less stringent parental rules in one of their homes, general dislike of changes in routine, etc.), however, most parents are sufficiently competent to ensure their children go where directed. Common examples of this are parents who can get their children to the pediatrician's office (even when the child might get a shot or have other unpleasant procedures), or the dentist (where many children deeply dislike routine cleanings, to say nothing of having cavities filled), or even school (where children may be at odds with teachers or peers they would rather not deal with). In these cases, parents understand both the short and long-term consequences of failing to have their children's needs met. They may not understand the need to have their children spend time with their other parent, even when a court has found it is also in their children's best interests to do so. In cases where alienating behavior is unintentional, or even in cases of mild but intentional alienation, rapid enforcement of clear court orders may produce rapid change. While the alienating parent may not understand why contact with the child's other parent is necessary (or indeed, may disagree with the court on this issue), rapid enforcement can produce compliance with the court's order before the alienation dynamic becomes fully entrenched. While a child might be no more interested in that contact, or might even be somewhat resistant, this does not escalate to outright refusal. In mild cases where children have previously refused contact, rapid enforcement of the court orders can motivate an alienating parent to change their approach and secure the child's compliance as the parent now makes contact with the child's other parent no more optional for the child than school attendance or dental checkups. Rapid court response is critical as without it the alienating parent may see that they can ignore the court's order with impunity and feel empowered to continue doing so. Whether theirIons are naive or intentional, the lack of corrective action on the court's part endorses such behavior. It is also clear, from studies of compliance with court orders, that the existence of mild consequences that are applied in a predictable in swift fashion are the most effective approach to gaining compliance. When court decisions are long-delayed or the possibility of consequences for failure to follow through on orders is uncertain, compliance is less likely as people are simply not as sensitive to the possibility of some vague future consequence, no matter how dire that might be.

At the same time behavioral interventions may be helpful in addressing the underlying issues for both children and parents. It is important that interventions be targeted toward the level of issues that are occurring. In theIest and most naive cases, basic parent education courses (as required in many jurisdictions for divorcing parents) may be effective at helping parents see past their obvious dislike (as generally one does not divorce when one is happy with one's spouse) of their coparent. As these parents learn of the normal reactions of children to divorce and how to help transition to a healthy post-divorce coparenting relationship, they may come to understand the long-term issues that make healthy coparenting as important for their children as a good educational experience or physical health. In cases where the alienating behaviors are less mild or more intentional therapy may be helpful for both parents and children involved. Often parents challenge the basic notion that there is a need for treatment, however it is clear from decades of research that children caught in difficult post-separation conflicts may neglect their own needs to foster a relationship with the favored parent. This is particularly true as such children age and fail to establish identities separate from the conflict dynamic. Poorly managed parental conflict results in other negative child outcomes, and there is increased risk of long-term behavioral health issues such as depression due to parental absence. Particularly when there are issues of negative behavior from both parents, the favored parent can gain insight into how their alienating behaviors are damaging to their child, while the resisted parent can gain insight into how their suboptimal responses fuel the child's resistance. Both parents can learn new skills and techniques for addressing their children's issues in a healthy manner, and they can be taught to work together for their mutual goal of raising healthy children in a post-divorce family system. In egregious examples of intentionally alienating behavior traditional family therapy approaches are generally not recommended. This stems from the essential fact that a parent who is intentionally alienating is generally disinterested in the insight-oriented change process of traditional therapy. When the goal for a parent is not correcting behavioral problems that exist, but rather removal of the other parent (who has been defined the problem), more specialized treatment may be necessary. Here is where the greatest controversy exists in the field, as logistical approaches with these families may be quite limited in traditional outpatient settings, and most therapists are not forensically trained to deal with such profound issues. While some specialized treatment programs have been developed to deal with the most extreme cases of alienation, the quality of the information on the effectiveness of these programs varies greatly.

In extreme situations, where both court intervention and behavioral health services fail to ameliorate alienating behaviors, there are a handful of profound interventions which are discussed in the professional literature. One of these extreme options is the change of parenting time by the court so that the preferred parent has no contact with the child and the rejected parent cares for the child full time ("rejected" parent is used here, as such cases involve far more negative behaviors than simple resistance to contact). Such an arrangement may be for a pre-defined short period of time, or it may be conditioned on various longer term therapeutic interactions. Such an approach may remove some of the family tensions by profoundly altering the dynamic between child and preferred parent but may be difficult on the child as their social ties and routine are significantly disrupted. Along the same lines when children cannot be placed in the care of the rejected parent an additional option is placement of the child away from both parents in a therapeutic boarding school or similar program. In such a setup the rejected parent has a supportive environment through which to reestablish a healthy relationship with the child, while the child has a chance to

separate from an alienating parent and establish a more reality-centered view of their family system. Finally, some alienated parents choose a strategy of "letting go" in the hopes of re-establishing a relationship when their children once the children reach adulthood. While there are some initial accounts of the successes and challenges with such an approach, studies of their population are limited, with outcomes that seem highly situationally dependent.

Aaron Robb

See also: Child Abuse; Maternal Gatekeeping; Toxic Relationships

Further Reading
American Professional Society on the Abuse of Children (APSAC). 2016. *APSAC position paper on allegations of child maltreatment and intimate partner violence in divorce/parental relationship dissolution.* Columbus, OH: Author. Retrieved from www.APSAC.org

Darnall, Douglas. 2008. *Divorce casualties* (2nd ed.). Lanham, MD: Taylor Publishing Company.

Eddy, Bill. 2010. *Don't alienate the kids!* Scottsdale, AZ: HCI Press.

Warshak, Richard. 2010. *Divorce poison* (2nd ed.). New York: HarperCollins Publishers.

Warshak, Richard. 2015. "Parental alienation: Overview, management, intervention, and practice tips." *Journal of the American Academy of Matrimonial Lawyers* 28: 181–248.

Parenthood, Transition

The transition to the parenthood is the timeframe from when the child's arrival is anticipated until the end of the child's first year of life. The transition can come in many forms. A couple may have their own biological child through the pregnancy of one partner or a surrogate. In the United States, there are almost 4 million children born each year (Martin et al. 2018, 3). Individuals or couples may also adopt a child domestically or internationally, with adoptions being open (where the biological parents are known, and some contact is maintained) or closed.

For many couples, the transition will be one of many normative transitions they will experience over the course of their lives. Normative transitions, such as the transition to parenthood, are often expected transitions that tend to occur at similar times for those in the same peer group. These types of transitions are ones in which individuals have time to prepare, are associated with rites of passage or rituals to celebrate them, and lead to changes in one's status (Grant and Ray 2018, 166). While the age at which one may become a parent may vary widely for men, most women experience parenthood at a similar time, with their peak reproductive years occurring during their 20s and early 30s (Martin et al. 2018). The transition for men and women may be a non-normative transition, if, for example, they unexpectedly experience becoming parents as teenagers. However, for many, the transition to parenthood is a planned event, with approximately half of all pregnancies being planned (Finer and Zolna 2016, 843). Parents expecting their own biological children also have 40 weeks of pregnancy to prepare for the transition. However, the transition may be non-normative if a couple unexpectedly takes on the custody of a family member's child in the case of a parent's sudden death. Finally, in modern society, a variety of rituals and rites of passage accompany the transition including gender reveal ceremonies, baby showers, and religious ceremonies such baptisms, christenings, bris, and naming ceremonies. Hence, for many, becoming a parent is a normative life transition.

While bringing a child into a family may bring a great deal of excitement and joy, it can also bring new challenges to the individual and the couple. Murray Bowen's family systems theory examines how changes in the family system influence the family unit, including individual expectations, roles, boundaries, and behavior (Kerr 2000). As individuals or partners become parents, they may have expectations regarding what it will be like to be a parent, including what it may be like to be a mother or a father. They may also have expectations or an idealized view of what their baby will be like, visualizing a "Gerber baby" with a big smile and an easy temperament. Individuals and partners may also have their own roles and responsibilities, both individually and as part of the couple, which need to be modified or adapted with the addition of a child to the family. Before having a child, both parents may work full-time and make equal financial contributions to support the couple and family. However, data from the U.S. Census Bureau (2017) finds that while most work during pregnancy, anywhere from 38.6–71.2% of new mothers, depending on their educational level, return to the workforce within 12 months. Hence, prior to the baby's arrival couples may have had an even division of household chores and responsibilities. As individuals and couples, they may also be free to pursue a variety of hobbies and leisure-time activities. However, as changes in roles, time demands, employment status, career focus, and earning potential occur, adjustments may need to be made.

Having a new baby may make it difficult to maintain these roles, responsibilities, and commitments. The developmental changes that characterize infancy make the ability to successfully adapt to change paramount, as this developmental period brings with it the most rapid period of growth and change in human development. While the transition may bring with it joy and excitement, it also brings with it a host of physical demands, emotional stresses, and an increased financial burden for individuals and couples. Having a new baby brings restrictions on your personal behavior, as individuals need to work together to meet the demands of a small creature who is dependent on them for their survival. With a lack of spontaneity, a couple's romantic and sexual relationship may also suffer. With no national policy for paid maternity leave, couples often need to negotiate the transition without the support of the other partner or coupled with financial hardships.

Deiner (2009) discusses several reasons the transition to parenthood is difficult, examining individual, dual, and social factors associated with the transition. For individuals, the transition to the parenting role and its demands may hurt their emotional functioning, including heightening their risk for depression, irritability, and fatigue. Hormonal changes women experience during the transition from pregnancy to the postpartum period may worsen these issues. For couples, the transition involves lifestyle changes that are permanent rather than temporary, including a loss of spontaneity and decreased time available to spend with one another. Socially, new parents may

experience changes in their relationships with friends, especially if they do not have children themselves. As couples establish their own family units, there may also be disagreement with family members regarding their parenting and caregiving choices, especially if they differ from other members of the family's practices.

They may also have trouble meeting expectations for parenting, both their own and societal ones. In modern U.S., societal expectations and perceptions put a great deal of pressure on parents to be "perfect." Parents of infants and toddlers are particularly affected, with survey data indicating 90% of mothers and 85% of fathers feel judged by others for their parenting behavior (Zero to Three and the Bezos Family Foundation 2016). How they manage this pressure is dependent upon whether the family system is open, adaptive to change, and willing to receive assistance (Kerr 2000). The quality of the couple's relationship before the child was born may also influence their adaptation. Bronfenbrenner's bioecological systems theory highlights the interplay between child, parent, and couple relationships. How one weathers the change and transition is determined by the quality of the couple's relationship before the transition and characteristics of the child. Research suggests having similar values or ideals, effective communication, and a positive, constructive perspective on their partner and solving problems bodes well for parental adaption (Brooks 2008). Hence, relationships that are stressed are not likely to be "saved" by having a baby. Having a child who is born premature, medically fragile, with a disability, or with a challenging temperament may make it more difficult for new parents to adapt. Those who adopt or have a child born prematurely may experience the transition abruptly and with less time to prepare (Brooks 2008).

Having a child involves changes to the individual, family, and life course (White and Klein 2008). Individuals and families need strong support networks, communication skills, and problem-solving strategies as they make the transition to parenthood. Brooks (2008) reviews a variety of different models of intervention to assist families with the transition including childbirth education and parenting classes offered through local hospitals and community service agencies and couples' groups, such as those utilized in Cowan and Cowan's (2000) Becoming a Family Project. A national policy supporting both paid maternal and paternal leave may also decrease some of the stresses associated with the transition, allowing parents to have the time to negotiate the transition and bond with their infant without experiencing financial hardship.

Patricia Hrusa Williams

See also: Parenthood, Unmarried; Planned Parenthood; Relationship Education

Further Reading

Brooks, Jane. 2008. *The Process of Parenting* (7th ed.). New York: McGraw-Hill.

Cowan, Phillip and Carolyn Pape Cowan. 2000. *When Partners Become Parents: The Big Life Changes for Couples.* Mahwah, NJ: Erlbaum.

Deiner, Penny Low. 2009. *Infants and Toddlers: Development and Curriculum Planning* (2nd ed.). Clifton Park, NY: Delmar Cengage.

Finer, Lawrence B., and Mia R. Zolna. 2011. "Unintended Pregnancy in the United States: Incidence and Disparities, 2006." *Contraception* 84, no. 5: 478–485. https://doi10.1016/j.contracecption

Finer, Lawrence B., and Mia R. Zolna. 2016. "Declines in Unintended Pregnancy in the United States, 2008–2011." *New England Journal of Medicine* 374, no. 9: 843–852.

Grant, Kathy B. and Julie A. Ray, eds. 2018. *Home, School, and Community Collaboration: Culturally Responsive Family Engagement.* Sage Publications, 2011.07.013.

Kerr, Michael E. 2000. "One Family's Story: A Primer on Bowen Theory." The Bowen Center for the Study of the Family. http://www.thebowencenter.org.

Martin, Joyce A., Brady E. Hamilton, Michelle J. K. Osterman, Anne K. Driscoll, and Patrick Drake. 2018. "Births: Final Data for 2017." *National Vital Statistics Reports* 67, no. 8 (November): 1–49.

U.S. Census Bureau. 2017. *Labor Force Participation by Education, Women Ages 15 to 50 with a Birth in the Past 12 Months.* American Community Survey. Washington, DC: Author.

U.S. Census Bureau. 2022. "About the American Community Survey." Census.gov, June 2, 2022. https://www.census.gov/programs-surveys/acs/about.html.

White, James M., and David M. Klein. 2008. *Family Theories* (3rd ed.). Thousand Oaks, CA: Sage.

Zero to Three and the Bezos Family Foundation. 2016. *Parents of Young Children Tell Us What They Think, Know, and Need.* Washington, DC: Author.

Parenthood, Unmarried

In 2017, 25% of parents were unmarried; this number has more than tripled since the 1960s (Pew Research Center 2018). Unmarried parenthood may occur due to childbearing outside of marriage or because of changes in family structure due to divorce. While it is commonly assumed that most unmarried parents function as single or solo parents, data from the Pew Research Center reports that 35% actually live or cohabitate with a partner, with rates of solo or single parenting down from 88% to 53% since the 1960s. Some sources place the rate of unmarried, cohabitating parenthood as high as 58% (Child Trends 2014). Unmarried partnerships may be comprised of heterosexual or same-sex couples who live together or apart, varying in commitment to one another, and raising their children without being legally married.

Increases in unmarried parenthood in the United States may be due to several factors. First, there has been an overall increase in births to women who are not married. In the United States, 39.8% of births are to unmarried women (Martin et al. 2018, 5); this is 10 times higher than in 1940 (Congressional Research Service 2014, 24). However, these rates are not due to a rise in teen pregnancy as one might assume. Martin et al.'s (2018, 6) data show the rate of unmarried, teenaged pregnancy has been on the decline, with 7.7% of births to those ages 15–17 years old. However, their data also reveals the rate of unmarried childbearing for those between the ages of 35–39 has reached its highest point in history, with 36% of unmarried births to this age group. Increased access to contraception, family planning services, and sex education has led to decreases in unplanned pregnancy rates, especially for adolescents. However, reproductive technologies such as artificial insemination and in vitro fertilization have opened up the possibilities for parenthood to older women, especially those who have established their careers but have not yet found a partner.

They have also assisted same-sex families in their quest for parenthood.

Second, marriage rates have been on the decline in the U.S.; even when couples marry, they are also doing so later (Congressional Research Service 2014, 3; Pew Research Center 2018, 5). As such there may be less societal and family pressure for expectant couples to marry or for couples to have "shotgun weddings." This is a term popularized to denote marriages that were caused by a woman's pregnancy to protect her honor or reputation. These marriages often occurred due to family pressure, especially from the woman's father. Popular media depictions of expectant and parenting unmarried couples, such as those shown on television programs such as *16 and Pregnant, Teen Mom, Single Parents,* and *Murphy Brown* reflect changing views associated with unmarried parenthood.

Finally, significant increases in unmarried parenthood may be due to increased access to and acceptability of divorce in the United States. While the divorce rate may vary by the age and socioeconomic status of couples, 40–50% of marriages will end in divorce. there has been a dramatic increase in the number of children who will live with an unmarried parent from 13% in 1968 to 32% in 2017 (Pew Research Center 2018, 4). Hence, almost one-third of children will spend some of life living in a single-parent family. These rates reflect changes in America's ideas about marriage and the need for couples to "stay together for the sake of the children" (Congressional Research Service 2014, 3).

While it is important to remember that children can thrive in a multitude of different family structures and configurations, there are some concerns about unmarried parenthood and specific challenges faced by this population of parents and children. First, pregnancies, where the partners are not married, may be unplanned or unintended. Rates of unplanned pregnancy are higher in those who are unmarried (81%) or cohabiting (61%) than in those who are married (28%) (Finer and Zolna 2011). Unplanned pregnancies may bring with them financial challenges and change the school, career, and life plans for one or both partners, at least in the short-term. All of these factors may increase the stress experienced by couples who are not legally bound to one another.

Second, unmarried parenthood brings with it many challenges to the economic well-being of the newly formed family. A major research study by Princeton University has followed approximately 5,000 of these "fragile families." The study's goal was to better understand how non-marital childbearing affects parents and children. Findings from the study suggest greater overall economic disadvantage, including increased reliance on federal and state income assistance programs (McLanahan 2011). There are variations in the poverty rate for unmarried parents. Data reported by the Pew Research Center (2018) finds those parenting solo are at higher risk for living in poverty (27%) than those who are cohabiting (16%) or married (8%). Further, their data suggests that educational disparity potentially contributes to income disparity, with unmarried parents, whether solo or cohabiting, being two times less likely to have a bachelor's degree (15–20%) than those who are married (43%).

Finally, relationship instability and the role it may have on individual and children's well-being are concerns. Data from the Fragile Families Study finds that many unmarried couples are unable to maintain their relationships over time. McLanahan (2011) reports that five years after a child's birth only 35% of unmarried couples in the study remained living together, with 40% of mothers entering other relationships and 14% having a child with a different partner. With the dissolution of these relationships, there are also financial and legal challenges, especially for same-sex partners. When a married couple (whether heterosexual or same-sex) has a child, both partners are assumed to be parents. However, the same stipulation may not apply when the couple is unmarried. The National Center for Lesbian Rights (2019) discusses the need for fathers and non-biological same-sex parents to obtain a parentage judgment or maternity/paternity action to ensure their legal rights as a parent are protected. In some cases, they suggest second-parent adoption as a means to ensure both have a voice in visitation, child support, medical decision-making, and guardianship.

To promote the healthy development of relationships for both unmarried couples and their children, programs such as the Building Strong Families (BSF) program have been introduced. The goal of the BSF initiative is to develop programs that can help to prevent relationship dissolution and strengthen low-income, unmarried parents' relationships. Dion and Hershey's (2010) reviewed the relationship education curriculum used as part of Building Strong Families (BSF) programs. The curricula focused on the development of couple skills in the areas of communication, conflict resolution skills, and empathy, all skills needed to maintain healthy relationships.

Patricia Hrusa Williams

See also: Child Custody; LGBTQ Parenthood; Premarital Pregnancy; Shared Custody

Further Reading

Child Trends, Data Bank. 2014. *Births to Unmarried Women, Indicators on Child and Youth.* Washington, DC: Author.

Congressional Research Service. 2014. *Nonmarital Births: An Overview.* Carmen Solomon-Fears. Report No. 7-5700. Washington, DC: Author.

Dion, M. Robin and Alan M. Hershey. 2010. "Relationship education for unmarried couples with children: Parental responses to the Building Strong Families Project." *Journal of Couple and Relationship Therapy* 9, no. 2, 161–180. doi: 10.1080/15332691003694919

Finer, Lawrence B. and Mia R. Zolna. 2011. "Unintended pregnancy in the United States: Incidence and disparities, 2006." *Contraception* 84, no. 5: 478–485.

Finer, Lawrence B. and Mia R. Zolna. 2016. "Declines in untended pregnancy in the United States, 2008–2011." *New England Journal of Medicine* 374, no. 9: 843–852. doi: 10.1056/NEJMsa1506575.

Martin, Joyce A., Brady E. Hamilton, Michelle J. K. Osterman, Anne K. Driscoll, and Patrick Drake. 2018. "Births: Final data for 2017." *National Vital Statistics Reports* 67, no. 8 (November): 1–49.

McLanahan, Sara. 2011. "Family instability and complexity after a nonmarital birth: Outcomes for children in fragile families." In *Social Class and Changing Families in an Unequal America,* edited by Marcia Carlson and Paula England. Stanford, CA: Stanford University Press, pp. 108–133.

National Center for Lesbian Rights. 2019. *Fact Sheet: Legal Recognition of LGBT Families.* Washington, DC: Author.

Pew Research Center. 2018. *The Changing Profile of Unmarried Parents.* Gretchen Livingston. Washington, DC: Author.

Parenting Plans and Custody Arrangements

When parents decide to parent separately (i.e., in cases of divorce or nonmarital separation), family courts typically require a parenting plan to outline the specific details of how the parents will raise their children. The parenting plans will include details that center on legal decision-making authority, where the child(ren) will reside, and how the parents will communicate or resolve disagreements about the details of parenting. Once ordered by a judge, the parenting plan becomes the agreement that parents are required to follow. Violation of the rules may come with a penalty issued by the judge (e.g., contempt).

Parenting plans are often developed by lawyers, by the parents independently or jointly, with a divorce mediator, with a therapist, or when contested, ultimately by a judge. Parenting plans are intended to be created in the best interests of the child(ren) (Kisthardt 2004, 225). The clarity in the details of the plan can keep unnecessary communication and subsequent opportunities for debate or conflict to a minimum (Saposnek 2013). Parenting plans provide overall guidance for numerous areas of parenting such as reminding the child that the divorce is not their fault, limiting child exposure to parent conflict, allowing a child to have uninhibited phone contact with each parent, and how to handle birthdays. Given the increased need for stability for children of divorce (Sun and Li 2008), the ultimate goal of a parenting plan is to create a cohesive plan for how the parents will raise their child(ren) to increase that stability.

Changes to Parenting Plans

Though not frequently modified, due to the ever-changing family system, parenting plans may need to be renegotiated over time. Fears of conflict or drawn-out legal processes can deter many parents from considering changes; however, unique family or child needs may necessitate changes to the plan. Key factors include the age and stage of development as well as the unique cognitive or developmental needs of the child (e.g., intellectual and developmental disabilities). Researchers suggest special consideration be given to specific needs related to infants and toddlers and children diagnosed with ADHD, Autism Spectrum Disorder, or depression with attention to not only the parent's capability to meet the unique needs of the child but also to the sequencing of transitions between households that accounts for the developmental capacity of the child or for extra bonding or child adjustment time (Pickar and Kaufman 2015, 118). Other factors such as new living arrangements, parent changes in jobs, remarriages, child educational needs, changing parent salaries/child support, or boundary clarification are important to adjusting the parenting plans. The goal is for the parenting plan to provide structure but leave room for flexibility and review annually as needed. Other areas where a change may be needed would entail safety factors to address patterns of abuse (Jaffe et al. 2008, 504) with a clear call for parenting plans to screen/assess for and limit child exposure to parent and child abuse and/or neglect.

Custody Arrangements

One of the most important and, unfortunately, most fought-over areas of the parenting plan involve the decision for legal custody of the child(ren). The secondary component of custody involves physical custody, or where specifically the child will reside. Though not always awarded for numerous reasons, research demonstrates that children who reside with both parents between 35–50% of the time do best in terms of emotional health, academics, and behaviors (Nielsen 2014, 621). The main benefit for children in a shared custody arrangement is that they have a more active opportunity to form a bond and parent-child attachment with both parents. The parenting plan will often specify a schedule between the two parents' homes that may vary across families and needs but typically specifies consistency in the days, times, and details for transition.

Children in sole custody arrangements may live primarily with one parent and have standardized visitation (now termed "parenting time" to emphasize the process of parenting and the fact that the child has two homes over simply "visitation") with the other parent (e.g., spend every other weekend, extended holidays, or longer time during summers) or have a modified standardized visitation schedule if possible that, for example, includes a mid-week overnight stay. Other less common options for parenting time may include the child residing in the same home and the parents rotating in and out is called Bird's Nesting.

Principles of Parenting

Given the negative outcomes related to children's exposure to parent conflict (Amato and Cheadle 2008, 1), parenting plans should outline the basics of do's and do not's for parents. These principles may include details about not engaging in conflict in front of the child, not making derogatory remarks in front of the child, not putting the child in the middle, not quizzing the child about their other parent, and respect factors such as keeping each parent informed of changes to phone numbers, emails, etc., not using illegal substances in the presence of the child(ren), and informing the other parent about parent-teacher conferences or sharing school-related information (e.g., school picture orders, report cards).

Details for Coparenting

With regards to outlining the specific sections of the parenting plan and the agreements, specific details related to the availability and living arrangements of each parent, relationships between children and siblings or extended family/caregivers, and even parenting ability should be taken into account. From there, the parenting plan will outline how parents will manage the following details and unique considerations for each area:

- Specific parenting time scheduling and transition details: Clarifying rules for scheduling vacations each year (e.g., each child is provided one week with each parent during the summer) or other holidays (e.g., splitting spring break week; the child should be with their respective parent on Mother's Day and Father's Day; rotate Thanksgiving and Christmas holidays; etc.).

The parenting plan would do well to include details about how, when, and where visitation exchanges will take place. Parents can choose a neutral location or use the school schedule (e.g., official transition is at 8:30 am when the child goes to school) to assist in minimizing potential conflict (Warshak 2014).

- Rules for childcare (right of first refusal): How the parents will negotiate a parent temporarily unavailable to provide care for the children and when the other biological parent should have the first option to provide care for their child before any other caregiver (e.g., babysitter, family member).
- Education plans: How parents will decide where the child(ren) will attend school; how they will participate in parent-teacher conferences; how they will handle communication with the school/teachers and share school information (e.g., report cards, school picture order forms) with one another.
- Extracurricular activities: How parents will decide on which activities the child(ren) will participate in; how they will handle practices; how they will share expenses for activities.
- Child support payment details and schedule: How much a parent will pay the other parent to cover child-rearing expenses and when the payments are due.
- Health care guidelines/rules for managing insurance: Rules for which parent is required to carry the children's health insurance; how/when reimbursement for child healthcare expenses is made; specifics for coverage for minor (e.g., routine doctor visits) and major health issues (e.g., psychological

services, orthodontics, etc.); provisions for both parents to have to access to the child's medical records.

- Rules for social mores (no overnight guest): Clarifying rules for limiting children's exposure to parents' intimate relationships with new partners.
- Relocation clauses and travel restrictions: Rules for limiting each parent from relocating (e.g., outside of a radius) and limiting parent access to the child as well as rules for child travel out of the country, passport access, etc. Many parenting plans also reference the Uniform Child Custody and Jurisdiction Act, which includes details and rules for interstate custody and visitation.
- Other areas for parenting plan consideration: Rules for filing tax returns and claiming dependents; Rules for parent-child phone contact; consideration for children's birthday on neutral territory (rather than one of the parent's homes) or rules for including both parents; clarity on rules for discipline methods, the amount of computer/screen time, access to cell phones, the timing of dating, driving, college planning; equal access to child's birth certificates and social security cards; consideration for details after the child becomes a legal adult (e.g., financial support for college, continued health insurance coverage).

In sum, parenting plans are to clarify the rules for how parents will manage the details of coparenting. When parents struggle to develop the rules together, the courts will intervene and create a plan for the parents. However, parents can use available options for completing a parenting plan (e.g., online software, fact

sheets, divorce mediation, etc.). As a general rule, parents should be willing to informally review the parenting plans annually to ensure that the needs of everyone are being met adequately. Formal changes to the plan may include the need to have a judge review and finalize the order, but if done without disagreement between the parents, costs can be kept to a minimum.

Matthew Brosi, Ethan Jones,
and Todd Spencer

See also: Child Custody; Child Support Calculations; Shared Custody

Further Reading

Amato, Paul R. and Jacob E. Cheadle. 2008. "Parental divorce, marital conflict, and children's behavior problems: A comparison of adopted and biological children." *Social Forces* 86, no. 3: 1139–1161. doi: 10.1353/sof.0.0025

Fabricius, William V. and Linda J. Luecken. 2007. "Postdivorce living arrangements, parent conflict, and long-term physical health correlates for children of divorce." *Journal of Family Psychology* 21, no. 2: 195. doi: 10.1037/0893-3200.21.2.195

Jaffe, Peter G., Janet R. Johnston, Claire V. Crooks, and Nicholas Bala. 2008. "Custody disputes involving allegations of domestic violence: Toward a differentiated approach to parenting plans." *Family Court Review* 46, no. 3: 500–522. doi: 10.1111/j.1744-1617.2008.00216.x

Kisthardt, Mary Kay. 2004. "The AAML model for a parenting plan." *Journal of the American Academy of Matrimonial Lawyers* 19: 223.

Nielsen, Linda. 2014. "Shared physical custody: Summary of 40 studies on outcomes for children." *Journal of Divorce & Remarriage* 55, no. 8: 613–635. doi: 10.1080/10502556.2014.965578

Pickar, Daniel B. and Robert L. Kaufman. 2015. "Parenting plans for special needs children: Applying a risk-assessment model." *Family Court Review* 53, no. 1: 113–133. doi: 10.1111/fcre.12134

Saposnek, Donald T. 2013. "Ten tips for developing and drafting effective parenting plans in mediation." https://mediate.com/ten-tips-for-developing-and-drafting-effective-parenting-plans-in-mediation/

Sun, Yongmin and Yuanzhang Li. 2008. "Stable postdivorce family structures during late adolescence and socioeconomic consequences in adulthood." *Journal of Marriage and Family* 70, no. 1: 129–143. doi: 10.1111/j.1741-3737.2007.00466.x

Warshak, Richard A. 2014. "Social science and parenting plans for young children: A consensus report." *Psychology, Public Policy, And Law* 20, no. 1: 46. doi: 10.1037/law0000005

Planned Parenthood

The transition to parenthood is an eventful time that is both rewarding and burdensome for many families. Pregnancy circumstances may increase the demands of parenthood; some research suggests that potential stressors that couples face are associated with pregnancy planning. Past research suggests that one of the variables that could explain how couples manage the transition to parenthood is whether the pregnancy was planned or unplanned (Bouchard, Boudreau, and Hébert 2006). In 2012, there were a total of 213 million pregnancies with 40% being unplanned and 60% being planned (Sedgh, Singh, and Hussain 2014).

Researchers have used several terms to describe a pregnancy status. Barrett and Wellings (2002) proposed that the term *planned to* be used when four criteria are met: intending to become pregnant, stopping contraception, agreeing with a partner, and reaching the right time in terms of lifestyle or life stage. Other researchers refer to planned pregnancies as *intended* pregnancies. The terms *planned, unplanned, intended, unintended, wanted,* and *unwanted* are most commonly used to describe a pregnancy status (Barrett and Wellings 2002). These labels are used about pregnancy in health policy, health services, and health research (Barrett and Wellings 2002). The terms *planned, intended,* and *wanted* are used to describe a pregnancy in which a woman and her partner had discussed and agreed beforehand, that there had been a conscious decision to become pregnant, and/or it was a pregnancy where a long-term view had been taken into account with how the baby will fit into the mother's/couple's life (Barrett and Wellings 2002). Planned behavior framework informs pregnancy decision-making research. According to this framework, pregnancy intention is often associated with fertility-related behaviors (Ajzen 1991). Borrero and colleagues state, pregnancy planning "was described by most women as a very deliberate act in which both partners discuss and reach consensus about the timing of pregnancy, and then take steps to prepare for a potential pregnancy" (Borrero et al. 2015, 5). Couples planning a pregnancy often report striving for ideal circumstances, such as stability with finances and relationships (Borrero et al. 2015).

Researchers have examined trajectories of change for couples with planned and unplanned pregnancies for several years; previous research on the association between pregnancy planning and parenthood suggests variability among couples. Pregnancy intention (Buist, Morse, and Durkin 2003) may impact the outcomes of the transition to parenthood. Some research suggests that an unplanned pregnancy predicts greater declines in marital reports because of this being a time of stress and challenge (Cox et al. 1999). In contrast, it was found that in the case of planned pregnancies, women may have strong positive expectations of what it could be like to have a child (Cox et al. 1999). Similarly, a planned pregnancy is often perceived as a positive experience by couples (Bouchard 2005). Moreover, couples facing a planned pregnancy may have simple and romanticized expectations about what parenthood will be like (Pancer et al. 2000). To this end, some "couples facing planned pregnancies experience lower levels of functioning following than before the birth" (Bouchard et al. 2006, 1512). Past research suggests that couples facing planned parenthood may have underestimated the impact of the transition to parenthood on their life by having simple and romanticized expectations about parenthood (Bouchard et al. 2006, 1526). Research also indicates that couples with planned pregnancies had more positive pre-pregnancy marital satisfaction which can protect a marriage from marital declines (Lawrence et al. 2008). Additionally, it was found that husbands and wives who reported being satisfied with their marriages before pregnancy also present greater pregnancy planning (Lawrence et al. 2008). It was speculated that the couple who are oriented toward valuing strong social relationships may be more likely to invest in their marriage and make plans for when they want to have children and become parents (Lawrence et al. 2008). When a pregnancy is planned, couples can prepare themselves and discuss issues relevant to the impending birth (Theisen et al. 2019). These couples tend to have more positive interactions in contrast to those with unplanned pregnancies have more negative ones (Cox et al. 1999).

There are many common demographic trends seen in mothers who plan their pregnancies. They are typically older, married, and more educated (Kost and Lindberg 2015). Additionally, those who have planned their pregnancy may be more conscientious, agreeable, and less neurotic (Bouchard 2005). The women's characteristics are predictive of beneficial maternal behaviors and the health of the infant at birth (Kost and Lindberg 2015). The planning status of pregnancy may impact a woman's prenatal behaviors and the health of her newborn (Ayoola et al. 2010; Kost, Landry, and Darroch 1998). Early pregnancy recognition is correlated with increased odds of initiating prenatal care early on in the pregnancy (Ayoola et al. 2010). The planning status of a pregnancy can influence infant outcomes. For example, research shows a correlation between those who plan their pregnancy being carried out to full term and the baby being born with a normal birth weight. In contrast, those with an unplanned pregnancy are more likely to have premature births and the baby has a low birth weight (Ayoola et al. 2010; Kost, Landry, and Darroch 1998). A planned pregnancy has many benefits to the health of the infant both in and out of the womb as well as the mother's health. Pregnancy intention may be a contributing factor to postpartum depression (Mercier et al. 2013). Women with an unplanned pregnancy had an increased risk of postpartum depression when compared with women with a planned pregnancy (Mercier et al. 2013).

Borrero et al. (2015) completed a study with low-income women due to their high rates of unintended pregnancy. The study found four factors impeding the public health goal of increasing planned pregnancies. The first factor is that many women do not always formulate clear pregnancy intentions. This includes scenarios in which women had spontaneous (unplanned) sex and were under the influence of alcohol or drugs. More commonly, however, the lack of intention stemmed from the perceptions of their own reproductive control, meaning they felt as if they do not have agency over their reproductive outcomes. The most commonly used phrase to describe their experiences with pregnancy is "It just happened." Second, women in their study described pregnancy planning as an unattainable ideal for many women. This is explained further by saying that the women who participated in the study had strong feelings about ideal circumstances (financially stable and in a committed relationship) in which pregnancy should be planned and these women felt as if those circumstances were unattainable. The third factor is that since planning may not occur, decisions about the acceptability of a pregnancy are often determined after the occurrence of the pregnancy. Finally, there is an unclear relationship between the desire to avoid pregnancy and contraceptive behaviors.

In conclusion, a planned pregnancy has many benefits to the health of the baby and mother, marital satisfaction, and helps with the transition to parenthood. There should be a goal of improving the health and well-being of mothers, infants, and families. It is suggested that public health policy should focus on efforts to assist women and men with the support and services they need to avoid unplanned pregnancies and empower them to choose the time and circumstances of becoming a parent (Kost and Lindberg 2015).

Donna Hoskins and Clara O'Connor

See also: Donor Insemination; Planned Parenthood (Organization)

Further Reading

Ajzen, Icek. 1991. "The Theory of Planned Behavior." *Organizational Behavior and Human Decision Process*es 50, no. 2: 179–211. https://doi.org/10.1016/0749-5978(91)90020-t.

Ayoola, Adejoke B., Mary D. Nettleman, Manfred Stommel, and Renee B. Canady. 2010. "Time of Pregnancy Recognition and Prenatal Care Use: A Population-Based Study in the United States." *Birth* 37, no. 1: 37–43. https://doi.org/10.1111/j.1523-536x.2009.00376.x.

Barrett, Geraldine and Kaye Wellings. 2002. "What Is a 'Planned' Pregnancy? Empirical Data from a British Study." *Social Science & Medicine* 55, no. 4: 545–557. https://doi.org/10.1016/s0277-9536(01)00187-3.

Borrero, Sonya, Cara Nikolajski, Julia R. Steinberg, Lori Freedman, Aletha Y. Akers, Said Ibrahim, and Eleanor Bimla Schwarz. 2015. "'It Just Happens': A Qualitative Study Exploring Low-Income Women's Perspectives on Pregnancy Intention and Planning." *Contraception* 91, no. 2: 150–156. doi:10.1016/j.contraception.2014.09.014.

Bouchard, Geneviève. 2005. "Adult Couples Facing a Planned or an Unplanned Pregnancy: Two Realities." *Journal of Family Issues* 26, no. 5: 619–637. doi:10.1177/0192513X04272756.

Bouchard, Geneviève, Jolène Boudreau, and Renée Hébert. 2006. "Transition to Parenthood and Conjugal Life." *Journal of Family Issues* 27, no. 11: 1512–1531. https://doi.org/10.1177/0192513x06290855.

Buist, Anne, Carol A. Morse, and Sarah Durkin. 2003. "Men's Adjustment to Fatherhood: Implications for Obstetric Health Care." *Journal of Obstetric, Gynecologic & Neonatal Nursing* 32, no. 2: 172–180. https://doi.org/10.1177/0884217503252127.

Cox, Martha J., Blair Paley, Margaret Burchinal, and C. Chris Payne. 1999. "Marital Perceptions and Interactions Across the Transition to Parenthood." *Journal of Marriage & Family* 61, no. 3 (August): 611–625. doi:10.2307/353564.

Kost, Kathryn, David J. Landry, and Jacqueline E. Darroch. 1998. "The Effects of Pregnancy Planning Status Of Birth Outcomes and Infant Care." *Family Planning Perspectives* 30, no. 5 (September): 223–230. doi:10.2307/2991608.

Kost, Kathryn and Laura Lindberg. 2015. "Pregnancy Intentions, Maternal Behaviors, and Infant Health: Investigating Relationships with New Measures and Propensity Score Analysis." *Demography* 52, no. 1 (September): 83–111. https://doi.org/10.1007/s13524-014-0359-9.

Lawrence, Erika, Rebecca J. Cobb, Alexia D. Rothman, Michael T. Rothman, and Thomas N. Bradbury. 2008. "Marital Satisfaction Across the Transition to Parenthood." *Journal of Family Psychology* 22, no. 1: 41–50. doi:10.1037/0893-3200.22.1.41.

Mercier, R. J., J. Garrett, J. Thorp, and A. M. Siega-Riz. 2013. "Pregnancy Intention and Postpartum Depression: Secondary Data Analysis from a Prospective Cohort." *BJOG: An International Journal of Obstetrics & Gynaecology* 120, no. 9: 1116–1122. doi:10.1111/1471-0528.12255.

Pancer, S. Mark, Michael Pratt, Bruce Hunsberger, Margo Gallant, S. M. Pancer, M. Pratt, B. Hunsberger, and M. Gallant. 2000. "Thinking Ahead: Complexity of Expectations and the Transition to Parenthood." *Journal of Personality* 68, no. 2: 253–280. doi:10.1111/1467-6494.00097.

Sedgh, Gilda, Susheela Singh, and Rubina Hussain. 2014. "Intended and Unintended Pregnancies Worldwide in 2012 and Recent Trends." *Studies in Family Planning* 45, no. 3: 301–314. doi:10.1111/j.1728-4465.2014.00393.x.

Theisen, Jaclyn C., Brian G. Ogolsky, Jeffry A. Simpson, and W. Steven Rholes. 2019. "Dyad to Triad: A Longitudinal Analysis of Humor and Pregnancy Intention during the Transition to Parenthood." *Journal of Social & Personal Relationships* 36, no. 11–12: 3611–3630. doi:10.1177/0265407519831076.

Trillingsgaard, Tea, Katherine J. W. Baucom, and Richard E. Heyman. 2014. "Predictors of Change in Relationship Satisfaction during the Transition to Parenthood." *Family Relations* 63, no. 5: 667–679. doi:10.1111/fare.12089.

Planned Parenthood (Organization)

Planned Parenthood is a non-profit organization that provides a variety of services, including but not limited to birth control, abortions and referrals for abortions, HIV care, general health care, and health-related specifically to men and women such as prostate or pelvic exams (Planned Parenthood 2021d). Their website also includes information and portals for enrolling in health insurance plans via the Marketplace (Planned Parenthood 2021c). Planned Parenthood has been active for more than a century and provides a wealth of information through its website and in person for those who need sex education, information on sexually transmitted diseases, birth control, or other general health questions (Planned Parenthood 2021b). For the last several decades, there have been executive orders, policy changes, and case laws that have affected the way that Planned Parenthood operates.

Various presidential administrations have removed or reinstated federal funding from agencies that provide abortion services. Most recently, President Biden signed an executive order on January 28, 2021, reversing the previous administration's ban on such funds. The Mexico City Policy, first developed in 1984 under President Reagan, prohibited any federal or foreign monies to provide abortions or information about abortion limiting some of the referral and educational capabilities of Planned Parenthood (Kaiser Family Foundation 2021).

Roe v. Wade (1973) was essentially a privacy case—stating that a woman's right to choose whether or not to have children was a private decision, not a government one—it is anecdotally referred to as the abortion case. However, there have been multiple court cases, directly and indirectly, involving Planned Parenthood and the services the agency provides including legal proceedings dealing with issues such as giving married couples the right to choose contraceptives (*Griswold v. Connecticut,* 1965), giving unmarried individuals the same right (*Eisenstadt v. Baird,* 1972), making it possible for agencies other than pharmacists to advertise and sell or provide contraceptives to minors (*Carey v. Population Services International,* 1977), and allowing allowed the distribution of unsolicited advertisements regarding contraceptives (*Bolger v. Youngs Drug Products Corporation*, 1983).

With specific regards to abortion, local offices of Planned Parenthood have

successfully pursued cases in Missouri and Pennsylvania (*Planned Parenthood of Central Missouri v. Danforth* (1976), *Planned Parenthood of Kansas City, Missouri v. Ashcroft* (1983), and *Planned Parenthood of Southeastern Pennsylvania v. Casey* (1992) challenging laws designed to take the choice from a pregnant woman either through giving another person unilateral veto power over her or presenting legal obstacles that could prevent a woman's choice. Even in *Babbitt v. Planned Parenthood of Central and Northern Arizona* (1986), justices were firm that a woman's right to choose could not be legally proscribed without a solid foundation for the statute.

The extant research shows that when women are given the right to choose whether to terminate a pregnancy and when contraceptives are easily and readily available, the rate of performed abortions actually decreases. Both of these findings demonstrate the need for agencies such as Planned Parenthood for counseling and referral services, as well as contraceptives and women's health services. Leaving all talk of abortion aside, though, advocacy and its effects on policy make Planned Parenthood invaluable in providing services related to cancer screenings and general preventative care for both men and women. This agency has achieved many of its goals in policy decisions through social media campaigns and educating the public about how funding cuts could adversely impact women's health services, specifically breast cancer screenings, in response to the Susan G. Komen for the Cure Foundation's 2012 decision to terminate funding to Planned Parenthood for such screenings.

Social media issues did not end in 2012. From 2015 to 2016, there was a "Planned

Parenthood Controversy" that played out on the social media platform, Twitter, following a later discredited video of Planned Parenthood executives selling aborted fetal tissue for research. The storm that followed on Twitter, though, was skewed significantly by the number of hashtags used and the fact that as users of social media, we self-select who were follow and interact with, which can allow the rapid spread of information—true or false (Han et al. 2017). Other research has shown that companies whose philanthropic efforts result in donations and contributions to social organizations such as Planned Parenthood show increased revenue, possibly through increased support of the companies by the very public that these social organizations support (Olson 2019), so the Twitter controversy did not hurt Planned Parenthood too much in the long run.

In 2020, Planned Parenthood served over two million patients and over 10 million services. Nearly 25% of those services were for birth control or information regarding birth control, a little over half were for the testing and treatment of sexually transmitted illnesses, and over half a million breast exams and pap smears. Further, there were services for transgender individuals in 31 states, more than 300,000 male patients, and providing sex education for 3.65 million people nationally (Planned Parenthood 2021a).

Jennifer M. Miller

See also: Donor Insemination; Premarital Sex

Further Reading

Babbitt v. Planned Parenthood of Central and Northern Arizona. 789 F. 2nd 1348 (9th Cir. 1986).

Bongaarts, J. and Westoff, C. 2000. "The potential rule of contraception in reducing abortion." *Studies in Family Planning* 32, no.1: 105–118.

Bolger v. Youngs Drug Product Corporation. 463 U.S. 60. 1983.

Carey v. Population Services International. 431 U.S. 678. 1977.

Deschner, A. and Cohen, S. 2003. "Contraceptive use is key to reducing abortion worldwide." *The Guttmacher Report on Public Policy* 6, no. 4: 7–10.

Dorfman, L. and Krasnow, I. D. 2014. "Public health and media advocacy." *Annual Review of Public Health* 35: 293–306.

Eisenstadt v. Baird. 405 U.S. 428 1972.

Griswold v. Connecticut. 381 U.S. 479. 1965.

Han, L., Han, L., Barney, B., and Rodriguez, M.I. 2017. "Tweeting PP: An analysis of the 2015–2016 Planned Parenthood controversy on Twitter." *Contraception* 96, no. 6: 388–394.

Kaiser Family Foundation. 2021, January 28. *The Mexico City Policy: An explainer*. Global Health Policy. https://www.kff.org/global-health-policy/fact-sheet/mexico-city-policy-explainer/

Olson, K. 2019. *The mystery of values to value: An examination of share price performance to an announcement of a contribution to Planned Parenthood*. [Doctoral Dissertation, Creighton University]. https://dspace2.creighton.edu/xmlui/handle/10504/122570?show=full.

Planned Parenthood. 2021a. *Planned Parenthood: 2019–2020 Annual Report*. Planned Parenthood.

Planned Parenthood. 2021b. "About us." https://www.plannedparenthood.org/get-care/our-services

Planned Parenthood. 2021c. "Health insurance." https://www.plannedparenthood.org/get-care/our-services

Planned Parenthood. 2021d. "Our services." https://www.plannedparenthood.org/get-care/our-services

Planned Parenthood of Central Missouri v. Danforth. 428 U.S. 52. 1976.

Planned Parenthood of Kansas City, Missouri, v. Ashcroft. 462 U.S. 476. 1983.

Planned Parenthood of Southeastern Pennsylvania v. Casey. 505 U.S. 833. 1992.

Roe v. Wade. 410 U.S. 113. 1973.

Polyamory

When it comes to relationships and sexuality, monogamy has socially dominated and constructed what is acceptable in romantic relationships in contemporary western culture. Monogamy serves as the binary model by which all relationships are analyzed, perceived, and experienced (Allen and Mendez 2018; Rothschild 2018). Polyamory, on the other hand, is defined as consensual non-monogamy, or "the desire for or state of having multiple loving relationships" (Manly, Diamond, and van Anders 2015, 168). Polyamory does not subscribe to the notion that there is only one person that should fulfill all of one's romantic and sexual needs. Understandably, this is sometimes considered a controversial concept (Rothschild 2018, 30).

While polyamorous relationships are not considered typical in mainstream Western culture, according to Rubin, Moors, Matsick, Ziegler, and Conley (2014, 3), approximately 4–5% of the U.S. population report that they engage in polyamory. Rubin et al. argued that due to factors such as social desirability and retrospective research methods, it is likely that this figure is an underestimate. Polyamorous relationships are not legal in the United States at the time of this writing even though they have existed since biblical times (Manly et al. 2015, 168).

At the heart of polyamory are four basic assumptions: (a) that it is possible to love more than one person at the same time, (b) it is possible to maintain multiple sexual relationships, (c) openness, and (d) honesty. Ideally, all partners involved in a poly relationship are aware of one another and their sexual and romantic attachments with different partners (Barker 2005, 77). However, there is a great deal of variability within polyamory, and it is not required that all partners in a polyamorous relationship be involved in a sexual relationship with all of the partners in the group. There can be triads, quads, or other configurations in polyamory and the type of relationship each member has with the others is self-defined by the group (Manly et al. 2015, 169). These guiding principles help to manage the dynamics of polyamory, including any potential jealousy.

While polyamory is not immune from cheating, the concept is defined differently in polyamorous relationships. Whereas cheating is typically defined as a sexual and/or emotional betrayal in monogamous relationships, cheating in poly circles happens when partners lie, sneak around, and/or break previously agreed-upon rules with their partners. Polyamorists are not immune from jealousy, but they use previously agreed-upon scripts and rules to channel and control their feelings to stop the individual from destroying the relationship. By following these rules, jealousy is accepted and explored, and used to further cement the connections within the polyamorous relationship.

Polyamory, or consensual non-monogamy, is based on the belief that people are capable of loving more than one person at a time. The best estimates indicate that around 4–5% of the U.S. population self-identifies as polyamorous, although the actual number is likely higher (Rubin et al. 2014). Within the poly community, cheating and jealousy are controlled by channeling negative feelings into positive outcomes with the use of scripts and rules. Contrary to myths about polyamory, there is a great deal of variability in how relationships are constructed and enacted; polyamorists self-define these constructs in ways that work best for the group.

Lisa Moyer

See also: Infidelity; Polygamy

Further Reading

Allen, Samuel H., and Mendez, Shawn N. 2018. "Hegemonic Heteronormativity: Toward a New Era of Queer Family Theory." *Journal of Family Theory & Review* 10: 70–86. doi:10.1111/jftr.12241

Barker, Meg. 2005. "This Is My Partner and My Partner's Partner: Constructing a Polyamorous Identity in a Monogamous World." *Journal of Constructivist Psychology* 18, no. 1: 75–88. doi: 10.1080/10720530590523107

Klesse, Christian. 2018. "Theorizing Multi-Partner Relationships and Sexualities: Recent Work on Non-Monogamy and Polyamory." *Sexualities* 21, 7: 1109–1124. doi: 10.1177/1363460717701691

Manly, Melissa H., Diamond, Lisa M., and van Anders, Sari M. 2015. "Polyamory, Monoamory, and Sexual Fluidity: A Longitudinal Study of Identity and Sexual Trajectories." *Psychology of Sexual Orientation and Gender Divers*ity 2, no. 2: 168–180. https://doi.org/10.1037/sgd0000098

Rothschild, Leehee. 2018. "Compulsory Monogamy and Polyamorous Existence." *Graduate Journal of Social Science* 14: 28–56. Retrieved from http://gjss.org/sites/default/files/issues/chapters/papers/GjSS%20Vol%2014-1%20Roths child.pdf

Rubin, Jennifer D., Moors, Amy C., Matsick, Jes L., Ziegler, Ali, and Conley, Terri D. 2014. "On the Margins: Considering Diversity Among Consensually Non-Monogamous Relationships." *Journal fur Psychologie* 22: 19–37. Retrieved from https://digitalcommons.chapman.edu/psychology_articles/133/

Sheff, Elisabeth. 2006. "Poly-Hegemonic Masculinities." *Sexuality* 9, no. 5: 621–642. doi: 10.1177/1363460706070004

Polygamy

Polygamy is the practice of plural marriage or simultaneous marriage to more than one spouse. The three main forms of polygamy are polygyny, polyandry, and polygynandry. The most prevalent type of polygamy is polygyny in which one man is married to multiple wives. In polyandry, one woman is married to multiple husbands. In polygynandry, multiple husbands are married to multiple wives. Both polyandry and polygynandry are extremely rare in the United States; therefore, the term *polygamy* generally refers to the more common case of one man married to multiple wives.

Although the origins of polygamy are unknown, it has been practiced by many cultures throughout history. In agrarian societies dependent on human capital for subsistence, there was a distinct advantage to having large families. Considering that women can carry only one pregnancy at a time, polygamous marriages may have been advantageous, especially when infant mortality rates were high. Polygamy might also have been a way to address large numbers of men dying in wars by providing a means to take care of widowed women with few other economic opportunities for survival. In patriarchal societies where women were considered commodities, polygamous marriages might also have been a status symbol for wealthy men.

Since 1862, polygamy has been illegal in the United States under federal law. All 50 states have also criminalized polygamy under their respective state laws. Nevertheless, some groups, including Fundamentalist Mormons, Muslims, and others, continue to practice polygamy discreetly. There is no official record of polygamous marriages; therefore, it is difficult to estimate the prevalence of the practice. Scholars have estimated that between 40,000–50,000 Fundamentalist Mormons and 50,000 to 100,000 Muslims are currently in polygamous marriages in the United States (Bennion and Joffe 2016). Local law enforcement generally does not intervene in these marriages unless they involve minors or other criminal behavior.

In the United States, polygamy is often associated with the Church of Jesus Christ of Latter-Day Saints (LDS), or Mormonism. In the 1830s, the founder of LDS, Joseph Smith, asserted divine revelation in support of polygamy. By 1852, polygamy became the official doctrine of the LDS; however, it was not a widespread practice. At any given time, no more than about 20–30% of Mormon families practiced polygamy. In 1890, LDS's then leader, Wilford Woodruff, ended the practice in the Church. Mainstream Mormons today do not practice polygamy; however, several breakaway fundamentalist sects continue to do so.

Polygamy is also practiced among some Muslim groups in the United States, including some communities of African Americans and immigrants from Africa, the Middle East, and Asia. According to Islamic religious doctrine, Muslim men are permitted to be simultaneously married to up to four wives. Although polygamy is not a widespread practice among Muslims in the United States, some Muslims do practice polygamy discreetly, with second, third, and fourth marriages conducted through religious contracts.

In recent years, Fundamentalist Mormons in polygamous relationships have been featured in popular culture on television programs like HBO's *Big Love* and TLC's *Sister Wives*. Media representation has resulted in greater awareness, tolerance, and even acceptance of polygamous lifestyles, with some even advocating for the decriminalization of polygamy, though decriminalization remains unlikely given that the majority of the general public continues to disapprove of the practice.

Julie Ahmad Siddique

See also: Infidelity; Polyamory

Further Reading

Bennion, Janet, and Lisa Joffe. 2016. *The Polygamy Question*. Boulder: University Press of Colorado.

Bernstein, Nina. 2007. "In Secret, Polygamy Follows Africans to N.Y." *New York Times*, March 23, 2007. https://www.nytimes.com/2007/03/23/nyregion/23polygamy.html.

Cox, Savannah. 2017. "The Ins and Outs of Polygamy and the Mormon Church." *All Things Interesting*. Last modified February 10, 2017. https://allthatsinteresting.com/mormonism-and-polygamy.

Haggerty, Barbara. 2008. "Philly's Black Muslims Increasingly Turn to Polygamy."

All Things Considered, NPR. https://www.npr.org/templates/story/story.php?storyId=90886407.

Haggerty, Barbara. 2008. "Some Muslims in U.S. Quietly Engage in Polygamy." *All Things Considered*, NPR. https://www.npr.org/templates/story/story.php?storyId=90857818.

Jacobson, Cardell, and Lara Burton. 2011. *Modern Polygamy in the U.S.: Historical, Cultural, and Legal Issues.* New York: Oxford University Press.

Pornography

Sexually explicit material or "pornography" is defined as content that can evoke erotic feelings, thoughts, and behaviors (Allen, Kannis-Dymand, and Katsikitis 2017) from its consumers. This content can include literature, photographs, or visual media. With recent technological advances, online pornography is now easily accessible while helping viewers retain anonymity. Past literature has explored the effects of pornography consumption on individuals. However, more recently, researchers have been interested in the effects of pornography consumption on couples. While the advantages of pornography consumption have been discussed (e.g., increased sexual and relational satisfaction), disadvantages of pornography use have been discussed as well (e.g., conflict, marital separation). Due to the sexual nature of pornography consumption, effects of consumption are largely based on individual and couple self-reports.

Those specializing in sexuality research have explored the advantages of pornography use for couples. When used individually, partners can explore self-pleasure, often in conjunction with masturbation. When individuals discover what feels pleasurable, they can verbalize this to their partner. Therefore, this may lead to increased sexual satisfaction within the marriage. Pornography can also be used conjointly during sexual activities. When utilized together, couples can engage in open conversation about exploring new ideas to enhance their sexual relationship. Discussion can often lead to new sexual experimentation (Kohut, Fisher, and Campbell 2017). Lastly, consumption of pornographic content during a couple's sexual activity may increase arousal from visual and auditory stimulation, therefore, leading to increase sexual satisfaction. Increased sexual satisfaction may also contribute to couples' overall satisfaction with their relationship.

Researchers have also studied the disadvantages of pornography use for couples. For some viewers, they may engage in conscious or subconscious comparisons of their partner to adult film actors/actresses. Individuals may compare the bodies of those they are viewing to their own romantic partner. They may also compare the sexual acts depicted to the sexual acts in their own relationship. Such comparisons may lead to dissatisfaction with their marital partner. In addition, pornography consumption has also been associated with marital conflict related to infidelity. While each couple's interpretation of infidelity varies, some may believe their partner's use of pornographic content is considered cheating. These feelings of betrayal and distrust may lead to conflict. While pornography consumption can produce strains on the marital relationship, these strains can ultimately be a contributing factor to divorce (Perry and Schleifer 2018). Future research should also consider the effects of consumption for couples in the LGBTQ+ community.

Rachael Elizabeth Farina

See also: Addictions, Drugs and Alcohol; Exhibitionism; Infidelity

Further Reading

Allen, Andrew, Lee Kannis-Dymand, and Mary Katsikitis. 2017. "Problematic Internet Pornography Use: The Role of Craving, Desire Thinking, and Metacognition." *Addictive Behaviors* 70: 65–71.

Kohut, Taylor, William Fisher, and A. Campbell. 2017. "Perceived Effects of Pornography on the Couple Relationship: Initial Findings of Open-Ended, Participant-Informed, 'Bottom-Up' Research." *Archives of Sexual Behavior* 46, no. 2: 585–602.

Perry, Samuel L. and Cyrus Schleifer. 2018. "Till Porn Do Us Part? A Longitudinal Examination of Pornography Use and Divorce." *Journal of Sex Research* 55, no. 3: 284–296. doi:10.1080/00224499.2017.1317709.

Postnuptial Agreement

A postnuptial agreement, also known as a marital agreement, is a private contract between spouses to change their prenuptial agreement, or if they do not have one, to make new provisions regarding their rights and responsibilities during the marriage or upon divorce or death. A postnuptial agreement is similar in substance and procedure to a prenuptial agreement, except that it is contracted during the marriage instead of before the wedding. The arrangements that couples make in prenuptial and postnuptial agreements replace the relevant state legal defaults.

Postnuptial agreements can be particularly useful when spouses move between two states with different default property regimes. Specifically, if spouses move from a community property state like California to a separate property state like New York, or vice versa, they may prefer to choose their approach to the character of their property. Postnuptial agreements are also commonly requested after there has been infidelity in the marriage, with the unfaithful spouse offering concessions in such agreements. Finally, a new business or financial situation, such as a decision to become a stay-at-home parent, might prompt a postnuptial agreement. However, any change in circumstances during the marriage may make a married couple agree to a postnuptial agreement.

States differ in their approaches to postnuptial agreements. For example, in some states, postnuptial agreements may receive more judicial scrutiny at divorce than prenuptial agreements. This is due to the nature of the marital relationship at the time of the postnuptial agreement, which may cause spouses to lack the caution and bargaining power that they would have had when executing a prenuptial agreement before the marriage.

Postnuptial agreements must survive procedural and substantive review by a court before being enforced. Although the exact legal requirements differ by state, generally postnuptial agreements must be fair and made voluntarily, without undue influence, fraud, coercion, or duress. In other words, one spouse cannot force the other to enter into a postnuptial agreement. Each spouse must also disclose the amount, character, and value of property and financial obligations.

Many people are unaware of postnuptial agreements or reluctant to request them of their spouses out of fear that the agreement might signal divorce. In addition, many people do not want to pay the several thousands of dollars in attorney fees for such an agreement, although free online guidance on creating such agreements is available. As a result, postnuptial agreements are not very common.

Margaret Ryznar

See also: Marriage and Legal Planning; Marriage Certificate/License; Prenuptial Agreement

Further Reading

Atwood, Barbara A. 2012. "Marital Contracts and the Meaning of Marriage." *Arizona Law Review* 54, no. 1: 11–42.

Atwood, Barbara A. and Brian H. Bix. 2012. "A New Uniform Law for Premarital and Marital Agreements." *Family Law Quarterly* 46, no. 3: 313–344.

Uniform Premarital and Marital Agreements Act. 2012.

Williams, Sean Hannon. 2007. "Postnuptial Agreements." *Wisconsin Law Review* 2007, no. 4: 827–888.

Premarital Counseling

While the divorce rate is currently leveling off, its current rate—40–50% for first marriages—is still extremely high, and represents a drastic spike when compared to the rates in the 1960s (Olson 2015). Premarital counseling, also referred to as premarital education, is a broad-spectrum, primary intervention approach for engaged couples and/or committed couples. The primary goal of premarital counseling is to prevent divorce. Due to the relative spike in divorce rates, premarital counseling has received increasing attention.

Who seeks premarital education? Religious people—specifically, those who wed in a religious setting—are most likely to attend premarital education. Additionally, people who have higher levels of education are significantly more likely to attend than people with lower levels of education. Recipients of public financial assistance, on the other hand, are significantly less likely to attend premarital programs than people who do not receive public assistance. Overall, the percentage of people who participate has risen steadily from the 1950s (12%) to the 1990s (44%) (Stanley et al. 2006).

Couples who want to participate in premarital counseling have many programs to choose from. These programs differ to varying degrees in setting, assessment, structure, theoretical approach, etc., but largely share the goal of divorce prevention by focusing on couples' relationship satisfaction, communication skills, and conflict resolution skills. For example, some programs (PREPARE/ENRICH, Olson, Olson, and Larson 2012; RELATE, Busby, Holman, and Taniguchi 2001) are assessment-focused; typically, couples first complete a comprehensive couple questionnaire, followed by several sessions where a trained facilitator guides the couple through their results. Other programs are more skills-based; for example, in PREP (Prevention and Relationship Education Program; Stanley, Markman, Jenkins, and Blumberg 2006), couples are offered one of two formats—either several hour-long sessions or a single, intensive weekend—and receive psychoeducational presentations on specific couple skills (e.g., communication; faith), followed by time to practice these skills with a trained facilitator (weekly format) or together in their hotel room (weekend format).

Approximately 75% of marriages in the United States occur within religious organizations, and as a result, couples commonly seek out premarital counseling at their religious institution, putting clergy and church members on the front lines of premarital prevention efforts (Stanley et al. 2001). These services are usually provided by Christian-based clergy and/or lay people with varying degrees of formal counselor training. Programs provided in these settings range in format from informal meetings (i.e., one or a series of facilitated conversations about marriage) to assessment and/or curriculum-based programs such as FOCCUS (Facilitate Open, Couple, Communication, Understanding and Study; Catholic orientation; Markey, Micheletto, and Becker 1985) and SYMBIS (Saving Your Marriage Before it Starts; Parrott and Parrott 2013). Compared to premarital counseling in secular (non-religious) settings, premarital counseling in religious settings has been found to be equally effective in preventing divorce (Stanley et al. 2006).

Is premarital counseling effective? Most signs point to "yes" but with some qualifications. For example, one study (Carroll and Doherty 2003) examined results from 26 premarital counseling effectiveness studies and found that couples who participated in premarital counseling reported higher levels of relationship satisfaction and positive communication and were less likely to divorce. The researchers were optimistic about the results, but cited important limitations of their study: namely, that the studies were not experimental, contained non-diverse samples, and did not track participant outcomes past five years, making it difficult to conclude whether or not they were truly helpful in preventing divorce. Three years later, researchers (Stanley et al. 2006) sent out surveys to a diverse sample of Americans and found that participation in premarital programs was associated with higher relationship satisfaction, relationship commitment, and lower levels of conflict and divorce. While these results are promising, it appears that some exploration is still needed. A 2010 meta-analysis (Fawcett et al. 2010) found that premarital counseling significantly improved couple communication but did not reduce the probability of divorce and reiterated the need for experimental and longitudinal studies with more diverse samples. Additionally, while studies have shown research-based programs to be more effective than naturally occurring (i.e., more informal) premarital services (Stanley et al. 2001), not much has been done to compare the effectiveness of specific programs. Overall, while there are limits to understanding "what works" and "what doesn't," participating in premarital therapy appears to be advantageous for any couple committed to wed.

Richard S. Dell'Isola

See also: Divorce, Causes/Risk Factors of; Marriage and Education Level; Marriage Counseling

Further Reading

Busby, Dean M., Thomas B. Holman, and Narumi Taniguchi. 2001. "RELATE: Relationship evaluation of the individual, family, cultural, and couple contexts." *Family Relations* 50, no. 4: 308–316.

Carroll, Jason S. and William J. Doherty. 2003. "Evaluating the effectiveness of premarital prevention programs: A meta-analytic review of outcome research." *Family Relations* 52, no. 2: 105–118.

Fawcett, Elizabeth B., Alan J. Hawkins, Victoria L. Blanchard, and Jason S. Carroll. 2010. "Do premarital education programs really work? A meta-analytic study." *Family Relations* 59, no. 3: 232–239.

Markey, Barbara, Marie Micheletto, and A. Becker. 1985. "Facilitating open couple communication, understanding, and study (FOCCUS)." Omaha: Archdiocese of Omaha.

Olson, R. 2015. "144 years of marriage and divorce in 1 chart." Retrieved from http://www.randalolson.com/2015/06/15/144-years-of-marriage-and-divorce-in-1-chart/

Olson, David H., Amy K. Olson, and Peter J. Larson. 2012. "Prepare-Enrich program: Overview and new discoveries about couples." *Journal of Family & Community Ministries* 25: 30–44.

Parrott, Les, and Leslie Parrott. 2013. "Preparing couples for marriage: The SYMBIS model." In *Case Studies in Couples Therapy*. Routledge, pp. 51–66.

Stanley, Scott M., Paul R. Amato, Christine A. Johnson, and Howard J. Markman. 2006. "Premarital education, marital quality, and marital stability: Findings from a large, random household survey." *Journal of Family Psychology* 20, no. 1: 117.

Stanley, S. M., H. J. Markman, N. H. Jenkins, and S. L. Blumberg. 2006. *PREP for strong bonds leader's manual*. PREP Educational Products.

Stanley, Scott M., Howard J. Markman, Lydia M. Prado, P. Antonio Olmos-Gallo, Laurie Tonelli, Michelle St. Peters, B. Douglas Leber, Michelle Bobulinski, Allan Cordova, and Sarah W. Whitton. 2001. "Community-based premarital prevention: Clergy and lay leaders on the front lines." *Family Relations* 50, no. 1: 67–76.

Premarital Pregnancy

Premarital pregnancy results from an unmarried couple engaging in sexual intercourse without the use of, or with improper or ineffective use of, contraceptives. Although the term *premarital* may imply that the parents will eventually marry each other, this entry is not limited to such couples. The rate of premarital pregnancies is increasing worldwide, and the two groups most likely to experience a premarital pregnancy are adolescents and cohabiting couples. Premarital pregnancies among cohabitating couples more frequently take place in developed countries, especially the United States. The largest at-risk group consists of female adolescents aged 15–19 (U.S. Department of Health and Human Services 2017), who likely lack understanding of or access to contraceptive methods. Cohabitating couples, by contrast, are more likely to have a planned premarital pregnancy, though many are unplanned. Common contributors to unplanned premarital pregnancy include low socio-economic status (SES), lack of education, and few job opportunities.

Worldwide, 23 million 15–19-year-old females have an unplanned or unwanted pregnancy and approximately 16 million of them give birth annually. Adolescent pregnancy is considered a global health concern in high-, middle-, and low-income countries. However, adolescents in developing/low-income countries are at particularly high risk due to factors that limit access to contraceptive methods (e.g., restrictive laws and policies, financial barriers, and lack of education on obtaining and using contraception). Moderately educated, working-class couples are more likely to experience a premarital pregnancy compared to college-educated, middle-class couples. Middle-class cohabiting couples are more likely to consistently use effective contraceptive methods, whereas working-class couples tend to be more ambivalent about contraception and use it infrequently. One explanation could be that couples who do not feel financially ready to have a child may not have family planning foremost on their mind and possibly also not the resources to pay for contraceptives (Sassler and Miller 2014).

Teen pregnancy is considered a global health concern due to the potentially negative emotional and physical risks (e.g., depression, anxiety, maternal and child mortality, eclampsia, puerperal endometritis, and systemic infections) for female adolescents and their infants. Some individuals with unintended pregnancies consider, and possibly follow through with, terminating their pregnancy. Reasons for abortion include lack of financial resources and inability to provide a good life for the child, concerns about one's future, quality of the relationship with the partner, and bad timing of the pregnancy (Biggs, Gould, and Foster 2013). In developed/high-income countries, there are more opportunities to receive a safe abortion. In developing countries, women aged 15–24 comprise more than

40% of unsafe abortions (World Health Organization 2018).

Teenage pregnancies are associated with lower birth rates, increased infant mortality, greater likelihood of the child's later hospitalization, and poorer childhood cognitive development. These risks most likely stem from teen mothers having fewer social connections, higher likelihood of mental-health problems, and fewer educational and employment opportunities (Langille 2007). Support systems and access to resources decrease the potentially harmful effects of early childbearing for both infants and mothers.

The field's knowledge of premarital pregnancy comes substantially from research on teen pregnancy. However, findings on premarital pregnancy in older, cohabiting couples are emerging. Romantically partnered cohabiting couples often have a long-term relationship resembling a marriage. Among younger couples, cohabiting often leads to marriage. As cohabitation has increased in the United States and worldwide, premarital pregnancies among such couples have also increased. Indeed, cohabiting families are increasingly common. Between 2006 and 2010, 56% of all nonmarital United States births occurred to women cohabiting with a partner. Among those who became pregnant during cohabitation, 20% were pregnant within one year of their first such union. Although most cohabiting women were between ages 25–29, one in four who became pregnant within one year of their first cohabitation were 20 years old or younger (Copen, Daniels, and Mosher 2013).

Many 1980s and 1990s research studies link premarital conception and birth to subsequent marital instability in those who wed. According to Sylvia Niehuis and her colleagues (Niehuis, Huston, and Rosenband 2006), one explanation is that premarital pregnancy deviates from the expected or normative sequencing of life-cycle events in the United States and carries negative consequences for women (e.g., lower SES; less social/psychological support from family, friends, and society), all of which predict marital instability. The impact of premarital conception and birth appears to be stronger for white women (particularly younger ones) than for Black women, regardless of the mother's age at conception. These racial differences suggest different norms and expectations, with white women's premarital births deviating from their respective subcultural norms to a greater degree than Black women's premarital births (Niehuis, Huston, and Rosenband 2006). Even though fewer people today than in prior decades feel the need to begin to cohabit or to marry prior to the birth of a child as a result of a conception outside of a relationship, cohabiting and marital relationships formed during pregnancy continue to be at an elevated risk of instability and those formed after the birth of a baby are even more likely to dissolve (Guzzo 2018). However, as United States norms have changed over the last 30–40 years, so have the effects on marital instability, with recent cohorts of premaritally pregnant women who marry being less likely to divorce the father of the child than in earlier cohorts.

Although there are potential negative impacts to teen pregnancy and births, especially regarding health and child outcomes, some research suggests many of society's views on teen mothers may be exaggerated. One study found that society

and folk wisdom overestimate the negative impacts of teen pregnancy, such as the belief in low-birth rates, higher risks of cognitive delay, and economic stresses. Rather, early childbearing only has a "slightly negative" impact on educational and economic outcomes for society and the individual (Germonious 2003).

Emma Willis and Sylvia Niehuis

See also: Divorce, Causes/Risk Factors of; Marital Success; Premarital Sex

Further Reading

Biggs, M. Antonia, Heather Gould, and Diana Greene Foster. 2013. "Understanding why women seek abortions in the U.S." *BMC Women's Health* 13, no. 1: 1–13.

Copen, Casey E., Kimberly Daniels, and William Mosher. 2013. "First premarital cohabitation in the United States: 2006–2010 National Survey of Family Growth." *National Health Statistics Reports 64.* U.S. Department of Health and Human Services.

Geronimus, Arline T. 2003. "Damned if you do: Culture, identity, privilege, and teenage childbearing in the United States." *Social Science & Medicine* 57: 881–893.

Guzzo, Karen B. 2018. "A research note on the stability of coresidential unions formed postconception." *Journal of Marriage and Family* 80: 841–852.

Langille, Donald B. 2007. "Teenage pregnancy: Trends, contributing factors and the physician's role." *Canadian Medical Association Journal* 176: 1601–1602.

Niehuis, Sylvia, Ted Huston, and Reva Rosenband. 2006. "From courtship to marriage: A new developmental model and methodological critique." *Journal of Family Communication* 6: 23–47.

Sassler, Sharon, and Amanda J. Miller. 2014. "'We're very careful . . .': The fertility desires and contraceptive behaviors of cohabiting couples." *Family Relations* 63: 538–553.

U.S. Department of Health and Human Services. 2017. "About teen pregnancy." Retrieved from https://www.cdc.gov /teenpregnancy/about/index.htm

Waldfogel, Jane, Terry-Ann Craigie, and Jeanne Brooks-Gunn. 2010. "Fragile families and child wellbeing." *Future of Children* 20: 87–112.

World Health Organization. 2018. "Adolescent pregnancy." Retrieved from https://www.who.int/news-room/fact-sheets /detail/adolescent-pregnancy\

Premarital Sex

With increasingly liberal attitudes toward varying aspect of society, such as dating, sexual liberation, the availability and use of contraceptives, views and rates of divorce, and the portrayal of sexual behavior in media and entertainment, the ubiquity of premarital sex has grown over time. Sexual activity among unmarried people has become common place. Research indicates premarital sex is a rising trend around the globe. Premarital sex is consensual sexual activity that people engage in before marriage. While there is some discourse on exactly what behaviors or acts fall in the category of premarital sex, i.e., oral sex, anal sex or masturbation, many agree with the philosophy that vaginal sex before marriage is considered premarital sex.

Views of Premarital Sex

There are many views held regarding premarital sex and what exactly constitutes premarital sex. Behavioral standards regarding sexual intercourse vary from person to person. Anal sex, oral sex, masturbation and heavy petting have all been included in the discourse on what acts are considered premarital sex. Religious and cultural variations play a factor in the varying standards people hold. Many, both in the secular world and those who hold religious views, have engaged in public discourse on this subject matter. Those within the secular world are understood to engage socially with little to no religious or spiritual foundation. While public opinions vary from conservative to liberal and premarital sex has become significantly less taboo and quite common, there are some that hold on to more traditional values. Historically, premarital sex was viewed in a negative light, frowned upon and considered forbidden from a religious perspective. Historically, social norms dictated that premarital sex was highly inappropriate and unsafe.

Many in the secular arena are considered more permissive and hold views that have little to no restrictions. Many, with what is often referred to as a worldly view, see sexual activity as a personal and private choice. A worldly view posits that by in large any type and frequency of consensual sexual acts, with as many partners as one desires is permissible, in or out of marriage. This choice is left to the individual and for some, does not include religious consideration. However, some who engage in premarital sex value religion and its doctrine. While there are those who hold this view, some are selective in their choice of sexual activity and do choose to abstain from sexual intercourse before marriage, but this is often still considered a permissive attitude, as room remains for autonomous choice in whether to sexual engage or not. While spiritual views and level of practice vary from person to person, those with worldlier views are considered to be less spiritual and thus give less or possibly no consideration to the spiritual implications of intercourse outside of marriage. Implications such as unwanted pregnancies or risk of disease are often noted when premarital sex is discussed. While these can be remediated with interventions such as birth control and condoms, the moral implications introduced by religious doctrine remain.

Sexual Liberation
While there are some that strictly adhere to their respective religious doctrine, many consider premarital sex less taboo and it is considered more widely accepted. While premarital sex has been around for thousands of years, the sexual liberation movement, also known as the sexual revolution, saw a rise in premarital sex and more liberal attitudes emerged. The sexual revolution started in the 1960s and lasted well over a decade. Implications of this movement were far reaching. As the sexual revolution was one of the social movements of that time, this movement sought to diminish or abolish public judgments and the guilt associated with freely engaging in sexually gratifying behavior, in or out of marriage. This time period is credited with dramatically changing the public view of sex and the freedom to engage in it, regardless of relationship status. Further, this period also gave rise to other another movement of sexual freedom. Sexual freedom among gay and lesbian people also became more visible during this period of time.

Modern medicine in the 1960s and 1970s played a noteworthy role in the rise of premarital sex with the introduction of oral contraceptives and other forms of contraceptives. Also, during this time other forms of contraception, such as condoms, became more easily accessible and affordable. Additionally, changes in attitude and views on marriage and timing of marriage also have also impacted decisions on whether to engage in premarital sex (Wellings et al. 2006).

Jahaan R. Abdullah

See also: Premarital Counseling; Premarital Pregnancy; Unmarried Cohabitation; Unplanned Pregnancy

Further Reading
Harding, D. J. and C. Jencks. 2003. "Changing attitudes toward premarital sex: Cohort, period, and aging effects." *Public Opinion Quarterly* 67, no. 2: 211–226. https://doi.org/10.1086/374399

Leiblum, Sandra R., et al. 1993. "Sexual attitudes and behavior of a cross-sectional sample of United States medical students: Effects of gender, age, and year of study." *Journal of Sex Education and Therapy* 19, no, 4: 235–245.

Pampel, F. C. 2016. "Cohort changes in the social distribution of tolerant sexual attitudes." *Social Forces*, 95, no. 2: 753–777. https://doi.org/10.1093/sf/sow069

Regnerus, Mark and Jeremy Uecker. 2011. *Premarital sex in America: How young Americans meet, mate, and think about marrying.* Oxford University Press.

Scott, Jacqueline. "Changing attitudes to sexual morality: A cross-national comparison." *Sociology* 32, no. 4: 815–845.

Sejati, Putri Eka and Riza Tsalatsatul Mufida. 2021. "The effect of sex education on premarital sex among adolescents; literature review." *Journal for Quality in Public Health* 5, no. 1: 363–366.

Wellings, Kaye, et al. 2006. "Sexual behaviour in context: A global perspective." *The Lancet* 368, no. 9548: 1706–1728.

Wright, P. J. 2015. "Americans' attitudes toward premarital sex and pornography consumption: A national panel analysis." *Archives of Sexual Behavior* 44, no. 1: 89–97. https://doi.org/10.1007/s10508-014-0353-8

Prenuptial Agreement

A prenuptial agreement, also known as a premarital agreement, is a private contract between prospective spouses effective upon marriage. The prenuptial agreement allows couples to make their own arrangements in case of divorce or death. Without a prenuptial agreement, state legal defaults apply.

Parties to a prenuptial agreement have much discretion over the contents and scope of their agreement, enabling them to dictate the terms of their marriage and divorce absent any enforceability issues. For example, parties may waive their rights to share property in community property states such as California. However, certain topics fall outside the scope of permissible contracting for public policy reasons, including some child-related matters.

Historically, prenuptial agreements were unenforceable because they were viewed as encouraging divorce, but the Florida Supreme Court in 1970 upheld the validity of prenuptial agreements in *Posner v. Posner.* Other American states followed in enforcing such agreements at divorce, with some modeling their laws on the Uniform Premarital Agreement Act promulgated in 1983 by the National Conference of Commissioners on Uniform State Laws.

Different states have different requirements for prenuptial agreements. Generally, a prenuptial agreement must survive substantive and procedural review, or it is overturned by the courts. In terms of substantive review, judges often examine the fairness of the terms of the prenuptial agreement. In terms of procedural review, judges examine the parties' conduct in obtaining the prenuptial agreement. For example, the parties must have voluntarily entered into the agreement, absent fraud, overreaching, sharp dealing, or duress. The parties must also have disclosed their financial situation at the time of entering the agreement.

Due to the various legal requirements for prenuptial agreements, many couples seek legal assistance before entering into these agreements. To avoid conflicts of interest and enforceability issues, each member of the couple should be represented by a different lawyer. This costs a few thousand dollars, and some couples may instead decide to draft their own prenuptial agreement or use forms available on the internet.

Many people do not seek prenuptial agreements because they are optimistic about their upcoming marriage or worry about signaling doubt about its success. Thus, despite judicial and social gains in the acceptance of prenuptial agreements, such agreements are not common. Often, the people most likely to seek prenuptial agreements are wealthy or have been previously divorced.

Margaret Ryznar

See also: Marriage and Legal Planning; Marriage Certificate/License; Postnuptial Agreement

Further Reading

Bix, Brian. 1998. "Bargaining in the Shadow of Love: The Enforcement of Premarital Agreements and How We

Think About Marriage." *William and Mary Law Review* 40, no. 1: 145–208.

Mahar, Heather. 2003. "Why Are There So Few Prenuptial Agreements?" *Olin Center Discussion Paper No. 436.* Available online at http://www.law.harvard.edu/programs/olin_center/papers/pdf/436.pdf.

Posner v. Posner, 233 So. 2d 381. Fla. 1970.

Ryznar, Margaret and Anna Stepień-Sporek. 2009. "To Have and the Hold, For Richer or Richer: Premarital Agreements in the Comparative Context." *Chapman Law Review* 13, no. 1: 27–62.

Uniform Premarital Agreement Act. 1983.

R

Registry (Bridal and Wedding)

The gift registry is a tool created by retailers to help soon-to-be brides specify to their potential guests what gifts they would like to receive at their bridal shower and/or wedding ceremony. Although the act of gift-giving during bridal and wedding ceremonies has occurred far back into history, the creation of bridal and wedding gift registries began in the 19th century and became standardized in the early 20th century. Since then, registries have changed considerably, taking on different forms and revolving around different people and purposes. Registries were first created by elites in the middle of the 19th century, where brides-to-be would include in their wedding invitations a list of items they would like to receive on their wedding day. Silver, linen, fine china, and crystal were among the gifts most often included in these early registries, reflecting the fact that registries were meant to help build the new family's home. By the early 20th century, middle-class people began creating registries, as well.

The first record of an in-store registry was in 1901, where the clerk Herman Winkle placed brides' names and preferences on index cards (Otnes and Pleck 2003, 75). By the middle of the 20th century, businesses caught on and began creating blueprints. They would go as far as to connect with guests and select gifts from their department for them, mailing the receipt and ensuring that nothing was bought twice. According to Otnes and Pleck (2003, 76), between 1984 and 1997, the number of brides saying that they planned to use a registry increased, as did the number of registry gifts given. This may be because registries were beginning to have looser norms and guidelines. Brides have historically created registries, but now both parties are often involved in the process, and couples usually follow current social norms and/or websites' suggestions in selecting items. Registries today often include traditional items such as crystal and fine china, as well as items like small kitchen appliances, cookware, and bed and bath linens.

In addition, almost all registries are now housed on retailers' websites, and couples simply include a link in bridal and wedding invitations. It is popular for couples to have multiple registries to diversify the items and prices, and there are options online for "universal registries" which include registries from multiple stores on one list. Retailers have also created standardized registries that couples can easily choose from, and there are over 500 registries they can pick from. This diversification of gifts is not only convenient for the couple but also provides guests with the ability to choose gifts usually ranging from $50–$200 (Hanlon 2020). The bridal gift is usually less expensive than the wedding gift, and in recent years, guests have spent an average of $150 on wedding gifts, and claim they are willing to spend up to $350 on all gifts; these numbers are projected to rise with millennials (those born between 1981–1996) (Renter 2018).

Furthermore, registries are now more varied because some couples do not need traditional gifts for beginning a new family or home. For example, couples who cohabited before marriage may not need basic household items and thus include non-traditional items on their registry, such as payments toward their honeymoon, charitable donations, or even just cash. An important aspect about the gift-giving process is that registries are set up to make easy exchanges for the couple with no obligation for them to keep the gift if it does not fit their needs. Apart from helping with the start of a new family or home, the act of giving registry gifts also symbolizes the status of the gift-giver. When one is giving a gift, they are symbolizing their relationship with the couple, as well as their economic standing. For instance, if they give a gift, they know the couple will like that is not on the list, but it shows that they are close to the couple. Conversely, if they give a gift, they personally think is nice but is not on the list, it can show their distance from the couple.

Today, couples can make their way onto the internet for tips and tricks for creating the "best" registry, as well as how to communicate to their guests that they have created a registry and would like them to contribute. With this growing change, it allows space for partners to get creative in thinking about what their new family will need for their future.

Jori A. Nkwenti

See also: Bridal Showers; Wedding Party; Wedding Reception

Further Reading

Bradford, Tonya and John Sherry. 2013. "Orchestrating Rituals Through Retailers: An Examination of Gift Registry." *Journal of Retailing* 89, no. 2: 158–175.

Hanlon, Sara. 2020. "The Ultimate Wedding Registry Checklist for Every Couple." Wedding Registry. Last modified December 10, 2020. https://www.weddingwire.com/wedding ideas/registry-checklist.

Montemurro, Beth. 2002. "'You Go 'Cause You Have to': The Bridal Shower as a Ritual of Obligation." *Symbolic Interaction* 25, no. 1:67–92.

Otnes, Cele and Elizabeth Pleck. 2003. *Cinderella Dreams: The Allure of the Lavish Wedding.* California: University of California Press.

Renter, Elizabeth. 2018. "The Secret World of Wedding Gift Giving: NerdWallet Study." Nerd Wallet. Last modified April 26, 2018. https://www.nerdwallet.com/blog/wedding-guest study/.

Relationship Education

Relationship education (RE) provides individuals and couples with the knowledge and skills needed to achieve their aspirations for healthy romantic relationships and strong marriages. It is an educational approach to strengthening relationships and is different from marriage or couple therapy with licensed therapists. Typically, participants receive 8–20 hours of face-to-face instruction in small-group settings. The earliest RE efforts were offered through religious organizations; engaged couples preparing for marriage were a primary target. While faith-based efforts continue to be an important part of RE offerings today, secular options have grown dramatically since the 1970s. Several marriage and family therapist scholar-practitioners played an important role in the secular growth of RE beginning in the 1970s and 1980s, emphasizing the prevention of serious relationship problems.

"Relationship education" is a generic term that covers a variety of educational interventions (Hawkins 2015). Some curricula target youth and young adults to help them achieve basic relationship literacy and avoid relationship pitfalls. Given the lengthening time between puberty and marriage for most young people today and the significant challenges they face in forming and sustaining healthy relationships, this form of RE has become increasingly important. Most young couples now live together before marriage but many of them—especially less educated couples—tend to slide into relationship transitions rather than make clear decisions and commitments. Because many of these couples have children in their unions, some RE programs target these unmarried parents, most of whom want to provide a stable future together for the sake of their children (Halpern-Meekin 2019). Many couples begin marriage with significant relationship problems and baggage. Accordingly, there is a strong case for helping engaged couples—even those who have lived together before marriage—strengthen their relationship skills before marrying (or sometimes end their relationship when serious red flags are discovered) (Clyde, Hawkins, and Willoughby 2019).

While divorce rates have gradually declined since the early 1980s, risks remain historically high, especially for less educated couples (National Marriage Project 2019). Accordingly, many RE programs target married couples, trying to help them maintain and strengthen their relationships. Some of these programs are designed specifically for couples making the challenging transition to parenthood when life gets more complex and energies are drained by childcare

demands and heightened financial needs (Pinquart and Teubert 2010). Other programs are designed for the unique challenges that remarried couples and blended families face (Lucier-Greer and Adler-Baeder 2012). With recent changes in the legal status of same-sex unions, programs designed specifically for same-sex couples are emerging (Whitton et al. 2017). Also, there are educational programs for highly distressed couples who are thinking about divorce. These are usually offered as weekend retreats and sponsored by religious organizations.

Additional research is needed on participation rates in formal RE. One study suggested that about 30% of married couples had participated in premarital education (Stanley et al. 2006). A recent study with a nationally representative sample of early-married couples finds that about 38% of individuals reported some kind and level of involvement with relationship help-seeking (White et al. 2019). But this figure included formal counseling and some of the help-seeking was self-directed (e.g., self-help books, websites). Digital delivery of RE is showing promise and could increase overall participation rates (Doss et al. 2019). Many RE studies report that substantial proportions of participants come to RE already in some relationship distress; this is especially so for programs serving lower-income individuals and couples (Bradford, Hawkins, and Acker 2015).

There is a strong and growing evidence base for RE. There have been more than 300 evaluation studies over the years. Early on, these studies were almost exclusively looking at samples of educated, middle-class individuals. A handful of studies that synthesized this body of research documented moderate positive effects on relationship quality and communication skills (Hawkins 2015). Over the past decade, studies of RE programs with more disadvantaged, less educated samples have dominated the field (Hawkins 2019). The results here are more mixed, with some studies showing no effects, some showing small-to-moderate effects, and some showing more complex patterns of effects. However, a consistent finding across nearly two dozen studies that have examined who benefits the most from RE programs is that more distressed and disadvantaged individuals and couples derive the most benefit. While most studies show some positive impact on relationship quality, fewer have shown positive effects on relationship stability. It appears that RE programs may reduce the risk of divorce somewhat among married couples, but studies have not shown an ability to increase marriage rates for unmarried couples. RE shows evidence of reducing abusive behaviors. More evidence is needed on the long-term effectiveness of RE for youth (Simpson, Leonhardt, and Hawkins 2017). Finally, an important set of studies is finding small but significant positive effects of RE on children's well-being, probably through reduced parental stress (Cowan and Cowan 2019).

The substantial and growing body of research on the effects of RE on more disadvantaged families is a direct result of recent government support for these programs. The federal government began funding demonstration projects and evaluation studies of RE programs in the mid-2000s (Randles 2017). This controversial new policy initiative was spurred by the public costs of family instability. These programs, funded by the federal Administration for Children and Families, have reached nearly 200,000 lower-income individuals a year (Hawkins 2019). Parallel to the federal policy initiative, several states also began supporting RE programs but all but one or two of those formal state initiatives have ended or been suspended. Some communities have formed coalitions of religious and secular organizations to support and increase RE services. However, almost all of these are privately funded.

Despite the noteworthy successes of the RE field since the 1970s, significant challenges remain. Perhaps the biggest is moving beyond a focus on individual program success to population impact to reduce family instability and social poverty in society. This is the ultimate goal of RE efforts. To achieve this goal, the field will need to spur innovations that improve the effectiveness and reach of RE (Hawkins 2019).

Alan J. Hawkins

See also: Parent Education Programs

Further Reading

Bradford, Angela B., Alan J. Hawkins, and Jennifer Acker. 2015. "If we build it, they will come: Exploring policy and practice implications of public support for couple and relationship education for lower income and relationally distressed couples." *Family Process* 54, no. 4: 639–654.

Clyde, Tiffany L., Alan J. Hawkins, and Brian J. Willoughby. 2019. "Revising premarital interventions for the next generation." *Journal of Marital and Family Therapy.* https://doi.org/10.1111/jmft.12378

Cowan, Carolyn Pape and Philip A. Cowan. 2019. "Enhancing parenting effectiveness, fathers' involvement, couple relationship quality, and children's development: Breaking down silos in family policy making and service delivery." *Journal of Family Theory & Review*, 11, no. 1: 92–111.

Doss, Brian D., McKenzie K. Roddy, Kathryn M. Nowlan, Karen Rothman, and Andrew Christensen. 2019. "Maintenance of gains in relationship and individual functioning following the online relationship program." *Behavior Therapy*, 50, no. 1: 73–86.

Halford, Kim W. 2011. *Marriage and relationship education: What works and how to provide it.* New York: Guilford.

Halpern-Meekin, Sarah. 2019. *Social poverty: Low-income parents and the struggle for family and community ties.* New York: New York University Press.

Hawkins, Alan J. 2015. "Does it work? Effectiveness research on relationship and marriage education." In James Ponzetti (Ed.), *Evidence-based approaches to relationship and marriage education.* New York: Routledge, pp. 60–73.

Hawkins, Alan J. 2019. *Are federally-supported relationship education programs for lower income individuals and couples working? A review of evaluation research.* American Enterprise Institute, Washington, D.C.

Lucier-Greer, Mallory and Francesca Adler-Baeder. 2012. "Does couple and relationship education work for individuals in stepfamilies? A meta-analytic study." *Family Relations*, 61, no. 5: 756–769.

National Marriage Project. 2019. *State of our unions: 2019.* Charlottesville, VA: National Marriage Project.

Pinquart, Martin, and Daniela Teubert. 2010. "Effects of parenting education with expectant and new parents: A meta-analysis." *Journal of Family Psychology* 24, no. 3: 316–327. https://doi.org/10.1037/a0019691

Randles, Jennifer M. 2017. *Proposing prosperity: Marriage education policy and inequality in America.* New York: Columbia University.

Simpson, David M., Nathan D. Leonhardt, and Alan J. Hawkins. 2017. "Learning about love: A meta-analytic study of individually oriented relationship education programs for adolescents and emerging adults." *Journal of Youth and Adolescence*, 47, no. 3: 477–489.

Stanley, Scott M., Paul R. Amato, Christine A. Johnson, and Howard J. Markham. 2006. "Premarital education, marital quality, and marital stability: Findings from a large, random household survey." *Journal of Family Psychology*, 20, no. 1: 117–126.

White, Thomas, Stephen F. Duncan, Jeremy B. Yorgason, Spencer L. James, and Erin K. Holmes. 2019. "Marital interventions: Participation, helpfulness, and change in a nationally representative sample." *Family Relations* 69, no. 1: 125–137.

Whitton, Sarah W., Shelby B. Scott, Christina Dyar, Eliza M. Weitbrecht, David W. Hutshell, and Amanda D. Kuryluk. 2017. "Piloting relationship education for female same-sex couples: Results of small randomized waitlist-control trial." *Journal of Family Psychology*, 31, no. 7: 878–888.

Relationship Self-Sabotage

Relationship sabotage has long been loosely defined in empirical and popular literature. The terminology has been used as a synonym for self-handicapping. Self-handicapping is a cognitive strategy employed with the overall aim of self-protection (Jones and Berglas 1978, 200–206; Rhodewalt 1990, 1255–1268). However, the term self-handicapping does not fully account for intrinsic self-defeating attitudes and behaviors, such as fear of intimacy and rejection sensitivity, which are commonly observed as contributors for the dissolution of intimate engagements (Peel et al. 2019, 1–9). This is because the concept of self-handicapping is limited to physical barriers employed to explicitly hinder performance-driven activities, such as excessive drinking or eating, constantly feeling sick, or feeling easily distracted (Strube 1986, 211–224; Peel et al. 2019, 1–9).

Many individuals who report either actively searching for love (or having searched for love in the past), report experiencing failure or negative outcomes. Individuals testify to being stuck in a continuous cycle of relationship sabotage (Peel 2020). It is observed that "some are no longer entering romantic relationships; others move through relationships too quickly searching for 'the one' and making quick assessments of their romantic partners; while others stay in their relationships but 'check out' or do not work on their issues" (Peel and Caltabiano 2021a). Thus, a better use of the term "self-sabotage" is employed to explain attitudinal or behavioral expressions of individuals dealing with intrapersonal struggles (Post 1988, 191–205).

The evidence to suggest that patterns of attitudes and behaviors characteristic of insecure attachment (i.e., anxious and avoidant) lead to the dissolution of romantic engagements is strong and well documented. Typically, anxious individuals fall in love frequently, experience extreme self-doubt, excessive need for approval, and distress when others are unavailable or unresponsive (Harper, Dickson, and Welsh 2006, 435–443; Hazan and Shaver 1987,

511–524). Whereas, avoidant individuals mostly do not believe in love, repress feelings of insecurity, are reluctant to engage in self-disclosure, and express an excessive need for self-reliance. Accordingly, investigations have linked self-defeating traits such as rejection sensitivity (i.e., anxious expectation of rejection in situations involving significant others; Downey and Feldman 1996, 1327–1343) to anxiously attached individuals and fear of intimacy (i.e., the lack of ability to exchange feelings or thoughts with significant others; Descutner and Thelen 1991, 218–225) to avoidant attached individuals. However, previous research has failed to consider whether the stressors which are often inherent in the maintenance of an intimate relationship may trigger defensive functioning among people who are insecurely attached, leading to the use of self-defeating behaviors, and in turn resulting in self-sabotage (Peel and colleagues 2018, 98–116; 2019, 1–9; 2021a, 1–17; 2021b, 99–131).

Rusk and Rothbaum (2010, 31–43) have explained how patterns of insecure attachment and insecure relationship views can trigger defensive functioning in individuals. This means that in stressful moments in the relationship, individual's attachment system will activate, determining how they respond to situations and set goals (Rusk and Rothbaum 2010, 34). Peel, Caltabiano, Buckby, and McBain (2019, 1–9) have offered examples of how these interactions might take place in romantic settings. For instance, if the individual has a secure attachment system, they might resort to an adaptive response and set learning goals informed by constructive strategies (e.g., "to improve communication to deal with relationships stressors"). However, if the attachment system is not secure, the individual might resort to a maladaptive response and set self-validation goals informed by defensive strategies (e.g., "to avoid new relationships to prevent from getting hurt"; Peel, Caltabiano, Buckby, and McBain 2019, 1–9). Overall, Rusk and Rothbaum's (2010, 31–43) theoretical model, based on attachment and goal orientation theories, proposed a possible path to explain self-sabotage in romantic relationships.

Peel and colleagues (2018, 98–116; 2019, 1–9; 2021a, 1–17; 2021b, 99–131) introduced a new approach and model to explain how self-defeating attitudes and behaviors in romantic relationships might lead to relationship sabotage. Individuals who sabotage relationships are often committed to portraying a win-win outcome. They typically hold insecure views of romantic relationships and although they might be doing all they can to maintain the relationship (Ayduk, Downey, and Kim 2001, 868–877), failure is an expected outcome (Rusk and Rothbaum 2010, 31–43). Individuals are not always aware of self-defeating patterns of attitudes and behaviors. Therefore, in the context of romantic relationships, "the individual guarantees a win if the engagement survives despite the employed defensive strategies or if the engagement fails, in which case their insecure beliefs are validated." Altogether, self-sabotaging behaviors in romantic relationships are expressed as impeding success or withdrawing effort and justifying failure (Peel and colleagues 2018, 98–116; 2019, 1–9; 2021, 1–17; 2021, 99–131).

The definition for relationship sabotage was coined from interviews with practicing psychologists specializing in romantic relationships (Peel, Caltabiano, and McBain 2019, 1–9) and the lived experiences of individuals in relationships (Peel and Caltabiano 2021b, 99–131). Furthermore, Peel and Caltabiano (2021a, 1–17) developed a scale to measure self-sabotage in romantic relationships, the Relationship Sabotage Scale (RSS), with three confirmed factors (1) Defensiveness, (2) Trust Difficulty, and (3) Lack of Relationship Skills. Defensiveness is a counter-attack to a perceived threat. An example of defensiveness is feeling criticized and misunderstood by a partner. Trust difficulty involves struggling to believe romantic partners and feeling jealous of their attention to others. People who feel this way might not feel safe and avoid feeling vulnerable in relationships. Lack of relationship skills involves having limited insight or awareness into destructive tendencies in relationships. This may be a result of poor relationship role models, or negative interactions and outcomes from previous relationships. Examples of lack of relationship skills are not being open to finding solutions and working out issues in the relationship, and not admitting fault for issues in the relationship (Peel and Caltabiano 2021a, 1–17).

The way people might arrive at relationship sabotage is best demonstrated in a "circular manner." It was noted that while "insecure attachment leads to self-sabotage; sabotaging relationships are reinforcing existing insecure attachment styles or establishing new vulnerable styles." Furthermore, sabotaging tendencies are influencing how people perceive quality and stress in the relationship, which essentially means that the individual's own actions are what keeps them from maintaining successful relationships (Peel 2020; Peel and Caltabiano 2021a, 1–17).

A novel finding resultant from the series of studies conducted by Peel and colleagues highlighted that lack of relationship skills also contributes to self-sabotage and perception of relationship quality. Therefore, the focus should shift to improving the skills of people in relationships to increase their understanding of what it entails to be in a couple engagement and the expectations of a romantic partnership (Peel 2020; Peel and Caltabiano 2021a, 1–17).

Future research in this area will benefit from further exploring lived experiences of relationship sabotage across several relationships and the long-term effects of self-defeating attitudes and behaviors. Another recommendation includes testing the RSS with more people in same-sex relationships and couples. For instance, a worthy investigation will be to compare the responses from each of the partners where relationships are broken or have been sabotaged. Lastly, individual differences such as gender, age, and sexual orientation need to be further explored regarding its effect on self-sabotage in relationships. Support already exists for mean differences between age categories, gender, and sex orientation groups. Also, cultural expectations are expected to come into effect (Peel 2020; Peel and Caltabiano 2021a, 1–17).

Regardless of how people sabotage their relationships, the pattern to self-sabotage is breakable. Overall, findings from the research conducted by Peel and colleagues highlighted that sabotage does not have to lead to relationship dissolution. Lived experiences of relationship sabotage suggest that insight into relationships, managing relationship expectations, and collaboration with partners toward better communication and commitment, are essential steps toward breaking the cycle of self-sabotage and maintaining successful future relationships. Conclusively, individuals should seek insight into how best to engage with romantic partners toward shared relationship goals. The key finding is that only the individual can engage in pursuing what the self wants, as opposed to self-sabotaging.

Raquel Peel

See also: Relationship Education

Further Reading

Ayduk, O., G. Downey, and M. Kim. 2001. "Rejection sensitivity and depressive symptoms in women." *Personality and Social Psychology Bulletin* 27, no. 7: 868–877. https://doi.org/10.1177/0146167201277009.

Descutner, C. J. and M. H. Thelen. 1991. "Development and validation of a fear-of-intimacy scale." *Psychological Assessment: A Journal of Consulting and Clinical Psychology* 3 no. 2: 218–225. https://doi.org/10.1037/1040-3590.3.2.218.

Downey, G. and S. I. Feldman. 1996. "Implications of rejection sensitivity for intimate relationships." *Journal of Personality and Social Psychology* 70, no. 6: 1327–1343. https://doi.org/10.1037/0022-3514.70.6.1327.

Gottman, J. M., and N. Silver. 2015. *The seven principles for making marriage work*. New York: Harmony Books.

Harper, M. S., Joseph W. Dickson, and D. P. Welsh. 2006. "Self-silencing and rejection sensitivity in adolescent romantic relationships." *Journal of Youth and Adolescence* 35, no. 3: 435–443. https://doi.org/10.1007/s10964-006-9048-3.

Hazan, C. and P. Shaver. 1987. "Romantic love conceptualized as an attachment process." *Journal of Personality and Social Psychology* 52, no. 3: 511–524. https://doi.org/10.1037//0022-3514.52.3.511.

Jones, E. E. and S. Berglas. 1978. "Control of attributions about the self through self-handicapping strategies: The appeal of alcohol and the role of underachievement." *Personality and Social Psychology Bulletin* 4, no. 2: 200–206. https://doi.org/10.1177/014616727800400205.

Knee, C. Raymond. 1998. "Implicit theories of relationships: Assessment and prediction of romantic relationship initiation, coping, and longevity." *Journal of Personality and Social Psychology* 74, no. 2: 360–370. https://doi.org/10.1037/0022-3514.74.2.360.

Peel, Raquel. 2020. *Relationship sabotage: An attachment and goal-orientation perspective on seeking love yet failing to maintain romantic relationships.* PhD Thesis, James Cook University.

Peel, R. and N. Caltabiano. 2021a. "The Relationship Sabotage Scale: An evaluation of factor analyses and constructive validity." *BMC Psychology* 9, no. 146: 1–17. https://doi.org/10.1186/s40359-021-00644-0

Peel, R. and N. Caltabiano. 2021b. "Why do we sabotage love? A thematic analysis of lived experiences of relationship breakdown and maintenance." *Journal of Couple & Relationship Therapy* 20, no. 2: 99–131. https://doi.org/10.1080/15332691.2020.1795039

Peel, R., N. Caltabiano, B. Buckby, and K. A. McBain. 2018. "Mental health diagnoses and relationship breakdown: Which is the chicken and which the egg?" *International Journal of Innovation, Creativity and Change* 4, no. 3: 98–116. http://www.ijicc.net/images/Vol4_iss3_spec_ed_nov_2018/Raquel_Peel_et_al.pdf

Peel, R., N. Caltabiano, B. Buckby, and K. A. McBain. 2019. "Defining romantic self-sabotage: A thematic analysis of interviews with practicing psychologists." *Journal of Relationship Research* 10 (e16): 1–9. https://doi.org/10.1017/jrr.2019.7.

Post, R. Dee. 1988. "Self-sabotage among successful women." *Psychotherapy in Private Practice* 6, no. 3: 191–205. https://doi.org/10.1300/J294v06n03_29.

Rhodewalt, F. 1990. "Self-handicappers. Individual differences in the preference for anticipatory self-protective acts." In *Self-handicapping. The Paradox That Isn't,* edited by R. L. Higgins, C. R. Snyder and S. Berglas, 69–106. https://doi.org/10.1007/978-1-4899-0861-2.

Rusk, N. and F. Rothbaum. 2010. "From stress to learning: Attachment theory meets goal orientation theory." *Review of General Psychology* 14, no. 1: 31–43. https://doi.org/10.1037/a0018123.

Strube, M. J. 1986. "An analysis of the self-handicapping scale." *Basic and Applied Social Psychology* 7, no. 3: 211–224. https://doi.org/10.1207/s15324834basp0703_4.

Relationships, Technology and

Technology has evolved significantly since the 1990s, particularly in the context of relationships. With romantic partners and family members, we can communicate digitally like we never have been able to before. We can text on our phones, share a picture on Instagram or Facebook, or send a funny video on Snapchat. We can also meet potential dating partners and spouses using technology, such as dating applications or online dating websites. As a result of this increased use and reliance on technology, many studies have examined how technology impacts family and romantic relationships.

Generally, the use of technology has supplemented face-to-face relationships. Although we generally enjoy spending quality time with our friends and family members in person, we also have an opportunity to feel close to them using technology. Media multiplexity theory provides an easy way to understand how the use of technology can impact relationships. According to this theory, the more digital connections we have with someone, the stronger the relationship (Haythornthwaite 2005). In other words, in our strongest relationships, which are usually family and romantic relationships, we are often connected through multiple digital platforms. We might be connected with them over multiple social media networks, we might text them, we might Skype or Facetime them, or even e-mail them, mostly using a mixture of these methods. It is important to note that few studies have examined the consequence of having a partner or family member who is not on social media, although theoretically these relationships may be weaker according to media multiplexity theory. On social media, we can communicate with our romantic partners and family members directly through messaging or posting on their content, or indirectly by "liking" their material. We can also share our relationships with others by posting pictures or other content of the relationship on social media. The more digital connections we have with someone, the more opportunity we have to talk with them, feel close with them, and increase our interdependence, which increases the strength of the relationship. However, it should be noted that what matters the most for the satisfaction of our close relationships is spending quality time in person. Individuals commonly prefer to spend time face-to-face with someone, compared to digital interactions, and more time spent in person is associated with increases in satisfaction with that relationship. Spending time in person provides a "3D" experience of a relationship, where we are able to analyze various nonverbal cues and expressions, whereas interaction via technology only provides a "2D" experience, where we are only given a certain amount of information, in which we have to concentrate on in order to discern context.

Additionally, the impact that technology has on relationships depends on the behavior that is being engaged. Certain behaviors are associated with benefits for family and romantic relationships, whereas other behaviors are associated with negative consequences for these same relationships. Generally, active behaviors on technology, which are behaviors that represent direct communication between individuals, such as texting, messaging, commenting on posts, and video chatting, appear to be beneficial for relationships, whereas passive activities, such as monitoring others' content on digital content, may be bad for relationships. Studies have shown that interaction via social media not only increases the amount of time that family members can spend together (albeit virtually) but also strengthens family ties. Also, sharing information about a relationship on social media (through a picture or post) is typically beneficial for close relationships, unless too much information is shared. Individuals who over-share relationship information on social media typically link their self-esteem to the quality of their relationships. By over-sharing, individuals are boasting about their relationship (even if the relationship isn't the best) in order to boost the quality of that relationship, which in turn helps individuals feel better about themselves. This research also reveals that posting positive information about a relationship on social media, even when that may not be the case, is also associated with self-esteem. For instance, if someone got into a fight with a family member, they might post a picture illustrating the strength of the relationship on social media because they feel guilty and/or because they want to remediate the conflict, which subsequently promotes interpersonal and relational self-esteem. In other words, over-sharing information about a relationship, or sharing information that is not genuine, are ways to help promote self-esteem.

Next, many studies demonstrate that communicating directly with someone, including a family member or romantic partner, through digital means is beneficial for those relationships. The pace of life has increased steadily over time, where there seems to be less free time available to spend in person with friends, romantic partners, or family members. Technology provides an opportunity to spend time with these individuals without actually physically being with them. Texting with a family member when you might have been busy all day with school activities helps strengthen and maintain that relationship. Sharing a romantic post on Facebook or Instagram when you haven't seen your partner for a while increases satisfaction and commitment within these relationships. Even married couples capitalize on the benefits of talking to each other via technology, as they can communicate about practical issues (such as who is going to pick up the kids from school) and romantic issues (sending an "I love you" text message, for instance). Technology is particularly beneficial for relationships that are long distance, like living far away from a friend, family member, or romantic partner, as digital communication is the predominant method to see and interact with each other. Compared to relationships that didn't use any or spent less time talking with someone via social media, those who use social media for communication in their close relationships commonly report more satisfaction with their family and romantic relationships. Although data illustrates that women are more likely to communicate than men on social media, the benefits of self-disclosure appear consistent regardless of gender. Currently, there is debate about technological saturation, meaning an overreliance on social media in relationships. Some researchers argue that spending too much time on social media is unhealthy for relationships as it detracts from engaging in quality time face-to-face, whereas others say that spending time on social media is simply replacing communication mediums of the past (i.e., phone, letters, etc.). Generally, using technology to actively communicate is associated with higher quality relationships, but relationships should continue to value and spend time together face-to-face.

Technology also has the potential to hinder relationships. First, the most common behavior associated with increases in conflict are passive behaviors such as monitoring, also known as "Facebook stalking" or "creeping." Through this behavior, an individual may come across information that is likely to upset them, make them feel jealous, or hurt their feelings. For example, someone's romantic partner shared a post on Facebook, and someone "likes" the post that this person doesn't know. Not knowing the source of the "like" could induce jealousy or make them upset, particularly if that person is a threat to the relationship, like an ex-partner (Tokunaga 2011). Additionally, sharing inappropriate content on social media is associated with negative consequences for families, friendships, and couples, prompting declines in social approval and increases in conflict within those relationships. If someone posts an embarrassing picture or creates a post that makes an individual feel uncomfortable, then the individual typically feels less satisfied in that relationship (Seidman, Langlais, and Havens 2017). Another negative consequence from media use is non-reciprocal digital communication, otherwise known as "ghosting." It is possible that an individual sends a message to a romantic partner, spouse, or family member, and that person doesn't respond. The lack of response is usually predictive of conflict in relationships (Punyanut-Carter and Wrench 2017). When forming romantic relationships, ghosting even predicts the end of a relationship (LeFebvre, Allen, and Rasner 2019). Although research on the consequences of ghosting is ongoing, some researchers suggest that a way to cope with ghosting is through the continuation of the relationship on social media by simply monitoring the others' content. For instance, someone who was ghosted may continue to maintain a connection with the individual who ghosted them, and use the connection to illustrate

that they are fine or potentially better as a result of the ghosting experience. Subsequently, if an individual spends too much time on technology, whether it's video games, social media, texting, etc., individuals are spending less time face-to-face with others. The lack of face-to-face time is predictive of declines in the quality of those relationships. To promote relationship maintenance, we should find ways to maximize time spent together, and use social media in ways to assist and promote relationship quality, rather than hinder our relationships.

Technology has illustrated some benefits and drawbacks for our close relationships. It is important to remember that technology can be beneficial when it's used to supplement face-to-face communication in family and romantic relationships. The more ways we connect to others we are close with, the stronger those relationships are. However, technology shouldn't be used as a substitute for these relationships. Spending too much time on technology, particularly through passive activities, is likely to hinder the quality of our relationships with others.

Michael Langlais

See also: Dating and Courtship 2000–Present; Relationships, Technology and

Further Reading

Haythornthwaite, Caroline. 2005. "Social Networks and Internet Connectivity Effects." *Information, Communication & Society* 8, no. 2: 125–147. https://doi.org /10.1080/13691180500146185.

LeFebvre, Leah, Mike Allen, and Ryan Rasner. 2019. "Ghosting in Emerging Adults' Romantic Relationships: The Digital Dissolution Disappearance Strategy." *Imagination, Cognition and*

Personality: Consciousness in Theory, Research, and Clinical Practice. https://doi.org/10.1177/0276236618820519.

Punyanut-Carter, Narissra M. and Jason S. Wrench. 2017. *The Impact of Social Media in Modern Romantic Relationships.* Lanham: Lexington Books.

Seidman, Gwendolyn, Michael R. Langlais, and Amanda Havens. 2017. "Romantic Relationship-Oriented Facebook Activities and the Satisfaction of Belonging Needs." *Psychology of Popular Media Culture* 8, no. 1: 52–62. http://dx.doi.org/10.1037/ppm0000165.

Tokunaga, Robert S. 2011. "Social Networking Site or Social Surveillance Site? Understanding the Use of Interpersonal Electronic Surveillance in Romantic Relationships." *Computers in Human Behavior* 27, no. 2: 705–713. https://doi.org/10.1016/j.chb.2010.08.014.

Remarriage

The practice of remarriage is common in the United States; however, during the 20th century, most remarriages followed widowhood. Remarriage after divorce became the predominant form of remarriage. A reason for the increase in remarriages is due to the greater number of divorced individuals in the general population. Fifty-six percent of men and 59% of women that have ever been married have divorced (Brown and Porter 2013). From 2008–2021 about 34% of men between the ages of 60–69 had two or more marriages, this is compared to 30% of women that had ever been married (Smock and Schwartz 2020).

Caucasians are the most likely to remarry after divorce compared to Latinas, African Americans, and Asians who are less likely to remarry after divorce. In 2012, six-in-ten whites who were previously married had remarried, this is compared to 51% of Latina, 48% of Blacks, and 46% of Asians (Livingston 2014). From data obtained from the mid-2000s showed that Black and Latina women took a longer time to remarry compared to white women. After marital dissolution, 25% of white women remarried (Smock and Schwartz 2020).

Remarriages are on the rise and have shown higher levels of satisfaction than the previous marriage. Unfortunately, remarriage does not receive as much attention as the first marriage; there is little research available that discusses religious variations in the propensity of remarriage.

There appears to be factors that contribute to the timing of when someone remarries. One of the factors that contribute to the timing of remarriage is religious capital. Religious capital is measured by the attendance of worship services, which can be helpful to the idea of remarriage. When a person attends worship services on a regular basis, it will help provide an opportunity to nurture and increase religious capital through interaction with co-religionists to improve their views of remarriage and even find a remarriage partner. Additionally, when an individual attends frequent worship services, it shows that the individual has a continued religious commitment and is devoted to remarriage. Another religious component that has an impact on remarriage is spiritual capital. Spiritual capital can be developed through the manifestation of investment in "non-institutionalized or individualized religious activities, such as in-home devotional efforts, private prayers, personal scripture study, or religious salience" (Xu and Bartkowski 2017, p. 4). Spiritual capital affects the timing of remarriage because it shows how important religion is to the individual and the extent to which they have internalized the religious values, norms, and teaching that are geared toward remarriage.

Remarriage also has an impact on children. It is not uncommon for children to exhibit adjustment issues when their parents have decided to divorce or remarry. One factor that is not given much attention in relation to children's adjustment is the child's attachment to their parents. Children may see the introduction of a new parent and possible stepsiblings as a threat to the bond that they share with their parents. The threat of the bond could be due to the child feeling that their parents are being less supportive, which could make the child feel abandoned or experience anxiety about separating. It was reported that adolescents expressed not being able to talk to their parents about their feelings. It must be noted that not all children or adolescents experience adjustment issues when their parents' divorce or marry. Although this can be a painful process, 75–80% of children and adolescents do not experience psychological problems, achieve their educational and career goals and go on to have healthy interpersonal relationships (Pino 2001).

La Toya L Patterson

See also: Blended Families; Half-Siblings and Stepsiblings

Further Reading

Brown, Susannah M., and Jeremy Porter. 2013. "The Effects of Religion on Remarriage Among American Women: Evidence from the National Survey of Family Growth." *Journal of Divorce & Remarriage* 54, no. 2: 142–162.

Cherlin, Andrew J. 1981. *Marriage, Divorce, Remarriage.* Cambridge: Harvard University Press.

Livingston, Gretchen. 2014. "The Demographic of Remarriage." Retrieved from https://www.pewresearch.org/social-trends/2014/11/14/chapter-2-the-demographics-of-remarriage/

Pino, Christopher J. 2001. *Divorce, Remarriage, and Blended Families: Divorce Counseling and Research Perspectives.* San Jose: Authors Choice Press.

Smock, Pamela J., and Christine Schwartz. 2020. "The Demography of Families: A Review of Patterns and Change." *Journal of Marriage & Family* 82, no. 1: 9–34.

Teachman, Jay, Lucky Tedow, and Gina Kim. 2013. "The Demography of Families." In G. W. Peterson and K. R. Bush (Eds.), *Handbook of Marriage and Family.* New York: Springer, pp. 39–65.

Xu, Xiaohe and John P. Bartkowski. 2017. "Remarriage Timing: Does Religion Matter?" *Religions* 8, no. 160: 1–13.

S

Second Shift

The "Second Shift," as Arlie Hochschild described it in her 1989 book of the same name, is the extra household work and childcare done by women after working outside the home. When both the husband and the wife have paying jobs, the wife works a "second shift" at home because she is the one who takes care of the children and does the chores that a household requires on a daily basis (e.g., doing dishes, cooking, laundry, cleaning), while the husband attends to occasional house repairs or mows the lawn every other week. Men's participation in household labor and childcare has increased over the years, but much of the work inside the house still falls on women's shoulders.

Traditionally, women stay home with children while men are working outside the home, but industrialization and changes in economy and gender roles have led to a steady increase in the number of women in the workforce, creating two-job marriages. The transition of women into the workforce has not been smooth because workplaces have remained inflexible about the demands of women in their family, and the husbands have not adapted to the changes. Hochschild coined the term a "stalled revolution," referring to the stagnated changes in government, corporate, and men's attitudes and help despite the changes in or the "revolution" of women.

There is absolutely nothing wrong with making conscious decisions to embrace traditional gender roles in adulthood, but a problem arises when there is a mismatch in ideologies between a couple. If the man is traditional and the woman is egalitarian, the man will expect the woman to do more housework, but the woman will expect the man to do equal work. A problem also arises when a couple's ideology does not fit their circumstances. If both the man and the woman are traditional, but they cannot afford to live with only one paycheck, they are both "forced" to work even though this is not their ideal.

The second shift is associated with a variety of problems in the family. Hochschild found that women were over-tired, sleep-deprived, emotionally drained, and even physically ill. As the wife does most of the housework, she feels resentment and perceives unfairness in the arrangement, which in turn creates personal and marital distress (Claffey and Mickelson 2009, 819–831). Other couples may manage their tension by creating "myths" of the reality, for example by convincing themselves that they are sharing housework equally, even if that is not true. In fact, in a more recent book on the second shift, Darcy Lockman (2019) states that men doing 35% of the housework felt that it was a fair share and that women doing 66% of the housework reported that it was the fairest arrangement.

The marital relationship is not the only family subsystem affected by the second shift. Children are away from their parents all day and feel resentment toward their parents for not spending enough time with them even while at home. They may even act out in efforts to receive attention from their parents. In turn, parents may feel guilty and indulge their children by forgoing discipline. Two-job parents may also face criticism from members of the extended family who may interfere in family decisions. For example, Hochschild described that when a well-educated woman and mother of three-year-old twin boys applied for a job, her mother expressed her disapproval because she believed that the job would get in the way of her daughter adequately raising her two young children.

At a family level, one way to eliminate or at least lessen the second shift for mothers is to not devalue the role of a homemaker and to share this role between the man and the woman. Indeed, when the husband and the wife share similar gender role attitudes that are primarily egalitarian rather than traditional, they show the highest levels of marital satisfaction and the most egalitarian division of housework (Helms et al. 2010, 568–577). Another way is to hire domestic helpers and/or nannies if couples can afford it, though doing so often creates emotional and interpersonal complexities among all parties involved (Stack 2019). At a societal level, one way to reduce the second shift is profamily reforms. For example, the government could give tax credits to developers who build affordable housing and family services near places of work. The government could also create policies that offer paid parental leave to both mothers and fathers.

Multiple studies have provided evidence for the "second shift" of women across different racial/ethnic groups in the United States though the inequality in the division of housework seems more pronounced among Hispanic and Asian households than their Black and white counterparts (Sayer and Fine 2011, 259–265; Wight, Bianchi, and Hunt 2013, 394–427). The second shift is prevalent among Black and white couples even when the husband and the wife earn comparable salaries (Kamo and Cohen 1998, 131–145). The second shift goes beyond the U.S. border. A European cross-national study (Ruppanner 2010, 963–975) demonstrated that regardless of gender empowerment levels (akin to egalitarianism), women did more housework than men in all 25 countries. However, women spent less housework hours if countries had higher parliamentary representations of women, higher percentage of women employed as professionals, and more equal female-male wage ratios. Another study with data from 29 nations (Tai and Baxter 2018, 2461–2485) showed that more than a half of the women perceived the division of household labor to be unfair and that when they did, they were more likely to report disagreements with their spouses about housework divisions than when men did. This finding suggests that women hold the key to any potential change, because if women perceive housework division to be fair even when it is not, they will not be motivated to change it. However, if women perceive unfairness in household labor, they will express disagreement, which will potentially lead to changes.

Ultimately, the second shift does not only concern women but also men; even though women are the main "victims" of this phenomenon, its effects on women have repercussions on husbands and children as well. With increases in women's participation in the workforce around the world, governments, workplaces, and men should actively support women inside and outside the home. If we regarded the second shift as a larger, societal problem rather than a private one, we may be able to create a true "revolution" in the family and beyond.

Anastasia Giorgoudi and Aya Shigeto

See also: Economic Independence; Gender Roles

Further Reading

Blakemore, Judith E. Owen. 2003. "Children's Beliefs about Violating Gender Norms: Boys Shouldn't Look Like Girls, and Girls Shouldn't Act Like Boys." *Sex Roles: A Journal of Research* 48, no. 9–10 (05): 411–419. https://doi.org/10.1023/A:1023574427720.

Claffey, Sharon T. and Kristin D. Mickelson. 2009. "Division of Household Labor and Distress: The Role of Perceived Fairness for Employed Mothers." *Sex Roles: A Journal of Research* 60, no. 11–12: 819–831. https://doi.org/10.1007/s11199-008-9578-0.

Helms, Heather M., Jill K. Walls, Ann C. Crouter, and Susan M. McHale. 2010. "Provider Role Attitudes, Marital Satisfaction, Role Overload, and Housework: A Dyadic Approach." *Journal of Family Psychology* 24, no. 5: 568–577. https://doi.org/10.1037/a0020637.

Hochschild, Arlie Russell. 2003. *The Second Shift*. New York: Penguin Books.

Kamo, Yoshinori and Ellen L. Cohen. 1998. "Division of Household Work between Partners: A Comparison of Black and White Couples." *Journal of Comparative Family Studies* 29, no. 1: 131–145.

Lockman, Darcy. 2019. *All the Rage: Mothers, Fathers, and the Myth of Equal Partnership*. New York: Harper, an imprint of HarperCollins Publishers.

Ruppanner, Leah E. 2010. "Cross-National Reports of Housework: An Investigation of the Gender Empowerment Measure." *Social Science Research* 39, no. 6: 963–975. https://doi.org/10.1016/j.ssresearch.2010.04.

Sayer, Liana C. and Leigh Fine. 2011. "Racial-Ethnic Differences in U.S. Married Women's and Men's Housework." *Social Indicators Research* 101, no. 2: 259–265. https://doi.org/10.1007/s11205-010-9645-0.

Stack, Megan K. 2019. *Women's Work: A Reckoning with Home and Help*. New York: Doubleday

Tai, Tsui-o and Janeen Baxter. 2018. "Perceptions of Fairness and Housework Disagreement: A Comparative Analysis." *Journal of Family Issues* 39, no. 8: 2461–2485. https://doi.org10.1177/0192513X18758346.

Wight, Vanessa R., Suzanne M. Bianchi, and Bijou R. Hunt. 2013. "Explaining Racial/Ethnic Variation in Partnered Women's and Men's Housework: Does One Size Fit All?" *Journal of Family Issues* 34, no. 3: 394–427. https://doi.org/10.1177/0192513X12437705

Sexual Compatibility

Sexual compatibility is described as "similarities in the emotional, cognitive, and behavioral components of a sexual relationship" (Apt et al. 1996). The emotional part of sexual compatibility is reached when both members in the sexual relationship feel "sexually close" to one another, and the cognitive component is achieved when individuals share the same "beliefs, desires and attitudes" (Offman et al. 2005, 31). Sexual compatibility and sexual satisfaction are positively associated with one another by the ways in which an individual evaluates their own satisfaction, their partner's satisfaction, and the sexual relationship overall.

However, there are two forms of sexual compatibility that are important to distinguish from one another. *Actual sexual compatibility* is when partners share similarities between turn-ons and turn-offs. *Perceived sexual compatibility* is when individuals believe their partner possesses the same "sexual needs, preferences, and desires" as them (Mark et al. 2013, 202). Perceived sexual compatibility is most commonly achieved when sexual satisfaction is reached for a member of the sexual relationship. Perceived sexual compatibility is not equivalent to actual sexual compatibility because if only one member of the sexual interaction achieves sexual satisfaction, it does not guarantee the other member has. Therefore, when both partners do perceive that they are compatible, actual sexual compatibility, sexual functioning, and relationship satisfaction are likely to be reached.

Much of the research surrounding sexual compatibility only observes one partner in heterosexual relationships and is significantly gendered, focusing on women's sexual satisfaction and sexual desire because women are considered most sensitive to sexual functioning in relationships. They relate most significantly to emotional compatibility among the components of sexual compatibility (Hurlbert et al. 1993, 325–347). In multiple studies, researchers found that: women's perceived sexual compatibility is associated with sexual desire, women with hypoactive sexual desire experience less depression and stress, and women who feel compatible with their partner feel sexually motivated (Hurlbert, Apt, and Rombough 1996, 7–14; Hurlbert, Apt, Hurlbert, and Pierce 2000, 325–347; Hurlbert, Apt, and Rabehl 1993, 3–13). While male sexual compatibility is

lacking exploration, the current research shows that men also experience less depression and anxiety when they perceive sexual compatibility.

To understand sexual compatibility, researchers use The Hurlbert Index of Sexual Compatibility (HISC), a self-reported survey consisting of 25 statements (e.g., "I think my partner understands me sexually," "My partner and I share similar sexual fantasies," "My partner enjoys doing certain sexual things that I dislike"), which are scored using a scale. The index of statements allows researchers to understand how members of sexual relationships understand their sexual compatibility with their partner; however, this information can only help to understand perceived sexual compatibility because it measures one member of the sexual relationship. Therefore, both members of that specific relationship would need to take the HISC to understand actual sexual compatibility.

Madison P. Tincha

See also: Marital Success; Premarital Sex; Value Theory/Role Theory

Further Reading

Apt, Carol, David Farley Hurlbert, Gabriel R. Sarmiento, and Melissa K. Hurlbert. 1996. "The Role of Fellatio in Marital Sexuality: An Examination of Sexual Compatibility and Sexual Desire." *Sexual and Marital Therapy* 11, no. 4: 383–392.

Hurlbert, David Farley, Carol Apt, Melissa K. Hurlbert, and Aaron Paul Pierce. 2000. "Sexual Compatibility and the Sexual Desire–Motivation Relation in Females with Hypoactive Sexual Desire Disorder." *Behavior Modification* 24: 325–347.

Hurlbert, David Farley, Carol Apt, and S. M. Rabehl. 1993. "Key Variables to Understanding Female Sexual

Satisfaction: An Examination of Women in Non-distressed Marriages." *Journal of Sex & Marital Therapy* 19: 154–165.

Hurlbert, David Farley, Carol Apt, and S. Rombough. 1996. "The Female Experience of Sexual Desire as a Function of Sexual Compatibility in an Intimate Relationship." *Canadian Journal of Human Sexuality* 5: 7–14.

Hurlbert, David Farley, Cynthia L. White, David R. Powell, and Carol Apt. 1993. "Orgasm Consistency Training in the Treatment of Women Reporting Hypoactive Sexual Desire: An Outcome Comparison of Women-Only Groups and Couples-Only Groups." *Journal of Behaviour Therapy & Experimental Psychiatry* 24: 3–13.

Mark, Kristen P., Robin R. Milhausen, and Scott B. Maitland. 2013. "The Impact of Sexual Compatibility on Sexual and Relationship Satisfaction in a Sample of Young Adult Heterosexual Couples." *Sexual and Relationship Therapy* 28, no. 3: 201–214. doi:10.1080/14681994.2013.807336.

Offman, Alia and Kimberly Matheson. 2005. "Sexual Compatibility and Sexual Functioning in Intimate Relationships." *The Canadian Journal of Human Sexuality* 14, no. 12: 31–39.

Shared Custody

Shared custody is an increasingly common custody arrangement following divorce. Arrangements can vary, and may be determined by parents and signed off by a judge or determined solely by a judge. Custody arrangements are often implemented in families facing divorce; however, custody arrangements should be implemented in any family structure change in which there are children involved, such as nonmarital unions or cohabitating relationships that end with children present. There are advantages and disadvantages for parents and children with a shared custody arrangement.

The term "shared custody" is used interchangeably with the term "joint custody." Shared custody is divided into two categories: legal shared custody and physical shared custody. Legal custody determines who will make important decisions that affect the children on topics such as education, health, and religion. Shared legal custody allows both parents to have continued decision-making authority in their child or children's lives. Physical custody determines where and with whom the child will reside. In some cases, a child will have two homes and divide his or her time between the two residences.

Determination of custody varies in each state. Standards-based on each state's custody laws are provided to judges to be used when making decisions regarding the parenting of children following a divorce. These standards are used not only in the legal system, but also in mediation and custody arrangement negotiations between parents. The current standard used in determining custody arrangements is referred to as the "best interest of the child" standard. This states that the legal system (courts and judges) must consider relevant information regarding both the parents and children, and make decisions that are in the best interest of the child. The needs of the children are the focus when determining custody, parenting time, and child support.

There is great variation in the definition of shared custody. Previous definitions of shared custody defined it as a 50/50 division of time by each parent, such as "one week on, one week off."

However, this proved difficult in practice, so many creative and complicated options are used today. For example, a child may spend Monday and Tuesday with one parent, then every Wednesday and Thursday with the other parent, and then alternate weekends with each parent. The ratio of shared physical custody is not limited to 50/50; a child can spend 33% of his or her time with one parent and 66% of the time with the other parent. Other states, court systems, judges or practitioners may more broadly define shared physical custody as 25% parenting time, or roughly 90 overnights per year.

Researchers have studied factors associated with parents who shared custody, including income, education, legal representation, age, and employment outside of the home. Families with higher incomes are more likely to share physical custody than parents with lower income levels. The income of a family is influential in the determination of custody arrangements, as maintaining two living spaces for children can be expensive. A shared physical custody arrangement is three times more likely when the total income of family is $80,000 when compared to other families with a total income of $20,000 (Cancian and Meyer 1998, 154–156). In addition, shared physical custody is more likely if parents own their home.

Parents with higher education levels are more likely to share physical custody when compared to parents with only a high school education. Individuals with higher education levels tend to have more resources to prepare themselves for the divorce process. Higher-educated parents may also have more enhanced negotiation skills and may be more likely to supervise their legal counsel by asking questions and voicing their wishes

regarding the custody arrangement. Parents with higher education levels than their former partners have been found to be more likely to gain sole physical custody than their less educated former partners (Kelly, Redenbach, and Rinaman 2005, 35–37).

Legal representation also impacts the custody arrangement determined among parents. When fathers are the only parent with legal representation, a shared custody or father-sole-custody arrangement is more likely to be the result than mother-sole-custody (Cancian and Meyer 1998, 154–156). If the father does not have legal representation and the mother does, the final arrangement is also more likely to be shared custody or mother-sole-custody. Previously, mothers were given the preference of custody as society saw them as the nurturer of the family (Demo and Fine 2010, 66).

The age of the mother has also been linked to the likelihood of shared physical custody arrangements. Teenage mothers and mothers over the age of 33 were more likely to share physical custody then mothers in their 20s and early 30s. Other research has found that shared physical and/or legal custody arrangements are more likely among older mothers. A shared physical custody arrangement is more likely to occur when both parents are employed outside of the home. If fathers are unemployed, the likelihood of them receiving shared physical custody of the children drastically decreases.

One advantage of a shared custody arrangement is for continued contact to be maintained between the children and parents. The function of a shared custody arrangement allows the opportunity for a balance to be maintained for both parents regarding time with children and time without. A successfully shared custody arrangement may provide children with a stronger sense of security and a lower likelihood of feeling abandoned by one parent. Parents with shared custody often cite greater satisfaction regarding their custody arrangement. In addition, shared custody arrangements are found to have lower rates of relitigation when the arrangement is chosen by parents instead of being court imposed.

Disadvantages are also present with shared custody arrangements. If one parent would like to relocate, a shared custody arrangement poses a potential challenge for the parent. When parents do not reside in the same state it is more difficult for the parent residing out of state to arrange time with the child or children. Facilitating travel to visit the other parent can also be expensive as well as time-consuming. In addition, children may feel shuttled between households and faced with differences in household rules, parental expectations, and socioeconomic statuses. For parents, a shared custody arrangement continues to connect the parents. This could be especially difficult depending on the feelings the parents have toward one another, the amount of conflict they might tend to have, and their willingness or desire for a different type of custody arrangement.

Jaimee L. Hartenstein

See also: Child-Inclusive Mediation

Further Reading

Cancian, Maria, and Daniel R. Meyer. 1998. "Who Gets Custody?" *Demography* 35, no. 2: 147–157.

Clarke-Stewart, Alison, and Cornelia Brentano. 2008. *Divorce: Causes and Consequences.* New Haven, CT: Yale University Press.

Demo, David H. and Mark A. Fine. 2010. *Beyond the Average Divorce.* Thousand Oaks, CA: Sage Publications.

Emery, Robert E. 2012. *Renegotiating Family Relationships: Divorce, Child Custody and Mediation.* New York: Guilford Press.

Kelly, Robert F., Laura Redenbach, and William C. Rinaman. 2005. "Determinants of Sole and Joint Physical Custody Arrangements in a National Sample of Divorces." *American Journal of Family Law* 19, no. 1: 25–43.

Socioeconomic Status and Marriage

Marriage has long played a centrally important role in American culture, and for much of American history, marriage has been a near universal experience (Cherlin 2010a). However, beginning in the mid-20th century, marriage rates started to drop for some groups—specifically, individuals who were lower in socioeconomic status. Socioeconomic status (SES) refers to one's social standing and is usually conceptualized as a combination of an individual's income, level of education, and type of occupation. Marriage rates for low-SES individuals began decreasing around 1960, while at the same time staying high for high-SES individuals. Today there is a large gap in marriage rates; for example, of individuals age twenty-five or older, 50% of those with a high school degree or less are married, whereas 65% of those with a college degree are married (Pew Research Center 2017).

It is not the case that low-SES individuals are less interested in marriage than high-SES individuals. In fact, quite the opposite seems to be true: low-SES individuals hold marriage in such high esteem that they want to be sure that they are prepared to live up to it, rather than setting themselves up for divorce. Thus, concerns about their financial well-being and the ability to provide for a family seem to be contributing to low-SES individuals choosing not to marry. Low-income unmarried adults are much more likely than high-income unmarried adults to say that not being financially secure is a major reason why they are not married (Pew Research Center 2017), and interviews with low-SES unmarried parents indicate that they want to be able to afford a wedding and house before getting married (Edin and Kefalas 2007). Even if low-SES individuals do get married, the stress and financial strain of their situation can have negative effects on their relationship. For example, low-SES married couples report financial concerns as one of the top problems in their relationship (Jackson et al. 2016), and married couples with high levels of financial strain communicate more negatively with each other, even if they are happy in their relationship (Williamson, Karney, and Bradbury 2013). And, it turns out that low-SES couples do go on to divorce at a much higher rate than high-SES couples, indicating that concerns about their ability to maintain a stable marriage in the face of poverty and financial strain were not unfounded.

Though low-SES individuals are often choosing not to marry, this does not mean that they are not partnering and forming families. Instead, low-SES individuals are living together and having children without being married. Not surprisingly, rates of cohabitation and nonmarital childbearing have been increasing over the past few decades, at the same time that marriage rates have fallen. Non-marital childbearing has now reached its highest ever in the United States, with 40% of children born to unmarried parents, the majority of whom are low-SES (Child Trends Databank 2016).

Turning toward high-SES individuals: although lifetime marriage rates have remained high for these individuals, their marital patterns have also been shifting over the past few decades. High-SES individuals have been delaying the age at which they get married, choosing to spend their twenties going to college, getting established in their careers, and building their financial stability before getting married (Cherlin 2010b). These individuals are engaging in "capstone marriages" in which marriage comes after a great deal of personal development and achievement. This is in contrast with "cornerstone marriages," which were the norm in the first half of the 20th century, in which individuals got married at a young age, then went to school or built their career, with their marriage as the foundation to their adult life.

At the same time that marriage rates were changing by socioeconomic status, married couples were becoming more similar to each other. In particular, educational homogamy in marriage was increasing, which means that individuals are now more likely to marry someone with the same level of education than they were in the past (Schwartz and Mare 2005). The cutoff seems to be college: individuals with a bachelor's degree or higher are very unlikely to marry someone else who does not have a bachelor's degree or higher, and individuals with only a high school diploma are very unlikely to marry someone with a college degree. Income equality between husbands and wives has also increased over time, which is partly a reflection of educational homogamy: individuals with similar levels of education are likely to have similar incomes. However, income equality within couples also reflects the fact that more women are staying in the workforce after having children, whereas in the past, even those with a college degree would often leave the workforce after becoming a mother (Sweeney and Cancian 2004). This means that high-SES individuals are marrying each other and creating high-SES families, while low-SES individuals are partnering or cohabiting with other low-SES individuals, or staying single, both of which create low-SES families.

In the past, there was one pathway to family formation that nearly everyone in the United States followed: marriage, career, and kids, in that order. Now, there are two distinct pathways to family formation in the United States that are clearly separated by socioeconomic status. In the first pathway, high-SES individuals go to college, start a career, get married, then have kids. In the second pathway, low-SES individuals go to high school, cohabitate with their partner, have kids, and may or may not end up getting married.

Hannah C. Williamson

See also: Unmarried Cohabitation

Further Reading

Cherlin, Andrew J. 2010a. *The Marriage-Go-Round*. New York: Alfred A. Knopf.

Cherlin, Andrew J. 2010b. "Demographic Trends in the United States: A Review of Research in the 2000s." *Journal of Marriage and Family* 72, no. 3: 403–419. https://doi.org/10.1111/j.1741-3737.2010.00710.x.

Child Trends Databank. 2016. *Births to Unmarried Women: Indicators of Child and Youth Well-Being*. Bethesda, MD.

Edin, Kathryn, and Maria Kefalas. 2007. *Promises I Can Keep: Why Poor Women Put Motherhood before Marriage*. Berkeley, CA: University of California Press.

Jackson, Grace L., Thomas E. Trail, David P. Kennedy, Hannah C. Williamson, Thomas N. Bradbury, and Benjamin R. Karney. 2016. "The Salience and Severity of Relationship Problems among Low-Income Couples." *Journal of Family Psychology* 30 (February): 2–11. https://doi.org/10.1037/fam0000158.

Pew Research Center. 2017. "As U.S. Marriage Rate Hovers at 50%, Education Gap in Marital Status Widens." Washington, DC. https://www.pewresearch.org/fact-tank/2017/09/14/as-u-s-marriage-rate-hovers-at-50-education-gap-in-marital-status-widens/.

Schwartz, Christine R. and Robert D. Mare. 2005. "Trends in Educational Assortative Marriage from 1940 to 2003." *Demography* 42, no. 4: 621–646. https://doi.org/10.1353/dem.2005.0036.

Sweeney, Megan M. and Maria Cancian. 2004. "The Changing Importance of White Women's Economic Prospects for Assortative Mating." *Journal of Marriage and Family* 66, no. 4: 1015–1028. https://doi.org/10.1111/j.0022-2445.2004.00073.x.

U.S. Census Bureau. 2017. "Current Population Survey Detailed Tables for Poverty." https://www.census.gov/data/tables/time-series/demo/income-poverty/cps-pov/pov-02.html.

Williamson, Hannah C., Benjamin R. Karney, and Thomas N. Bradbury. 2013. "Financial Strain and Stressful Events Predict Newlyweds' Negative Communication Independent of Relationship Satisfaction." *Journal of Family Psychology* 27: 65–75. https://doi.org/10.1037/a0031104.

Spousal Support

Spousal support, also known as spousal maintenance or alimony, is the payment by one spouse for the future support and maintenance of the other spouse after their divorce, either in a lump sum or on a continuing basis. Most often, it entails sharing the future income of one person with a former spouse who lacks an earning capacity. This is distinguishable from property division, which is the division of existing property between the couple at divorce, and from child support, which is the financial support for the children of the couple.

The concept of spousal support arrived to the American colonies from England, where it was available in a divorce from bed and board, a legal separation wherein the husband was still held accountable for financially providing for the wife. Spousal support eventually became gender neutral and available in divorces that completely severed the legal ties between spouses, stemming from the common law duty to support a spouse. Justifications for spousal support included compensation, the need for damages for breach of the marriage contract, the unpopularity of using taxpayer support for the lower income spouse, and the division of the economic benefits that the marriage created.

Spousal support is a state law issue, but many states have modeled their spousal maintenance law on the Uniform Marriage and Divorce Act (UMDA), offered by the National Conference of Commissioners on Uniform State Laws in 1970. The UMDA recommends that courts consider the following factors in making decisions about spousal support awards without considering fault for the divorce: (1) the financial resources of the party seeking spousal support; (2) the time necessary to acquire sufficient education or training to enable the party seeking spousal support to find appropriate employment; (3) the standard of living established during the marriage; (4) the duration of the marriage; (5) the age and the physical and emotional condition of the spouse seeking maintenance, and 6) the ability of the spouse to meet both spouses' needs. However, under the UMDA, a court may award spousal support in the first place only if the spouse seeking maintenance: (1) lacks sufficient property to provide for reasonable needs and (2) is unable to support himself or herself through appropriate employment or is the custodian of a child whose circumstances make it appropriate not to seek employment.

The UMDA breaks away from the traditional reliance upon maintenance as a primary means of support for divorced spouses. Spousal support has become less popular in many states over time, with limits being placed on its availability. For example, in Indiana, spousal support is available only for as long as a spouse cannot support himself or herself due to a personal physical or mental incapacity or due to a physically or mentally incapacitated child. Alternatively, up to three years of "rehabilitative maintenance" is available in Indiana based on (1) the educational level of each spouse; (2) interruptions in a spouse's education, training, or employment based on homemaking or caregiving responsibilities; (3) the earning capacity of each spouse; and (4) the time and expense necessary to acquire sufficient education or training to enable the spouse who is seeking maintenance to find appropriate employment. This represents the trend of limits placed on spousal support by the states in recent years. Many states also prefer property division to spousal support because it allows divorcing spouses to receive a clean break from each other instead of creating future obligations.

While it is not always easy to receive a spousal support award today, modification of the award by the payor may be difficult. Whether former spouses seek modification of spousal support varies. The standard for modification typically is whether a substantial and material change in circumstances justifies the modification of a spousal support award. Many states take the view that spousal support terminates when the recipient remarries because the new spouse takes on the duty of support. It is more controversial whether spousal support ends when a former spouse cohabitates with another.

There are instances when the payor minimizes income in order to avoid paying spousal support, such as choosing not to work. It is then possible for the court to award spousal support orders exceeding the payor's income by imputing income to the payor. For example, a court can examine a person's income from previous years if it was higher, or impute income according to what that person is capable of earning. Courts have also imputed income from a second job or another source when that income was previously earned on a recurrent or steady basis.

For decades prior to the 2017 tax reform, spousal support played a role in tax planning during divorce because spousal support was deductible by the payor and included in the gross income of the recipient. Paying spousal support, therefore, lowered the tax bill of the higher-income spouse, providing an

incentive to pay spousal support. However, a compliance issue arose because more people deducted their spousal support than included it in their gross income, which created a loss of tax revenue. After the 2017 tax reform, however, payors can no longer deduct their paid spousal support and recipients no longer must include it in gross income.

In sum, spousal support is a type of financial transfer at divorce, which allows a more vulnerable spouse to receive future support payments. However, there is no guarantee of receiving it, and states have been trending toward reducing it in favor of property division at divorce.

Margaret Ryznar

See also: Child Support Calculations; Division of Assets; Divorce and Legal Planning

Further Reading

Morgan, Kiley. 2011. "How Ubiquitous Are Alimony Awards? A Call for Current Data." *Journal of Contemporary Legal Issues* 20, no. 1: 95–102.

Starnes, Cynthia Lee. 2011. "Alimony Theory." *Family Law Quarterly* 45, no. 2: 271–292.

Willick, Marshal S. 2014. "A Universal Approach to Alimony: How Alimony Should Be Calculated and Why." *Journal of the American Academy of Matrimonial Lawyers* 27, no: 1: 153–244.

Stepfamilies

Stepfamilies form when at least one adult in a new committed opposite-sex or same-sex relationship brings a child or children from a previous relationship (Ganong and Coleman 2017). "Simple stepfamily" is a term commonly used to describe a stepfamily in which only *one* adult in a new committed relationship brings a child or children from a previous relationship. The term "complex stepfamily" is often used to describe a stepfamily in which *both* adults bring a child or children from previous relationships. These distinctions are important, as they highlight different stepfamily experiences.

A variety of terms have been used in place of *stepfamily* over time. Such labels include "blended family" and "remarried family." These alternative labels are generally unsuitable, as they do not necessarily reflect the reality of stepfamily experiences (Ganong and Coleman 2017). For instance, the term "blended family" presupposes that a stepfamily must somehow blend together in a prescribed way. "Remarried family" cannot be universally applied, as an increasing number of stepfamilies form through cohabitation rather than through marriage (Kreider and Ellis 2011). Consequently, the term *stepfamily* generally is used and favored among family scholars and practitioners (Ganong and Coleman 2017; Papernow 2013).

Stepfamilies represent an increasingly common family experience in the United States and beyond. Family demographers have estimated that nearly one-third of all children in the United States will live in a stepfamily household at some point before reaching adulthood. Data collected by the U.S. Census Bureau in 2021 indicated that 11% of minor children were living in a married or cohabiting stepfamily household—a nearly 4-point increase from 7.5% in 2009 (Kreider and Ellis 2011; Westrick-Payne and Wiborg 2021). Moreover, a survey conducted by the Pew Research Center found that 42% of adults in the United States had at least one step relative (Pew Research Center 2011). Taken together, stepfamilies clearly have become commonplace and warrant ongoing acknowledgment from family scholars, family practitioners, and policymakers.

The experiences of stepfamilies differ in important ways from other family types. For one, the pathways to stepfamily life often include demanding transitions, such as the death of a partner or the end of a committed relationship. Stepfamilies also face negative responses from society, either by being ignored by policymakers or by being stigmatized. Indeed, stepfamilies often have been viewed, either explicitly or implicitly, as functionally inferior to biologically related, two-parent families (Ganong and Coleman 2018). These societal responses can pressure stepfamilies to appear and function as though they are first-time, biologically related, two-parent families—a generally unrealistic and unproductive expectation (Papernow 2013).

Stepfamily formation also introduces intricate dynamics that stem from structurally merging existing family relationships with new, often ambiguous, stepfamily ties (Jensen 2021). On this front, family practitioners have highlighted five specific demands common to stepfamilies: (a) stuck insider and stuck outsider positions; (b) children experiencing high levels of change; (c) polarization of parenting tasks between parents and stepparents; (d) creating a new family culture; and (e) ex-partners being a part of stepfamily life (Papernow 2013). Each of these five demands is summarized below.

When stepfamilies form, parents often experience the role of "stuck insider" with their children, whereas stepparents often experience the role of "stuck outsider"

(Papernow 2013). That is, parents possess existing connections to their children and feel pulled toward maintaining norms and interactions that existed prior to the entrance of a new stepparent. Stepparents, on the other hand, can struggle integrating into the family and feel isolated or rejected. These insider and outsider positions can create tensions within the new couple relationship and inhibit the development of mutually satisfying stepfamily relationships. Building the new couple relationship and sustaining strong parent-child bonds are both important features of stepfamily functioning.

Stepfamily formation can also introduce significant change into the lives of children. Changes can include relocating to a new home and neighborhood, whereby children are displaced from their peer groups and other social networks. Many children in stepfamilies also experience loyalty binds, or situations in which children worry about being disloyal to a nonresident parent when connecting with a new stepparent. Children can also struggle with their resident parent drawing close to a new partner, especially if the parents' separation was relatively recent. Overall, children benefit from ongoing support from and connections with their parents and others amid the transition to stepfamily life and the changes it introduces.

Couples in stepfamilies must also navigate parenting tasks, which can yield disagreements and polarization. In an attempt to protect and advocate for their children, parents in stepfamilies can revert to a permissive style of parenting, marked by high levels of parental warmth and low levels of parental control. This might especially be true when stepparents adopt an authoritarian approach to parenting, marked by low levels of parental warmth and high levels of parental control. Research indicates that stepfamilies function optimally when stepparents do not assume parenting responsibilities, especially early on in stepfamily formation or when stepchildren are in their teenage years (Ganong and Coleman 2017). Instead, stepfamilies should allow space and time for children and stepparents to cultivate relationships that are mutually satisfying and that meet the needs of the family. Stepparents can assume a variety of roles, such as being academically involved in stepchildren's lives, being more casually connected, or eventually, being involved in many aspects of stepchildren's lives (Jensen 2019).

Another demand common to stepfamilies is establishing a new family culture. Even in the best of cases, it can take four or more years for stepfamilies to cultivate a new family identity and culture (Papernow 2013). Indeed, becoming a stepfamily is a process that unfolds over time; it is not an event that occurs instantaneously. Consequently, stepfamily formation requires patience and benefits from realistic expectations.

Many stepfamilies must also navigate connections with nonresident parents. That is, many parents continue to coparent their children with an ex-partner. As a result, stepfamily dynamics transcend the boundaries of a single household to include a larger network of parents. Children tend to fare best when their parental figures are cordial, cooperative, and avoid open conflict. Resident parents and non-resident parents should resist forming alliances with their children to retaliate or conspire against the other parent or stepparent. Instead, stepfamilies should seek to build a cooperative parenting team, with a focus on promoting the development and well-being of children.

Research indicates that the transition to stepfamily life is relatively less demanding when children are younger compared to when children are older (Jensen and Howard 2015). Older children have more time than younger children to grow accustomed to particular family routines and interactions. Consequently, when stepfamilies form, older children can respond with a greater amount of hesitation and resistance, favoring family conditions that predated the structural change. Young children, on the other hand, might not remember the transition to stepfamily life—for these children, stepfamily life simply is family life.

In addition to demands, stepfamilies can possess important strengths and opportunities. Foremost, stepfamily formation invites opportunities to cultivate unique and satisfying step relationships. As one example, family practitioners have highlighted the "intimate outsider" role that stepparents can assume (Papernow 2013). When stepparents become intimate outsiders, children can engage their stepparents as trusted advisors and confidants, holding conversations around topics that might be too charged for parents to address calmly or objectively (e.g., conversations about sex and career choices). High-quality stepfamily relationships are beneficial to children. Research suggests that when youth perceive high-quality stepfamily relationships, they are more likely to report high levels of psychological, behavioral, and even physical well-being (Jensen and Harris 2017; Jensen, Lippold, Mills-Koonce, and Fosco 2018).

In terms of stepfamily research, stepfamilies began drawing significant attention from scholars in the 1970s when stepfamily formation became more likely to follow parental divorce or separation rather than the death of a parent (Ganong and Coleman 2018). Much of this early research focused on how stepfamily experiences and outcomes differed from those of other family types, particularly first-time, biologically related, two-parent families. More recently, family scholars have advocated for research that focuses on what aspects of stepfamily life yield optimal outcomes for adults and children (Coleman, Ganong, and Russell 2013; Jensen and Sanner 2021). This new focus is productive because it identifies what works well and what does not work well in the specific context of stepfamily life. Information of this kind can enrich efforts to develop and implement programs and policies that aim to support stepfamilies.

With respect to existing resources and services, a variety of options currently exist for stepfamilies. An increasing number of self-help materials have been produced over time, allowing stepfamilies to gain new knowledge and insights related to stepfamily life. Formal education programs have also been developed that bring together stepfamilies in the community to help stepfamily members acquire helpful knowledge and develop new skills that can facilitate stepfamily functioning. Some stepfamilies benefit from more in-depth professional counseling, which can help stepfamily members resolve issues that are inhibiting stepfamily functioning. The use of technology (e.g., social media, smartphone applications) to educate, support, and connect stepfamilies has also become more common—a trend that will likely continue moving forward (Ganong and Coleman 2017).

Todd M. Jensen

See also: Dating after Divorce; Remarriage; Shared Custody; Stepfamilies, Developmental Stages; Stepfamily Education

Further Reading
Coleman, Marilyn, Lawrence Ganong, and Luke Russell. 2013. "Resilience in Stepfamilies." In *Handbook of Family Resilience*, edited by Dorothy Becvar. New York: Springer, 85–103.

Ganong, Lawrence and Marilyn Coleman. 2017. *Stepfamily Relationships: Development, Dynamics, and Interventions* (2nd ed.). New York: Springer.

Ganong, Lawrence, and Marilyn Coleman. 2018. "Studying Stepfamilies: Four Eras of Family Scholarship." *Family Process* 57, no. 1: 7–24.

Jensen, Todd M. 2019. "A Typology of Interactional Patterns Between Youth and Their Stepfathers: Associations with Family Relationship Quality and Youth Well-Being." *Family Process* 58, no. 2: 384–403.

Jensen, Todd M. 2021. "Theorizing Ambiguous Gain: Opportunities for Family Scholarship." *Journal of Family Theory & Review* 13, no. 1: 100–109.

Jensen, Todd M., and Kathleen Mullan Harris. 2017. "A Longitudinal Analysis of Stepfamily Relationship Quality and Adolescent Physical Health." *Journal of Adolescent Health* 61, no. 4: 486–492.

Jensen, Todd M. and Matthew O. Howard. 2015. "Perceived Stepparent–Child Relationship Quality: A Systematic Review of Stepchildren's Perspectives." *Marriage & Family Review* 51, no. 2: 99–153.

Jensen, Todd M., Melissa A. Lippold, Roger Mills-Koonce, and Gregory M. Fosco. 2018. "Stepfamily Relationship Quality and Children's Internalizing and Externalizing Problems." *Family Process* 57, no. 2: 477–495.

Jensen, Todd M. and Caroline Sanner. 2021. "A Scoping Review of Research on Well-Being Across Diverse Family Structures: Rethinking Approaches for Understanding Contemporary Families." *Journal of Family Theory & Review* 13, no. 4: 463–495.

Kreider, Rose M. and Renee Ellis. 2011. *Living Arrangements of Children: 2009.* Washington, DC: U.S. Census Bureau.

Papernow, Patricia. 2013. *Surviving and Thriving in Stepfamily Relationships: What Works and What Doesn't.* New York: Routledge.

Pew Research Center. 2011. *Pew Social & Demographic Trends Survey.* Washington, DC: Pew Research Center.

Westrick-Payne, Krista and Corrine Wiborg. 2021. *Children's Family Structure, 2021.* Family Profiles, FP-21-26. Bowling Green, OH: National Center for Family & Marriage Research.

Stepfamilies, Developmental Stages

Stepfamilies are an increasingly common family structure in the United States and abroad and are typically formed following a divorce. Although a typical family form, stepfamilies are likely to experience challenges as they develop. Stepfamily researcher and psychologist Patricia Papernow proposed a seven-stage model in 1993 to help members of stepfamilies better make sense of the challenges they experience. Papernow originally conceived this model in her dissertation work, where she drew upon both family systems theory and Gestalt theory to develop the model (1984).

Papernow makes a point to note that it is difficult for family members themselves to identify when they transition into a new stage, and that different families likely exhibit very different patterns as they move through the model. Nonetheless, Papernow's model describes typical stepfamily development and illuminates the common family challenges due to remarriage. For example, a common challenge to newly developed stepfamilies is how to change and modify old rituals such as birthday or holiday traditions. This model can explain how a family adapts to such a challenge as it develops over the years.

Papernow's Model of Stepfamily Development includes the following stages: *Fantasy Stage, Immersion Stage, Awareness Stage, Mobilization Stage, Action Stage, Contact Stage,* and *Resolution Stage.* These seven stages represent the *individual development* of stepfamily members, but the model also categorizes these seven individual stages within three larger stages of *family development.* In order for the model to reflect how individual family members progress through three developmental time periods, each of the seven stages is identified as being part of the early, middle, or later stages of stepfamily formation. The model's seven stages are therefore organized within these larger time stages (Early Stages: Fantasy Stage, Immersion Stage, and Awareness Stage; Middle Stages: Mobilization Stage and Action Stage; Later Stages: Contact Stage and Resolution Stage).

In the *Early Stages*, a stepfamily is likely still divided along biological lines, meaning biologically related siblings and parent-child dyads are prone to share the same rituals, rules, and expectations. Stepsiblings or stepchild–stepparent dyads have greater difficulty accomplishing these same tasks early on in stepfamily development. The first stage in this developmental period is the *Fantasy Stage*, where stepfamily members likely hold unrealistic, idealized, or even fantasy-like expectations. Stepparents may expect to immediately be welcomed into the family by their stepchildren. Biological parents may expect the new stepparent to help equally share the load of parenting duties. Stepchildren may fantasize that the new stepparent is only temporary, and that their biological parents will soon get back together. Many of these fantasized expectations are then shattered in the *Immersion Stage* when stepfamily members are confronted with the daily challenges of stepfamily life. Confusion due to uncertain roles, rules, and boundaries in the new stepfamily are likely to occur as family members become "immersed" in everyday family life. These challenges lead stepfamily members to enter the *Awareness Stage,* where they attempt to make sense of their unmet expectations and confusion. During this stage, family members gain more confidence in understanding their experiences, because they can make more psychological sense of their previously unfulfilled fantasies and the challenges currently present in their stepfamily.

In the *Middle Stages*, the stepfamily begins to loosen boundaries that once were only connected by biological relatedness, and instead the family attempts to strengthen step relationships as well. As the first middle stage, the *Mobilization Stage* is likely characterized by heightened conflict between stepfamily members as they try and make efforts to change boundaries. Family members are likely to speak up about difficulties in the stepfamily and express their true feelings about either wanted or unwelcomed family changes in this stage. Changes in discipline, communication, and rituals may be tried out by stepfamily members (stepparents especially) but are likely to be resisted, leading to conflict. Through trial and error, stepfamilies hopefully enter into the *Action Stage* where stepfamily members come to new agreements, work together, and take action to navigate previous challenges. Workable solutions have finally been reached in this stage through mutual effort. The stepfamily now has an established foundation in which to build upon and resulting changes may include a mix of old traditions prior to the remarriage and new traditions created as a new stepfamily. The stepparent and biological parent are also likely to take action and communicate the importance of their marital relationship to their children, being strategic in appearing as a unified front in the eyes of their children to help build a strong foundation for present and future family changes. Papernow argues that unsuccessful stepfamilies are those who remain in the Mobilization Stage and do not progress to the previously mentioned Action Stage.

In the *Later Stages*, the new boundaries established in the previous few stages become clear and stepsibling and stepchild–stepparent communication and contact become regular and reliable. This begins with the *Contact Stage*, which sees stepfamily members forming emotional bonds with one another and building more intimate family relationships. The intense challenges in the Mobilization Stage compared to the improved changes made in the Action Stage likely lead stepparents to be more authenticated in the eyes of their stepchildren in the present stage. Communication in this stage likely leads stepfamily members to feel genuine in their contact with one another, satisfied in their exchanges, and experience an overall sense of well-being. As a result, the stepfamily enters the *Resolution Stage* where family members not only experience satisfaction, but stability. Stepfamily members no longer feel a need for constant boundary negotiation or maintenance, but instead feel confident in a solid and established family foundation and history to draw upon when needed. This final stage is characterized by members holding a shared family identity, one that is integrated and not divided along step and biological lines. Unfortunately, stepparents may also experience grief in this final stage where the awareness of their established and emotional bond with their stepchildren causes them to be sharply aware that they must share this bond with another (potentially more entitled) biological parent.

Since Papernow's original development of this model, other researchers have validated its usefulness, replicating findings of these distinct stages in stepfamilies. However, some researchers, such as communication scholars Leslie Baxter, Dawn Braithwaite, and John Nicholson (1999), warn stepfamily stage models such as this one may be too prescriptive, linear, and ambiguous. Researcher criticism also notes Papernow's model does not fit all of the varying trajectories of modern stepfamily development (Baxter, Braithwaite, and Nicholson 1999, 19–20). Nonetheless, Papernow's model helps illuminate the challenges and development of many stepfamilies today.

Bailey M. Oliver-Blackburn

See also: Half-Siblings and Stepsiblings; Stepfamilies; Stepfamily Education; Remarriage

Further Reading

Baxter, Leslie A., Dawn O. Braithwaite, and John H. Nicholson. 1999. "Turning Points in the Development of Blended Families." *Journal of Social and Personal Relationships* 16, no. 3:291–314.

Bonnel, Karen S. and Patricia L. Papernow. 2019. *The Stepfamily Handbook: From Dating, to Getting Serious, to Forming a "Blended Family."* Kirkland: CMC Publishers.

Papernow, Patricia L. 1984. "The Stepfamily Cycle: An Experiential Model of Stepfamily Development." *Family Relations* 33, no. 3:355–363.

Papernow, Patricia L. 1993. *Becoming a Stepfamily: Patterns of Development in Remarried Families.* San Francisco: Jossey-Bass Publishers.

Papernow, Patricia L. 2013. *Surviving and Thriving in Stepfamily Relationships: What Works and What Doesn't.* New York: Routledge.

Stepfamilies, Laws and Policies

Stepfamilies have become increasingly common in the United States. Roughly half of all Americans report having a step relative and stepfamilies are more prevalent in the United States than in any country in the world. U.S. laws and policies regulating family life have not kept pace with this growth. Stepfamilies remain what Andrew Cherlin (1978) famously referred to as an "incomplete institution." According to Cherlin, unlike original two-parent families, stepfamilies lack clear social norms and guidelines needed to navigate relationships with one another and our language, customs, and laws do not adequately accommodate stepfamily relationships. Incomplete institutionalization is associated with greater stress, poorer relationship quality, lower levels of closeness, and overall lower well-being in stepfamilies than in traditional nuclear families.

In 1995, Mason and Simon (p. 447) wrote of the "ambiguous stepparent" and "a lack of coherent federal policy toward stepchildren." Stepfamilies seeking legal rights must navigate a "patchwork quilt" of federal laws, state laws, and court precedents (Pollet 2010). The situation is further complicated by a distinct *absence* of laws that would guide judges' and policymakers' decisions. The result is that stepparent and stepchildren's rights and responsibilities depend on largely on where they happen to reside, individual judges' definitions of family, and their ability to understand the law, pay for court costs, and retain an attorney. Without explicit instructions on how to act, teachers, public officials, social workers, and others who interact with stepfamilies are forced to make quick case-by-case decisions that are likely to be influenced by personal opinions, leading to inconsistent treatment.

Laws and policies governing stepfamily relationships are based on three legal concepts. First, stepparents are considered "legal strangers" to one another under the law, which attaches no significance to the stepparent–stepchild relationship. This concept is based on the outcome of the 1988 worker's compensation case, *Mendoza* v. *B.H.L. Electronics*. The judge ruled that the stepparent's benefits, after getting hurt on the job, would not go to his stepchildren. The result of *Mendoza* is that stepparents have almost no legal say in the education, health, religion, and welfare of stepchildren, even if they raised their stepchildren since birth. The majority of states do not require a stepparent to financially support a stepchild, even during their marriage. Adult stepchildren are typically not allowed to make medical or financial decisions for a stepparent who is ill or incapacitated. Employers are not required to extend health insurance to stepchildren. Should the parent and stepparents' relationship dissolve, stepchildren have no legal right to visitation or child support from their stepparent and stepparents have no legal right to see their stepchildren or gain custody. Stepchildren and stepgrandchildren are not considered "heirs" and can be denied inheritances even if the deceased designates them in their will. In hospitals, whether stepfamily members are allowed to be in areas designated "just family" can depend on the views of individual administrators, nurses, and doctors. Hundreds of thousands of children reside with a stepparent and no biological parent. They too are considered legal strangers under the law even if the stepparent is their sole caretaker.

The second legal concept affecting stepfamilies is "the rule of two," which means that children cannot have more than two legal parents. With few exceptions, the only way for stepparents to establish a legal relationship with their stepchild is to adopt them, which, in most cases, requires the child's other biological parent to relinquish their parental rights. Stepchildren can change their last name to match their stepparent's but there is no legal significance attached to doing

so. The "rule of two" permeates our educational system. School and extracurricular activity forms and on-line systems of communication typically allow space for two parties and teachers may be unprepared for meetings and correspondence with multiple parental figures.

The third concept guiding the legality of stepfamily relationships is the *de facto* ("in the place of") parent. A *de facto* parent under federal law is defined as "those stepparents legally married to a natural parent who primarily resides with their stepchildren or provide at least 50% of the child's support" (Mason and Simon 1995, 468–469). There have been cases in which the stepparent was granted custody in the case of the death of the custodial parent and several states have statutes that allow stepparent visitation if they are found to be *de facto* parents during the marriage. Yet, in the case of *Troxel v. Granville* (2000), the Supreme Court struck down a Washington state law that allowed a third party to petition the courts for child visitation over parental objections.

How federal policies regard stepfamilies is highly inconsistent. FERPA, the Family Education Rights and Privacy Act (1974), utilizes the *de facto* parent status. Under FERPA rules, a stepparent has rights to educational records but only if they are married to the child's natural parents and are present on a "day-to-day" basis. The Health Insurance Portability and Accountability Act (HIPAA) is the federal law that protects people's private health information. Under this 1996 law, a court order granted by a judge and/or a statement signed by a biological parent is required for stepparents to access a stepchild's information or make medical decisions for them.

Under U.S. federal income tax rules, stepfamily members can be claimed as dependents (if they meet certain criteria) and stepchildren can be claimed for the Earned Income Tax Credit, as long as the stepparent's household is the stepchild's primary place of residence. Temporary Assistance for Needy Families (TANF) provides cash assistance to poor families and stepchildren are included in benefit calculations. The Supplemental Nutrition Assistance Program (SNAP) provides food benefits to all household members who share food expenses and includes stepchildren. Supplemental Security Income (SSI) provides financial support to disabled adults and children whose parents are unable to support them financially. SSI, TANF, and SNAP assume stepchildren are supported by their stepparents and benefits are reduced in relation to stepparent's income. In contrast, Medicaid, a federal program that provides health care for low-income individuals and families, does *not* assume stepchildren are supported by their stepparents and benefits are not reduced.

Stepchildren can receive social security income in the event of their stepparent's death, but only if the stepparent and natural parent were married and it can be proven that the stepparent provided at least 50% of their support before their death. The rules of federal government employee benefits programs (e.g., retirement, life insurance) vary with some imposing conditions on stepparent–stepchild relationships and some excluding stepchildren outright. With few exceptions, military benefits (e.g., housing, death benefits) are not extended to anyone other than spouses and biological or adopted children. On the other hand, the 1993 Family and Medical Leave Act (FMLA) defines "child" without qualification.

The federal student loan program provides grants and low interest loans for college. The Free Application for Federal Student Aid (FAFSA) assumes stepchildren are financially supported by their stepparent as long as the parents are married, and the child lives with the stepparent at least half the time. The U.S. immigration system defines families broadly and stepfamily relations are considered "immediate relatives" for the purpose of family reunification if certain criteria are met (Gubernskaya and Drebey 2017).

Many states have laws regarding stepfamilies which can override federal ones. The number of states with laws specifically referring to "stepparents" and "stepchildren" is increasing and as of 2017, 12 states (Alaska, California, Delaware, Florida, Louisiana, Maine, New Jersey, New York, North Dakota, Oregon, Pennsylvania, Washington) had specific laws or court cases that allow children to have more than two parents (Kazyak et al. 2018; Peltz 2017). However, most of the time stepparents' rights and responsibilities are decided in the courts. For example, *Spells v. Spells* (1977) in Pennsylvania was the first appellate court decision to address stepparent visitation rights and stated that "rejection of visitation privileges cannot be grounded in the mere status as a stepparent" (Gregory 1998, 364).

Stepfamilies have always confounded our social institutions. In times past, stepmothers and new half-siblings disrupted the transmission of wealth and the line of succession. Compared to other Western countries, the United States has been slow to recognize and incorporate stepfamily relationships into its laws, policies, and programs. It is important to educate public officials, administrators, judges, and lawmakers on how stepfamilies' ambiguous legal status negatively affects their well-being.

Susan D. Stewart and Elcy E. Timothy

See also: Stepfamilies; Stepfamilies, Developmental Stages; Stepfamily Education

Further Reading

Cherlin, Andrew. 1978. "Remarriage as an Incomplete Institution." *American Journal of Sociology* 84, no. 3: 634–650.

Gregory, John DeWitt. 1998. "Blood Ties: A Rationale for Child Visitation by Legal Strangers." *Washington & Lee Law Review* 55: 351.

Gubernskaya, Zoya and Joanna Dreby. 2017. "U.S. Immigration Policy and the Case for Family Unity." *Journal on Migration and Human Security* 5, no. 2: 417–430.

Kazyak, Emily, Brandi Woodell, Kristin Scherrer, and Emma Finken. 2018. "Law and Family Formation Among LGBQ-Parent Families." *Family Court Review* 56, no. 3: 364–373.

Mason, Mary Ann and David W. Simon. 1995. "The Ambiguous Stepparent: Federal Legislation in Search of a Model." *Family Law Quarterly Review* 29: 445.

Peltz, Jennifer. 2017. "Courts and 'Tri-Parenting': A State-by-State Look." Last Modified November 15, 2018, https://www.boston.com/news/national-news/2017/06/18/courts-and-tri-parenting-a-state-by-state-look.

Pollet, Susan L. 2010. "Still a Patchwork Quilt: A Nationwide Survey of State Laws Regarding Stepparent Rights and Obligations." *Family Court Review* 48, no. 3: 528–540.

Spells v. Spells. 378 A. 2d. 879 1977.

Troxel v. Granville. 530 U.S. 57 2000.

Stepfamily Education

Stepfamily education began in the 1970s as a resource for remarried couples in which one spouse, or both, already had children. Today, stepfamily education is offered to married and unmarried couples with children from previous relationships. Offerings tend to be group-based, multi-session classes with a facilitator following a lesson guide. The facilitators are usually trained family-life educators, human service professionals, or therapists. The lessons cover topics related to the couple relationship, the coparenting relationship, and the parent-child relationships and how they influence each other in a stepfamily. The goal of the programs is to promote a healthy family environment through improving each relationship within the stepfamily as well as the relationship of coparents in different households.

The reason that stepfamily-specific education exists is because of the growing number of stepfamilies and unique issues in these blended households. Recent surveys find that over 40% of people in the United States report having a stepfamily member. This can occur through a first marriage, a remarriage, or cohabitation. Stepfamily experiences are even more common for young adults, certain ethnic minorities, and those without a college degree (Pew Research Center 2011).

Like couples in other family forms, couples in stepfamilies benefit from family life education that teaches "basic" interpersonal skills (e.g., communication, conflict and stress management). However, stepfamilies face unique stressors because of their complex structure. Children and adolescents often struggle with having a "new" parent, while new spouses or partners often struggle with establishing a relationship with their stepchild. There can also be challenges in the coparenting relationship between ex-partners who share biological children. These issues can be addressed in family life education classes specifically for stepfamilies. Recommended topics for stepfamily education include effective stepparenting practices, positive parenting practices between biological parent and child(ren) in a stepfamily, cooperative coparenting practices with past partners that help keep conflict low during transitions across households, financial management skills for issues related to stepfamilies (e.g., navigating child support), stepfamily rules and roles, appreciation of stepfamilies' unique characteristics, and the development and effective use of support networks (Adler-Baeder and Higginbotham 2004; Ganong and Coleman 2017).

A distinction between stepfamily education and general couples education (also known as marriage or relationship enhancement programs) is the target audience. Rather than recruiting couples, the target of stepfamily education is the entire family. Drawing upon ecological systems theories (Bronfenbrenner 1997), the design of popular stepfamily education programs allows for the participation of adults and their children and stepchildren. Having a child from a previous relationship is the defining characteristic of a stepfamily and one of the defining features of stepfamily education is the opportunity for adults and children to learn together.

Stepfamily education has documented multifaceted benefits. Evaluation research on stepfamily education found improvements in individual, relational, and family functioning; in some cases, the benefits are documented for up to one-year post-program (Lucier-Greer and Adler-Baeder 2012). Specifically, for the adults, there are reports of increased stepfamily skill development, family time, and awareness of common stepfamily issues. For the children, there are reports of interpersonal skill development including anger management and empathy. For both adults and child attendees of group stepfamily education there is evidence of increased social support and normalizing of stepfamily life. These results have been found in studies using samples of married, unmarried, same-sex couple, Caucasian, and Latino stepfamilies.

Not all stepfamilies are able or interested in attending group stepfamily education programs. Common reasons for non-use include thinking it is not needed and unavailability in communities. Those who are interested in attending as a family may still face logistical barriers, such as couples with joint custody or low-income families needing transportation. Alternatives to group stepfamily education include reading resources at home or participating in online programs, although less is known about the research foundation and effectiveness of these options. Professionally facilitated in-person stepfamily education (i.e., courses or counseling) is infrequently used; however, these are the forms of stepfamily education that are most frequently funded by the government, evaluated by researchers, and shown to improve relationship skills and knowledge. This suggests a need for practitioners to offer formal stepfamily education in ways that are viewed as accessible and relevant to stepfamilies (Higginbotham and Goodey 2016).

There is also a need for long-term evaluation studies of stepfamily education as well as more research that considers whether existing programs meet the needs of all types of stepfamilies. In a conceptual model for community-based stepfamily education, Robertson and colleagues (2006), highlight three categories that may affect people's specific needs: individual characteristics (e.g., age, ethnicity, gender, mental health, race and ethnic background, substance use), stepfamily characteristics (e.g., children's age, stepfamily complexity), and community characteristics (e.g., cultural customs). More research that tests whether existing stepfamily programs should be adapted for different types of individuals and different types of stepfamilies is needed to inform best educational practices for diverse stepfamilies.

Brian J. Higginbotham
and Francesca Adler-Baeder

See also: Coparenting and Divorce; Parent Education Programs; Remarriage; Stepfamilies

Further Reading

Adler-Baeder, Francesca, and Brian Higginbotham. 2004. "Implications of Remarriage and Stepfamily Formation for Marriage Education." *Family Relations* 53, no. 5: 448–458.

Bronfenbrenner, Urie. 1997. "Ecological Models of Human Development." In M. Gauvain and M. Cole (Eds.), *Readings on the Development of Children* (2nd ed.). (pp. 37–43). NY: Freeman. (Reprinted from *International Encyclopedia of Education*, Vol. 3, 2nd. ed., pp. 1643–1647, 1994, Oxford, England: Elsevier.)

Coleman, Marilyn, and Lynette Nickleberry. 2009. "An Evaluation of the Remarriage and Stepfamily Self-Help Literature." *Family Relations* 58, no. 5: 549–561.

Ganong, Larry H., and Marilyn Coleman. 2017. *Stepfamily Relationships: Development, Dynamics, and Interventions.* New York: Springer.

Higginbotham, Brian, and Sheryl Goodey. 2016. "Relationship and Marriage Education for Stepfamilies." In *Evidence-Based Approaches to Relationship and Marriage Education,* edited by James J. Ponzetti, 301–316. New York: Routledge.

Higginbotham, Brian, Julie Miller, and Sylvia Niehuis. 2009. "Remarriage Preparation: Usage, Perceived Helpfulness, and Dyadic Adjustment." *Family Relations* 58, no. 3: 316–329.

Lucier-Greer, Mallory, and Francesca Adler-Baeder. 2012. "Does Couple and Relationship Education Work for Individuals in Stepfamilies? A Meta-Analytic Study." *Family Relations* 61, no 5: 756–769.

Papernow, Patricia. 2018. "Clinical Guidelines for Working with Stepfamilies: What Family, Couple, Individual, and Child Therapists Need to Know." *Family Process* 57, no 1: 25–51.

Pew Research Center. 2011. "A Portrait of Stepfamilies." Retrieved from http://pewsocialtrends.org/2011/01/13/a-portrait-of-stepfamilies/

Reck, Katie, Brian Higginbotham, Linda Skogrand, and Patricia Davis. 2012. "Facilitating Stepfamily Education for Latinos." *Marriage & Family Review 48,* no. 2: 170–187.

Robertson, Anne, Francesca Adler-Baeder, Ann Collins, Donna DeMarco, David Fein, David Schramm. 2006. *Meeting the Needs of Married, Low-Income Stepfamily Couples in Marriage Education Services.* Final Report Prepared for Office of Planning, Research and Evaluation, Administration for Children and Families. Washington, DC: Abt Associates Inc.

Styles of Love (John Lee)

Styles of Love, initially "Colours of Love," were proposed in 1973 by John Alan Lee (1933–2013) as a typology to explain the various ways that people approach love relationships. His ideas were later expanded and refined by Susan and Clyde Hendrick, who referred to these as "love styles." The Hendricks created a self-report scale, the Love Attitudes Scale (LAS), which has been widely utilized in close relationship research. Studies exploring love styles have found partial support for the typology as well as tested associations with various personal and relational characteristics, experiences, and outcomes.

John Alan Lee, a Canadian scholar-activist, is known for this theory of love and his activism for gay rights. Most of his work centered on experiences of love and sex in both same- and other-sex relationships. In *Colours of Love: An Exploration of the Ways of Loving*, Lee's aim was to propose multidimensional "styles" of loving that would describe various expressions of love by individuals in romantic relationships. Utilizing the color wheel to describe the styles along with Greek words regarding love to label them, Lee (1973/1976) proposed a typology that would become one of the more widely known theories of love.

Similar to our understanding of color, there are three primary (Eros, Ludus, Storge) and three secondary (Mania, Agape, Pragma) styles. Secondary styles are "compounds" of two primaries but have properties and characteristics unique from them (Hendrick and Hendrick 1986). Each color/style was conceptualized to have a specific place in relation to the others, with adjacent styles sharing associations between them. Lee also proposed nine tertiary love types that were combinations of these six, each with one primary and one secondary. However, he did not find supporting evidence in his later work to fully distinguish these. Numerous studies by other scholars have provided confirmation of the six styles and their relation to various individual and relational factors. However, one central aspect, the circular nature of these colors and their presentation in a disc, has been seldom studied (Cassepp-Borges and Ferrer 2019, 1).

Individuals are said to exhibit all styles to some extent at the same and/or various points in their relationships, but one or more styles are dominant. Further, the dominant style (or styles) can change over time as well, i.e., demonstrating behavior and attitudes reflective of eros at one point but exhibiting storgic qualities later (Lee 1977, 173–174). Style descriptions are:

- **Eros (Red).** Passionate, romantic, with a physical focus on the relationship and fascination of one's partner with intense attraction, quickly felt and expressed.
- **Ludus (Blue).** Game-playing, casual, with little commitment, emotional involvement, or even monogamy as well as sex and love being seen as for short-term fun.
- **Storge (Yellow).** Friendship, companionship, with feelings unfolding over time and a focus on commitment in the long term.
- **Mania (Purple; eros and ludus combined).** Dependent, possessive, jealous, with an obsession for a partner and constant need for reassurance from

them. Immediate passion for partner as with eros and from ludus a desire to control feelings but encounter greater difficulty in doing so.

- **Pragma (Green; ludus and storge combined).** Practical and objective, with calculating thoughts and actions being central in approach to finding a partner that is deemed to be compatible with them and suitable by logical criteria. Control of thought processes and emotion comes from ludus with an expectation that this process will take time from storge.
- **Agape (Orange; storge and eros combined).** Unselfish, kind, self-sacrificing with a focus on a partner and giving of oneself completely to meet their needs with little thought of reciprocity. Focus on the partner comes from eros and low importance of physicality by storge.

Lee's systematic development of these styles first involved analysis of romantic-themed literature and then later research with individuals utilizing the "Love Story Card Sort." This approach consisted of 1500 cards in 170 sets. Each of the 170 sets had a card with a phrase about a thought, emotion, or experience one might have in a love relationship with several corresponding cards containing possible answers to the statement. For instance, "On our first date the closest we got to being intimate . . ." had optional cards with "holding hands" or "kissing several times" (Lee 1973; Lee 1977, 176). Participants were to choose the card or cards that reflected their experiences. The selection of certain cards would affect the sequence of subsequent sets. When done with sorting, the selected options would reflect their "love story." From these stories, Lee identified factors that distinguished the various love styles from each other.

While Lee preferred this approach for examining love styles, the vast majority of studies use rating scales. While several scholars have created scales to measure these styles, Clyde and Susan Hendrick's Love Attitudes Scale is the most known and utilized. The LAS was initially six subscales each with seven items but short versions with three and four items per subscale have been developed. The three-item scale omits items that would exclude individuals who are in relationships with same-sex partners or are not able to have children (Hendrick, Hendrick, and Dicke 1998).

In the Hendricks' review of studies focusing on love styles (both their own and that of others), several patterns between these and individual and relational factors emerged (Hendrick and Hendrick 2019, 227–233). Gender of participants was found to be an influence, with men endorsing ludic and agapic styles and women of storge and pragma. However, the correlational pattern of love styles with other variables was similar for men and women. Personality and temperament have also demonstrated consistent links with various styles. Endorsements of styles do not seem to differ greatly by age, but by relational status. While there were variations by ethnicity and country of residence, more similarities than differences existed in endorsements of love styles and their impact on relationships. Notably, across sex, age, ethnicity, and relational status, eros was consistently found to be positively linked with relationship or marital satisfaction and ludic negatively. Self-esteem was positively related to eros but negatively to mania. Greater sensation seeking correlates with ludus, as well as the endorsement of casual sexual attitudes. However, sexual attitudes involving idealized and responsible sex were related to eros. Lastly, while initial studies indicate that style endorsement and relation to various factors do not differ greatly by sexual orientation, there does appear to be variation within as a result of relational status. In one study men who were gay and "in love" were more likely to endorse mania and pragma styles than men who were not.

Shannon E. Weaver and Tong Shen

See also: Attachment Theory of Love; Five Love Languages; Love, Connection, and Intimacy; Triangular Theory of Love

Further Reading

Cassepp-Borges, Vicente and Emilio Ferrer. 2019. "Are We Missing the Circumplexity? An Examination of Love Styles." *Journal of Relationships Research* 10, no. e21: 1–10.

Hendrick, Clyde and Susan Hendrick. 1986. "A Theory and Method of Love." *Journal of Personality and Social Psychology* 50, no. 2: 392–402.

Hendrick, Clyde and Susan Hendrick. 2019. "Styles of Romantic Love." In *The New Psychology of Love*, edited by Robert J. Sternberg and Karin Weis. New York: Cambridge University Press, pp. 223–239.

Hendrick, Clyde, Susan Hendrick, and Amy Dicke. 1998. "The Love Attitudes Scale: Short Form." *Journal of Personal and Social Relationships* 15, no. 2: 147–159.

Lee, John Alan. 1973/1976. *Colours of Love: An Exploration of the Ways of Loving.* Toronto: New Press.

Lee, John Alan. 1976. "Forbidden Colors of Love: Patterns of Gay Love and Gay Liberation." *Journal of Homosexuality* 1, no. 4: 401–418.

Lee, John Alan. 1977. "A Typology of Styles of Loving." *Personality and Social Psychology Bulletin* 3: 173–182.

Swingers

Couples that identify as *swingers* are one type of consensual non-monogamous (CNM) relationship. Swingers include a primary—typically married—couple that engages in physical relationships with an outside person or couple. The commitment to the primary relationship remains the primary focus with outside partners typically fulfilling physical, non-emotional desires. For a swinging couple to be successful, rules are formed to protect the primary relationship (e.g., not engaging in physical relationships when the primary partner is not present).

The ability to remove secrecy and dishonesty within the primary couple is attributed to the continuation of this group. Specifically, swinger relationships reduce the problems resulting from infidelity because partners agree on sexual boundaries and rules to guide their physical interactions outside of the primary relationship, diminishing the likelihood of deception and violation of trust between the couple. Successful swingers also have the ability to balance this lifestyle with their day-to-day lives. In fact, swingers have been referred to as the group closest to traditional marriages when compared to other CNM types because of how they typically portray themselves publicly as heteronormative and monogamous.

The emphasis on presenting themselves as a "normal" couple causes challenges with gathering accurate statistics on the number of swingers. The North America Swing Club Association estimated that there were around three million swingers in the United States while other sources give the range of 4 to 15 million (Marino 1999; Richardson 2015). Additional research has been conducted on the demographic characteristics of this group. A majority of swingers identify as Caucasian, male, Democrat, and have at least a bachelor's degree (Jenks 2014). When compared to the general population, swingers tend to be politically liberal, satisfied with their relationship, and have more sex with their partner (Kimberly and McGinley 2018, 228).

Noted benefits of being a part of the swinging culture, when compared to monogamy, includes an invigorated sex life; an absence of anxiety about fantasizing or acting upon physical desires with someone outside of the primary marriage; improved communication within the primary relationship, particularly with regard to sexual self-disclosure, openness, and honesty; and a heightened level of self-awareness. There are also known challenges associated with engaging in a relationship that deviates from the social norm. These challenges include loss of time and energy for the primary relationship due to engagement with secondary partners; navigating non-traditional sex and gender roles that may form within the unique dynamics of non-heteronormative, non-monogamous relationships; feelings of exclusion from family and friends who disapprove, do not understand, or are unaware of the non-monogamous

relationship boundaries; and potentially feelings of guilt or shame for engaging in a relationship viewed as deviant by the larger society. Moreover, reactions to a spouse engaging in sex with someone outside of the primary relationship can result in a wide range of emotional responses including insecurity, sadness, fear, anger, or jealousy. There has been an increase in the number of people approving of non-monogamous relationships in the United States, reducing some of the aforementioned challenges for the group.

Claire Kimberly

See also: Diversity in Marriage; Divorce, Alternatives to; Infidelity; Monogamy; Open Marriage; Polyamory; Polygamy

Further Reading

Bergstrand, Curtis R., and Jennifer Blevins Sinski. 2010. *Swinging in America: Love, Sex, and Marriage in the 21st Century.* Santa Barbara, CA: Praeger.

Gould, Terry. 1999. *The Lifestyle: A Look at the Erotic Rites of Swingers.* Toronto, ON: Vintage Canada.

Jenks, Richard. 2014. "An On-line Survey Comparing Swingers and Polyamorists." *Electronic Journal of Human Sexuality* 17. www.ejhs.org/volume17/swing.html

Kimberly, Claire, and Robert McGinley. 2018. "Changes in the Swinging Lifestyle: A National and Historical Comparison," *Culture, Sexuality, and Health* 21, no. 2. https://doi.org/10.1080/13691058.2018.1460692

Marino, Jacqueline. 1999. "Full Swing." *Scene.* https://www.clevescene.com/cleveland/full-swing/Content?oid=1472240

Richardson, Rachel. 2015. "Reality Show about Warren Co. Swingers Sparks Controversy." Cincinnati.com. Last

modified March 2, 2015. https://www
.cincinnati.com/story/news/2015/02/27
/swingers-tv-reality-show-sparks
-community-controversy/24147723/

Rubin, Roger. 2004. *Alternative Lifestyles
Today: Off the Family Studies Screen.*
Thousand Oaks, CA: Sage.

Ryan, Christopher, and Cacilda Jethá.
2010. *Sex at Dawn: The Prehistoric Origins of Modern Sexuality.* New York:
HarperCollins Publishers.

T

Tender Years Doctrine

The Tender Years Doctrine is the legal practice of awarding custody of infants and young children to their mothers in divorce proceedings. This doctrine was based on the belief that custody of infants and young children should be awarded to their mothers because mothers held nurturing abilities superior to those of fathers.

The Tender Years Doctrine originated in England at a time when women and children in the household were considered the property of the male head of the household and children, in particular, were seen as economic assets in a primarily agricultural-based society. Therefore, in cases of divorce, the custody of the children was granted to the father. However, as farming was replaced with more industry-based work, fathers left the home for work, children played less of a role in the workforce, and mothers were primarily responsible for the home and the upbringing of the children. It was this shift and a new focus on women's rights that led to the creation of the Tender Years Doctrine which emphasized the role of the mother in the upbringing of her children, particularly in their early years. Under this doctrine, it was presumed that in all cases, the mother had an ability to care for her children during their "tender" years (which is generally regarded as age four and under but has been interpreted by different courts as up to age six or even age 13) that was superior to that of the father's. As a result, preference was given to mothers in custody matters at the time of a divorce.

Under this practice, all custody disputes began with the presumption that the mother was superior in caring for the children. This automatically placed the mother and father on unequal ground in the eyes of the court with the father being viewed as the inferior parent. Therefore, the father then had the burden of disproving this presumption not by proving his ability to care for the children, but by proving that the mother was "unfit" to care for the children. If the father was unable to prove that the mother was unfit (which predominantly occurred), custody was awarded to the mother.

The Tender Years Doctrine gained popularity in the United States and remained the predominant practice in custody disputes of young children until the 1960s when the courts found that this doctrine violated the Equal Protection Clause of the Fourteenth Amendment to the Constitution. The Equal Protection Clause states: "No State shall . . . deny to any person within its jurisdiction the equal protection of the laws." Therefore, it prohibits states from denying individuals the equal protection of the law and requires states to treat individuals in the same manner as other individualsImilar conditions and circumstances. This includes discrimination based upon gender. Under the Tender Years Doctrine, males were presumed to be inferior to females with regard to raising young children.

Because the Equal Protection Clause prohibits discrimination based on gender, the Tender Years Doctrine was found to be a violation of fathers' rights under the Fourteenth Amendment. This was specifically noted in *Watts v. Watts* (1973) when the court held that the Tender Years Doctrine would deprive a father of his Fourteenth Amendment rights.

The presumption that the mother was superior to the father at raising children was seen as discriminatory against fathers, and therefore, the Tender Years Doctrine was abolished in most states in the 1970s and replaced with a gender-neutral "best interests of the child" practice. This practice requires courts to analyze a variety of factors when making a determination of custody, such as each parent's relationship with the child, the physical and mental health of the parents, the child's age and developmental status, the child's wishes regarding the custody arrangement, which parent has been the primary caregiver, each parent's willingness to foster the child's relationship with the other parent, extrafamilial support, etc. Examining gender-neutral factors such as these aligns with the requirements of the Equal Protection Clause and eliminates the gender discrimination found under the Tender Years Doctrine. Further, in *Pusey v. Pusey* (1986), the court held that a presumption of maternal superiority "perpetuates outdated stereotypes" and was "unnecessary."

Today the "best interests of the child" approach is the norm that is used in most states. However, the previous preference for awarding custody to mothers and the presumption that the mother is the superior parent is still an unwritten approach practiced in many courts when determining custody cases. Research has indicated that despite the "best interests of the child" approach, judges in custody cases tend to award physical custody to the mother of the children. So, despite the law "on the books" being gender-neutral, the law "in action" still has the presumption that the mother is the preferred parent in custody disputes. As a result, in some courts, fathers and their legal counsel are still faced with the presumption that the mother is the preferred parent and are required to prove the mother to be unfit in order to be granted custody despite this approach being in clear violation of the Equal Protection Clause of the Fourteenth Amendment.

However, critics of the "best interests of the child" approach (that presumes gender equality) note that while gender discrimination is unfair in many institutions (such as the workforce and education), the roles of the mother and father are gendered and by nature are unequal, so attempting to treat a custody case between a father and mother as gender-neutral is inappropriate. These critics believe that the mother does possess some unique parenting skills that the father is unlikely to be able to contribute, so a gender-blind approach puts the mother at a disadvantage. Therefore, there are still advocates for a legal presumption that mothers have a superior parenting ability.

The Tender Years Doctrine arose out of a desire to increase women's rights but was abandoned due to its inherent discrimination against males. However, some supporters of the doctrine believe that parenting is not a gender-blind endeavor so a gender-neutral approach cannot be taken. Further, even though the "best interests of the child" approach is primarily used by courts, there may still be an unwritten presumption of maternal superiority in custody cases.

Carolyn L. Carlson

See also: Child Custody; Parenting Plans and Custody Arrangements; Shared Custody

Further Reading

Artis, Julie. 2004. "Judging the Best Interests of the Child: Judges' Accounts of the Tender Years Doctrine." *Law & Society Review,* 38: 769–786.

Fineman, Martha Albertson. 1991. *The Illusion of Equality: The Rhetoric and Reality of Divorce Reform.* Chicago: University of Chicago Press.

Pusey v. Pusey, 728 P.2d 117. Utah 1986.

Wallace, Sara and Susan Koerner. 2003. "Influence of Child and Family Factors on Judicial Decisions in Contested Custody Cases." *Family Relations,* 52, no. 2: 180–188.

Watts v. Watts, 77 Misc.2d 178, 350 N.Y.S.2d 285. 1973.

Toxic Relationships

According to Lillian Glass (1995), a toxic relationship is an emotionally damaging interaction between at least two people where there is little to no support for one participant. There is high conflict, and one strives to undermine their partner. Glass goes on to say that there is high competition in toxic relationships, lack of respect, and an absence of cohesiveness. Toxic relationships can occur in many forms including romantic partners, family, friends, co-workers or anyone with whom one is engaged in an interpersonal relationship. Characteristics of toxic relationships can be but are not limited to arguments, rejection, manipulation, and contempt. In the following paragraphs, characteristics as well as an explanation of dynamics and symptoms of toxic relationships are discussed.

Arguments in and of themselves are not necessarily toxic. It is normal for partners to argue and disagree. Arguments in toxic relationships become problematic when there is no resolution or reparative experience. A reparative experience is where partners are able to admit when they are wrong or are able to be held accountable for their hurtful words and actions. Sometimes repair after arguments includes an apology or acknowledgment of a relational violation. In toxic relationships, arguing crosses boundaries and can spin out of control. There can be name-calling, cussing, insults, and threats. Oftentimes, there is no acknowledgment of pain or the hurt caused.

Rejection in toxic relationships has to do with refusing the partner's bids for attention, dismissing the partner's need for emotional connection, and turning down the partner's requests for physical or emotional closeness. The act of rejection is a disruption in balance of power in the relationship. When one partner rejects a bid for attention, it starves the other's needs and desires. For example, a partner in a relationship asks the other partner to take a walk with them. What that partner is bidding for, or seeking is to fulfill a desire for closeness. When the partner turns down the bid for closeness, an unfair power dynamic is created and the partner who made themselves vulnerable and made the bid for closeness is left feeling powerless, alone, and sad.

Manipulation in toxic relationships is an intentional act where partners attempt unfairly influence the other for selfish reasons. Manipulation, like rejection creates an unbalanced power dynamic whereby one partner is left with unfulfilled needs, lonely and perhaps resentful. Gaslighting is a manipulation tactic that is often found in toxic relationships. Manipulation takes place when one partner denies or invalidates the other partner's perception or memory of events and feelings. The partner being gaslit may begin to question their memories and not trust their emotions. Oftentimes, when one is being gaslit, they experience anger and rage as a protective mechanism against the manipulation. One may not like themselves in this manner. They may feel disappointed in themselves for lashing out at their partner. They may feel emotionally drained and psychologically exhausted and start to develop negative feelings toward their partner. These emotions add to the existing toxic patterns within the relationship.

Contempt is another element of toxic relationships where partners believe the other partner is beneath them, worthless and deserving of scorn. According to Ellie Litisia in 2013, the Gottman Institute found that when partners communicate with contempt, their intent is to be mean and hurt their partner. Contempt can look like mocking, mimicking, hostile humor, defamation of character, name calling or cold body language such as eye rolling and sneering. Contempt is one of the most dangerous aspects of a toxic relationship because partners treat the other with disgust. The partner possesses a deep seeded belief that they are morally, ethically or characteristically superior.

The dynamics of being in a toxic relationship inflict emotional pain onto partners. A toxic relationship erodes the self-confidence and self-worth of partners. In contrast to healthy relationships that are characterized by mutual respect, interest, affection, and support, toxic relationships are just the opposite. A toxic relationship is one where there is little or no mutual respect, or regard for the partner's emotional or physical wellbeing. Being in a toxic relationship drains one's emotional and physical energy, damages self-esteem and negatively influences one's beliefs of being happy. Toxic relationships taint the experience of being loved and living without tension or grief.

It is important to note that it takes at least two people to be in a toxic relationship. It is not that an individual in and of themselves is toxic within a relationship. Rather, it is the dynamic between two people that create an unhealthy, emotionally damaging relationship. An individual in and of themselves can be toxic. However, in order for there to be a toxic relationship, there has to be two people with an interactional pattern that is malicious. Toxic relationships can leave a person feeling unworthy, unlovable, and undeserving of good things and positive experiences. A toxic relationship can lead an individual to believe hateful lies about themselves. A person can feel helpless, hopeless, powerless and trapped, leaving them feeling as though they are unlovable. A toxic relationship can cause someone to question their value and self-worth. A person in a toxic relationship may feel as though everything is their fault. They may believe they deserve bad things or that they deserve emotional punishment or ridicule.

In conclusion, it is important to note that an individual may be toxic, however, in order for there to be a toxic relationship, there has to be at least two people in relationship with one another. The dynamics between the two are problematic, dysfunctional, and malicious that give rise to a relationship that is toxic. Toxic relationships are characterized by arguments, rejection, manipulation, and contempt. Finally, persons in the relationship may experience symptoms such as hopelessness, helplessness, low self-esteem, and self-worth.

Jessica M. Moreno

See also: Cycle of Violence; Intimate Partner Violence; Relationship Self-Sabotage

Further Reading

Glass, L. 1995. *Toxic People: 10 Ways of Dealing with People who Make Your Life Miserable.* Simon & Shuster.

Listisa, E. 2013. "The Four Horseman: Contempt. The Gottman Institute, A Research Based Approach to Relationships." https://www.gottman.com/blog/the-four-horsemen-contempt/.

Triangular Theory of Love (Sternberg)

Over the past few decades, love has become a prominent focus in social science research. One of the more well-known and studied models is the Triangular Theory of Love by Robert J. Sternberg who has also been credited with helping to establish love as a respectable area of study in psychology. In the theory, Sternberg proposed that love has three components: intimacy, passion, and decision/commitment. He presented these as vertices of a triangle ("The Love Triangle"). These three components are present or absent to varying degrees in different (and the same) love relationships and the combinations of them create various love types people experience throughout life (Sternberg 1997).

According to this theory (Sternberg 1986, 119–135), intimacy involves "feelings of closeness, connectedness, and bondedness" that often lead to experiencing a sense of warmth in relationships. One could have this feeling when giving or receiving support from a loved one or when self-disclosures lead to a greater sense of trust and connection. Passion refers to inner motivational drives that transform arousal into physical or sexual desire. Sexual needs are often main drives in romantic relationships, but for others such as parent-child, nurturance and other needs could be the contributors to passion. Decision/commitment, the third component, has two aspects: (1) the decision or recognition that one loves another and (2) the commitment one makes to stay in that relationship. The two aspects are not necessarily both present in this component as one can have decided that they love another but are not committed to maintaining this love in the future just as one can be committed to continuing a relationship with someone they do not recognize as loving.

Sternberg asserted intimacy, passion, and decision/commitment are separate but interactive components where the presence (or absence) can affect the other. For instance, feeling greater intimacy can lead to a stronger sense of commitment and passion. While all three are considered central to love, their presence, degree, and importance differ in various relationships and life stages. These variations can be the result of relationship duration or length as well as the stability and commonality of various components across relationships. In the short-term or new romantic relationships, passion is a significant presence while intimacy levels are moderate and decision/commitment little to none. With relationships of longer duration, intim,acy and decision/commitment have a greater presence with passion declining over time. Intimacy and commitment are also perceived to be more stable in relationships as these components are ones in which people have some conscious control over, that is, they can do things to influence their presence. Passion, on the other hand, is viewed as more unstable because people have less control over their own physiological arousal. The commonality of these components across relationship types also differs with intimacy being at the core of most love relationships (friend, parent-child, partner, sibling, etc.) but with less frequency in other areas. Decision/commitment is more variable as it is often high in a parent's love for a child but lower for friends or relational partners who come and Io over time.

The presence of these three components in relationships creates different "types" of love. Sternberg proposed eight types but caution that relationships can fall between types as well as change over time. This is because the expression of the components falls along a continuum; that is, they are present in degree rather than complete absence or presence with levels varying over the duration of the relationship.

1. Nonlove (absence of all components). Most relationships fall into this category such as a classmate or coworker seen only at school/workplace with limited interaction.
2. Liking (intimacy). This love type is frequently found in friendships. People care about friends and want to spend time with them, but do not feel

intense passion or commitment to love them for a lifetime .
3. Infatuated love (passion). A "crush" or "love at first sight" where one desires to go out with or hook up with a person even though they do not really know each other. It can also be seen in casual dating or sexual relationships.
4. Empty love (commitment). The love seen in a long-term relationship in which neither feels cared for or understood by the other and passion has dissipated but the relationship is maintained due to a sense of obligation or constraints (e.g., "for the sake of the kids"). It can also be observed in early stages of arranged marriages, where commitment to the relationship comes first, with passion and intimacy expected to follow and grow over time.
5. Romantic love (intimacy and passion). This type is typical in dating or romantic relationships. There is physical attraction and emotional closeness; however, partners may not be ready for or want to make a commitment yet or perhaps ever.
6. Fatuous love (passion and commitment). This love is where commitment is quickly made based upon passion felt for another. Examples include whirlwind courtships where couples who have just met quickly marry before they know much about the other and intimacy has not yet had the time to develop.
7. Companionate love (intimacy and commitment). Often found in long-term marriages where physical attraction has declined as well as close friendships; passion is not the driving force behind the relationship at this point, but there is a great deal

of understanding and caring along with commitment to each other.

8. Consummate love (all three components). In Sternberg's eyes, as well as many of ours, this is the ideal love type, especially in romantic relationships, and likely what most hope for in marriages and lifelong partnerships. In romantic relationships, attaining consummate love is easier than the maintenance of it. For consummate love in parent-child relationships, passion includes motivational needs such as nurturance, self-esteem, and self-actualization, and is less difficult to maintain than such love for romantic couples.

A last, and less discussed, part of this theory deals with the geometry of the triangle and the match of triangles between relational partners. The amount of each component and the balance between them could produce different triangles (e.g., equilateral, isosceles, etc). Furthermore, love could include many triangles, such as real, ideal, and perceived with such triangles also possibly differing between relational partners. The (mis)match of these can impact satisfaction in relationships. Comparing the love triangles of partners can highlight issues with over, under, and mis-involvement when mismatches occur. More recently, Sternberg (2019) proposed the Duplex Theory of Love, which combines the triangular theory with his more current work on love as a story with a focus upon the development of love in relationships.

Shannon E. Weaver and Tong Shen

See also: Attachment Theory of love; Love, Connection, and Intimacy; Love at First Sight; Styles of Love

Further Reading

Cornell Human Development—A.P. Psychology Partnership. "Robert J. Sternberg—Everyone Loves to Learn About Love." Youtube video, December 14, 2017. https://www.youtube.com/watch?v=pwD-dL5cDFg

Sternberg, Robert J. 1986. "A Triangular Theory of Love." *Psychological Review*, 93, no. 2: 119–135.

Sternberg, Robert J. 1997. "Construct Validation of a Triangular Love Scale." *European Journal of Social Psychology* 27, no. 3: 313–335.

Sternberg, Robert J. 2019. "A Duplex Theory of Love." In *The New Psychology of Love*, edited by Robert J. Sternberg and Karin Weis. New York: Cambridge University Press, pp. 184–199.

Trophy Husband

The original term "trophy wife" can easily coincide with the term "trophy husband," referring to a young, attractive man who is married to an older and/or wealthier woman. It also refers to a man recognized for his physical attributes versus his other qualities. This situation tends to regard the husband (or long-term partner) as a status symbol for his wife (or equivalent), although this concept is far more common with trophy wives. A wife with a trophy husband is often referred to as a "honey gal" or "sugar momma," who is involved with a rich, but less attractive man, who parades him around when she seeks his physical and emotional affection in exchange. However, the ironic wordplay in the 21st century suggests that the term refers to husbands who leave their careers to take care of their households and support their wives' ambitions. This trend seems to be more of the norm when "trophy husband" is used in contemporary society, and remains separate from "trophy wife."

The current meaning evolved when "trophy husband" was introduced in *Fortune Magazine* of 2002. Betsy Morris, the journalist, reintroduced the term in 2002, referring to the husbands of headstrong career women, or prominent CEOs of leading companies and organizations; they are "powerful women in the United States" with loyal husbands, cheerleaders, helpmates, and fathers. The 2002 book *Househusband* by Ad Hudler tells the story of Lincoln Menner who leaves his job to support his wife in pursuit of her dream job. Both authors document the gender role shift of well-educated men who depart from their successful careers to support their families. It is believed that they deserve a "trophy" for managing these responsibilities.

The husbands, according to Burkstrand-Reid (2011), do not align with the original meaning of "trophy husband." Rather, the term was used to humble men, who were unconditionally supportive of hardworking wives in dominant roles. Burkstrand-Reid pinpointed why the term was used with a double-standard, based on gender: Taking care of the household for women was a given, but such a role for men was something considered "unusual," "rare," "extraordinary," and a "sacrifice." Family care is not a free choice, regardless of how societal expectations change, yet, trophy husbands are in a "stay-at-home" role of their own choice.

The term is not meant to minimize husbands (Copland 2015). It is often used to honor these men, who fulfill women in their physical and emotional needs by being well-educated but still stay at home. The meaning of "gold digger"

coincides with that of trophy wife—if one refers to a man married to a rich woman for financial security. Trophy husband also refers to an older, caring man, associated with a woman who is socially respected; however, he does not pursue a career equivalent to his spouse, yet, her social merit continues to help him flourish. This practice continues to exist, and is more common, as couples shift family care roles and arrangements.

Seungyeon Lee

See also: Trophy Wife; Work Wives and Work Husbands

Further Reading

Burkstrand-Reid, Beth. 2011. "Trophy Husbands & 'Opt-Out' Moms." *Seattle University Law Review,* 34: 663–677. https://digitalcommons.unl.edu/lawfacpub

Copland, Jill. 2015. "Meet the New Trophy Husbands." *Fortune.* https://fortune.com/2015/02/26/trophy-husband (accessed on February 20, 2015)

Hudler, Ad. 2002. *Househusband.* Rochester, NY: Ballantine Books.

Morris, Betsy. 2002. "Trophy Husbands: Arm Candy? Are You Kidding? While Their Fast-Track Wives Go to Work, Stay-at-Home Husbands Mind Their Kids. They Deserve a Trophy for Trading Places." *Fortune.* https://archieve.fortune.com/magazines/fortune/fortune_archieve/2002/10/14/330033/index.html (accessed on October 14, 2002).

Trophy Wife

The term "trophy wife" refers to a young, attractive woman married to a significantly older man, who is recognized as a powerful figure. This situation tends to regard the wife (or long-term partner) as a status symbol for her husband (or equivalent).

Trophy husbands also exist, but they have rarely been compared to a trophy wife. A husband with a trophy wife is often referred to as a "sugar daddy," which is a rich, older man who bestows wealth and luxury on his companion for offering physical and emotional affection.

The origin of the term "trophy wife" was derived from the historical practice of male warriors claiming the most physically attractive women to bring home as "trophy" wives. The current meaning evolved when "trophy wife" was introduced in *The Economist* in 1950. Adam LeBor, the journalist, reintroduced the term in 1965, while referring to the wife of Bernie Madoff, who was a non-executive chairperson of the NASDAQ stock market. Another journalist, William Safire, wrote a cover story, "On Language: Trophy Wife," in the *New York Times* in 1994, based on its common usage, but the term has become less popular.

The term is often used to disparage women, whose physical attractiveness (but lack of notable intelligence) leads to a convenient marriage to wealthy men. The meaning of gold digger, to an extent, coincides with that of trophy wife—if one refers to a woman who is married to an older man for money. Trophy wife also refers to a young, beautiful woman being the wife of a man who is socially respected; however, she does not pursue a career equivalent to that of her spouse, but her husband's social merit continues to help her flourish. This practice still exists, but the phenomenon has become less and less common.

Seungyeon Lee

See also: Trophy Husband; Work Wives and Work Husbands

Further Reading

Bell, Caroline. 2019. "Trophy Wife." *The Prairie Light Review,* 42, no. 1: 39. https://dc.cod.edu/plr/vol42/iss1/39

LeBor, Adam. 2009. "The Believers: How America Fell for Barnard Madoffs $65 Billion Investment Scam." *Phoenix.* Accessed on September 26, 2016.

Linker, Harry. 2010. "Buying into the Hype: Trophy Antiques and Collectibles." *Today.* Accessed on May 7, 2010. https://worthpoint.com

Macrossan, Mark. 2016. "Augmented Sonnet for a Trophy Wife." *Meanjin* 75, no. 1: 95.

Safire, William. 1994. "On Language: Trophy Wife." *The New York Times.* Accessed on May 1, 1994.

Schwarz, Sascha and Hassebrauck, Manfred. 2012. "Sex and Age Differences in Mate-Selection Preferences." *Human Nature* 23, no. 4: 447–466.

Vranich, Belisa and Grashow, Laura. 2008. *Dating the Older Man: Consider Your Differences and Decide if He's Right for You.* Massachusetts: Adam Media.

U

Unmarried Cohabitation

Unmarried cohabitation is when a couple lives together without being married. In the United States, cohabitation has a relatively short history: 7.5 million heterosexual couples cohabitated in 2010, versus fewer than half a million in 1960. Certain socioeconomic groups, such as those who are low-income or without a college degree, are currently experiencing higher levels of cohabitation and lower levels of marriage than others.

There are no standard practices when it comes to cohabitation. Some people drift into living together, while others carefully plan to cohabitate. Couples cohabitate for various reasons, such as minimizing living costs or avoiding marriage. Cohabitants also have different preferences for their relationship based on their gender, age, background, and level of commitment. Their expectations for cohabitation may also depend on whether they are in marriage-like trials, in long-term cohabitations with shared children, or are older cohabitants with adult children from previous relationships. Cohabitants may experience an easy transition to cohabitation or face challenges caused by differing lifestyles that become more pronounced when living together.

Cohabitations may be short or indefinite. While some cohabitants may eventually marry each other, others may hope to marry someone else. Some people may have lower standards for cohabitation than marriage, with lower levels of commitment and relationship quality than married couples. Other people have the same standards for cohabitation as marriage, objecting to the state's role in marriage and choosing cohabitation instead.

In a few states, cohabitation, when coupled with other elements such as an intention to be married, may qualify as a common law marriage. States currently allowing common law marriages include Colorado, District of Columbia, Iowa, Kansas, Montana, Rhode Island, Oklahoma, Utah, and Texas.

Some cohabitants have children together. Should they later separate, state child support and custody laws apply once paternity is established.

Many cohabitants comingle their assets, provide money for house down payments, or forgo professional opportunities, believing that such investments are compensated if the relationship were to end. Although this may be true upon divorce, it is not necessarily true at the end of a cohabitation. While divorce law governs the separation of married couples, it does not apply to cohabitants. Instead, cohabitants must have cohabitation agreements if they want a framework to govern their separation.

Cohabitation agreements usually address property distribution if a cohabitating couple separates. However, most cohabitating couples do not enter into a cohabitation agreement before moving in together. Often, they do not even know about cohabitation agreements or are too optimistic about their relationship to seek such a contract. A few states also do not allow cohabitation agreements and will not enforce them at the breakup of a cohabitation.

The first American case recognizing cohabitation agreements was *Marvin v. Marvin* in California in 1976, which led the majority of American states in their approaches to cohabitation. To reach its decision, the *Marvin* court rejected the historical reasons against the enforcement of cohabitation agreements: that nonmarital relationships should be punished, cohabitants could have no reasonable expectations outside of marriage, services provided without a contract are gifts, and enforcement of cohabitation agreements would discourage marriage.

Most states have adopted the *Marvin* approach. Thus, in the majority of states today, express contracts between cohabitants on earnings and property will generally be enforced at their separation. Implied contracts are more difficult to enforce because they are more difficult to prove, and some states may not allow them as a result.

Without an enforceable contract, courts may still be able to grant a remedy at the end of a cohabitation based on theories of constructive trust, resulting trust, or quantum meruit. The theory of unjust enrichment permits courts to order restitution in an unjust situation where one cohabitant has obtained a benefit at the other's expense.

In contrast to the *Marvin* approach, a few American states still do not enforce cohabitation agreements. The leading state taking this approach is Illinois. In 1979, the Illinois Supreme Court explained in its decision *Hewitt v. Hewitt* that division of property between cohabitants is a reinstitution of common law marriage,

which was outlawed by the Illinois legislature in 1905. The Illinois Supreme Court reaffirmed this position on cohabitation in *Blumenthal v. Brewer* in 2016. Historically, opposition to cohabitation was rooted in public policy reasons that ranged from disapproval of sexual relationships outside of marriage to concern for women in, and children of, unstable cohabitations. Cohabitation agreements were also previously viewed as contracts for sex and therefore unenforceable.

In sum, cohabitation is becoming an alternative to or substitute for marriage, but the law provides little remedy at the end of the relationship. Therefore, people should consider entering into a cohabitation agreement outlining the terms of their cohabitation if they live in the majority of states that recognize such contracts.

Margaret Ryznar

See also: Common Law Marriage; Division of Assets

Further Reading

Blumenthal v. Brewer, 69 N.E.3d 834. Ill. 2016.

Garrison, Marsha. 2008. "Nonmarital Cohabitation: Social Revolution and Legal Regulation." *Family Law Quarterly* 42, no. 3: 309–332.

Hewitt v. Hewitt, 394 N.E.2d 1204. Ill. 1979.

Marvin v. Marvin, 557 P.2d 106. Cal. 1976.

Ryznar, Margaret and Anna Stępień-Sporek. 2019. "Cohabitation Worldwide Today." *Georgia State University Law Review* 35, no. 2: 299–328.

Unplanned Pregnancy

Unplanned or unintended pregnancies are those that are mistimed (occurring when women did not intend to be pregnant) or unwanted (occurring for a women who had no plans to become pregnant) (Centers for Disease Control and Prevention 2019; Guttmacher Institute 2019). Determining the prevalence of unplanned pregnancies is difficult. For example, data from the National Survey of Family Growth (NSFG) has been used to measure unintended pregnancy using abortion, birth, and miscarriage information. However, obtaining accurate data on abortions using an in-person survey is difficult; some women may not feel comfortable reporting that they had an abortion due to the social stigma attached. Hence, they are likely to be underreported (Finer, Lindberg, and Desai 2018, 522). Finer et al. also noted the measure examines conception and pregnancy information after women have become pregnant and may not accurately assess an individual's pregnancy desire before its occurrence.

Even with these limitations, U.S. data indicates that approximately half of all pregnancies are unplanned (Finer and Zolna 2016, 843). The reasons for unplanned pregnancies are complex. Not using birth control, not using it reliably, or birth control failure all directly contribute to unexpected or unintended conception. Birth control may not be used due to religious or moral reasons, assumed infertility, poor access to family planning services, lack of sex education regarding reproduction and pregnancy prevention, or sexual assault. However, there are some groups who are at increased risk for unplanned pregnancies. They include adolescents (80% of pregnancies are unplanned), women who are cohabiting with their partners, women of color, those living in poverty, and those with lower educational

attainment (Finer and Zolna 2011; 2016; Guttmacher Institute 2019).

Those who are victims of domestic or intimate partner violence are at increased risk for unplanned pregnancy. National data finds that 30% of women who have been raped by an intimate partner also have experienced reproductive coercion in their relationship with that partner. Reproductive coercion is when the intimate partner either tries to block the women from using birth control or refuses to wear a condom, intentionally trying to get them pregnant (Basile et al. 2018).

Increased access to contraception and family planning services have led to decreases in unplanned pregnancy rates over the past 50 years. There are also a wider range of options for birth control available to women, including long-acting reversible contraceptives (LARCs) which include intrauterine devices and hormonal implants. These devices can provide long-term protection from pregnancy, decreasing the likelihood that contraception is not used. Women who fear they may become pregnant after unprotected sex or birth control failure can also access "morning after pills" from most pharmacies which can be used prevent pregnancy. However, there are some public misconceptions about the pill, with many perceiving it to be an abortion pill. The pill actually contains some of the same hormones found in birth control pills to either prevent release, fertilization, or implantation of a fertilized egg. The drug's role in preventing the implantation of a fertilized egg is considered by some as the termination of a life. Hence, some pharmacists have refused to dispense the pill on moral and religious grounds. There has also been controversy regarding the age at which women can access the pill without a prescription. The cost of medication, which can range from $40–50, can be a barrier to access as not all insurance companies cover the cost.

Women who experience unintended pregnancies also have more options or choices regarding their pregnancy. Data suggests approximate 40% choose to terminate their pregnancies (Finer and Zolna 2016). Those who give birth may choose to raise the child alone, with their partner, or with family members who support them and provide some caregiving. They may also put the child up for adoption, with the adoption being closed (there is no contact between the biological parent, child, and adoptive family) or open (where they have some contact with the child and adoptive family).

Unplanned pregnancies may bring with them changes in relationships with intimate partners such as the child's father. There may be a disruption in intimate relationships, especially if one or both partners disagree as to the options to pursue regarding the pregnancy. The pregnancy may bring with it financial challenges and change the school, career, and life plans for one or both partners, at least in the short-term. All of these factors may increase the prenatal stress experienced by mothers. Research confirms a wide variety of negative effects can be attributed to prenatal stress, from miscarriage to a range of children's developmental disorders (DiPietro 2004). Unplanned pregnancies carried to term have their risks for both mother and child. Since women were not planning to become pregnant, they may not be aware of the pregnancy in its early stages. They may also not choose to acknowledge the pregnancy until later due to fear, shame, depression, and anxiety regarding how the father, family, and friends may respond. Women may also not be in optimal health or may continue engaging in practices such as smoking, drinking, and using drugs which may harm the developing fetus. Late access or no access to prenatal care, especially during early pregnancy, may increase risk of complications such as low birthweight and premature birth which may result from untreated health issues in the mother.

There is controversy in the United States as to how best to prevent unplanned pregnancies. Developing unified strategies to address the issue are complicated by differences in moral and religious views regarding an individual's sexual activity choices, contraception, and women's reproductive choices. Some groups do not support comprehensive strategies to preventing pregnancy using birth control due to concerns that it will encourage early sexual activity outside of marriage which they view as morally wrong. Sawhill and Guyot (2019) discuss several strategies which have been tried by states to help prevent unintentional pregnancy. They include Medicaid expansion efforts which provide increased access to family planning and contraceptives at federal and state-level, improved training of women's health providers, and social media campaigns to increase awareness of contraceptive options and their effectiveness. However, the content of sex education programs, especially those aimed at adolescents, has long been debated as to whether the emphasis should be on abstinence or sexual health and contraception.

Patricia Hrusa Williams

See also: Abortion; Intimate Partner Violence; Parenthood, Unmarried

Further Reading

Basile, Kathleen C., Sharon G. Smith, Yang Liu, Marcie-jo Kresnow, Amy M. Fasula, Leah Gilbert, and Jieru Chen. 2018. "Rare-Related Pregnancy and Association with Reproductive Coercion in the U.S." *American Journal of Preventive Medicine*, 55, no. 6: 770–776. https://doi.org/10.1016/j.amepre.2018.07.028

Centers for Centers for Disease Control and Prevention (CDC). 2019. *Unintended Pregnancy Prevention*. Atlanta, GA: Author.

DiPietro, Janet A. 2004. "The Role of Prenatal Maternal Stress in Child Development." *Current Directions in Psychological Science*, 13, no. 2: 71–74. doi:10.1111/j.0963-7214.2004.00277.x

Finer, Lawrence B., Laura D. Lindberg, and Shelia Desai. 2018. "A Prospective Measure of Unintended Pregnancy in the United States." *Contraception* 98, no. 6: 522–527. https://doi: 0.1016/j.contraception.2018.05.012.

Finer, Lawrence B., and Mia R. Zolna. 2011. "Unintended Pregnancy in the United States: Incidence and Disparities, 2006." *Contraception*, 84, no. 5: 478–485. https://doi10.1016/j.contraception.2011.07.013.

Finer, Lawrence, B., and Mia R. Zolna. 2016. "Declines in Untended Pregnancy in the United States, 2008–2011." *New England Journal of Medicine*, 374, no. 9: 843–852. doi: 10.1056/NEJMsa1506575.

Guttmacher Institute. 2019. *Fact Sheet: Unintended Pregnancy in the United States*. New York: Author.

Sawhill, Isabel V. and Katherine Guyot. 2019. *Preventing Unplanned Pregnancy: Lessons from the States*. Washington, DC: Economic Studies at the Brookings Institute.

V

Value Theory/Role Theory

Value or role theory attempts to describe the process of mate selection and partner retention in romantic relationships. Through successive stages of *stimulus, value,* and *role,* people in search of romantic partners attempt to find an ideal mate that both matches the values they seek in a mate and presents those values throughout the relationship. The presentation of desired values and roles (e.g., caring or parental) ultimately leads potential partners to decide to marry. The *stimulus* stage refers to the first contact with a potential mate and the first impressions they present (e.g., assessing a potential partner based solely on visual stimuli and attractiveness). The *value* stage refers to assessing whether a potential mate shares particular values expected of a mate (e.g., partners comparing and contrasting their compatibility on views of politics and religion). Finally, the *role* stage refers to how well mates continually present these values throughout the progress of the romantic relationship, which leads individuals to the decision to marry (e.g., a partner displaying that they are a good husband or wife).

Bernard I. Murstein (1929–2020) first put forth stimulus-value-role theory in 1970. Murstein was attempting to a provide a comprehensive and general explanation for why people choose particular mates over others, how held values impact mate selection, and the factors that held values play in maintaining relationships and retaining mates.

Prior to Murstein's theory, some psychologists offered theories that attempted to explain mate selection but were ultimately scientifically untestable. For example, Sigmund Freud's (1949) classic theory of the Oedipal or Electra complex as a means for mate selection detailed how the childhood formation of envy for parents of the opposite sex influenced later choices of marital partners, offered no scientific evidence or data to support the theory. Moreover, sociologists put forth ideas that the values of a certain culture influenced psychological choices of potential marital partners, but these theories offered little scientific evidence as to how societies shape romantic values and individual choices.

Murstein sought to bridge the sociological factors, or societal influences and cultural values, with the psychological outcomes, or individual choices for specific marriage partners. In an empirical study of pre-marital couples, Murstein analyzed trends and patterns (e.g., initial attraction, compatibility of values, and role validations) that arose between individuals at different stages before they decided to get married and used this evidence to formulate his stimulus-value-role theory of marital partner selection.

Murstein acknowledged that his theory of mate selection could only occur in societies where individuals had the free choice to decide their potential spouses. In appropriate situations (e.g., at a party or after class), individuals can approach and interact with potential mates. During this interaction, people enter into the *stimulus* stage. In the stimulus stage, upon first contact with a potential mate, individuals can only perceive external attributes, such as hairstyle, dress, and physical features, and they use this information and compare it to their desired values for a mate. Moreover, individuals also use *their* own perceived self-image to determine whether the person they are interacting with will find them attractive. If they believe that the other person fits their values of attractiveness and will reciprocate this feeling, they will continue interacting and attempt to further the relationship.

If individuals continue interaction with their selected partner based off of the initial attraction, the second stage, or *value* stage begins to develop. In the value stage, individuals begin to learn more about their partners than what appeared at face-value. Partners begin to develop a sense of each other's political, moral, and ethical values, and they use this information, and continued interaction, to compare their partner's values to their own. If both partners share an appreciation for each other's core values, they will continue to maintain and deepen their relationship.

If both partners agree and validate each other's core values, they move on to the final or *role* stage. In the role stage, partners discern whether or not their significant other can fulfill each other's desired roles, such as a potential parent or spouse. If these role perceptions satisfy both partners, then they have good evidence of how their significant other should behave in the future under specific consequences. Murstein also noted the importance of self-acceptance in assessing their partner's role fulfillment and that partners higher in self-acceptance are more likely to regard their significant other as similar to them. Murstein theorized that following the role stage, if both partners are still satisfied with each other, they will be much more likely to decide to marry.

Murstein found overall that similarities between partners were important to partner selection, especially in the stimulus and value stages. However, similarities in the role stage did not matter as much unless the individuals reported high self-acceptance. If individuals reported low-self acceptance they were more likely to perceive their partner as dissimilar from themselves, hindering partner selection (p. 479).

Implications of role/value theory continue to influence research on social psychological theories of relationships. Echoing Murstein's original theory, recent empirical research supports that partner similarity largely affects mate selection and relationship satisfaction. For example, researchers have found support that the initial perceptions of others at the beginning of relationships (as Murstein described in the *stimulus* stage) predict partner selection (George et al. 2015, 130).

Expanding on Murstein's originally theory, current research also supports that different types of similarities and values are more important to different stages in the progression of a relationship. For example, it appears that similarities in beliefs, attitudes, and values tend to be more important early on in relationships, but qualities such as partner personality seem to predict partner satisfaction later on in the relationship (Luo and Klohnen 2005, 322–323).

Moreover, broad research supports the importance of role and value verification in overall relationship functioning and stability, in addition to the importance of overall identity relations between partners (Stets and Burke 2005, 173–175). However, many current researchers focus more on nuanced processes of accumulated intimacy disclosure between partners in relationship growth, rather than generalized stages that characterize what partners seek throughout relationships (Laurenceau, Barrett, and Pietromonaco 1998, 1249; Reiss and Shaver 1988, 387–389).

Alexander L. Smith

See also: Attachment Theory of love; Triangular Theory of Love

Further Reading

Freud, S. 1949. *An Outline of Psychosis.* W.W. Norton.

George, Darren, Shanhong Luo, Jared Webb, Jennifer Pugh, Alan Martinez, and Jeremy Foulston. 2015. "Couple Similarity on Stimulus Characteristics and Marital Satisfaction." *Personality and Individual Differences* 86: 126–131.

Laurenceau, Jean-Philippe, Lisa Feldman Barrett, and Paula R. Pietromonaco. 1998. "Intimacy as an Interpersonal Process: The Importance of Self-Disclosure, Partner Disclosure, and Perceived Partner Responsiveness in Interpersonal Exchanges." *Journal of Personality and Social Psychology* 74, no. 5: 1238–1251.

Luo, Shanhong, and Eva C. Klohnen. 2005. "Assortative Mating and Marital Quality in Newlyweds: A Couple-centered Approach." *Journal of Personality and Social Psychology* 88, no. 2: 304–326.

Murstein, Bernard I. 1970. "Stimulus—Value—Role: A Theory of Marital Choice." *Journal of Marriage and Family* 32, no. 3: 465–481. https://doi.org/10.2307/350113

Reiss, Harry T., and Phillip Shaver. 1988. "Intimacy as an Interpersonal Process." In *Handbook of Personal Relationships,* edited by S. W. Duck. John Wiley & Sons, pp. 377–389.

Stets, Jan E., and Peter J. Burke. 2005. "Identity Verification, Control, and Aggression in Marriage." *Social Psychology Quarterly* 68, no. 2: 160–178.

Visitation

Visitation rights may be granted to the non-custodial parent, sometimes called a non-residential parent, following the adults' break up. Nonmarital parents have the same rights as marital parents, but visitation may be awarded in different proceedings depending on whether the parents married—if unmarried, this may occur in conjunction with a paternity proceeding and if married, with a divorce proceeding.

The parents often negotiate a division of time with the child or children through a device known as a parenting plan. Where parents cannot agree, a judge may determine the visiting schedule guided by the best interests of the child.

Visitation is a natural right flowing from parentage and may not be denied absent a showing of unfitness or risk to the child (Wadlington, O'Brien, and Wilson 2013, 904–905). The right to access children is premised on the fact that parents have a fundamental right to direct the upbringing and education of their children (Wilson 2010, 1115).

Visitation can enhance the bond between the children and the parents following divorce or separation by promoting frequent, meaningful and continuing contact between the children and parents. Children will feel connected and loved rather than abandoned by one parent. A body of social science suggests that children are harmed when denied the opportunity to know both parents when the parent-child relationship is otherwise positive (Difonzo 2015, 1003–1023).

A significant body of literature emphasizes the need for parents to have similar rules and approaches when parenting separately. Children report feeling divided between households and faced with differences in household rules, parental expectations, and socioeconomic status (Marquardt 2005, 19–32). Different standards may confuse the children and make it difficult for them to adjust to the different environments, most especially with the non-custodial parent who spends less time with the children.

Concerns for child welfare sometimes warrant restrictions on visitation, which may be supervised, unsupervised, or even virtual. Supervised visitation requires a showing of risk to the child meriting a restriction on the parent's parental prerogatives since it introduces another adult during the visit. The supervising adult is usually appointed by the court and may be another relative, a friend, a social worker, or court personnel. Supervised visitation may be warranted in instances of domestic violence in order to ensure that a child is safe during the visit. Supervised visitation may result when violence has been directed at the child, but it also may be imposed when violence has been directed at the child's other parent and the court is concerned for the child's safety. In instances of demonstrated abuse and neglect, Court Appointed Advocates (CASA) may be directed to attend the visitation between the parent and child. The rationale of including the CASA is to ensure that children are safe and have an opportunity to thrive (Atwood 2008, 85–87).

In cases of domestic violence, abusers sometimes use the exchange of the child for visitation as an opportunity to harass or harm the child's parents. Where the risk of violence to the parent exists, courts will sometimes institute "supervised drops" at public locations like restaurants or at police stations (Hardesty et al. 2012, 318–331).

Unsupervised visitation follows a particular schedule without further restrictions. Virtual visitation facilitates contact between the noncustodial parent and child through video conference technology, allowing continuity when the child lives elsewhere (Wadlington, O'Brien and Wilson 2013, 890).

The process and substantive rules for determining visitation rights vary by state. In some states, courts will appoint a lawyer for the child or a guardian ad litem (GAL), who may or may not be a lawyer, to advocate for the child's best interests (Wadlington, O'Brien, and Wilson 2013, 955). The child's attorney or GAL may interview the child, both parents, and others with knowledge of the child's circumstances and report to the court orally or in writing what they have observed. In some states, GALs may make recommendations regarding the child's placement and whether visitation should be supervised (Wadlington, C. O'Brien and Wilson 2013, 970). In other states, recommendations made by GALs do not, and should not, carry any greater presumptive weight than other evidence in a case (In the matter of Choy and Choy, 154 N.H, 707 [N.H 2006]).

Substantive rules guide judges in awarding visitation to the non-custodial parent. As previously stated, judges in granting visitation are guided by the welfare of the child. In assessing welfare promotion, they consider relevant information regarding both the parents and child to arrive at a decision that promotes the child's welfare.

A visitation schedule may be modified by the court upon application of the one or both parties. Often, the child's living situation will change between the time an original visitation order is entered and when child attains the age of majority, which is typically 18 years and may be as old as 26 (Wadlington, O'Brien, and Wilson 2013, 450–451). For example, courts may modify a visitation order when there is a change of circumstances not contemplated by the original order. For instance, the custodial parent changes residence, making travel between locations less practicable. The judge may exercise discretion when revising visitation to ensure that the best interest of the child is promoted. Some parents may seek to relocate to better their financial situation or because they have formed a new family. In such instances, courts will interrogate whether the parent seeking relocation in good faith or is attempting to thwart the other parent's visitation (In re Heinrich and Curruto, 7 A.3d 1158 (N.H 2010)). Courts have used relocation as grounds for shifting custody to the non-relocating parent, something that is the subject of great critique, especially for the difficulties posed to custodial parents, usually women (Weiner 2007, 1747–1834).

The right to grant visitation to the non-custodial parent is not absolute and therefore can be denied if it does not safeguard the welfare of the child. Though rarely denied, visitation can be denied completely in extreme situations. For example, in a situation where

extraordinary circumstances exist over a long period of time, visitation may be denied (Wadlington, O'Brien, and Wilson 2013, 934). Such extraordinary circumstances include 24 months separation of parent and child, parent's voluntary relinquishment of care and control over a child, or when the child lives in the grandparent's or another parent's home.

The granting of visitation rights to non-parents over the parent's wishes has resulted in litigation in many states (Wilson 2020, 7). Much of this litigation involves claims for visitation by adults who have been present in the child's life by virtue of their relationship to the child's legal parent, such as stepparents, live-in nonmarital partners, grandparents, and others. The awarding of visitation over the legal parent's objection raises significant constitutional questions when the parent is fit, has not abandoned or neglected the child, and other extraordinary circumstances are not present. Special factors that justify interference with parents' fundamental rights concerning the rearing of children must be present before granting visitation rights to third parties (Troxel v. Granville, 530 U.S. 57, 67). In the 1990s, states enacted statutes allowing award of visitation to grandparents in a variety of circumstances (Averett 1998, 355–377). Some permit visitation to be awarded to any interested person if the court determines that a continued relationship with the child would be in the child's best interest or, more narrowly, to prevent detriment to the child (Wilson 2020, 7).

The grant of visitation rights to third parties is often advantageous to the child because it preserves generational contact and connects children to adults who have been present and positive in their lives.

In the context of sole custody, the non-custodial parent will be given a visitation schedule which facilitates continued contact, most often arrived at by an agreement with the custodial parent. Under "friendly parent statutes," the custodial parent in many states has a duty to foster a good relationship between the non-custodial parent and child—or at the very least not to undermine that relationship. Interference with visitation rights should be avoided since it may be grounds for modification or loss of custody (Wadlington and O'Brien 2001, 174–178).

Remedies to interference of visitation rights by the custodial parent can include an action for civil contempt and statutory remedies. Contempt may arise when a person violates a court order. The court will issue a compelling order to the offending custodial parent requiring them to comply with the court order and absent compliance, or they may move custody to the wronged parent.

Often, disputes over visitation arise between parents living in different states or countries. Complicated laws govern which body of law will oversee the dispute. Some states have adopted versions of the Uniform Child Custody Jurisdiction Act 1 and others follow the Uniform Child Custody Jurisdiction Enforcement Act of 1997 (Gregory, Swisher, and Wolf 2001, 434–440). Federal law and treaties, including the Parental Kidnapping Prevention Act and the Hague Convention, also come into play. These laws facilitate and enforce cooperation between states and countries when resolving visitation issues.

Visitation has been criticized for assigning the drudgery of day-in-and-day-out parenting to the custodial parent while permitting the non-custodial parent to indulge their child with gifts and good times during visitation, leaving most or all the disciplinary responsibilities to the custodial parent (Stewart 1999, 539). This "Disneyland parent" phenomenon may be muted with thoughtful visitation schedules that allocate "parenting functions" (Difonzo 2015, 1003–1023). Parenting functions are broadly defined to include aspects of the parent-child relationship in which the parent makes decisions and performs functions necessary for the care and growth of the child.

When parents do not reside in the same state, it may be more difficult for the non-custodial parent to arrange parenting time with the child. Traveling to visit the child may be expensive and time consuming. One way to maintain contact is to utilize visual visitation using technology.

In conclusion, visitation optimally enhances active participation of both parents in the growth and development of the child. While parents often arrive at the arrangements themselves, judges are entrusted to assess the circumstances and make the most well-informed decisions for each child based on their specific and special needs.

Elsa Zawedde and Robin Fretwell Wilson

See also: Child Custody; Parenting Plans and Custody Arrangements; Shared Custody

Further Reading

Atwood, Ann Barbara. 2008. "The Uniform Representation of Children in Abuse and Neglect, and Custody Proceedings Act: Bridging the Divide Between Pragmatism and Idealism." *Family Law Quarterly* 42, no. 1 (Spring): 85–87.

Averett, Stephen E. 1998. "Grandparent Visitation Statutes." *Brigham Young University Journal of Public Law* 13, no. 2: 355–377.

Difonzo, Herbie J. 2015. "Dilemmas of Shared Parenting in the 21st Century: How Law and Culture Shape Child Custody." *Hofstra Law Review* 43: 1003–1023.

Gregory, John Dewitt, Peter N. Swisher, and Sheryl L. Wolf. 2001. *Understanding Family Law.* Ohio: LexisNexis.

Hardesty, Jennifer L., Marcela Khaw Raffaelli, Lyndal Mitchell, Elissa Thomann, Megan L. Haselschwerdt, and Kimberly A. Crossman. 2012. "An Integrative Theoretical Model of Intimate Partner Violence, Coparenting After Separation, and Maternal and Child Well-being." *Journal of Family Theory and Review* 4: 318–331.

Marquardt, Elizabeth. 2005. *Between Two Worlds: The Inner Lives of Children of Divorce.* New York: Crown Publishers.

Stewart, Susan D. 1999. "Disneyland Dads, Disneyland Moms?" *Journal of Family Law Issues* 20 no. 4: 539–556.

Wadlington, Walter and Raymond C. O'Brien. 2001. *Family Law in Perspective.* New York: Foundation Press.

Wadlington, Walter, Raymond C. O'Brien, and Robin Fretwell Wilson. 2013. *Domestic Relations: Cases and Materials.* Minneapolis: West Academic Publishing.

Weiner, Merle H. 2007. "Inertia and Inequality: Reconceptualizing Disputes over Parental Relocation." *U.C. Davis Law Review* 40, no. 5 (June): 1747–1834.

Wilson, Robin Fretwell. 2010. "Trusting Mothers: A Critique of the American Law Institute's Treatment of De Facto Parents." *Hofstra Law Review* 38, (January 1): 1103.

Wilson, Robin Fretwell. 2020. "Relational Parents: When Adults Receive Rights in Children Because of Their Relationship with a Parent." *The Oxford Handbook of Children and the Law* 1–32.

W

Wedding Industry

The wedding industry aspects are important in giving a foundational understanding of a typical wedding. In addition, the wedding industry was impacted by COVID-19 and resulted in modifications, such as weddings being postponed to a later date or holding the ceremony virtually. The wedding industry encompasses a social and cultural expression of how the couples see their wedding day. Each couple sees this important day from a religious, social, cultural, racial/ethnic, and/or religious perspective.

A wedding is a ceremony between two people that unites them in marriage.

The wedding-planning industry began in the United States around the late 1970s and early 1980s (Blakely 2007, 639). In 2014, wedding industry revenues were projected to exceed $50 billion in the United States (IBISWorld 2021; Francis-Tan and Mialon 2015, 1919). The wedding industry has grown substantially by selling the idea of romance and love in a consumer society. The wedding industry constantly tries to correlate wedding spending with marriage duration (Francis-Tan and Mialon 2015, 1919). In other words, the wedding industry routinely fuels the myth that spending an astronomical amount on a wedding is a signal of the level of commitment that the groom and bride have for the marriage and each other. Happily married couples indicate that commitment is one of the most important factors contributing to the success of their marriages (Robinson and Blanton 1993; Weigel, Bennett, Ballard-Reisch 2006). The wedding industry is making the idea that "forever love and commitment" is a deserving possibility that is worth the financial investment. This financial investment is reflected in pre-and-post wedding rituals, such as purchasing the ring to purchasing a nice home.

There is no such thing as a "typical" wedding because the couple has the freedom to incorporate their personal thoughts and values. For example, some weddings may be extravagant with a large attendance while some weddings may be simple and attended by close friends and family members. Weddings have long incorporated religious and racial/ethnic identification of the wedded couple. For example, jumping the broom is an African American tradition that originated in Africa when Africans were enslaved and could not marry legally in the United States (African American Registry 2020). Typically, weddings have traditional components such as the DJ (Disc Jockey), caterers, wedding favors, bridesmaid gifts, food, various beauty suppliers such as hair and makeup, honeymoon related, videographers, and so forth. This is not to say that all couples must incorporate these components into their wedding. The wedding components supports tradition and the festive and joyful nature of the wedding. The idea is to create a pomp and circumstance by grabbing attendee's attention that the legal, financial, spiritual, and emotional union of two people is in the process of taking place.

The COVID-19 pandemic, which began in 2020, has affected the wedding industry in many ways including social gatherings, entertainment venues, and dining establishments. These restrictions are mandated by state law, so restrictions differ depending on the state. However, common requirements have included social distancing, wearing masks, enforcement of sanitation through hand-washing and hand sanitizers, and so forth. Guetto, Vignoli, and Bazzani (2020) believe that given the long-term socioeconomic consequences of the COVID-19 pandemic, uncertainty will continue to be important in shaping union formation practices in the years to come. Puhak (2021) points out that COVID-19 negatively impacted the wedding industry last year, resulting in thousands of couples across the United States altering their wedding plans. For example, Puhak (2021) reports that nearly half of couples (47%) postponed their reception to a later date, with 32% still legally tying the knot in 2020 while 15% decided to postpone the entire wedding altogether with the majority setting their eyes In a date in 2021.

The wedding industry is subject to internal and external changes. Internal changes originate with the couple themselves. This includes the type of wedding, location of wedding, honeymoon site, and components incorporated in the wedding. External changes include changes beyond the couple's control such as the COVID-19 pandemic or natural disasters such as monsoons or hurricanes. The wedding industry is a compilation of various components that serve to create the desired effect for the couple. Weddings are a time for two couples to symbolically become one and that begins with navigating through the storms of uncertainty which can include aspects of the wedding.

Damon J. Bullock

See also: Destination Wedding; Wedding Party; Wedding Reception; Wedding Rituals; Wedding Venues; Wedding Vows

Further Reading

African American Registry. 2020. "Jumping the Broom: A Short History." March 6, 2021. https://aaregistry.org/story/jumping-the-broom-a-short-history/

Blakely, Kristin. 2007. "Busy Brides and the Business of Family Life." *Journal of Family Issues*, no. 5 (November): 639–662. https://doi:10.1177/0192513x07309453

Francis-Tan, Andrew and Mialon, Hugo. 2015. "A Diamond Is Forever and Other Fairy Tales: The Relationship Between Wedding Expenses and Marriage Duration." *Economic Inquiry*, no. 4 (October): 1919–1930. https://doi: 10.1111/ecin.12206

Guetto, Raffaele, Vignoli, Daniele, and Bazzani, Giacomo. 2020. "Marriage and Cohabitation Under Uncertainty: The Role of Narratives of the Future During the COVID-19 Pandemic." *European Societies*, no. 1 (October): S674–S688. https://doi: 10.1080/14616696.2020.1833359

IBISWorld, Inc. 2021. "IBISWorld: Industry Market Research, Reports, and Statistics." Ibisworld.com. https://www.ibisworld.com/.

Merrill Edge. March 3, 2021. "How Marriage Can Bring Financial Benefits to Newlyweds." https://www.merrilledge.com/article/marriage-and-your-finances

Puhak, Janine. 2021. "National Wedding Planning Day 2021: Expert says COVID Changed Industry Forever, Makes Big

Prediction for 2021." March 7, 2021. https://www.foxnews.com/lifestyle/national-wedding-planning-day-2021-expert-coronavirus-industry-predictions

Robinson, Linda C., and Blanton, Priscilla W. 1993. "Marital Strengths in Enduring Marriages." *Family Relations*, 38–45.

Stanton, Glenn. 2020. "The Health Benefits of Marriage." March 3, 2021. https://www.focusonthefamily.com/marriage/the-health-benefits-of-marriage/

Weigel, Daniel, Bennett, Kymberley, and Ballard-Reisch, Deborah. 2006. "Roles and Influence in Marriages: Both Spouses' Perceptions Contribute to Marital Commitment." *Family and Consumer Sciences Research Journal*, no. 1 (September): 74–92. https://doi:10.1177/1077727X06289423

Wilcox, Bradford. 2005. "Why Marriage Matters Twenty-Six Conclusions from the Social Sciences." March 3, 2021. https://pol285.blog.gustavus.edu/files/2009/08/CMF_Why_Marriage_Matters.pdf

Wedding Officiant

A wedding officiant is the person who performs a couple's wedding ceremony. Most American states require a wedding officiant for a valid marriage. A few states allow couples to self-unite or self-solemnize their marriage, which does not require a wedding officiant in order to enter into a valid marriage.

Wedding officiants must be authorized to perform weddings. Historically, wedding officiants have been ordained religious figures, such as Catholic priests, or certain civil servants, such as judges. Modern couples increasingly hire a wedding officiant through the internet for approximately $500 or request a friend to serve as the wedding officiant. If not already ordained, the chosen wedding officiant must get ordained, which can be done online for free or a nominal fee at a non-denominational ministry's website, such as that of Universal Life Church.

The wedding officiant has discretion in how to perform a wedding ceremony. He or she may follow the couple's suggestions for themes and topics for the ceremony or rely on more standardized practices. Before the wedding ceremony, the officiant may decide to meet with the engaged couple in order to better personalize the ceremony and tailor it to the couple. The wedding officiant may also help the couple seek a marriage license. Finally, as the wedding date nears, the officiant typically participates in a wedding rehearsal with the couple and the bridal party.

At the wedding ceremony, the officiant commonly leads the couple through the exchange of wedding vows and speech acts that unite the couple in matrimony during the wedding ceremony, such as through words that may include: "I take thee to be my lawful wedded wife or husband." Couples may instead respond "I do" to the wedding officiant's inquiry "Do you take this person to be your lawful wedded wife or husband?" Often near the end of the ceremony, the wedding officiant states, "I now pronounce you husband and wife."

Although the exact requirements vary by state, the wedding officiant usually must sign the couple's marriage license after performing the wedding and deliver it to the appropriate local government office. This license is then recorded and filed. Without it, a marriage may not be valid. Overseeing this documentation is therefore an important task of the wedding officiant, in addition to performing the wedding ceremony.

Margaret Ryznar

See also: Marriage and Legal Planning; Marriage Certificate/License

Further Reading

Adler, Andrew N. 1998. "Can Formalism Convey Justice?—Oaths, 'Deeds,' & Other Legal Speech Acts in Four English Renaissance Plays." *St. John's Law Review* 72, no. 2: 237–290.

Francesca, Lisa. 2014. *The Wedding Officiant's Guide: How to Write and Conduct a Perfect Ceremony.* San Francisco: Chronicle Books LLC.

Wedding Party

With the bride(s) and groom(s) as the foundation, parents, siblings, sometimes extended family, are all those who may be involved in the wedding party. The history of those commonly in the wedding party can be traced back to the start of the 1900s and earlier. An Italian artist, Henri-Julien-Félix Rousseau (1844–1910) completed a portrait of a wedding party he observed. Done in 1904 or 1905, the portrait contained the bride, the groom, as well as both individuals' parents and grandparents outlining what Rousseau viewed as the traditional wedding party (Southgate 2007). Modern wedding parties, in addition to the bride and groom, still include parents or guardians, grandparents at times, and other family members. Additionally, it is also more common now to have friends or confidantes who participate in the role of best man and maid of honor, as well as other friends who fill the roles of groomsmen, bridesmaids, flower girls, and ring bearers.

The function of the various members of the wedding party can vary depending on specific roles given. Family members such as parents and grandparents may take part in a formal wedding line where attendees can come and congratulate each individual for the occasion. Some couples tend to only want themselves, bride and groom, to be the primary participants in these kinds of interactions, though, and let their family be more involved as guests. Some couples may invite individuals to join the wedding party as bridesmaids and groomsmen to help with the different tasks of hosting the wedding itself or to participate in toasts and speeches about the couple, with toasts and speeches being primarily reserved for parents and closest friends. The drive around having these individuals included in aspects of the wedding is often attributed to helping build meaning in the experiences for the couple being wed as well as for those who are able to participate (Chesser 1980).

There are difficulties with wedding parties, especially for those who have mixed families or larger families. With these situations, there is a pressure on the couple to find ways to include each family member in the wedding party. There is no set number of people to include in the wedding party, but typically most weddings have a group of five for the bridesmaids and an equal number for the groomsmen (The Knot 2019). Families who have a history of dysfunction may also experience what could be considered moments of drama from those in the wedding party if expectations of the individuals involved are not met as they anticipated. Aside from the pressure the couple may feel, friends who are selected as groomsman, bridesmaids, best men, and maid of honor can often experience their own stress and pressure toward making the couple's wedding a good experience. Because of this pressure, there are those who feel it is better to skip including friends in the wedding party (Sloss 2018). Ideally, a couple will be able to find a balance between building a meaningful wedding party while not placing too much pressure on themselves and on those they choose for the roles in the wedding party.

Research has argued that marriage is a significant role transition surrounded by various amounts of uncertainty. Couples can be uncertain about the decision to get married, what their married life will look like in the future, the timing of their marriage, etc. While the wedding celebration in general is considered to be a reinforcer for the couple's transition into their new roles, research also argues that the couple specifically looks to their social circle within the celebration for approval and encouragement. Creating an audience to be a witness for their wedding transition further cements for the couple their decision to go through this life transition together, reducing the uncertainty they may feel (Kalmijn 2004). The implications for the importance of the individual members of the wedding party cannot be overlooked, as it provides insights into the potential behavioral-cultural role for the wedding party, that is, being a secure base for the anxious wedding couple.

Brendan Ewell, Michael Anderson, and Todd Spencer

See also: Bachelor Parties; Bachelorette Parties; Bridal Showers; Wedding Industry; Wedding Reception; Wedding Rituals

Further Reading

Brent Berry. 2006. "Friends for Better or for Worse: Interracial Friendship in the United States as Seen through Wedding Party Photos." *Demography* 43, no. 3: 491–510.

Chesser, Barbara Jo. 1980. "Analysis of Wedding Rituals: An Attempt to Make Weddings More Meaningful." *Family Relations* 204–209.

Kalmijn, Matthijs. 2004. "Marriage Rituals as Reinforcers of Role Transitions: An Analysis of Weddings in the Netherlands." *Journal of Marriage and Family* 66, no. 3: 582–594.

The Knot. 2019. "9 Must-Know Tips for Choosing Your Wedding Party." *The Knot.* https://www.theknot.com/content/tips-for-who-to-pick-as-bridesmaids

Sloss, Lauren. 2018. "Make the Friends Happy. Don't Have a Wedding Party." *The New York Times.* https://www.nytimes.com/2018/02/06/fashion/weddings/no-wedding-party-no-bridesmaids-no-groomsmen.html.

Southgate, M. Therese. 2007. "The Wedding Party." *JAMA.* https://jamanetwork.com/journals/jama/article-abstract/207499?casa_token=ZcdJ2QMUesQAAAAA%3AyI6XR8T7ENw20mDsqbByWe0J-nS781eZ9I7U27-L37ibWRQ9_iMBpcS_ZhLOQD-S0yh4WFn1xGBD.

Wedding Reception

Receptions are an important part of a couple's wedding day. The wedding reception is a time for the couple to celebrate their union with family and friends, while also exhibiting their unique style. The decisions a couple makes about their reception and how they make those decisions provide important information about a couple's future together including their marital happiness and the likelihood of staying together.

Prior to World War II, wedding receptions in the United States were typically held in the family home and accompanied by a small lunch where the bride, groom, and their parents stood in a receiving line to greet every guest. In the 1950s, as dance halls became more popular venues and guest lists began to grow, wedding receptions began to evolve. Today wedding receptions take place in a variety of venues, including hotel ballrooms, banquet halls, backyards, or even public parks and zoos. Many couples have also streamlined their day by forgoing a religious venue and holding the ceremony and reception in the same location.

In the United States, the wedding industry is thriving. According to data from research firm IBISWorld, in 2016 wedding industry revenue exceeded $70 billion. Much of the marketing from the wedding industry implies that the more a couple spends on a reception, the more likely they are to have a happy, successful marriage; however, researchers Andrew M. Francis and Hugo M. Mialon of Emory University have found the opposite might be true. In a study focused on the relationship between the amount a couple spends on a wedding and marital longevity, they found that the more a couple spends on a wedding and reception, the more likely they are to divorce. Based on the answers of 3,151 heterosexual couples, the study found that women with wedding costs of $20,000 or greater were more likely to divorce than women who spent between $5,000 and $10,000 on a wedding. Couples who spent $1,000 or less had a lower-than-average rate of divorce (Francis-Tan and Mialon 2015).

For many couples, the wedding reception has become a chance to showcase their personalities and style. In a 2019 survey of more than 25,000 couples by the prominent wedding website The Knot, 55% of couples stated that their celebration being a true reflection of their relationship was a top priority (The Knot 2019). With nearly half of all couples marrying someone from a different background, couples frequently incorporate blends of cultural and religious traditions into their wedding receptions.

When planning the reception, the way a couple makes decisions together may provide insight into how long-lasting or happy their marriage will be. According to data from the National Marriage Project at the University of Virginia, couples who decide to have a formal wedding celebration are, on average, more likely to stay together and report higher marital quality than those who have no formal celebration (Rhoades and Stanley 2014, 13). The authors believe there are multiple factors contributing to this statistic. The first is how the wedding reception ritualizes the commitment a couple is making. The second is that the decision to hold a formal celebration may align with a couple's relationship satisfaction prior to the wedding, for example, a couple who is distressed may be less likely to want a celebration.

Wedding receptions are an opportunity for the couple to publicly celebrate their love and commitment. The same report from the previously mentioned National Marriage Project found that in addition to the amount a couple spends on a wedding, the number of guests they invite is associated with marital satisfaction. When controlling for education, personal income, race, and other demographic factors, the research found that the more guests a couple invites to their wedding, the more likely they are to stay together. While the direct causes of this association are unknown, researchers hypothesize that more guests at a wedding (150 or more) represent a larger social support network for a couple. It also may be that a large declaration of love might increase a couple's desire to stick with their commitment.

The COVID-19 pandemic, which began in 2020, forced many couples to cancel their receptions or dramatically downsize. Many couples redirected money that would have been used on a big reception to other areas such as larger engagement rings or putting the money into savings. Wedding receptions will continue to evolve, especially in the wake of the COVID-19 pandemic.

Whitney Sanchez, Brendan Ewell, and Todd Spencer

See also: Registry; Wedding Party; Wedding Venues

Further Reading

Bhattarai, Abha. 2021. "Smaller Cakes, Shorter Dresses, Bigger Diamonds: The Pandemic Is Shaking up the $73 Billion Wedding Industry." *The Washington Post.* https://www.washingtonpost.com/road-to-recovery/2021/02/11/zoom-weddings-covid-diamond-rings/.

Francis-Tan, Andrew, and Hugo M. Mialon. 2015. "'A Diamond Is Forever' and Other Fairy Tales: The Relationship Between Wedding Expenses and Marriage Duration." *Economic Inquiry* 53, no. 4: 1919–1930. https://doi.org/10.1111/ecin.12206.

"Industry Market Research, Reports, and Statistics." IBISWorld. Accessed April 5, 2021. https://www.ibisworld.com/united-states/market-research-reports/wedding-services-industry/.

The Knot. 2019. "Real Weddings Study: The Knot." *WedInsights.* Accessed April 5, 2021. https://www.wedinsights.com/report/the-knot-real-weddings.

Rhoades, Galena K., and Scott M. Stanley. 2014. "Before 'I Do' What Do Premarital Experiences Have to Do with Marital Quality Among Today's Young Adults?" *The National Marriage Project.* www.virgina.edu/marriageproject.

Wedding Rituals

Rituals are an important aspect of all cultures that celebrate or mark significant events in people's lives. These repeated, organized behaviors and patterns of interaction have symbolic meanings that transcend beyond the actual experience. By providing such meanings, they can foster a sense of connection not only to important others but also to something larger than oneself. There are three main categories of family rituals: *celebrations* involving observation of holidays and rites of passage, *traditions* including birthdays and family reunions, and *patterned routines* such as family dinners (Fiese 2006). Rituals surrounding weddings fall into the celebration category as weddings are rites of passage. Wedding rituals reflect cultural values and mores, not only in the meanings they possess but the manners in which they are practiced and perpetuated.

Family rituals, including weddings, enable us to assess the means by which cultures and societies regulate families (Fiese et al. 2002, 381). While rituals surrounding weddings and the events leading up to them vary both between and within cultures, they all possess symbolism that reflect dominant ideologies. Rites and rituals of weddings often contain metaphors, concrete objects or activities that are symbols of more abstract ideas regarding marriage and family (i.e., exchange of rings as a sign of commitment to another, lighting a unity candle to represent joining of two lives). Themes of symbolism present in wedding rituals include:

- **Fertility/Fecundity and physical consummation of relationship**. The oldest wedding rituals are related to symbolism surrounding procreation. These include the use of fruit and grains for decoration as well as young children serving various roles in the ceremony and the throwing of rice or birdseed. Sexual activity is also represented by actions such as the joint cutting of the wedding cake.
- **Importance of marriage to family and broader community**. Symbols related to this theme in wedding rituals include an emphasis on how marriage ties the couple to something bigger than themselves. It can also involve the offering of gifts which reflects the economic arrangement of marriage that is important to both families and society.
- **Family approval as well as joining of families and membership**. With these, emphasis is on how marriage redefines identities of those involved as well as the boundaries of broader family systems. Rituals can include welcoming speeches and toasts by specific family members and friends given during wedding events, presentation of special gifts between families, and escorting of those getting married by family members into the ceremony as well as lighting of unity candles, sand pouring, and mixing and consumption of ceremonial beverages.
- **Marriage as a sacred union**. This appears to be the most universal meaning present in marriage rituals around the world. This theme of symbolism can be seen in rituals that represent the lifelong commitment and serious nature of marriage as well as responsibility to spouse and any children may have. Instances include joining of hands, exchange of rings, and handfasting or tying of ribbons/cords/garments to represent solemn bond of marriage; jumping of a broom to symbolize new beginning and life with another; foot washing to represent commitment service to another; and breaking of a glass with meaning that varies but usually reflects a blessing for stability of the marriage and a reminder of one's cultural past and their place within it.

The sources of wedding rituals include religious beliefs and practices seen in the rites for ceremonies officiated by religious leaders, family traditions that may be particular to that family or similar to broader social practices, cultural ideologies and structures, and economic systems. Many practices also have roots in past customs, superstitions, or laws that, while no longer as relevant as in the past, are still performed today as part of tradition such as bridal parties dressing alike and the wearing of veils.

Wedding rituals are reflective of societal norms for family and couple relationships, but more so for injunctive norms that prescribe what *should be done or how to behave* rather than what most people *actually do* (i.e., descriptive norms; Strano 2006, 31–32). Rituals, because they are seen as special events with behaviors that, while repeated, are viewed as not typical daily experiences but extraordinary ones. As such, they enable the perpetuation of expressions of abstract ideologies that can persist even when people hold values that contrast with or live their lives differently than what is reflected in these rites. Further, as these rituals are often in public settings, they can have a greater influence because people adapt their behavior to fit with what they perceive to be expected of them by others (Strano 2006, 33–35). Therefore, these injunctive norms are codified, and even celebrated, through wedding rituals. For instance, weddings can reinforce traditional gender norms present in such rituals; heterosexual couples with egalitarian views may still participate in practices (e.g., giving away of bride) reflective of gender inequality. Same sex couples also negotiate these gendered, heteronormative traditions in ways that can both perpetuate and counter them. In one study, couples were observed to display behavior that reflected strategic compliance to these norms as well as playful appropriation, annexation, and conspicuous absence or omission of them (Mamali and Stevens 2020, 994–999). However, injunctive norms reflected in wedding rituals that emphasize gendered, heterosexual relationships can serve to alienate participants and attendees at these events whose lived lives (descriptive norms) differ.

The work to create these rituals also reflects social and cultural norms, particularly related to gender. Family rituals are important areas for examination of how couples negotiate and perform domestic labor related to these celebrations (Humble, Zvonkovic, and Walker 2008). Despite changes in egalitarian ideologies, the actual gendered practice in rituals may be difficult to alter as these events are so entrenched within familial and social institutional standards; women still do a greater proportion of the work to plan, prepare, and host these.

Lastly, wedding rituals reflect, and are influenced by, broader economic systems. They create significant income for businesses involved with special events (hotels, restaurants, reception halls, catering companies, florists, clothiers, travel specialists). From one nationwide survey of several thousand couples, average wedding costs in 2019 (including all expenses surrounding wedding, reception, engagement ring, etc.) was $28,000. While averages dropped due to COVID in 2020 ($19,000), it was more from couples having smaller ceremonies and indications for 2021 are that expenditures are closer to pre-pandemic levels (Forest 2021). Gift giving at wedding events and use of a wedding registry are part of many rituals (showers, parties, receptions) to mark the event as well as assist in setting up of the household. The giving of gifts is significant to the economy as revenues from weddings are second only to those during the Christmas holiday shopping season (Bradford and Sherry 2013, 158).

Shannon E. Weaver and Rachael Elizabeth Farina

See also: Wedding Industry; Wedding Officiant; Wedding Party; Wedding Reception; Wedding Venues; Wedding Vows

Further Reading

Bradford, Tonya W. and John F. Sherry. 2013. "Orchestrating Rituals Through Retailers: An Examination of Gift Registry." *Journal of Retailing* 89, no. 2: 158–175.

Fiese, Barbara H. 2006. *Family Routines and Rituals.* New Haven, CT: Yale University Press.

Fiese, Barbara H., Thomas J. Tomcho, Michael Douglas, Kimberly Josephs, Scott Poltrock, and Tim Baker. 2002. "A Review of 50 Years of Research on

Naturally Occurring Family Routines and Rituals: Cause for Celebration?" *Journal of Family Psychology* 16, no. 4: 381–390.

Forest, Kim. 2021. "This Is How Much a Wedding Actually Costs." https://www.weddingwire.com/wedding-ideas/wedding-cost

Humble, Aine M., Anisa Zvonkovic, and Alexis J. Walker. 2008. "The Royal We: Gender Ideology, Display, and Assessment in Wedding Work." *Journal of Family Issues* 29, no. 1: 3–25.

Mamali, Elizabeth and Lorna Stevens. 2020. "When Same-Sex Couples Say 'I Do': Display Work and the (Re)Production of the Wedding Rite." *Sociology* 54, no. 5: 987–1003.

Strano, Michele M. 2006. "Ritualized Transmission of Social Norms Through Wedding Photography." *Communication Theory* 16: 31–46.

Wedding Venues

For many couples, a wedding is a special event that serves as a celebration of their commitment to one another. Although wedding attendees observe the outcome, the couple must make several decisions prior. Wedding-based decisions are often driven by cultural and religious influences. However, common decisions across culture and religion include those regarding attire (e.g., bride and groom's wear) and guest invitations (i.e., deciding who to invite). Cost also plays a role in these decisions. Some couples may also carefully consider inclusion of traditional cultural or religious practices such as specific music or dance.

When considering the plethora of decisions before the wedding, a couple must also decide where to host their wedding. For couples opting in to both a traditional wedding ceremony and a reception (i.e., the celebration for guests after the ceremony), one of the first choices they must make is whether to host them both at the same or separate locations (Lau and Hui 2010). Some couples may prefer to have their ceremony and reception at the same venue while others may prefer to have them at different locations. Those who choose to separate the location of the ceremony and reception may feel strongly about having the ceremony at their preferred place of religious worship (e.g., church, temple, mosque). Although limited, current literature on wedding venue selection has focused on the reception. In other words, researchers are interested in what factors influence a couple's decision to select the venue of the reception where the celebration takes place as opposed to the wedding ceremony. Reception venues may include banquet halls, hotel ballrooms, or restaurants (Daniels, Lee, and Cohen 2012). First, many couples carefully consider their budget when deciding which venue to choose. Available finances, whether provided by the couple and/or their respective families, inevitably influences which venue they select. Once deciding what is within budget, couples also select venues based on location availability for the selected date(s) of their choosing. Additionally, selection is also based on the location of the venue (Daniels, Lee, and Cohen 2012). Geographical location may include consideration of both preference and ease of accessibly for wedding guests.

Couples also prioritize interactions with reception employees when considering which venue to select. Interactions with reception venue employees includes the quality of service the employees have been known to provide in the past and communication with venue employees regarding booking the reception and the ease associated with doing so (Napompech 2014; Lau and Hui 2010). Lastly, a factor that remains consistent across literature is the emphasis on food and beverage in the venue selection process. Many couples are not only concerned about the pricing of food and beverages offered at the venue (Mahmoud 2015) but also about the variability in options offered and the perceived quality (Lau and Hui 2010; Napompech 2014).

Future research should more carefully examine the factors influencing the selection process for couples residing in the United States specifically. Although current literature has focused on couples from various geographic locations such as Hong Kong and Egypt (Lau and Hui 2010; Mahmoud 2015), examining couples in the United States, where there is quite a variation in culture and religion, may provide novel and richer insights. Additionally, research should examine these factors for LGBTQ+ couples who may prioritize or value different components of both ceremony and reception venues.

Rachael Elizabeth Farina

See also: Wedding Industry; Wedding Officiant; Wedding Party; Wedding Rituals

Further Reading

Daniels, Margaret J., Seungwon Lee, and Tessa Cohen. 2012. "The Attributes Influencing Wedding Reception Venue Selection." *Event Management* 16, no. 3: 245–258. https://doi.org/10.3727/1525995 12x13459279626845.

Lau, Chloe K.H., and Siu-Hung Hui. 2010. "Selection Attributes of Wedding Banquet Venues: An Exploratory Study of Hong Kong Prospective Wedding Couples." *International Journal of Hospitality Management* 29, no. 2: 268–276. https://doi.org/10.1016/j.ijhm.2009.10.008.

Mahmoud, Eman A. 2015. "Modern Wedding Industry in Egypt: The Influence of Key Wedding Venue Attributes on Newlywed Couple Satisfaction and Future Intention." *International Journal of Hospitality and Event Management* 1, no. 3: 244. https://doi.org/10.1504/ijhem.2015.074724.

Napompech, Kulkanya. 2014. "Factors Affecting Wedding Banquet Venue Selection of Thai Wedding Couples." *Journal of Applied Sciences* 14, no. 19: 2258–2266. https://doi.org/10.3923/jas.2014.2258.2266.

Wedding Vows

Wedding vows, often viewed as a fundamental component of a wedding ceremony, are the solemn promises, oaths, or declarations partners make to one another at the time of their marriage. Typically done publicly in the presence of family and friends, wedding vows are declarations usually made with the intent of being together for a lifetime and for better or worse within their union. Wedding vows are often sacred, intimate, and heartfelt. Frequently they are a covenant, meaningful expression of love, commitment, passion, respect, and devotion among other sentiments for the present and succeeding relationship. Wedding vows customarily detail what commitment and partnership uniquely look like for the individuals reciting them, and many hold vows as a moral obligation to those they commit to. However, it should be noted that for many, wedding vows are an obligation but not an unconditional one (Martin 1993). While many go into marriage with dedication, for many people when vows have been broken, so has the commitment and in some cases the relationship. Some of those who have experienced violations of their vows feel little to no duty or commitment to the marriage, even in some cases where people hold vows as a moral obligation, divorce is still present (Lambert and Dollahite 2008, 594). An indication of this is the divorce rate at roughly 14.0 divorces per 1,000 married women in the United States.

It is said that marriage vows date back to medieval times in Europe. While wedding vows are not understood to be solely a religious practice, many couples choose to reference religious doctrine in the recitation of their vows to one another. As marriage vows are a sentimental choice for many, they look different from union to union and such dynamics as race and religion often influence the use or lack in use of vows and how they are carried out. Hermeneutically, the use of wedding vows varies for many, from preapproved vows by the Vatican for Catholics, to not using wedding vows for those who practice Islam, as they are not compulsory in this faith. While Islam and Christianity are the two biggest religions in the world, it is noted that there are many religions and forms of spirituality, as well as individuals who do not have any religious affiliation, and within these groups, the use of wedding vows varies as well.

Commonly used and familiar to many are the traditional Catholic vows (United States) approved by the Vatican. These vows read: "I, (name here), take you, (name here), for my lawful wife/husband, to have and to hold, from this day forward, for better, for worse, for richer, for poorer, in sickness and in health, until death do us part." Another example is from the Protestant perspective: "I, (Name here), take thee, (Name here), to be my wedded husband/wife/spouse, to have and to hold, from this day forward, for better, for worse, for richer, for poorer, in sickness and in health, to love and to cherish, till death do us part, according to God's holy ordinance; and thereto I pledge thee my faith [or] pledge myself to you." However, many develop unique vows that are a reflection of their relationship and what they want for the future.

Jahaan R. Abdullah

See also: Destination Wedding; Wedding Party; Wedding Reception; Wedding Rituals; Wedding Venues

Further Reading

Dannenberg, Jorah. 2015. "Promising Ourselves, Promising Others." *The Journal of Ethics* 19, no. 2: 159–183.

Lambert, Nathaniel M. and David C. Dollahite. 2008. "The Threefold Cord: Marital Commitment in Religious Couples." *Journal of Family Issues* 29, no. 5: 592–614.

Martin, Mike W. 1993. "Love's Constancy." *Philosophy* 68, no. 263: 63–77.

Smith, Robin L. 2006. *Lies at the Altar: The Truth About Great Marriages.* Hachette Books. https://www.catholic weddinghelp.com/topics/catholic -wedding-vows.htm

Work Wives and Work Husbands

A work spouse is a co-worker or colleague with whom one has a distinctively good relationship (i.e., confidence, trust, support, respect). Although the concept of a work spouse has been around since the 1930s, it was not until around 1987 that the terms "work wife" and "work husband" were created (Jackson 2017). Today, the concept of having a work spouse is fairly common. The idea has predominantly been popular in media, blogs, and internet articles with titles such as *Key to Success!, Is it Healthy?,* and *Want to Succeed at Work? Find a Work Spouse.* These articles and blogs often provide information about the pros and cons of a work spouse, managing the relationship, and how to know if you have a work spouse. One article published through CNN mentioned these seven ways to know if you have a work spouse: you depend on them for items such as aspirin; you have inside jokes with them; you can be open and honest with them or comfortable to share uncomfortable information; you seek them out first for debriefing; they know your dietary preferences; you finish each other's sentences; and they are familiar with your personal life (Erwin 2008). Other advantages to having a work spouse include an increase in work productivity, reduced stress, and trusted reassurances (Everwise 2016). There are also some disadvantages to having a work spouse, i.e., damaged reputation based on how others perceive your relationship, could lower productivity, and professional boundaries could be blurred. In addition, those in a work spouse relationship need to be careful of not cutting off other relationship opportunities in the workplace (Everwise 2016).

In 2015, communication researchers Chad McBride and Karla Bergen surveyed 269 participants about their work-spouse relationships and found five domains that emerged from the responses: characteristics of a work spouse, conditions for the work-spouse relationship, characteristics of the work-spouse relationship, functions of work spouses, and ways of managing the work-spouse relationship. They defined a work spouse as having high levels of disclosure and support, and mutual trust,

honestly, loyalty, and respect (McBride and Bergen 2015). Despite a belief that those who have work spouses are likely to be sexually active with one another, only two people in the study reported to have been romantic with one another and about 80% reported not being romantically attracted to one another. Instead, a major theme that emerged in the research was how work spouses enjoyed having someone valuable that they could trust (McBride and Bergen 2015). Aside from the work of McBride and Bergen, there is not much evidence-based information about having a work spouse. Most of what is known about having a work spouse has been based on opinion pieces and information learned through media.

Audrey Besch

See also: Economic Independence; Individualized Marriages; Marriage and Military Families

Further Reading

Day, Arla and Trina Chamberlain. 2006. "Committing to Your Work, Spouse, and Children: Implication for Work-Family Conflict." *Journal of Vocational Behavior* 116–130.

Erwin, Patrick. 2008. "Seven Signs You Have a Work Spouse." http://www.cnn.com/2008/LIVING/worklife/11/10/cb.seven.signs.work.spouse/index.html.

Everwise. 2016. "Company Culture: The Benefits and Pitfalls of Work Spouses." *Everwise.* June 16, 2016.

Jackson, Christine. 2017. "'Til 5 p.m. Do Us Part: the 'Work Spouse' and Why You Need One." https://www.rewire.org/work/work-spouse-relationships/.

McBride, Chad, and Karla Bergen. 2015. "Work Spouses: Defining and Understanding a "New" Relationship." *Communication Studies* 487–508.

About the Editor and Contributors

EDITOR

Jaimee L. Hartenstein is an associate professor in Child and Family Development at the University of Central Missouri. She serves as both the undergraduate and graduate program coordinator. She is a Certified Family Life Educator. Hartenstein received her Bachelor of Science degree in Human Ecology and Mass Communications and her master's and PhD in Family Studies from Kansas State University. Her primary areas of research are divorce and child custody; representation of diversity and disability in children's literature; and teaching effectiveness.

CONTRIBUTORS

Jamie R. Abrams is a professor of Law and Assistant Dean for Intellectual Life at the University of Louisville Louis D. Brandeis School of Law. She teaches Family Law, Torts, Legislation, and Women and the Law. She received her LL.M. from Columbia University School of Law and her JD from American University Washington College of Law, receiving the highest academic honors at both institutions. She has published numerous articles and book chapters on topics relating to reproductive rights, gender-based violence, and feminist legal theory.

Jahaan R. Abdullah is an assistant professor at Chicago State University.

Dr. Abdullah has significant mental health experience and has published and presented nationally and internationally on social justice issues, issues impacting women and marginalized groups, counseling marginalized populations, disparities in mental health diagnosis, and other topics relating to and impacting mental health for marginalized people.

Francesca Adler-Baeder is a professor in the Department of Human Development and Family Studies at Auburn University. She has a master's degree and PhD in Human Development and Family Studies from the University of North Carolina, Greensboro.

Sara Albuquerque received her European Doctorate in Clinical Psychology from the University of Lisbon and the University of Coimbra, and during this period she was a research visitor at VU University, Amsterdam. Her doctoral research focused on the individual and marital adjustment of bereaved parents. She has published several papers in peer-reviewed journals and book chapters. Her research interests include grief, trauma, dyadic coping, posttraumatic growth, and continuing bonds. She has clinical experience working with a variety of areas, such as anxiety, depression, grief, divorce, chronic illness, trauma, and drug addiction. She is also a licensed trainer, conducting regular workshops regarding grief and emotional regulation, and also collaborates with a yearly module on grief and family from the Integrated Master of Psychology of the Faculty of Psychology of the University of Lisbon.

Sarah Alkire holds a master's in Business Administration and is employed at Carnegie as a Senior Slate Strategist.

Kimberly Allen, PhD, BCC, CFLE, is an associate professor and Director of Graduate Programs in Youth, Family, and Community Sciences at North Carolina State University. Dr. Allen has coached and educated hundreds of families, has research expertise in parenting and family life coaching, and is the author of the book *Theory, Research, and Practical Guidelines for Family Life Coaching.*

Michael Anderson is a licensed Associate Marriage and Family Therapist. Michael graduated with his master's in Marriage and Family Therapy from Utah Valley University and is providing services for individuals, couples, and families at Utah Family Therapy in American Fork, Utah.

Melissa Barton has a master's degree in Marriage and Family Therapy from Utah Valley University. She has researched the "Sexual attitudes, beliefs and behaviors of women" and presented this at UCUR (National Conference on Undergraduate Research). She works at Covenant Sex Therapy and is seeking her certification as a Sex Therapist.

Rachel Baumann, MA, SYC., NCSP, is a nationally and state-certified school psychologist. She graduated from Fairfield

University's Graduate School of Education and Allied Professions in May. Her research interests include chronic illness in children and adults, grief and resiliency, and evidence-based treatments addressing trauma.

Elaina K. Behounek is an assistant professor in Sociology and Criminal Justice at Middle Georgia State University. She studies intimate partner violence, sexual assault, fear of crime, and educational inequality.

Julia M. Bernard is the Vice President for Diversity, Equity, and Inclusion at Norwich University. She is a licensed Marriage and Family Therapist in Vermont, a Clinical Fellow of the American Association of Marriage and Family Therapists, a Certified Clinical Trauma Professional, and a Certified Family Life Educator.

Audrey Besch, MS, CTP, received her master's degree in Human Services from East Tennessee State University in 2018. She is a certified trauma professional and her professional/research interests include trauma, internal family systems, adults with dyslexia and recollection of family climate, working with adults with disabilities, and advocating for animal welfare.

Kay Bradford, PhD, is a professor in the Department of Human Development and Family Studies at Utah State University. His research focuses on processes and outcomes in relationship education targeting youth, adults, and couples. He is active in family therapy scholarship and training. Dr. Bradford received his PhD in Marriage, Family, and Human Development from Brigham Young University.

Melissa A. Bray, PhD, is a professor and Director of the School Psychology program at the University of Connecticut in the Neag School of Education. She is a licensed psychologist, holds national and state certifications in school psychology, and has licensure in speech-language pathology. She has 200 publications and 150 presentations. Her research interests are mind-body health.

Candace Forbes Bright, PhD, is an associate professor and faculty affiliate of the Applied Social Research Lab in the Department of Sociology and Anthropology at East Tennessee State University in Johnson City, Tennessee.

Matthew Brosi is a professor of Marriage and Family Therapy at Oklahoma State University and State Specialist with the Oklahoma Cooperative Extension Service. He has a long history of leadership and teaching in MFT, co-authoring the Coparenting for Resilience program, and developing programs addressing rural mental health, fatherhood, and the opioid epidemic.

Kristina S. Brown, LMFT, is a professor and Chair of the Couple and Family Therapy Department at Adler University. Both in Marriage and Family Therapy, Dr. Brown earned her PhD from Syracuse University and her MA from the University of San Diego. She is the Editor-in-Chief of the *Journal of Feminist Family Therapy* and Editor of the upcoming *AAMFT Systemic Ethics Textbook.*

Joseph R. Budd is an assistant professor of Criminal Justice at Campbellsville University in Campbellsville, Kentucky.

Damon J. Bullock, PhD, is an associate professor of Criminal Justice at Western New Mexico University, the author *of How Wars Are Won: Leadership, Friendship, Family, and Unit Cohesion* (2016), and was a participant in the Vuelo Verano Global Program in Mexico from 2016–2020.

Carolyn L. Carlson is an associate professor at Washburn University in Kansas. She holds two doctorates (a PhD in Literacy Education and a JD [Law]), a master's in Literacy Education, and a bachelor's in Japanese. She teaches undergraduate- and graduate-level courses in literacy education, research, and education law. She is the author of numerous journal articles, has spoken at numerous national and international conferences, and has earned multiple awards recognizing her research.

Kristie Chandler serves as the chair and professor for the Department of Human Development and Family Science and the Department of Educational Leadership at Samford University. Dr. Chandler is a Certified Family Life Educator and a recipient of the Outstanding Teaching Award for the School of Education.

I. Joyce Chang is a professor in the Human Development and Family Science program at the University of Central Missouri. Dr. Chang received her doctorate in Human Development and Family Sciences and master's degree in Interdisciplinary Studies (Psychology, Women Studies, & Statistics) from Oregon State

University. Her primary research interests are high-risk behaviors, relationship development, and the impacts of technology on families. Dr. Chang is a legacy member of the National Council on Family Relations and has received awards for teaching, research, and service from UCM and professional organizations. In addition to Oregon and Washington, Dr. Chang has taught/lectured in Sweden, Taiwan, and the Netherlands.

Megan L. Chapman, PhD, is an adjunct faculty at Grand Canyon University and Touro University.

Koriann B. Cox, PhD, is a licensed psychologist in Washington State and an acting assistant professor at the University of Washington Medical Center. She provides clinical care to individuals as part of inpatient, intensive outpatient, and general outpatient care clinics. Her clinical and research interests focus on co-occurring mental health and addiction, with a particular focus on co-occurring trauma and addiction as well as reproductive mental health.

McKenzie L. Cox-Zimmermann has a BS in Family Studies and a master's in Applied Family Science from Kansas State University. She is the 4-H Enrollment, Evaluation, and Data Management Program Coordinator for Kansas State Research & Extension. McKenzie has focused her research career on family, divorce, and fathers. She is a member of the executive team for the Divorce Education Assessment Collaborative.

Ming Cui is a professor of Family and Child Sciences at Florida State University.

René Dailey, PhD, is an associate professor at the University of Texas at Austin in Communication Studies. Her research focuses on how communication in on-again/off-again relationships differs from other dating relationships. Her work has appeared in the *Journal of Social and Personal Relationships* and *Communication Monographs.*

Shannon N. Davis is a professor of Sociology and Associate Dean for Faculty and Academic Affairs at George Mason University Korea. Her research focuses on the reproduction of social inequality through unpaid labor within families, higher education, and the labor market. In addition to numerous publications in scholarly journals such as the *Journal of Family and Economic Issues, Social Science Research, Community, Work, & Family, Sex Roles,* and *Research in Social Stratification and Mobility,* she is co-author (with Theodore N. Greenstein) of *Methods of Research on Human Development and Families,* co-author (with Theodore N. Greenstein) *Why Who Cleans Counts: What Housework Tells Us About American Family Life,* and co-editor (with Sarah Winslow and David J. Maume) of *Gender in the Twenty-First Century: The Stalled Revolution and the Road to Equality.*

Patrice Delevante is an author and independent scholar who graduated from the University of Virginia, Universidad de Valencia, and Simmons University. Her research and teaching interests include 19th- and 20th-century American, Native American, and African American literature and culture, transnational studies, and feminist theory. Her work appears in the *Oxford Encyclopedia of Women in World History* (2008), *Battleground:*

Women, Gender, and Sexuality (2009), *Conspiracies and Conspiracy Theories in American Literature* (2019), *Race and Ethnicity* (2019), among others.

Richard S. Dell'Isola, PhD, LMFTA, is an assistant professor of Psychology at Belmont Abbey College. Richard is a marriage and family therapist who has published on factors that promote positive relationship outcomes for young couples.

Tuba Demir-Dagdas, PhD, is a postdoctoral research scholar at UC Davis School of Medicine, Department of Public Health Sciences. She received her doctoral degree in Medical Sociology from the University of Alabama at Birmingham. Her work has appeared in numerous journals including *Health Education and Behavior, Journal of Divorce & Remarriage,* and *Vulnerable Children and Youth.*

Rachel M. Diamond, PhD, LMFT, is an assistant professor and the Clinical Training Director in the Department of Couple and Family Therapy at Adler University in Chicago, IL. Dr. Diamond has a clinical and research interest in divorce and is a certified family mediator. She is the co-creator of the Divorce Initiator Inventory-Revised, a comprehensive assessment of divorce initiation.

Theresa E. DiDonato is a professor of Psychology at Loyola University Maryland. She writes the popular *Psychology Today* blog "Meet, Catch, and Keep" and is anticipating the forthcoming publication of her first textbook, authored with Brett Jakubiak, titled, *The Science of Romantic Relationships.*

Gayle T. Dow, PhD, is an associate professor of Psychology at Christopher Newport University. She received her PhD in Educational Psychology from Indiana University, Bloomington, an MA in Cognitive Psychology from the University of California, Santa Barbara, and an MA in Experimental Psychology from California State University, Fullerton. She has taught courses on Research Methodology, Educational Psychology, and The Science of Evil. Her research on the Dark Triad (Psychopathy, Narcissism, and Machiavellianism) and Malevolent Creativity has been published in several journals including *Creativity Research Journal, Journal of Educational Psychology,* and *Educational Psychologist.*

Patricia Drentea is a professor of Sociology at the University of Alabama at Birmingham. She authored the book *Families and Aging* (2019).

Melanie L. Duncan, PhD, is the Assistant Diversity and Inclusion Officer and Deputy Title IX Coordinator at the Indiana University of Pennsylvania.

Ashley E. Ermer is an assistant professor in the Department of Family Science and Human Development at Montclair State University.

Brooks Evans graduated with a bachelor's degree in Business Administration from the Conover Education Center of Campbellsville University in Harrodsburg, Kentucky.

Brendan Ewell is a Marriage and Family Therapist practicing in Utah. He focuses on the treatment of relationship and family dynamics and conducts research in these areas. Brendan also teaches Psychology at Utah Valley University. Brendan has completed a bachelor's degree in Psychology from Utah Valley University, a master's in Human Resources from Utah State University, and a master's in Marriage and Family Therapy from Utah Valley University.

Rachael Elizabeth Farina, LMFT, ADS, is a licensed marriage and family therapist in Glastonbury, CT, who specializes in sex therapy. She is also a PhD student at The University of Connecticut in the Department of Human Development Family Sciences. Her research interests include sexual health and sexuality.

Nickole Durbin Félix graduated with her JD with honors from the University of Louisville Louis D. Brandeis School of Law. She then went on to graduate with honors in 2021 with her LLM in Litigation and Alternative Dispute Resolution from the Universidad InterAmericana de Puerto Rico.

She represents people convicted and sentenced to death in collateral postconviction proceedings in South Florida. She is also admitted to practice in DC and New York.

Anthony J. Ferraro holds a PhD in Human Development and Family Science from Florida State University and is an associate professor in the Department of Applied Human Sciences at Kansas State University. He is Co-Director of the Divorce Education Assessment Collaborative, the Chair of the Family Policy section of the National Council on Family Relations, and sits on numerous journal editorial boards. His work focuses on adjustment to divorce, program evaluation, and coparenting relationships.

Clara Gerhardt, MBA, PhD, is a Distinguished Professor and past Chair of Human Development and Family Science at Samford University. She is licensed both as a clinical psychologist and a marriage and family therapist. She is the author of two textbooks: one on parenting and the other on family dynamics.

Patricia E. Gettings, PhD, is an associate professor of Communication at the University at Albany, State University of New York. She received her PhD from Purdue University.

Anastasia Giorgoudi graduated from Nova Southeastern University with a BS in Psychology. She is in a master of science program in Clinical Psychology at the University of Nicosia, Cyprus.

Eric T. Goodcase, PhD, LMFT, is a postdoctoral fellow in the Human Development and Family Studies Department at the University of Alabama. His research interests include adolescent and emerging adult romantic relationships including the role of technology. He is also involved in projects that utilize technology to improve the relational and mental health of others.

Stevi Gould, MA, AMFT, is a doctoral student at Adler University in Chicago, IL, studying Couples and Family Therapy. She is also a therapist working at a private practice in Chicago where her clientele is a combination of couples, families, and individuals.

Jordan E. Greenburg is a PhD student in Applied Development Psychology at George Mason University. She received her MA in Applied Developmental

Psychology from George Mason University in 2019. Jordan is an academic advisor, graduate student teaching assistant, and graduate research assistant for the Psychology department.

Erin Guyette is a master's student in Couples and Family Therapy at the School of Family Studies and Human Services at Kansas State University. Erin attended the University of Minnesota, Twin Cities, for her bachelor's degree where she majored in Psychology and minored in Family Social Science. Her clinical interests include working with families in transitions of divorce or separation. Similarly, her primary research interests include coparenting, parenting coordination, blending families, custody decision-making, and mediation.

Cadmona A. Hall, PhD, LMFT, FT, is a professor in the Department of Couple & Family Therapy at Adler University in Chicago, IL. Dr. Hall is a licensed Marriage and Family Therapist in the states of New York and Illinois. She is a Clinical Fellow of the American Association of Marriage and Family Therapists and an AAMFT Approved Supervisor. She is also a Fellow in Thanatology (the study of death, dying, and bereavement) through the Association of Death Education and Counseling. Through Hall Consultation & Therapy Services, Dr. Hall sees couples, families, and individuals. She also provides professional consultation, training, seminars, and executive coaching related to social justice and diversity, equity, and inclusion.

Tara Katherine Hammar, PhD, LMFT, is an associate professor in the Department of Human Services and Counseling

at the Metropolitan State University of Denver.

Brian Hannigan is a doctoral student at Antioch University New England, Keene, NH, studying couple and family psychotherapy. As a clinical mental health counselor, he focuses on clinical interventions in school settings, integrated care clinics, and residential programs.

Amber Harkey, BCC, is the owner and coach at Carolina Family Life Coaching as well as a Graduate Researcher at North Carolina State University. Amber's research focus is on divorce coaching and blended family coaching and she specializes in working with families going through the Collaborative Divorce process.

Meredith Marko Harrigan, PhD, is a professor in the Department of Communication at the State University of New York College at Geneseo. She received her doctorate from the University of Nebraska-Lincoln, and her research centers on the intersection of communication, family, and identity and seeks to understand how members of discourse-dependent or nontraditional families communicatively construct and negotiate personal and relational identities.

Carrie Hatch is a doctoral candidate at Antioch University New England, Keene, NH, and is a Licensed Marriage and Family Therapist. In her private practice, she specializes in gender-affirming therapy, trauma, grief, and attachment. Her research focuses on clinical work through a social justice and feminist framework. Carrie also teaches as an adjunct professor for two graduate clinical training programs.

Alan J. Hawkins, PhD, is the Camilla E. Kimball Professor of Family Life and Director of the School of Family Life at Brigham University. His scholarship focuses on educational and policy interventions to help couples form and sustain healthy marriages and relationships.

Brian J. Higginbotham is a professor and Extension Specialist in the Department of Human Development and Family Studies at Utah State University. He has a master's degree in Marriage and Family Therapy and a PhD in Human Development and Family Studies from Auburn University.

Amanda J. Hill is an Attorney at Law and Founding Partner of Khosroabadi & Hill, APC, Alumni of California Western School of Law.

Kevin Hogg is a high school law and English teacher in British Columbia. He holds an MA degree in English Literature from Carleton University. His research focuses on world religions, sports history, race relations, and the summer of 1969.

Donna Hoskins, is an associate professor and Department Chair of Health and Human Sciences at Bridgewater College. She earned a PhD from the University of Georgia. Her human development and family science research focuses on the consequences of parenting on adolescent outcomes.

Aaron Hoy, PhD, is an assistant professor of Sociology at Minnesota State

University, Mankato. His research and teaching interests include families, sexualities, aging, and the life course. He is the editor of *The Social Science of Same-Sex Marriage: LGBT People and Their Relationships in the Era of Marriage Equality* (2022).

Rashida Ingram is a doctoral candidate at Antioch University, Couple and Family Therapy Program. Rashida is the owner of Innergy Connections, LLC, an online wellness and international consulting center dedicated to providing women and couples with the experience of feeling grounded, self-aware, and confident as they reset, redefine, and rebuild their lives after a significant life-altering event. Rashida's current research focuses on relationship satisfaction among African American couples using a strength-based perspective. She is also an adjunct professor for two universities in their MFT programs.

Seyma Intepe-Tingir is an assistant clinical faculty member in the Special Education Department at the University of Maryland, College Park. She received her PhD with a Special Education major from Florida State University and her master's degree in Learning Disability/Behavioral Disorder from The University of Texas at Austin. Her research interests include students with Autism Spectrum Disorder, literacy skills, vocabulary intervention, reading comprehension, and early intervention. She teaches undergraduate and graduate courses on an introduction to special education, reading instruction, severe disabilities, literature review of evidence-based practices, action research, assessment, and diversity.

Chelsea-Alexis Jackson, MA, is an academic advising and retention specialist at Christian Brothers University. Her teaching and research interests include romantic relationships, mental health, race and ethnicity, cultural competency, and young adults in transition.

Todd M. Jensen, PhD, MSW, is a research assistant professor in the School of Social Work at the University of North Carolina at Chapel Hill. Dr. Jensen's scholarship focuses on promoting family well-being in diverse contexts; strengthening family-serving systems; and prioritizing equity in family research, practice, and policy. His work attends to families experiencing relationship transitions and shifts in parental structure, family maltreatment prevention among military-connected families, promoting the use of evidence in family-serving systems, advocating for inclusive definitions of family, and centering equity in the theory and methods used to study and support families. He is also co-founder and co-chair of the Diverse Family Structures Focus Group of the National Council on Family Relations, which has amassed over 120 scholars across the country and globe who are interested in aligning research and intervention programs with the complex and rich realities of family relationships.

Denzel L. Jones, PhD, LMFT, is an assistant professor in Marriage and Family Therapy at Antioch University New England. In addition to teaching, Dr. Jones engages in multiple professorial, clinical, supervisory, scholarship, and community engagement and service roles. His primary research interest is on social processes that impact relationships and identity with a secondary interest in relationship education.

Ethan Jones, PhD, is a licensed Marriage and Family Therapist and AAMFT-approved supervisor.

Archana Kamaal holds an MBA (Finance/Marketing) from Symbiosis, Pune. She is associated with Emeritus as a Senior Associate, Academic Delivery (Grading). Her role revolves around working as an academic grader and contributor for e-learning modules, assessment, providing learners with constructive feedback on graded assignments and collaborating with subject matter experts to understand module expectations.

Most recently, she set the strategic training direction for designers comprising of United States, APAC, and India team to facilitate and train for best practices on "Rubric Designing and Instructional Gaps" based on the needs assessment. In the past, Archana worked as an assistant professor at the Institute of Management and Computer Studies, delivering lectures as per UGC Norms in General Management, Finance, and Marketing. She also worked as a student/career counsellor for MBA students, playing a key role in assessing the student interest and guiding them to choose the right specializations. Her corporate stint includes working as an Investor Relations Executive with Suzlon Energy Ltd, Mumbai. Before joining Suzlon Energy, she worked in the capacity of a Credit Risk Analyst with companies like Deutsche Postbank Home Finance Limited, Reliance Capital, First Data and Manba Finance.

Youngjin Kang, PhD, received her doctorate in Human Development and Family Science from the University of Missouri-Columbia. She is an assistant professor of Human Services at the University of Illinois at Springfield. She teaches classes related to child and family studies. Her research interests include family processes and family dynamics in post-divorce families.

Falon Kartch, PhD, is an associate professor in the Department of Child and Family Science at California State University, Fresno. She received her doctorate from the University of Wisconsin-Milwaukee. Her research centers on how various populations define what it means to be "family," particularly in the context in which "family" occurs outside of social and cultural conventions, and the application of relational justice frameworks to understand, develop, maintain, and terminate close relationships.

Sam Kendrick is a PhD candidate in the Department of Sociology at the University of Kansas.

Claire Kimberly, PhD, is a research coordinator in the Department of Internal Medicine at Virginia Commonwealth University. Previously, she was an associate professor in the Department of Child and Family Studies at the University of Southern Mississippi. She earned her doctorate in Family Science and a certificate in Family Life Education from the University of Kentucky.

Kwangman Ko is an assistant professor in the Department of Counseling and Human Services at East Tennessee State University.

Olena Kopystynska, PhD, is an assistant professor at Southern Utah University in the Department of Family Life and Human Development. She was previously a post-doctoral fellow in the Department of Human Development and Family Studies at Utah State University. Her research focuses on interparental conflict and parenting across diverse family environments. Dr. Kopystynska received her PhD in Family Studies and Human Development from The University of Arizona.

Shane W. Kraus, PhD, is an assistant professor of Clinical Psychology at the University of Nevada, Las Vegas. Dr. Kraus studies psychopathology, sexual trauma, substance use disorders, problem gambling, and compulsive sexual behavior disorder. He has co-authored over 125 publications on the topics of addiction, mental health, sexual behavior, and trauma.

Michael (Mickey) Langlais is an assistant professor at the University of North Texas in the Department of Educational Psychology.

Elizabeth Laughlin is a graduate student at the University of Central Missouri studying human development and family science with a specialization in marriage and family therapy.

Seungyeon Lee is an associate professor of Psychology at the University of Arkansas at Monticello. She received her PhD in Educational Psychology from the University of Kansas in 2014. She teaches a wide range of psychology courses, with research interests involving the impact of technology on cognition as well as how technology influences spatial abilities, in terms of retained memory of the navigated environment.

Gordon Limb, PhD, is Director of the School of Social Work at Brigham Young University. He received his PhD in Social Welfare from the University of California at Berkeley. Prior to joining the faculty at BYU, he had served as an assistant professor of Social Work at Arizona State University and as Assistant Director of the Kathryn M. Buder Center for American Indian Studies at the Brown School of Social Work, Washington University in St. Louis. Dr. Limb concentrates his research activities around Native American families and children with much of the focus on American Indian child welfare issues.

Dr Limb's practice experience includes working with adolescents in a wilderness survival program, as a clinical social worker at a social service agency, and as a counselor at a community college. He has articles published in a wide range of top social work journals.

Gina Marie Longo, PhD, is an assistant professor in the Sociology department at Virginia Commonwealth University. Dr. Longo's work has been featured in publications such as *Gender & Society, Migration Politics, Sociological Imaginations*, the *Journal of Family Relations*, and the London School of Economics' U.S. Centre.

Eunice Makunzva, MA, LPC, is a doctoral candidate in the Couples and Family Therapy Program at Adler University. She has presented at several domestic and international conferences and focuses on increasing accessibility to clinical services for students at universities and professional schools.

Melinda Stafford Markham, PhD, CFLE, is an associate professor and Associate Director of Academic Affairs in the School of Family Studies and Human Services at Kansas State University. Markham earned her master's and a doctorate in Human Development and Family Studies with a certificate in Women's and Gender Studies from the University of Missouri. Her primary research interest is post-divorce relationships, principally coparenting relationships between former partners.

Yehezkel Margalit is a senior lecturer of Law at the Netanya Academic College and Bar-Ilan University. He received his LL.B., MA (Law), and PhD (Law) from Bar-Ilan University. He was a Visiting Research Scholar at New York University Law School from 2011–2012 and is the author of the books *The Jewish Family—Between Family Law and Contract Law* (2017) and *Determining Legal Parentage—Between Family Law and Contract Law* (2019).

Jaclyn S. Marsh earned her PhD from the University of Nebraska-Lincoln. Her teaching focuses on Family Communication, Interpersonal Communication, and classes that help students better understand themselves. Her primary research interest looks at the interplay between family members and their influence on our overall health and well-being.

Katie E. Matthew is an active-duty officer in the U.S. Army and a doctoral student in Sociology at George Mason University, specializing in work and family studies. She has a master's in Business Administration and Organizational Psychology from Kansas State.

Jennifer M. Miller earned her PhD in Criminal Justice at the University of Arkansas at Little Rock, and her dissertation focused on sentencing outcomes in Arkansas. She is an assistant professor of Criminal Justice at the University of Arkansas at Monticello, where she began her career teaching college in January 2015.

Rachel D. Miller, LMFT, is a Marriage and Family Therapist working in private practice in Chicago, IL. She is also a PhD candidate at Adler University whose research focuses on adult children who experienced intimate partner violence and a high-conflict divorce or custody battle in the family court system while growing up.

J. Kale Monk, PhD, is an assistant professor in the Department of Human Development and Family Science at the University of Missouri. He researches romantic relationship instability and how couples develop and maintain commitment and satisfaction across critical transitions (e.g., the transition to marriage). Dr. Monk is the co-editor of *Relationship Maintenance: Theory, Process, and Context.*

Beth Montemurro is a professor of Sociology at Penn State University, Abington. Her current research focuses on the development of heterosexual men's sexual selves. She is the author of *Deserving Desire: Women's Stories of Sexual Evolution* (2014) and *Something Old, Something Bold: Bridal Showers and Bachelorette Parties* (2006), as well as numerous journal articles related to gender, sexuality, and popular culture.

Jessica M. Moreno is an assistant professor within the Counselor Education Program, Marriage Couple Family Counseling concentration at California State University, Sacramento. Dr. Moreno is a licensed Marriage and Family Therapist in the state of California.

Lisa Moyer, Lecturer, Auburn University.

Felicia Law Murray, PhD, LCSW, is an assistant professor in the Department of Social Work at Tarleton State University. Her research interests include father engagement and involvement, intergenerational transmission of parenting practices, and the scholarship of teaching and learning.

Makena Nail is a PhD student at the University of Nebraska-Lincoln studying quantitative methodologies.

Katie Nick, LMFT, is a Chicago-based relationship and sex therapist with a background in journalism. She received her MA from Adler University and her Bachelor of Journalism from the University of Missouri.

Bonnie M. Nickels, PhD, is a visiting assistant professor in the School of Communication at Rochester Institute of Technology. Dr. Nickels' research in interpersonal communication is particularly focused on difficult conversations within the contexts of family and health. She has presented and published research related to relational maintenance behaviors used by women with their incarcerated partner, end-of-life communication in veterinary medicine, and depictions of end-of-life in film and television and how these scenes can facilitate discussions of end-of-life within families. Her work has been published in the *Journal of Family Communication, Health Communication,* and *Omega: Journal of Death and Dying.*

Sylvia Niehuis is an associate professor in the Department of Human Development and Family Studies at Texas Tech University.

Jori A. Nkwenti, is a graduate student at Minnesota State University, Mankato. Their interests include intermarriages, family, culture, empathy, and international studies.

Ismail Nooraddini holds a PhD in sociology from George Mason University and is an international research methodology consultant for the U.S. Department of State. He is a mixed-methodologist interested in immigration and family studies.

Sharon N. Obasi, PhD, is an associate professor of Family Studies at the University of Nebraska at Kearney.

Clara O'Connor graduated from Bridgewater College, Magna Cum Laude, in May of 2020 with a Bachelors of Science in Family and Consumer Sciences with concentrations in Child Development and Family Life Education. Upon graduating, she earned the Major of the Year award and Excellence in Leadership and Service award in the Department of Health and Human Services. Clara resides in Martinsburg, West Virginia, and after several years in the workforce, she is a full time mom and wife with hopes to provide parenting and infant development education to those in her community in the future.

Matthew A. Ogan is a PhD student in Human Development and Family Science at the University of Missouri. His research focuses on the influence of stress in romantic relationships, with a particular emphasis on relationship functioning and instability as both precursors and outcomes of stress.

Taylor Ogden graduated with a master's degree from the University of Akron.

Bailey M. Oliver-Blackburn, PhD, is an assistant professor in the Department of Applied Communication at the University of Arkansas at Little Rock. She holds a PhD in Human Communication, with a focus on restructured family communication. She is a published researcher, professor, and certified group facilitator in the fields of conflict transformation and family resilience.

M. L. Parker, PhD, LMFT, is an assistant professor in the Department of Human Development and Family Science at Florida State University. Dr. Parker's research has been published in prominent journals such as the *Journal of Marital and Family Therapy* and *Family Process.*

La Toya L Patterson received her bachelor's in Psychology and an MA in Clinical Professional Psychology from Roosevelt University. Dr. Patterson went on to receive her second MA in Forensic Psychology from Argosy University and her PhD in Counselor Education and Supervision from Adler University. She is also a licensed Clinical Professor Counselor and a National Certified Counselor. Dr. Patterson has worked as a therapist for 12 years, providing individual therapy for individuals that have co-occurring disorders. Dr. Patterson works as an assistant professor.

Raquel Peel is a senior lecturer at the Royal Melbourne Institute of Technology, in Australia. Dr. Peel is an internationally recognized relationship expert and an award-winning educator and researcher. Her TEDx talk on relationship sabotage was featured as one of the most popular talks in the TED series "How to Be a Better Human" and TEDxShorts. Raquel has also spoken at high-profile events such as the World of Science Festival and is a prolific contributor to The Conversation. She is regularly interviewed by the media to provide expert commentary on relationship matters at national and international outlets such as The Project, ABC, Forbes, The Guardian, Psychology Today, Channel News Asia, and the Deutsche Welle German Broadcaster. Her current research program encompasses studies on interpersonal relationships, mental health, suicide, and education. For a complete portfolio, please visit: www.RaquelPeel.com

Vanessa Perocier is a doctoral student at Antioch University New England, New Hampshire, studying couple and family psychotherapy. After six years of clinical experience as an associate marriage and family therapist, she loves working with underserved families coping with severe mental illness and helping them create healthier futures.

Daniel W. Phillips III, PhD, is an instructor of Sociology and Criminal Justice and Regional Coordinator of Faculty Development at the Conover Education Center of Campbellsville University in Harrodsburg, Kentucky. His research and teaching interests include the intersection of mental illness and criminal justice as well as sexual abuse.

Courtney A. Polenick, PhD, is an assistant professor in the Department of Psychiatry at the University of Michigan and a Faculty Associate in the Aging & Biopsychosocial Innovations Program of the Survey Research Center at the University of Michigan Institute for Social Research. Dr. Polenick's research focuses on later-life family relationships and caregiving in the context of complex care needs including dementia and multimorbidity.

James J. Ponzetti, Jr., is a professor emeritus at the University of British Columbia, Vancouver, BC, Canada. As a Certified Family Life Educator (CFLE), he is committed to the promotion of family life education. He edited *Evidence-Based Relationship and Marriage Education*, *Evidence-Based Parenting Education,* and *Evidence-Based Approaches to Sexuality Education: A Global Perspective.* He has also investigated indigenous grandfamilies, governance in communal groups, the use of theater in sexuality education, and marital preparation programs.

Amy J. Rauer, PhD, is an associate professor in Child and Family Studies at the University of Tennessee at Knoxville. Dr. Rauer's work focuses on how intimate relationships develop as the individuals within them grow and change over their lifespan.

Abiodun Raufu is an assistant professor in Criminal Justice at Southern University and A&M College. Dr. Raufu holds an M.Sc. in Political Science from the

University of Lagos and a BA in Philosophy from Obafemi Awolowo University both in Nigeria. A former journalist, Raufu is a parole officer with the Texas Department of Criminal Justice in Houston. Raufu is a recipient of the 2019 Academy of Criminal Justice Sciences (ACJS) Doctoral Summit Scholarship.

Tonya Ricklefs, PhD, LMSW, is an assistant professor and Chair of the Department of Social Work at Washburn University. She has a Graduate Certificate in Conflict Resolution from Kansas State University and is trained in Elder/Healthcare decision-making by Elder Decisions, Newton, MA. She studied International Conflict and Trauma in Northern Ireland and hosts a faculty-led study abroad with Social Work and Human Services in Colombia. She is a board member of the Heartland Mediator Association and the Kansas Chapter of the National Association of Social Workers, and the Vice President of the Kansas Council on Social Work Education.

Anthony Rivas is a faculty member in the Counselor Education program at California State University-Sacramento (CSUS).

Dr. Rivas began his career in academia at the director level in academic advising, student retention, and student disability services before moving on to faculty roles at both the community college, baccalaureate, and graduate levels. Prior to teaching at CSUS, he taught at the undergraduate level at MSU Denver and prior to that, at the graduate level at the University of Colorado, Colorado Springs (UCCS) in the Department of Counseling and Human Services. At UCCS, he taught: clinical mental health counseling, substance abuse counseling,

student development theory, educational psychology, educational leadership, and within the Air Force Officer Commanding Leadership program. Dr. Rivas is an approved trainer for Clinical Supervision for the State of Colorado.

Dr. Rivas has clinical experience providing mental health and substance abuse counseling in both private practice and with community agencies working with court-mandated offenders and individuals with chronic and severe mental health diagnoses. Dr. Rivas holds clinical licensure in Colorado as both an Addiction Counselor and Marriage and Family Therapist with the national credential of Master Addiction Counselor. His research interests focus on equity and access to care, disparity in treatment for those with SUD, and the effect of socioeconomic status on clinical relationships, diagnosis, and prognosis.

Bita Ashouri Rivas, Ed.D, LPC, LMFT, LAC, NCC, MAC, ACS, is an assistant professor of Marriage, Couples, and Family Counseling at California State University Sacramento. Dr. Rivas' research areas of interest include substance use disorders and has recently submitted a manuscript for a book chapter titled, "The Causes and Implications of the Opioid Crisis in Rural America" in the *Handbook of Research on Leadership and Advocacy for Children and Families in Rural Poverty*. In addition, she is serving as the Chair of the Legislative and Advocacy Committee of the California Association of Licensed Professional Clinical Counselors (CALPCC) for which she is also a board member, advocating for all counselors and therapists in California.

Aaron Robb, PhD, is the Program Director of Forensic Counseling Services, based in the Dallas-Ft. Worth metro area. His practice focuses on child custody evaluations and intervention services for high-conflict family law cases. He is the author of numerous publications and serves on the editorial boards of the journal *Family Court Review* and the *Journal of Family Trauma, Child Custody, and Child Development.*

Shannon Roddy is an associate law librarian and adjunct professor at American University, Washington College of Law. Before entering academia, she clerked for a family court judge in the Superior Court of the District of Columbia and practiced family law in Washington, DC and Maryland.

Katya Ruiz is a student double majoring in Child Development and Family Studies and Family Life Education at California State University, Long Beach.

Margaret Ryznar is a Family Law professor at Indiana University McKinney School of Law.

Whitney Sanchez is a Marriage and Family Therapy graduate student at Utah Valley University.

David G. Schramm, PhD, is a professor and Extension Specialist in the Department of Human Development and Family Studies at Utah State University. He has a master's degree in Family, Consumer, and Human Development from Utah State University and a PhD in Human Development and Family Studies from Auburn University.

Arielle A. J. Scoglio, PhD, is a postdoctoral Research Fellow at Harvard T. H. Chan School of Public Health in Boston, MA. Her research focuses on functioning, psychopathology, and resilience following interpersonal violence, particularly in marginalized populations. She has co-authored over 30 publications on topics of trauma recovery, mental health, and resilience.

Amber J. Seidel, PhD, CFLE, is an associate professor of Human Development and Family Studies at The Pennsylvania State University. Dr. Seidel's research focuses on family involvement such as providing and receiving support or control across the lifespan with a health context.

Tong Shen is a PhD student in Business Administration (Concentration: Information Systems), at the University of Connecticut.

Aya Shigeto, PhD, is an associate professor in the Department of Psychology and Neuroscience at Nova Southeastern University. She has published journal articles and encyclopedia entries in the areas of family science and developmental psychology.

Julie Ahmad Siddique is an associate professor of Criminal Justice at the University of North Texas at Dallas. She specializes in interpersonal violence and victimization and her research has been published in *Violence and Victims, Victims and Offenders*, and the *Journal of Interpersonal Violence.*

Jefferson Alan Singer, PhD, is the Dean of the College, Faulk Foundation

Professor of Psychology at Connecticut College in New London, Connecticut. He is the co-author with Karen Skerrett of *Positive Couple Therapy: Using We-Stories to Enhance Resilience* and a Fellow of the American Psychological Association.

Lisa A. Singleton, PhD, is an assistant professor of Business at Campbellsville University.

Karen Skerrett, PhD, is a psychologist, consultant, and, most recently, an associate clinical professor at the Family Institute at Northwestern University, Evanston, IL. She is the co-author with Jefferson Singer of *Positive Couple Therapy: Using We-Stories to Enhance Resilience* and the co-editor with Karen Fergus of *Couple Resilience* (2015).

Christine Slovey is a freelance writer, editor, and researcher.

Alexander L. Smith is a graduate student and teaching associate in the Department of Sociology and Anthropology at East Tennessee State University. His research interests include social psychology, identity, social theory, religion, public health, and quantitative methodology. His thesis work is on religion, spirituality, and health outcomes.

Amy M. Smith is an associate professor of Media & Communication at Salem State University. She is the author of *Tracing Family Lines: The Impact of Women's Genealogy Research on Family Communication.*

Todd Spencer, PhD, is an assistant professor in the Behavioral Science Department at Utah Valley University. He is a licensed Marriage and Family Therapist, Certified Family Life Educator, and an AAMFT-approved supervisor.

Susan D. Stewart, PhD, is a professor of Sociology at Iowa State University. She has published extensively on divorce, remarriage, and stepfamilies. Dr. Stewart served as keynote speaker at *Old Bonds, New Ties: Understanding Family Transitions in Re-Partnerships, Remarriages and Stepfamilies in Asia* at the National University of Singapore. Her most recent work on the subject is the book, *Multicultural Stepfamilies* (with Gordon Limb).

Nicholas L. Syrett is a professor of Women, Gender, and Sexuality Studies at the University of Kansas. He is a co-editor of *Age in America: The Colonial Era to the Present* and author of *The Company He Keeps: A History of White College Fraternities* and *American Child Bride: A History of Minors and Marriage in the United States.*

Eman Tadros is an assistant professor at Governors State University in the Division of Psychology and Counseling. She received her PhD from the University of Akron's Counselor Education and Supervision: Marriage and Family Therapy program. She is a licensed Marriage and Family Therapist, MBTI certified, and an AAMFT Approved Supervisor. She is the Illinois Family TEAM leader advocating for MFTs and individuals receiving systemic mental health services. Her research follows the trajectory of incarcerated coparenting, incorporating family therapy into incarcerated settings, and the utilization of family systems theories within these settings.

Sarah Taylor is an assistant professor of Child Development and Family Studies at California State University, Long Beach.

Elcy E. Timothy is an undergraduate student at Iowa State University pursuing a bachelor's degree in Sociology with minors in Political Science and Data Science. Ms. Timothy is involved in a range of social causes and is the president of the Iowa State chapter of UNICEF.

Madison P. Tincha, MA, NCC, holds a master's degree in Sociology from George Mason University and a master's degree in Counseling from Marymount University. She is a couples and sex therapist and National Certified Counselor practicing in the Washington, D.C. area.

Joshua Turner is a postdoctoral fellow at Utah State University. He received his PhD in Human Development and Family Sciences from Mississippi State University. His research interests include family demography, relationship education, remarriage and stepfamily issues, health and aging, and survey design.

S. Thomas Valentine is an associate professor of Theology and Pastoral Ministries and the Director of the Chapel at the Conover Education Center, Campbellsville University. Tommy served as a senior minister for 28 years and is the editor of the book, *Questions of the Soul*, a collection of sermons from the 2014 Academy of Preachers.

Amber Vennum, PhD, CFLE, LMFT, is an associate professor of Couple and Family Therapy at Kansas State University focused on early prevention and intervention. As a scholar and practitioner, Dr. Vennum is interested in increasing young people's life-long chances for establishing healthy romantic and familial relationships through interventions during adolescence and young adulthood.

Alicia M. Walker is an assistant professor of Sociology at Missouri State University. She is credited with developing a sociology of infidelity. Her research interests include intimate sexual relationships, gender and sexuality, and sexual identity.

Michelle Washburn-Busk, MS, LMFT, is a doctoral student in the Couple & Family Therapy program at Kansas State University. She specializes in couples therapy with clients who have a history of on-again/off-again cycles. Michelle's research focuses on helping clinicians prevent and intervene in the risks posed by chronic instability and conflict in couples.

Karen Washington, LMFT, MEd, CST, is an adjunct faculty and PhD candidate with Adler University in Chicago, IL. She is also a practicing sex therapist at Relationship Reality 312.

Shannon E. Weaver, PhD, is an associate professor in the Department of Human Development and Family Sciences at the University of Connecticut.

Sarah White is a master's candidate in Human Services at East Tennessee State University. Sarah is also the co-director is RISE: Healthy for Life whose mission is to provide and promote comprehensive sexuality education to humans throughout their lifespan.

Patricia Hrusa Williams, PhD, is a professor of Early Childhood Education at the University of Maine at Farmington. Her teaching and scholarship focus on infant-toddler education, family and parent engagement in education, family support programs, and higher education's role in communities. She holds a PhD in Applied Child Development from Tufts University.

Emma Willis is a doctoral student in the Department of Human Development and Family Studies at Texas Tech University.

Hannah C. Williamson is an assistant professor of Human Development and Family Sciences at The University of Texas at Austin. She received a PhD in Clinical Psychology from the University of California, Los Angeles. Her research focuses on the effect of socioeconomic status on marriage.

Robin Fretwell Wilson is the Associate Dean for Public Engagement and the Roger and Stephany Joslin Professor of Law at the University of Illinois College of Law, where she directs the College of Law's Family Law and Policy Program and the Epstein Health Law and Policy Program. She specializes in family law and health law, and her research and teaching interests also include biomedical ethics, law and religion, children and violence, and law and science.

Adam Winsler is a professor of Psychology and an Applied Developmental Psychologist at George Mason University. Dr. Winsler earned his PhD in Child and Adolescent Development from Stanford University. He has authored over 100 journal articles and book chapters. Dr. Winsler is known for his research in early childhood education, private speech, and the school readiness and academic trajectories of low-income, ethnically diverse children.

Emily Winter, MA, SYC, NCSP, is a nationally and state-certified school psychologist. She is a PhD student in the school psychology program at the University of Connecticut within the Neag School of Education. Her research interests are eating disorders, mind-body health, and supporting student-athletes.

Jeremy B. Yorgason, PhD, is a professor in the School of Family Life and Director of the Gerontology Program at Brigham Young University. Dr. Yorgason's research interests are in the area of later-life family relationships, with a specific focus on health and marriage.

Elsa Zawedde is a lawyer from Uganda. She specializes in health law and human rights law, and her research interests include reproductive health rights, preventive health, and medical ethics. As a legal advocate, she has contributed to many areas of the law regarding maternal health, law reform of the tobacco bill and regulations of Uganda, and the sexuality education policy. Elsa is also a JSD candidate at the University of Illinois. She researches medical–legal partnerships in Uganda.

Index

Bold page numbers indicate the location of main entries.

resolution, 166
retirement, 22, 145
Roe v. Wade (1973), 1, 209–210
role theory, 450–452
Rolfe, John, 27
Roman Catholic perspective, abortion from, 1
romantic break-up, pornography as factor in, 10–11
romantic disillusionment, 131–132
romantic love (intimacy and passion), 441
romantic love, pre-1950, 112
romantic partner, gambling impact on, 9
romantic partner, search for, 4, 6
romantic relationships
  age differences in, 22–24
  dimensions underlying, 36
  partner retention in, 450
  sex-related behaviors impact on, 10
  Triangular Theory of Love applied to, 440–441
Rousseau, Henri-Julien-Félix, 460

same-sex couples, 105–106, 130
same-sex divorce. *See* LGBTQ divorces and separations
same-sex dyads, online dating by, 117
same-sex marriage, 20, 205
Sample, Ian, 23
Sandusky, Jerry, 53
"sandwich generation," 64
Savage, Dan, 353
school dropout rate, 58
school-age children
  childcare for, 65
  chronic illness among, 70
screen time, restricting, 7
second marriages, divorce rate for, 159
Second Parent Adoption for unmarried persons, 20
second shift, **408–410**
secondary traumatic stress, 21
secure attachment style, 36, 38

self-advertising, 116
self-advocacy for children with chronic illness, 71
self-determination, 67
self-esteem, relationship information over-sharing and, 403–404
self-selected marriage, 30
self-understanding, 36
semi-open adoptions (defined), 16
sensitivity, 37
separated parents and children, educators working with, 32
separation as alternative to divorce, 140
serial monogamy, 283
sex education, 448
sex frequency, factors affecting, 49–50
sex outside of marriage, 112, 114, 115, 390–391
sex outside of relationship, 11
sexless marriage (defined), 49
sexless relationships, addressing issues in, 50
sex-related behaviors, 9–10
"sexting," 103
sexual abuse, 51, 53
sexual behaviors, 10
sexual compatibility, **410–412**
Sexual Configurations Theory, 353–354
sexual connection in marriage, 141
sexual double standard, 115
sexual experience, first, 113–114, 115
sexual imprinting, 224
sexual intimacy, 37, 50
sexual liberation, 391
sexual minority individuals. *See* terms beginning with LGBTQ
sexual orientations theory, 353
sexual revolution, 115
sexuality
  attitudes toward, shift in, 103
  expression of, 102–103, 112
  role in marriage, 135
Shag and Bachelor Party (film), 41
shared custody, 54–55, 357–358, **412–414**

www.ingramcontent.com/pod-product-compliance
Lightning Source LLC
Chambersburg PA
CBHW080409270326
41929CB00018B/2949